IN MY TIME

A Personal and Political Memoir

———◦———

DICK CHENEY

with Liz Cheney

THRESHOLD EDITIONS

New York   London   Toronto   Sydney   New Delhi

THRESHOLD EDITIONS
A Division of Simon & Schuster, Inc.
1230 Avenue of the Americas
New York, NY 10020

Copyright © 2011 by Richard B. Cheney

All rights reserved, including the right to reproduce this book or
portions thereof in any form whatsoever. For information, address Threshold
Editions Subsidiary Rights Department, 1230 Avenue of
the Americas, New York, NY 10020.

First Threshold Editions hardcover edition August 2011

THRESHOLD EDITIONS and colophon are trademarks of
Simon & Schuster, Inc.

For information about special discounts for bulk purchases,
please contact Simon & Schuster Special Sales at 1-866-506-1949
or business@simonandschuster.com.

The Simon & Schuster Speakers Bureau can bring authors to your live event. For
more information or to book an event, contact the Simon & Schuster Speakers
Bureau at 1-866-248-3049 or visit our website at www.simonspeakers.com.

Designed by Joy O'Meara

Manufactured in the United States of America

1 3 5 7 9 10 8 6 4 2

Library of Congress Cataloging-in-Publication Data is available.

ISBN 978-1-4391-7619-1
ISBN 978-1-4391-7623-8 (ebook)

To Lynne, who helped me write my life

CONTENTS

IN MY TIME

———◄◦►———

September 11, 2001

Special Agent Jimmy Scott burst through the door. "Mr. Vice President, we've got to leave now." Before I could reply he moved behind my desk, put one hand on my belt and another on my shoulder, and propelled me out of my office. He rushed me through narrow West Wing hallways and down a stairway toward the "PEOC," the Presidential Emergency Operations Center, located underneath the White House.

We stopped at the bottom of the stairs in a tunnel outside the PEOC. I watched as Secret Service agents positioned themselves at the top, middle, and bottom of the staircase, creating layers of defense in case the White House itself should be invaded. Agent Scott handed out additional firearms, flashlights, and gas masks. He'd evacuated me from my office, he said, because he'd gotten word over his radio that an inbound, unidentified aircraft was headed for "Crown," code name for the White House.

Within moments another report came in. "Sir," Scott said, "the plane headed for us just hit the Pentagon." Now I knew for certain that Washington as well as New York was under attack, and that meant that

President Bush, who had been at an elementary school in Florida, had to stay away. I turned to one of the agents in the tunnel. "Get me the president." He picked up the handset of a phone on the wall to patch through a call.

This was the second call I had made to President Bush since hijacked airliners flew into the World Trade towers, and he'd been trying to reach me as well. A communications glitch had cut us off earlier, and as I waited to talk to him now, I watched images of the burning towers on an old television set that had been set up in the tunnel. When the president came on the line, I told him that the Pentagon had been hit and urged him to stay away from Washington. The city was under attack, and the White House was a target. I understood that he didn't want to appear to be on the run, but he shouldn't be here until we knew more about what was going on.

My wife, Lynne, had been in downtown D.C. when the planes hit, and her Secret Service detail brought her to the White House. She arrived in the tunnel shortly before 10:00 a.m., and when I finished talking to the president, she went with me into the PEOC. I took a seat at the large conference table that occupied most of the wood-paneled room. Underneath the table telephones rested in drawers. On the wall across from me were two large television screens and a camera for videoconferencing. A side wall contained another video camera and two more TV screens. The wall behind me was blank except for a large presidential seal.

We hadn't been in the PEOC long when the television sets showed the South Tower of the World Trade Center collapsing. Both Lynne and I knew we had just watched hundreds, maybe thousands, of innocent people die.

Transportation Secretary Norm Mineta, who'd been one of the first in the PEOC, was making lists of airline flight numbers, trying to figure out which planes were confirmed hijacked and crashed, and which might still be threatening us in the air. Norm was working two telephones, with the FAA on one and his chief of staff on the other, trying to get the skies cleared until we knew just what we were dealing with. A commercial airline pilot usually has wide discretion to handle his aircraft in an emergency, and apparently someone said something to Norm about pilots deciding when and if to bring their planes down. I heard him say in no uncertain terms that pilot discretion would not be the rule today. "Get those planes down now," he ordered.

In those first hours we were living in the fog of war. We had reports of six domestic flights that were possibly hijacked, a number that later resolved to four. We had conflicting reports about whether the Pentagon had been hit by a plane, a helicopter, or a car bomb. We started getting reports of explosions across Washington, at the Lincoln Memorial, the Capitol, and the State Department. We heard there was an unidentified, nonresponsive plane headed for Camp David and another headed for Crawford, Texas; we also received word of a threat against Air Force One.

At about 10:15, a uniformed military aide came into the room to tell me that a plane, believed hijacked, was eighty miles out and headed for D.C. He asked me whether our combat air patrol had authority to engage the aircraft. Did our fighter pilots have authority, in other words, to shoot down an American commercial airliner believed to have been hijacked? "Yes," I said without hesitation. A moment later he was back. "Mr. Vice President, it's sixty miles out. Do they have authorization to engage?" Again, yes.

There could have been no other answer. As the last hour and a half had made brutally clear, once a plane was hijacked it was a weapon in the hands of the enemy. In one of our earlier calls, the president and I had discussed the fact that our combat air patrol—the American fighter jets now airborne to defend the country—would need rules of engagement. He had approved my recommendation that they be authorized to fire on a civilian airliner if it had been hijacked and would not divert. Thousands of Americans had already been killed, and there was no question about taking action to save thousands more. Still, the enormity of the order I had just conveyed struck all of us in the PEOC, and a silence fell over the room. Then Deputy Chief of Staff Josh Bolten leaned forward in his chair and suggested we get in touch with the president to let him know what had just happened. At 10:18, I picked up the secure phone in the drawer beside me and called Air Force One, which had left Florida and was heading west as the president's aides looked for a secure location from which he could address the American people. When the president came on the line, I told him about the shootdown order.

There soon followed some tense moments when we got word that an aircraft was down, south of Johnstown, Pennsylvania. Had it been forced down? Had it been shot down by one of our pilots following the authorization I'd conveyed? Eventually we learned that an act of heroism had brought United Airlines Flight 93 down in the fields near Shanksville. Aware of the fates of the other planes hijacked that morning, the passengers on Flight 93 stormed the cockpit. By sacrificing their own lives, those brave men and women saved the lives of many others, possibly including those of us in the White House that morning.

Eric Edelman, my deputy national security advisor and a veteran foreign service officer, entered the PEOC with a message for me from Steve Hadley, the president's deputy national security advisor. "Mr. Vice President," he said, "Steve believes you should evacuate." I told Eric I wasn't going anywhere. I knew the president was safe. And I knew I had to maintain my ability to communicate, as frustrating as our communications challenges were that day. "Eric, if we leave here and get on a helicopter to evacuate, it will be at least forty-five minutes before I can be back in touch with anyone. That's valuable time we can't afford to lose. Tell Hadley we're staying put."

Lynne, who'd been sitting at the end of the conference table, brought me news of our family. She had heard from the Secret Service that they were getting our kids and grandkids to secure locations. At 10:28, the second tower came down, and there was a collective gasp in the room. Mothers and fathers were in that building, and wives and husbands, sisters and brothers, sons and daughters. They weren't combatants in a war, but people going about their lives. They had been killed, and their families would be plunged into grief by terrorists who had no regard for innocent lives.

Within minutes of the tower collapsing, I was told that another plane headed in the direction of Washington had hit the ground on the border of Ohio and Kentucky. Then came word of another hijacked plane, this one just five miles out from the White House. "Take it out," I said. "If it looks threatening, take it out."

At 10:39 I had a chance to update Secretary of Defense Don Rumsfeld, who was in the National Military Command Center in the Pentagon. A transcript exists of our conversation:

> **VP:** There's been at least three instances here where we've had reports of aircraft approaching Washington—a couple were confirmed hijacked. And, pursuant to the president's instructions, I gave authorization for them to be taken out. Hello?
>
> **SecDef:** Yes, I understand. Who did you give that direction to?
>
> **VP:** It was passed from here through the operations center at the White House, from the shelter.
>
> **SecDef:** Okay, let me ask the question here. Has that directive been transmitted to the aircraft?
>
> **VP:** Yes, it has.
>
> **SecDef:** So, we've got a couple of aircraft up there that have those instructions at this present time?
>
> **VP:** That is correct. And it's my understanding they've already taken a couple aircraft out.
>
> **SecDef:** We can't confirm that. We're told that one aircraft is down but we do not have a pilot report that did it.

As the 9/11 Commission would later find, the Northeast Air Defense Sector of NORAD had not passed the shootdown order to the fighter pilots as they scrambled out of Langley Air Force Base, although pilots out of Andrews Air Force Base did have permission to shoot. And only one aircraft had crashed into the ground—Flight 93, near Shanksville, Pennsylvania. The plane we had thought was down on the Ohio-Kentucky line was actually American Flight 77—the plane that had been headed in the direction of the White House. It had circled away from us, then back toward the White House, prompting my evacuation. Then it set on its deadly course for the Pentagon.

TWO THOUGHTS WERE UPPERMOST in my mind that morning: preventing further attacks by getting planes out of the skies and guaranteeing the continuity of a functioning United States government. We began immediately taking precautions to ensure that any attack on Washington would not decapitate the leadership of our nation. The president stayed away from the city until things clarified. We evacuated key leaders in the House and Senate to a secure location away from D.C. I had trouble getting hold of House Speaker Dennis Hastert, but finally reached him at Andrews Air Force Base, where his security team had taken him. I brought him up to date and urged him to move to a secure location, which he did. I called him at least once more that day. It was crucial that he know what was happening since he was second in line to succeed to the presidency.

The president pro tempore of the Senate, Robert Byrd, who was next in the presidential line of succession after the Speaker, refused to move to a secure location. He went home instead. Others who did evacuate were anxious to return to Washington as soon as possible. At one point my friend Senator Don Nickles of Oklahoma asked why the executive branch had the right to decide when members of Congress, a coequal branch of government, could come back to Washington. "Because we've got the helicopters, Don," I told him.

With all air traffic to and from the continental United States being grounded, requests began to come in for planes to fly senior officials who had been stranded. Alan Greenspan, the chairman of the Federal Reserve, was stuck in Zurich, Switzerland. The magnitude of the economic impact of the attack would be significant, and we needed Alan back in the United States to help us manage it. We asked the Pentagon to get him a plane.

While we were managing things from the PEOC, another meeting was under way in the White House Situation Room. The PEOC staff attempted to set up a videoconference to connect the two rooms, and we managed to get images of the Situation Room meeting up on one of our screens, but we couldn't get any audio of the meeting. We were getting better real-time information from the news reports on TV, but because of a technical glitch, I couldn't hear those reports when the video of the Sit Room meeting was on display. Finally I asked that the videoconference to the Sit Room be turned off so we could follow the reporting on TV. I told Eric to get on the phone and try to listen in on the Sit Room meeting, but after a few minutes he described the audio quality as "worse than listening to Alvin and the Chipmunks at the bottom of a swimming pool." I told him to hang up. If something important was happening upstairs, they could send someone down or call us direct.

In the meantime, Secretary Rumsfeld had made the decision to take our nation's military alert level from the peacetime Defense Condition 4 to DefCon 3, higher than we'd been since the 1973 Arab-Israeli war. Scooter Libby, my chief of staff, and Eric Edelman pointed out that someone needed to tell the Russians that we were going to a higher alert level. They were at that moment conducting major military exercises, and we didn't want them to be surprised or think our alert level had been raised because of them. We had all lived through the Cold War and knew the possibility of a mistaken nuclear launch had to be kept in mind. National Security Advisor Condoleezza Rice made the call, got through to Russian President Vladimir Putin, and reported back his expressions of support. The Russians agreed to halt their military exercises in light of the attacks on the United States.

A decision had been made to set Air Force One down at Barksdale Air Force Base in Louisiana, where the president would tape a brief message to the American people. Shortly before he landed, we began to get word in the PEOC of international flights in trouble. The Coast Guard was receiving distress calls from United, Air Canada, and Continental planes, all over the Atlantic. Within a half hour, we were told that those flights were no longer cause for concern, but there was a Korean Air flight over the Pacific inbound for Anchorage with its hijack code squawking. Fighter jets had been scrambled from Alaska's Elmendorf Air Force Base to shadow it.

Condi Rice asked me where I thought the president should go from Barksdale. "Strategic Command at Offutt Air Force Base near Omaha," I told her. From my time as secretary of defense, I knew that the U.S. military has facilities throughout the country that offer a combination of high security and state-of-the-art communications. STRATCOM was one. The president would be safe there, and on a day when the weaknesses of our communications capability had become painfully obvious, he could be in close touch with the key members of his government in Washington, D.C.

BY EARLY IN THE afternoon, we had gotten most of the planes out of the sky. We had learned that many of the reports of attacks and hijacked airliners were false. The situation and the flow of information about it were stabilizing. I knew that the president was anxious to get back to Washington, and during a call with him as he was on his way to Offutt, I recommended he begin thinking about a time to return. He had scheduled a secure videoconference at Offutt so he could talk to his National Security Council, but I had no doubt that after that he'd be on his way to D.C.

As the day progressed, it became clear that someone from the executive branch who was fully briefed on our early responses to the attack needed to go on the air to reassure the American people and the world that the president was safe and that the U.S. government was functioning. The attack had not succeeded in shutting us down. As we watched television reports in the PEOC, it seemed that none of the reporters had been in contact with anyone in the executive branch who could talk authoritatively about what we were doing. Several members of Congress had been on the air, but they were all removed from the business of actually running the country.

Someone needed to make a formal statement to the nation—and I knew it couldn't be me. My past government experience, including my participation in Cold War–era continuity-of-government exercises, had prepared me to manage the crisis during those first few hours on 9/11, but I knew that if I went out and spoke to the press, it would undermine the president, and that would be bad for him and for the country. We were at war. Our commander in chief needed to be seen as in charge, strong, and resolute—as George W. Bush was. My speaking publicly would not serve that cause.

Presidential Counselor Karen Hughes seemed to me to be the right one to talk to the press. She'd taken a rare day off, but had made her way to the White House and soon started working with Vice Presidential Counselor Mary Matalin to draft a statement. For a range of security reasons, the Secret Service did not want Karen to use the White House press briefing room, so they arranged for her to be driven to FBI head-quarters, where she briefed reporters.

In the meantime I was starting to think about our response to this act of war. I had managed to get my general counsel, David Adding-ton, back into the White House after he had been forced to evacuate. Almost as soon as he arrived in the PEOC, he began coordinating by phone with a team of the president's staff who were in the Roosevelt Room thinking through what kind of legislative authorities we would need in the days and months ahead.

We suspected early on that this was an al Qaeda attack. There were few other terrorist organizations capable of organizing and carrying out an attack of this scale. We'd certainly go after those responsible, but that wasn't enough. There were organizations that financed terrorist activity and provided weapons and arms. There were states that provided the terrorists with safe harbor. Those who supported terrorism also needed to be held accountable.

During the National Security Council meeting that the president convened by means of secure teleconferencing from Offutt, the con-tours of the Bush Doctrine began to emerge. We would go after the ter-rorists who had done us harm—and we would also go after those who made their murderous attacks possible.

The president returned to the White House and at 8:30 p.m. ad-dressed the nation from the Oval Office. "We will make no distinction between the terrorists who committed these acts and those who harbor them," he said. Afterward he chaired a National Security Council meeting inside the PEOC. When it was over, Lynne and I left the bunker and walked out the diplomatic entrance of the White House onto the South Lawn, where a white-top helicopter was waiting to take us to an undisclosed location. It was the first of many times that I would leave for a location different from the president's that we did not reveal publicly. If the terrorists tried an attack to decapitate our government, we wanted to make sure they didn't get both of us.

As Marine Two gained altitude, we could see the Pentagon. The building was lit up for the rescue teams still at work, and smoke was rising from it. All day I had seen images of the World Trade Center and the Pentagon on TV. Seeing the site of an attack firsthand brought home the vulnerability of the United States and the dangers that America faced. I thought about the fact that the city of Washington had come under attack in 1814 at the hands of the British. Now, 187 years later, al Qaeda had demonstrated they could deliver a devastating blow to the heart of America's economic and military power. On this day all our assumptions about our own security had changed. It was a fundamental shift.

We flew toward the Catoctin Mountains and Camp David, the presidential retreat that would be our undisclosed location on the night of September 11. When we arrived we were taken to Aspen Lodge, where I stayed up into the morning hours thinking about what the attack meant and how we should respond. We were in a new era and needed an entirely new strategy to keep America secure. The first war of the twenty-first century wouldn't simply be a conflict of nation against nation, army against army. It would be first and foremost a war against terrorists who operated in the shadows, feared no deterrent, and would use any weapon they could get their hands on to destroy us.

CHAPTER ONE

Beginnings

When I was born my granddad wanted to send a telegram to the president. Both sides of my family were staunch New Deal Democrats, and Granddad was sure that FDR would want to know about the "little stranger" with whom he now had a birthday in common. My parents had been married in Lincoln, Nebraska, and I was born there, at Bryan Memorial Hospital, on January 30, 1941—the same day that Franklin D. Roosevelt turned fifty-nine. My mother, who had a penchant for keeping scrapbooks, saved the bill for my delivery—exactly $37.50.

My first memory is of riding on a crowded bus with my mother. I'm seated beside her, and my younger brother, Bob, about two, is on her lap. It's wartime, and even the aisles are packed with servicemen. One of them leans over and offers my mother a cigarette. She takes it and he gives her a light, which is the most amazing thing I have ever witnessed. I'm not quite four years old, and I have never seen her smoke before.

Mother and Bob and I have just left our home in Lincoln and are heading halfway across Nebraska to live with my father's parents in Sumner. Dad had received his draft notice in 1944, and after training at Great Lakes Naval Station, he was sent to San Diego with the expectation of being shipped out to the Pacific. Instead he was stationed there and assigned to a shakedown unit, which made sure that ships headed out were seaworthy and ready for combat. We'd have gone to be with him, but San Diego was a nearly impossible place to find wartime housing. My mother had tried to stay on in Lincoln, but after an attack of appendicitis, she decided she couldn't manage with two small boys on her own.

We couldn't move in with her folks, David and Clarice Dickey, because when the war began, David had closed the small restaurant he owned and signed on as a cook for the Union Pacific Railroad. Now his and Grandma's home was the railroad car next to the one in which they cooked for repair crews up and down the UP line in Kansas, Nebraska, and Wyoming. After the war Bob and I loved visiting them. Grandpa Dickey knew how to turn the most ordinary day into an adventure. He would take us fishing for catfish, using a special combination of blood and chicken guts for bait. For dinner he'd fry up our catch, or on the rare occasions when the blood and guts failed to get a bite, he would make a big batch of spaghetti. Afterward he and Grandma would bed us down on the oilcloth-covered tables where we'd just eaten, and we would fall asleep to the raucous laughter of my parents and grandparents playing cutthroat games of pitch by lantern light in the railroad car next door.

But those good times lay ahead. Right now we were headed to Sumner, population 296, to stay with Grandfather and Grandmother Cheney, and Mom must have known that the cigarette she was enjoying—the one that had so astonished me—was going to be her last one for a long while.

My mother had grown up in a laughing, card-playing family, with a dad who drank bourbon, smoked Camels, and had an endless store of jokes. My Cheney grandparents, Thomas and Margaret, on the other hand, had probably been staid even in youth. Thomas had been a schoolteacher before going to work in a bank. Margaret was the product of a rigorous Baptist upbringing and did not believe in tobacco, alcohol, or gambling. Nor, as we were about to learn, did she believe in comic books for her grandsons. Grandmother Cheney, her hair pulled back in a bun, was sixty-eight, and my white-haired grandfather, his back ramrod straight, was seventy-five. They had been enjoying the tranquility their years had earned them before my mother arrived accompanied by two rowdy little boys.

THE CHENEY FAMILY HAD originally come to America from England as part of the great Puritan immigration of the 1630s. For seven generations, the family lived in and around Massachusetts, but in the middle of the nineteenth century, Samuel Fletcher Cheney broke the mold, moving west to Defiance, Ohio. Right after Fort Sumter he signed up to defend the Union, and he served all four years of the Civil War. He was at Stones River and Chickamauga and in the campaign for Atlanta. He marched with Sherman to the sea. In May 1865 he camped with his 21st Ohio Regiment just outside Washington, D.C., in Alexandria, Virginia, and he was among the one hundred and fifty thousand soldiers who took part in the Grand Review of the Armies. He marched past the White House, where President Andrew Johnson and his cabinet, along with Generals Grant and Sherman, saluted the brave men who had just won the war.

Samuel had remained unscathed through thirty-four battles and had managed to avoid the terrible sicknesses that plagued most and killed many of his comrades. But not long after he returned home to his wife and two daughters in Defiance, Ohio, he stumbled into a circular saw and lost all the fingers of his left hand.

In 1883, as the country struggled through a long economic depression, the sash and door factory he co-owned had to be sold to pay its debts. At the age of fifty-four, Samuel Cheney had to start over. He gathered his wife and his four youngest children, all sons, and moved eight hundred miles west to a homestead claim in Buffalo County, Nebraska.

The Cheneys built a sod house, planted trees and crops, and slowly began to build a new life on the Great Plains. Within two years they had proved up their 160-acre claim and acquired an adjacent one to plant trees. The properties flourished until the early 1890s, when drought struck. Then the crops withered and the trees died, and finally, in economic circumstances even harder than those that had driven him under before, Samuel found himself unable to pay his debts. As he testified, despite his excellent record, "The banks will not loan to anyone at present." In 1896 he saw all his possessions auctioned off on the steps of the Kearney County Court House.

In 1904, after spending several restless years cooped up in Omaha, he claimed a second homestead in the Nebraska Sand Hills. A friend who fought beside Samuel at Stones River had written that "Cheney is clear grit," and he showed it to the very end: He proved up the Sand Hills homestead before he died in 1911 at the age of eighty-two.

Samuel named his second son Sherman, after the general with whom he had marched to the sea, and his third son, my grandfather, was Thomas, after the great Civil War general George H. Thomas—the "Rock of Chickamauga"—under whom Samuel had served. My granddad's middle name was Herbert, so everyone called him Bert for short. A teenager when his father first homesteaded, young Bert helped cut the sod bricks from the prairie for their house. He helped plant the cottonwood trees that died when the rain didn't come. He resolved to live a different kind of life—one in which he wouldn't have to get up every morning and anxiously scan the skies to figure out his fate.

In Sumner he prospered, becoming cashier and part owner of Farmers and Merchants Bank. After his first wife died of tuberculosis, he married a teacher and church leader, who was, like him, a pillar of the community. On June 26, 1915, forty-six-year-old Bert and thirty-eight-year-old Margaret Tyler Cheney became the parents of my father, Richard Herbert Cheney.

Despite all his plans and success, Bert Cheney found that, like his father, he couldn't escape the terrible power of nature. When drought struck in the early 1930s, farmers couldn't pay their debts, storekeepers had to close their doors, and Farmers and Merchants Bank went under.

Years later my dad would tell me about the day the bank failed. He'd been in downtown Sumner and had run into the bank examiner. It was 1:00 p.m. and the bank still hadn't opened its doors. The examiner asked my dad where his father was. People were starting to talk, the examiner said, and somebody better do something fast. My father ran home and found his father and the bank board in the living room, making the painful decision to close the bank down. My grandparents lost everything except for the house in which they lived.

Richard was a bright kid who taught himself to type and then paid his way at Kearney State Teachers College by cutting stencils and running the mimeograph machine. He majored in commerce and got good grades, but having to work while going to school meant that it was going to take him five years to graduate. Impatient and strapped for funds, he took the Civil Service Exam and was offered a job as a senior typist with the Veterans Administration in Lincoln, the state capital. After scraping by for so long, he found the prospect of a $120 monthly salary and the security of a government job too good to turn down.

Before long he was offered a job with another federal agency, the Soil Conservation Service. The SCS taught farmers about crop rotation, terraced planting, contour plowing, and using "shelter belts" of trees as windbreaks—techniques that would prevent the soil from blowing away, as it had in the dust storms of the Great Depression. My dad stayed with the SCS for more than thirty years, doing work of which he was immensely proud.

He was also proud of the pension that came with federal employment—a pride that I didn't really understand until as an adult I learned about the economic catastrophes that his parents and grandparents had experienced and that had shadowed his own youth. I've often reflected on how different was the utterly stable environment he provided for his family and wondered if because of that I have been able to take risks, to change directions, and to leave one career path for another with hardly a second thought.

The SCS moved my father from Lincoln to Syracuse, a small town in the southeastern part of Nebraska. As a young bachelor living in a rented room, he took most of his meals at Dickey's Café, where one of the waitresses was Marjorie Lorraine Dickey, daughter of the café's proprietor. My father was, like his parents, somewhat reticent. He didn't give away a lot on a first meeting—or a second or even a tenth—but that wouldn't have mattered to my mother, an open, outgoing person, who probably engaged my father in conversation the first time he walked through the door of Dickey's Café. It's easy to imagine her taking his order for chili and talking to him as though she'd known him forever.

Mom was something of a star in her small town. She was one of the famed Syracuse Bluebirds, a female softball team that had been state champions for two years in a row and had gone all the way to the national semifinals in Chicago. Syracuse loved the Bluebirds. They gave people something to hope for and cheer about in the lingering gloom of the Great Depression.

My pretty, high-spirited mother and my quiet, handsome father fell for one another and got married on June 1, 1940. I was born the next year, and my brother, Bob, followed fourteen months later. Our sister, Susan, joined us in 1955.

WHEN WE ARRIVED IN Sumner in 1944, my mother was given the bedroom my grandparents usually rented to a teacher, and Bob and I slept on cots in a storage room. The house was small, and the weeks must have seemed endless to the grown-ups until on Sundays both sides got a break. In some kind of dispensation from my grandmother, my grandfather would start the day by reading the Sunday funnies to Bob and me. Then after church, my father's half sister, Mildred, and her husband, Elmer Ericson, would pick us up and take us to their farm just outside town. There were horses and cows—big Holsteins for milking—and two white collies and several cats. There were also platters of food I think about to this day. Mildred's specialty, fried chicken, began in the backyard, where she'd chase down a chicken and chop off its head with the hatchet she kept stuck in a tree stump for precisely that purpose. A few hours later the chicken would appear all fried up on the table, together with biscuits and gravy, all of it topped off with rhubarb pie.

At the end of January 1945, my father was given a week's leave, and he arrived in Sumner just in time for my fourth birthday. I had never seen him in his uniform, and when I asked him why he had been gone, he pointed to the patch on his arm—an embroidered white eagle above a red chevron—and said that now he was a yeoman. I still remember trying to process the startling information that my father had apparently spent the last several months as a bird.

A few months later, my mother decided to visit my father in San Diego. Aunt Mildred and Uncle Elmer, good and gracious people with no children of their own, offered to look after Bob and me. We had a fine time, chasing chickens, floating corncob ships in the horse tank, and following Elmer everywhere. The farm wasn't mechanized, and Bob and I got to ride around on the horse-pulled wagon. Uncle Elmer took naps in the afternoon, and I would lie down beside him, hooking a finger in his belt loop so that I would know if he got up. Every afternoon I would wake to find he was gone, and I'd run out of the house looking for him. I'd find him someplace in the farmyard, wearing his big straw hat, smiling, and holding out his arms, ready to lift me into the air.

My mother loved San Diego. She got to see her husband and had a great adventure, traveling farther than she ever had, seeing the ocean for the first time, and watching the San Diego Padres play. Her scrapbook is full of red and white Padres programs in which she carefully kept score.

What had been planned as a two-week visit turned into a two-month stay, and wonderful as life at Mildred and Elmer's was, Bob and I missed our mom. One hot August day we decided that she had been gone entirely too long, and we were going to hitchhike to California to see her. We made it to the highway, but were intercepted before we managed to catch a ride. In fact, our adventure was interrupted at just about the time she was starting home. While she was changing trains in Ogden, Utah, she heard the news that Japan had surrendered. The war was over, and the Cheney family would soon be reunited.

DEMOBILIZATION PROCEEDED ON A last in, last out basis, so my father wasn't discharged until April 1946. When he got back to

Lincoln, he found there was a severe postwar housing shortage, and we were lucky to have friends offer us their unfinished basement. My mother cooked on a hot plate, and we shared a single bathroom with the family upstairs until my folks found a five-room tract house that was going up in the suburb of College View. We would drive out in the '37 Buick that Dad had inherited from an uncle and impatiently watch our new home being built.

Our street in College View dead-ended in a woods that had what we called a stream running through it. In fact, our "stream" was really a drainage ditch for storm sewers, but it provided some fine crawdad fishing for the many neighborhood kids. The woods also provided opportunities to explore and climb, and there were hours when we covered considerable distances by stepping or jumping from tree to tree without ever touching the ground. In the winter a long, wide, sloping street in College View provided a terrific hill for sledding.

Granddad Dickey visited, one time pushing a stray mutt he'd found into our living room and letting my mother get used to the idea before he came inside himself. We named the dog Butch, and his claim to fame was his ability to sit up in a variety of places, from a bicycle seat to the palm of your hand. Our neighbors gave us a cat that was nearly as big as Butch, and the two developed a wary relationship. There was a throw rug on the hall floor, and whenever Butch saw the cat positioned just right, he'd run for the throw rug, landing on it so that he would slide down the hall and smack into the cat.

I don't remember much of my early schooling, but a kindergarten report card my mother saved notes that I seemed "a little self-conscious when speaking before the group." As the year progressed, I was "speaking more confidently," asking "worthwhile questions," and, apparently, showing persistence. "Richard does not give up easily," Miss Korbel wrote. She also noted that I had good health habits. "He always tries to sit and stand correctly and to use his handkerchief in the right way." My third-grade teacher, Miss Duffield, gave me top-notch grades in English, arithmetic, reading, and social studies, and although she noted that my work in art and music wasn't all it could be, she still concluded,

"I have enjoyed working with Dicky this year. He has the qualifications for a good leader."

All the kids in College View rode bikes everywhere. I used to ride home from school each day for lunch. Even after my mother started working for the state health department downtown in the Nebraska State Capitol, I would ride the ten blocks home and cook myself a hamburger. Bob and I joined Pack 54 of the Cub Scouts. Mom was the den mother of Den No. 2, sponsored by the Sheridan Boulevard Baptist Church, which met in our unfinished basement. When we were older, the Boy Scout who was our troop leader would sometimes bring a pack of cigarettes, and after our meetings, we would go outside and light up.

I supplemented my allowance by mowing lawns during the summer. I also had a paper route delivering the *Lincoln Star,* from which on a good month I could clear thirty dollars, very good money for a twelve-year-old in those days. My enterprise even led to my debut in newsprint in a short feature headlined "*Star* Carrier Dick Cheney." I told the interviewer that I had bought a clarinet with a portion of my earnings, but I was saving for college, where I planned to become an architectural engineer. For most of the year, I enjoyed those early morning rides, when the sun was just coming up and everything was quiet. But there were some cold mornings when even my thick gloves weren't enough, so I bought a small hand warmer at an army surplus store. It was about the size of a pack of cigarettes with holes poked all around it. You pulled out the innards, doused them with lighter fluid, and put them back in the small tin box. Once ignited the wick would burn slowly without any flame. I'd steer with one hand through the frozen postdawn streets and keep the other in the pocket with the warmer.

In the summer we all played Little League baseball, and in the fall it was Pop Warner football. I was probably seven or eight when my dad started taking me to some of the farm ponds and slow-moving creeks just outside Lincoln. We fished for bullhead and carp with bamboo poles, using worms for bait. I remember a trip to visit my mom's brother Ward in Idaho Falls, which was the first time I used spinners.

I read a lot. Arthur Draper's *Wonders of the Heavens* explained the shooting stars we saw in the vast Nebraska sky. Other books introduced heroes like George Washington, Kit Carson, and Lou Gehrig. The whole family listened to the radio, and very early in the fifties we acquired one of the first television sets in the neighborhood. When President Eisenhower was inaugurated on January 20, 1953, the entire sixth-grade class of College View Elementary crowded into our living room to watch the event on our small black-and-white screen.

In 1952 both my parents had voted for Adlai Stevenson, the Democratic candidate, but it was the new Republican president who was responsible for a major change in the Cheney family's life. One of Eisenhower's earliest initiatives involved a reorganization of the Department of Agriculture, which included the Soil Conservation Service. My father was given a choice of new assignments, and he chose Casper, Wyoming, over Great Falls, Montana. Casper, which was known as "the Oil Capital of the Rockies," was in the central part of Wyoming. With a population of about twenty-five thousand, it was the second-biggest city in the state. Only the capital, Cheyenne, was larger—and not by much. We had driven through Wyoming on a few car trips west. We'd seen the mountains and fished the trout streams. We remembered the crisp morning air of the high plains and the sunny afternoons, one after another. As much as we liked College View, the Cheney family couldn't wait to get to Casper.

THE SPRING BEFORE WE moved, I began following the Battle of Dien Bien Phu in Vietnam. I'd sit on the floor of our living room, the newspaper spread out in front of me, and pore over maps of the battle as it unfolded week after week. I'd watch the nightly news reports of the communist Viet Minh besieging French forces and the French driving them back until ultimately the Viet Minh overran the garrison, delivering the French a terrible defeat.

When we first arrived in Casper in 1954, I read a lot about World War II. I checked *Guadalcanal Diary* and *Those Devils in Baggy Pants* out of the Carnegie Library, a redbrick building with a white dome on Second Street. I didn't know anybody yet, so I was a regular patron.

Our house was the last one on the east side of town, and Bob and I loved to go out on the prairie. To a casual observer the landscape might have seemed barren and boring, but my brother and I, out there for hours, knew its different grasses, the sagebrush, the scrub pine, and all the animals that lived there—antelope, deer, jackrabbits, cottontails, and an occasional rattlesnake. We took our .22s along and usually returned with at least a couple of rabbits, which Mom would fry up for our lunchboxes the next day.

In Casper we were living in the heart of the old West, in a town on the Oregon Trail that traced its beginnings to a ferry that the Mormons established to take pioneers across the Platte River. As the number of wagon trains rolling down the trail increased, so did conflicts with the Plains Indians, and the U.S. Cavalry came riding into the West—often at their peril. In 1865, not far from the site of the old ferry on the Platte, there was a battle that took the life of young Lieutenant Caspar Collins, after whom the town would be named, with the spelling only slightly altered. The following year, a few hours north at the foot of the Bighorn Mountains, Sioux and Cheyenne warriors wiped out an army column of some eighty men, including their commander, Captain W. J. Fetterman. And ten years later, just over the border in Montana, Sitting Bull's warriors killed General George Armstrong Custer and more than two hundred men of the 7th Cavalry in a battle near the Little Bighorn River.

I became fascinated with the stories of the men who came before the pioneers, such as John Colter, who broke off from the Lewis and Clark expedition and in the winter of 1807–1808 made his way to what we now call Yellowstone National Park. People accused him of lying when he reported on the geysers and boiling pools he had seen, and although he wasn't telling tall tales, exaggeration was part of the mountain man tradition—as were independence and self-reliance. Whiskey and profanity were part of it too—except maybe in the case of Jedediah Smith, a man of religion, who traversed vast sections of the West with his Bible and an unbelievable threshold for pain. When an encounter with a grizzly left him with his scalp and ear hanging off, he had one of his fellow mountain men sew them back on, and within a few weeks, he was back blazing trails. Hugh Glass was another great story. In an encounter with a grizzly, he was so badly wounded that his traveling companions left him for dead. His leg broken, his body gashed and torn, he crawled a hundred miles to a river, where he constructed a raft and floated to Fort Kiowa. When he had recovered, he set out to kill the men who had left him.

A. B. Guthrie's novel *The Big Sky* re-created not only the era of the mountain men, but the remarkable land of high plains and higher mountains that was now my backyard, a place where "there was more sky than a man could think, curving deep and far and empty, except maybe for a hawk or an eagle sailing." Guthrie's book was a favorite of my teenage years, surpassed only by Bernard De Voto's telling of the mountain men's story in *Across the Wide Missouri*. De Voto knew well the land that the pioneers traveled as they approached the Platte River ferry, and vast stretches of it still existed, "gullies, knife-edges, sage, greasewood, and alkali, . . . covered with flowers in June, relieved by small sweet creeks flowing among cottonwoods." I've reread *Across the Wide Missouri* many times since my youth. It's one of those books I've never really put away.

DURING OUR FIRST SUMMER in Casper, I signed up for Pony League baseball, and at the end of the season I was picked for an all-star team that got to travel on a chartered bus to Richland, Washington, for a regional tournament. Although we had more fun than success, I made some good friends, including Tom Fake, who would be my best friend all through high school. When I got home and saw the newspaper stories about the trip that my mom had clipped from the local papers, I began to get an inkling of the support that a small town gives to its sports teams. A lot of adults wanted a bunch of thirteen-year-olds to succeed, and when we didn't quite live up to their hopes, they were with us anyway, confidently predicting that next year would be our time.

Life in Wyoming was turning out to be everything we had expected and more. In 1954 my granddad Dickey joined us for a family fishing outing to Dubois. We stayed in a motel with a kitchenette so we could save money by cooking our own meals, but its main attraction was that it was right on the banks of the Wind River. We thought it was great to be able to walk outside the room right in the middle of town and start fishing. We didn't know that some of the best water in Wyoming was only a few miles away in the winding streams that fed into the Wind River. We used nightcrawlers as bait occasionally, but in those days we were mostly hardware fishermen, using metal spinners and lures.

Granddad Dickey was the life of our small party, but he had had a couple of heart attacks and seemed to grow frailer with each visit. When he came to see us again in the spring of 1955, it was clear that he wasn't doing well. One morning when I was in the living room and my parents were outside working in the yard, I heard him calling from his bedroom down the hall. "Dicky, come here, I need you." I found him sitting on the edge of his bed, clearly in pain. He told me that he thought he was having another heart attack. I ran outside to get my folks, and they called for help. I ran down to the street corner to flag down the ambulance and make sure it came to the right house. In those days there wasn't much the drivers could do except put Grandpa on oxygen and rush him to the hospital. I held the screen door open as they carried him out on a stretcher. My folks followed the ambulance to the hospital, but they were back home within an hour and told Bob and me that Grandpa had died.

He was buried next to Grandma Dickey in Lincoln, but we couldn't go to Nebraska for the funeral because Mom was nine months pregnant and couldn't travel. One week later, my sister, Susan, was born.

ALTHOUGH CASPER WAS A small town, it had a big high school. The next city of any size to the south of Casper was one hundred twenty miles away. You had to go west a hundred miles before encountering anything larger than a gas station. The towns east and north were very small. So Natrona County High School drew from all over central Wyoming, and there were nearly five hundred kids in my freshman class. When Casper athletic teams wanted to compete with schools of comparable size, some pretty big distances were involved. We thought nothing of loading into a school bus and traveling two or three hundred miles to Rapid City, South Dakota; Scottsbluff, Nebraska; or Grand Junction, Colorado.

I played football in the fall and American Legion baseball in the summer. I tried basketball my freshman year, but gave it up when our coach, Swede Erickson, told me I had two problems: I couldn't shoot and I couldn't jump. Swede also once paid me a compliment about my football ability. "Cheney, you're the finest 'mudder' on the NCHS team," he said. Trouble was, it never rained in Wyoming during football season.

Our coaches had a big impact on us. They worked us hard on the field and made sure we kept up in the classroom. Two of my coaches, Bob Lahti and Don Weishaar, were also my teachers, and very good ones, of chemistry and calculus. Harry Geldien taught biology until he took over as head football coach in 1957. He'd been a star tailback at the University of Wyoming, and the whole town counted on him to bring our team out of its doldrums. He didn't let us down. We tied with Sheridan for the state championship that year, which made us celebrities in Casper and shined a bright light on Geldien. He was soon as much loved by the community as he was by those of us he coached. He taught us about competition, focus, and discipline.

When I was vice president, I was invited to address the Wyoming legislature, and my friend Joe Meyer, the Wyoming state treasurer, whom Geldien had also coached, arranged for a small reunion with Geldien and another of our teammates, Mike Golden, justice of the Wyoming Supreme Court. The best part of our get-together was seeing how proud we had made the coach.

Except during football season I always had a part-time job, everything from delivering newspapers and cutting lawns, to working as a janitor at Ben Franklin, a five-and-dime store, and Donell's, a candy store in the Hilltop Shopping Center. One summer I loaded hundred-pound bags of bentonite onto railway cars at a plant west of town and another I worked as a laborer at the Central Wyoming Fair and Rodeo grounds. That last job ended about a week before football started, and I joined three friends and football teammates, Tom Fake, T. J. Claunch, and Brock Hileman, on a fishing trip in the upper reaches of the Middle Fork of the Powder River.

By this time I had done a fair amount of fishing. Sometimes with my mom and dad and sometimes with friends, I had fished the Alcova Reservoir, about thirty miles southwest of town. I'd also gotten to know a stretch of river above Pathfinder, a dam about fifty miles to the southwest, which always gave up lots of big trout. The stretch is called "miracle mile," and it was where I fished for the first time using streamers instead of hardware or bait, although I was still using a casting rod instead of a fly rod.

Now, along with Tom, T.J., and Brock, I was headed to the upper reaches of the Middle Fork. The section we wanted to fish was in a very rugged deep canyon, so we camped on top and climbed down to the stream every day. With a used fiberglass fly rod and a handful of flies I'd purchased at the local hardware store, I tried fly-fishing for the first time in my life. We had a magnificent trip, and it was my introduction to a sport that has since taken me all over the world.

THE MOST IMPORTANT THING that happened to me in high school was that I fell in love. I'd known who Lynne Vincent was since I'd arrived in Casper as a thirteen-year-old in the eighth grade. She was blonde, very smart, and very attractive, in addition to being the state champion baton twirler. I didn't summon up enough courage to ask her out until we were juniors, at the end of January 1958, just before my seventeenth birthday. She agreed to go to a formal dance with me, and after that there was no looking back.

That summer I was selected by my high school teachers to attend a five-week program for promising students at Northwestern University. One of the local service clubs raised enough money to pay for my round-trip ticket, and Dad drove me down to Rawlins to catch the Union Pacific train. I went to Northwestern with the idea that I was going to become an engineer, and while I liked the summer program, I discovered I didn't like engineering. I saw my first Chicago Cubs baseball game at Wrigley Field that summer, but my best day was when Lynne came down from Wisconsin, where she was competing in a baton-twirling competition, to spend an afternoon with me.

Our senior year was like a classic fifties movie. I was class president, Lynne was homecoming queen, and as co-captain of the football team for homecoming, I got to crown her. Everything seemed possible through that fall of football games, movie dates, and going to the Canteen, a town-sponsored teen hangout where the jukebox played the Everly Brothers, Fats Domino, and Elvis Presley. By the early months of 1959, Lynne had figured out that she would go to Colorado College in Colorado Springs. While I knew I'd go somewhere, I hadn't given a lot of thought to the details when an independent oilman in Casper, Tom Stroock, approached my friend Tom Fake and me about applying to his alma mater, Yale. Stroock thought that based on our grades, our athletic records, and the fact that we were both class officers, we'd be accepted. He said that coming from Wyoming would also help because Yale was interested in geographical diversity. Neither the Fakes nor the Cheneys could begin to pay for four years in the Ivy League, but both Tom and I were accepted and awarded scholarships that covered full tuition, room, and board. We'd have to work as part of the arrangement, but otherwise all we had to do was get ourselves there.

I'D NEVER SEEN YALE before I showed up in the fall of 1959 to begin my freshman year. In fact, I'd never been farther east than Chicago, and when I got off the train in New Haven, Connecticut, it felt a little like arriving in another country. At home in Wyoming, I had a great sense of wide-open spaces. You could see for miles in any direction. In New Haven everything was jammed together—people, buildings, trees. The most distant horizon was no farther than a few blocks away.

Many of my fellow students had gone to prep school. They had had experiences very different from mine and knew things I did not. I sometimes felt they were speaking another language—and they certainly played at least one sport I found strange. Students arriving at Yale took a series of physical tests, one of which involved going through a door so small you had to stoop over. On the other side, a fellow handed me a racquet like the one he was holding and immediately began smacking a small, hard rubber ball against the wall. I had no idea what I was supposed to do or how I was supposed to score. And that was my introduction to squash.

I was no longer a big fish in a small pond. Instead of being president of my class and hanging out in the student council office, I was waiting on my classmates in the dining hall. Most of all, I missed Lynne. I spent most of my time thinking about the next time I would see her and trying to scrape together a couple of bucks so that I could afford a long-distance call to Colorado Springs.

Plenty of scholarship students, finding themselves in a totally new environment, manage to get themselves together, apply themselves to their studies, and succeed. Instead, I found some kindred souls, young men like me, who were not adjusting very well and shared my opinion that beer was one of the essentials of life. At the beginning of our second year, twelve of us roomed together in Berkeley College, which with the benefit of hindsight I understand wasn't a great idea. We created a critical mass that led to several encounters with the dean. My parents began to get letters, one of which began, "Dick has fallen in with a group of very high-spirited young men."

I wasn't entirely unaware of Yale's intellectual attractions. One professor in particular stood out: H. Bradford Westerfield, who taught a political science course on the diplomatic history of the Cold War. It covered the foundation of NATO and the Marshall Plan, the war in Korea, the creation of post–World War II foreign policy. It was absolutely intriguing—probably more history than political science, though I didn't understand that at the time. But even though the course was fascinating, I didn't exert myself to get more than a C in it.

The university tried to motivate me by shifting the terms of my scholarship and making me financially responsible for my education. Beginning with my sophomore year, I was to consider all future financial aid as a loan. When that failed to get my attention, the dean asked me to take a year off and come back only if I was willing to pay my own way. I managed to do that for one semester, during which I continued to accumulate bad grades and disciplinary notices. In the spring of 1962, Yale and I finally parted ways.

WHEN I GOT BACK home to Wyoming in 1962, I returned to what I'd been doing off and on since high school—"working in the tools" as a union member on jobs across Wyoming, Utah, and Colorado. I helped build electrical transmission lines and coal-fired generating plants. I worked on bringing power to oil fields. One of my assignments was to work on Minuteman missile sites around Cheyenne's Francis E. Warren Air Force Base, laying communications cable between silos in the middle of a Rocky Mountain winter.

As a member of Local 322 of the International Brotherhood of Electrical Workers, I started as a groundman, or "grunt." Later, as I got more experience, I became an "equipment operator." At one point I gave serious thought to taking out my apprenticeship papers and working up to "journeyman lineman." These were the men who climbed the wood or steel towers to string power line.

The work we did was sometimes dangerous, and everyone had tales of spectacular accidents. While working on adding capacity to the Dave Johnston Power Plant outside Glenrock, I saw an equipment operator drive a truck mounted with a front-end boom close enough to a live transmission line to cause the power to arc, sending a large fireball down the line toward Casper and frying the truck. The equipment operator was frozen with fear and stayed where he was, which was a good thing. If he had tried to get out of the truck, that would have been the end of him.

On another job we were using dynamite, and after the charges were in place and the electrical blasting cap attached, I watched the crew foreman uncoil a roll of wire from the charge back to his pickup truck. He raised the hood on his pickup, leaned across the fender, and touched the wire to the truck battery to detonate the charge. The blast blew a large rock high in the air, and it came down right on top of the pickup's hood, driving it down onto the foreman and seriously injuring him. We were in the Black Canyon of the Gunnison, a rough, mountainous area in western Colorado, and it took us several hours to get him to the hospital.

Stories like these were a reminder of what happened when you weren't alert and careful. They illustrated why the spirit that prevailed in line work—cultivating competence and taking pride in your performance—was essential. If you were a groundman and you tied your knot right, the heavy crossarm you winched up to the lineman would make it to the top safely, and he'd be able to release it from the rope with ease, but if you fashioned the knot so securely that he had trouble releasing it, you complicated his job enormously, and if you didn't get the knot tight enough and a crossarm or a string of insulators fell, you could kill somebody.

The culture and lore of line work were captured in a book, *Slim,* that the crews I worked on passed around. Written by William Wister Haines in the early 1930s and later made into a movie starring Henry Fonda, *Slim* told the story of a young man who joined a line crew and learned how great it felt to do work he was good at and could take pride in, how satisfying it was to have the money he earned in his pocket. He was free to pick up and move on whenever he wanted. It was a point of pride with Slim that when he was asked for his address, he pointed to the license plate on his car.

I was earning $3.10 an hour, which was good pay in those days, and picking up a lot of overtime at time and a half. I traveled from job to job with one large suitcase, driving a 1949 Chevy for a while. When it had to be junked, I hitched a ride or caught a bus until I managed to buy a '58 Ford. Living accommodations were never fancy, usually a room in an old hotel or roadside motel. For ten or fifteen dollars a week, these places didn't offer any amenities or impose any demands. I wasn't tied down to one location or any particular job or anyone's expectations. Whenever I wanted, I could pick up and move on.

After work, the guys on the crew would spend considerable time in one of the local bars, ideally a place that would cash our checks or carry a tab until we made our first payday. We consumed vast quantities of beer. If something stronger was called for, we'd drink shots of bourbon with beer chasers—a combination that helps explain how I managed to get arrested twice within a year for driving while under the influence.

The first time was in Cheyenne, and I managed to brush it off. But the second time, in the summer of 1963 in Rock Springs, was a different matter. Many of my friends had just graduated from Yale. Lynne, after spending a semester in Europe, had graduated summa cum laude from Colorado College. And I was sleeping off a hangover in the Rock Springs jail.

It had taken a lot to drive the message home, but I realized the morning I woke up in that jail that if I didn't fundamentally change my ways, I was going to come to a bad end. As soon as I was released, I drove home to Casper. I remember spending the better part of a day on Casper Mountain, up near the top where you can see all the way to the Bighorns. It was a good place to get perspective on life and to figure out what I was going to have to do to get off the self-destructive path I was on. I talked to Lynne and my folks, and although they would have been fully justified if they'd stopped speaking to me then and there, they seemed to believe that even after all the false starts, this time I really meant it about turning my life around.

I went back to Rock Springs, to the apartment I was sharing with Tom Ready, a journeyman lineman and crew foreman, who had been drinking with me the night I was arrested. The job we were on— building a 115,000-volt line from Rock Springs to the new Flaming Gorge Dam, on the Green River—was the third we'd worked together. Tom was an interesting guy, good enough on a horse to rodeo on the weekends. I considered him a friend but told him he would have to get a new roommate. I was moving out and camping at the job site. When he asked me why, I told him I'd decided to clean up my act and go back to school in the fall. "I'm going to make something of myself," I said. "Who in the hell do you think you are?" he responded. "You're no better than the rest of us." It was the last time we spoke.

———

I MOVED OUT TO the job, where my crewmate Bob Lieberance and I had the assignment of going ahead of the other crews, drilling and dynamiting holes for the wooden structures they would follow along and build. Bob had a fascinating and complicated history. The way he told it, after he'd gotten in a scrape in Tennessee in the late 1930s, he had moved to Canada, and when the war started in Europe, he'd joined the Royal Air Force and flown missions against Hitler. After Pearl Harbor he'd transferred to the U.S. Eighth Air Force and been badly wounded on one of his missions. By the time I got to know him, he was something of a loner. For most of the year he worked as a "powder monkey," dealing with all the explosives on a site, but in the winter he would leave and hole up in the mountains.

Bob lived out at the job site, sleeping in a camper on his four-by-four truck and stowing his gear in a big wall tent he used for cooking. He considered a stray dog he'd picked up as his best friend, and he didn't have many others, but he and I got along. After I spent a night in my sleeping bag in the open, he told me I could set up a cot in his cook tent.

Except for once-a-week trips to town to buy groceries, shower, and hit the laundromat, I spent the rest of the summer out on the job and far from the bars. Bob and I would work hard all day and share the cooking at night. After dinner I began reading Churchill's six-volume history of World War II by the light of a Coleman lantern.

In the fall, I moved to Laramie and enrolled at the University of Wyoming. UW is a school with many virtues, not least of which in my day was that, regardless of my previous academic record, they had to accept me because I had graduated from a Wyoming high school. The tuition was $96 a semester, and I moved into a $45-a-month, one-bedroom furnished apartment that fronted on an alley. I saved on expenses by getting my high school classmate Joe Meyer, who was now going to law school, to sign on as a roommate. Eventually Joe would have one of the most distinguished political careers in Wyoming history, serving as attorney general, secretary of state, and state treasurer, but while we were rooming together he was best known for being one heck of a jazz clarinet player and for dating Miss Wyoming.

I got a part-time job reading to a retired air force colonel who had lost his sight. He was getting the credits he needed to become a counselor for the blind, and four nights a week I read his textbooks to him for $1.75 an hour, paid for by the Veterans Administration. I also spent a fair amount of time studying and got very good grades, almost all A's—as I would do for the rest of my years in higher education.

In late September 1963, not long after I'd started back to school, President Kennedy came to Laramie to deliver a speech at the university's War Memorial Field House. I stood among the crowd of thousands and listened to him deliver an eloquent call to public service. He talked about the Greek definition of happiness—the full use of one's powers along lines of excellence—and said that working for the public good could provide that kind of satisfaction. He talked about the importance of bringing what we were learning to the task of building a better nation and a better world. When he had finished I left the field house by a back door and saw his motorcade pulling away. He was riding in an open convertible and hundreds of students were running after him, wanting a last glimpse as he departed the campus. He had inspired us all, and at a time when I was trying to put my life back together, I was particularly grateful for the sense of elevated possibilities he described. When he was killed only two months later, the mood at the university was especially somber. Everyone remembered that he had been with us so short a time before.

DURING MY FIRST YEAR at the University of Wyoming, I spent most of my weekends in Boulder, where Lynne was working on her master's degree at the University of Colorado. At Easter we went home to tell our parents we were going to get married, and we set a date—August 29, 1964.

While Lynne and her mother worried about flowers and silver patterns, I went back to work building power line. One of the things I was saving for was the honeymoon Lynne and I were planning at Jackson Lake Lodge in Grand Teton National Park. But I came down with a terrible case of food poisoning and had to be hospitalized for a week.

I had no health insurance, so in addition to losing seventeen pounds, I spent all the money I had been saving on medical bills. We still had a nice wedding, complete with bridesmaids and groomsmen, with my little sister, Susie, as our flower girl and Lynne's brother, Mark, as the ringbearer. But our honeymoon afterward was one night in the Holiday Inn in Laramie, Wyoming.

Our first home was in a yellow, cinder-block apartment on the edge of campus. It was a real bargain at $53.65 a month furnished, but it lacked any kind of insulation—something of a drawback when the temperature dropped to 30 below. With an elevation over seven thousand feet, Laramie was known for its challenging winters. If you had a car, you had to install a head bolt heater and plug it in at night or else the engine block would freeze. Still, the natural setting was beautiful, with the Snowy Range and some good trout streams close by. When the fishing season opened, it was possible to get up early, drive up into the mountains and catch a few trout, and still make it back in time for morning classes.

As graduation neared, I decided to stay on and earn a master's degree, and it was as a graduate student that I got my first taste of politics by working as an intern in the Wyoming state legislature. Half my stipend was paid for by the National Center for Education in Politics, an organization that went back to the 1940s and a belief on the part of Judge Arthur Vanderbilt, dean of New York University School of Law, that student participation in politics should be encouraged. The other half was paid for by the Republican Party, which was then under the enlightened leadership of Stan Hathaway, who would become one of Wyoming's most popular and influential governors. I'd get up early in the morning and drive fifty miles over the pass from Laramie to Cheyenne, where the legislature met. After working all day, I'd turn around and drive the fifty miles home at night, often through some pretty brutal weather.

The legislative session lasted forty days, and it was a fascinating experience for me. The Republicans, usually dominant in Wyoming politics, were getting a lot of pushback from Democrats in the wake of the

1964 Goldwater debacle, and that made the session especially lively. The report I wrote on my internship won a Borden Award from the National Center for Education in Politics, and I received a check for one hundred dollars—an amount not to be scoffed at since that was nearly two months' rent.

One of my professors gave me an application for another program run by the NCEP. This one, which was funded by the Ford Foundation, placed political science graduate students in mayors' and governors' offices across the country. I filled out the application and pretty much forgot about it until one Sunday night in late November when Lynne and I got back from a weekend at home in Casper and I found a telegram waiting. It informed me that I had been selected for the program and was expected at an orientation in Columbus, Ohio, on Wednesday morning. I had to hustle, but I made it in time to the Stouffer's Inn where the group was gathering. I met graduate students from Yale, Columbia, Cornell, Ohio State, Ball State, and Penn State, all planning field assignments that would begin after the first of the year.

One of the most important people I met at the orientation was Maureen Drummy, assistant director of the NCEP. She would play a crucial part in my life over the next few years, and we became good friends. Maureen persuaded me that the best place for me to work would be in Madison, Wisconsin, in the office of Governor Warren Knowles. Lynne liked the idea because the main campus of the University of Wisconsin was located in Madison and had a fine English department, where she could begin work on her Ph.D. We packed up the '65 VW bug we had acquired and headed for Wisconsin through memorably cold January weather. Along about Dubuque, Iowa, the car became difficult to steer because the grease in the steering column had stiffened with cold, and we had to put the VW in the garage at a gas station to thaw it out. Despite the freezing weather, we faithfully stopped the car every few hours so that Lynne could get out and walk around, per doctor's orders. She was pregnant with our first child, Elizabeth, who would be born in Madison on a warm day at the end of July.

WARREN KNOWLES LOOKED LIKE a governor. Tall, with wavy silver hair, he had been elected in spite of the Democratic sweep of 1964. I became an all-purpose aide, traveling with him all over the state. My pockets were filled with buttons emblazoned with "We Like It Here," which was the slogan of a campaign he had initiated to promote the state. We hit all the county fairs, and my job was to follow the governor up and down the midway, handing the buttons out. I also carried a Polaroid instant camera, and I snapped pictures as we went along. When the photo slid out, I'd rip the cover paper off it and give it to the fairgoer the governor had just shaken hands with.

When I wasn't traveling with the governor, I often worked at my desk, which someone had thoughtfully put in the center of the staff office so I could see everything going on. I participated in staff meetings and learned a valuable lesson early on. I don't remember the problem we were discussing, but I do recall that I saw the answer with crystal clarity and offered it right up, using a tone of some authority, as I remember. There was silence, then the group went on talking, eventually ending up with the solution I had proposed, though it was as if I'd never offered it. As I thought about what happened, I realized that it's often better to listen than to speak, particularly if you are the junior person around. Moreover, when a group has a problem to solve, they usually need to grapple with it for a while. If you have a solution, wait until people are ready for it, and then present it in a cool and collected way that makes the answer to the problem be about the answer—and not about you.

One night when we had been in the northern part of the state, the governor gave Mel Laird a ride to Chicago on the state's official twin-engine plane. Mel was the congressman from Wisconsin's 7th District, and he would become Richard Nixon's secretary of defense during the height of the war in Vietnam. As the three of us, the governor, the congressman, and I, flew through the night, I listened to Laird warn his old friend to be very careful what he said about the war in Southeast Asia. It was 1966, and the American presence had just begun to expand. The antiwar movement had yet to gain much momentum, but Laird was concerned that the Johnson administration didn't have a coherent policy on the war and that things would get much worse before they got any better. I remember being impressed by the way Laird was looking beyond the moment, and, as it turned out, he offered good advice.

I hit it off with the governor, and when my fellowship was over, he asked me to stay on. He even offered me a paycheck. At the same time, I'd decided to begin my Ph.D. at Wisconsin. Lynne and I both wanted to be college professors, and while we looked at other places where we might both do graduate work, there were few universities where both the political science and the English departments were as good as the ones at Wisconsin. We had also applied for and received teaching and research assistantships at Madison, which, combined with my part-time salary from the governor's office, would pay our way.

Shortly after I began work on my Ph.D., I turned twenty-six and was no longer eligible for the draft. In the days when I had been, I had received deferments as a student and father. Earlier, when I was doing line work, I had been classified 1-A, but draft numbers were low and I wasn't called. If I had been, I would have been happy to serve.

MY MAJOR PROFESSOR AT Wisconsin was Aage Clausen, who was working on a study of roll call voting in the U.S. Senate and House of Representatives. The work was highly statistical, and I spent a lot of time on the university's computer, which in those days filled most of a big room, running calculations to show the various factors that played into a member's vote. Our assumption—that political behavior could be understood scientifically—was very much the trend of the time, and the *American Political Science Review,* a prestigious academic journal, published a long article we wrote about our research. Professor Clausen, a generous man, shared authorship of the paper with me.

But in 1967 many days were a reminder of a far messier politics. In October the presence on campus of recruiters from Dow Chemical Company, which made the napalm being used in Vietnam, precipitated what became known as the Dow Riot. When students blocked the entrance to the building where the recruiters had set up, the police were called in to remove them by force. In the resulting free-for-all, tear gas was fired off, and demonstrators as well as police were bloodied. Prancing through the whole chaotic scene, urging the demonstrators on, was a mime troupe from San Francisco. Lynne encountered the white-faced mimes, who were carrying animal entrails over their heads, as she tried, but failed, to get to a classroom where she was supposed to teach freshman composition.

I strongly disagreed with the protestors trying to shut down the university and portray Ho Chi Minh as a hero. As a general proposition, I supported our troops in Vietnam and the right of the Kennedy and Johnson administrations to make the decision to be involved there.

Early in 1968 I got a job offer to manage a congressional campaign. The Republicans had a candidate who needed some help running in the 2nd District against the popular five-term Democratic incumbent, and a friend in the governor's office called to see if I'd be interested. It sounded like something I'd enjoy doing, and it paid well, a thousand dollars a month as I recall. Taking the job would require delaying my preliminary exams—the comprehensive tests that had to be passed before starting a Ph.D. dissertation—but I saw no harm in that. When I approached the powers that be in the political science department, however, they were far from enthusiastic. It wasn't just that I would have to delay the prelims, one senior professor said, but that working in a campaign would send the wrong professional signal. "If you get involved in politics," he said, "you will not be taken seriously by political scientists." That gave me a lot of pause, since I was pretty sure that real-world experience would be an asset whether I was doing research or in the classroom, but what did I know about how the academic world worked?

I decided to turn down the campaign job and return to school full-time. Before long, however, another interesting opportunity presented itself, and this one had the political science department's approval. Senator Joe Tydings, a Maryland Democrat, had contacted the university about establishing a fellowship in honor of his grandfather, Joseph E. Davies, who had been born in Wisconsin and had served as FDR's ambassador to the Soviet Union. Tydings wanted to make the fellowship part of the American Political Science Association's congressional fellowship program, and the political science department suggested me as the first recipient.

Years later, after I became vice president, one of the trustees of the Davies Foundation sent me the letter of recommendation that the chairman of the political science department wrote to Tydings, which noted that I was married and the father of a two-year-old daughter and described me as "a very bright, hard-working, wholly personable, and attractive young man of twenty-seven." The chairman quoted Aage Clausen saying that I was "the most cooperative, capable, and helpful assistant" he had ever worked with. When I read that letter thirty-seven years later, what struck me most was to think that in 1963, just five years before the letter was written, I had been sitting in a jail cell with my life pretty much in ruins around me. I'd gotten a second chance, and I'd made pretty good use of it.

Senator Tydings was scheduled to come to Madison in April to speak at a rally on behalf of Bobby Kennedy, who had entered the Democratic presidential primary for president and was slugging it out with Hubert Humphrey and Gene McCarthy. I attended the rally and afterward met the senator in a bar on State Street, where we had a beer and a long conversation. He offered and I accepted the congressional fellowship that would take me to Washington, D.C., for a year.

More than thirty years later, when I was vice president, I attended a dinner at the University of Maryland where former Senator Tydings, now a trustee, was among the guests. I made a point of going over to thank him for what he had done for me all those years before. He was gracious, but seemed a little puzzled. Later he told a writer that he didn't have the slightest idea what I was thanking him for. He didn't remember our meeting on that cool spring night in Madison—although I have never forgotten it.

CHAPTER TWO

Anybody Here Named Cheney?

On a muggy Friday afternoon at the end of July 1968, I got behind the wheel of our black Volkswagen and headed south out of Madison. My goal was to drive to Washington and rent an apartment for Lynne, Liz, and me for when my American Political Science Association congressional fellowship started in September. Because I was cramming for my upcoming preliminary exams, I was determined to complete the whole process, including the 1,700-mile drive and finding and renting the apartment, over the weekend and be back studying by Monday morning.

I'd done a lot of long-distance driving and I enjoyed it. I listened to the radio as I drove through Illinois, Indiana, Ohio, Pennsylvania, and Maryland, stopping every now and then for food and gas and once to sleep for a few hours. When I finally hit Interstate 495, the Capital Beltway that surrounds Washington, I had to decide which way to go. So I turned right and continued south until I saw a sign that said "Annandale," which I thought sounded pretty good, and I exited onto Little River Turnpike, a major thoroughfare that despite housing developments and apartment buildings hadn't entirely lost its rural character. I turned into the driveway of an apartment complex—the Americana Fairfax—and found the rental office. Less than an hour later, I had signed a year's lease on an unfurnished two-bedroom apartment for $130 a month.

Before heading back to Madison, I decided to see D.C., a city I knew was still reeling from the riots and fires following the assassination of Martin Luther King, Jr., only four months earlier. Twelve people had been killed, hundreds injured, and President Johnson had called in fourteen thousand federal troops to restore order. But as I crossed over the Potomac on the Theodore Roosevelt Bridge and caught my first glimpse of Washington, the turmoil I'd seen on the evening news dissolved into the background. Off to my right were the Washington Monument and Lincoln Memorial, white and gleaming in the summer haze. They were an impressive sight, as was the White House, when I drove by it, and the Capitol, shining at the top of the hill. I did a slow loop around the Capitol building, trying to take it all in, then drove down Independence Avenue along the Mall and headed out of town. I was back in Madison for Sunday lunch.

LYNNE AND I BOTH passed our preliminary exams, putting us a step closer to our Ph.D.s, and by mid-September we were unpacking our books and papers, a few clothes, and Liz's crib in the Annandale apartment. Not long after we arrived, I had a meeting scheduled on Capitol Hill. I put on the only suit I owned, an electric blue one that had caught my eye at Jon-N-Jax Men's Shop in Laramie, kissed Lynne and Liz goodbye, and caught the bus on Little River Turnpike. Forty-five minutes later, I was downtown in front of the Old Post Office at Eleventh Street and Pennsylvania Avenue.

I was still a long way from the Capitol, but since I didn't have the slightest idea how to do a bus transfer, I decided to walk. Within a few blocks, I realized that my suit, which had been fine for winters in Wyoming and Wisconsin, didn't function so well on a sweltering September day in Washington, D.C. I was also wearing shoes made of Corfam, a kind of synthetic leather, and they began to produce a swamp-like climate zone of their own.

Half an hour and an uphill mile or so later, completely drenched, I was in Wisconsin Congressman Bill Steiger's office in the Longworth House Office Building. I was there to see his chief of staff, Maureen Drummy, whom I'd met when she worked at the National Center for Education in Politics. She was one of the few people I knew in Washington, and I'd come to seek her counsel about the congressional fellows program, which, from her vantage point in Steiger's office, she had seen in operation. Kind and generous as always, she overlooked my disheveled state and gave me her best advice. During the ten-week orientation that began the program, I'd have a chance to participate in seminars and listen to speeches by congressmen and senators. The idea was not only to look for members I might like to work for and arrange interviews with their offices, but also to figure out what they expected of fellows and to see if it matched what I wanted to do.

One of the most impressive orientation speakers was a young Republican congressman named Don Rumsfeld, from Illinois. I had never heard of him before, but I learned he had a great reputation for allowing—in fact, demanding—his fellows' participation in the work of the office. By the time he had finished speaking to us, I had decided that this was the man I wanted to intern for.

I arrived early for my interview with Rumsfeld in the Cannon House Office Building and was ushered in to meet with him exactly on time. And exactly fifteen minutes later I was ushered out. In answer to his invitation to tell him something about myself, I had talked about how I was working on my doctoral dissertation on congressional voting patterns and planned to return to the University of Wisconsin at the end of my fellowship in order to pursue a career as a professor of political science. He described the setup of his office and mentioned the need for someone who could write press releases. After a little more back-and-forth, he stood up, extended his hand, and said, "This isn't going to work, but thanks for coming in."

The next thing I knew, I was standing in the corridor outside his

office. I didn't have a swelled head, but since I had gotten my act together, I'd become a fairly good judge of what was going to work for
me and what wasn't, and this interview had ended in a pretty surprising way. Thinking back on it now, I realize I didn't have the foggiest
idea what a congressman needed, and Rumsfeld was probably right to
view me as a fuzzy-headed academic. He had sized up the situation
within the first few minutes and knew he was wasting his time. There
was nothing personal about it. I just wasn't what he was looking for.
While some people might have spent some time chatting and softening
the blow, that was not how Don Rumsfeld did things.

I wasn't feeling so magnanimous as I walked back over to Bill
Steiger's office in Longworth. I recounted my experience to Maureen
Drummy, who smiled sympathetically and then proposed the perfect
solution. She suggested I sign on with Bill Steiger when the fellowships
started in January.

WORKING FOR BILL STEIGER was a brilliant idea that had been
hiding in plain sight. I had gotten to know him while I was working for
Governor Knowles. He had been elected to the state legislature shortly
after graduating from the University of Wisconsin, and the first time
I saw him I understood the stories about the new assemblyman being
mistaken for an intern. He was young and looked younger, and he had
formidable political skills. I watched him campaign with Governor
Knowles, and seeing how he loved meeting people and what a phenom-
enal memory he had for their names and concerns, I wasn't surprised
when he was elected to the U.S. House of Representatives in 1966.
Although he was still in his first term, Bill's obvious intelligence, easy
personality, and deep integrity had already made a strong mark on his
colleagues. He was known in the APSA program for placing his fellow's
desk in his own office. The months I spent working for Bill Steiger were
the best introduction I could have possibly had to the Congress of the
United States.

Members of my family had been Democrats going back quite a
way. My grandfather Cheney had been a Democratic committeeman

in Sumner, Nebraska. My grandfather Dickey considered it a point of pride that I'd been born on FDR's birthday. But I was moving into Republican ranks, and as I did, I got a kick out of teasing my folks about it. "Sure will be sorry to see Nixon win the election," I wrote to them on October 28, 1968. "Never can tell—Humphrey might edge him out yet." But he didn't, of course. On November 5, Nixon pulled it out by half a million votes, 43.4 percent to 42.7 percent, and became the thirty-seventh president of the United States.

A few weeks later, while Lyndon Johnson was still president and Nixon was president-elect, the APSA fellows were given a special tour of the White House. After going through the public rooms of the mansion, we went over to the West Wing. This was truly hallowed ground, and I can still remember looking inside the Oval Office—the guards wouldn't allow anyone to cross the threshold—and seeing President Johnson's desk. It was in front of the windows at one end, and to the left of it was a low, white-painted console housing three TV sets so the president could watch each of the national networks' news broadcasts. There were also two news tickers, with glass tops to mute the teletype clacking and the bulletin bells, so the president could have everything fresh from the Associated Press and United Press International. These were interesting examples of modern technology, but I was most impressed by the small box with three buttons that was next to the large phone console on the president's desk. The guard explained that they were for ordering coffee, Coke, or Fresca (LBJ's favorite) for the president and his guests.

RIGHT AFTER THE NEW year, I began work in—literally in—Bill Steiger's office. With my desk right there I either monitored or participated in all his meetings and phone calls. He also included me along with his staff members at many of his committee meetings.

On January 14, 1969, President Johnson came to Capitol Hill, the site of his rise to power and so many of his triumphs, to deliver his last State of the Union message. Steiger was able to get me onto the floor of the House, and I stood at the back watching this impressive but rather melancholy ceremony unfold. The usually confident and dynamic president seemed restrained and ruminative as he spoke about what he had tried to accomplish and about how he hoped history would view him. I had the strong impression that in his mind he was already back at the LBJ Ranch in Johnson City, Texas.

A couple of days later, I was attending a meeting of the House Education and Labor Committee at which a Johnson administration official was testifying. I noticed that one part of his testimony directly contradicted something that the president had said in his speech. Bill Steiger wasn't there at the moment, so I got a copy of Johnson's text, circled the difference, and pointed it out to one of the committee staffers. He told me to show it to Al Quie of Minnesota, the ranking Republican in attendance that day. I walked up and slid it onto the desk in front of Quie. He looked up, and although he clearly had no idea who I was, he took the paper, read it, and then used it to ask the witness some very pointed questions. I savored the moment. It was the first time I had actually been engaged, in however peripheral and minor a way, in the great process that I was observing.

Of course most of the work of a congressional office is far less exciting and dramatic. One of my main assignments was Dutch elm disease, which by then had blighted much of the country, killing elm trees that had been a hallmark of the American landscape for centuries. By the late 1960s the epidemic had reached Wisconsin, and Steiger's office was deluged with letters and calls, many of which I answered.

ON APRIL 21 President Nixon nominated Don Rumsfeld to be the director of the Office of Economic Opportunity. OEO had been created by Lyndon Johnson as part of his Great Society program to provide grants and economic development aid to lower-income areas of the country. The announcement of Rumsfeld's nomination was met with skepticism and surprise. Nixon had campaigned against OEO and Rumsfeld had voted against it. It was widely thought that Nixon wanted someone to oversee the dismantling of the agency, but that was a mistaken assumption.

Rumsfeld immediately asked Steiger to join the informal brain trust he was mobilizing to help him prepare for Senate confirmation. Because of the reading and work I had been doing for Steiger for the Education and Labor Committee, I was up to speed on OEO. Over a weekend I wrote a long memo about how I thought Rumsfeld should handle his confirmation hearings and how he might organize and manage the place once he was in charge. Steiger was very complimentary about the memo and asked if I would mind if he passed it along to Rumsfeld. Of course I had no objections. Then I heard nothing more about it.

AS LYNNE AND I knew well from our time at the University of Wisconsin, American college campuses were being rocked by demonstrations. In 1969 congressmen and senators, besieged by angry constituents who wanted them to do something, began to consider proposals that would cut off federal funds to colleges and universities that didn't move against the protestors. Bill Brock, a young congressman (and future senator and cabinet member) from Tennessee, was concerned that cutting off federal funds could seriously damage American education, and he organized a group of twenty-two Republican congressmen, including Steiger, to visit campuses across the country in order to understand better what was happening. Steiger took me with him to one of the group's organizational meetings, and it was there I met George H. W. Bush of Texas, who would play a big role in my life. He was smart, personable, and a war hero, altogether a very impressive person.

Steiger was in the group that was to visit the University of Wisconsin, and I was chosen to advance the trip. I'd been at the university so recently that I was familiar with the situation in Madison. There had been protests in February in support of black students' demands for a black studies department. When police were unable to cope with the demonstrators' hit-and-run tactics, Governor Knowles sent in two thousand troops from the National Guard. Their appearance swelled the ranks of the protestors to some ten thousand. Guardsmen used tear gas and smoke bombs. Students rampaged through campus, destroying property. The protest finally abated, but not the unrest behind it, and a few weeks before the congressional visit in May 1969, students threw rocks and bottles at police trying to shut down a party on Mifflin Street. The police responded with clubs and tear gas, and it was three days before peace was restored.

On the night the congressmen arrived, Students for a Democratic Society was holding a campus rally with the controversial Black Panther firebrand Fred Hampton as the guest speaker. A friend from one of my political science classes was one of the SDS organizers, and I had asked him if he could arrange for us to attend. I can say without hesitation that we were the only people there wearing jackets and ties. We got some hostile looks and a little verbal abuse, but once we took our seats nobody paid us much attention. Everyone was too busy shouting support for the increasingly inflammatory rhetoric of the speakers leading up to the guest of honor.

Hampton turned out to be a skillful orator and a very charismatic individual. He distanced himself from the students who wanted a black studies department, declaring that revolution had to be the goal—and violence the means. He worked the crowd into a frenzy by shouting about how satisfying it was to "kill pigs" and how much more satisfying it was to kill a lot of them. I noted to myself that Hampton was fascinating to listen to—as long as you ignored the content of his message.

The congressional group interviewed students ranging from the editor of the *Daily Cardinal*, the campus newspaper, which was egging on the demonstrators, to a group called Hayakawas, who were protesting the protests and had named themselves after S. I. Hayakawa, the English professor who had famously stood up against demonstrators at San Francisco State College (San Francisco State University today). They also attended a faculty meeting that was held every week on campus. It was a gathering of senior professors, who tried to keep their meetings private and had largely succeeded. Although I had been a student at the university for three years, I'd never known about the group. When I came to campus with the visiting congressmen, the chairman of the political science department got us an invitation to sit in on one of their sessions.

They set some ground rules: We weren't allowed to ask questions or say anything; we could only observe. The faculty in the room that day had a long list of concerns—about students, about the administration, about the chaos—but no one addressed the larger context. As we met, college campuses all across the country were in an upheaval, and it was a traumatic time in American politics. Martin Luther King, Jr., and Bobby Kennedy had been assassinated the year before; the war in Vietnam was raging. We'd just lived through the Tet Offensive, the presidential election of 1968, Lyndon Johnson's decision not to run, and the election of Richard Nixon. There were many incredibly intelligent people in that room whose scholarly achievements had given the University of Wisconsin its sterling reputation. But the meeting could hardly have been further removed from the experience I was having in Washington, and I was beginning to realize that it was the political life that I preferred.

Back in D.C., the congressmen briefed the president on their campus visits and issued a public report that offered a number of ideas, including lowering the voting age to eighteen. While condemning violence on campuses, the group stood united behind the idea of "no repressive legislation," and the powers that be in Washington seemed to listen, because the move to deny federal aid died.

There were a few footnotes to our visit to the Wisconsin campus. Six months after we saw Fred Hampton at the SDS rally, he was killed in a police raid on a West Side Chicago apartment. The next summer in Madison, a van loaded with explosives blew up the Army Mathematics Research Center in Sterling Hall, where as a student I had often used the computer in off-hours when the time was cheap. The four student bombers had chosen the middle of the night, thinking that the building would be deserted, but a graduate student with a wife and three young children was there working. He was killed and three others seriously injured.

———

AFTER ONLY A COUPLE of months of working for Steiger, it was, according to APSA rules, time to begin planning for the switch to the other house and the other party. Having begun the fellowship with a Republican congressman, I would be expected to complete it with a Democratic senator. In my case, it wouldn't be just any Democratic senator, because there was a slot waiting for me in Ted Kennedy's office.

Ordinarily this half-and-half arrangement made great sense. Most fellows were assigned to a member of the staff and given the kinds of projects that could be completed in a couple of months; few had any direct contact with the boss except in an occasional staff meeting. But Steiger had kept me working closely with him from my first day on the job. I didn't want to leave such a unique position just when I was starting to get up to speed.

I had a good relationship with Bob Bates, the APSA intern assigned to Senator Kennedy's office, and I knew that he felt the same way about working there. He had been assigned to the press secretary and had been given some significant responsibilities. We had lunch and hatched a plot to make the switch on paper and show up for a day at our "new" jobs before returning to the old ones.

It took another lunch (and a couple of martinis) to convince the APSA program director that our intentions were as pure as our logic was sound. After I met briefly with Senator Kennedy, who was polite but distracted, and Bob Bates met with Steiger, each of us went back to the offices where we had started our fellowships. I never really worked for Senator Kennedy, though for the rest of my political career, I expected that any day someone was going to turn up paperwork saying that for four months I did.

DON RUMSFELD WAS SWORN in as director of OEO on May 26, 1969. That same afternoon I got a call from Frank Carlucci, who said Rumsfeld had asked him to help get OEO up and running. He wanted to know if I would be part of a task force they were setting up. I said I would be happy to be there, and the next morning I went to the OEO building at Nineteenth and M Streets, where I was welcomed by Carlucci and then joined about fifty other people jammed into a conference room.

Carlucci, who would quickly become a friend (and, years later, would be my predecessor as secretary of defense), was a compact, wiry man whom Rumsfeld had met when they were both varsity wrestlers at Princeton. Although not yet forty he'd already had a storied career in the Foreign Service, including an assignment in the Congo during which he had been stabbed. He had been on his way to a sabbatical at the Massachusetts Institute of Technology when Rumsfeld asked him to help out at OEO.

Rumsfeld came into the meeting and talked for half an hour, completely enthusiastic about OEO's starting to make a real difference in the lives of the poor. This was not a man who had been sent to dismantle the agency. As soon as he left, a young woman came in. "Is there anybody here named Cheney?" she asked. I raised my hand and she motioned me out of the room and down a couple of corridors. "Mr. Rumsfeld would like to see you," she said, opening a door and ushering me in.

Rumsfeld was seated at a desk and poring over a thick file. He didn't look up, so I had a chance to observe his office. It had windows on two sides, none of them too clean, as I remember it. There was a desk, a sofa, and a coffee table that had clearly seen better days. A couple of cans were strategically placed under dark spots on the ceiling.

Finally he looked up and pointed at me. "You, you're congressional relations," he said. "Now get the hell out of here."

Back in the corridor, it took me a minute to process what had just happened. It was harsher than my first encounter with Don Rumsfeld, but this time I had been offered a job. Accepting it would mean delaying my return to Wisconsin and the work on my Ph.D., but I told myself that it was only for a year, and I'd have a chance to be where the action was, where things were getting decided. I set out down the hall to find the congressional relations office, not realizing what a life-altering decision I was making. I didn't know I was saying goodbye to the academic world forever and signing up for a forty-year career in politics and government—but it was exactly the right call.

———

THE OEO CONGRESSIONAL RELATIONS office was small and leaderless, and although I was still a congressional fellow, I found myself working with the House and Senate in Washington as well as with governors and legislatures across the country. The state-level relationships were frequently more complicated—and far more testy—because many governors felt that OEO's reason for being was to make things difficult for them. Governors had the right to veto OEO programs, and the director of the agency had the right to overrule those vetoes. This situation guaranteed a lively and contentious time.

One morning soon after I arrived, I got an irate call from the governor's office in Juneau, Alaska, about an OEO grant that was in the works. If it went forward, I was warned, the governor would veto it and we would have a real mess on our hands. I assured the voice on the phone that I would look into the situation, and after a few calls, I found the individual in our building responsible for the grant. I asked him to bring me the package so I could study it. Half an hour later, it had been delivered by hand and was locked in my desk drawer, where I intended it to stay until I could sort things out.

A couple of days later Juneau was back on the phone. The grant, which was still locked in my desk, had just been announced, and the governor was about to hold a press conference condemning the project and proclaiming his veto. I learned that there were multiple copies of the grant package and that my request for one of them had triggered an alarm that led to the speeding up of the announcement. Thus in my first days I learned a valuable lesson about dealing with bureaucracies: There is always more than one copy.

One morning I got a call from Bill Bradley, who said that Rumsfeld had asked him to meet with me. Bradley's arrival at OEO, another example of Rumsfeld's Princeton connection, had created a minor stir. Although he was in only his second season as forward for the New York Knicks, Bradley's background as an Olympic champion and Rhodes scholar had already made him a national figure, and his interest in politics was widely known.

Rumsfeld had given Bradley the task of finding him an all-purpose assistant, a job I was certainly interested in. Since my peremptory hiring I'd had the opportunity to spend some time with Rumsfeld, and it turned out that our different personalities and temperaments actually worked well together. He was certainly a tough and demanding boss, but no tougher or more demanding of others than of himself, and that was a quality I greatly respected. Beneath the gruff exterior he was as thoughtful as he was focused, and he had developed an intensely loyal team of which I already considered myself a part.

Bradley interviewed a number of people, and at the end of that process, I had the job. Since Rumsfeld was not only OEO director, but also an assistant to the president, I now had a desk in the West Wing of the White House. There was nothing fancy about my White House office. It was more like a closet, and I shared it with Don Murdoch, another Rumsfeld assistant. But a desk in the West Wing was a prime piece of Washington real estate, and I'll confess I was pretty proud of it.

I now started each morning with Rumsfeld at the White House. While he attended the senior staff meeting, I got a head start on his day. Then we were driven over to the OEO building, where we worked until early evening. Then it was back to the White House for a few more hours before we headed home, he to what had to be Georgetown's smallest row house and I to the apartment in Annandale.

When I moved onto the federal payroll at OEO, I had to fill out a number of very comprehensive forms. One of them asked about prior arrests, and I listed my two DUI incidents in 1962 and 1963. Apparently this had raised no alarms at OEO, but when the FBI conducted the usual full field investigation for anyone who would be working in the West Wing, red flags went up.

Rumsfeld called me into his office and asked if it was true I had been arrested twice. I said I had. He asked if I had put the arrests on the original form. I said I had. He asked his secretary to bring the file in, and he studied the form closely. Then he closed the file. "Okay, that's good enough for me." There were plenty of young people with outstanding records that Rumsfeld might have turned to once he became aware of the blemishes on mine. But he stood by me, and I have never forgotten that.

IN SEPTEMBER, KENTUCKY GOVERNOR Louie Nunn vetoed renewed OEO funding for an antipoverty program in the mountainous eastern part of his state, charging corruption and claiming that federal funds were being used to entrench the local Democratic Party and the Turner family that controlled it. Nunn, a Republican governor, had been an early and strong supporter of Nixon, and the White House naturally wanted to be responsive. But the program was in the home district of Democratic congressman Carl Perkins, one of the most powerful men in Washington and chairman of the Education and Labor Committee, which authorized OEO's budget. Moreover, the Turners weren't the kind to buckle under pressure, as I learned when Rumsfeld sent me to Breathitt County to see if I could figure out what was going on.

Treva Turner Howell, whose parents had established the Turner dynasty, took me around to show me all the good works OEO was funding. At the end of the day she drove me back to her house, sat me down at the kitchen table, and poured us both stiff bourbons. With great charm and even more insistence, she restated her case, reminded me of Chairman Perkins's interest in her work, and indicated that as far as corruption was concerned, she had the goods on Louie Nunn.

OEO funds were, without doubt, strengthening the political hold of Breathitt County's Democratic machine, headed by Jeff Davis Howell, Treva's husband, and while it could be argued that this was improper, my job was to find out whether it was illegal. When I got back to Washington and Rumsfeld wanted to know whether the program was corrupt, my answer was: possibly, but there doesn't seem to be enough evidence to charge illegality. That was enough for him. He overrode Governor Nunn's veto.

Louie Nunn went through the roof, and Rumsfeld found himself in a meeting with Nixon's domestic policy chief, John Ehrlichman, who had taken Nunn's call. Ehrlichman conveyed the governor's particular unhappiness that some interloper named Cheney had undercut his au-

thority, and he suggested sending a White House team to investigate, a
step Rumsfeld argued against. Because the basic question was whether
the operation was illegal, Rumsfeld suggested sending the FBI. I was
not surprised when I heard that the FBI reached the same conclusion I
had, and the veto override stood.

ON APRIL 30, 1970, President Nixon announced that he was sending
troops into Cambodia, where the North Vietnamese had been stock-
piling ammunition and staging troops for the war in South Vietnam.
Shortly after that, on May 4, Ohio National Guardsmen, sent into Kent
State University after protestors burned down the ROTC building, shot
and killed four students and wounded others. A hundred thousand protestors, mostly students, descended on Washington, causing enough apprehension that the Secret Service arranged to ring the White House
complex with D.C. Transit buses parked so closely together that no one
could squeeze between them. Someone decided that it would be a good
idea if some young White House staffers could be found to go out beyond the wall of buses, talk to some of the demonstrators, and judge
their mood.

And so it was on a mild May afternoon that Rumsfeld and I, our
jackets and ties left in the West Wing, walked the few blocks to the
National Mall. We had a few intense discussions with protestors along
the way, but this was not a threatening crowd. As we got close to the
long Reflecting Pool, we noticed a commotion, as though someone had
fallen in. On closer inspection we could see that a few young women,
naked from the waist up, were cavorting in the shallow water and being
cheered on by a fast-growing audience.

We soon realized that one of the cavorters worked for us at OEO.
We had inherited her as a photographer in the press office, and she
had made an impression as a free spirit even before the day she photo-
graphed the ceremony in which Rumsfeld awarded a grant to the Navajo
Tribal Council. She arrived dressed head to toe as a Native American in
a costume straight out of a thirties Hollywood western, complete with a
fringed beaded dress and feathers in her hair.

Now here she was, topless in the Reflecting Pool. In those days, there were free spirits everywhere, it seemed, even in a bureaucracy like the OEO.

IN SEPTEMBER 1970 Gamal Abdel Nasser, the president of Egypt, died of a heart attack while hosting a summit of the Arab League. President Nixon appointed an official delegation to his funeral that included Rumsfeld, Secretary of Health, Education and Welfare Elliot Richardson, veteran diplomat Robert Murphy, and the distinguished lawyer and banker John McCloy.

Rumsfeld called and asked if I would like to accompany him as his staff member. I'd have to pack a bag and get out to Andrews Air Force Base, which was easy to do, but the fact that I didn't have a passport was a bit of a problem. The solution was to get a letter on State Department letterhead signed by the country director for Egypt. Dated September 30, 1970, it certified that I was an employee of the U.S. government and that I'd been born in Lincoln, Nebraska. It also said I was "the bearer of Office of Economic Opportunity Identification card No. 6427, which bears a photograph." I folded the letter neatly and tucked it inside my coat pocket, not sure it would work if put to the test, but more than willing to take the risk.

This was my first time ever outside the United States. Stepping off a plane with "United States of America" written on the side at the Cairo airport and then driving into the crowded streets of this ancient city was unlike anything I had ever experienced. Teeming with people in normal times, Cairo was packed to overflowing with mourners who had arrived from all over the country for the funeral. We stayed in a top-floor suite at Shepheard's Hotel on the banks of the Nile, and after the principals in our party left to participate in official ceremonies, the other staffers and I gathered on the balcony. A helicopter flew overhead, carrying Nasser's body to the headquarters of his Revolutionary Command Council on Gezira Island in the middle of the river. As the helicopter passed there was a wave of noise, a wall of high-pitched trilling coming from the crowd such as I had never heard before. By the time the body was placed on a caisson and the funeral cortege started across the Qasr al Nil Bridge, the police had lost all control of the mourning crowd. We watched people surging toward the coffin, mad with grief. Later we learned that many had been killed.

I also learned later that Rumsfeld had been down in the crowd. Ignoring all official warnings, he had followed the coffin carrying Nasser's body across the bridge. He made it back to Shepheard's, none the worse for wear, and the next evening our group drove out to the Mena House hotel. Rumsfeld, Elliot Richardson, and I rented camels, and wearing our dark business suits, rode out to the pyramids.

The plane ride home turned out to be just as memorable as those few days in Egypt. I got a chance to spend several hours listening to Robert Murphy and John McCloy talk and reminisce, and I realized that I was hearing history. Murphy had been an ambassador in many key posts, and he had known Nasser well. His memories, his insights, and his thoughts about how this death would impact American relations across the Middle East were fascinating. McCloy, who had been assistant secretary of war during World War II, had helped shape the postwar world as president of the World Bank and U.S. high commissioner in Germany. He was one of the "Wise Men," the storied handful of advisors whose counsel was sought by presidents from Truman through Nixon.

Between the two of them, they had about a hundred years of diplomatic and military history and experience. Murphy described being in the room when General Omar Bradley called to fire General George Patton and relieve him of his command of the Third Army. McCloy talked about his time in the horse cavalry in the days before World War I. Listening to them was like having the history book you're reading come to life and tell you its story.

IN DECEMBER 1970 RUMSFELD turned over the reins to Frank Carlucci and left OEO. In his nineteen months there, he had imposed management criteria and intellectual standards, ending programs that were failing and encouraging those that showed promise with the idea of eventually spinning them off. He kept the agency going and succeeded in getting it reauthorized, while he and the team around him tried mightily to carry out the president's charge "to ask new questions and find new answers." One of the ideas the agency tried to nurture was for school vouchers that would introduce an element of competition into education. The fierce opposition from the teachers' unions at the idea that we would even test such a program was instructive. People with entrenched interests often like the status quo. You can find good ideas but not necessarily be able to implement them.

At OEO I also learned about the unintended consequences of government intervention in the marketplace. I remember, for example, one OEO proposal that promised to help migrant workers by moving them from Florida to South Carolina and teaching them to grow azaleas. It sounded great until someone asked how many azalea growers there already were in South Carolina and how many azalea growers South Carolina could realistically support. The answer was that the market was already operating efficiently and at full capacity. The proposed plan could have wiped out the entire azalea industry in the state.

We had more success with a program in Alaska that Rumsfeld and I inspected personally. We flew in a chartered Aero Commander, a twin-engine plane, to the village of Tanana, on the Yukon River, where native Alaskans had abundant salmon catches but no markets. With a grant from OEO, the fishermen of Tanana and several other villages were able to take advantage of a growing demand for salmon in Japan, delivering their catches to a factory ship, where the fish were quick-frozen and then shipped.

As our twin-engine plane took off from the gravel strip at Tanana, there was a loud bang, and we found ourselves without the engine on the left wing. Our pilot, a fellow in his twenties, didn't want to try for Nome, where we were supposed to spend the night, but he was sure we could make it to Kotzebue, above the Arctic Circle. I've had many a hairy plane ride since, but our one-engine flight that day over miles of Alaskan wilderness still stands out in my memory.

———

ONCE RUMSFELD LEFT OEO, we spent all day at the White House, where he was being tapped for domestic policy advice and used as a troubleshooter on specific projects. My life was somewhat more orderly, but I still missed dinner at home most nights, including on one particularly memorable evening, when Lynne had arranged a celebration for my thirtieth birthday. Although OEO was in the past, a crisis there on January 30, 1971, over the legal services program in California, drew me back in and delayed most of the guests whom Lynne had invited. People who were supposed to arrive at 7:00 p.m. began dribbling in around 10:30 p.m. Lynne responded to the mass tardiness by publicly declaring that her days as a Washington hostess were definitely over. It was a line that got a lot of laughs, since, as our friends knew well, she did not place hostessing high on her list of priorities.

Lynne had nearly finished her dissertation, an accomplishment that reflected her incredible drive and focus. Our family had grown. Mary Claire was born on March 14, 1969, and, like her sister, she was good-natured, beautiful, and smart. But now we had two young children and I was working long hours. Especially during these early years, I operated on the assumption that the more time you put in, the better you were doing in meeting your responsibilities and achieving your potential. I hadn't figured out it was important to pace yourself and accept that sometimes less produces more.

My being gone so much wasn't ideal, but as Lynne and I discussed our options, we both had the attitude "Who could walk away from something like this?" I was having a heck of a good time, and I did what I could to bring Lynne into the experience. Many nights when I got home late, we'd stay up for hours as I recounted my tales from the day.

I also tried to keep Sundays clear. I didn't always succeed, but when I did I'd combine giving Lynne a break with spending time with my daughters. I'd take them for daylong outings, frequently to Civil War battlefields and once or twice to reenactments. We lived in an area rich with history, and we went to Antietam, Manassas, Gettysburg, Chancellorsville, Fredericksburg, and Harpers Ferry. After we'd been at this awhile, Liz and Mary started greeting Sundays by groaning, "Daddy, do we have to do another battlefield?" But the lesson stuck. Today they are both avid readers of history and have even been known to take their own children to visit the Civil War sites.

After Mary was born our Annandale apartment became too cramped, and we rented a town house nearby in Falls Church. One night, when I came home late after having been on a trip, I stumbled over something lying on the floor in the hall. It was a puppy that Lynne had acquired while I was gone, a long-nosed basset hound, whom she named Cyrano.

From that first encounter, when I woke him up by stepping on him, Cyrano and I became close friends. We have had several great dogs since, and as I write this, our labs Jackson and Nelson are keeping me company, but I think that Cyrano and I had a special understanding. I took him along when the girls and I went on our Civil War excursions. He'd stick his head out the car window, ears flapping in the wind, and when we got to where we were going, he, unlike my other companions, would jump out of the Volkswagen, totally enthusiastic about tramping around the countryside.

WITH THE 1972 PRESIDENTIAL election now less than two years away, I began to do a little work on some campaign-related projects, mostly with Bart Porter, who, along with Jeb Magruder, had moved from the White House staff to the Nixon reelection committee. The campaign's strategy was to keep the president above the fray while others blanketed the country making his case and singing his praises. Porter asked for my help setting up the recruitment and scheduling of these presidential surrogates, who would include Republican congressional leaders, cabinet officers, and administration officials.

I enjoyed the world of elective politics, and it was interesting to work with so many different people. Our roster of political surrogates read like a Who's Who of heavy hitters. Our ranks of celebrities, however, were somewhat thinner. While the McGovern campaign was working with Paul Newman, Warren Beatty, Julie Christie, Shirley MacLaine, Carole King, Barbra Streisand, James Taylor, and Quincy Jones, we were scheduling immensely talented but lesser-known luminaries such as Buddy Ebsen, Chad Everett, and Ruta Lee.

As the reelection operation began moving into higher gear, I had conversations with Porter about the possibility of my moving over to the campaign. It was an interesting idea. The campaign was clearly going to be where all the action was for the next year.

About this time the president announced a plan to fight inflation and named Rumsfeld to run the Cost of Living Council, the organization that would be in charge. When Rumsfeld asked me to go with him as an assistant director, he emphasized that the decision was mine to make and that he would fully understand if I chose to work with the campaign.

I sometimes think about how different things would have been if I hadn't gone with him to the Cost of Living Council. Although the Committee to Re-Elect the President raised unprecedented amounts of money and delivered a landslide, it was a troubled and troubling place. All that money turned out to be the root of many evils, and both Porter and Magruder ended up serving prison sentences. None of this touched the surrogate and scheduling operations, but within a few years, association with the CRP would be an albatross on anyone's résumé.

RICHARD NIXON'S REELECTION WAS far from a sure thing. It looked very much as though the war in Vietnam, which he had said when he was campaigning in 1968 he knew how to end, would be an issue again in 1972. Meanwhile, the hefty bills for Lyndon Johnson's determination to fight the war in Vietnam and fund his Great Society at home had come due. The inflation rate that had hovered comfortably around 1.5 percent at the beginning of the 1960s had climbed to 5 percent. The unemployment rate had nearly doubled to 6 percent.

The Democratic majority in Congress was urging the president to use powers they had given him when they passed the Economic Stabilization Act, legislation that effectively authorized him to commandeer the economy by imposing controls on wages, prices, salaries, and rents. The Democrats voted these extraordinary powers confident that no Republican president, much less a solid free market one named Richard Nixon, would ever use them, and in the meantime, they could criticize him for not taking action. But Nixon took them up on their offer, and on Sunday night, August 15, 1971, he announced a freeze for ninety days on all wages and prices. The Cost of Living Council was created to monitor the freeze and to achieve an orderly return to the free market when the ninety-day period was over.

The freeze was simple enough. Nobody was to raise wages or prices. But the follow-on, which became known as Phase Two, would have to have rules covering all sorts of things, from permitted increases in union contracts to the price of dill pickles, for the period until market forces ruled again. The deadline for moving from the freeze to Phase Two came fast, and the two entities that were supposed to write the regulations, the Pay Board and the Price Commission, wrangled and dithered. When it looked as though they were going to miss a crucial deadline for getting regulations published in the *Federal Register,* Rumsfeld decided to take things in hand. He assembled Jack Grayson, the chairman of the Price Commission, and about a dozen of our CLC staff and said that we wouldn't be leaving until we had the regulations ready for the printer. We set up in Rumsfeld's outer office, and as others paced and dictated, I sat at one of the secretary's desks and typed everything on an IBM Selectric typewriter. By nine the next morning, when the secretaries arrived and emptied the ashtrays and replenished the coffee, we had written the regulations that would now be governing a major share of the U.S. economy. The degree of detail we achieved during our overnighter was truly impressive. We drew distinctions between apples and applesauce; popped and unpopped corn; raw cabbage and packaged slaw; fresh oranges and glazed citrus peel; garden plants, cut flowers, and floral wreaths. We regulated seafood products "including those which have been shelled, shucked, iced, skinned, scaled, eviscerated, or decapitated." We covered products custom-made to individual order, including leather goods, fur apparel, jewelry, and wigs and toupees.

REGULATING ENERGY PRICES WAS one of the most complex and complicated tasks the CLC had to address. At one point, when we were up against a deadline to set prices for the coming week on oil, we discovered that there was no one available with expertise in that area. Then someone mentioned that Chachi Owens was from Texas and that Texas had a lot of oil, so we called Chachi and asked him to stop by. At that time he was working for the public affairs office. If the CLC was going to permit the price of bread to rise by two cents the following week, it was Chachi Owens who would bring you that news.

Aside from his resonant voice, his claim to fame was that he had played fullback for Darrell Royal at the University of Texas. He turned out to be a very bright young man. Perhaps it was his Texas confidence, or perhaps it was the result of the coaching he'd received, but he had no hesitation about sitting down and writing the oil regs we needed.

As assistant director for operations, I oversaw some three thousand IRS agents tasked with enforcing wage and price controls. At one point I sent a team of them to visit the major food chains, such as Safeway and Giant, and report on how they were complying with our regulations. The agents reported back that, depending on how a single regulation was applied, any one of several different prices might result, from one high enough to give the chain a significant profit to one low enough to cause a terrible loss. It was pretty clear which option the chains would pick—and who could blame them? They were dealing rationally with the arbitrary rules we were trying to impose.

As a junior staffer in the White House, I didn't see that much of the president, but occasionally I attended meetings at which he presided, usually so I could flip charts as Rumsfeld made a presentation. One day at a meeting in the Cabinet Room, I sat in one of the chairs lining the wall as the president's economic advisors debated reimposing a freeze on food prices. After letting the discussion continue for a while, Nixon finally spoke. He recalled a conversation he had had with Nikita Khrushchev at the Soviet premier's dacha back in 1959. After a long lunch, Khrushchev became expansive. He said that sometimes in order to be a statesman, you have to be a politician. If the public sees an imaginary river in front of them, the politician doesn't tell them there's no river. A politician builds an imaginary bridge over the imaginary river. Nixon told the story as though there was guidance to be found in it, and I took his point to be that if the public thought food prices were a problem, the politician should offer a solution, thereby preserving his ability to make statesmanlike decisions another day.

A year after I heard President Nixon tell the Khrushchev story, he imposed another price freeze, apparently hoping in the midst of Watergate for some political benefit. But he didn't get it. Among other things, the freeze made raising animals for market unprofitable. A Texas hatchery drowned forty-three thousand baby chicks. Pigs and cows were slaughtered—and the president announced an early end to his 1973 effort to freeze prices.

By this time I had grown wary of government economic control. At the start of my tenure at the Cost of Living Council, when I had been immersed in getting things going, I hadn't had much time to think about it, but by now I realized that every day millions of people were making millions of economic decisions, and it didn't matter how smart we were or how many regulations we wrote. There wasn't any way we could intervene without doing more harm than good.

These thoughts confirmed my innate skepticism about what government could and couldn't do. We could write checks, and we could collect taxes. We could run the whole military and defense side of things. But when something as big and ham-handed as the federal government tries to run something as complex and dynamic as the American economy, the result is sure to be a train wreck.

AT CLC RUMSFELD CONTINUED his usual pace, in early, out late, and cramming more into his average day than many manage in a busy week. And he was sending out hundreds of small notes, requests for information or demands for action that were so numerous we called them "snowflakes." His secretary, Brenda Williams, would type them up in memo form for forwarding to the relevant departments or individuals. Lest the whole place be overwhelmed, however, she would bring the snowflake memos to me first, so I could try to put them in some kind of realistic priority, based on my knowledge of what Rumsfeld really wanted and needed. I would decide which ones should be sent and which could probably be safely ignored. Brenda kept copies of both in separate files.

One morning my direct line from Rumsfeld rang. "Get down here now," he said. When I rushed in, Brenda was already there. Rumsfeld was looking at two substantial piles of paper on his desk. I could see that they were the carbon copies of the snowflakes and I could figure out what the two piles represented—what we'd sent and what we hadn't.

After a moment of silence, he said calmly, "I just want you to know that I know what you're doing." That was it. And that was all. We were dismissed and we returned sheepishly to our desks—and continued exactly as before. But we had shared what I think of as a classic Don Rumsfeld moment. He had somehow figured out what we were doing. He didn't say that we had been wrong. And he didn't tell us not to do it anymore. But he wanted us to know that he knew. So he told us and let us draw our own conclusions.

ON JUNE 12, 1972, George Shultz, who had been director of the Office of Management and Budget, was sworn in as secretary of the Treasury. On his first day in his new office, Secretary Shultz scheduled a meeting with the CLC senior staff. He closed the door, sat down, and said, "Okay, gentlemen, the first thing we're going to do is get out of these controls."

And that is what we did. We put together a strategy for moving into Phase Three (which would depend on voluntary self-restraint by business and labor regarding increases in prices and wages), and, finally, into Phase Four (which was intended to complete the return to the free market). Rumsfeld and I left the Cost of Living Council before these strategies were fully implemented. Others would oversee the process by which a massive interference with the American economy ended nearly three years after it had begun. Or mostly ended. In the oil industry, the price controls that went on in 1971 didn't come off until President Reagan removed them in 1981. For nearly a decade, price controls on oil and gas acted as a disincentive to achieving the fuel efficiency that we finally came to recognize as crucial.

———

ON NOVEMBER 7, 1972, Richard Nixon was reelected in one of the biggest victories in presidential history. Lynne and I stood near the front of the crowd that gathered to celebrate his victory in the ballroom of the Shoreham Hotel. People were excited—at least until the president took the stage. He was subdued, not at all like a man who had just been reelected to the presidency with forty-nine out of fifty states. It was almost as though he were anticipating the scandal and tragedy that would soon engulf his administration.

Over the last several months in the White House and during the campaign, Rumsfeld had become increasingly disenchanted with the president and his senior staff; and, at least on the part of the senior staff, I think the feeling had been reciprocated. If they saw him as a non–team player, he saw them as out of touch and riding for a fall. He turned down the domestic positions they offered him, including head of the Republican Party, and accepted an appointment as ambassador to NATO, which was headquartered in Belgium.

Rumsfeld asked me if I would like to go to Brussels with him, but it didn't seem right for me and my family, and I had another opportunity. A group of friends, Alan Woods, Bruce Bradley, Tony Brush, and Paul Ripp, had set up an investment advisory business in Washington. Alan was getting ready to leave, and I was asked to join the firm as a partner. At Bradley Woods we gave political and policy advice to clients, which were mostly big banks, insurance companies, and mutual funds. We deciphered legislation and explained how it might impact portfolios and investment strategies. Having been a behind-the-scenes man for so long, I found that I actually enjoyed getting up in front of groups and talking about what I knew and thought and answering questions.

I quickly got used to relatively normal working days, having weekends off, and moving beyond a government salary. Lynne and I bought our first house, a three-bedroom in Bethesda, Maryland, with a fenced-in yard for the kids and the dog.

LIKE EVERYONE ELSE, I was first surprised and then appalled as the details of the Watergate scandal reached critical mass in the spring of

1973. I had known some of the people involved. I had attended meetings with them and eaten lunch with them at the round staff table in the White House Mess.

I had very few direct dealings with Haldeman or Ehrlichman on a daily basis when I was working for Rumsfeld. But one incident was perhaps emblematic of the attitude that led to some of the problems. In February 1970, Rumsfeld took a few days to go skiing with his family in Colorado. When an urgent meeting was scheduled in Washington, we decided that I would ride out on the military plane that was going to pick him up, so that I could bring all the necessary documents and briefings and we could work together on the flight back to D.C. Then I got a call asking if I would mind leaving early enough to make a detour to deliver an important package to Ehrlichman, who was skiing in Sun Valley, Idaho.

A White House car picked me up at home and brought me to the West Wing, where the package—a securely taped manila envelope— was waiting. We continued on to Andrews Air Force Base, where I boarded a small government jet. When we landed in Idaho, a car sped out on the tarmac. Two armed MPs emerged and boarded the plane. One introduced himself as the courier who would deliver the package to Ehrlichman. I handed it to him and figured that my assignment was now completed.

"Sir, do you know what the contents are?" he asked. I told him that I didn't know. He asked if I minded whether he opened it, and I told him to go ahead if he thought it was important. He slit the tape, opened the flap, and removed copies of the most recent issues of *Time, Newsweek,* and *U.S. News & World Report.* I hid my dismay as the MPs carefully put the magazines back in the envelope, saluted, and disembarked. Rumsfeld ran such an obsessively frugal and ethical operation that I could hardly believe someone would send a government plane eight hundred miles out of the way to deliver magazines. I later wondered if this episode didn't reveal some of the arrogance that led to Watergate.

FROM THE OPENING OF the Senate Watergate committee hearings in May 1973 until the House Judiciary Committee voted out three articles of impeachment in July 1974, the flow of stories and leaks and charges went on day after day, week after week, month after month. The scandal unfolded like a novel, with one stunning revelation after another, most of them coming by way of the *Washington Post*. Many mornings Lynne and I didn't want to wait for the newspaper to be delivered to our door, so one of us would leave our Bethesda house in the predawn hours and walk to a nearby street corner, where a delivery truck dropped off bundles of the *Post*. We'd extract a copy, leave a note for the paper boy telling him not to deliver us another one, and then head home to read about the unraveling of the Nixon administration. It was a sad and amazing spectacle, and as I watched the story unwind, I felt a sense of relief in being away from the whole thing.

Deciding to get out of government when Don Rumsfeld departed for Brussels was turning out to be one of my wiser choices in life. I had no idea that I was soon to be drawn back in.

A phone call was my first indication. It came on August 8, after I'd had dinner at the northwest Washington home of our friends Bill and Janet Walker. My family was in Wyoming, so the Walkers had invited me over, and we watched President Nixon announce that he would resign the next day. When I got back to my empty house in Bethesda, the phone was ringing. It was Lee Goodell, Don's assistant, telling me that Don had been asked to come back to Washington by Vice President Gerald Ford. Would I meet his flight, she asked?

The next day I watched President Nixon's farewell address on a television set in my H Street office. I watched the Fords walk him out to the helicopter and saw Gerald Ford sworn in at noon. Then I headed for Dulles International Airport, where Rumsfeld's plane would soon be landing.

———◄◦►———

CHAPTER THREE

Backseat

While I waited for Rumsfeld's flight, I was joined by a White House driver carrying a message for Don. The new president wanted Rumsfeld to head up his transition team. As we left the airport and headed for D.C. in the White House car, Don showed me the message and asked me if I would take a few weeks off from my job to help him out. It wasn't a question I had to think twice about. A president had just resigned under the most extraordinary circumstances, another had been sworn in, and I had a chance to assist in the changeover.

As we drove into the White House complex through the southwest gate, I couldn't help but think with amazement that I had left government eighteen months ago, and now here I was right back in it. I was fully aware that the fact that I had left before Watergate erupted was one of the reasons I was here, and the same was true of Don. He and I had one other advantage. We were both young and foolish enough to think there wasn't anything we couldn't do.

The transition office was in the basement of the Old Executive

Office Building, and I spent the next ten days there, writing and reviewing sections of the transition report. I wasn't senior enough to be in the meetings with the president, but the orders I got secondhand were unequivocal and unmistakable: We were to stick to organizational and domestic matters. President Ford didn't want any recommendations for changing foreign policy. He believed that continuity there was essential. Indeed, on the night before he became president, he had stepped outside his house in Virginia to announce that Secretary of State and National Security Advisor Henry Kissinger would be staying on.

Perhaps the new president's most pressing decision involved the selection of his vice president—and that was also to be outside the purview of the transition committee. Bryce Harlow, an old Washington hand trusted by all, was instrumental in the process. Harlow prepared a tally sheet on a yellow legal pad, listing all the possible vice presidential choices down one side and their qualifications on the other. Ford later told me that his choice had really come down to three individuals: Nelson Rockefeller, George H. W. Bush, and Don Rumsfeld.

Ford said he viewed Bush and Rumsfeld as the future of the party, and Rockefeller as the establishment candidate. He went with Rockefeller, in large part because the unique circumstances of Ford's sudden accession to the presidency called for a vice president who needed no introduction to the world.

On the evening of August 19, 1974, Don happened to be at our house in Bethesda. We listened to the kitchen radio as news reports described the unfolding scene at Rockefeller's New York estate, where aides and family members were gathering. A fleet of sedans was lined up, and Rockefeller family jets stood by ready to fly the whole entourage to Washington. Don laughed at the superior resources Rockefeller brought to the competition. "Here's Nelson Rockefeller with planeloads of people flying down from New York," he said, "and all I've got is you, Cheney."

Shortly after the Rockefeller announcement, the transition team presented its report to the president. Rumsfeld and I went our separate ways, he back to his NATO post in Brussels and I back to Bradley

Woods. Thus, like most of America, I was surprised a few weeks later when on September 8 President Ford announced that he was granting a "full, free, and absolute pardon" to Richard Nixon. He described his action as a way to "shut and seal" the matter of Watergate and to mitigate the suffering of Richard Nixon and his family.

All these years later, the wisdom and generosity of Gerald Ford's instincts have been recognized for their courage and honored for their rightness. But at the time the pardon was controversial and unpopular. I was among the majority of Americans who thought then that it was a mistake. While I was prepared to believe that it might be justified eventually, I was sure that it would cost Ford too much of his support in the near term.

The immediate result was indeed a firestorm of controversy and criticism. According to a Gallup poll, Ford's approval rating dropped from 71 percent to 49 percent. The press corps declared the pardon indefensible. They condemned the president and lionized their former colleague Jerald terHorst, whom Ford had just named as the White House press secretary. When terHorst was informed about the pardon, he resigned in protest just as the president was about to go on camera. Across the country people who had been relieved by Ford's becoming president turned negative. There were widespread rumors about a secret deal, with Ford being elevated to the presidency in return for promising to pardon his predecessor. News of all this was accompanied by stories of bitter turmoil and conflict between Nixon and Ford people in the White House—at least some of which were true.

In addition to the negative impact on the president's own approval rating, the pardon clearly hurt us in the 1974 elections, which followed less than two months after the pardon was issued. Many commentators believe it ultimately cost Ford reelection. The impact of the pardon was intensified by the fact that it was a total surprise to everyone. Ford announced it on a Sunday morning at a time when not many people were watching television, so few Americans heard his explanation directly. Additionally, the announcement was made without any notification to the Congress or discussion in the press. I always believed that the negative impact could have been lessened if more thought had been given to how the pardon was announced.

While I was unfortunately accurate in my assessment of the negative political impact, I was wrong about the wisdom of the pardon itself. It was clearly the right decision, and over the next few years in the White House, I was thankful that Watergate was behind us rather than hanging over our heads with a former president facing trial.

A week or so after the pardon, I was in Florida on a business trip when I got a call from Rumsfeld. Once again the president had asked him to come back from Europe, and once again he wanted to meet with me before he went to the White House. On Saturday night, September 21, we met in his room at the Key Bridge Marriott, just across the Potomac River from Georgetown, and he said he believed President Ford was going to ask him to be White House chief of staff. If he took the post—and given the serious disarray at 1600 Pennsylvania Avenue, that was a big if—he wanted to know whether I would agree to sign on with him. I said I would. When he called me the next morning, he had accepted the job and asked me to be his deputy.

A week later, on Sunday, September 29, I met President Ford for the first time. Rumsfeld had a meeting at the White House, so I went with him to look around the chief of staff's West Wing suite in preparation for moving in. I remember being particularly fascinated with the desk that Nixon's chief of staff, Bob Haldeman, had designed especially to meet his needs. It was enormous, covering an entire wall, and it was an electronic masterpiece that included the ability to record office conversations. The phones were all equipped with "cutout" buttons that permitted a secretary or an aide to pick up an extension and listen in without the outside party hearing any telltale clicks.

When Don came back from his meeting in the Oval Office, he brought the president with him. Ford was extremely pleasant and gracious, which I knew took some effort because he was clearly preoccupied with the condition of his wife, Betty, who had undergone surgery for breast cancer the day before. What I remember most about that first encounter was how quickly and completely Jerry Ford accepted me. I was thirty-three years old, just six years out of graduate school, with a résumé that wouldn't necessarily rise to the top of anyone's pile. All I really had going for me was the good opinion of Don Rumsfeld. And suddenly I had the confidence of the president of the United States. At the time I felt very lucky and grateful to them both, and the feeling has never changed.

When Don and I started work on Monday morning, it was clear that the task at hand was enormous. We made a preliminary decision not to get bogged down in any of the projects that were already under way or any of the turf wars or personnel problems that were beginning to reach critical mass in the West Wing. Our job was to concentrate on laying the groundwork for future efforts by reorganizing and staffing the White House. It was obvious that many of the carryover Nixon people needed to go so that we could put a fresh face on the new administration.

Jerry Ford was very different from Richard Nixon—to put it mildly—and it was important that the administration reflect the man it served. At the same time it was important not to be indiscriminate, unfair, or vindictive. Nixon had attracted many able and exceptional men and women, and it would be unfair to them and a disservice to the country to make them suffer from guilt by association. One of them, speechwriter and communications expert Pat Buchanan, chose to quit, and we were sorry to lose him. Others like Red Cavaney, Jerry Jones, and Terry O'Donnell agreed to stay on in key posts. The point was to make decisions on individuals and on the merits. After all, if everyone who had worked for Nixon were to be automatically terminated, Don and I would have to be among the first to go.

We knew that many of the new people coming on with Ford had little or no experience in the executive branch, and we didn't think that on-the-job training in the White House was a good idea. One of the bright exceptions was Jack Marsh, whom Ford had named counselor to the president, with cabinet rank. Jack had served in Congress for eight years as a Democratic representative from Virginia. Nixon had appointed him assistant secretary of defense for legislative affairs, and when Ford was named vice president, he brought Jack on board as his national security advisor. In the Ford White House, Jack would take on many difficult assignments and handle them all with skill. He was a pillar of strength for the president—and for me.

But for the most part, the new people were green. And being green in Washington—as I had discovered when I thought I had solved the Alaska OEO grant problem by locking the paperwork up in my desk—can create problems. The mechanism, for example, by which material and memos were circulated for comment and review before going to the president was still entirely in the hands of Nixon holdovers. The new Ford staffers, many of whom were still isolated across the street from the White House in the Old Executive Office Building, didn't even realize that they were out of the information loop.

One obstacle to bringing order to the White House in the early months was President Ford's preferred model of White House organization, a design he described as the "spokes of the wheel" model, which was based on the way he had structured his congressional and committee staffs. The idea was to have eight or nine senior advisors each reporting directly to him, without any one having authority over the rest. It was a collegial style of doing business that had served him well for twenty-five years on the Hill as a representative from Michigan, and he assumed it would work in the White House. There was also a widespread belief that Watergate had been caused in part by Bob Haldeman's domination of the White House staff, and Ford saw "spokes of the wheel" as a healthy break from the past. The problem was that it soon became clear it didn't work. It took a while, but the president finally agreed that he needed someone on the staff who could wield real authority, a conclusion that all his successors have ratified.

In the last days of the Ford administration, among the gifts given me by my staff was a bicycle wheel with all the spokes destroyed except one, and it came with a plaque: "The 'spokes of the wheel,' a rare form of management artistry as devised by Gerald Ford and modified by Dick Cheney." When the Carter people came in, I passed it along to my successor, Hamilton Jordan.

My desk in the West Wing was a cubbyhole outside Don's office, nothing to impress visitors, but I didn't have time to worry about that. Don was the toughest boss I'd ever had—or ever would have. He demanded a high level of performance, and if you came through, your reward was more work. He expected loyalty, but he also knew it is a two-way street. And you could count on his word. Don had assured me when I accepted the job as his deputy that he would do everything he could to give me a real piece of the action, to see that I had regular access to the president, and to share as much as possible his own responsibilities. And that's exactly the way it worked out. From the beginning I was in the Oval Office almost every day, sometimes with Don and sometimes not. Partly to dramatize the change of leaders and partly just to introduce himself to the American people, Ford made many trips around the country. Don and I quickly figured out that given all there was to do, it didn't make much sense for both of us to accompany the president. Within weeks I was traveling with the president on my own.

One problem we had was allocating and optimizing the president's time. His longtime executive secretary, Mildred Leonard, had run the Ford congressional office for a quarter century, and she still felt free to commit him to seeing anyone who called her and passed her muster. One time, as I was leaving the Oval Office with a high-level foreign official, we had to make our way through a crowd of Grand Rapids Rotarians eagerly waiting to see their "Jerry." Such informal drop-bys had been routine on Capitol Hill, and Mildred saw no reason to change things now. The president understood that this couldn't continue, and at his request, we arranged a suite of offices for Mildred on the second floor, where she continued to handle the mail from his old congressional district.

A much more serious staff problem was presented by Bob Hartmann. Bob was much closer in age to the president than either Don or I and had gone to work for him in 1966, after twenty-five years as a reporter for the *Los Angeles Times*. His manner was brusque on good days and abrasive on bad ones, and if others found him difficult to deal with, that was fine by Bob. He was comfortable in that role and even cultivated it. Bob had been Ford's principal advisor and speechwriter in the vice president's office, and particularly in the latter position, had done some very fine work. Ford's truly memorable swearing-in remarks and his statement explaining Nixon's pardon were examples of Hartmann at his very best.

Unfortunately, when he wasn't writing speeches, Bob's contributions to the overall enterprise were mixed at best. His certainty that he was the man to continue running the show after August 9 led him to make a move that was admirable only in its audacity. Amid the confusion that followed Nixon's sudden departure, Bob simply moved his things into the office directly adjacent to the Oval Office. The space, which included a door opening directly into the Oval Office, had been vacated only hours earlier by Nixon's personal secretary, Rose Mary Woods. With that beachhead secure, Hartmann was hard to manage. He adopted the practice of stepping through his door into the Oval Office when the president was away. He would go through the inbox to treat himself to an exclusive look at all the presidential business and add new material as he saw fit.

One of our major management goals was to make sure that all the paperwork going to and from the president's desk passed through the staff secretary's office. This would enable us to keep records of everything the president had seen and signed and to make certain that documents given to him were circulated and vetted among senior officials. In addition, as another check, I reviewed everything going in and out of the Oval Office. But Bob's connecting door gave him a way around the system. We discovered this when documents that the president returned to the staff secretary included some that no one else had ever seen before. Bob's visits to the Oval Office could also be discerned in the appearance of some strategically leaked information in a newspaper item by Rowland Evans and Robert Novak. Finding an internal memo whose drift he had not cared for, Bob simply conveyed its contents straight from the president's desk to the appreciative hands of Washington's most read columnists.

President Ford had a lot to attend to in late 1974, including the continuing controversy over the pardon, which he tried to tamp down by testifying before the House Judiciary Committee. I accompanied him to the Hill and sat with Jack Marsh in the hearing room in the Rayburn Building as the president told the committee members and the nation, "There was no deal. Period. Under no circumstances." I hadn't been involved in the debate or discussions leading up to the pardon, but it was—and remains—my firm conviction that he granted it because he believed it was the right thing for the country.

Also on his plate was the confirmation of a new vice president, a bad economy, and the unraveling of America's effort in Vietnam. For him to move forward on these many fronts, it was clear to me that the chief of staff had to get a handle on the day-to-day operations of the White House, and that was never going to happen as long as Bob Hartmann remained just a few unobstructed steps from the Oval Office.

I urged Don to suggest to the president that he needed a private office where he could work and think in more relaxed and comfortable surroundings than the magnificent but very formal Oval Office. President Nixon had used a spacious private hideaway in the Old Executive Office Building. But why, Rumsfeld and I argued, trudge all the way over there when the perfect space was only a few steps away through a convenient connecting door? Ford quickly warmed to the idea. All that remained was to decide who would break the news to Hartmann, and Ford accepted our recommendation that, while either of us could do it, only he could make it stick. And that is how the problem was solved. When the president of the United States asks if you wouldn't mind making room for him, the only answer is the one Bob gave. He vacated what is arguably the second most prime piece of real estate in the Western Hemisphere as quickly and efficiently as he had commandeered it. And by any measure it was a very soft landing, just down the hall into the spacious office between Rumsfeld and Kissinger. A few years later, Bob Hartmann's new digs became the West Wing office of the vice president, and it has remained so ever since.

Hartmann's move marked an immediate improvement in the functioning of the staff system that Rumsfeld and I were trying to put into place. We now had better control over the paper flow and the foot traffic. Now the only way for staff to enter the Oval Office was through the main door, where all visitors would be met by Nell Yates, who had served in the White House since Eisenhower, and by Terry O'Donnell, the president's personal aide, who reported to me and to Rumsfeld. Ford instantly recognized the smoother-running operation, although he continued to maintain a modified separate track for aides like Mildred and Bob. In fact, until the end of his term, he kept a separate box on the credenza behind his desk for materials they brought to him. He had spent twenty-five years looking after the interests of Michigan's 5th Congressional District, and he never shook the habit even when bigger things came along. The practice was an understandable and even admirable example of his loyalty.

BEFORE DON AND I had moved into the chief of staff suite in the West Wing, the president had presided over an economic summit to discuss ways of combating inflation, which was now running at 12 percent. The program that came out of it involved a surcharge and budget cuts, but little is remembered about them because Bob Hartmann and his staff persuaded the president that he needed some sort of special appeal to capture the attention of the American people and enlist them in the struggle to hold down the cost of living. They created a theme and gave it a slogan, "Whip Inflation Now," which provided the acronym WIN, emblazoned on campaign-style buttons that we were all expected to wear—up to and including the president himself. More WIN buttons were ordered in anticipation of the campaign's rollout in a televised address to a joint session of Congress.

On October 7, a week after Rumsfeld and I arrived and the day before the president was to launch the WIN program, Alan Greenspan, our new chairman of the Council of Economic Advisers, came to me to express his deep concern. I took him to see Don, who, never faint of heart, urged the president to postpone his trip to Capitol Hill.

The last-minute intervention didn't succeed, and twenty-four hours later, wearing his WIN button on his lapel, the president delivered the speech naming inflation as "public enemy number one" and calling for a tax surcharge combined with a cut in federal spending and government services. That would be strong medicine at any time. But administering it without even the slightest sugarcoating less than a month before the midterm elections—when every congressman and one-third of the senators in the audience would be submitting themselves to the voters—was just asking for trouble.

The press and the Democrats fastened on the packaging and dismissed the whole thing as half-baked and PR-driven. The president was offended, and instead of retooling the presentation and getting rid of the buttons, he doubled down a few days later at the convention of the Future Farmers of America in Kansas City. In this speech, which was also televised nationally, he urged the young people to be bargain hunters, to "save as much as you can," and—the pièce de résistance—to "clean up your plate before you get up from the table." Around the Ford White House, the FFA address was forever after known as the "lick your plate clean" speech.

With no political traction or public support, the WIN campaign was quietly abandoned. The buttons and "lick your plate clean" lived on only as inside jokes among the staff and the press. Before long, President Ford was good-natured enough to take a little teasing about them. I'd nearly forgotten about the WIN campaign until Inauguration Day in 1977. President Ford had come over to say goodbye and take one last look around the Oval Office. After he returned to the residence, where the Carters would soon be arriving for coffee before driving to the Capitol, I stayed behind to help gather the last of his personal effects. I opened one of the drawers in his desk and found it filled with red and white WIN buttons as fresh as the day they had been minted at the very beginning of the administration.

The WIN embarrassment was only one of the burdens we carried into the 1974 congressional elections. The greatest, by far, was Watergate and President Ford's pardon of Richard Nixon. But there was also a growing view in the press that Jerry Ford, though he might be a very decent and well-meaning man, just wasn't up to the job of president.

Unfortunately, Ford's easygoing manner and casual demeanor supplied some ammunition for this attitude. After a campaign stop in Grand Junction, Colorado, press attacks on the issue of competence took on a new edge. The president, at the end of a long and grueling campaign swing, crowned the homecoming queen of La Mesa Junior College and bestowed presidential kisses on her and her court. Finding that task a pleasant one, he kissed all the young women again and then delivered a rambling speech. This shaky performance inspired a snide piece in *New York* magazine, with Ford depicted on the cover as Bozo the Clown.

The November elections dealt us a big setback. The Democrats ultimately picked up forty-nine House seats and four in the Senate, adding to their already decisive majorities in both chambers. This left the new president with a tough hand to play. As a man whose experience on Capitol Hill reached back to 1949, he knew better than any of us that legislative successes were going to be few and far between.

It was in the wake of our loss that Don Rumsfeld and I had dinner one night at the Two Continents restaurant in the Hotel Washington with economist Art Laffer, a creative guy who certainly captured my imagination with a curve he drew on the back of my napkin. What it showed was that you can raise taxes only so high before people become disinclined to work. On the other hand, it's possible to create incentive—and economic growth—with tax cuts. The Laffer Curve subsequently became one of the hallmarks of supply-side economics. I wish I had known how historic my napkin would become so that I could have saved it.

The idea of cutting taxes certainly suited the times, because the country was now heading into a recession. The president called his economic team together for a two-day meeting in Vail, Colorado, where he was spending his Christmas holidays with the family. The team at the time included assistant for economic affairs Bill Seidman, Treasury Secretary William E. Simon, and chairman of the Council of Economic Advisers Alan Greenspan, who was fast becoming first among those equals. Alan combined economic expertise with an appreciation of practical politics. No less important, he had a real knack for capturing large and complicated ideas in a few well-chosen words. The president liked him and put a lot of stock in his judgment. After I became chief of staff, I would take Alan into the Oval Office, as Don had before me, for lengthy discussions of economic policy.

The Vail meeting generated many of the policies that President Ford announced in his State of the Union message on January 15, 1975. Among them was a $16 billion cut in taxes. He would advocate tax relief again at the end of 1975, insisting on fiscal discipline as well. That didn't come naturally to the liberal Democrats who dominated the House of Representatives, but they were dealing with a president who had recently been one of their own. Jerry Ford had served on the House Appropriations Committee starting in the Truman administration and he knew the budget as well as any modern president before or after him. I once heard him correct a staff member on how many rangers were employed by the National Park Service. Late in his term, when the time came to brief the press corps on the new budget—a task usually falling to the top people at the Office of Management and Budget—the president decided to handle it himself. He laid out his priorities, his numbers, and his reasoning, then submitted to cross-examination by the press corps. The relevant policy aides and cabinet members were all there and ready to supply any details he needed. Later on, deputy OMB director Paul O'Neill told me that after witnessing a couple of these performances, many of the experts became scared of being called on. They realized that if Jerry Ford didn't know the answer they probably wouldn't either.

Having been on the receiving end of it for so many years, President Ford was well acquainted with Article I, Section 7 of the Constitution, conferring the veto power. Few presidents have put it to better use. In all he sent back sixty-six pieces of legislation to Congress, preventing billions of dollars in unnecessary spending and helping lay to rest any assumptions on Capitol Hill that the executive branch had been cowed into submission by Richard Nixon's impeachment crisis.

The president also laid down a rule for the executive branch stating that with very few exceptions there would be no new spending initiatives. We called this mandate "No New Starts," and it fell to me to be the enforcer. I had to defend this policy many times, and against no one more often than the vice president.

Quite apart from his personal advantages, which had instilled in him little fear of large price tags, Nelson Rockefeller had been governor of New York from 1959 to 1973. In that capacity he had conceived and executed a series of huge projects. When President Ford placed him in charge of domestic policy, new federal initiatives seemed to the vice president like the natural order of the day.

Ford held a weekly meeting with his vice president, and Rockefeller often used the time to lobby for his latest ideas. Listening to a few of those pitches myself, I could see why Ford liked and admired this man, who had natural charm and a forceful personality. After his meetings with the vice president, Ford would often call me into the Oval Office, hand me Rockefeller's latest proposal, and say, "Dick, what do we do with this?" And each time I would reply, "Well, Mr. President, we'll staff it out." This meant that the idea would be circulated for general review, including a cost assessment by OMB, and that it would invariably come back with the answer that the proposal had been found inconsistent with our policy of No New Starts.

That got the job done, but in time Rockefeller came to feel frustrated with limits that struck him as arbitrary and unimaginative. Despite the serious assignments Ford gave him in such matters as reassessing CIA programs and methods, in the end Rockefeller seemed to feel, as other vice presidents had before him, that the work of the office hadn't measured up to the title.

Ford was always sensitive to Rockefeller's situation, having counted his months as vice president as a generally miserable experience. But Rockefeller never blamed Ford for his disappointments in office. He decided that the cause of his troubles was elsewhere—with Don Rumsfeld and that deputy of his. In my case, I suppose it must have been a little galling to see his grand ideas sandbagged by some staff aide who was exactly half his age and who had never been elected to anything.

Rockefeller let loose on me only once, later on at the 1976 Republican National Convention, after the sound system had mysteriously gone dead in the middle of his speech. Protocol issues earlier in the week—debates about whether it should be Rocky, the sitting vice president, or Bob Dole, the running mate, who joined Ford onstage after his acceptance speech—had left him feeling slighted one too many times. On the final night he spotted me in the corridor beneath the rostrum and saw a fitting target for all his frustrations. He leaned in close and really let me have it, even accusing me of sabotaging his speech. I took my verbal pounding, assured the vice president of my innocence, and got out of there as fast as I could.

A FEW DAYS BEFORE Christmas in 1974, the *New York Times* ran a front-page story reporting that the Central Intelligence Agency had engaged in illegal operations inside the United States, including placing wiretaps on American citizens and journalists. Within a matter of weeks, the Senate (the Church Committee) and the House (the Pike Committee) and the White House (the Rockefeller Commission) had all launched inquiries into the CIA's activities.

Jack Marsh kept me apprised of the Rockefeller Commission's progress and the work of the two committees on the Hill. The president was often irate about the congressional committees—and with good cause. At times their sensational proceedings seemed sure to cripple America's intelligence capacity, if not destroy it. In the end, the result of the various CIA investigations was the disclosure of many unsavory activities that had taken place in the past, the correction of some very serious abuses that were still being committed, and a regularized procedure for congressional oversight that in ten years I would find myself a part of.

By the time President Ford came into office, the United States was unwinding its commitment in Vietnam. The Paris Peace Accords had been signed in January 1973 and American combat forces had been removed. The South Vietnamese government had been promised economic assistance to build up its defense forces, as well as renewed U.S. military action if the North Vietnamese violated the terms of the peace.

The violations began almost before the ink was dry and slowly continued, until at the beginning of 1975 the North Vietnamese had sent some three hundred thousand troops into South Vietnam and seized control of fourteen provinces. By the beginning of April, they were in a position to conduct a strike on Saigon. President Nixon had given his assurance that the U.S. would help the South Vietnamese resist a renewed enemy attack, but the antiwar forces in both houses of Congress were able to cut off funding that would have been necessary to support—or save—our South Vietnamese ally.

Faced with the lack of funds, President Ford could do nothing but evacuate, first from Cambodia, which fell on April 17, 1975, and then from Saigon. The night of April 28, when President Ford ordered the final evacuation of Saigon, I was at the White House. While the dramatic news footage kept the focus on the thousands of Americans and Vietnamese we were airlifting by helicopter off the roof of the American Embassy, I found it impossible to ignore the fact that we were leaving tens of thousands of Vietnamese who had cast their lot with us.

After that final unraveling, there was debate in the White House over what was left to be said about the conflict, and Ford's instinct, as with the pardon after Watergate, was to let go of the past and find a way to bring the people and the country forward. In a speech at Tulane University in April, he declared the war "finished as far as America is concerned." I was with him in New Orleans that night. I remember distinctly that when he spoke those words, some people in the audience wanted to cry and some wanted to cheer, but there was an unmistakable sense of relief for all of us that transcended one's view of the war. Indeed, even for me, and I had supported the effort, hearing the president say those words was welcome in a way it is hard to describe. We had lost more than fifty-eight thousand young Americans in the war, and Vietnam had divided us as a nation for so long. The war in Southeast Asia had ended in an awful way, but at least it had ended. It was over.

From that low point onward, the great foreign policy challenge of the Ford presidency was to shake off the effects of a searing defeat.

Here was the first American president never elected to national office, overseeing the final withdrawal of American forces from a foreign theater of war in defeat. Ford was left to deal with the consequences of this devastating setback for America's interests and morale. He faced a crucial test just a few weeks later, when communist forces in Cambodia seized the unarmed American merchant ship *Mayaguez* in international waters and captured its crew of thirty-nine men. The *Mayaguez* was anchored offshore, and President Ford ordered that U.S. naval aircraft should interdict any boat traffic between the mainland and the American ship.

When a small boat was spotted departing the *Mayaguez,* a naval aviator believed he saw some members of the U.S. crew aboard and had the good sense to confirm his order before firing. His request, relayed up his chain of command, made it all the way to the Pentagon and then to the commander in chief. We were in a meeting monitoring the crisis in the Cabinet Room when the president was informed he had a call. He picked up the handset of the telephone that hangs at the president's spot underneath the cabinet table, listened to the request, and conveyed the order that the pilot should hold his fire. It was the right decision. The crew had been on board the small boat. It was also the only time in all the hours I have spent in meetings in the Cabinet Room that I recall seeing any president use the phone at his place.

All these years later, few people even remember the *Mayaguez* and to those who do, it may seem like a very small incident in the greater scheme of things. But President Ford's swift action at the time—demanding the release of the crew and sending in the Marines and air strikes to ensure their safety and reclaim the vessel—had a lasting effect for the good. It said to our enemies and to the world that while America might have withdrawn from Vietnam and been forced to acquiesce in the hostile takeover of that nation, our adversaries would make a mistake to think that we would ignore provocation, particularly when American lives were involved.

Throughout the *Mayaguez* crisis, Henry Kissinger was constantly on the phone monitoring the situation and demanding information. When I think of all that Henry had been through in that same room with President Nixon, I still marvel at the energy and focus he brought to the service of President Ford. He'd been with Nixon from 1969 until the very last day—seeing all the highs and lows of the Vietnam peace negotiations, the great breakthrough with China, the endless exertions of Cold War diplomacy, the shuttle diplomacy in the Middle East— and still showed no sign of weariness or passivity in his service to the president or his defense of America's interests. Even while acting as both national security advisor and secretary of state, he was remarkably clear in mind and purpose. Henry was one of America's higher-profile secretaries of state and not exactly the kind to resist the pull of celebrity. But all that was part of a very impressive package. If ever there was a Washington heavy hitter whose actual talents and achievements justified his star billing, it's Henry. Nothing about him is overrated.

Of course Henry and I were far from peers in the Ford years when it came to our grasp of international affairs, and I was usually content to be a learner and listener in his company. This was the recommended practice for staff generally, as Henry was alert to his prerogatives and tolerated no intrusions. Indeed the only time I ran into trouble with him was because he suspected larger designs and far more guile than were in me at the age of thirty-four. In August 1975, after signing the Helsinki Accords, the president visited Poland and Yugoslavia. After Ford and the official delegation had settled into the hotel in Warsaw, I broke off from the group and was driven to a private home on the edge of the city. There, by prior arrangement, I met with our ambassador to East Germany, John Sherman Cooper. After a lengthy and highly useful conversation, Ambassador Cooper and I parted, and I returned to the business of the president's trip.

A few days later, I was working aboard Air Force One when I found myself confronted by an extremely agitated secretary of state. Just who did I think I was, going off on my own to meet with one of "his" ambassadors? He was furious over this breach of hierarchy. And in no uncertain terms he told me that whatever nefarious things were going on with

my secret meetings and back channels, they were completely unacceptable. He wanted a stop to it at once. The president would hear about
this. Cooper ought to be fired on the spot. And so on.

It took some doing, but I got Henry calmed down and explained
that the president had asked me to see the ambassador because he'd
been thinking ahead to next year's primary elections. John Sherman
Cooper had been involved in Kentucky Republican politics since the
1920s, had been one of the state's United States senators for more than
three terms, and had served as an ambassador under Eisenhower before Ford had made him a diplomat several months before. Kentucky's
thirty-seven delegates would be up for grabs in the upcoming primary,
and where Republican politics in the Bluegrass State were concerned,
the man to see was John Sherman Cooper. So it was all perfectly innocent, and I assured Henry that I wasn't doing any diplomatic maneuver-
ing behind the master's back. That ended my upbraiding, and it turned
out that my perilous mission to the Warsaw suburbs was worth it. With
a lot of good advice from Cooper, President Ford managed a come-
from-behind victory in the Kentucky primary.

Actually, the closest I ever came to acting as a diplomat in those days
was in my occasional role as mediator between Henry and others in the
administration. One day in early 1976, the offending party, as Henry
saw it, was Daniel Patrick Moynihan. Pat was our ambassador to the
United Nations and as his counterparts there could attest, was not the
sort to keep his complaints to himself. Both men knew how to work
the press too, and for some time had been taking shots at each other
through unattributed quotes fed to James "Scotty" Reston of the *New
York Times.*

The final straw came on the last day of January. I'd gone with the
president to Williamsburg, Virginia, where he was going to kick off the
1976 bicentennial celebration with a speech in the old colonial House
of Burgesses. Ford was in the very chamber where Patrick Henry, protesting the Stamp Act, had denounced King George III. But instead
of sitting in the gallery witnessing this moving and historic event, I
was upstairs in a cramped, stuffy closet where a White House phone

line had been installed, listening to Henry Kissinger and Daniel Patrick Moynihan have at it. I must have spent an hour in that closet refereeing the fight, with my brief interjections mostly only allowing the smoke to clear so they could both reload and take aim again. It all ended with Moynihan's resignation.

ALMOST FROM THE BEGINNING, our thoughts were never very far from the impending presidential election. Ford had announced on July 8, 1975, that he would run for a full term in 1976. Although that was a fairly early start for an incumbent's campaign, here again he was on new ground, and none of us doubted that we were going to need every bit of that time to get things up and running. Ford had never run for office outside Michigan's 5th District, so we would have to build a national political organization virtually from scratch in less than twelve months.

The '74 midterm elections, reflecting the fallout from Watergate and the pardon, had been a train wreck for the Republican Party and the new president. Looking ahead to 1976, Ford did not feel presumptuous in believing he deserved a united party and a clear path into the general election campaign. But many conservatives had another idea and plenty of reservations about a full term for Ford. They were upset for one thing about the Helsinki Accords, which had been signed by thirty-five nations and included provisions mandating respect for human rights and affirming the recognition of national boundaries. Ford's critics emphasized the latter, viewing any affirmation of Cold War borders as legitimizing the Soviet Union's control of satellite states. The president and his foreign policy advisors placed greater value on Helsinki's unprecedented human rights language, which legitimized the right of the United States and other Western countries to insist upon universal standards of human rights, even within the Soviet sphere. American presidents and diplomats would thereafter be as entitled to raise human rights issues as they were to raise matters of arms control or trade preferences with our communist adversaries. Ford believed that Helsinki would open the door to a debate the Soviets could never win, while giving courage to dissenters and protestors across the Soviet empire. And time would show that he was right.

Conservatives who viewed Ford as too prone to compromise with the Soviets also pointed to an episode involving Aleksandr Solzhenitsyn, the great Russian novelist and historian. Solzhenitsyn had won the Nobel Prize for Literature in 1970, but it wasn't until 1974 that an English translation of *The Gulag Archipelago* was published. This three-volume masterpiece about the brutal life in Soviet forced labor and concentration camps, some of it based on his firsthand experience, made him famous in America. Having been expelled from his homeland, Solzhenitsyn had recently settled in Vermont and had expressed a wish to meet the president. I thought it was a great idea and advised Ford that by all means a man of such standing should be received in the Oval Office.

But Kissinger and his deputy, Brent Scowcroft, argued strongly against it. While they respected Solzhenitsyn's courage and genius, they felt that such a meeting, which was being championed by Senator Jesse Helms of North Carolina, could become an irritant in our dealings with the Soviets at a time when delicate arms control negotiations were under way and a summit meeting with General Secretary Leonid Brezhnev was under consideration. So, initially at least, Ford decided against the meeting with Solzhenitsyn. And though the decision seemed minor at the time, we paid a heavy price for it. That refusal to see the most powerful witness against Soviet tyranny became a centerpiece of the conservative foreign policy case against Ford.

Oddly enough, one decision of the greatest consequence was scarcely remarked on by Ford's critics. In the fall of 1975, he nominated Chicago federal judge John Paul Stevens to succeed Supreme Court Justice William O. Douglas. Here was a chance to fill a seat on the high court that had last been vacant in 1939, and yet in the Ford White House there was remarkably little discussion as to how to proceed. The president turned the matter over to Attorney General Edward H. Levi. Ed, in turn, conducted a brisk search and settled on a well-regarded judge whom he had known for years. With that, the Senate put the nomination on the calendar and Stevens was confirmed unanimously less than three weeks later. This was just how things were done in those days. Justice Stevens went on to serve nearly as long as Douglas did, with a record equally pleasing to liberals. I like and respect John Paul Stevens a lot more than I do his judicial philosophy, but I've wished we had not simply left the choice up to Ed Levi. For his part, however, Ford never regretted the choice he made, and his opinion mattered more than mine. In any case, his sole Supreme Court nomination came and went with practically no objection.

What did wear us down month after month was the portrayal of the president as a hapless, clueless bumbler. The ridicule in the media really took off after the president, deplaning on a rainy day in Salzburg, Austria, slipped on the wet stairs and tumbled to the tarmac. After that, even a very ordinary spill on the ski slopes became a subject of scrutiny and hilarity for the press corps. For the public, the sight gag was immediately understandable, and there was little to be gained by pointing out that Jerry Ford, the former star athlete, had remained a strong and graceful man well into middle age. He was far more athletic than any of his predecessors since Theodore Roosevelt, and the fact that the press witnessed the occasional spill was partly because he was so active.

The bumbler image had become one of those stock jokes that was too good to let go of. Before long, it became a mainstay of the weekly comedy show *Saturday Night Live*. The president took it all good-naturedly and even played along with the jokes on occasion, but I could never say the same about my own attitude. I thought it was deeply unfair, and it still bothers me when I think about it. The image of President Ford as some sort of dimwitted stumbler hurt badly in the general election, and the press was not above keeping the gag going just for that reason.

Of course, it didn't help that our rival for the Republican nomination looked so surefooted and was always camera-ready. I had my first glimpse of Ronald Reagan in October 1974 when both he and Ford were attending a black-tie dinner at the Century Plaza Hotel in Los Angeles. I was in the room when the president received him beforehand. The two of them settled into deep armchairs in front of the window of the presidential suite with a nighttime backdrop of high palms and the lights of the Hollywood Hills.

I remember thinking that the former movie star cut a very impressive figure. Tanned and tailored in a way I'd never seen matched in Washington, this was a guy who knew how to carry himself. People as far back as the 1950s had sized up Ronald Reagan as presidential material and now for the first time, I could see why. On that evening in 1974, neither man knew for sure what 1976 would bring for them and their presidential ambitions, and they cordially chatted about everything except the possibility that they would soon be rivals.

Our initial strategy in the White House was to try to put pressure on Reagan not to challenge the president in the first place. It seemed worth attempting because even well into 1975 no one knew for sure whether Reagan would get into the race. We kept in touch with him through intermediaries, chiefly Tom Reed, who had been California's Republican national committeeman and would become air force secretary. Tom was a Ford man but he knew Reagan well, and the Reagan people listened to him. The same was also true of Stu Spencer, a campaign strategist who had helped Reagan win the governorship and was now signed up with Ford.

AS THE 1976 ELECTION played an increasingly important part in our day-to-day lives, Rumsfeld assigned me responsibility for campaign-related activities. As I looked at the task ahead, I became convinced there was no way Ford could win election without first making some fairly dramatic changes in his administration. Part of the problem, as I saw it, was that in the national security area we were still operating with the same structure and personnel we had inherited from the Nixon administration. The president had never clearly established the perception that he was in charge of national security policy. Henry Kissinger's continued position as both secretary of state and national security advisor created the impression that he had more control over foreign policy than the president did.

There was also the crucial matter of the vice presidency. Rockefeller had been very loyal to the president, but I believed he would be a huge liability in the upcoming battle with Ronald Reagan. The only way Ford could win was by capturing part of the conservative base that leaned toward Reagan. That would be impossible if his running mate were Nelson Rockefeller, the same man who had tried to stop Barry Goldwater in 1964. And if it became known that Rockefeller would not be on the ticket, we could expect a number of Republican leaders to support Ford with an eye to being chosen as his running mate.

I wasn't shy about making my point of view known, but having handed over the campaign portfolio to me, Don was more focused on improving the internal functioning of the White House. He began working on what turned out to be a very long memo to the president, urging him to remedy such matters as lack of accountability on the part of White House staff and lack of coordination across policy areas. I had some ideas for it too, and it grew into a pretty frank document.

In order to convey how seriously we viewed the situation and to give the president complete freedom to make necessary changes, we both wrote out and signed resignation letters. This wasn't a matter of saying unless you accept our recommendations, we will quit; rather, we were telling Ford that if his idea of changes included moving us out, we'd make it easy for him.

Near the end of October 1975, the president caught a bad cold and spent a couple of days upstairs in the White House residence instead of coming to work in the West Wing. Don and I took advantage of the opportunity to go see him and lay out our concerns and recommendations. It was clear that the president himself had come to some of the same conclusions, and within days he would carry out a sweeping set of changes.

He personally told Rockefeller that he would not be on the ticket in 1976. The vice president was obviously disappointed, but he remained loyal to the president to the end and delivered New York's delegates to Ford at the convention. Henry Kissinger agreed to step down as national security advisor while continuing as secretary of state—there being no question that he retained the full confidence of the president as his chief foreign policy advisor. His deputy, Brent Scowcroft, moved into the NSC job.

Jim Schlesinger was relieved of his position as secretary of defense. Although Jim was a very talented man with an impressive résumé, he had not endeared himself to the president. As we were pulling out of Vietnam, miscommunication between the Pentagon and the White House had resulted in an announcement that all Americans had been safely evacuated from Saigon, when in fact sixty-one marines remained on the grounds of the embassy. The president had never forgotten that embarrassment, nor had he ever forgiven Schlesinger for launching a verbal assault on the chairman of the House Appropriations Committee. After Congress had rejected our defense budget, the president asked Schlesinger to make an unapologetic case for it, but Ford was stunned when he got reports of his defense secretary going after the chairman, George Mahon of Texas. Mahon was a longtime colleague of Ford's on the Defense Appropriations Subcommittee and one of his dearest friends.

Schlesinger did not go quietly. The president later told me that his parting with Jim was one of the most unpleasant sessions he ever had.

Another change came at the CIA, where Director Bill Colby had become something of a liability because of all the controversy surrounding allegations of wrongdoing by the agency. Bill had begun his intelligence career in the Office of Strategic Services, the precursor to the CIA. He was the station chief in Saigon during most of the Vietnam War. In 1973 Nixon chose him to replace Schlesinger when he moved Jim from the CIA to the Pentagon. Now Bill clearly knew another change was coming. In fact, I had a feeling he was relieved to step down. George H. W. Bush was brought back from China to take his place.

Elliot Richardson, ambassador to the United Kingdom, was made secretary of commerce and later replaced in London by Counselor to the President Anne Armstrong. Rogers Morton, who had been secretary of commerce, became both a counselor to the president and Ford's campaign manager.

The president clearly wanted Rumsfeld to replace Schlesinger at the Defense Department, but Don did not immediately agree. On the Sunday before the president was to announce the cabinet changes, he still had not heard back from Don. En route to Florida for a summit meeting with Egyptian president Anwar Sadat, Ford called me up to his cabin on Air Force One. He told me to get Don on the phone and get him to agree to take the Defense job, which I did. I leaned pretty hard on Don to say yes, and he finally relented. Twenty-five years later, I would again find myself, on behalf of another president, urging Don Rumsfeld to serve as secretary of defense.

The next morning, as the president prepared to announce all of these changes to the press, he reviewed a stack of note cards with questions likely to come up, including one about the incoming chief of staff that somebody had slipped in for a laugh. It asked, "Mr. President, just who the hell is Richard Cheney?"

MY PROMOTION TO WHITE House chief of staff brought a minor flurry of media attention, but it didn't last long and that was fine with me. I had come to know and like a lot of the reporters covering President Ford, and to this day I count some of them as friends. But I had never been much impressed by presidential aides who cultivated a high public profile, and I didn't intend to become one of them. When the Secret Service assigned me the code name "Backseat," I took it as a real compliment.

In the White House, the top staff guy is still a staff guy, which is why, when President Ford offered to attach cabinet status to my job, I turned it down. I also tried to turn down having a White House car and driver pick me up in the morning and take me home at night. I liked driving my VW Beetle, though it was missing a front fender since I had been clipped by a Mrs. Smith's pie truck in one of the traffic circles that make driving in D.C. a real adventure. But Jack Marsh, the Ford White House's wise man, convinced me that with the hours I was working and all I had to do, I should take advantage of the extra time I'd gain each day for work if I weren't driving myself.

The main reason I wanted to keep a low profile was so that I could be an honest broker. If the chief of staff is out giving interviews every day and advocating a particular point of view, he loses credibility with those in the administration who disagree with him. Cabinet members begin looking for ways to go around the system instead of going through the process. They need to know that you'll go to the president and present their views fairly and won't tilt it to get a particular outcome.

By the time I became chief of staff, Ford was so used to having me around that there wasn't much of a transition involved. I've sometimes wondered if he realized exactly how young I was when he put me in charge of his White House. One time when he felt that his son Jack, then in his early twenties, needed an adult talking-to, the president asked me to sit the young man down for a Dutch uncle session. He wanted me to share with Jack the wisdom of my years—overestimating, I think, how much I really had of either. Another time, I brought my folks into the Oval Office for a photo, and afterward the president went on and on about how remarkable it was that my father was in such fine shape for a man his age. I think he assumed Dad and Mom were senior citizens. I didn't bother to tell him that they were both younger than he was.

I didn't feel the need for a deputy of my own when I succeeded Rumsfeld, but I did hire some really smart assistants, including Jim Cavanaugh, Mike Duval, Terry O'Donnell, Jerry Jones, Jim Connor, and Red Cavaney. There was also a very young man who has a special place in memory among Ford White House alumni. Foster Chanock was only twenty-three, but he helped me with just about everything I did, from follow-through on presidential orders to the analysis of issues and trends in the '76 election. He had graduated from the University of Chicago, where he, like most of his classmates, had been a man of the left. But some postgraduate travel in Eastern Europe opened his eyes. Foster started out as a gofer, and before long, with his unflagging energy and brilliant mind, he was participating in some of the toughest decisions we had to make. He was one of the finest, most talented people I knew in those years. His death from cancer in 1980 left me and many others to wonder about all that might have been.

I was pretty good at hiring and apparently not bad at firing, either, since I was so often given the responsibility. Along the way I had to relieve the White House social secretary, the head of the Federal Aviation Administration, the agriculture secretary, Ford's campaign manager, and a few others of their duties. My method was direct: no hints, cold shoulders, or slow, agonizing departures. Those were not good for anyone—neither the president nor the person being fired. Anyone failing to serve the president's interests, intentionally or not, simply needed to move along.

One internal problem that never did get entirely fixed was in the speechwriting shop, which had remained the preserve of Bob Hartmann even after his relocation from alongside the Oval Office. During the transition from Nixon to Ford, in part because Bob was involved and in part because we had no alternative clearly in mind, we had passed too quickly over the question of where to place authority for speechwriting. As a result, it had never become fully integrated with the policy and political elements of the White House staff. It went its own way, following its own agenda and its own rules. The rule that Hartmann tried hardest to impose, for example, held that a speech draft could not be reviewed by staff until the president had seen it, and after that no changes could be made because, of course, the president had already seen it.

Even in the very last week of the 1976 campaign, when you would expect every man with an oar to be rowing in the same direction, we were still having to deal with this problem. In late October we were flying with the president to Pittsburgh, where he was to deliver a policy speech the next morning. A familiar disagreement over competing drafts prompted Hartmann to fire Pat Butler, one of the junior members of his staff. Bob and I had it out, right then and there—rather loudly as I recall—while Pat went off to ponder the prospects of a young man who had just been fired aboard Air Force One. When things quieted down, the speech question was settled in my favor, and I told Pat that if Hartmann had fired him, then I was now rehiring him, and throwing in a raise.

I LED THE WHITE HOUSE staff for a total of fourteen months. I stepped into the job just as the '76 campaign was beginning to dominate our schedule, and thinking back on those days, the memories are mostly of being with President Ford on Air Force One or in a motorcade or some hotel suite somewhere.

We got off to a good start by squeaking out a victory in the New Hampshire primary. Even more crucial than the prize of seventeen out of twenty-one delegates was the gain in morale. New Hampshire was widely considered Reagan country. Despite the widely anticipated and projected results, Ford had defied expectations and shown that Reagan was not unbeatable after all. It was Ford's first electoral victory anywhere outside of greater Grand Rapids, and it was Reagan's first electoral defeat anywhere.

In fact, as it turned out, one of the things we had going for us in New Hampshire was the widespread assumption that we had no chance there. The state's governor, Meldrim Thomson, had said as much a few weeks before the vote, when he was campaigning for Reagan and had pretty much guaranteed a Reagan victory. Even if that statement were true—which it may well have seemed when he made it—the last thing you want to do is talk about a sure thing or convey an impression of overconfidence. Ford was in the unique position of entering an election battle as both an incumbent president and an underdog, and we tried to make an advantage out of being both.

An unbroken string of early primary victories turned things around, and suddenly Ford was the clear front-runner. By late March we had won decisively in Florida and Illinois, and we were sure that if Reagan didn't get a win of his own very soon, he would be out of the running. Sure enough, he dug in hard in North Carolina, borrowed money for a statewide TV broadcast, and came out six points ahead of us in the primary on March 23. With that victory under his belt, the contest was now moving into Texas, Georgia, and Indiana, and suddenly it was his turn to run the table. We stayed on our feet with a couple of narrow and much-needed wins—including Kentucky, thanks at least in part to the advice I received from John Sherman Cooper in Warsaw. All through the late spring and summer, and right up to the Republican convention in August, the nomination battle was being fought house to house and vote by vote, making us scratch and claw for every last delegate.

Whenever the president or I wanted to know how we stood in the hunt for delegates, the man with the answer was Jim Baker. Back then James A. Baker III was as new to national politics as I was. The Houston attorney and former marine had cut his Republican teeth in Texas working for his good friend George H. W. Bush. Jim is the kind of guy you want around when things get tense and complicated, and even in the mid-seventies, anyone watching him in action at the President Ford Committee could observe the calm and shrewd turn of mind that future presidents, including Reagan himself, would depend upon. As our man in charge of delegate hunting, Jim was part of a core group that also included pollster Bob Teeter, political director Stu Spencer, and admen John Deardourff and Doug Bailey. Jim was in charge of every detail and knew the precise state of play at any given moment; he knew who was with us and who was against us and who was uncommitted.

Being an uncommitted delegate had its benefits, including friendly notes and phone calls from the president, who was just checking in to see how you were doing. One afternoon we flew the entire Pennsylvania delegation down to Washington for cocktails with the president. A woman from Brooklyn, who kept switching sides, wanted a White House meeting with Ford, if that wasn't asking too much. Too much? Why of course not, she was assured. And could she bring her whole family? By all means. The president was hoping she'd ask.

The quest for delegates was on everyone's mind as we neared the Republican convention. One night a crazed intruder jumped the White House fence and raced across the North Lawn with a three-foot length of pipe in his hand. He ignored shouted orders to stop, disregarded a warning shot fired in the air, and left the Secret Service with no choice but to shoot to bring him down. In the ensuing chaos, as sirens from every corner of town converged on the White House, one of the older Secret Service agents was heard to say, "Gentlemen, if that fellow we just shot was an uncommitted delegate, we're in deep trouble."

I even did some delegate scouting myself a few weeks before the convention, including a trip to Mississippi to try turning a few votes there in Ford's direction. Harry Dent, a longtime South Carolina politico and one of the key staffers who had organized the South for Nixon in 1968, believed we had a shot to take the Mississippi delegation. Mississippi operated under the "unit rule," so if we got a majority of the votes of their delegates, we'd get the votes of their entire delegation. Not everyone on the campaign took Harry's advice to heart, but I did, and it paid off.

He got me invited to two key events. The first was a meeting of the southern state Republican chairmen in North Carolina. I had the chance to meet them all and make a strong case that they ought to support Gerald Ford. Dent also advised me that it would be well worth my time to make a trip to Jackson, Mississippi, to attend a meeting of all the Mississippi Republican convention delegates. I had the chance to spend time with their chairman, Clarke Reed, and I spoke to the assembled group. As a conservative stronghold, Mississippi was leaning Reagan, and we wanted to show them we would fight for their votes.

When I got off the plane at National Airport back in Washington, I heard the news that Ronald Reagan had announced that if he were nominated, liberal Pennsylvania Senator Richard Schweiker would be his running mate. Reagan's selection of Schweiker had been a gambit to take Pennsylvania's delegates away from Jerry Ford. I made a quick call to Drew Lewis, the Ford campaign chairman in Pennsylvania. He assured me I didn't have to worry. He would deliver Pennsylvania for Ford. I knew we should take advantage of the moment and lock down Mississippi.

I went directly to the Oval Office and recommended that President Ford place a call to Clarke Reed. He did and the timing could not have been better. Clarke had just heard that Reagan had selected a northeastern liberal to be his running mate. Even in the anger of the moment, Clarke had trouble bringing himself to give up on Reagan. But Ford wouldn't let him buy any more time and leaned on him hard until he got a commitment. Two days later Air Force One appeared in the skies over Jackson, and with a final direct appeal to delegates from the president himself, Mississippi was ours. We had managed to deny Reagan the extra delegates he was hunting in Pennsylvania and had nailed down our own additional votes in Mississippi.

Political historians still speak of the Schweiker move as a fatal miscalculation, although in retrospect, it's probably closer to the truth that Reagan by then had already lost his chance at the nomination. The early announcement of a running mate merely showed a realistic understanding that desperate measures were in order. After that failed, the only options the Reagan people had left were more in the nature of throwing roadblocks in Ford's path than actually adding to their own delegate total. Having made some serious mistakes going into the convention, the best they could hope for was to force us into committing some calamitous error of our own.

THE CONVENTION AT KEMPER ARENA in downtown Kansas City was the last one ever to begin in a state of genuine uncertainty about who would leave town with the nomination. Even the glossy programs hedged their bets, with pictures of both Ford and Reagan as the party's "standard bearers," to allow for either outcome. The numbers were holding for Ford, but at conventions back then you never knew what might happen on the floor before delegates finally got around to casting their votes on the third night. The Reagan camp was determined to stir up some last-minute drama, and their chosen vehicle was Rule 16-C.

Apparently dreamed up by Reagan's campaign manager, John Sears, a bright guy who had kept us on our toes all year, 16-C would have required that before the balloting began, each candidate must declare whom he would choose as his running mate. On Ford's team, we called this the "misery loves company" rule because the sole purpose was to drag Ford into the same no-win situation Reagan had created for himself by choosing Schweiker. No matter whom Ford chose for the ticket, it was bound to annoy at least some of our delegates, and if the choice

turned out to be really controversial or unpopular, it might even inspire enough eleventh-hour conversions to tilt the convention toward
Reagan.

The floor fight over 16-C created a real moment of exposure for us,
and we treated the vote on it as a proxy battle for the nomination itself.
When we prevailed on Tuesday night, everybody knew Ford would be
the nominee.

There was one last obstacle thrown in our path that night, and here
we decided that the best course was just to take the hit and move on. It
made things a little easier that the actual target was not so much Ford
as Kissinger, who at the time was not a beloved figure among conservatives. After the vote on Rule 16-C, the convention turned to a debate
over the party platform, with special attention to a plank on "Morality
in Foreign Policy" drawn up by Senator Jesse Helms. It was a thing of
beauty, in its own way, a ringing affirmation of all that was good and
pure in American foreign policy, mixed in with expressions of disdain
for those connivers and compromisers who had given us détente. The
draft language didn't mention anyone by name, but everyone knew who
the target was.

Naturally, Kissinger was livid. He assumed that we all shared his
indignation, which was mostly true. But he also assumed that we would
fight this affront at all costs, which was definitely not true. With the
exception of Henry's old friend and mentor Vice President Rockefeller,
the consensus in the Ford high command was to let it go. We had won
the important battle. Why make a big fuss over some little passage in a
platform that nobody was going to read anyway?

This gave no comfort to Henry, and he and Rockefeller were still
fired up for battle when we all gathered in Ford's suite at the Crowne
Plaza Hotel to make a final decision. This was an outrage, they said, a
deep insult that must not be allowed to pass. Ford heard them out and
then went around the room for advice from the rest—Stu Spencer, aides
Bill Timmons and Tom Korologos, and me. None of us saw the point
in fighting. Our view was, look, we just had a big win on Rule 16-C, it's
late at night, and our people are in bars all over Kansas City; if we go to

a vote on this we could actually lose, and that would reverse the whole dynamic of the convention. If we just let it pass, nobody will even remember it a week from now.

Not acceptable, said Henry. If we didn't wage a fight to keep that insulting language out of the platform, then he would have no choice but to resign. For a moment after this threat, nothing was said. Then Tom Korologos piped up with a wisecrack that quickly settled the entire matter and left even Kissinger laughing. "Henry," he said, "if you're going to quit, do it now. We need the votes."

The next night, August 18, I sat with President Ford and his family as they watched television coverage of his victory on the first ballot, scraping by in a vote of 1,187 to 1,070. It was one more moment in their lives that they could scarcely have imagined just a few years earlier, and I felt as happy for Betty and the kids as I did for my boss.

As they celebrated, I attended to the matter of bringing Ford and Reagan together for the traditional laying-down-of-arms meeting, and placed a call to John Sears. We had already agreed that the winner would visit the loser's hotel suite; they would then appear before the press in a show of unity. In the planning stage and again that night on the phone, Sears set down just one condition for the encounter: Under no circumstances, he made clear, was the president to ask Reagan to be his running mate.

At the time I really regretted this, and on my own had put out some feelers to make absolutely certain that the firm "no" we were hearing from Sears and others reflected Reagan's own wishes. By all indications, it was so.

A Ford-Reagan ticket made obvious sense to me. I'd started to think about the possibilities even before our victory in Kansas City and a few times tried to turn the president's own thoughts in the same direction. I had to be rather careful in bringing it up because I knew Ford was cold to the idea, and under the circumstances he was becoming more and more immune to the charms of Ronald Reagan. What I needed was hard evidence that Reagan would help us, regardless of personal feelings. So in the early summer of '76 I asked Bob Teeter to poll it: As discreetly as possible, ask a sampling of voters how they would respond to a Ford-Reagan ticket in the general election.

Not long afterward, Bob returned with some favorable numbers, and I wanted Ford to hear the case directly from him. On Friday, August 6, we sat down at Camp David and Bob laid it out for the president, demonstrating beyond any doubt that Reagan would add more support than any other potential running mate. As a purely political proposition, it was a winner. Ford listened patiently, and I don't remember him disputing anything we said. Even so, our pitch went nowhere. He just didn't want to hear it.

Of course, there would be consolations ahead for conservatives, and reading the story backward it's probably fair to say that Ford and Reagan were both wise to rule out the vice presidential spot, and the governor was lucky that things played out as they did. After all, how do you get a Reagan presidency without a Ford loss in '76 and four years of Jimmy Carter?

When Ford and Reagan met in Kansas City, in any case, there was no chance the conversation might wander toward talk of joining of forces in the fall. We arrived at the Alameda Plaza Hotel just after 1:00 a.m. and went into Reagan's suite. The president and the governor then met alone, and as Ford recounted the meeting to me afterward, he moved quickly to the names he was considering for the second spot. Reagan had responded most favorably to the mention of Senator Bob Dole of Kansas, which was a big plus for Dole, but the choice wasn't settled there and then. Ford left the meeting with Reagan still needing to think it over.

In the way that many past running mates had been settled upon, there was a long, middle-of-the-night meeting, with an announcement due by morning and all the political world waiting on a name. Among those we had tossed around were Dole, Senator Howard Baker of Tennessee, John Connally, the former governor of Texas, and Ambassador Anne Armstrong, who had been a highly regarded figure in the party for years. The idea of a woman on the ticket held a lot of appeal, and Ford that night probably came closer to that choice than any other presidential nominee had up to then. The problem was that generic polls showed that a female running mate would cost him 12 points. Being way down already, we couldn't afford to deepen that deficit.

Another name reluctantly crossed off the list was George H. W. Bush, although the reasons for that would need clearing up for years to come. As much as Ford liked Bush and wanted to consider him for the '76 ticket, he ruled Bush out for one reason alone: When Ford made him director of central intelligence a year earlier, as part of the same shakeup that had removed Rockefeller as a candidate for VP, Democrats on Capitol Hill suspected a fast political move. They wanted assurances that Bush would not simply serve ten months at the agency and then end up as Ford's running mate. After talking it over with Bush, Ford gave the Democrats their guarantee, and now, in Kansas City, he was bound by that promise.

No decision about a running mate had been reached by the pre-dawn hours when we finally packed it in. From the general feel of that meeting, I left the president in his suite with the strong impression that Howard Baker would be the one. The next morning, Ford called me down to his suite to tell me his choice. Mrs. Ford was in her bathrobe sitting at the vanity when I arrived, and the president was putting on his tie. We had a short discussion about the candidates, in particular Baker and Dole, and then the president told me he had decided to go with Dole. He asked me to get him on the phone.

What strikes me most when I think back on the selection is that right in the middle of our deliberations on the vice presidency was Nelson Rockefeller. Here we were talking about who was best to replace Rockefeller, and there was Rocky himself offering counsel on which of the prospects would help Ford the most. It speaks well of him that he would do that—although I have a feeling that part of his motivation was to make darn sure the second spot didn't go to Reagan. No doubt the team spirit Nelson showed in Kansas City was one of the reasons why, even decades later, the decision to drop his vice president still gnawed a little at Ford. He felt he had let down a friend, although for my part I never shared his second thoughts. Our goal was to get Gerald Ford elected, and there was simply no way to do that with Nelson Rockefeller on the ticket.

WE LEFT KANSAS CITY on Friday, August 20, feeling pretty good, although with not much of a postconvention "bounce." On the strength of his untainted, outsider image—and with Watergate and the Nixon pardon still fresh enough to exploit—Jimmy Carter led in the Gallup poll 50 percent to 37 percent. For us that spread was actually an improvement over what we'd seen following the Democratic convention in mid-July, when Ford trailed Carter by 33 points.

When you're that far down in the polls, at least you can assume you've established a floor. Any movement at all is likely to be in your direction. Being way down can also give a campaign a certain spark and provide the candidate the fighting edge he needs. In this case, the underdog was a fellow who had never ended a competition in any place but first. As friendly and easygoing as Jerry Ford was known to be, on the field of political battle he was focused, intense, and accustomed to winning. Whatever the pollsters had to say about the general election, he had just bested the former governor of California and felt he could handle the former governor of Georgia.

As it turned out, he almost did. In the electoral count, the Carter-Ford election of 1976 ended up closer than any other presidential election since 1916, when Woodrow Wilson edged out Charles Evans Hughes. And America wouldn't see another contest so tight until the Bush-Gore race in 2000.

Having had a stake in both the Ford and George W. Bush campaigns, I'm struck by how much the map changed in the quarter century between them. For one thing, in '76 the Democrats counted on and got the entire South, excluding only Virginia. Most of those states have rarely gone Democratic since. It was a race in which the Democrat took Texas and Missouri, the Republican took New Jersey and most of New England, and California was still reasonably solid Republican territory. The layout in 2000, when I found myself on the ticket, presented a different world. The lesson I draw is never to pay much heed to any talk of a party having a "lock" on one or another state or region. In the space of a generation, a political map can be practically inverted. When you hear any presidential election outcome described as "transformational," altering the political world forever, you can put that analysis down as true and valid for exactly four years.

In the general election campaign of 1976, of course, our goal wasn't to "transform" anything except the very depressing poll numbers in front of us. It took everything we had just to stay in the game. Week after week, Ford slogged away, and little by little he closed in on his opponent. We knew we were gaining ground on Carter, who was also in his first national campaign and making a few mistakes of his own. But it was slow going across a big field. My nagging fear throughout was that in the end the clock would beat us.

A campaign plan drafted by Mike Duval, Foster Chanock, Bob Teeter, and Jerry Jones recommended that the president engage Carter in a series of debates. The president liked the idea of going on the offense and issued the debate challenge in his convention speech. It was a bolder move than it might sound today, when presidential debates are a given and even the running mates are expected to square off. There hadn't been any debates since Kennedy and Nixon in 1960, and no sitting president had ever agreed to, much less proposed, a joint televised appearance with his opponent.

The Ford-Carter debates are remembered now for one exchange that cost us dearly. It seems almost beside the point to note that our man came out of the first exchange looking great and climbing in the polls. It was that next encounter, in San Francisco on October 6, that broke our momentum.

The trouble came with a question to the president from Max Frankel of the *New York Times*. It concerned America's dealings with the Soviets, and Frankel implied that the Helsinki Accords constituted acceptance of Soviet domination of Eastern Europe. That hit a sore spot with Ford, who felt that Helsinki had been misrepresented, and in the course of his answer the president declared, "There is no Soviet domination of Eastern Europe, and there never will be under a Ford administration." When Frankel pressed him again, the president clarified his answer some: "The United States does not concede that those countries are under the domination of the Soviet Union."

Watching this on television from the green room behind the stage, I thought it sounded odd, but I didn't expect it to be much of a problem. In fact, when the full ninety minutes were up, I thought that apart from that one misstep, Ford had put in another solid performance. Not long afterward, however, when Stu Spencer and I paid the usual post-event call on the press corps, I knew something bad was up when my friend Lou Cannon of the *Washington Post* saw me and called out, "Hey, Cheney, how many Soviet divisions are there in Poland?"

The president's slip-up, which some were already calling the "liberation" of Eastern Europe, was the only story of the night. Our field poll conducted during the debate registered no adverse impact from Ford's statement. But the press and the Carter campaign were working on that, and by the next day we were hurting badly. As we boarded Air Force One for the hour-long flight to Los Angeles, I was sure that nothing short of a retraction would do. Ford would simply have to admit that he misspoke, offer a clarification, and get this thing behind us.

The moment we were in the air, I made straight for the president's cabin and laid it on the line. He was unconvinced, insisting it was an innocent mistake that voters wouldn't hold against him—*of course* the leader of the free world understood that Soviet forces were not in Eastern Europe by invitation. When Ford sent me away, I went for reinforcements and came back with Stu Spencer, who helped explain to the president that this was bigger than he thought.

Okay, Ford finally agreed. He'd try to clear it up at the next stop. But even the statement he offered soon afterward at the University of Southern California and yet another statement the next morning to a San Fernando Valley business group did nothing to get us out of the fix we were in. Someone had to tell the president that his two "clarifications" were just not clear enough. He needed to face the problem and the press directly, and it had to happen immediately, before he left Southern California.

When Spencer and I finally got him cornered and the president agreed to meet the problem head-on, we were in the mayor's office at the city hall in Glendale. Ford had just addressed a rally outside, and I'd been back talking to reporters, who were enjoying all of this a little too much. By now they were writing about almost nothing else. I told the president that we could set up the press in the back parking lot and he could clean things up once and for all right there.

Even then he needed persuading, but we didn't let up, until finally he said, "Oh, all right, I'll do it." As press secretary Ron Nessen shepherded the press into place, we went carefully over what Ford was going to say. When it was time to go out, I was still worried that he wouldn't be as blunt and direct as the moment required, so I said, "Mr. President, do you have firmly fixed in your mind what it is you want to say?" He spun around on me and said, jabbing a finger in my chest with every word, "Poland is not dominated by the Soviet Union!" The tension broke with a good laugh, and his performance with the press a few moments later showed the candidate at his best.

There was no getting around the setback the Ford campaign had suffered, but in the closing days of the election the president drew roughly even with Carter. Gallup even had him ahead by one on the day before the election. We were hopeful of victory, but realistic enough to know that everything would have to break our way in the end. And accomplishing that, in those final hours, seemed a tough proposition.

I suppose that's why we all found ourselves so emotional on the very last stop of the campaign, in Ford's hometown of Grand Rapids. On the morning of Election Day, the citizens of Grand Rapids unveiled a special tribute. It was a mural in the local airport terminal, showing scenes of Ford's life from boyhood to the presidency. Seeing it for the first time, he got pretty choked up and spoke of his mother, Dorothy, and adoptive father, Gerald R. Ford, Sr., and all they had done for him. It was as sincere and sweet a moment as you're likely to see during a campaign, and the genuine feeling in the room—a town's pride in a favorite son, and a man's loving gratitude to his parents—was lost on no one. I recall looking over to the press area and seeing a few tears even there. For all of us, it was a reminder that however the fates played that day, the career that began here in Grand Rapids was quite a story, and the vote we awaited could take nothing away from all that had been achieved in the life of this good man.

I HAD ONE MORE unexpected part to play in the election of 1976. Wednesday morning, after the results were in, it was time to call President-elect Carter. Having just about lost his voice by then, all Ford could manage were a few words of congratulations before turning the phone over to me to read his formal statement conceding the election. If Jimmy Carter ever enjoyed the sound of my voice, that would have been the time. I didn't care for the task, but it was surely a great moment in Carter's life, and he had earned the satisfaction and title that were now his.

The truest glimpses of democracy in action don't always come during a presidential election, but often right afterward, when suddenly one team places itself at the service of the other. Overnight, you go from "How do we beat them?" to "How can we help them?" The finality of defeat has a way of awakening goodwill all around, sometimes more than the losing side might have thought possible.

So it was with the transition from Ford to Carter. To my own surprise, I had no trouble at all showing the ropes to Jack Watson, Carter's transition chief, and the rest of the incoming staff. Under orders from Ford and with the details ably handled by Jack Marsh and military aide Major Bob Barrett, my job was to make sure the Carter people had the calm and orderly transition into power that Ford never got. The whole Ford team took pride in carrying out the president's wishes.

On January 20, 1977, after a breakfast with senior White House staff and some final sorting and packing in the West Wing, I hopped in the motorcade to the Capitol. I figured it would be the last time I would have a close view of an inauguration, and the plan from there was to leave with former President Ford on the helicopter ride to Andrews Air Force Base. From just inside the doorway to the Capitol Rotunda, I watched Jimmy Carter take the oath of office and then in a gracious touch, thank Gerald R. Ford "for all he has done to heal our land." Moments earlier, I had also made a point of watching the real transfer of power. At the very instant Carter had finished reciting the oath of office, I watched as the "football"—the heavy briefcase containing nuclear launch codes—was passed from the hands of Ford's military aide to Carter's.

There were handshakes and goodbyes on the way to the chopper, and as we lifted off and circled the Capitol dome, there was not much to say. Waiting for me at Andrews were Lynne and the girls; we joined a big crowd there to see the Fords off on their journey to California. And what next for us? Well, with no work to do, not much of a plan, and just ten days to go before my thirty-sixth birthday, we piled into our silver station wagon and decided to get something to eat. Just outside the gates of Andrews is a McDonald's I'd passed a hundred times in White House vehicles, always with better things to do than pull in for a Big Mac and fries. Now it was a different story, and the afternoon was given over to a leisurely lunch under the golden arches.

There would be plenty of time down the road for taking stock of the Ford years and my part in the story. Better still, our thirty-eighth president would live well into his nineties, and as the years advanced so would our friendship. In the winter of 1977, however, it was hard to shake the feeling of disappointment at having come so close to earning a full term for Jerry Ford and not quite making it.

In the way of consolations, my colleagues and I knew at least that the presidency of Gerald Ford was incomplete only in its count of 895 days. It had been filled with testing and trial enough for a much longer stay. And we who had worked for this president knew he had proved as worthy of that office as any who had ever come before. I've always liked the late columnist David Broder's observation that Ford was exactly the kind of person Americans say they want in a president, but didn't know it when they had him.

My own debt to the man is beyond my power to settle, though he was not the type to make you feel indebted. Just about everything that followed in my career I trace back to the break he gave me and the confidence he placed in me. Many others will tell you the same story about themselves. Among veterans of the Ford years, there is also a warmth and camaraderie you don't always find among the alumni of administrations past. To a person, they'll all tell you that this good spirit began with our leader.

The disappointment I felt in the winter of 1977 has long since given way to sheer gratitude for one of the greatest and happiest experiences in my life. My favorite memento from the period is a letter from my mother that I've kept in a frame for years. She wrote it the day after the '76 election, saying, "It's hard to put down what I feel—much love, much pride, and I know you will come out of this knowing that you did your best." Sometimes in life that's all you're left with, the knowledge that you gave a job your best shot. And sometimes that's enough.

———◄○►———

CHAPTER FOUR

The Gentleman from Wyoming

While the Carters were settling into the White House, the Cheneys and the Rumsfelds were on Eleuthera, a small island in the Bahamas, vacationing in a borrowed cottage. We swam and sailed, played tennis, and enjoyed conch soup, a local delicacy. We also spent several evenings dining off an enormous roast that Joyce Rumsfeld, who'd learned to be thrifty on a government salary, had cooked at home and brought along in her luggage.

After two and a half very intense years, our time in the Bahamas was a most welcome break, but when we got back to Washington, I had to figure out what to do with the rest of my life. Age thirty-six was too young to retire. I had lost all desire to return to the academic world, which appeared pretty tame after a tour in the Ford White House. There were some private sector possibilities, but most involved becoming part of the permanent Washington establishment, and that held no attraction for me.

In the end I decided that what I really wanted to do was run for office. I wanted to put my name on the ballot, and if I was going to do that, the best place for me was Wyoming. It was not at all certain that the opportunity to run would occur anytime soon, but once I had decided I wanted to pursue a career in public office back home, it made no sense to hang around Washington. As I have told many an aspiring candidate since, if you want to run for office, you have to get out of D.C. and establish yourself someplace around the country where you may someday have the chance to run. Washington is full of people who would like to hold office and would be good at it, but they can't bring themselves to take that first step.

In June 1977, as soon as school was out, I loaded up a rental truck and drove to Casper, then came back to Washington, rented another truck, and repeated the trip, taking eight-year-old Mary with me this time. I hitched our Volkswagen Beetle behind the moving truck, and at Lynne's insistence, filled it with houseplants. Mary, armed with an old Windex bottle full of water, was given the job of spraying down the houseplants every time we stopped for gas.

Back home in Casper, we moved into a comfortable old house with a big porch across the front. White with green shutters, it had been built in 1916 by one of the original ranch families in central Wyoming. It needed a lot of work, most of which Lynne and I did ourselves, everything from stripping wallpaper to repairing the roof. I joined the board of a local bank and did a little work for my old firm, Bradley Woods and Company. Lynne got a part-time teaching job at the community college.

The family thrived. Daughters Liz and Mary immediately settled into new schools, rode their bikes around our tree-lined neighborhood, and learned to camp out and fish. Their grandparents were delighted to have their only grandchildren living just five minutes away. Lynne and I renewed old friendships and made new ones.

NINETEEN SEVENTY-EIGHT WAS SHAPING up to be a big political year in Wyoming, with every statewide office from the governorship on down up for grabs. In addition, Cliff Hansen, the former Republican governor and two-term U.S. senator, had announced that he would not stand for reelection, causing a lot of stirring around in both parties about his seat. About the only office not open was Wyoming's single seat in the House of Representatives. Democratic Congressman Teno Roncalio, a ten-year veteran of the House, was expected to win an easy reelection.

Shortly after we returned to Casper, I drove to Cheyenne to seek advice from former governor Stan Hathaway about the political outlook in the state. Stan had helped me get my first political job as an intern in the Wyoming Senate in 1965, when he was GOP state chairman, and was revered as a great governor and grand old man of the Republican Party. I knew I could count on him for candid advice on my prospects—or lack thereof—and he didn't disappoint. When I told him that I was giving some thought to seeking the U.S. Senate seat being vacated by Cliff Hansen, he said, "You could do that. You could run for that Senate seat, but if you do, Al Simpson's going to kick your butt."

Al was the ideal candidate for whatever office he wanted. He was just completing twelve years in the Wyoming Legislature, the last two as Speaker pro tem. His family had deep roots in Wyoming, his father having been governor and a U.S. senator. The Simpsons were held in high regard by people all over the state, and Al—tall, gangly, and very funny—knew how to win a crowd over with both humor and substance. Stan Hathaway was right. Everyone who ran against Al—in 1978 and in his two subsequent campaigns—got their butts kicked.

My conversation with Stan Hathaway ended any idea I'd had of running for the Senate, and since I wasn't interested in state office, it looked as though I was going to have to put my political aspirations on hold for a while. But all that changed on a sunny mid-September day when Congressman Roncalio went up to the press box at a University of Wyoming football game and told the radio audience that he didn't plan to run for reelection. Teno's announcement opened the way for me to put my name on the ballot in hopes of returning to Washington as a member of the U.S. House of Representatives.

THE FIRST MEETING OF the "Cheney for Congress" Committee was a small affair, just four of us: Lynne, Dave Nicholas, Celeste

Colgan, and me. Dave was a high school classmate who had been the best man at our wedding. He'd attended Harvard and the University of Wyoming College of Law and was now practicing law in Laramie. He and his wife, Karen, another high school classmate, who was now teaching at the university, were two of our closest friends. Dave agreed to be my campaign chairman. We recruited Lynne's brother, Mark, to be campaign treasurer, responsible for keeping track of the money and filing all the required federal reports.

Celeste Colgan had shared an office with Lynne when they were both English instructors at the University of Wyoming. As the only four-year college in the state, the university is in many ways the common denominator of the state's politics. I was lucky that after my detour to New Haven, I got my undergraduate degree at UW.

Celeste was from Riverton, in Fremont County, where her brother Bruce McMillan, a state legislator, ran the local feed elevator and farm implement store. The first time I went to Riverton, Bruce was my only contact. He wasn't willing to commit to support me at that point, but he walked me around and introduced me to people—which was a start.

Over in Lander, Fremont County's other main town, I went to see Jack Nicholas, Dave's brother, who was the local county judge. Jack and his wife, Alice, introduced me to Judy Legerski, an active Republican and an ardent Catholic who was willing to support me because of my pro-life stance. Every time I went to Lander, I would stay with Jack and Alice and meet more of their friends and neighbors.

I arrived in Cody with only the name of the Republican county chairman, who kindly agreed to make some calls and get several women over to her house to meet this guy they had never heard of who wanted to run for Congress. One of the women was Mildred Cowgill, a former schoolteacher who had outlived two husbands, was tough as nails, and had a heart of gold. Mildred was one of the most respected people in northwestern Wyoming. If she vouched for you, you were good in Park County. She took me under her wing, and we stayed in her house whenever we were up there. She put me together with Gordon Brodrick, her stepson, who owned the General Motors dealership over in Powell, the next town. Gordon and his wife, Esther, hosted an event for me to meet all their friends. That's the way things work in a state where a population of fewer than five hundred thousand is spread out over a hundred thousand square miles.

I knew that my campaign had to look and feel like Wyoming. The last thing I wanted was to import a lot of out-of-state guns for hire, who would cost me a lot of money, ride roughshod over the locals, and end up losing me more votes than they would gain. Friendship and professional expertise justified a few exceptions to that rule. I had worked with Bob Teeter during the Ford campaign, so I asked him to help us do our polling from his base in Michigan. And I asked Bob Gardner, another Ford alum and friend, to moonlight from his agency in San Francisco and help with our media and advertising. Kathie Berger, my White House staff assistant, had gone home to Pittsburgh, but when I called she agreed to drop everything and move to Casper. It was great to have her running the campaign headquarters, supervising volunteers, and managing my schedule.

Finally, I decided to do something the experts always tell you not to do, and that was to be my own campaign manager. While it was true that I was a first-time candidate, I was not exactly a neophyte where campaigns were concerned. I had done every job from passing out buttons for a governor to setting poll questions for a president. I couldn't imagine hiring someone to tell me what to do.

EVERY MEMBER OF CONGRESS will tell you his congressional district is special, but that is really true for Wyoming. It's big and it's beautiful, with high mountains and prairies that go on forever. And the small population means that you can often drive a long way without seeing a soul. I once took Pulitzer Prize–winning photographer David Kennerly, whom I had gotten to know in the Ford White House, on a campaign trip between Casper and Laramie. "It's a long way between voters," he said after we'd gone an hour or so without seeing a town. And he was right, and the fact that there are so few people means that politics is very personal. Voters want to meet you, look you in the eye, and hear what you have to say. It's a kind of campaigning that I feel totally comfortable with, though, as Kennerly observed, the ratio of miles traveled to voters met can be pretty high. I once traveled three hundred miles to attend a two-person coffee—and one of the two people was my local chairman who had organized the event.

That first election—the 1978 contest for the GOP nomination for Congress—turned out to be the toughest of my six campaigns for the House of Representatives. It was a three-way contest among me, the incumbent state treasurer Ed Witzenburger, and Jack Gage, an attorney who was the son of a former Democratic governor. Witzenburger and Gage were both from Cheyenne and could be expected to split the vote there. If I could run up a respectable total in Casper and at least be competitive in Cheyenne, I had a good chance of getting the nomination. Of course, it was also important to work hard in the rest of the state. If I won the primary, I wanted to have a foundation for a strong showing statewide in the general election.

AS A CANDIDATE I was not without liabilities. Between graduate school and working in Washington, I had been away from Wyoming for a dozen years. The last time I had voted there was in 1964. Even having served in the White House as President Ford's chief of staff was a mixed blessing. On the one hand it was by far the most impressive entry on my résumé, but few Wyoming voters would be all that impressed. I would have to be careful not to come across as some hotshot from Washington who thought he was entitled to the House seat. I had to earn it by persuading Wyoming voters that I was really from Wyoming and the best man for the job.

Wyoming was also one of those states where Ronald Reagan had an early and loyal following. The Wyoming delegation to the 1976 GOP convention had been evenly split between Ford and Reagan, and the Reagan state chairman, Dick Jones, a trucker from Cody, was so angry about Reagan's loss that he stormed out of the convention. At the start of my campaign I tried to patch up the relationship by asking to meet with Jones, but he refused to see me. I worked around the problem with the Reagan people by recruiting Peggy Mallick, a Reagan delegate to the '76 convention, to be my county chairman in Casper.

I was also lucky enough to recruit Toni Thomson, a Reagan supporter, who had worked in Washington in the seventies, and her husband, Bill, a prominent attorney, to head up my campaign in Cheyenne. I met them, as I did so many people, through friends. Both Thomsons were about as politically savvy as they come and had deep connections in the state. Paul Etchepare, Toni's father, owned one of the largest ranches in Wyoming. Thyra Thomson, Bill's mother, was Wyoming's secretary of state, and Keith, his father, had been Wyoming's congressman. He was elected to the Senate but died before he could be sworn in. With Bill and Toni on my side, I had good prospects for taking a healthy number of votes out of Cheyenne.

Jimmy Carter also came to my aid by announcing his plans for the Panama Canal. During the Ford-Reagan battle in 1976, ownership of the canal had been a major issue, with Reagan going after Ford for supporting its return to the Panamanians. I hadn't agreed with President Ford on the canal, and when President Carter announced that he would initiate the diplomatic and legislative process of transferring it to Panama, it gave me an opportunity to demonstrate my independence and validate my conservative credentials.

I denounced the giveback of the Panama Canal in the first campaign speech I ever made. It was late fall in 1977, and the Republicans of Lusk, Wyoming, had invited everybody who was even thinking about running to come to a rally and speak. Lusk was a small town named after a local rancher, and the event was modeled after *The Gong Show,* a weekly TV program popular at the time. Each speaker was allotted eighty seconds, and the instant anyone ran over, a tall cowboy with a handlebar mustache would bang a large gong.

This format turned out to be quite a draw, and there were hundreds of people in the Lusk gymnasium that night. It looked like the whole town had turned out. Talking fast, I managed to work in the Panama Canal and several other issues, and if I didn't bring the house down, at least I got through it all without being gonged to a halt.

I formally announced my candidacy on December 14, 1977, and in a rented Ford Mustang began driving all over the state. It had a tape deck on which I could listen to the Carpenters and Anne Murray when I was out of range of a radio station. Later on when Lynne and the girls came along, there would be a chorus of groans from the backseat every time "Close to You" or "Son of a Rotten Gambler" began to play. I had thought that my musical taste was actually pretty with it, but my pre-adolescent passengers enlightened me. And I suspect at least one of them had something to do with leaving the Carpenters tape on the car dashboard to melt in the hot midday sun during one of our campaign stops.

I'd go into a town, introduce myself to key party officials, visit with local newspaper editors and radio talk show hosts, and speak to any group that would have me. I met a lot of nice people and saw a strange sight or two. One was in Evanston, Wyoming, where I walked into the local radio station and found it empty. "Hello, anybody here?" I called out. A large man wearing bib overalls walked out of a back room, holding a very big knife that was dripping blood. It was the station manager, who'd just poached a deer out one of the station's windows and was in the process of butchering it in the back room. He promised to interview me next time I stopped by.

I talked to the Rotary clubs and Kiwanis clubs and Chambers of Commerce. Yes, I had been White House chief of staff, I would say, after I'd been introduced, and the guy who held the job before me was Don Rumsfeld. He'd gone on to be secretary of defense. And before that it had been Al Haig, who'd gone on to be supreme Allied commander in Europe. And the guy who'd held the job before that was Bob Haldeman. He'd gone on to do time in a California penitentiary. It was a good way to describe my credentials in Riverton, Wyoming—or most places for that matter.

I soon discovered that in almost every community there was an informal gathering on weekday mornings at the local diner that usually included the main street merchants who were the economic backbone of the town and senior citizens who paid attention to what was going on and had time to think about things. I learned a lot just by showing up, sipping my coffee, and listening.

Some places what you weren't was more important than who you were. In the Ramshorn Bar in Dubois, when I was introduced as Dick Cheney, candidate for Congress, an old cowboy at the bar looked me over and asked, "Son, are you a Democrat?" I said, "No sir." "Are you a lawyer?" he asked. I said nope, and he said, "Then I'll vote for you!"

PRESIDENT FORD HAD OFFERED to come to Wyoming and appear on my behalf, but particularly in light of the hard feelings left over from the 1976 campaign, we agreed we didn't want it to look as though he were trying unduly to influence the state's choice of a congressman. He agreed to deliver the keynote address at the Republican state convention in Jackson. He neither mentioned my name nor endorsed my candidacy. But everyone knew that the reason he was there was that I had asked him.

The day before his speech, he came to Casper, spoke at the local community college, and then spent the night as our houseguest. We put him in the master bedroom upstairs, thinking maybe we should warn him about the eccentricities of the master bath, but in the end, neither Lynne nor I could bring ourselves to tell a former president to be sure to close the shower curtain tight. The next morning, as we sat around the breakfast table waiting for the thirty-eighth president of the United States to come down and join us, water began to drip into the dining room just under the bath. We enlisted the kids, and the four of us ran around trying to catch the drips in kitchen pans and dry up the ones we missed.

We hosted a small coffee for friends and neighbors to come meet our distinguished houseguest. Edness Kimball Wilkins, a longtime Democratic state legislator, lived across the street. She brought a photograph taken around the turn of the century showing two couples on a stagecoach in front of the local Casper bank. One couple was her parents and the other was President Ford's grandparents, Mr. and Mrs. C. H. King, who had been Wyoming residents. Their son Leslie was the president's biological father, from whom he was largely estranged. He did tell me about stopping to see King in Riverton one summer when he was in college on his way to work as a park ranger in Yellowstone. But he always considered Gerald Rudolph Ford, his mother's second husband, to be his real father.

IN MID-JUNE 1978 LYNNE and I drove to Cheyenne for a few days of campaigning. As usual we stayed with our old friends, Joe and Mary Meyer. Joe had been a high school classmate, my roommate at the University of Wyoming, and an usher at our wedding. Mary, a former Miss Wyoming, was introducing me to people all over the state, including in her hometown of Sheridan.

About 2:00 a.m. I was awakened with a tingling sensation in two fingers of my left hand. I wasn't in any pain, and there were no other symptoms, but my cousin, a physician in Idaho, had suffered a major heart attack just a few weeks before. Thinking of his experience, I decided to have a doctor take a look at me. Joe drove Lynne and me to the Cheyenne Memorial Hospital. On the way I said that I really felt fine and that it was probably a false alarm—although my fingers were still tingling. When we got to the hospital, I walked into the emergency room, sat down, and immediately passed out. When I came to I noticed that there was a great deal of activity in the ER. Then I noticed that it was all focused on me. That was when I was pretty sure I had suffered a heart attack.

I couldn't help but think of my grandfather, my mother's father, who had had heart disease and had suffered his last heart attack in our home. Heart attacks ran in my family, and I knew that they were serious business.

I had been warned by an internist shortly after I left the White House that I was a prime candidate for a coronary. I had a family history on my father's side as well as my mother's. I had been smoking for nearly twenty years. The tobacco companies supplied free cartons of cigarettes to the Nixon and Ford White Houses, with each pack in white and gold boxes bearing the presidential seal. For the last few years

I had been going through two or three packs a day. I found they went especially well with the unlimited supply of strong black coffee provided by the navy stewards in the White House Mess.

But I'd ignored the warnings, and so here I was, thirty-seven years old and a heart patient, wondering if I might have to give up my campaign and my hoped-for career in politics. There were no cardiologists in Cheyenne, but I was blessed to have a fine young internist named Rick Davis handling my case. When I asked him whether I could—or should—resume my campaign, he said, "Look, hard work never killed anybody. What takes a toll is spending your life doing something you don't want to do." He encouraged me to plan on continuing my campaign after a suitable period for rest and recovery and gave me strict orders: Get some exercise and get rid of the cigarettes. Rick and his wife, Ibby, remain good friends and strong supporters to this day.

Out of the hospital and back in Casper, I took it easy for a month and followed doctor's instructions to the letter. I quit smoking and began to watch my diet. I walked to restore my strength, each day going a little farther, and I read. We had a big beautiful old spruce tree in our backyard and I spent most of each day in a comfortable chair under that tree reading President Nixon's memoirs. A friend of mine, Frank Gannon, had helped Nixon write his memoirs and managed to ship me an early copy.

In the meantime the campaign continued with Lynne filling in for me at meetings, rallies, and speeches. She was so good at it that many friends suggested my vote totals would have been higher if I'd just stayed in the backyard and let Lynne do all the rallies.

I had plenty of time to think about how my heart attack was likely to impact voters. My friend Bob Teeter flew in from Michigan, and we talked about a poll to assess voter attitudes, but concluded that the situation had so few precedents we wouldn't even be able to figure out what questions to ask.

We shot a TV commercial of a group of people sitting around talking about prominent political leaders, including Dwight Eisenhower and Lyndon Johnson, who had suffered heart attacks and still served productively in office. But my instinct was that the finished product would make people uncomfortable, and we never put it on the air.

In the end we decided that I should send a letter to every registered Republican in the state explaining why I was running in spite of the heart attack. I described some of the reasons why I had decided to run—the public policy and budgetary issues that had motivated my decision. At the top of the second page I became more personal:

> *But a man's political beliefs are only a part of what motivates him, and in June an event in my life gave me reason to evaluate why I am running for Congress from a different perspective. While I was campaigning in Cheyenne, I suffered a mild heart attack. At thirty-seven years old, I had hardly expected such a thing to happen.*

I noted that doctors in both Cheyenne and Casper had told me that I could expect a full and complete recovery. I reflected Rick Davis's diagnosis when I wrote, "They saw no reason why I should not return to an active schedule in August. I have worked hard all my life, and the doctors said, after a period of rest, I could continue to do so—as long as I take proper care of myself."

I continued with more personal thoughts:

> *An event like a heart attack, however mild it might be, causes a man to reflect upon himself and what is important to him. I must admit that when I found out what had happened, it occurred to me that there are certainly easier ways for a man to spend his life than in running for Congress and being a public official, ways of life which are easier on his family, on his privacy, on his pocketbook.*
>
> *But as I talked to my family, it became clear to me that while public life is sometimes difficult, it is also, for the Cheneys at any rate, immensely satisfying. All of us, Lynne, our two daughters, and myself, like being involved in an effort which goes beyond our own personal interests. Trying to achieve goals which benefit many people gives all of us a good feeling, an uplifting sense of purpose.*

The letter was an unusual campaign document because it didn't ask for anything. The heart attack gave me an opportunity during a political campaign to talk to people on an important subject, with politics set aside.

In time I came to think that the heart attack, much as I might have wished it had not happened, helped from a political point of view. It increased my name identification in the months before the primary election and even helped raise a little money. Wags joked about forming a "Cardiac Patients for Cheney" group, but Foster Chanock, my young assistant from the Ford White House, actually took it upon himself to contact my friends and tell them to send campaign contributions in lieu of flowers. In a typically generous gesture, Bill Steiger, who didn't face much of a challenge in his race for reelection to his Wisconsin congressional seat, urged supporters of his to contribute to me.

The heart attack had occurred on June 18, 1978. One afternoon at the end of July I walked over to a nearby park where some senior citizens were having a picnic. I worked the tables, shaking hands and chatting—and thus relaunched my campaign.

After my heart attack, the campaign became even more a family affair. I turned in the Mustang, and we rented an RV with room for all of us, including my parents and the girls. Dad drove, and Mom made sure I ate regularly and sensibly. The kids took it all in stride. Mary would later write that she thought everyone grew up walking door to door, handing out campaign buttons, and worrying about what was going to happen on the first Tuesday in November. She also claimed that her proudest assignment was standing outside our headquarters wearing a "Honk for Cheney" sandwich board. Liz showed formidable political skills, pressing Cheney buttons and literature upon everyone in sight. She also provided one of the key stories in the archives of Cheney campaign lore when she took a wrong turn in the state fair parade in Douglas, Wyoming, and got lost for several hours.

As the September 12 primary approached, we found ourselves, despite the generosity of many friends, running out of campaign funds, but we did have some personal savings, thanks to Lynne's father, who had left us money from his civil service retirement when he died. It was enough so that we could either buy another round of advertising or pay for a poll, but we couldn't do both. We decided on the advertising, figuring that the poll wouldn't do us any good anyway if we had no money left to act on the results. We were confident that if we won the nomination, we would be able to raise sufficient funds to repay our loan to the campaign, and we managed not to think about the alternative.

Primary election night was a very special time. We waited for the returns to come in at our home on Beech Street, and when the votes were tallied, I had won the Republican primary with 42 percent of the vote to 31 percent for Ed Witzenburger and 27 percent for Jack Gage. That first election victory was an emotional high, topped by few things in life, not just because of all the hard work, although there was plenty of that, but because of the ups and downs and the risks we had taken. In the end, it had all worked out, and Lynne, Liz, Mary, and I celebrated with family and friends into the wee hours of the next morning.

I BELIEVED THAT ONCE I won the primary, I could be confident of winning the general election in the fall. My Democratic opponent was Bill Bagley, longtime aide to Congressman Roncalio, who was from Star Valley. He could expect to capture some GOP votes in that area of the state, but overall it was going to be a tough year for Democrats in Wyoming. With seven statewide seats including the governorship on the ballot, the Democratic Party was going to be stretched for resources. The GOP had advantages in registered voters and in finances, and the Democrats had the added disadvantage of having Jimmy Carter in the White House. He was a definite liability in Wyoming.

Because of the late primary, the fall campaign was mercifully short, just eight weeks, and for part of it, the GOP candidates traveled together. This was a tradition based on necessity, since most communities in Wyoming were small and couldn't possibly host separate events for every statewide office seeker.

The star of the '78 GOP road show was Al Simpson, our candidate for the United States Senate. His father, Governor Milward Simpson, had unexpectedly been defeated for reelection in 1958, and Al worked hard on that first campaign and every one after to make sure that never happened to him. He kept precise notes of all the people he met and how their families were doing and carefully filed the cards away after each event. He was a diligent politician, which I think most people never guessed because they were so taken with his sense of humor. It wasn't that the jokes he told were so great, but the way that he told them brought the house down every time. In fact you could hear his jokes many times (and, believe me, I have) and still find yourself laughing.

Al and his wife, Ann, also have a gift for friendship, and Lynne and I have been lucky to know them for more than thirty years. Al has campaigned with me every time my name has been on the ballot, including when I was running for vice president. Altogether we've done six statewide campaigns and two national ones, and we've never lost an election when one of our names was on the ballot.

One of the most memorable days of the 1978 campaign came near the end. We had been in Sheridan in northern Wyoming for an event the night before, and my dad was driving Lynne and me back to Casper and Cheyenne for the closing events of the campaign. It was one of those glorious Indian summer days that Wyoming is famous for. All of the aspen and cottonwood leaves had turned to gold. The sky was a brilliant, cloudless blue. We stopped, threw an old quilt on the ground, and spent a couple of hours sitting at the foot of the Bighorn Mountains reminiscing about all we had seen in the last twenty years. Now, some thirty years later, that day still stands out as a very special moment in our lives.

When the vote was tallied on November 7, I had 59 percent of the vote. It would be my narrowest victory in six general election campaigns—and the sweetest one. For the next ten years I would be recognized on the floor of the United States House of Representatives as "the Gentleman from Wyoming." I would have a lot of titles after that, but never one of which I was prouder.

SHORTLY AFTER THE ELECTION, there was a weeklong orientation for all the new GOP members at a hotel just outside Washington. It was designed to make us more effective as legislators and to get us thinking, even before we were sworn in, about our campaigns for reelection. The sessions covered everything from our salary ($57,500) to how to get mail answered. We heard from the leadership and senior floor staff about the House rules and procedures. And we spent a lot of time on the question of committee assignments. Many freshmen had unrealistic expectations, fully believing they could claim a seat on one of the most important committees, such as Ways and Means or Appropriations, when those assignments were hotly contested among more senior members and almost never given to newcomers.

I had already called Republican leader John Rhodes of Arizona the day after the election to put in a bid for an assignment to the Interior Committee. With the federal government controlling some 50 percent of the surface and 65 percent of the mineral wealth in Wyoming, public lands policy issues were vital to the state. Whether you were involved in the energy business or ranching or tourism and recreation, the rules set by the federal government for access to and the use of federal lands were vitally important to your economic success. My time and work on the Interior Committee would be rewarded in 1984 with the passage of the Wyoming Wilderness Act, which was my most significant piece of legislation and the one of which I'm proudest. I worked closely with both my Wyoming colleagues on the Senate side, Al Simpson and Malcolm Wallop, and we were able to add almost a million acres to the state's wilderness areas.

When I'd first sought a slot on Interior, Leader Rhodes said he would support my request and that he had a request of me in return. He wanted to assign me to the Ethics Committee, which I thought was pretty unusual. Freshmen are almost never assigned to Ethics, which deals with some of the most sensitive issues to come before the House, including whether a member should be sanctioned or even expelled for misconduct. The leadership of both parties was very selective about whom they appointed to Ethics, and most members, reluctant to judge their colleagues, did whatever they could to avoid service on it. But I agreed and decided to take the request as something of a compliment to my responsibility and judgment rather than the result of Rhodes having been refused by all the more senior and wiser members. Besides, I thought it might be challenging, which turned out to be both true and an underestimate. During the 96th Congress, the committee would be busier than it had been for many years. And we would be responsible for expelling a member for the first time since the Civil War.

After the election, Lynne, the girls, and I spent several days in Hawaii relaxing and enjoying the wonderful weather. Bill Steiger and I had both been invited to speak to a convention of realtors in Honolulu, and since his and Janet's son Bill was the same age as Mary, the four of us sat around the pool at the Hawaiian Village, talking and watching the kids play. The conversation was wide-ranging, as it always was when we had time to spend with Bill and Janet. I looked forward to working alongside Bill in the House and expected to be one of the growing company of members who looked to him for leadership. His conduct and contributions to the work of the Ways and Means Committee had attracted attention and gained him widespread and bipartisan respect. Although he was only forty, his influence was steadily growing, and there was already talk about his presidential potential.

I HAD SPENT ENOUGH years in Washington to know the importance of hiring the right staff. They should have knowledge of Congress and how to get things done on Capitol Hill, but just as important was having some feel for and understanding of Wyoming.

As my administrative assistant (the equivalent of a chief of staff) I hired Dave Gribbin, who had graduated from high school in Casper and was a good friend. He'd served a tour in the U.S. Army, was working for the National Automobile Dealers Association, and was an ordained Methodist minister. He and his wife, Lori, had been our neighbors in student housing at the University of Wyoming when we were first married.

I was able to persuade Patty Howe to come work for me as my top legislative aide. The Laramie native was a twelve-year veteran of Cliff

Hansen's staff, and she was intimately familiar with all of the federal issues that would have an impact on my constituents and our state. A single mother with only a high school education, she had started work for Cliff as a secretary. By the time she came to work for me she was recognized as one of the finest legislative assistants on the Hill.

Kathie Embody (formerly Kathie Berger) was like part of our family after the months she had spent with us on the Wyoming campaign, and I was pleased when she agreed to come to Washington. There were many others who made significant contributions in those first days and during the early years, including Jim Steen, Pete Williams, Cece Boyer, Ruthann Norris, Norma Fletcher, Sue Benzer, and George Van Cleve. One of the things I always felt good about was the low rate of turnover among the people who worked for me. Once someone signed on they rarely expressed a desire to move on. Many were still working for me long after I left the Congress.

On December 4, 1978, the House Republicans who would serve in the 96th Congress convened to elect our leadership for the coming Congress. I had an appointment scheduled with a photographer from *U.S. News & World Report* to take a picture for an upcoming issue on new members of Congress, and at the appointed hour I left the caucus. As I stepped outside, I noticed that the U.S. flags over the Capitol and the House office buildings were being lowered to half-staff, and when I asked why, I was told it was to honor a member who had just died.

I asked who it was and was stunned to be told it was Bill Steiger. After living with diabetes for many years, he had died of a heart attack at the age of forty.

A few days later, I was granted permission to fly out to Oshkosh, Wisconsin, for the funeral with the official delegation from the House, even though I had not yet been sworn in as a member. I've attended a great many funerals over the years, but few have rivaled the Steiger service for the sense of loss about what might have been.

AMONG HOUSE REPUBLICANS THERE were a number of informal social groups that a member might be invited to join, including

SOS (Society of Statesmen) and the Chowder and Marching Society. Neither group had official standing or function, but they were invaluable in developing relationships with colleagues. When I was invited to join SOS, I did so eagerly. We met every Tuesday afternoon at 5:00 p.m. in a member's office, with the host providing snacks and drinks. During the course of the meeting each member would take the floor for a few minutes and talk about whatever he chose, everything from politics back home in the district to a report on a recent congressional trip overseas—or maybe just the latest gossip. On Wednesday mornings SOS and Chowder and Marching held a joint breakfast and invited an outside guest, a cabinet member, perhaps, or a columnist or senior White House official.

There was also a third group, known as the Wednesday Group, which had more of an ideological edge. Its members were moderate Republicans, such as Jim Leach of Iowa, Bill Green of New York, Pete McCloskey of California, and John Anderson of Illinois, and there was some overlap with SOS and Chowder and Marching. When I was invited to join the Wednesday Group, I turned down the invitation because I considered myself a conservative and saw little value in being identified with liberal Republicans, but Barber Conable of New York, ranking Republican on Ways and Means and one of the most respected members of the House, called me to his office and suggested I reconsider. Not many members got an invitation to join the Wednesday Group, he said, and it was a "dumb move" on my part to reject it. He said as a conservative I would automatically get to know all the conservatives in the GOP caucus. Joining the Wednesday Group would give me a chance to know and understand the liberal Republicans. He was right and I joined. It was a good thing to do, and because of it I had support from the moderate camp as well as conservatives as I moved up in the leadership ranks.

From my earliest days in the House I was involved with various outside groups, including think tanks and academic institutes, that took a scholarly, analytical, and bipartisan approach to the House's past and present. I was invited by senior Democrat Dick Bolling, the chairman of the powerful Rules Committee and an old ally of Speaker Tip O'Neill, to join a small breakfast group he occasionally summoned. Bolling was one of the most brilliant historians and tacticians in the history of the House, and every time I was around him I learned something new and important. Among the others in his group were Dick Gephardt and Steny Hoyer.

I was also invited to join a small group that was being assembled at the American Enterprise Institute by scholars Norm Ornstein and Thomas Mann. They chose seven freshmen, four Republicans and three Democrats, and every few months would invite us to sit down over dinner and talk on a background basis about everything we were seeing and doing. In the monograph that was subsequently published, called *Congress Off the Record: The Candid Analyses of Seven Members,* we were not identified. Today the discerning (and dedicated) may be able to put the names Cheney, Gingrich, Martin Sabo, and Geraldine Ferraro to some of the sentiments on those pages.

I participated in several events sponsored by the Aspen Institute, which ran seminars for congressmen and senators as well as two annual retreats. Lynne and I enjoyed a few midwinter days of great conversation and food at sunny places such as Bermuda and Round Hill in Jamaica. It was at Round Hill that I met Condoleezza Rice for the first time. She was at Stanford and had been invited to lead a seminar on Soviet military policy.

The Center for Strategic and International Studies, which was then connected with Georgetown University, used to hold an annual retreat at Williamsburg, Virginia. That was where I met Sam Nunn, a Democratic senator from Georgia, who would later head the committee that considered my nomination to be secretary of defense.

During my time in the House, I also participated in continuity-of-government exercises. They dealt with contingency responses to an attack on the United States that decapitated our government. What were our plans if both the president and vice president should be killed? If the Congress were wiped out? These were Cold War exercises, premised on the nuclear threat that the Soviets represented, and according to press reports, they were ended during the Clinton administration, discontinued as relics of another day. But the risk of mass-casualty attacks did not disappear with the dissolution of the Soviet Union, and years later, on

9/11, the possibility of the government's being decapitated would seem a real and present danger.

I WAS OFTEN ASKED by people why in the world I wanted to be a freshman member of the House, serving in the minority party, after I'd already been White House chief of staff. I used to explain that there was something very special about having your name on the ballot and convincing thousands of voters to support you. That running and winning the right to cast your state's vote in the U.S. House of Representatives was politics at its best. That being elected in accordance with our Constitution meant you had earned the right to cast that vote and no one could take it away except by defeating you at the polls. Your political fate didn't depend upon someone else's success in an election.

It would also be accurate to say that I was heavily influenced by my experience with men such as Jerry Ford, Don Rumsfeld, and Bill Steiger. An institution that could attract men like these had to be one that I could be proud to be part of. The fact is I loved the House of Representatives and had every intention of spending the rest of my career as a "Man of the House."

Every new class of House members arrives in Washington with the conviction that they are going to "clean out the stables" or "drain the swamp"; that at long last they are going to be the "reformers" the Congress so badly needs. Most of the time this phase passes, and the new members become established senior members with all the privileges and opportunities that entails. But every once in a while, a class does have an extraordinary impact. It may be because the class is especially large or they affect a particular issue or they stick around longer than most, thus gaining seniority, or because they have an unusual degree of cohesion and vote as a block larger than most. The 1974 Democratic class of "Watergate Babies" is often cited as an example.

The 1978 class of which I was a part produced leaders who would shape Washington for decades: Jerry Lewis, who would become chairman of the Appropriations Committee; Bill Thomas, future chairman of the Ways and Means Committee; and Jim Sensenbrenner, who would one day chair the Judiciary Committee. On the Democratic side were Geraldine Ferraro, who would be the Democratic vice presidential nominee in 1984, and Phil Gramm, who would become a Republican and a United States senator from Texas. Another Texan in the class of 1978, Democrat Kent Hance, had won his seat by defeating a future president, thirty-two-year-old George W. Bush.

But no one in our class stands out in memory as much as Newt Gingrich of Georgia. An academic with a Ph.D. in history from Tulane, Newt decided in 1974 to run for Congress in Georgia against the incumbent Jack Flynt, a longtime member of the House Appropriations Committee. Nineteen seventy-four, of course, was the Watergate election, not a good time to begin a career in elective office as a Republican, and Newt was defeated.

Two years later Newt again ran against Flynt and lost again. Nineteen seventy-six, it turned out, was a tough year to win in Georgia as a Republican, because the state's own Jimmy Carter was running as the Democratic candidate for president. When Newt announced that in 1978 he would be running a third time against Jack Flynt, Flynt quit. It was said he just couldn't take any more. Newt was nothing if not tenacious.

I first met Newt at the orientation session for freshman Republicans in 1978, and he was fascinating to watch. He had tremendous energy, a head full of ideas, and an absolute, unwavering conviction that we Republicans could once again become the majority in the House. But to do it, he argued, we had to quit being polite to the Democrats and go after them—a tactic that drove some of our more senior members right up the wall. Many House Republicans were comfortable in the minority and not eager to go to war against our Democratic colleagues.

One of the innovations Newt came up with was for him and many of the other new Republicans to use the "one-minutes," which were short speeches at the beginning of each day's session, to really go after Jimmy Carter and his administration. Using one-minutes to go on the attack was typical of Newt: clever, creative, and very successful. It fired up the troops and fed the media. It was not, however, my personal cup of tea.

My style was more restrained, and I was reluctant to speak unless I had something I really wanted to say—and then I'd save it for debate. I didn't garner a lot of publicity this way, but I found that at least some of my colleagues appreciated what I wasn't doing. I was at the rail at the back of the chamber, leaning over, watching one of my freshman colleagues give a barnburner of a speech—pounding on the podium and really letting the Democrats have it—when one of the senior Republicans came over, put his arm around my shoulder, and said, "You know what I like about you, Cheney? You are the only member of your whole class who doesn't drool when he speaks!" I took that as high praise.

I wasn't part of Newt's Conservative Opportunity Society, the group with which he plotted the takeover of the House, but he encouraged my chief of staff, Dave Gribbin, to sit in on the regular meetings. And on occasion, when Newt would push too hard or take some action that angered the senior members of the caucus or the leadership, he would come to my office and seek my counsel on what he'd done to ruffle so many feathers and how best to patch things up. Our relationship was useful in maintaining some degree of peace among the Republicans in the House. For the leadership I served as a bridge to the younger, more aggressive members. For Newt I provided knowledge of which lines he shouldn't step over if he didn't want to get in a pile of trouble. And for me, my role allowed me to be identified on the one hand as part of the Republican establishment and on the other as someone who had close ties to that younger generation, eager to overthrow the establishment.

I REMEMBER WELL THE afternoon when I sought recognition by the Speaker and then rose to address the House of Representatives for the first time as a member. I was less than thrilled with the subject matter, which dealt with one of the many sad cases the Ethics Committee had to pass judgment on. Charles Diggs was a longtime congressman from Michigan's 13th District. He had been one of the bright young men of the civil rights movement, and he had been elected the first chairman of the Congressional Black Caucus. Now he had been convicted of taking kickbacks from his congressional staff, but while he was appealing his case, his Michigan constituents had reelected him.

An incensed group of members, mostly Republican and led by Newt Gingrich, were demanding his expulsion, but the Ethics Committee recommended censure instead, a decision I was happy to defend. As I pointed out in my speech, the Constitution clearly gives the House the right to expel a member, but it also bestows upon the people the right to choose their representatives, and the people of Michigan's 13th had chosen Diggs even after he was convicted. "Much as I deplore Mr. Diggs' unethical behavior," I said, "much as I believe that he should no longer serve in the House of Representatives, I cannot support the contention that this body should now take the unprecedented step in these circumstances, of setting aside the right of the voters of Michigan's 13th District to select the congressman of their choice." The vote to censure rather than expel Diggs passed by an overwhelming majority.

The most important cases considered during my term on the Ethics Committee stemmed from the so-called Abscam scandal. The "Ab" in *Abscam* was short for Abdul Enterprises—the name of the phony company the FBI set up supposedly representing the interests of an Arab sheikh who was prepared to pay bribes to obtain U.S. government help. What began as an FBI sting operation targeting corrupt local officials in the Philadelphia area ended up ensnaring six congressmen and a U.S. senator.

Most of those convicted in Abscam lost their bids for reelection or resigned after their trials, but Ozzie Myers of Pennsylvania insisted on taking his case before the entire House and forcing a vote on the question of whether he should be expelled. In his case, there was no intervening election, as there had been for Diggs, and there was an absolutely damning videotape that showed him telling undercover agents, "Money talks in this business and bullshit walks." I joined in the overwhelming vote in both the Ethics Committee and the House to expel him, but it was painful business for everyone, not because Congress should protect its own or its members should expect special treatment, but because the Constitution provides for the direct election of representatives by the people. The only qualifications are age, citizenship, and residence. At the time of Abscam, Myers was only the fourth member in history to be expelled. The previous three expulsions had been during the Civil War, and the grounds were treason.

One of the members caught up in Abscam was John Murtha of Pennsylvania, a former marine and the first Vietnam veteran to be elected to Congress. He made an appearance on one of the FBI's undercover surveillance tapes that was embarrassing, but not, in my opinion, illegal. Still he was being tarred with the same brush as the others, which I didn't think was fair, so one afternoon I talked to him on the House floor and told him I thought he was getting a bum rap. I said that if he needed any help on our side, he should let me know. He thanked me, and we never mentioned it again. In July 1981, the Ethics Committee cleared him.

DURING MY FIRST YEAR in the House, Republican leader John Rhodes of Arizona announced that he would not run for that position again after the next election. This immediately set off a major succession battle within the Republican caucus. One of the major contenders for the post was Guy Vander Jagt of Michigan, a charismatic individual and an impressive orator, who had worked closely with most of the new members in his capacity as chairman of the National Republican Congressional Committee. Many of them felt they owed their election to Guy, and he had a considerable following. The other contender was Bob Michel of Illinois, Leader Rhodes's second in command as minority whip. He was widely liked and universally respected, though some of the younger members in the Vander Jagt camp criticized him for being too comfortable in the minority, too unwilling to take on the Democrats.

Only two members of the '78 class, Tom Loeffler of Texas and I, supported Bob Michel. I liked both him and Guy Vander Jagt, but I had run my campaign without any help from the NRCC. I knew Bob Michel from my earlier work in the Nixon and Ford administrations— and I thought he would win the Leader's job. I signed on early.

Shortly before the 1980 election I was approached by one of Bob's key floor assistants, Walt Kennedy. There were certain people, Walt said, who thought I should run for a leadership position—in particular the chairmanship of the Republican Policy Committee, the fourth-ranking position behind the Leader, the whip, and the chairman of the House Republican Conference (or caucus). I responded cautiously, telling Kennedy I'd think it over. There were already two announced candidates for the post, Marjorie Holt of Maryland and Eldon Rudd of Arizona, both senior to me and holding commitments from a number of members.

I figured Bob Michel was behind Kennedy's suggestion, but I couldn't really talk with Bob about it. His contest with Guy Vander Jagt was close and hard-fought, and if word got out that he was actively recruiting me to run against more senior members for policy chairman, it might well cost him support from their backers and lose him the contest for Leader. On my own I took some quiet soundings, and when I determined I could marshal enough support to win, I announced for the race.

Some years later Bob Michel confirmed that he had asked Walt Kennedy to suggest that I run for policy chairman. One of his rationales was that my candidacy would attract support and energy among my fellow freshmen and thereby lessen their fervor for Vander Jagt. He was also thinking about putting together a leadership team that he could count on and work with in the years ahead.

When the voting was over in that 1980 caucus, Michel was the GOP Leader, Trent Lott of Mississippi was the newly elected whip, Jack Kemp of New York was Conference chairman, and I was policy chairman. It was an effective team, and we worked well together throughout the 1980s, the Reagan years.

Because of the way the House is organized and its rules are written, individual members of the minority typically have little impact on the overall work of the House, but being in the leadership took me into the meetings where legislative and political strategy were decided and the relationship with the administration was managed. From my personal standpoint, being in the leadership made a world of difference.

———

MY FIRST TERM IN the House coincided with the last half of President Carter's administration. The 1976 campaign had not left me a fan of President Carter, nor had his first two years in office. I found his administration singularly unimpressive.

Despite the fact that the Democrats had an overwhelming margin of more than one hundred House seats during 1979 and 1980, the Carter White House found it difficult to achieve legislative successes. In 1979, faced with serious shortages in fuel, partly as a result of the Iranian Revolution and other unrest in the Middle East, President Carter pushed hard to enact energy legislation in the Congress. At the end of a House debate on one of the administration's energy-related initiatives, Tip O'Neill made the dramatic gesture of coming down from the Speaker's chair—where custom prohibited him from taking a position for or against any piece of legislation—in order to speak from the well of the House on behalf of the administration's bill. On this day Tip was particularly eloquent in his remarks. He talked about how, as a young man visiting Washington, he had been sitting in the gallery of the House on the day in the fall of 1941, not long before Pearl Harbor, when the House was asked to extend the Selective Service System. He argued that now, in 1979, we were faced with a crisis of similar magnitude, and the stakes of the vote were no less high.

It was an extraordinary performance, and when he finished, all of us, Democrats and Republicans alike, rose and gave the Speaker a standing ovation. Then we voted—and beat him decisively. Tip O'Neill was much loved and highly respected, but he couldn't transfer either of those sentiments to the president, and he couldn't translate them into votes when we were considering the president's proposals.

President Carter encountered difficulties as well in trying to project American power. When the Shah was toppled in Iran and the Saudis asked for a demonstration of U.S. commitment to the Kingdom, President Carter responded dramatically by sending a squadron of F-15 fighter aircraft to the Persian Gulf. Then, when the planes were in the air, he announced that they were unarmed. The Iranian hostage crisis plagued him for his last year in office. A bungled and failed attempt to rescue the American hostages—code-named Desert One—seemed to symbolize his administration's ineptitude.

His difficulties with Congress stemmed in part from a lack of understanding about how to manage relations with Capitol Hill. Speaker O'Neill, after being treated cavalierly by the president's chief of staff, Hamilton Jordan, took to referring to him as "Hannibal Jerkin," and the Georgians never achieved any kind of détente with the powers that be at the other end of Pennsylvania Avenue. Carter made a big deal of getting rid of the presidential yacht *Sequoia*. He didn't realize that far more than being an expendable perk for the man in the Oval Office, the historic vessel was a great tool for lobbying Congress. One of the most sought-after invitations in Washington during the Ford years had been for drinks and dinner with the president on an evening cruise on the Potomac. It was a tradition that when the *Sequoia* sailed past Mount Vernon, all aboard came on deck to join the crew in an official salute to the first president. Many votes were quietly won on those evening cruises.

My biggest frustration with President Carter arose while I was serving as secretary of defense. President George H. W. Bush and Secretary of State James Baker were working to get U.N. Security Council approval of a resolution authorizing the use of force to eject the Iraqis from Kuwait in 1990–91. We found out that former President Carter was actively lobbying against the U.S. position. He had contacted heads of government with seats on the Security Council and urged them to oppose our resolution. His intervention was ineffective—and also totally inappropriate for a former president.

Many years later, long after they had both left office, President Ford developed a strong friendship with the man who had handed him the only electoral defeat in his long career. He used to take a certain delight in letting me know that he disagreed with my rather harsh judgment of his successor. Near the end of his days, President Ford spent a good deal of time planning the details of his state funeral. He must have had a good laugh setting down the arrangements for the burial near his presidential museum in Grand Rapids, which required the Cheneys and the Carters, together with the Rumsfelds, to spend the afternoon in close quarters.

THE PENDULUM CAN SWING fast in presidential politics, and it looked as if 1980—only six years after Nixon's resignation and four years after Jimmy Carter's election—was going to be a very good year for Republicans. Ronald Reagan was the clear front-runner for the GOP nomination, and nearly every Republican officeholder was now a Reaganite, including many of us who had supported Jerry Ford four years earlier.

President Ford had briefly considered the possibility of making another run for the White House. Early in the year he asked a group of us who had worked for him to visit Palm Springs, California, to discuss the subject. Among those attending were Jack Marsh, Stu Spencer, and Bob Teeter. We spent the better part of a day discussing the possibility of mounting a campaign at this relatively late date and his prospects of capturing the GOP nomination.

At the end of the day, he said he wanted to sleep on it. The next morning when he reconvened the group of advisors, he announced that he really did not want to be a candidate in 1980. He said that he simply wasn't prepared to subject himself to the rigors of another national campaign. By this time he had acquired a very nice home on a golf course in the desert near Palm Springs and built a new home in the mountains in Beaver Creek, Colorado. He was earning a good living in the private sector. I always believed that he felt an obligation to consider the possibility of mounting a campaign in 1980, in part because he was still smarting from the closeness of his defeat in 1976, and in part because he really didn't like the idea of Ronald Reagan as the nominee. But when he focused on what a national campaign would require of him, he had little interest.

IN WYOMING I HAD worked hard to build a strong political base and to head off any serious opposition, and I pretty much succeeded. I had no Republican challengers in 1980, and the four-man Democratic primary was won by Jim Rogers, a bartender from Lyman, a small town in the remote southwest corner of the state. Rumor had it that he had meant to run for the state legislature but checked the wrong box when filing his papers. I had to go through the motions of a campaign—fundraising, advertising, and making public appearances—but I coasted to an easy victory with 69 percent of the vote.

In 1976 I had played a major role in the Republican convention in Kansas City. I had a spacious suite next to President Ford's and cars and drivers to whisk me around. But in 1980, as a freshman congressman, I was only one member of the Wyoming delegation. Reflecting our state's population and general role in the proceedings, we were assigned a motel about half an hour outside Detroit, and if I didn't catch the delegation bus each morning, I was looking at a fifty-dollar cab ride.

The 1980 Detroit convention was basically a coronation for Ronald Reagan. Although there had been several candidates for the party's nomination, the former California governor's victory was never really in doubt. For one brief moment in Detroit, I found myself back in the action, when attention turned to our nominee's choice of a vice presidential running mate. A number of Reagan's top advisors, foremost among them campaign manager Bill Casey, believed that a Reagan-Ford ticket would be the strongest possible combination. In the Ford camp Henry Kissinger, Jack Marsh, and Bryce Harlow were among those urging President Ford to give serious consideration to joining his former rival's ticket.

Bryce Harlow in particular was a strong advocate of a Reagan-Ford ticket. The little-known Harlow, who had first served in the Eisenhower administration, was one of the wisest, most respected, and most influential men in Washington for three decades. In 1976 he believed that Ford would win if he could put the wounds of the nomination fight behind him and invite Reagan to join his ticket. Harlow considered the electoral logic no less compelling four years on. Reagan and Ford were the unrivaled leaders of their wings of the Republican Party. At the time, before Carter's extreme unpopularity and Reagan's great appeal were fully appreciated, a Reagan-Ford ticket looked like the best way to bring the party together and enter the race with a united front.

On the third day of the convention, I was invited by Howard Baker and John Rhodes, the Senate and House minority leaders, to join them and representatives of Governor Reagan and President Ford at the Renaissance Hotel to discuss the proposal. President Ford had made it clear that he would consider the vice presidency only if there was an agreement giving him significant responsibilities in a Reagan-Ford administration. At the meeting Bill Casey indicated they were willing to go a long way toward meeting the Ford demands, including giving the former chief executive a major role in foreign policy, the budget, and personnel. I realized that what was being discussed all but amounted to a co-presidency, with the president and vice president dividing and sharing the powers of the office.

I was stunned at the extent to which Bill Casey, and presumably Governor Reagan, were willing to share the power of the president. After the meeting Bob Teeter and I joined Baker and Rhodes in discussing the proposal. It was clear that none of us thought the arrangement being discussed was even remotely workable. There can be only one president at a time, and certain presidential powers cannot be delegated.

Fortunately, later that evening the Reagan people arrived at the same conclusion and offered the second spot on the ticket to George H. W. Bush, who readily accepted. On reflection, I don't think President Ford had any intention of being vice president a second time. He often told me over the years that the months he spent as vice president were the most miserable of his career. I think he deliberately made demands that he fully expected to be rejected and that he was surprised at how far Reagan was prepared to go to persuade him to accept the vice presidential nomination.

AFTER THE 1984 ELECTION, Speaker O'Neill, at the recommendation of Bob Michel, appointed me to a seat on the House Intelligence Committee. I regarded my assignment as an honor—though I realized it was not an honor that all members sought. The committee requires a tremendous amount of time, work, and study. Because of the sensitivity of the subject matter, much of the work can't be delegated to staff members and the material can't be duplicated or distributed outside the committee's high-security offices. That means going over to the offices in person and spending hours reading the reports that pour in daily from all over the world and the detailed analyses prepared by the professional staff. Further, the very nature of the committee's work requires absolute confidentiality and secrecy. There can never be a press conference to claim credit or even a passing mention in a newsletter to constituents with respect to most of what a member on the Intelligence Committee does.

I burrowed into the work, spending many hours in the offices. The committee staff responded to my interest by giving me even more material. I was fascinated by all the information, which was sometimes conflicting, and by the challenge of assimilating and assessing it.

I visited the various intelligence agencies—the CIA headquarters at Langley were just a few miles from our house in Virginia—and many of the private sector companies that produced the equipment that was such an important part of the intelligence business. I went to a National Reconnaissance Office ground station to watch the real-time downloads of feeds from the worldwide network of intelligence satellites.

One night in the Nevada desert, I became one of the first civilians to see the new F-117 stealth fighter. I was flown on a small shuttle plane into a completely blacked-out facility, where a jeep with driver and guide met me and drove me to a hangar—a huge, dark shadow against the desert sky. Inside, in the center of the vast and empty football-field-length interior, was one of the most magnificent—and weirdest—sights I have ever seen: a stealth fighter. Today the sleek, delta-shaped aircraft are familiar through photos and films and video games, but that night in the desert it was still a complete secret, and I was literally in awe.

The House Permanent Select Committee on Intelligence was small: ten Democrats and six Republicans. The chairman when I went on the committee was Lee Hamilton of Indiana, a Democrat for whom I have a great deal of respect. Bob Stump of Arizona, the ranking Republican, was solid, dependable, and totally reliable. Henry Hyde of Illinois, who succeeded Stump, was a close personal friend, someone I had known and respected for more than a decade.

At one point I became ranking member on the Programs and Budget Authorization Subcommittee, where I was ably assisted by two talented staffers, Marty Faga and Duane Andrews. My position allowed me to survey the entire range of our intelligence activities and operations and to get a practical sense of how things worked—and how they didn't work. This was knowledge that would turn out to be very useful when I became secretary of defense and later vice president.

During my time on the Intel Committee, we dealt with Soviet adventurism in the Middle East and Latin America, and the regional aftermath of the invasion of Afghanistan. On one Intel trip we went to the Khyber Pass in Pakistan and met with several leaders of the Afghan mujahideen. We also met with Pakistani president Zia in Islamabad. At home the committee had to deal with some very serious and very sensitive espionage cases. Edward Lee Howard was a CIA officer who defected to Moscow with the names and covers of many agents all around the world. And the Walker family—retired navy officer John Anthony Walker and his older brother and son and a friend—sold our secret naval codes, thus allowing the Soviet Union to read secret military communications.

There was an intriguing coda to my time on the Intelligence Committee. In May 1987 I received a call from the legendary CIA counterintelligence director James Jesus Angleton. He said that he had something of vital importance to tell me and that it could be conveyed only in person. I knew that Angleton's resignation from the CIA in 1975 had enabled him to avoid prosecution on charges of illegal surveillance, and I knew that he had a reputation for being obsessed by the belief that the Soviets had managed to infiltrate a mole into the highest levels of American government. But many who had worked with Angleton regarded him as brilliant, and I wanted to hear what he had to say.

I called Henry Hyde, the Intel Committee's ranking Republican, and invited him to sit in on the meeting. A few days later, before our scheduled meeting, Jim Angleton died. I never learned what it was he wanted to tell me.

I WAS REELECTED IN 1986 with 69 percent of the vote. I hadn't had tough opposition, but I had worked hard in the campaign and was looking forward to a postelection elk hunt with my friend Al Simpson and his sons, Colin and Bill. Our lottery applications for elk tags had been successful, and I had packed my bags for the flight home when I got a call from Bob Michel. Apparently I was the only member of the House Republican leadership still in Washington during that postelection period, and Bob wanted me to attend a hastily called meeting at the White House. On November 12, when I arrived at the West Wing, I was ushered into the Situation Room in the basement. The majority and minority leaders of the Senate, Bob Dole and Robert Byrd, were there, along with Speaker Jim Wright and key members of the administration's national security team. The whole thing had the air of a crisis about to unfold, and I suspected I wouldn't be going elk hunting.

National Security Advisor John Poindexter briefed us, revealing the story of a secret administration initiative that would soon result in a firestorm. In hopes of improving our relationship with supposedly moderate elements in Iran, the United States had begun to sell arms—at first indirectly, then later directly—to these factions. The United States also wanted help from the Iranians in securing the release of American hostages whom Hezbollah was holding in Lebanon, and after the arms sales commenced three Americans were freed. Less than a week before our Situation Room briefing, President Reagan had appeared in the Rose Garden with David Jacobsen, who had been released after seventeen months in captivity in Beirut.

The freeing of hostages was undeniably a good thing, but it was clear to me that the initiative was ill-conceived. It violated the arms embargo that we had imposed on Iran and that we were insisting other nations observe, and it undermined our strict policy against negotiating with terrorists. Congress had not been told about the operation, as we should have been.

The situation grew exponentially worse in late November when Attorney General Ed Meese disclosed in a press conference that profits from Iranian arm sales had been diverted to insurgents known as the Contras, who were fighting against the pro-communist government in Nicaragua. The Congress had passed the Boland Amendments, measures aimed at constraining the president from pursuing his policy of aiding the Contras. After President Daniel Ortega of Nicaragua made a much-publicized trip to Moscow, the fierce resistance on the part of the Democrats to aiding the Contras had abated somewhat, but the Boland Amendments were still on the books, so the stage was set for a confrontation.

On December 2 I made my way through a downpour to an 11:00 a.m. meeting the president had called with the Republican leadership in the Cabinet Room. He assured us he'd had no knowledge of the diversion of funds to the Contras, and after we departed he made the same point in a four-minute televised speech. He also said he would welcome the appointment of a special prosecutor and endorsed congressional inquiries into the matter.

The next day the president called another meeting with the Republican leadership, this time in the Oval Office. The president sat in a chair on one side of the fireplace and Senate Majority Leader Bob Dole in the chair on the other side. I was on a cream-colored sofa between House Republican Whip Trent Lott and Vice President George Bush. Across from us were House Minority Leader Bob Michel, president pro tem of the Senate Strom Thurmond, and my friend Alan Simpson, the Senate whip. The president was emphatic that the administration had not traded arms for hostages. The terrorists who had done the kidnapping had gotten nothing, he said. He went on to explain that the arms had been sold to moderate Iranians who in turn helped convince the terrorists to release the hostages. Reagan leaned forward in his chair and asked, "Now, what exactly is wrong with that?"

He emphasized again that he had not known about the diversion of funds to the Contras, which was better than if he had known, but troubling nonetheless. Iran-Contra wasn't Watergate, though plenty of Democrats were trying to make it seem that way, but as I noted on

NBC's *Meet the Press* in late December, "Clearly something went haywire at the White House," and the president's "lack of involvement in some of those details is at the root of the problem."

President Reagan did not have to wait long for the congressional inquiry he said he would welcome. In the first week of January 1987, both the Senate and the House formally appointed investigative committees. Bob Michel named me the ranking Republican on the House side, passing over more senior members. I suspect he chose me in part because I was already involved, having been his representative at the initial meetings when everyone else was out of town. But he also knew of my deep interest in national security issues, and I suspect he trusted me to do what needed to be done without any grandstanding.

In preparation for the hearings, I hired some top-notch people, including Tom Smeeton, who was minority counsel for the Intelligence Committee, to be minority staff director, and George Van Cleve, a lawyer who had worked in my congressional office, to be minority counsel. For the minority editor and writer, I chose Michael Malbin, who had a Ph.D. in political science from Cornell University and had also worked for several years as a reporter at the *National Journal.* He had recently been studying conflicts between the executive and legislative branches of the government, giving him particularly valuable expertise.

The most dramatic moments of the hearing began on July 7, when Oliver North, who had been on Reagan's National Security Council staff from 1981 to 1986, was sworn in. He rose to take the oath in the hearing room wearing the beribboned and bemedaled uniform of a U.S. Marine lieutenant colonel. The majority had planned to use his testimony to tie the president to illegal activities. Suddenly it was confronted with the possibility that Lieutenant Colonel North, with his earnest manner and unabashed patriotism, might coalesce national support behind the efforts to free hostages in Iran and fight communists in Nicaragua.

Colonel North had a slide show he had presented many times to mobilize support for the Contras, but the Democrats, seeing how persuasive he could be, prevented him from making the presentation. As the ranking minority member, I chose to question him last, and I used the opportunity to ask him to talk through his slide show, which he did in a twenty-minute tour de force. Of course I had serious concerns with North's conduct. He had shredded documents and operated without proper authority. It was later judged he had acted illegally, though in the end his conviction was reversed on the grounds that his immunized testimony had affected his trial. If the majority was determined to present him as a man who had purposely broken the law and subverted the Constitution, I felt that he had the right to defend himself as a man who was trying to save lives and protect democracy in the face of congressional vacillation.

In my closing statement at the hearings, I made the point that Iran-Contra represented serious errors on the administration's part, but that there were mitigating factors—"which, while they don't justify administration mistakes, go a long way to helping explain and make them understandable." Among them were "congressional vacillation and uncertainty about our policies in Central America" and "the vital importance of keeping the Nicaraguan democratic resistance alive until Congress could reverse itself and repeal the Boland Amendment." I also noted that the administration's failure to notify Congress, while inexcusable, needed to be set against "a Congressional track record of leaks of sensitive information sufficient to worry even the most apologetic advocate of an expansive role for the Congress in foreign policy-making."

The majority report on the Iran-Contra affair was a sensational story of rogue operatives within the administration willing to skirt the law and subvert the Constitution in their determination to carry out their own foreign policy. In the minority report we tried to present a more balanced view, one that took the long history of struggle between the executive and the legislative branches over foreign-policy making into consideration. As the report noted:

> *The boundless view of Congressional power began to take hold in the 1970s, in the wake of the Vietnam War. The 1972 Senate Foreign Relations Committee's report recommending the War Powers Act,*

and the 1974 report of the Select Committee on Intelligence Activities (chaired by Senator Frank Church and known as the Church Committee), both tried to support an all but unlimited Congressional power.

The tendentious majority report was part of the same pattern, resting as it did "upon an aggrandizing theory of Congress' foreign policy powers that is itself part of the problem."

The minority report continued:

> *The country's future security depends upon a modus vivendi in which each branch recognizes the other's legitimate and constitutionally sanctioned sphere of activity. Congress must recognize that an effective foreign policy requires, and the Constitution mandates, the President to be the country's foreign policy leader. At the same time, the President must recognize that his preeminence rests upon personal leadership, public education, political support, and interbranch comity. . . . No president can ignore Congress and be successful over the long term. Congress must realize, however, that the power of the purse does not make it supreme. Limits must be recognized by both branches, to protect the balance that was intended by the Framers. . . . This mutual recognition has been sorely lacking in recent years.*

Iran-Contra was part of what the report called "an ongoing state of political guerrilla warfare over foreign policy between the legislative and executive branches," and while the Democrats had tried to turn the scandal into another Watergate, no evidence emerged that the president was guilty of anything except inattention or absentmindedness. Those of us in the committee's minority noted many times that we were critical of the administration's conduct, but we nonetheless worked vigorously to defend the president against the extreme charges made by his critics. I thought it was also crucial to defend the presidency itself against congressional attempts to encroach on its power.

Shortly after the hearings and investigation were completed, I received a phone call at home on a Saturday from First Lady Nancy Reagan, who was at Camp David with the president. They both got on the phone and thanked me for the role I had played in the investigation.

DURING MY CONGRESSIONAL YEARS, I frequently took either Liz or Mary with me on trips back to Wyoming. These one-on-one excursions were a good chance to talk, an opportunity for me to find out what was going on in their lives. It was on one of these trips—in the Denver airport, to be precise—that Mary told me she was gay. I told her that I loved her dearly and that what was important to me was that she be happy.

Both Liz and Mary became interested in and knowledgeable about politics, which did not mean that they always responded the same to political events. Liz was a page at the 1984 Republican convention in Dallas and was thrilled to march into Reunion Arena for opening ceremonies each evening, carrying a flag and wearing a cream-colored robe covered with red, white, and blue elephants. Mary, who was a page at the 1988 convention in New Orleans, took one look at that year's page uniform—khaki pants or skirt, white shirt, and red kerchief around the neck—and resigned, declaring that she had no intention of dressing up in something that Soviet youth in the Young Pioneers might wear.

Lynne, meanwhile, was teaching English courses at George Washington University and Northern Virginia Community College. She had established herself as a writer and journalist, published a couple of novels, and contributed frequent freelance articles to different newspapers and magazines. She became a contributing editor at *Washingtonian* magazine, where she wrote a monthly column about D.C. history. In 1985, President Reagan appointed her to the Commission on the Bicentennial of the Constitution. In 1986 he chose her to succeed Bill Bennett as chairman of the National Endowment for the Humanities.

A few years after I'd been elected to Congress, Lynne and I both read *The Proud Tower*, Barbara Tuchman's book about the period before

World War I, and we had been particularly struck by Tuchman's profile of the acerbic and autocratic House Speaker Tom Reed. We knew there must be more stories like that and decided to write a book about Speakers of the House, who have been generally underappreciated. Our subjects were Henry Clay, James Blaine, Thomas Reed, Joseph Cannon, Nicholas Longworth, Sam Rayburn, and James K. Polk, the only Speaker to become president. We also included Thaddeus Stevens, who led the charge for the impeachment of President Andrew Johnson.

One afternoon after the book came out, I was standing at the rail at the back of the House chamber when a page came over and told me that Speaker O'Neill would like a word with me. It turned out that he wanted to talk about *Kings of the Hill.* I had sent him a copy as a courtesy, but I was frankly surprised that he had not only read it but had some strong and detailed opinions about it.

For the next half hour—while he effortlessly presided over the business of the House—we discussed the book. He was interested in the reasons for our choice of subjects and the way we had divided the writing chores. His only criticism involved our chapter on Sam Rayburn. He did not think that we had sufficiently praised "Mr. Sam," whom he had known and loved.

I WAS IN THE basement of our house in Virginia watching TV when the first reports of the bombing of the Marine barracks in Beirut were broadcast on October 23, 1983. Early that morning, two separate trucks carrying bombs broke through the security perimeter and crashed into the American and French barracks. More than two hundred marines and a number of sailors and soldiers were killed.

The Marines, first dispatched to Lebanon in August 1982 as part of a multinational peacekeeping force, were part of an attempt to settle the Lebanese civil war. I was one of many in Congress who had questioned the wisdom of what appeared to be America's ad hoc involvement in Lebanon. After the bombing there would also be questions about a decision-making process that had bunched all our marines into one building in the middle of a violent city only months after the American

Embassy had been bombed. The tragedy raised a number of questions about interservice rivalries in the American military and a convoluted chain of command.

The invasion of Grenada, two days after the bombing of the Marine barracks, was a successful effort, but also underscored disorganization. When I visited the Caribbean island as a member of Congress a few days after we'd gone in, I was told about an army officer who had needed artillery support. He could look out to sea and see naval vessels on the horizon, but he had no way to talk to them. So he used his personal credit card in a pay phone, placed a call to Fort Bragg, asked Bragg to contact the Pentagon, had the Pentagon contact the navy, who in turn told the commander off the coast to get this poor guy some artillery support. Clearly a new system was needed.

The result was the Goldwater-Nichols legislation, formally known as the Goldwater-Nichols Department of Defense Reorganization Act of 1986 and named after Republican Senator Barry Goldwater and Democratic Congressman Bill Nichols. The purpose of it was to streamline the chain of command and to emphasize "jointness" in an effort to mitigate interservice rivalries. Although the bill passed the Senate by a vote of 95–0 and the House by 383–27 and was signed by President Reagan on October 1, the administration was less than enthusiastic about the legislation. Caspar Weinberger, who was secretary of defense, called me to protest. I understood that no administration wants to be told how to run the Pentagon, but I felt this was one case where Congress had properly asserted itself.

As it would turn out—though I could not have guessed it at the time I was supporting and voting for Goldwater-Nichols—I would be the first secretary of defense to serve a full term under the act.

ON SEPTEMBER 10, 1984, while I was in the Capitol Building, I had a sense that something wasn't right with my heart. I had no pain. I've never had pain with a heart attack. But I knew enough to ride the elevator down to the physician's office. The doctors there put me in an ambulance to Bethesda Naval Hospital, where I spent several days recuperating from my second heart attack. I rested at home for about a month after that, going to Capitol Hill only once. On October 2, the Wyoming Wilderness Bill was up, and hard as I'd worked for it, I wanted to cast my vote. Two weeks later, I headed home to campaign for my fourth term in Congress.

After the election I decided it was time for me to find a doctor with whom I could establish a long-term relationship. I needed a guide through my coronary artery disease, and I wanted a good one. Lynne sought advice from John Pekkanen, an award-winning journalist at *Washingtonian* magazine who specialized in health. One of the cardiologists he recommended was Allan Ross at George Washington University Hospital, who agreed to take me on.

In 1988, after I had a third heart attack, Dr. Ross thought it was time for bypass surgery. I agreed and scheduled the operation for August 19, the day after the Republican convention. I'd been appointed chairman of the Rules Committee at the convention, a responsibility I definitely wanted to fulfill. I was on Spanish Plaza on the sweltering day when our nominee, George H. W. Bush, announced from the deck of the steamboat *Natchez* that Dan Quayle would be his running mate, and I was in New Orleans to get phone calls from political friends frantic at how badly the vice presidential nominee had been rolled out. One of my clearest memories, however, is of sitting with Larry King on the stairs in the convention arena that led up to the CNN booth. He had recently had open heart surgery, and at my request, he explained his operation and his recovery step-by-step.

I left the convention on August 18 and watched George H. W. Bush give a terrific acceptance speech while I was being prepped for surgery at George Washington University Hospital. The next day, Benjamin Aaron, a talented surgeon who had also operated on Ronald Reagan, performed quadruple bypass surgery. My recovery went well. In the fall I was back on the campaign trail running for my sixth term in Congress, and after the election, I ran unopposed to become minority whip, the second-ranking position in the Republican leadership.

By Christmastime I was skiing.

CHAPTER FIVE

Mr. Secretary

The Senate had never turned down a nominee to a new president's initial cabinet, nor had it ever turned down one of its own—and John Tower wasn't just any former senator. He had served in that body for nearly a quarter century and been chairman of the Armed Services Committee, the very committee in charge of his nomination. He seemed like a sure bet for confirmation when President-elect George H. W. Bush chose him to be secretary of defense.

But then came allegations of drinking and womanizing, and Tower's prospects sank. On Thursday, March 9, 1989, the day of the Senate vote on the Tower nomination, I got a morning phone call from John Sununu, President Bush's chief of staff. The White House knew it didn't have the votes for confirmation, Sununu said, and the president wanted to move forward quickly with a choice for the job who could be confirmed and get to work. Could I come by the White House and offer some advice on a Plan B?

Sununu wanted to meet at four in the afternoon, but I had a conflict, an appearance on the television show *Evans & Novak* that I had agreed to tape. I said I would stop by the White House afterward. At the *Evans & Novak* taping, the Tower nomination's imminent defeat and the question of whom the president would turn to next were the main topics. Neither Bob Novak nor Rowland Evans asked me who I thought the next nominee would be, but as I sat listening, cameras rolling, they discussed the next steps with each other. With an air of great authority, Novak declared, "I've got it, guaranteed, it's going to be Bobby Inman!" After the announcement of my nomination the next day, Evans and Novak had to scrap the show and scramble to tape a new one. Novak, whom I liked a lot, despite his irascibility, later said that he was furious with me, but, in my defense, it's worth noting that nobody had asked for my prediction.

After the taping I headed down Pennsylvania Avenue from Capitol Hill to the White House, where I met with Sununu and National Security Advisor Brent Scowcroft in John's office in the southwest corner of the West Wing, the same office I had occupied when I was chief of staff more than a decade earlier. By this time John Tower's nomination had been voted down, 53 to 47, and Brent began the conversation by asking my advice on possible replacements. "What about Rumsfeld?" I asked. Don had been secretary of defense before and was a man of enormous talent. That idea was quickly rejected, though, because there was a history of hard feelings that had been made worse by the New Hampshire primary in 1988. Rumsfeld had endorsed Bob Dole the weekend before the primary, which George H. W. Bush then won. I never heard Bush say anything negative about Rumsfeld, but Sununu made it clear at this meeting that Rumsfeld was a nonstarter.

Not long into the conversation, Scowcroft asked me directly, "What about you? Would you consider it?" I wasn't completely surprised. I had begun to catch on that there was something going on here beyond just consulting me for my views. We talked about the job of secretary of defense, its importance, and the president's priorities for the department. I told them I needed some time to think about it and to talk to my family, and we agreed I would call Sununu in the morning to tell him whether I wanted to take the next step. If I did, they would arrange for me to see the president. This was a pretty standard way of handling big personnel decisions such as this one. A president's staff never wants to put him in the position of offering someone a job until they know his offer will be accepted.

Lynne and I were scheduled to have dinner that night at La Colline restaurant, near the Capitol, with old friends from Wyoming, Tom and Marta Stroock. Tom had recommended me for admission to Yale thirty years earlier, and despite my less than stellar record there, we'd stayed close friends. I wasn't able to talk about the White House meeting at the dinner, and I couldn't talk about it with Lynne on the way home, either. As the House Republican whip I had a car and driver, and I didn't want to discuss something this sensitive in front of anyone except my family.

When we got home and I finally told Lynne, she was suitably impressed with the poker face I'd managed through the evening. Our daughter Mary, home from Colorado College on spring vacation, told us that while we had been at dinner, she had answered a call from a White House operator. Secretary of State Jim Baker was trying to reach me. As the three of us sat around the kitchen table, I called Jim back. He talked about how well we had worked together during the Ford years when I was chief of staff and he was running President Ford's 1976 campaign. He stressed the importance of the Defense job, told me he had recommended me to the president for it, and said he hoped I would take it. I appreciated the call and told him I would sleep on it and get back to him in the morning.

AS LYNNE AND I talked more that night, we went over the choice between staying in the House of Representatives or leaving to become secretary of defense. As the whip I was the second-ranking Republican in the House. Bob Michel, a mentor and a man for whom I have tremendous respect, was the minority leader. There was a good chance that I would become the GOP leader myself if I stayed in the House, but that might be a long time away. I was a buffer of sorts between the Old Guard, personified by Michel, and the New Guard, the Young Turks, led by Newt Gingrich. As long as I was there, Bob was comfortable staying where he was, so as I looked ahead at the next four years, the choice boiled down to spending them as Bob's understudy in the House or spending them as secretary of defense. As much as I loved the House and my time there, it really wasn't a tough decision.

I had no way to predict the magnitude of the historic events we were about to live through—the liberation of Panama, the disintegration of the Soviet empire and the collapse of the Berlin Wall, the defense of Saudi Arabia and the liberation of Kuwait in Desert Shield and Desert Storm—but issues of national security and defense were of great interest to me. In Congress I had served for four years on the House Permanent Select Committee on Intelligence, cosponsored the Goldwater-Nichols Act, which reorganized the Department of Defense, and been an active member of the Military Reform Caucus. I knew this would be a critically important job—and it also promised to be fascinating.

The prospect of being able to work for George H. W. Bush and with others such as Jim Baker and Brent Scowcroft, who were old friends and for whom I had a lot of respect, was also very appealing. I had to face the fact that if I went to the Pentagon my career in elective politics was probably over, but I was willing to accept that for the opportunity and high honor of leading the Department of Defense. I knew then what has been affirmed for me so many times in the two decades since—that the men and women of the U.S. military are among the finest Americans you will ever meet.

The next morning I called John Sununu and told him I was interested and wanted to take the next step. He arranged for me to meet privately with the president at noon. In order to keep the meeting a secret, Sununu asked me to come into the White House through the Diplomatic Entrance, which faces the South Lawn and doesn't ordinarily have news cameras focused on it.

A little before twelve I walked through the Diplomatic Reception Room, turned left down the ground-floor hallway past the portraits of former first ladies, and got on the small elevator that goes up to the White House's private quarters. At the top, one of the White House ushers met me and showed me to the Treaty Room, the president's second-floor office, a room where the cabinet had met before the West Wing was built, but that since the early twentieth century has been a sitting room or private office. The room was dominated by *The Peacemakers,* a large painting of President Lincoln meeting with Generals Sherman and Grant and Admiral David Porter in 1865 aboard the *River Queen,* anchored off City Point, Virginia. I thought for a moment of my great-grandfather who served under General Sherman and named one of his sons for the famous Civil War leader. What would he have thought of his great-grandson there in the White House residence meeting with the president about leading the nation's military?

As President Bush greeted me genially, I remembered when I'd first encountered him twenty years before. I'd been working for Congressman Bill Steiger of Wisconsin and Bush was a rising star in the House GOP. Our paths had crossed again during the Ford administration when he became CIA director the same day I became White House chief of staff. I remembered Jerry Ford singling out George Bush, as well as Don Rumsfeld, as the future of the Republican Party.

Some weeks earlier, about the time the Tower nomination's troubles were becoming apparent, President Bush had attended a meeting with the House Republican leadership in the Capitol. As the meeting was breaking up, the president had crossed the room to speak to me. "How are you doing, Dick? How are you feeling?" he asked. It had been eight months since my bypass surgery, and I told him I was feeling fine, fully recovered, and had spent a week skiing in Vail during Christmas. As I entered the president's private office that day, it occurred to me he might already have been thinking about me as a possible replacement for Senator Tower when he'd made those inquiries into my health.

President Bush began by talking about the importance of the job of secretary of defense, about what he was looking for in a defense secretary, about his priorities, and about some of the problems the next secretary would face. We discussed issues like Central America, arms control, and procurement reform. During the course of our conversation, I raised two issues I thought he needed to be aware of. The first was my academic record at Yale, and, in particular, the fact that I'd been kicked out twice. Second, I wanted him to know that I had a police record, that I'd been arrested twice for driving under the influence in my twenties. The president assured me that he didn't believe my misspent youth would cause any trouble for a potential confirmation. Governor Sununu and Brent Scowcroft joined us for the last part of what I thought was a very good meeting, but I left and headed for my office on Capitol Hill without having been offered the job.

Back at the Cannon House Office Building, I went ahead with my schedule and was being interviewed by an assistant professor from the University of Georgia, John Maltese, about my experiences as White House chief of staff, when Kathie Embody buzzed in to tell me the president was on the phone. I asked Maltese to excuse me, and when he was safely out the door, I picked up the phone.

"Dick," the president said, "I want you to be my secretary of defense. Will you take the job?" I said, "Yes, sir, Mr. President." "All right," he said, "get yourself back down here and we'll announce it right now." Not wanting word to get out about my new assignment before the president had a chance to announce it, I proceeded as though nothing extraordinary was going on and finished up my interview with Maltese. Then I headed downtown, and at 4:06 that afternoon walked into the briefing room with the president and became the secretary of defense-designate.

My loyal and longtime congressional staffers may have begun to suspect something was up because of my repeated trips to the White House, but most of them found out I was about to become secretary of defense from CNN, just like the rest of America. Then the phones started ringing off the hook, and the FBI showed up to begin a full-field background investigation on me.

My confirmation hearings started the following Tuesday, March 14, and the whole process was one of the speediest on record. The background investigation, committee hearings, and unanimous Senate vote to confirm me all took only seven days. The issue of my arrest record was handled in a closed session of the Senate Armed Services Committee. I had submitted the information in my written answers to committee questions, and Sam Nunn said he didn't see the need to bring it up in open session. Senator John Glenn of Ohio asked me in the closed session how I had managed to "clean up my act." I replied, "I got married and gave up hanging out in bars."

My official swearing-in ceremony was scheduled for the following week at the Pentagon. In the meantime, so that I could begin work right away, I needed to take the oath of office the day the Senate confirmed me. As a final tribute to the House of Representatives, I planned to have Jim Ford, chaplain of the House, swear me in, but moments after the Senate vote, I received a phone call from an Admiral Bill Owens at the Pentagon. He explained that he was going to be my military assistant and that he was on his way to my office with David O. "Doc" Cooke, who, Owens said, had sworn in every secretary of defense since Clark Clifford. Cooke, the senior career civil servant in the department and a much-revered figure, was popularly known as the Mayor of the Pentagon, and I decided that carrying on a Pentagon tradition would probably be a good thing.

Surrounded by my family and my congressional staff, I repeated after Doc Cooke the oath I had taken as a congressman and would later take as vice president, to "support and defend the Constitution of the United States against all enemies, foreign and domestic." Accompanied by military aides and a newly assigned security detail, I left my congressional office for the last time, walked down the marble halls of the Cannon House Office Building, and went out the door and into an armored limousine. It was a moment of real transformation—and it felt like it. I had arrived at work that morning as the lone congressman from the state of Wyoming, responsible really only for my own vote. I was leaving that afternoon as the secretary of defense, in charge of the world's most formidable military and the roughly four million men and women, military and civilian, who make up the Department of Defense. Fifteen minutes later, when I walked into the secretary's suite at the Pentagon, a nameplate had already been placed on the desk that read, "Richard B. Cheney, Secretary of Defense."

SATURDAY, MARCH 18, WAS my first full day on the job, and I had the limousine pick me up early. Accompanied by my military aide and security, I took the elevator from the Pentagon garage directly into my new office in the Pentagon E-ring, the outermost of the five concentric rings that make up the building. Inside the spacious office was a huge and ornate desk designed for General "Black Jack" Pershing, famed World War I commander, that the Pentagon inherited after Pershing's death in 1948. On the wall across the room was a large world map, one of many maps I would have in this office over the next four years. Behind the world map was a small bedroom where later I would spend nights during Desert Storm.

Next to my desk was a small round table, where a lot of important decisions would be made during my time in office. At the end of every day, when we were all in town, Colin Powell, chairman of the Joint Chiefs of Staff, Don Atwood, deputy secretary of defense, and I would meet, often with our military assistants, to go over the key issues we were facing. Sometimes we'd kick out the aides, so it was just the three of us. This was where we did the heavy lifting.

As I settled in behind Pershing's desk, Kathie Embody buzzed in to tell me that I was expected at a meeting in the White House residence later that morning. As the appointed hour approached, I got in the elevator to go down to the garage and pushed the wrong button, ending up in the basement of the Pentagon instead of in the garage. This would have been an easy mistake to remedy, except, as I discovered after I had gotten off and the doors had closed behind me, there was no button to call the elevator back to the basement. Someone had made a perfectly sensible security decision that people shouldn't be able to ride from the basement straight into the secretary's office, but what this meant for me was that the president of the United States was waiting, and I didn't have the slightest idea how to get to the garage and my limo.

I wandered around until I found some stairs headed up. At the top I could look through a glass window in a door out to where my limousine was parked and see a number of very upset aides running around, yelling, I was sure, "Where the hell's the secretary?" I straightened my tie, walked out, and got in my limousine, acting like nothing was wrong. I was driven to the White House for my meeting with the president— and no one ever had the nerve to ask me where I'd been.

ONE OF THE FIRST things I did at the Pentagon was ask to see an organizational chart of the Department of Defense. When I received it, I unrolled it and watched it fall off both sides of the Pershing desk. I rolled it back up and never looked at it again. I decided then and there that if I spent time trying to reorganize the Pentagon, I wouldn't get anything done.

I wanted to address questions of grand strategy. We couldn't yet be sure of the end result of glasnost and perestroika, the "openness" and "restructuring" that Soviet leader Mikhail Gorbachev was advocating, but we needed to address the matter of what changes in the Soviet Union might mean for our force structure and our strategy, from what we would need to fight an all-out global nuclear war to how to defeat anyone trying to dominate a region of the world vital to us.

I also wanted to focus on the operational command of the forces, the wartime system. When you go to the Department of Defense, you don't know if you're going to have to use the force, but it's something I wanted to be prepared for. Early on, I asked for the after-action reports from major uses of force since the end of the Vietnam War. They laid out our successes and failures in those previous engagements, and I spent time studying them. I've always been convinced that we don't do enough during the transition to a new administration to prepare those coming in for the possible use of the force. We spend a lot of time briefing on the SIOP—the Single Integrated Operational Plan—for launching our nuclear weapons, but any president is much more likely to have to use conventional or special operations forces, and we do little to prepare them for that.

I also wanted to spend significant time on intelligence matters, which had been a special interest of mine since my time on the House Intelligence Committee. As secretary of defense, I was in charge of a larger portion of the government's intelligence assets than the director of the CIA.

Finally, I had learned from long experience that nothing was more important than personnel. I could make the best possible policy decisions, but unless I had the people on board to execute those decisions, the policies wouldn't succeed. When I took over the Pentagon, there were forty-four presidential-level appointments requiring Senate confirmation in DOD. Ultimately I put new people into thirty-nine of those positions.

Perhaps the single most important personnel decision I would make during my first six months was for chairman of the Joint Chiefs of Staff, and I began to think about it the first night I was secretary. I was well aware that if I made a mistake, I would have to live with it for two years and maybe four. Brent Scowcroft had already indicated his preference for reappointing Admiral Bill Crowe, who would be completing his second two-year term as chairman on October 1, 1989, but I wanted to make my own selection for the chairman's job—a task that became easier when Crowe indicated to me that he wasn't all that enthusiastic about serving another term.

I was leaning toward Colin Powell, whom I had met when I was on an Intelligence Committee trip in 1986. We had stopped in Germany, where Powell was commander of the U.S. Army's V Corps. I subsequently had the opportunity to watch him work when he served as national security advisor in the aftermath of Iran-Contra at the end of the Reagan administration. I had been impressed enough with his abilities that I called him during the Reagan-Bush presidential transition and expressed the hope that we would have the opportunity to work together at some point in the future. I had no idea that that opportunity was just months away.

The weekend after the president had announced that I would be the secretary of defense, I paid a visit to an old friend, Frank Carlucci, who also happened to be my predecessor at the Pentagon. I sought Frank's advice about running the department, and knowing that he had worked closely with Colin Powell during tours at Defense and the National

Security Council, I also asked his opinion about Powell as the next chairman of the Joint Chiefs. Carlucci was enthusiastic.

General Powell was at that time in command of U.S. Forces Command, or FORSCOM, at Fort McPherson, Georgia, a post he'd gone to after leaving his Reagan White House assignment. I didn't have to make a decision right away, but I was increasingly attracted to the idea of him as chairman.

A crucial job I had to fill immediately was deputy secretary of defense, a post more important than most cabinet secretaries. Don Atwood of Michigan, formerly vice chairman of General Motors, had been slotted to be John Tower's deputy, and the president asked me to look at him. It was the only time the president weighed in with a suggestion, and it was a good one. Don was sometimes frustrated at the way Washington worked, especially the relations between the Defense Department and the Congress. He told me once that "at least at General Motors the board of directors wanted us to succeed." But Atwood brought great managerial strength to the Pentagon and got us through many of our toughest problems, from reform of the procurement system to the aftermath of Hurricane Andrew, which devastated Florida and Louisiana in 1992.

I chose Paul Wolfowitz as undersecretary of defense for policy. A former ambassador and assistant secretary of state for East Asia and the Pacific, Paul had the ability to offer new perspectives on old problems. He was also persistent. On more than one occasion, I sent him on his way after I had rejected a piece of advice or a policy suggestion, only to find him back in my office a half hour later continuing to press his point—and he was often right to do so.

As general counsel for the department, I recruited Terry O'Donnell, an Air Force Academy graduate and Vietnam veteran, whose wisdom and discretion I had first seen when he was President Ford's personal aide and I was deputy chief of staff. David Addington, a CIA-trained attorney with experience working at both the White House and on Capitol Hill, became my special assistant. Bright, completely discreet, and with tremendous personal integrity, Addington was an ideal choice.

Pete Williams, who had been press secretary in my congressional office, became assistant secretary of defense for public affairs. A Stanford graduate, Pete was from my hometown of Casper, Wyoming, where he had once been news director of KTWO television. He had the intellect and judgment to know what he could say to the press and what had to remain confidential. Others from my personal staff, including Dave Gribbin, Patty Howe, Jim Steen, Kim McKernan, and Kathie Embody, moved to the Pentagon with me.

WITHOUT QUESTION ONE OF the most significant posts is that of senior military assistant to the secretary of defense. During my tenure, the military assistant was usually the first person I saw each morning when I arrived for work, and he accompanied me to many of my meetings throughout the day. Inside his office, right next to mine, there was a photograph on the wall taken during the Civil War that showed the military assistant's supposed forebears. Called *Horse Holders,* the photo shows a number of junior officers holding the horses of Ulysses S. Grant's commanders while they meet with the general. If the young men in that photograph were the predecessors of the military assistants I knew, they must have gone on to distinguished careers. My three military assistants all went on to become four-star officers. Admiral Bill Owens would serve as vice chairman of the Joint Chiefs of Staff, Admiral Joe Lopez would command all U.S. naval forces in Europe, and General John Jumper would become air force chief of staff.

ON FRIDAY, MARCH 24, 1989, I held my first press conference. That morning a front-page story in the *Washington Post* reported that Air Force Chief of Staff, Larry Welch, had been negotiating directly with Congress about the future of U.S. intercontinental ballistic missile systems. Specifically, the issue was whether we should continue to fund the MX missile system based in silos at Warren Air Force Base, outside Cheyenne, Wyoming. The alternative to the MX was a smaller, single-warhead system called the Midgetman. Both systems had benefits and drawbacks, and choosing between them—or coming up with a compromise—was a major strategic decision for the secretary of defense and ultimately the president to make.

When I took the podium that morning, I knew I would be asked about the *Post* story. It was the first question out of the gate. "Are we in fact close to a compromise on those two weapons systems?" a reporter asked. "I have as yet made no decision," I answered. "To say that a compromise is near, I think would be premature."

Then the second question: "General Welch, the chief of staff of the air force, apparently has been up on the Hill working this program himself. Is that a change of policy for the Defense Department to have a service chief negotiate his own strategic system?"

I answered directly. "General Welch was freelancing. He was not speaking for the department. He was obviously up there on his own hook, so to speak." Then I was asked whether I accepted this. "No, I'm not happy with it, frankly. I think it's inappropriate for a uniformed officer to be in a position where he is in fact negotiating an arrangement. I have not had an opportunity yet to talk to him about it. I've been at the White House all morning. I will have the opportunity to discuss it with him and I will make known to him my displeasure. Everybody's entitled to one mistake."

My statement sent a clear message through the building about who was in charge. And that's what I had intended. I found out later that Welch believed he had gotten approval to go ahead with the Hill talks from Will Taft, the department's outgoing deputy secretary, who had been acting secretary until I was confirmed, and I came to regard Welch as a fine officer. But in the meantime I had signaled my intention to exercise control and authority over the Department of Defense.

I TOOK OFFICE EXACTLY thirty-nine days before I had to present my first defense budget to the Congress. Although I had inherited this first budget, I was determined to master it, knowing that being able to answer any and all questions about it was the best way to get off to a good start. Being knowledgeable about the budget during that first session with my former colleagues on the Hill helped set a tone for my long-term relations with the Congress.

For subsequent budgets, we established a unique arrangement for preparing the department's requests. Typically cabinet and agency heads negotiate for their budgets with the Office of Management and Budget (OMB), but during my time at Defense, the president and I would sit down at the beginning of the process with Dick Darman, the director of OMB, and agree on an overall top line for Defense. This arrangement allowed Darman to get a fix on the largest discretionary item in the budget so that he'd know what was left for everyone else. It allowed me to avoid the give-and-take with OMB and know exactly how much I had to work with. As long as I stayed within that agreed-upon top line, I was free, with few exceptions, to put together the defense budget.

My strongest ally in the Congress was Democrat Jack Murtha of Pennsylvania, whom I'd gotten to know when we served together in the House. Murtha was chairman of the Defense Appropriations Subcommittee, and at the beginning of each legislative session, I would invite him over for breakfast in my office at the Pentagon. We would discuss which items were high priority for each of us and put together a back-of-the-envelope outline of a bill.

Murtha was a master legislator. Once he got behind a proposal, it usually got approved. One year he arranged to pass the defense appropriations bill worth many billions of dollars on a voice vote without amendment. At the end of each session, the bill enacted was very close to what we had agreed to back in January at the beginning of the process.

The years I'd spent as a member of Congress, most of the time as a member of the leadership, were invaluable in working on the issues important to the Defense Department during my tenure as secretary. The friendships developed over ten years were vital in everything we did on the Hill, from the annual appropriations and authorization, to winning the fight over the resolution to go to war to liberate Kuwait. But I don't mean to suggest that all was always clear sailing with the Congress.

Every year, for example, I tried to kill the V-22 Osprey, a Marine

Corps aircraft, but the Congress funded it. The Marines had decided before I became secretary that they needed something to replace their Vietnam-era helicopters. The problem was, instead of buying new helicopters, they decided they needed the Osprey, which would take off and land like a helicopter, but once airborne its rotors would swivel so it could fly like a conventional airplane. The requirement used to justify this project was that when landing under fire on an enemy-held beach, the Marines needed an aircraft that could move from ship to shore faster than a helicopter could manage.

There were several problems with this approach. The tilt-rotor technology was difficult to develop and the cost was at least double that of a conventional helicopter. By the time I arrived at the Pentagon, the project was significantly behind schedule.

I realized early on as secretary that I wasn't likely to succeed in killing the Osprey, but I went ahead and knocked it out of my budget each year anyway. I figured that if the Congress was busy fighting to restore the Osprey, members wouldn't have time to go after something I really cared about.

Years later, when I was vice president, I landed in Air Force Two at New River Marine Corps Air Station in Jacksonville, North Carolina, where a large contingent of V-22 Ospreys is based. As I disembarked from my aircraft, the Marines arranged for two of their Ospreys to do a flyover, very low and very slow, right over my head. I smiled at the gentle reminder that the United States Marine Corps had prevailed in the battle of the Osprey.

AS I WRITE THIS, looking back twenty years and more, it's clear that 1989 was a turning point in modern history. The Cold War was ending, but the great historical change under way wasn't so clear from the vantage point we had in March of that year. As I took office, there was a strong push from some in Congress urging us to make significant cuts in our defense budget. I was wary of cutting too deeply. Although we had seen initial signs of change in the Soviet Union, there was no denying that they still had thousands of missiles aimed at the United

States. They had some six hundred thousand troops stationed in Eastern Europe. I felt strongly that it would be irresponsible to make deep cuts or changes to our strategic defense systems on the promise of change from the Soviets.

I was skeptical about whether Mikhail Gorbachev was the agent of change that many perceived him to be. When he had visited the United States in December 1987, Lynne and I were invited to the state dinner in his honor at the White House. I was seated on one side of First Lady Nancy Reagan and Gorbachev on the other, and I took the opportunity to ask him a few questions. Although he had begun making efforts to open up the Soviet Union's economy, he still seemed to think that communism was a workable system. He also bristled when I asked him how he came to be general secretary of the Party. I told him that in our system the job of secretary of agriculture, which he had held, wasn't normally a path to the presidency. He said he had been much more than an agriculture secretary and detailed his service in the Communist Party leadership structure. I came away from the evening thinking that he wasn't as serious a reformer as some believed.

My view hadn't changed by 1989. But the month after I took office, I learned an important lesson about the difference between sharing your view when you're a member of Congress and sharing it when you're secretary of defense. Appearing on CNN's *Evans & Novak,* I said I believed Gorbachev's efforts would "ultimately fail." I hadn't been off the air long when I got a call from Jim Baker telling me I was out of my lane, that my comments, now that I was a member of the administration, would have a direct impact on relations between the United States and the Soviet Union. Jim was right. I wouldn't make that mistake again.

Eight years later I was at a reception at Robert Mosbacher's home in Houston when George H. W. Bush, a former president now, told me he had someone he wanted me to talk to. He took me by the arm and walked me into the dining room, where a lone person sat at the table—Mikhail Gorbachev. The president said he thought we should know each other better, seated me next to Gorbachev, and left. On that fall afternoon for a half hour or so, the two of us, with help from an interpreter, talked about the bygone days when we had been adversaries.

I must give Gorbachev credit. He could have done as his predecessors did and used force to preserve the U.S.S.R. The fact that he did not is enough to make him one of the twentieth century's historic figures.

ONE OF THE FIRST challenges on my watch as defense secretary was a problem we had inherited from the Reagan administration—Panamanian strongman General Manuel Noriega. America had significant interests at stake in Panama. Although President Carter had signed the treaty turning over control of the Panama Canal to the government of Panama, the turnover would not take effect until 1999. In March 1989, America was still in charge, and protecting the rights of transit through the canal was our responsibility. We also had twelve thousand American troops stationed in Panama, and I was responsible for their welfare.

Noriega was a thug, guilty of a long string of outrageous actions, and he was under indictment by federal grand juries in Florida for money laundering and drug trafficking. In early May 1989, when Noriega's preferred candidates were defeated at the ballot box by presidential candidate Guillermo Endara and others, Noriega threw out the results of the election and sent his "dignity battalions" into the streets to bloody the opposition. Newscasts in the United States carried footage of one of the opposition's vice presidential candidates, Guillermo "Billy" Ford, trying to flee along a street in Panama City as he was beaten by Noriega's goons.

We weren't prepared at this point for a major military action in Panama, but we needed to generate options for the president. The Panama Canal was a strategic asset, there were American lives at stake, and President Bush wanted to make clear that our country's patience was running thin.

Our plan was to send a clear message by deploying an additional three thousand U.S. troops into Panama, but we ran into an obstacle in the person of our commanding general, Fred Woerner, who headed up Southern Command. He basically told us no thanks when we informed him we'd be sending reinforcements. His response was the same when we told him we would be sending some of our special operations forces into Panama to be ready in case we needed them. Not necessary, he said. Having a general who wouldn't accept reinforcements was clearly a problem.

After a conversation with Brent Scowcroft, I realized Woerner was going to have to be replaced. At about the same time my old friend Jack Marsh invited me for lunch. Jack was now the secretary of the army, a job he loved and was terrific at. He was a very effective back channel for me a number of times when I was secretary of defense. Marsh knew I would be looking for a replacement soon for the chairman of the Joint Chiefs, Admiral Crowe. "Have you thought about Max Thurman?" he asked. Thurman was currently serving as commanding general of the Training and Doctrine Command, getting ready to retire in two months. Although he wasn't well-known outside the army, he was a legend inside it. He was a bachelor, married to the army, really. He'd been heavily involved in creating our all-volunteer force. And he got things done. If you gave Max an assignment, he might break a lot of china along the way, but he would deliver. He carried the well-earned nickname Maxatollah.

I was intrigued and asked Marsh to set up a session where I could talk with Thurman face-to-face. A few weeks later, he joined us for lunch in Marsh's office, and he didn't disappoint. As secretary, I had run into plenty of general officers who told me what they thought I wanted to hear and, frankly, that wasn't very helpful. Thurman was something completely different. A combination of being near retirement and having a tell-it-straight personality made him direct and forceful. I appreciated it. As I sat in Jack's office eating my lunch and listening to Thurman, I thought to myself, here is the kind of guy we need in Panama.

Before we could offer him the job I would have to retire Woerner. Telling people they have to go is never pleasant, and firing a four-star general is not something that is done every day. But we had no choice.

I knew from experience that it was more responsible and more honorable to move quickly to make a change when it was clear things weren't working out. And I knew I owed it to General Woerner to deliver the news directly and in person. I asked my military aide, Admiral Bill Owens, to have Woerner make the trip to Washington.

A few days later Woerner and Admiral Crowe took seats at the round table in my office. Looking General Woerner in the eye, I told him, "General, the president has decided to make a change." He wanted to know why. I told him it wasn't personal, it was just time for a change. Though he was not pleased with the decision, he understood it was final and handled it with grace and dignity. On July 20 I announced that General Fred Woerner would be retiring and the new CINC, or commander in chief, for Southern Command would be General Max Thurman.

BY THIS TIME, THE summer of 1989, I had pretty well decided that I wanted General Colin Powell to be chairman of the Joint Chiefs of Staff, a job unique in the U.S. military. The chairman is not only the senior uniformed officer but also the key link to the civilian leadership, providing military advice to the secretary of defense, the National Security Council, and the president. For most of the post–World War II period, the chairman offered only military advice that all the members of the Joint Chiefs concurred in. Unless there was a consensus among the chiefs of the services, the chairman's hands were tied.

All of that changed with the enactment of the 1986 Goldwater-Nichols Act, which emphasized the importance of "jointness" (as opposed to service-centered advocacy) among the services and made the chairman the principal military advisor, freeing him from the constraint of offering only the consensus views of the chiefs. I had cosponsored the legislation in the House, believing it provided badly needed reforms.

Goldwater-Nichols also took the chiefs out of the chain of command. The air force and army chiefs as well as the Marine commandant and the chief of naval operations would no longer command forces when they were deployed. They were responsible for recruiting, training, and equipping the force, but not for using it in combat. That role was reserved for the CINCs, the commanders in the field. The secretary of defense may, at his option, send military orders to the field through the chairman, which I chose to do.

The chairman about to be appointed would be the first to serve his entire tenure in the consequential position that Goldwater-Nichols had created, and I wanted to make certain that the man I picked was not a "political" general, someone who'd had his head turned by the rarefied atmosphere of the White House. I needed to know that General Powell was happy to be back commanding troops and satisfied with the idea of serving out the rest of his career in uniform. To find out if that was the case, I made a stop at FORSCOM headquarters at Fort McPherson and visited with Powell face-to-face. I came away impressed, my mind made up to recommend him to the president.

I knew Scowcroft had some hesitation about Powell, based, I thought, on Powell's having been the national security advisor to President Reagan. Brent wasn't enthusiastic about having a chairman of the Joint Chiefs who knew as much as he did about running the National Security Council and advising the president, but I thought his reluctance could be overcome.

President Bush had worked closely with Powell when he was vice president and Powell was national security advisor, and I knew he was a fan. But I was also aware that the president was worried about jumping Powell, a brand-new four-star, over fourteen others in order to put him in the military's top job. Picking him would certainly ruffle some feathers, and when I made the case to the president that Powell was the man for the job, I said I would handle any blowback from those we passed over.

The president backed my decision about Powell and agreed to nominate him. On October 1, 1989, after confirmation by the Senate, Colin Powell became chairman of the Joint Chiefs of Staff. I knew we would have important work to do together. I believed we would be a good team. And for our time together at the Pentagon, we were.

ON HIS FIRST DAY on the job, General Powell woke me early in the morning with news that we were getting reports a coup might be about to get under way in Panama. We monitored the situation through the day, and I left the next morning to take my Soviet counterpart, General Dmitri Yazov, on a tour of Gettysburg National Military Park. On a previous visit to the Soviet Union, my hosts had taken me to see the mass graves from the siege of Leningrad; Hitler's troops had failed to capture the city, but more than a million Russians had died. I thought I would reciprocate for the tour the Soviets had given me by taking their official party to the site of one of the most important battles in American history. We got an expert from the U.S. Army War College at Carlisle, Pennsylvania, and loaded the delegation on a bus to tour the sites of the key events in the famous battle.

On the bus ride through the military park, I sat in the front row next to Yazov, a big, beefy guy, who had been chosen for his post by Gorbachev—and who would within two years be in jail for attempting a coup on the Soviet leader. We were well into our tour when my cell phone rang. Since this was 1989, the cell phone was bigger than a brick and my military aide carried it in his briefcase. Admiral Owens answered the call, leaned over the seat, and said, "Mr. Secretary, General Powell is on the phone, and he says he needs to speak with you." Reaching behind me, I took the phone, put it to my ear, and listened as General Powell told me it looked like the coup in Panama had begun. When the call was finished and I handed the phone back to Admiral Owens, I noticed that General Yazov was clearly curious—not so much about the content of my call, but about my phone. Apparently mobile technology was still pretty rare in the Soviet Union.

For our new national security team, this was a first test. How would we operate in a crisis? Would we be able to generate options for the president and a timely response? In this case, with hindsight, I would have to say we did not perform as well as we might have.

The first question for us was whether this was a legitimate coup. Our reporting was spotty, and we did not want to fall into some kind of trap Noriega might be setting, trying to get us to take the first step militarily only to find out later there hadn't been a coup. On the other hand, if the coup was real and American aid to the plotters could help unseat Noriega, intervening on the side of the plotters would be worth considering.

By around one in the afternoon, we had developed a list of options to recommend to the president, ranging from what to do if the coup plotters brought Noriega to an American base to the possibility of using U.S. forces to extract Noriega. By 2:30 p.m. the coup had failed. Reports were that Noriega, outsmarting his captors, was able to reestablish his control over the situation and kill the coup leader. Shortly after that Noriega went on TV to denounce the coup plotters and the United States. Within the week we were being criticized by Democrats and Republicans in Congress for failing to take advantage of the situation.

While I don't believe the United States would have benefited by siding with the coup plotters more openly in this instance, the truth is, we didn't move fast enough to make a decision. It was made for us by events on the ground. We learned from this experience that we needed a better system in place to stay on top of fast-moving developments and to get good intelligence that we could act on. These were lessons we put to good use a few months later when we invaded Panama.

AS WE MONITORED EVENTS in Panama throughout the fall of 1989, we were also dealing with a potential coup in the Philippines. On November 30 we started getting reports that rebels opposed to the rule of Corazon Aquino had seized air bases belonging to the Filipino government. We also received a request from President Aquino for the United States to use the F-4 Phantom jets stationed at Clark Air Force Base to bomb the rebel positions. I did not believe we should agree to this—nor did General Powell. For one thing, President Aquino made it clear that she would publicly deny having made the request. Asking the United States to bomb Filipino citizens, even if they were rebels, would not go over well inside her own country. But we were committed to defending the government of the Philippines and needed to come up with a show of strength to discourage the rebels.

As the crisis was coming to a head, President Bush, Jim Baker, and Brent Scowcroft made an evening departure for a summit meeting in Malta with Mikhail Gorbachev. Later that night, Vice President Dan Quayle convened a meeting of members of the National Security Council in the Situation Room at the White House. I stayed home in McLean, Virginia, where I had secure communications that enabled me to talk directly to Powell, who was in the National Military Command Center at the Pentagon, and to Air Force One. When Powell briefed me on the response to the Philippine situation that he and the Pentagon planners proposed—to put up a combat air patrol of American-flown aircraft over Manila—I called Air Force One directly. When I learned that the president agreed with the proposed response, I called Powell with the order to get the operation started. The plan was the right one. It worked to keep Aquino in power without our ever firing a shot.

While our communications ability allowed us to do things our predecessors could not have dreamed of, we also ran into glitches from time to time. During my conversations with Powell the night of the Philippines crisis, he expressed extreme frustration at being unable, despite all the fancy equipment in the National Military Command Center, to talk to Filipino defense officials. The solution, as he described it to me in colorful terms as it was happening, was to have the floor of the command center ripped up and a regular phone line brought in so he could dial out to the Philippines.

AFTER NORIEGA PUT DOWN the coup attempt in October, we took steps to be better prepared for the next crisis—and it wasn't long in coming. On December 15, the Panamanian legislature declared that Panama was at war with the United States, and the next day members of the Panamanian Defense Force, or PDF, shot and killed an unarmed United States Marine lieutenant, Robert Paz, when the car he was in took off in panic after being surrounded at a checkpoint. An American naval officer and his wife, witnesses to the shooting, were taken into custody by the PDF, harassed, threatened, and the husband beaten.

At ten the next morning, Sunday, December 17, I called a meeting in my office to review our options. General Powell, Paul Wolfowitz, Dave Addington, Pete Williams, and Admiral Owens were there, as well as General Tom Kelly, the smart, straight-shooting officer who was director of operations for the joint staff. I went around the table to give each man a chance to be heard. General Powell was particularly eloquent on the consequences of Noriega's PDF killing an American soldier in cold blood. This was not the kind of thing we could let go unanswered.

That afternoon, when we took our recommendations to the president, Christmas celebrations in the White House were in full swing. I made my way through hallways decked out for the season to the private elevator that goes up to the second-floor residence, where Generals Powell and Kelly briefed the president on our overall war plan, then called "Operation Blue Spoon," and described its objective—taking down Noriega and the PDF and restoring the democratically elected government of Panama. All around the room there was support for taking action, and at the end of the meeting President Bush gave us the order—"Do it."

Back at the Pentagon later that day, General Kelly and his deputy then, Admiral Joe Lopez, discussed the formal name of the operation. "Blue Spoon" just didn't seem right, a little too frivolous. The two batted around some options until Lopez said, "How about 'Just Cause'?" And the operation was named.

The next day was spent on a final check of plans that had been set in place weeks earlier. I knew as a student of history that in even the most successful military operations there are failures, but I also knew that it was the responsibility of those of us in command at the Pentagon to do as much as we could to plan for eventualities and minimize error. Civilian leaders also have to walk a fine line. You have a legal obligation to make certain the military is doing its job, that it assembles a force and puts together a plan to achieve the objective it has been given. But it's important not to cross into Lyndon Johnson territory, where civilian leadership picks bombing targets from the White House.

PANAMA WAS THE FIRST military operation where I had to decide how to handle the reporters who wanted to cover operations. I understood the press had a job to do, but I felt it was important that they not interfere with the job I had to do. In any military operation, the press will push for the maximum coverage possible, but we had to be aware, particularly in light of technology that now made instant reporting from the field increasingly possible, that their coverage could jeopardize the security of our operation.

For Panama, we used a pool system, which basically meant that certain reporters were selected to be on call at a given time. They would be the ones to go if something came up during their watch. We sent the pool to Panama, but they became frustrated when they got there and found themselves under the control of General Thurman. I understood the frustration, but we couldn't divert assets we needed to fight the battle to the task of escorting journalists, so they had to cool their heels for a while.

In addition there were a few reporters who had gotten down to Panama on their own, not as part of the pool system. When the fighting started, one group hid out in the basement of the Marriott hotel. They placed frantic calls to their home offices in New York, which were in turn putting tremendous pressure on the White House. There were thirty-five thousand American civilians in Panama, but the journalists at the Marriott became the center of attention, and finally Brent called and told us we had no choice. The president wanted us to rescue them. The problem wasn't only their superiors in New York calling in, but other reporters focusing on the stranded journalists. They were making it seem as though the military operation, which was generally going well, was somehow not succeeding.

We sent units from the 82nd Airborne to the Marriott, and they successfully freed the journalists as well as others who were there. But three American soldiers were wounded in the rescue, and a Spanish photographer covering the operation was killed.

Many at the Pentagon had a deep distrust of the media that was in part left over from Vietnam. There was a view—which I shared—that unduly negative reporting had helped sour public opinion on that war. The Tet Offensive, for example, was presented as a devastating blow to our side, when, in fact, we dealt out punishing losses to the North Vietnamese. Operation Just Cause deepened my conviction that the press ought not be the final arbiter of whether we have won or lost a war. When it came time for Desert Storm, I would try to be sure that we had maximum opportunity to communicate directly with the American people—without going through the filter of the press.

BEFORE WE WENT INTO Panama, the air force came to me with plans to use F-117s, our new stealth fighter. I wanted to know why. Surely the Panamanian air defense system wasn't sophisticated enough to require stealth capability. But the planes had never been used in combat before, and the U.S. Air Force wanted the opportunity to try them out—which seemed reasonable to me. They also recommended using AC-130 Spectre gunships, a very stable platform that has massive firepower and great precision. Because they are vulnerable to ground-to-air defenses and enemy fighter aircraft, we preferred to have air superiority before using AC-130s, but we planned to establish that quickly in Panama, then use these planes to take down Noriega's headquarters, the Comandancia.

At around 7:00 p.m. on Tuesday, December 19, we got word that Guillermo Endara would agree to be sworn in and restored to power by the United States. This was crucial. If he hadn't agreed, we would have had to rethink our entire operation. Later that night I headed down to the National Military Command Center, where Tom Kelly and the joint staff team presided. Kelly had set up a small conference room where Powell and I could work. We were close enough to monitor what was happening, but we had a quiet space away from everyone else if we needed to talk.

Shortly after midnight, Just Cause was under way. As reports came in, I stepped out of the conference room every half hour or so to use a secure line to the White House. My first call of the evening was to Scowcroft, but the president asked that I call him directly after that. He wanted as much information as we could give him, and as quickly as possible.

Most of the news that first night was good, although I did have to report the loss of four Navy SEALs, killed at Patilla airfield. We also failed to find Noriega. He wasn't seen until December 24, when he arrived at the Papal Nunciatura, the residence of the pope's representative in Panama. He stepped out of his car, carrying two AK-47s, strolled into the protected grounds, and requested political asylum. From this point forward, his capture was a certainty, the date of it hurried along by a plan devised by our troops to blast heavy metal music at earsplitting levels toward the Nunciatura. On January 3 Noriega walked out and surrendered to our forces. Operation Just Cause was a success.

CHRISTMAS IS A FAMILY time in the Cheney household. Liz and Mary, in their twenties by the time of Just Cause, would always make it home, and we would get up early on Christmas morning to open presents, eat a big breakfast, and start cooking the turkey—an effort that I customarily led. But Christmas 1989 was different. I flew to Panama on Christmas Eve, landing in blackout conditions for security, while Lynne, Liz, and Mary stayed in McLean under blackout conditions of their own. The power, notoriously fickle in Northern Virginia, went out, inspiring them to try to cook Christmas dinner in the fireplace—an effort that they have never chosen to repeat.

My host in Panama was Lieutenant General Carl Stiner, who had helped develop the plans for Just Cause and as commander on the ground done a superb job of seeing to their execution. On Christmas Day, we traveled from Panama City to Fort Amador, Rio Hato, Colón, and Patilla, and as I met with the troops who had participated in Just Cause, I stressed the importance of their achievement. "Democracy exists in Panama today because Panamanians voted for it," I said, "and each one of you has stood by them." I wanted them to know how proud their nation was of them, and I tried to convey my own high personal regard:

Every day that I'm in office as Secretary of Defense, my admiration increases for the men and women who have chosen to serve this nation. This thought is brought home to me each time I walk out of my door into the halls of the Pentagon. In the stairwell facing my office is a saying from the prophet Isaiah. It is a fitting reminder of what you mean to America.

Isaiah said, "I heard the voice of the Lord, saying, whom shall I send, and who will go for us?" And Isaiah said, "Here I am. Send me."

In the face of an unknown peril and in a dangerous world, each of you has answered, "Send me." I am proud to be with you all today.

THOSE OF US ON the National Security Council had come to our jobs with a lot of experience. I had been White House chief of staff and a member of Congress, in the leadership; Jim Baker had been chief of staff and Treasury secretary; Brent Scowcroft had been NSC advisor to President Ford, and Colin Powell likewise to President Reagan. But even with all that background, we had made mistakes when we first started working together. The lesson here is that while experience matters, it's not just each individual's experience that's important, but experience working together as a team. We learned a lot from our missteps during the failed coup as well as from our success with Just Cause. And I believe it was because we'd had real experience managing crises together that we were able to respond as well as we did eight months later when Saddam Hussein invaded Kuwait.

THE MOST MOMENTOUS EVENT of 1989 happened in Berlin. In October I had been there, and I was feeling greater optimism than I had earlier about the sincerity of Mikhail Gorbachev and the historic nature of the changes we were seeing. But even as thousands of East Germans were finding ways to flee to the West that fall, the Berlin Wall was still standing. The East German government was still trying to force people to live under a system and society they would not freely choose. "The biggest symbol of the inadequacy of the government in East Germany is the continued presence of the Wall," I said in West Berlin, and I noted that "the sooner it comes down, the better off it will be for everyone."

It is hard now to describe the elation when the Wall did come down in November 1989. I remember the nightly coverage of people who had been trapped for years in the communist bloc suddenly able to stream across the border. I remember Leonard Bernstein at Christmas conducting Beethoven's Ninth Symphony in both East and West Berlin. The words of "Ode to Joy" were changed so that it became "Ode to Freedom."

As I watched the celebrations on TV, I kept looking for a glimpse of my good friend Dave Nicholas. He'd been best man at my wedding, chairman of my first campaign for Congress, and was now my representative to NATO, and I knew that he and his family were in the middle of those happy crowds somewhere. Dedicated to the idea of freedom in Eastern Europe, Dave would later become an ambassador from the Organization for Security and Co-operation in Europe to Ukraine, where he helped in the movement for democratic reform. Before he died unexpectedly in Kiev in 2005, he would see the triumph of the Orange Revolution and thrill to it, as did we all.

After forty years, we were seeing the Iron Curtain lift and the Soviet threat diminish, and it was happening in a peaceful and promising way. I had no doubt that the United States military was the most effective single reason for the transformation we were witnessing. The victory of the West in the Cold War still stands as a preeminent historic example of peace achieved through strength.

But there was another dimension as well. Ronald Reagan's determination that people should live in freedom was part of it. His clear call in 1987 at the Brandenburg Gate—"Mr. Gorbachev, tear down this wall"—deservedly lives in history, as do the words of Pope John Paul II: "Be not afraid." When the pope visited his native Poland in 1979 he took that biblical message behind the Iron Curtain, where it inspired freedom-seekers such as Lech Walesa. I would have the honor of an audience with Pope John Paul II at the Vatican in January 2004, nine months after U.S. and coalition forces had liberated Iraq. I knew the pope had not favored our action; nevertheless, when everyone else had left the room, he took one of my hands in both of his and said, "God bless America."

CHAPTER SIX

Desert Shield

Cold War military planners looked at the Persian Gulf and envisioned a threat coming from the Soviet Union. As they saw it, the United States needed to be ready for Soviet tanks rolling south through Iran, headed for the oil-rich Arabian Peninsula. But as the Cold War was ending, Admiral Bill Crowe, chairman of the Joint Chiefs of Staff for the first few months of my term, decided that with a diminished Soviet threat, the Persian Gulf needed less attention, and in 1989 he published guidance for the military services that made the Gulf into an afterthought as far as America's strategic priorities were concerned.

I disagreed with this assessment. I thought it was too early to discount the Soviets entirely and a mistake to overlook the possibility of a threat arising from within the region. In January 1990, I put out revised guidance, making it clear that the Arabian Peninsula had high priority and that we should plan for a crisis in the Gulf. It came sooner than anyone—except, perhaps, Saddam Hussein—could have imagined.

SADDAM WAS IN A fury in the spring and early summer of 1990. He threatened chemical warfare, swearing to "let our fire eat half of Israel if it tries to wage anything against Iraq." He lashed out at Kuwait and the United Arab Emirates for driving down the price of oil and thus thrusting "their poisoned dagger into our back." His foreign minister and deputy prime minister, Tariq Aziz, zeroed in on the Kuwaitis for encroaching on Iraqi territory, stealing Iraqi oil, and ungratefully refusing to forgive loans made to Iraq at a time it was battling Iran and spilling "rivers of blood in defense of pan-Arab sovereignty and dignity." The accusations were harsh, but what followed was still a shock. In mid-July, Iraqi tanks began moving toward Kuwait, and by July 19 our satellite photos showed three heavy armored divisions within striking distance of the Kuwait border.

Word of what was happening was still not public when I received two visitors in my office, Moshe Arens and Ehud Barak. Arens, slight and studious, was the Israeli defense minister. General Barak, a future Israeli prime minister, was deputy chief of staff of the Israeli Defense Forces. A round-faced, unassuming man, he was also his country's most decorated soldier. On July 20, the two of them took seats at the small round table in my office, and pulling papers and maps out of their briefcases, they presented evidence of the advanced stage of the Iraqi nuclear program. Access to European technology, they believed, was helping the Iraqis speed completion of a uranium enrichment facility, and we had a narrow window of time in which to stop the program.

The Israelis had long considered a nuclear-armed Iraq a mortal threat, and in 1981 had bombed the reactor at Osirak, dealing a severe setback to the Iraqi program. I took very seriously what Arens and Barak had to say—particularly since they described a program much further advanced than the one portrayed in our intelligence assessments. After the war, we would find out that the Israelis had been closer to the truth than our own intelligence community was.

Barak and Arens were concerned about the growing danger of war in the Middle East and wanted to beef up their technology to counter the threat of ballistic missiles launched at Israel from Iraq. They had developed their own system, the Arrow, comparable to the U.S. Patriot antimissile system, but they needed U.S. assistance, particularly in the areas of radar and a more effective early warning system. This was a conversation to which we would return with increased urgency in the coming months.

As Saddam continued to mass elements of the Republican Guard— his best, most experienced units—on the Iraq-Kuwait border, we heard from many quarters that he was bluffing, saber-rattling to get the Kuwaitis and perhaps the United Arab Emirates to pay him off. Egyptian president Hosni Mubarak and other Arab leaders assured us that they would handle what they viewed as an intra-Arab dispute and urged us not to take any steps that would provoke Saddam. We got similar advice from the State Department and most of the intelligence community.

But at the end of July, when Saddam began moving his artillery forward, it looked increasingly as though he would cross the border and attempt to take Kuwait. On Wednesday, August 1, 1990, General Norman Schwarzkopf, the commander in chief of U.S. Central Command, which is in charge of most of the Middle East, came to the Pentagon to brief me. I'd met Schwarzkopf, a big, physically imposing man, apparently with a temper to match, but I didn't know him well. I took a close look at him, wanting to be sure that he was the right man to command our operations through what lay ahead. One of the most important things I could do in a crisis was make sure we had the right people in charge.

Schwarzkopf knew his brief, but his message was not reassuring. Saddam would probably go into Kuwait, he said, perhaps to seize the Rumaila oil field or to take two disputed islands just over the border, Warba and Bubiyan.

Later that night, I was at home in McLean when I got a call from my military aide, Admiral Bill Owens. The Iraqis had crossed into Kuwait.

By the time the National Security Council met the next morning, Iraqi troops had rolled across the desert and into downtown Kuwait City. They had another line of tanks moving south toward the Kuwait-

Saudi border. The White House press pool was brought in at the top of the meeting and reporters wanted to know what the United States was planning to do. Was the president going to use military force? "I'm not contemplating such actions," President Bush said. I suspect he responded in the way he did because we hadn't even begun to discuss the invasion. Was this a significant strategic event? Did it matter from the standpoint of the United States if Iraq had taken Kuwait, a small country out in the Persian Gulf? In the discussion that followed, Colin Powell indicated that he wasn't convinced that it did, but it sure seemed important to me. On a White House notepad I made notes about the enormous economic clout that Saddam would gain from Kuwait, how its wealth would enable him to acquire increasingly sophisticated capabilities, chemical weapons, nuclear weapons, and ballistic missiles. It was also clear to me that we needed to make a strong statement of commitment to Saudi Arabia, whose oil fields Saddam was surely thinking about. After taking Kuwait, he controlled 20 percent of the world's oil reserves. The eastern province of Saudi Arabia would give him 45–50 percent.

WHEN THE NSC MEETING broke up, the president prepared to depart for Aspen, Colorado, where he was scheduled to give a speech about America's post–Cold War military force. With the fall of the Berlin Wall and the collapse of the Soviet position in Eastern Europe, there was growing pressure in Washington to modify our national security strategy and defense budget. At the Defense Department we had focused on a new force structure called the "base force" and a regional strategy that would enable us to deny any adversary the ability to control a part of the world that was vital to our interests.

Powell and I went to Capitol Hill to brief members of Congress on the base force concept, but all anyone was really interested in was what was happening in Kuwait. After the session on the Hill, Powell and I headed back to my office, where we got an update from General Tom Kelly, head of operations for the joint staff, on the Iraqi invasion. When he had finished, I turned to Powell. "What options do we have to respond?" I asked. Powell said the options were being worked and began discussing domestic political concerns, public opinion polls, and the American public's view of Kuwait. It was a tiny nation, a monarchy six thousand miles away, he said, and the American people would not support military action to put the emir back on his throne.

Powell seemed more comfortable talking about poll numbers than he was recommending military options. Part of it was just Colin, the way he was attuned to public approval, but listening to him also made me think about how Vietnam had shaped the views of America's top generals. They had seen loss of public support for the Vietnam War undermine the war effort as well as damage the reputation of the military. There was a view in the Pentagon, for which I had a lot of sympathy, that the civilian leadership had blown it in Vietnam by failing to make the tough decisions that were required to have a chance at prevailing.

I understood where Powell was coming from, but I couldn't accept it. Our responsibility at the Department of Defense was to make sure the president had a full range of options to consider. No one else in the government could provide him with these options. He had plenty of people who could give him political advice. I brought the meeting to a close, and afterward, although we normally operated on a first-name basis, I addressed Powell formally. "General," I said, "I need some options." The business we were about was deadly serious, and I wanted him to understand he was receiving an order. "Yes, sir, Mr. Secretary," he replied.

As Powell walked out the door of my office, I picked up the phone, punched the extension for Admiral Owens, and asked him to step in for a moment. "I want you to pulse the system," I told him. "Find out what the navy's got, what they're thinking, how we might respond." A few minutes later I had the same conversation with my junior military aide, Air Force Lieutenant Colonel Garry Trexler, tasking him to pulse the air force planners. I wanted to know what carriers could be deployed, what air wings sent, how soon they could get there. General Powell wasn't pleased when he learned my military aides were working their own services, and he chewed both of them out. But the president needed options, and I wanted to send a message that I intended for him to have them.

Sitting at my desk that afternoon, I filled several pages of a yellow legal pad, going over the consequences of Saddam's move and listing questions I had about it. "Shouldn't our objective be to get him out of Kuwait?" I wrote. "Isn't that the best short and long term strategy?" I went over nonmilitary options, from diplomatic condemnation to economic sanctions, and concluded, "No non-military option is likely to produce any positive result." The key to the situation, I wrote, was "U.S. military power—the only thing Hussein fears." The key to our success would be "determination to use whatever force is necessary."

At the next NSC meeting, on Friday, August 3, it was clear that Scowcroft was about where I was. There was simply too much at stake, he said, for us to acquiesce in the Iraqi occupation of Kuwait. We needed forces in the area, and Saudi Arabia was the logical place, but, as I noted in the meeting, they had been traditionally reluctant to have an American presence on their soil.

But that might change if the Saudis understood that our forces were essential for their protection, and Scowcroft asked me to arrange a briefing for Prince Bandar, Saudi ambassador to the United States, on the threat to Saudi Arabia and what we could do to defend the Kingdom. A former fighter pilot, Bandar was a gregarious, larger-than-life presence in Washington, a uniquely effective ambassador known for his sense of humor, his cigars, and his friendships with everyone from George Bush to Jerry Jones, owner of the Dallas Cowboys. Scowcroft said the president wanted Bandar to have a full brief on Operations Plan 90-1002, the plan prepared by Central Command for defense of our interests in the Gulf. It hadn't been completed and, like all war plans, would be modified by events on the ground, but it would convey to Bandar how strong a response we were contemplating.

Later that day, before Bandar arrived, I had another private meeting with Powell. I wanted to be sure he understood that the purpose of our meeting was not to debate what the American public would accept, not to discuss strategic alternatives. "Our purpose is to give Bandar the full laydown on Op 1002," I said. "We want him to know the scale of the military commitment the president is willing to make."

Bandar was skeptical during the first part of our meeting. He reminded us of the story of the time when the Shah of Iran was overthrown and President Jimmy Carter provided the unarmed squadron of F-15s to the Kingdom, humiliating the Saudis and leaving a bitter memory of America as an unreliable ally. "We're serious this time," I told Bandar.

We showed him the satellite imagery of Iraqi troops now massing near the Saudi border. Then Powell briefed him on what the United States was prepared to do to defend the Kingdom, laying out divisions, tanks, artillery, ships. "How many forces are we talking about?" Bandar asked when the brief was done. One hundred and fifty to two hundred thousand, we told him. He was taken aback, but we had convinced him we meant business. This wouldn't be a rerun of the unarmed F-15s. I emphasized that we needed to begin deploying the force as soon as possible. We didn't have time to wait while Saddam gathered strength and planned his next move. Bandar said he would leave that night to brief King Fahd on the plan. He said he would support the deployment and convey a sense of urgency to his king.

The president called another meeting of the NSC for Saturday, August 4, at Camp David. We met in Laurel Lodge, a gathering place built by President Nixon. The main room, overlooking the woods, has a fireplace, TV, piano, backgammon board, and bar. There is also a dining room, a small study for the president, and a conference room for larger meetings. During George H. W. Bush's presidency, the conference table had aircraft models displayed down its center.

General Schwarzkopf briefed on Op Plan 90-1002—which forces we would use and how long it would take them to deploy. He stressed that it would be months before we had an effective force in place, which underscored a concern shared by many of us: that Saddam would move on Saudi oil fields before we had sufficient troops in place to stop him. Over the next few days, there would be several reports that Saddam was on the verge of moving across the Saudi border. Having missed Saddam's invasion of Kuwait, our intelligence analysts now seemed to see signs everywhere of his invading Saudi Arabia.

It became clear pretty quickly that if the Saudis didn't agree to accept U.S. forces, we had few options. Israel would likely have accepted our troops, but we couldn't launch military action against an Arab country from Israeli territory. Turkey was another option, with the large U.S. base at Incirlik, but the distances involved would have provided real logistical challenges. We got word while we were at Camp David that the Saudis were uncomfortable with the idea of U.S. forces in the Kingdom. As our meeting broke up, President Bush got on the phone to speak directly to King Fahd.

Several hours later, I was back at home in McLean when Scowcroft called to say we needed to send a team to brief the Saudis on the possible troop deployment. Scowcroft said he would lead the team and planned to take General Powell with him. "Brent, I want to lead that team," I told him. "The deployment of forces is my responsibility, and I ought to be the one to lead it." "Okay," Scowcroft said. "I'll take that to the president." As national security advisor, Scowcroft was an honest broker. I knew that even though he may have wanted to lead the trip himself, he would faithfully carry my request to the president. He called back awhile later to say the president agreed. I should lead the team.

I also had concerns about Powell's participating as the senior military official. He had been hesitant in discussions of military options, and we needed to convince the Saudis to accept troops—and accept them now. I wasn't sure Powell would deliver the strong message they needed to hear. Additionally, Powell and I tried not to be out of the country at the same time. I decided Powell would stay home, and General Schwarzkopf would provide the military brief to the Saudis.

It wasn't clear the Saudis would accept such a high-level team. Scowcroft worked the phones with them all afternoon and through the night. "If we send Cheney," he told them, "the answer better be yes." It would be a clear setback to have the U.S. secretary of defense make the trip and get turned down. Finally, on Sunday morning, they agreed to receive me.

We departed from Andrews Air Force Base that afternoon, Sunday, August 5, on one of a fleet of 707s I used as secretary of defense. Some of these planes had been used as Air Force One by Presidents Kennedy, Johnson, and Nixon. One of them, tail number 26000, was the plane that flew President Kennedy to Dallas on November 22, 1963, and flew his body back to Andrews Air Force Base at the end of that tragic day. After more modern aircraft were brought into the fleet to serve as Air Force One, 26000 and the other 707s were used to transport cabinet secretaries.

Just before taking off I received word of the strong statement the president had made to reporters on the South Lawn of the White House. "This will not stand, this aggression against Kuwait," he had said. Sitting in the cabin of the 707, I wrote notes for a presentation to King Fahd that echoed the president's words and laid out the dangers of acquiescence. Saddam Hussein "must not be permitted to get away with his aggression," I wrote in longhand on a yellow legal pad:

> *He will grow stronger—especially if he has all that Kuwaiti wealth. He will dominate the Gulf. He will dominate OPEC. He will acquire more, deadlier armaments—the kind that will allow him to totally dominate the region. At some point we will have to deal with him—it will be easier now—together—as part of an international effort.*

During the flight, I went back to the staff section of the plane and asked the CIA briefer to make the presentation he had prepared for the king. It was technical and equivocal, and it did not convey the urgency of the situation. I scrapped that part of the brief and decided that Schwarzkopf and I would handle it. Later I had our ambassador to Saudi Arabia, Charles Freeman, up to the cabin to brief me on what to expect. You have to be cautious, he told me. If you are too aggressive or talk about too large a force, you will scare the Saudis and they won't commit. Also, he said, you have to be prepared to wait around in Riyadh for hours or even days. They don't make up their minds quickly and certainly won't make a quick decision on something this important.

We landed in Jeddah at around 2:00 p.m. Saudi time and went to one of the king's guest palaces. Bandar came to see me while we waited for our meeting with the king. He had undergone a transformation, no longer wearing one of the Savile Row suits he was known for in Washington, but dressed in the traditional robes of a Saudi prince. "It's very important," he said, "that you demonstrate to the king that you are serious." He wanted me to make sure the king knew we would commit a large force and do it fast. I couldn't seem cautious or unwilling to do what was necessary, Bandar said. I was asking the king to take a big risk by allowing U.S. forces onto Saudi soil and had to convince him the United States was a worthy ally. In other words, Bandar was giving me advice 180 degrees different from the advice I had received hours earlier on board my plane from the U.S. ambassador. I decided to go with Bandar's guidance.

At about 7:00 p.m. we were ushered into our meeting with the king. Crown Prince Abdullah was there, along with Saudi Foreign Minister Saud al Faisal and Deputy Minister of Defense Abdul Rahman. Prince Sultan, the minister of defense and Bandar's father, was out of the country but would return the next morning. We sat in overstuffed chairs arranged in an L shape, my team—including General Schwarzkopf, Paul Wolfowitz, Ambassador Freeman, and Bob Gates, a future secretary of defense who was then Scowcroft's deputy—along one arm of the L and the Saudis on the other. The king and I sat in the center, with Bandar between us and slightly back to do the interpreting. Servants wearing holstered guns, carrying silver pots in one hand and tall stacks of small cups in the other, made their way around the room, pouring Arabic coffee for each of us.

Unlike all the other meetings I've ever had with Saudi royalty, there was no small talk. It was clear the king wanted us to get right to the business at hand, and I began by affirming the United States' commitment to Saudi Arabia and emphasizing the danger Saddam represented. The president was personally working to build international support for economic, diplomatic, and military action against the Iraqis, I said, but in the meantime we had to prevent an attack on Saudi Arabia. Military deterrence would be critical, I said, "as economic measures began to bite and Saddam, feeling the pain, might be tempted to lash out."

I asked General Schwarzkopf to brief our hosts in more detail on the forces Saddam had deployed along the border between Kuwait and Saudi Arabia. Saddam was in a position to launch in one or two days, Norm said. He also briefed on what the United States was prepared to do, the F-15s that would be deployed immediately and the air and ground divisions that would follow.

At the end of his briefing, I emphasized that we would stay as long as the Saudis wanted and leave when they wished us to, and I stressed the importance of acting quickly. If we waited for "unambiguous warning of attack," it would be too late. The Saudis began a discussion among themselves in Arabic. Bandar stopped interpreting. I learned later that there was some feeling among the Saudis that there was no need for a quick decision, that they could afford to wait. King Fahd ended that line of argument. "The Kuwaitis waited," he said, "and now they are living in our hotels."

The king turned to me. "Okay," he said. He knew that his decision was controversial, but he did not care, he said, since Saudi Arabia itself was at stake.

Back at the guest palace, I told Joe Lopez, my new military assistant, to connect me with the president. When the White House Situation Room was on the line, I picked up the handset of one of the dedicated U.S. government phones installed wherever the secretary of defense travels. The president came on the line from the Oval Office, with British Prime Minister Margaret Thatcher at his side. She had come back to Washington with him from Aspen. "Mr. President, the Saudis have agreed to accept our forces. Do we have your approval to begin the deployment?" "Yes, Dick. Go ahead." I thanked the president, hung up, and placed a call to General Powell. "Colin, begin the deployment." Within hours of my call, F-15 fighter jets from Langley Air Force Base arrived in Saudi Arabia and began flying combat patrols. The next day, the first elements of the Ready Brigade of the 82nd Airborne arrived; the U.S.S. *Eisenhower* started for the Suez Canal and the U.S.S.

Independence for the Gulf of Oman. In a week the first U.S. Marines were there, then the first three prepositioned ships, then the A-10 tank-killers, three thousand men from the 101st, and eighteen F-117s. It all started happening with a single phone call.

Defense Minister Sultan returned home that night, and we met the next morning. He wanted to be sure that it was clear to the world that Saudi Arabia had invited U.S. forces, and he wanted assurances that there would be no announcement of the deployment until our troops had arrived. I gave him my word on both counts.

I left Jeddah and headed for Egypt, where I was scheduled to meet President Mubarak in his summer home outside Alexandria, on the Mediterranean Sea. With the summer heat and a full load of fuel, my 707 required more runway to land and take off than was available at the Alexandria airport, so we stopped in Cairo, and I got on an old King Air Beechcraft propeller plane used by the U.S. Embassy for travel around Egypt. When we landed in Alexandria, we pulled up next to a much larger plane with an Iraqi flag on the side. Saddam's representative, his close aide Izzat Ibrahim al-Douri, was making the rounds of Arab governments trying to encourage them not to go to war over Kuwait, and I had to wait in a holding room at the presidential palace while he finished meeting with President Mubarak.

As the Iraqi representative exited one door, I entered another, and I found a very angry President Mubarak. The Iraqis had lied to him, he said. Just days before the invasion, all the Arab countries had been together for an Arab League summit, and at dinner one night, the Iraqis had made a big show of sitting next to the Kuwaitis, calling them "brother" and promising never to invade.

When I told President Mubarak that the Saudis had agreed to accept the deployment of U.S. troops, he was ready to help. "What do you need?" he asked. I asked him for overflight rights so our planes could fly through Egyptian airspace. He agreed. I told him we also needed permission for one of our nuclear-powered aircraft carriers, the U.S.S. *Eisenhower,* to pass through the Suez Canal. Normally the Egyptians did not like nuclear-powered ships going through the canal and permission could take weeks, but he agreed immediately. "When is it coming?" he asked. "Tonight," I said. Mubarak also told me he planned to convene an Arab League meeting to discuss the crisis, and he conveyed strong support for U.S. efforts to defend Saudi Arabia. Throughout the crisis King Fahd and President Mubarak would prove to be two of America's most important allies in the region.

That afternoon I left Egypt and headed for Washington. As my plane rose over the Mediterranean, I got a call on board from President Bush. He had just spoken with King Hassan of Morocco and asked me to stop there on my way home. He wanted me to brief the king on our plans and on my talks with the Saudis and Egyptians. Since the stop was unanticipated, our flight crew had to have landing charts faxed up to the plane.

We landed in Morocco in the middle of the night and took a motorcade to the king's palace. I asked to see the king one-on-one, which actually meant there were three of us: the king, me, and his interpreter. Hassan asked if the information I wanted to discuss was secret. "Yes," I told him. "It's highly classified." He removed a small box from within the folds of his robes and handed it to his interpreter, who held it in his hands while he and the king exchanged a few words in Arabic. Then the interpreter handed the box back to the king, who put it in a pocket in his robes. The king, who spoke some English, could see I was curious, so he explained to me that his interpreter had just sworn on a fragment of the holy Koran never to divulge the information he was about to hear. I was impressed. It seemed to be a pretty effective classification system—and conveniently portable too.

I told the king that the Saudis had agreed to accept U.S. forces and that President Mubarak was also supportive. I explained that President Bush would be announcing the deployment shortly and wanted King Hassan to know the details of our plans. When I finished, King Hassan told me he was prepared to send Moroccan forces to serve alongside the Americans.

I landed back at Andrews Air Force Base at 3:20 a.m. on Wednesday, August 8, 1990, and after a stop at the Pentagon, I went to the

White House for a 7:15 a.m. breakfast meeting with Baker and Scowcroft. At 8:00 a.m., the same hour the first U.S. planes were landing in Saudi Arabia, I went into the Oval Office to brief the president on my trip. At 9:00 a.m., President Bush addressed the nation and announced the deployment of U.S. forces to the desert of Saudi Arabia.

I believe it was in a meeting shortly after the president's announcement that I fell asleep while seated in the chair next to his in the Cabinet Room—not delicately asleep, but full-on, mouth-open, snoring asleep. Probably because Brent Scowcroft had gotten him used to such behavior by nodding off from time to time, the president didn't take offense, but he did take note and even called a photographer in. Later, at a cabinet dinner, he presented me with the Brent Scowcroft Excellence in Somnolence Award.

ON AUGUST 17 I left on my second trip to the Gulf in two weeks. On the way over I considered the implications of reports we were receiving about Saddam's readiness to invade Saudi Arabia. Should he launch an attack, he could capture or disable Saudi oil production, and he could disrupt U.S. deployments, handing our forces a defeat. There was every reason for him to do this. Saddam's forces were at their peak, unaffected as yet by the embargo we had put in place that would deny him such things as spare parts and munitions. U.S. and Saudi forces, on the other hand, were at their weakest and would only gain strength with the passage of time and increased U.S. deployments. I called both Colin and Brent to make sure that we were working this contingency—which they assured me we were. But we couldn't have done much had Saddam decided to keep right on rolling into the Saudi oil fields.

I flew first to Saudi Arabia, then headed to three other countries that lie on the western side of the Persian Gulf—Bahrain, the United Arab Emirates, and Oman. Saudi Defense Minister Sultan had helped arrange these visits, in which I intended to seek additional basing rights for U.S. forces and gain support for what was to become Operation Desert Storm. Sultan's help was key since Saudi Arabia is the dominant Arab state in the Gulf—the largest producer of oil, the biggest geographically, the strongest militarily. Without Saudi approval, it would have been virtually impossible to gain the full cooperation of the other Gulf allies. Once the Saudis had signed on, the others were eager to join the coalition that we were building to oppose Saddam. The only exceptions were Jordan, where the king was dependent on Iraqi oil, and Yemen, which had also thrown in its lot with Saddam.

I was welcomed warmly in Bahrain, a longtime ally of the United States and the headquarters of the U.S. Navy's activities in the Persian Gulf. When I stopped in the United Arab Emirates, I was the highest-ranking U.S. official ever to have visited. My host was the president of the UAE, Sheikh Zayed, a man held in high regard by all of his neighbors and revered by his people. He agreed to let us base C-130s and F-16s there. Oman, at the mouth of the Persian Gulf, also had an established relationship with the U.S. military. For some time we had prepositioned supplies and spare parts in Oman for just the sort of contingency we now faced. Sultan Qaboos, a graduate of England's Royal Military Academy at Sandhurst, was also willing to provide bases that were important to our air and naval forces.

I had not intended to stop in Qatar, another country on the west side of the Gulf, because of strained relations between our two nations. The Qataris had asked us to provide Stinger missiles to them, as we had to our close allies in Bahrain. When we said no, the Qataris purchased a Stinger on the black market and put a photo on the front page of their newspaper of the Qatari defense minister holding the shoulder-fired antiaircraft missile. This in turn had generated protests to the government of Qatar by our State Department.

But Prince Sultan, one of our most important allies in helping us gain agreement and cooperation from Arab countries, had been working the phones from Jeddah, and late in the day he called to report that he had been in touch with the Qataris and that they would welcome a visit. It was a memorable stop, where I was received in a beautiful palace by the emir and his son—who would in 1995 depose his father and become emir himself. Under the rule of the son, also a graduate of Sandhurst, Qatar would become the location of an important U.S. mil-

itary base, perhaps the most important in the region, although Qatari
actions would sometimes run counter to U.S. interests. At the end of
our conversation, I headed back to the airport, accompanied by the
minister of defense. He hadn't been in the meeting with the emir and
was clearly curious about our plans. He turned to me in the backseat of
the armored limo. "So," he asked, "are you going to nuke Saddam?" No,
I said, that was not the plan.

AS WE WERE BUILDING up forces in the operation we now called
Desert Shield, many senior military officers traveled to the Persian
Gulf. Air Force Chief of Staff Mike Dugan and several generals on his
staff flew to Saudi Arabia during mid-September. General Dugan had
been advised not to take press with him on the trip, but he ignored the
advice and spent many hours on the way over and back talking with
journalists.

On Sunday morning, September 16, 1990, I opened my front door
and retrieved the *Washington Post* off my front porch. Before I got back
inside, I saw the headline "U.S. to Rely on Air Strikes if War Erupts."
I read through the article, my anger rising. During the hours of plane
interviews, Dugan had apparently talked to journalists about specific
targets we would hit if war came—Saddam personally, his family, and
his mistress. He'd talked about numbers and types of aircraft deployed
in the region, declared "air power" to be "the only answer that's available
to our country" if we wanted to avoid a bloody land war, and said the
American public would support the operation in the Gulf—"until body
bags come home."

I called Scowcroft, who was scheduled to be on CBS's *Face the Na-
tion* in a few hours. He would be asked about the story. We agreed that
Brent would make clear Dugan did not speak for the administration.
Then I left and went for a walk alongside the C&O Canal to cool down.
A few hours later, back at home, I read the piece again. And I got angry
again. I picked up the phone and called the president at Camp David.
He was on the tennis court, but when he called back a short while later,
I told him I had decided I might have to relieve General Dugan based

on his comments in the piece. The president said I should do what I needed to do, and he would back me up.

I did not take the prospect of firing the air force chief of staff lightly. Dugan was a good man with a distinguished career, who had been in his job less than three months. But he had displayed terrible judgment. I worried that if I tolerated what he had done, other generals would step out of bounds, and as the nation prepared for the prospect of war, I couldn't tolerate loose cannons in senior ranks. I made notes on the article and a list of the most serious problems arising from what Dugan had done. I decided I would call Dugan in and ask him whether the news stories were accurate. If they were, I would relieve him.

I asked Joe Lopez to have Dugan report to my office at eight the next morning. Just before eight I met with my deputy Don Atwood and General Powell. I told them I planned to relieve Dugan. I think Powell was surprised. He knew Dugan had made a mistake in sharing so much information with the press, but I don't think he believed I would fire Dugan over it. He didn't object. He left my office, but I wanted a witness in the room and asked Atwood to remain. General Dugan came in and took a seat. I went through the major points in the articles and asked the general if he'd been accurately quoted. He said he had. I told him I needed his resignation by the end of the day. He took it like a man, saluted smartly, and left. I placed another call to the president to inform him that I had indeed relieved General Dugan.

I recommended General Tony McPeak, an F-15 pilot, as Dugan's replacement, and in short order the president nominated him and the Senate confirmed him. Some days later, McPeak introduced me to a group of retired air force four-stars. "This is Secretary of Defense Dick Cheney," he said. "He wasn't the president's first choice, either."

AS U.S. FORCES CONTINUED to flow into the desert, Colin Powell repeatedly pressed the case for long-term sanctions, for waiting and hoping that economic pressure would drive Saddam out of Kuwait. I had little faith in sanctions to begin with, and to think that Saddam would give up one of the world's great oil reserves—100 billion barrels, roughly, in Kuwait—because of sanctions struck me as foolish. More-over, we couldn't let our troops sit in the desert indefinitely, hoping that sanctions would squeeze Saddam. There was also the matter of the coalition of nations that the president had led the way in assembling. It was very impressive, but it would not hold forever.

On September 24, when Powell came to me to make the case for long-term sanctions one more time, I told him I thought he should make his argument directly to the president. It was important for President Bush to hear Powell's arguments firsthand, I believed—and I didn't want Powell, after the fact, to be able to say we hadn't listened to him. I took him to the Oval Office that afternoon, told the president that General Powell had something to say, and Powell said it. A week or so later, President Bush asked for a briefing on our plans to use force to evict Saddam from Kuwait.

On Wednesday, October 10, 1990, a small group gathered in the "Tank," the Joint Chiefs of Staff conference room in the Pentagon, to hear Schwarzkopf's representative, Major General Robert Johnston, brief us on their offensive war plan. General Schwarzkopf and the team of planners he had working with him in Riyadh had broken the war plan into four phases. The first three involved air attacks on Iraqi command, control, and communications; Iraqi supply and munitions bases; and the Republican Guard. The fourth phase would be the ground assault. As described that day in the Tank, coalition forces would be moving directly north into the heart of Iraq's most lethal forces.

It didn't make any sense. Why would we send our forces—some of which were only lightly armored—up against the heavily armored core of Saddam's defenses? Why not swing to the west? I wasn't the only one asking questions. No one in the Tank seemed happy with the ground assault plan. General Schwarzkopf himself wasn't happy with it. He had ordered that a final slide be included in the presentation that read, "Offensive Ground Plan Not Solid. We Do Not Have The Capability To Attack On Ground At This Time." The planners in Riyadh believed at least another corps would be needed to undertake an offensive ground operation.

I thought the president needed to see the brief right away. He needed to know, as commander in chief, what the forces in theater were and weren't capable of doing. I arranged for Schwarzkopf's briefers to provide the brief to the president and Brent Scowcroft in the White House Situation Room the next day. I opened with an overview for the president in which I explained that the first three phases of the offensive plan, all part of the air campaign, were well planned and ready to execute with three days' notice. We had a high degree of confidence in the air plan and our ability to execute.

Phase IV, the ground campaign, was a different proposition. We now had nearly 200,000 troops in theater, while the Iraqis had built up to well over 400,000. Saddam had not been idle. His troops had erected fortifications, laid down minefields, and established an effective logistics network. The bottom line, I said, was that while the plan showed how we might use the forces we currently had in theater to liberate Kuwait, it laid out a very high-risk proposition, one that depended on everything going perfectly—which it never does.

Briefing the air campaign to the president and the National Security Council was Buster Glosson, an air force one-star. Glosson had been working in legislative affairs when I first arrived at the Pentagon. When his tour was up, Larry Welch, then air force chief of staff, had assigned him to be deputy commander of the Joint Task Force Middle East. I suspected Glosson had crossed Welch at some point because being an air force officer assigned to duty on board a ship steaming around the Persian Gulf wasn't exactly career-enhancing. But if the intent had been to sideline Glosson, it didn't work. Saddam's invasion of Kuwait put him right in the center of the action. Here he was in the White House briefing the commander in chief.

When Glosson finished, General Johnston briefed the ground war and explained that no one in theater liked the straight-up-the-middle concept, but that it was all we could do with the numbers of forces deployed. The president and Brent were not happy with the plan. What would it take, the president wanted to know, to have a satisfactory offensive ground option? I told him we would get him answers ASAP.

The next morning I made clear to Powell that he needed to get with Norm Schwarzkopf and come back with a workable plan. What I didn't tell him was that I intended to push the system myself to make sure we got such a battle plan.

Undersecretary of Defense Paul Wolfowitz pulled together a small team to study and develop a plan that came to be called the "Western Excursion." The concept originally came from Henry Rowen, the assistant secretary of defense for international security affairs. Wolfowitz's team, headed by a retired army general, Dale Vesser, took Rowen's concept and expanded it into a plan to move coalition forces into the western desert of Iraq. Rather than go straight into the heart of Iraqi defenses in Kuwait, this plan would involve taking Iraqi territory, forcing the Iraqis to move key elements of their best troops to defend a potential threat to Baghdad, and perhaps acquiring for the coalition territory they could use to bargain for Kuwait. The team began working on the plan in secret as I left on a nine-day trip that would take me to London, Paris, and the Soviet Union.

IN LONDON I MET with Prime Minister Thatcher at Number 10 Downing Street. Shortly after our meeting began, she asked everyone to leave the room except for me and my British counterpart, Tom King, and the three of us spent more than an hour talking about the Gulf crisis. She drew on her own experience in the Falklands War in 1982 for lessons both in military strategy and how to build and maintain public support. She was eloquent and insightful, and my session with her, the single most valuable I had in the run-up to the war, illustrated why she deserves to be regarded as one of the most effective national leaders of the twentieth century. That session also came near the end of her political career. Little more than a month later, facing a growing challenge within her own Conservative Party, she would inform the queen that she did not intend to stand again for prime minister.

The next day, Tuesday, October 16, 1990, I landed in Moscow. In Red Square at dusk, I laid a wreath at the Tomb of the Unknown Soldier. It was a stirring moment for an American secretary of defense. Afterward I was driven to a dacha outside Moscow for a dinner hosted by Soviet Defense Minister Yazov. On that cold Russian night, there were many toasts, and I was struck by the historic moment. Here I was, the U.S. secretary of defense, exchanging toasts with men who a few years earlier had been our deadliest and staunchest enemies. I raised my glass: "To peace."

The next morning I had a formal meeting with Gorbachev in his Kremlin office. He emphasized that his government wanted a peaceful solution to the Gulf crisis, but in meetings with him, Foreign Minister Eduard Shevardnadze, and Defense Minister Yazov, I gained information that was important if we did go to war. Had the Soviets provided any weapons to the Iraqis that we didn't know about? I asked. In years past, the Soviets would surely have refused to enter into such a conversation, but now they assured me that we would encounter no surprises.

My hosts showed me the Moscow Air Defense Center, buried sixty-five feet beneath Moscow and entered through nine steel doors. Surrounded by Soviet generals, I sat at the computer console in the control room and watched as huge maps flashed on the wall, first of Moscow, then of the eastern Soviet Union, and finally, of all Europe. In the event of nuclear war, the Soviets would have overseen some of their defensive operations from this command post. I was the first American to see it.

I was also taken to the ancient Russian city of Tula, site of a training center for Soviet airborne forces that was roughly equivalent to our Fort Bragg in North Carolina, but a much less sophisticated facility. While I was there, elite Soviet troops staged an exercise, an airdrop of several hundred men in an impressive show—although it did not match what I'd seen our own forces do.

My host at Tula was Soviet General Alexander Lebed, commander of the 106th Division. A hero of the fighting in Afghanistan, he looked every inch the tough soldier he was, but he would oppose hard-liners like Yazov when they tried to overthrow Gorbachev for moving too quickly with reform, and he had an eye for politics. Later, as a civilian, he visited America, stopping to see me in Texas, where I was heading up Halliburton, and presenting me with his memoirs and a knife used by

Soviet fighters. For a time he was seen as Boris Yeltsin's successor, a position that eventually went to Vladimir Putin. Lebed was subsequently governor of Krasnoyarsk, a huge, mineral-rich region of Siberia, where he remained a political force until he was killed in a helicopter accident in 2002.

One of my last stops was at a large industrial site, a factory for MiG-29s, the top-of-the-line Soviet fighter. But the planes being produced were unfinished. Various key parts simply weren't available. Rather than shut the plant doors, plant managers continued to operate in order to keep the workforce employed, but the products coming off the assembly line were worthless from a military standpoint. The managers of the plant indicated they were working on converting to the production of food processors similar to those found in millions of American homes, but when they showed me their prototype, I realized their plan wasn't going to work. The food processor they so proudly showed me was the size of a small refrigerator.

The Soviets were clearly heading for a significantly diminished military capability. And what I saw, coming on top of the dramatic shifts that had occurred—the decision to free Eastern Europe peacefully and to allow Germany to reunify—convinced me that much of the talk about reform was real.

At a final meeting in Moscow, I found myself sitting across from members of the Supreme Soviet in an ornate room in the Kremlin, where I had attended a similar meeting in 1983. Then I had been a member of Congress and our delegation had had a very tense exchange with our Soviet counterparts over arms control, human rights, and Soviet treatment of dissidents. Now the feeling of standoff was gone, and the debates were mostly on the Soviet side as they argued over the merits and wisdom of different elements of economic reform.

AS I WAS FLYING home from Moscow, General Powell was departing Washington for Riyadh. His mission was to work with General Schwarzkopf to come up with a list of additional troops Schwarzkopf would need to go on the offense and liberate Kuwait.

In the meanwhile Paul Wolfowitz and his team had been working on the Western Excursion option, and it was time to staff it out. I called Admiral Dave Jeremiah, vice chairman of the Joint Chiefs of Staff, to my office on the morning of October 23, 1990, and had him briefed on the plan and given the work Paul's team had completed. I knew that as soon as the staff of the Joint Chiefs saw the plan, word would get around—and I was counting on that to convey my seriousness to the generals. We were going to provide the president with an offensive option, one way or another.

That task took on increasing importance the next day, when the president told me he was leaning toward action to remove Saddam from Kuwait. How many more troops would it require, he wanted to know. I told him that as soon as Powell got back from the Gulf, I would get to him with a report.

When I appeared on the morning television shows on October 25, I laid some groundwork. Asked by Harry Smith on *CBS This Morning* whether we were getting ready to send another hundred thousand troops to the Gulf, I responded that it was conceivable that we could end up with an increase that large. I also explained that we had never put an upper limit on our deployment and I wasn't prepared to do that now. My comments were intended to prepare the American people for what I believed was a likely new buildup, but I also wanted to send yet another message to our generals that we planned to continue to flow forces until we had provided whatever they needed to do the job. Schwarzkopf, in particular, seemed to need bucking up. The week I did the morning shows, he gave an interview in the Gulf to the *Atlanta Journal-Constitution* claiming that sanctions were working, "so why should we say . . . 'Let's get on with it and kill a whole bunch of people'?"

By October 30 Powell had returned from the Gulf with Central Command's troop requests. When I met with him at 8:00 that morning to review the bidding, he laid out a long and lengthy list—and I said that I fully supported it. That afternoon Powell and I went to the White House for a meeting in the Situation Room, and the president, Scowcroft, Baker, and I listened as Powell briefed us on what

Schwarzkopf wanted if he was ordered to carry out the offensive option—basically a doubling of the force. When Powell had finished, I told the president that I fully supported the request, and I went further. I was convinced the offensive option was the right one, and that we should give the generals whatever they thought it would take. The president agreed and signed off on Powell's and Schwarzkopf's requests.

Prior to the public announcement of the new deployment on November 8, 1990, I placed calls to congressional leaders to notify them it was imminent. Then, at 4:00 p.m., I joined President Bush at the White House as he announced, "I have today directed the secretary of defense to increase the size of the U.S. forces committed to Desert Shield to ensure that the coalition has an adequate offensive military option should that be necessary to achieve our common goals." After the White House briefing, I went directly back to the Pentagon, where, at 4:45 p.m., Colin and I briefed the Pentagon press corps. I set forth a long list of units to be deployed: the VII Corps Headquarters out of Stuttgart, Germany; the 1st Armored Division in Germany; the 3rd Armored Division in Germany; the 2nd Armored Division (forward); and the 2nd Armored Cavalry Regiment. In addition, we were taking 2nd Corps Support Command from Stuttgart and the Big Red One, the 1st Infantry Division, from Fort Riley, Kansas. The navy would be sending three additional aircraft carrier battle groups and their escorts; one additional battleship and another amphibious group. The Marine Corps would be sending the II Marine Expeditionary Force out of Camp Lejeune and the 5th Marine Expeditionary Brigade out of Camp Pendleton. I also announced that we would be calling up combat units of the Army National Guard.

On November 18, when I appeared on *Meet the Press,* there was interest in whether we had decided to seek congressional authorization for the use of force in Iraq. I told Garrick Utley that I loved the Congress. I had served there for ten years. But I also had a sense of its limitations. "I take you back to September 1941," I said, "when World War II had been under way for two years; Hitler had taken Austria, Czechoslovakia, Poland, Norway, Denmark, the Netherlands, Belgium, France and was halfway to Moscow. And the Congress, in that setting, two months before Pearl Harbor, agreed to extend . . . the draft for twelve more months, by just one vote."

I made clear the decision hadn't been made, but I also emphasized that putting a matter of the nation's security in the hands of the 535 members of the U.S. Congress could be a risky proposition. And I cautioned that a drawn-out debate in Congress could convey a sense to our allies and to Saddam that we weren't resolute in our commitment to liberate Kuwait.

By the end of the month, Congress was holding hearings, and Sam Nunn, chairman of the Senate Armed Services Committee, his mind on a presidential run, seemed intent on providing a forum for those opposed to using force to liberate Kuwait. Among the witnesses was Admiral Bill Crowe, former chairman of the Joint Chiefs of Staff, who said we needed to give sanctions another year to work before we considered force.

The day after Crowe's testimony, a United Nations Security Council resolution set a January 15, 1991, deadline for Iraq to get out of Kuwait and authorized "all necessary means" to accomplish that end. But this clear message to the world—and Jim Baker deserves enormous credit for it—was muddied when the president announced he was going to send Jim to negotiate with Saddam. Tariq Aziz was also going to be invited to the United States, and many of our allies were dismayed. The Saudis, in particular, felt as though we'd pulled the rug out from under them.

On a crucial front, we were making progress. The generals in the Pentagon were starting to believe we meant business. The president's approval of General Schwarzkopf's large additional troop request had been key, as had the successful vote in the UN Security Council. It also helped enormously when I issued an order in mid-November authorizing the services to call up additional reserve and National Guard forces as needed. This was another effort that the president supported unhesitatingly, overruling Chief of Staff John Sununu's political objections. Yes, communities across the country would be affected when their folks were called up to serve, but we were going to build the force the generals thought we needed.

These actions signaled to the military that the civilians now in charge had learned the lessons of Vietnam—and other steps we were taking did as well. We were embarked on a massive buildup, not a gradual one in hopes that Saddam would change his mind. We were deploying troops in units, not using the individual rotations that had created turmoil during Vietnam. I had issued a stop-loss order. Nobody was leaving the armed forces until this job was done. The president had meant it when he said, "This will not stand."

The execution of this war would be in the hands of the generals, but I wanted to be sure I understood as thoroughly as possible the details of what our troops were doing, and with that in mind I set up a series of briefings for myself, perhaps three dozen in all. Tom Kelly, the director of operations for the joint staff, was in charge of them. He would bring a team up to my office or sometimes I would go to the Tank, and I would be briefed on how a cruise missile works or on how to penetrate a minefield. We spent a lot of time on chemical weapons, which Saddam had used before, and on how we could defend our troops against them.

ON DECEMBER 18, POWELL and I left D.C. and headed for Saudi Arabia. In Schwarzkopf's headquarters, located in a bunker beneath the Saudi Ministry of Defense, Norm had assembled his command team to brief us on every aspect of the air and ground war planning. During our first morning session, we focused on intelligence—what did we know about Saddam's troops, their locations, their readiness—and the readiness of our own forces. One of my biggest concerns was that the planners not make overly optimistic assumptions. We needed to be ready, I told them, for the possibility of a long conflict. We needed to assume the worst.

The afternoon briefing covered the war plan itself. It had come a long way since our first session two months earlier, when the only option for a ground campaign had been the straight-up-the-middle approach. We now had three phases of an air campaign, followed by a ground campaign, which would involve a left-hook maneuver where our forces swung wide and then attacked Saddam from the side, rather than driving directly into the heart of his best troops.

This left-hook maneuver would put heavy logistical demands on our troops, as we moved the forces and their equipment hundreds of miles to the west. Our success would depend upon air superiority and on the element of surprise—we had to hope Saddam either would not find out about the plan or wouldn't believe it if he did.

Satisfied that Norm and his team had done a very solid job putting the plan in place, preparing for contingencies, and getting ready to move, Powell and I left for Washington. On the way home we got word that Israeli Defense Minister Moshe Arens wanted to meet me—anytime, anywhere. The Israelis had promised us they would not preemptively strike Iraq, but they were understandably nervous about the war planning and wanted to know what to expect.

I was concerned that if I left Saudi Arabia and went directly to a meeting with the Israelis, it would put real pressure on our coalition. It was important that we do everything possible to keep Israel out of the action. We did not want them to become an excuse for Saddam to divide our coalition. Instead of a meeting, we agreed to install a hotline, code-named Hammer Rick, which would connect my office in the Pentagon directly to Israeli Defense Minister Arens.

Back in Washington after the holidays, talk turned to whether we should seek congressional approval for a use of force against Iraq. I opposed the idea. We had all the authority we needed, because the United States Senate had previously ratified the United Nations Charter, including Article 51, which allowed us to go to the assistance of a member state, such as Kuwait, that had been invaded. Moreover, if we got turned down by the Congress, that would be a huge blow to our coalition and to our troops already deployed. If the military action was successful, it wouldn't matter whether Congress had supported us beforehand. If, on the other hand, we failed, even if we had a vote supporting the use of force we'd be faced with intense criticism, including from those who had voted with us. In other words, I thought there was significant risk in seeking their approval and very little to be gained.

I also thought it would set a dangerous precedent. As a legal and constitutional matter, the president had the authority he needed. If he sought congressional approval, that would surely be read by some as a message that he needed the congressional vote. It looked to me like a move that would diminish the power of the office. The president heard these arguments, but decided to go for a vote, and on January 8 he sent a letter to Congress seeking their approval for the use of "all necessary means to implement UN Security Council Resolution 678," which required that Saddam withdraw from Kuwait.

Meanwhile, in an effort to ensure that we had exhausted all possibilities for a peaceful resolution, the president sent Jim Baker to Geneva to meet with Saddam's foreign minister, Tariq Aziz. I had been concerned that Jim might broker a last-minute deal based on Saddam's promising to withdraw from Kuwait. What if Saddam used such a pledge to push us beyond the UN deadline? What if he pulled back into Iraq? Would we bring half a million troops home and wait for him to go over the border again? But when Baker called the president on the morning of January 9, it was to say that the Iraqis were determined to stay in Kuwait. The president, Brent, and I gathered around a small television set in the president's private office as Baker was about to address the press corps gathered in the Intercontinental Hotel in Geneva. As soon as he stepped in front of the cameras it was clear to the world from the look on his face that no deal had been struck. "Regrettably, ladies and gentlemen, . . . in over six hours I heard nothing that suggested to me any Iraqi flexibility whatsoever on complying with the United Nations Security Council resolutions."

Baker left Geneva to confer with our allies in Riyadh, and I went to work, lobbying hard for Congress to authorize the use of force against Iraq. On January 12, the resolution made it through the House handily, 250–183, but it was close in the Senate, 52–47. I called George Bush. "Mr. President," I said, "you were right." Years later, President Bush wrote that if the vote had been negative, he would still have ordered our troops into battle—and probably been impeached. Going to Congress was high-risk, no doubt about it, but it had worked.

Late in the afternoon of January 15, General Powell came to my office with an order for me to sign. As secretary of defense, I signed a lot of orders. All deployments required my sign-off, and I usually just initialed them. But this order was different. This was an execute order, authorizing war. I signed my full name, and then I asked General Powell to sign his.

CHAPTER SEVEN

Desert Storm

In the early morning hours of Wednesday, January 16, 1991, my limousine pulled to a stop on Constitution Avenue. Lynne and I got out and walked through a light rain down the sloping path to the Vietnam Veterans Memorial. We stood in front of the long black wall as visitors often do, silent and in awe. The fifty-eight thousand names etched on the wall are a reminder of the terrible cost of war. They were also a reminder to me, as operations in Iraq were about to begin, of the solemn obligation of America's civilian leaders to provide our soldiers with a clear mission and the resources to prevail. We bowed our heads in prayer, thinking of the young Americans who would soon be flying in combat over Iraq.

By 7:15 a.m. I was at the White House for a meeting with Jim Baker and Brent Scowcroft in Brent's West Wing office. We went over the details of what would unfold in the coming hours and walked through the list of world leaders whom we would call to notify in advance that operations would soon be under way. I made my first call of the day back in my Pentagon office to Israeli Defense Minister Moshe Arens, with whom I had been staying in touch. We had offered to send Patriot antimissile batteries to help protect Israel from missile attacks that Saddam might launch. Undersecretary of Defense Paul Wolfowitz and Deputy Secretary of State Lawrence Eagleburger had traveled to Israel with that offer, but the Israelis had declined. They had accepted our offer of early warning from our satellites of any missiles launched, and we had established the Hammer Rick hotline between my office and the Israeli Defense Ministry. In my 9:00 a.m. call to Arens, I told him that H-Hour, the hour when the operation would begin, was 7:00 p.m. Washington time, 3:00 a.m. in Baghdad. I urged him to use the secure communications link to call me anytime.

By the time I talked to Arens, seven B-52 long-range bombers had already taken off from Barksdale Air Force Base in Louisiana, armed with cruise missiles and headed for Iraq. As H-Hour approached, F-15E fighter-bombers, AWACS, KC-135 refueling planes, and F-117 stealth fighters prepared to take off from bases inside Saudi Arabia. Sailors on board ships such as the U.S.S. *Wisconsin* and the U.S.S. *Missouri* in the Persian Gulf ran through checklists, readying cruise missiles for launch.

Because our F-117s were stealthy, they would be able to penetrate Iraqi airspace without being detected by radar. As they were flying toward Baghdad, eight Apache gunships would fly in low in the dark and take out two of the key nodes of the Iraqi early warning system, opening up a hole in their air defenses so that we could start flowing the rest of our airplanes through to attack Baghdad. Desert Shield was about to become Desert Storm.

As H-Hour neared, I sent an assistant to my home in McLean to retrieve the suitcase I'd packed. I planned to spend the night in the small bedroom connected to my office, but I hadn't brought the suitcase in with me that morning out of concern that it might alert any close observers that the war was about to begin. By late afternoon, it was clear we had done all we could from Washington. The only thing left now was to wait. At 5:00 p.m. General Powell and Deputy Secretary Atwood joined me in my office for our daily evening wrap-up session. We turned the television to CNN, then the only twenty-four-hour news

channel. Bernard Shaw was on the air from Baghdad. He was interviewing Walter Cronkite in New York, who was telling stories about
covering World War II as a young correspondent. After the two talked
for a while, Shaw said he was heading back to the States. He said that
he'd be on the first plane out of Baghdad in the morning. We knew that
wasn't happening. Not long after, the night sky outside Bernie's hotel
room window lit up as Operation Desert Storm began. This would be
the first war Americans would be able to watch unfold, in real time, on
live television.

The president spoke to the nation from the Oval Office at 9:00 p.m.
to announce the beginning of military operations. At 9:30 p.m. General
Powell and I appeared in the Pentagon briefing room to hold a brief
press conference. I noted that great care was being taken to minimize
U.S. casualties and focus on military targets and that we were hitting
targets in both Iraq and Kuwait. We couldn't say a lot at this early stage,
but I wanted to establish the precedent of the American people hearing
information about our military operations directly from the Pentagon
briefing room. General Schwarzkopf would also conduct briefings from
Riyadh.

Before the war my assistant secretary of defense for public affairs,
Pete Williams, had gone to see Lieutenant General Tom Kelly, the director of operations for the joint staff. Pete told Tom we wanted to hold
daily briefings for the press once the war started and said that he, Pete,
thought Tom ought to conduct the briefings. Tom resisted mightily. He
told Pete there was absolutely no way, given his responsibilities in the
upcoming conflict, that he had time to brief the press every day. It just
wasn't going to happen, he said. Pete came to see me with the suggestion, and I backed him up. I thought it made tremendous sense to put
senior guys such as Tom Kelly and Rear Admiral Mike McConnell, the
director of intelligence for the joint staff, out in front of the press each
day. These were the same officers who briefed General Powell and me in
the morning. They were knowledgeable enough to answer tough questions and experienced enough to know what they could and couldn't
tell the press. When Pete went back to see Tom a few days later, he said,

"You know, Tom, *the secretary* would really like you to give the daily briefings." Kelly replied, "That's an excellent idea, Pete. I'd be thrilled to do that."

We had given a good deal of thought to ensuring the most accurate coverage of the war. Before Desert Storm began, Pete put together a plan that would have embedded reporters directly with our military units, an early version of the plan the Pentagon followed twelve years later. I supported Pete's concept and one evening had him come to my office to brief General Powell and me on it. General Powell was decidedly unsupportive. There was absolutely no way we could embed reporters without compromising operational security, he said, expressing robust views on the subject in very strong terms. As Pete was leaving I told him not to worry about it. "Good briefing, Pete. We're gaining on him," I said with a smile.

At the end of the day, though, it was clear that our commander in the field, Norm Schwarzkopf, shared Powell's strong resistance to having reporters embedded with the troops. Both Powell and Schwarzkopf and many of our senior officers had developed a deep distrust of the press based on their experiences in Vietnam. It was understandable, and I did not want to add to the already considerable pressure Schwarzkopf was under by insisting on the embed concept. So we agreed the war would be covered using a pool system, which ultimately had mixed results. Some reporters ended up with commanders who included them in key meetings and operational briefings. Others could barely get the time of day from the officers assigned to mind them.

It was also the case that most of the prewar action had taken place in Saudi Arabia—a country that wasn't issuing visas to journalists as a general matter. At first the only American journalists who could get into Saudi were the ones who flew in with me. The restrictions opened up a bit when King Fahd realized how much airtime Saddam Hussein was getting and determined to allow more Western journalists into the Kingdom to level the playing field.

Ultimately, no matter what the Pentagon does with the press during a time of war, the U.S. government is likely to be criticized for it. If they embed reporters and give them access to lots of information, the military is accused of trying to shape the truth or sugarcoat things. If reporters don't get access then the military is accused of trying to hide the truth. In some sense it's a no-win situation, but I think all in all we handled it pretty well.

One of my main concerns was not getting into a situation where the press was deciding whether or not we were winning. I wanted information about what was happening to come straight from the military and civilian leadership, not be filtered or skewed by the press in any way. Though we could not guard against this completely, I think our schedule of daily briefings and pool coverage helped ensure that plenty of accurate information did get through.

After Powell and I finished our briefing on the first night of the war, I called the president, a World War II veteran of carrier-based combat operations. "Mr. President," I told him, "we have sent fifty-six navy planes out and we've got fifty-six back. We have over two hundred air force planes out and no sign of any missing." Overnight, however, we would lose a pilot, Lieutenant Commander Scott Speicher, whose F-18 was shot down over Iraq.

ON THE SECOND DAY of the war, Saddam began launching Scud missiles at Israel. These were low-tech 1960s Soviet hardware, but in an urban setting they could cause considerable damage, and there were repeated rumors, all of which turned out to be false, that the Iraqis were putting chemical warheads on some of them. Shortly after the first Scuds struck, my phone rang. It was Israeli Defense Minister Moshe Arens. He was urgently requesting the Patriot missile batteries and crews we had offered before the war began. Arens said the Israelis also planned to launch retaliatory air strikes, and he asked for the Identification Friend or Foe, or IFF, codes that would allow Israeli pilots to avoid being shot down by allied planes. I told him I would get back to him. Then I called Scowcroft at the White House.

In discussions before the war began, we had agreed that we had to do everything we could to keep the Israelis out of the war, because once

Happy in Nebraska: On the front lawn in Lincoln at six months.

My great grandfather, Captain Samuel Fletcher Cheney, who served in the 21st Ohio from 1861 to 1865. A friend who fought with him at the Battle of Stones River said he was a man of "clear grit."

Below, left to right: My mom's parents, Dave and Clarice Dickey, who were cooks on the Union Pacific Railroad in the 1940s; My dad's parents, Thomas Herbert "Bert" and Margaret Cheney, on the front porch of their house in Sumner, Nebraska, 1946.

Clockwise from top left: My mother, Marjorie Dickey, with one of her softball teammates, in front of Dickey's Café in Syracuse, Nebraska. My mom's folks ran the café before they started to work for the Union Pacific; With my uncle Elmer and my brother, Bob, on Elmer's farm in Dawson County, Nebraska, where Bob and I stayed when our mom went to visit Dad in San Diego during the war; Bob and I showing off our catch. We're standing in front of the Cheney family 1947 Frazier; My dad home on leave from the navy during World War II with my mom, brother, Bob, and me in Sumner, Nebraska.

With Bob and our friends Ed and Vic Larson in our Little League uniforms in Lincoln, Nebraska, in 1952. I'm on the far right.

Left: With Lynne at the Natrona County High School senior prom in Casper, Wyoming, 1959.

Below: The Natrona Country High School football team—the Mustangs—Casper, Wyoming, 1958. I'm number 20.

Lynne Vincent and I traded senior year yearbook photos. One of the best decisions I ever made was asking her out on our first date, January 30, 1958.

Lynne and me on a scooter in front of my mom and dad's house in Casper, Wyoming, in the early 1960s.

Our wedding party. My sister, Susan, is the young attendant in the front row. Joe Meyer, far left, Dave Nicholas, third from the left, and Karen Nicholas, second from the right, later helped me run for Congress. My brother-in-law, Mark, far right, was the campaign treasurer.

Leaving the church, August 29, 1964. The best man, Dave Nicholas, is on the left and the maid of honor, Janet Rogers, is on the right.

Meeting President Nixon for the first time, with Don Rumsfeld, in the Oval Office in 1970. I had seen President Johnson at his last address to a joint session of Congress in January 1969. I'd also seen President Kennedy when he visited the University of Wyoming in 1963, and President Harry Truman in 1948, when he'd done a whistle-stop tour campaigning through Nebraska, but Nixon was the first president I'd ever actually met. *Official White House Photo*

Going over plans for the Republican National Convention with President Ford in Aspen Lodge at Camp David, August 1976. *Official White House Photo/David Kennerly*

With President Ford during one of our daily sessions in the Oval Office, November 1974. *Official White House Photo/Ricardo Thomas*

In the Cabinet Room of the White House on June 17, 1976, discussing plans for the evacuation of Americans from Lebanon with President Ford and members of his national security council, including CIA Director George Herbert Walker Bush, National Security Advisor Brent Scowcroft, and Secretary of State Henry Kissinger. *Official White House Photo/David Kennerly*

In the Oval Office on April 28, 1975, with President Ford and Don Rumsfeld, two men who changed my life. *Official White House Photo/David Kennerly*

With Secretary of State Henry Kissinger and National Security Advisor Brent Scowcroft in Vail, Colorado, in the summer of 1976. *Official White House Photo/David Kennerly*

Taking a break from the 1976 presidential campaign at the Texas State Fair with my aide, Foster Channock. *Official White House Photo/David Kennerly*

With Lynne, Mary, Liz, and our dog, Cyrano, on the front porch of our house in Casper, Wyoming, during my first campaign for Congress, 1978. *Photo by David Kennerly*

Meeting with a Wyoming voter on the campaign trail in 1978.
Cheney for Congress photo

GIVE CONGRESS
OUR BEST.

RE-ELECT
DICK CHENEY!

It's been six years since we first sent Dick Cheney to
cast our vote in the U.S. House of Representatives. When
he first ran for office, Dick was a talented, energetic
young Wyomingite with valuable experience as White
House Chief of Staff for former President Gerald Ford.
    During his six years in the House of Representatives,
he has combined that talent, energy and experience
with plain hard work to become a leader in the Congress —
an institution with 535 members where Dick is one of
the top four elected officials among House Republicans
and only the second Wyoming representative in history
to serve as an elected House leader.
    At home in Wyoming, Dick stays in touch with the
people he represents. Being a member of Congress is
a full-time job, often involving 12-hour days, yet Dick
effectively carries out his duties in Washington
while maintaining close contact with his
constituents. He has made more than
112 trips to Wyoming, traveled almost
half a million miles, and spent close to
575 days in his state since he first left
Casper to represent us in Congress. To put it
in more personal terms, he cares about
Wyoming people, and it shows in the way he
does his job.
    It isn't exaggerating to say that Dick
Cheney is probably the best Congressman
Wyoming has ever had.

Above: A campaign photo, taken on the road
between Casper and Rawlins, Wyoming, 1978.
Photo by David Kennerly; Right: One of my
campaign reelection brochures, 1980. *Official White
House Photo/David Kennerly*

With fellow members of the Wyoming congressional delegation Al Simpson and
Malcolm Wallop at a campaign rally with President Ronald Reagan in Cheyenne,
Wyoming, in 1984. *Photo by David Kennerly*

Leaving the White House residence in February 1991 with President Bush after reporting to him on one of my trips to the Middle East during Operation Desert Storm. *Photo by David Kennerly*

Atop an M-60 tank, talking with U.S. Marines deployed in Saudi Arabia during Operation Desert Shield, December 22, 1990. *Official Pentagon Photo/Pete Williams*

With President Bush in the White House residence on Sunday, February 24, 1991, the morning after we launched ground operations in Operation Desert Storm. I'm briefing the president on our progress in the first hours of the ground war. *Official White House Photo/Dave Valdez*

Left: In Saudi Arabia with Generals Powell and Schwarzkopf, preparing to brief the press during Operation Desert Storm, February 10, 1991. *Photo by David Kennerly*

Right: Ticker-tape parade in New York City to honor troops returning from Desert Storm. Lynne and I are in the first convertible, followed by Colin and Alma Powell and Norm and Brenda Schwarzkopf, June 10, 1991. © *Rick Maiman/Sygma/Corbis*

Receiving the Presidential Medal of Freedom from President George H.W. Bush, July 3, 1991. *Official White House Photo/Dave Valdez*

Rich — Congratulations! You Earned This Medal of Freedom By Steadfastly Leading our Armed Forces in War and to Your Wise Counsel to this Grateful President Gg Bsh

Getting ready to fish the Snake River with Mary and Liz during the Democratic National Convention in August 2000. *Photo by David Kennerly*

Our granddaughters Kate and Elizabeth joining us on the campaign trail in California, October 2000. © *Photo by M. Spencer Green/Associated Press*

Liz and Mary on election night 2000 reacting to the networks calling the election for George W. Bush and me. It was a premature—but nonetheless heartfelt—celebration. Jim Baker and Al Simpson are behind them. *Photo by David Kennerly*

In the governor's mansion in Austin, Texas, later that night after Al Gore had retracted his concession, with Lynne, George and Laura Bush, Jeb Bush, President Bush 41, Al and Ann Simpson, Heather and Mary, and campaign chairman Don Evans. *Photo by David Kennerly*

On the Bush ranch in Crawford during the thirty-seven-day recount.
Photo by David Kennerly

With Lynne, Liz, and Mary in the presidential reviewing stand at the inaugural parade, January 20, 2001. *Official White House Photo/Karen Ballard*

they got in, the conflict might look like an Arab-Israeli war, and Arab nations might well leave the coalition. Saddam, no fool, had launched the Scuds with that in mind. Scowcroft thought the best way to keep the Israelis on the sidelines was to hold them at arm's length. My assessment was that we should keep them close, tell them everything we were doing, and do everything we could to ensure Israel's safety, which did not include giving them IFF codes, but, I told Arens, we would go after the Scud launchers in the western desert. The Israelis had to know there was no reason for them to get into the conflict, because we were doing all that could be done.

In our discussions before the war, General Powell and the air commanders had assured me that we would have F-15E flights over the Iraqi western desert ready to take out any launch site from which a Scud was fired. As it turned out, the F-15Es had run into refueling difficulties and had not been flying the night of January 18. Nor did it seem—judging from CENTCOM's plans for the next day's air strikes—that General Schwarzkopf fully understood the importance of dedicating assets to hunting Scuds.

The next day Tel Aviv was hit again, and the Hammer Rick phone line got a workout. I could understand the Israeli anger. I myself was furious when I asked about the number of sorties that Central Command was flying against the Scuds and got a totally unsatisfactory answer. I knew the source of the problem. Norm Schwarzkopf didn't want to take assets away from bombing Baghdad and divert them to what he thought was a militarily insignificant mission. This was a misjudgment on his part. Not only was it militarily significant for us to keep the Israelis out of the war, but it would turn out that the heaviest American losses in a single attack during Desert Storm came from a Scud attack against our barracks near Dhahran, Saudi Arabia. The way our military commands are structured, Israel is part of European Command's area of responsibility, not part of Central Command, which was Schwarzkopf's area. This may have added to Norm's tendency not to factor Israel into his plans. Whatever the reason, I made it clear to Powell that going after the Scud launchers wasn't an option, it was a necessity. He passed the message to Schwarzkopf, and American sorties over the western Iraqi desert picked up the next night.

It was time for me to have a talk with Schwarzkopf, and when I got him on the phone, I told him he was doing a hell of a job, which he was, and that I understood his point: Civilians approve strategy and generals execute. But he needed to understand that the president considered this a strategic question. Whether our effort was successful or not could well depend on keeping Israel out of the war, and we had to devote resources to bombing Scud bunkers and launch sites. I also told him that he needed to understand my problem. "I'm the guy who gets to lean on the Israelis and who has to reassure them that we are doing everything we can. My credibility is crucial. If I tell them we are going to do something, then we will do it."

The air sorties over the western desert didn't bring an end to Scud attacks by any means, not on Israel nor on Saudi Arabia, which Saddam was also targeting. Part of the problem was that while we'd identified a number of fixed sites where we knew there were Scud launchers, the Iraqis were using mobile launchers instead. Although we weren't able to stop the launches, the diversion of air assets to the western desert did go a long way toward convincing the Israelis we were serious about doing all we could to stop the attacks. I'd call Arens with daily updates: twenty-four F-15s, cluster-bomb units, flying at midnight; four F-15s flying combat air patrol from 0300 to 1000; forty-eight A-10s during twelve hours of daylight; twelve F-16s on a fixed target at 1100; twenty-four on mobile units at 1400; twelve on bunkers at 1500.

Larry Eagleburger from the State Department and Paul Wolfowitz from the Pentagon went to Israel again, which helped enormously in letting the Israelis know what we were doing and understand the size and scale of our effort. The deployment of Patriot batteries out of Germany and into Israel, which we managed in about forty-eight hours, was another sign of our commitment—though the missile turned out to be less effective against Scuds than we first thought. One problem was that the Patriot was developed to defend a point target, something like an airfield, not a whole area, not a city. If you're protecting a base and you hit a Scud warhead coming in and knock it off target, that's a success. But if you're protecting Tel Aviv and you hit the incoming Scud and it goes down two miles away, that's not a success. It's also the case that Scuds are really crude devices. They'd break up as they came down, so that a lot of what we were shooting at was junk, not warheads.

We also sent special operations forces into western Iraq to work behind enemy lines to hunt down the Scud launchers. As theater commander, Norm had ultimate sign-off for anyone operating in his area of responsibility, and at first he did not want the special operators there. He shared some of the suspicion of others in the regular army that our special operations forces were overrated. I disagreed. I'd spent time learning about what they could do when I was in Congress, and after I was briefed by Wayne Downing, who commanded our joint special operations command and was an enormously capable officer and a true gentleman, I was convinced he and his men had an important contribution to make to our effort to shut down the Scud attacks. They did not disappoint. Once we combined special operations raids with air patrols, the number of attacks fell dramatically, and although they increased slightly as the Iraqis adjusted to our tactics, the Israelis did what we asked of them and stayed out of the war. It wasn't until after the war that I came to understand what a near-run thing it had been. A senior Israeli official told me that at one point Israeli commandos were loaded into helicopters ready to fly into Iraq, but their mission was canceled after one of the phone calls I made reporting on the extent of our efforts to go after the Scuds. I emphasized that since we already had people on the ground, Israeli intervention could endanger American forces.

THE SOVIETS HAD BEEN helpful in the early days after the Iraqis invaded Kuwait and had not opposed our efforts to liberate that country. However, once we launched operations, they began trying to arrange a cease-fire on terms we could not accept. They urged that we pause our bombing in response to a vague promise from Saddam to comply with UN Security Council resolutions. We knew that a pause would only give him time to rearm and regroup and we could not accept it. We had also been clear that Saddam had actually to withdraw from Kuwait, not simply make promises to do so.

On January 28, a little less than two weeks into the air campaign, the new Soviet foreign minister, Alexander Bessmertnykh, was in Washington for meetings with Jim Baker. I had the sense that the Soviets, their empire on its last legs, were desperate to make themselves seem relevant by attempting to negotiate a cease-fire between us and the Iraqis. It also seemed that they wanted to show the world they could prevent their former client state, Iraq, from being on the receiving end of a massive military defeat. To his credit the president bore the brunt of the Soviet efforts to negotiate a cease-fire, patiently responding to call after call from Gorbachev himself. But on January 29 Jim decided to issue a joint statement with Bessmertnykh on Iraq without clearing it with the White House or showing it to us at the Pentagon. The statement was a problem because it suggested that we would in fact agree to a cease-fire in exchange for a *promise* from Saddam to pull out. The statement also suggested a linkage between a cease-fire and the Israeli-Palestinian peace process. Although the language of the joint statement suggested this wasn't a change in our policy, it was in fact a change and caught all of us by surprise. It was released on the day of the president's State of the Union address, and it caused a flurry of questions from the press about our cease-fire conditions.

Jim, to his credit, apologized for the foul-up and said later it was one of his biggest mistakes as secretary of state. We all make mistakes. I had made my own with the Soviets two years earlier when I'd publicly predicted Gorbachev's demise shortly after I became secretary of defense. I do think, though, that Jim was more willing to try to find a negotiated settlement than the president was. And the president held firm.

ON FEBRUARY 7 Colin Powell and I flew to the desert. The trip gave us a chance to see the troops—and what an inspiration they were. We visited the 101st Airborne Division, and the atmosphere inside the tent where we gathered was electric. Colin had once commanded the second brigade of the 101st, and when he reached in his pocket and pulled out his coin—a souvenir he still had from his time in command—the place just went wild.

We also had a session with pilots flying missions over Iraq. One pilot, who had been hit by Iraqi antiaircraft fire while flying an A-10, a 1970s-era tank killer, showed us the huge hole in his airplane's wing and gave us a blow-by-blow of how he'd been hit and survived and made it back to base. I never tired of listening to the troops talk about their experiences. They were very, very good.

Killing Iraqi tanks was a key mission for our air campaign. In early February, some of our F-111 pilots had discovered that their planes, developed for long-range bombing missions during Vietnam, had an advantage when it came to finding and taking out Iraqi tanks. The F-111s were equipped with an infrared targeting system. Many of the Iraqi tanks had been hidden under sandbags or behind berms. Our air force planners discovered that often the Iraqis weren't turning them off at night, and even if they did, the heat the tanks had absorbed during the day would be released as night temperatures cooled. In either case, the F-111s could see the tanks, hotter than the surrounding sand, on their infrared systems and take them out. We started destroying a good number of Iraqi tanks this way. The pilots called it "tank plinking."

Although the method was successful, the kills were often difficult for the CIA to track using satellite photos. This meant their estimates of numbers of tanks destroyed varied widely from the CENTCOM estimates, which had the advantage of gun-camera footage from the F-111s and other planes firing on the tanks. Since we had agreed our aim was to degrade Iraq's tank force by 50 percent before we launched the ground war, the difference in estimates mattered. At one point CIA Director Bill Webster went to the president to tell him we had not met our target. This led to a meeting in Brent's office with Powell, Webster, Mike McConnell and me. We compared our estimates and convinced Scowcroft and the president that CENTCOM had it right and that we were, in fact, ready to begin the ground war.

On our February trip to the desert, Powell and I spent eight hours in meetings with Schwarzkopf and his team to get up to speed on preparations for launching the ground invasion. They walked us through the status of the air campaign and updated us on the bomb damage assessments for each category of strategic targets and the status of Iraqi forces in the Kuwait Theater of Operations. They briefed us on the current deployment of our ground forces, logistics issues, and our ability to guard against the possible use of chemical weapons against our troops.

One of the key pieces of information Powell and I needed from Schwarzkopf was a date when he would be ready to begin ground operations. He told us what he thought made sense—sometime around February 21, with a window of three days. When Powell and I returned to Washington, we met upstairs in the White House with President Bush in the Yellow Oval Room and gave him the word.

Those of us in charge of the war effort knew that the air campaign had succeeded in destroying much of Saddam's air force and sending much of the rest of it fleeing to Iran. We had also degraded his army, but we still thought we'd have a fight on our hands. And there were some very troubling predictions: An expert at the Brookings Institution said between a thousand and four thousand Americans were going to die. Others warned that ten thousand Americans would be killed.

A question in our minds all along had been whether Saddam would use chemical weapons. We made sure our troops had the gear for that, and we also made sure there was plenty of footage of our guys practicing the drill, putting those suits on. We wanted to be certain Saddam knew our guys would be much better prepared to deal with any chemical attack than his own troops would be. The president, Jim Baker, and I also made clear that the military had a wide range of options that could be used against Saddam Hussein if he used chemical weapons. I had warned that Saddam "needs to be made aware that the President will have available the full spectrum of capabilities. And were Saddam Hussein foolish enough to use weapons of mass destruction, the U.S. response would be absolutely overwhelming and it would be devastating."

After the war, Saddam's foreign minister, Tariq Aziz, said that our statements, which Iraq had interpreted as threats of nuclear retaliation, had deterred Iraq from using its WMD. General Wafiq al Sammarai, who headed Iraqi military intelligence during the Gulf War, said in an interview that some of the Iraqis' Scud missiles had been loaded with chemical warheads, but they were not used, "because the warning was quite severe and quite effective. The allied troops were certain to use nuclear arms and the price will be too dear and too high."

ON FRIDAY, FEBRUARY 22, largely in response to continued Soviet efforts to broker a cease-fire, President Bush went into the Rose Garden and gave Saddam an ultimatum. He said the Iraqis would have until noon on Saturday to begin an immediate and unconditional withdrawal from Kuwait. Forty-five minutes before the deadline expired the next day, Gorbachev called the president again with yet another proposal that fell short of immediate unconditional withdrawal. No, the president told Gorbachev, a deadline is a deadline.

ON FEBRUARY 24, THE morning after the ground war started, Lynne and I went to St. John's Church near the White House. President and Mrs. Bush were there and I knew he would be anxious for news from the desert. I passed him a note that said, "Mr. President, things are going very well." He invited Lynne and me to come up to the White House residence after church, and as we sat in the second-floor sitting room, I told him that there had been no major glitches so far. The campaign was going according to plan. Resistance was light all across the front. The most significant problem we were having was dealing with the Iraqis who were surrendering in droves to our forces.

Time magazine had published an excellent war map that I laid out on the president's coffee table. It showed the Iraqi forces arrayed along the Kuwait-Saudi border, the Republican Guard deployed on the Iraq-Kuwait border, and the general positions of the U.S. Army and Marines and our allies. It also showed our impressive naval assets: the aircraft carriers Saratoga, Kennedy, Theodore Roosevelt, and America in the Red Sea; the carriers Midway and Ranger and the battleships Missouri and Wisconsin in the Persian Gulf. Using a pen as a pointer, I walked the president through what had happened overnight.

The 1st and 2nd Marine divisions had breached the first line of Iraqi defenses and were now working through the second line. The first brigade of the 101st was approximately one hundred miles inside Iraq, at Forward Operating Base Cobra. The second brigade would be at Cobra within two to three hours. The third brigade would close on FOB Gold sometime during the morning. The 3rd Armored Cavalry Regiment was twenty miles into Iraq and had met no resistance. The VII Corps, which was scheduled to attack that night, was in position and had begun cutting through the berm the Iraqis had erected as a barrier. The 1st Cavalry, scheduled to go at H+26, might go early.

The Egyptians had crossed into Kuwait against light resistance. The Saudis on the coast were also meeting light resistance. Air operations were continuing as planned. The only major losses reported were two Apache helicopters that collided, but both crews were reported to be okay.

It was encouraging, I noted, that in these first hours when we had expected some of the heaviest fighting, the resistance had been so light. But after laying out all this good news for the president, I cautioned that these were only first reports, and we had not yet encountered the Republican Guard, Saddam's best troops.

By the next afternoon, February 25, we began to get word that Saddam was promising to withdraw in exchange for a UN-brokered cease-fire. Although we could see some of Saddam's troops heading toward the Iraqi border and out of Kuwait, others were continuing to engage our troops. Saddam had not given up, but he was clearly hoping for a UN cease-fire that would allow him to retreat while keeping most of his forces intact.

Events on the ground were moving too fast by then for Saddam to get help from the UN. On February 26, with Arab forces in the lead, the liberation of Kuwait City began. And as we gathered in the Oval Office on February 27, we were faced with an unexpected situation—the prospect of the war coming to an end much sooner than we anticipated. Our forces had moved with much greater speed than we had predicted, meeting much smaller resistance than we'd planned for. Faced with the might of the oncoming American forces, Iraqis were now fleeing, many of them headed north out of Kuwait on what came to be known as the Highway of Death. Images from burnt-out tanks and abandoned vehicles along the road were broadcast around the world.

As it became clear that our forces had delivered a massive defeat to the Iraqis, we addressed the question of when to order them to stop. After months of planning and dealing with issues of transportation and logistics to get our troops to the desert, it was a very sudden shift, after three days of ground operations, to be sitting in the Oval Office deciding when to call a halt. General Powell and the president were particularly concerned that we not ask our young soldiers to continue to fire upon an enemy that seemed to be retreating in defeat.

Powell, using a secure phone in a drawer in the president's desk, placed a call to Schwarzkopf in Riyadh. He told Schwarzkopf that the president wanted to know when we could bring things to an end. It was a question we all wanted an answer to. Schwarzkopf had just conducted a briefing in Riyadh in which he had told the press we'd accomplished our mission, and he was supportive of the idea of stopping as soon as feasible. He asked for some time to consult with his commanders. A few hours later we gathered again, and Schwarzkopf said his commanders agreed we could call a halt to hostilities. Someone came up with the idea of a hundred-hour war, which would mean stopping the fighting at midnight Washington time.

At the time the decision to end the war was made, there was confusion about how far coalition forces had advanced into Iraq. This led to calling a halt before the escape routes into Iraq had been blocked, and as a result, some Iraqi forces escaped, including armored units of the Republican Guard. There was further confusion when Schwarzkopf announced that cease-fire negotiations would be held in Safwan, just inside the Iraqi border with Kuwait. As it turned out Safwan was not under allied control. With the help of some low flyovers by A-10s, our forces were able to convince the Iraqis to abandon the site.

The Iraqis were represented at Safwan by Saddam's generals, which at the time seemed appropriate since Schwarzkopf, along with Saudi

Lieutenant General Khalid bin Sultan, represented the coalition. But one result was that Saddam never publicly admitted defeat, and we should have insisted upon that. We had been told repeatedly by our own intelligence services and by our Arab allies that Saddam would never survive after the blow the coalition had delivered, but he was able to turn the fact that he had stood up to and survived a massive assault into a personal victory. This would have been more difficult if we had demanded that he acknowledge having led his country to defeat.

Schwarzkopf was more accommodating of the Iraqis than he should have been as he sat down and agreed to terms of the cease-fire. When they argued that they needed their helicopters for official transport since we'd taken out most of the major bridges and roads in the country, he agreed that helicopters, even armed ones, could fly over Iraq.

In February before the ground war began and in March after the war was over, President Bush made public statements suggesting the Iraqis should "take matters into their own hands" and force Saddam Hussein "to step aside." We hoped that Saddam's military, in particular, might turn against him after the humiliating defeat we had just delivered them on the battlefield, but this failed to happen. There were public uprisings, especially among the Kurds in the north and the Shia in the south. In the north, six weeks after the war ended, the United States joined the British and French in establishing a no-fly zone and creating a secure Kurdish enclave to prevent Saddam from slaughtering the Kurds and to stop the significant flow of Kurdish refugees across the border into Turkey.

In the south, Saddam, using his helicopters, began a brutal crackdown on the Shia. At one point I learned that more than ten thousand refugees had fled to the part of Iraq where the U.S. Army was still in control and were pleading with our soldiers to take them with them. Schwarzkopf, I was told, had given orders that our forces should have nothing to do with the refugees. I sent word to Scowcroft's deputy, Bob Gates, that we couldn't leave Iraq until some honorable arrangement was made for these people. The Saudis agreed to set up a refugee camp.

A year and a half later we established a no-fly zone in southern Iraq, but Saddam continued his oppression of the Shia with ground forces.

He ordered the draining of the marshes near the confluence of the Tigris and Euphrates Rivers, displacing thousands of the predominantly Shiite Marsh Arabs. Our failure to do more to protect the Shia from Saddam contributed to a sense of betrayal and suspicion that affected our relationships twelve years later when America was confronting Saddam once again.

Our reaction to the Shia uprising was guided in part by a mistaken perception about the Iraqi Shiites—one that would persist until we were confronting Saddam again in 2003. Many in the U.S. government, and in the Department of State in particular, viewed the Iraqi Shia as natural allies of Iran—also a predominantly Shiite country. Iranians are Persian and Iraqis are Arab, but the State Department view held that sectarian ties among Shiite Muslims were stronger than cultural ties among Arabs. This notion overlooked the fact that thousands of Iraqi Shiites had fought Iran for eight years in the Iran-Iraq War. It also, I believe, misjudged the divide between Arabs and Persians. However, the fact that Iran began expressing overt support for the uprisings in 1991 seemed to confirm the State Department's view of the situation and highlighted the complexity of the choices we faced.

At the time we had accomplished a tremendous military victory and the impetus was to be good for our word. We'd told our Arab allies, the Saudis in particular, that we'd bring enough forces to liberate Kuwait and that we'd leave when we were done, that we were not interested in becoming an occupying power or leaving our combat forces in the desert for the long term. In addition, neither the United Nations nor the U.S. Congress had signed on for anything beyond the liberation of Kuwait. Now that our mission was done, we would begin to bring our troops home.

Twelve years later, when we did go all the way to Baghdad, toppled Saddam, and liberated Iraq, the world looked very different. We had suffered a mass casualty attack on the U.S. homeland. We worried that Saddam was a dangerous nexus between terrorists and weapons of mass destruction capability. We had attempted for twelve years, with sixteen UN Security Council resolutions and international sanctions, to contain the threat he posed. By 2003 that sanctions regime was crumbling, Saddam had corrupted the UN's oil-for-food program to buy prohibited materials and enrich himself, and he was biding his time planning, as soon as he could, to reconstitute programs that had been halted or slowed in the aftermath of Desert Storm. The calculation about the nature of the direct threat Saddam posed to America and the military action required to defend against that threat was very different in 2003.

But those decisions were many years ahead of us. No one on President George H. W. Bush's national security team was arguing in 1991 that we should continue on to Baghdad to oust Saddam. And though there were arguably some misjudgments at the end of the war, I think you would be hard-pressed to argue that they fundamentally altered the strategic landscape.

AS OUR TROOPS RETURNED home from the desert, there was a palpable sense that their magnificent performance had restored a feeling of pride we had lost in Vietnam. The country welcomed our servicemen and servicewomen home with the celebrations they deserved.

On June 8, 1991, we honored our troops in Washington. The day opened with a prayer service at Arlington National Cemetery, where we remembered those who had not returned and expressed our gratitude to the families who would mourn them forever. President Bush spoke about the dream of "a commonwealth of freedom" that is at the foundation of who we are as a people:

> America endures because it dares to defend that dream. That dream links the fields of Flanders and the cliffs of Normandy, Korea's snow-covered uplands, and the rice paddies of the Mekong. It's lived in the last year on barren desert flats, on sea-tossed ships, in jets streaking miles above hostile terrain. It lives because we dared risk our most precious asset—our sons and daughters, our brothers and sisters, our husbands and wives—the finest troops any country has ever had.

The president also talked about the yellow ribbons, perhaps one of the clearest signs that the stigma of Vietnam was gone. From the moment the conflict began, Americans across the nation began showing support for our troops by tying ribbons to trees and pinning them to lapels, joining, as President Bush said, "this nation's hands and souls."

I left Arlington National Cemetery and went to a reviewing stand on Constitution Avenue to watch our troops march by in a grand review. I couldn't help but think of my great-grandfather, Samuel Fletcher Cheney, who had marched in just such a parade after the Civil War. America had also welcomed her heroes home from World War I and World War II with parades through our beautiful capital city.

A few days later, New York City held a ticker-tape parade. Our troops marched through the Canyon of Heroes on a glorious spring day, and Colin Powell, Norm Schwarzkopf, and I were fortunate enough to join them along with our wives. American flags were everywhere, huge red, white, and blue balloons floated through the air, and the ticker tape and paper raining down on our troops soon got so deep that the street cleaners were darting into the street between the marching bands to try to clear the way.

Before the time of celebration was over, I placed two phone calls—one to David Ivry, who had been commander of the Israeli Air Force on June 7, 1981, when the Israelis conducted a daring raid to take out Iraq's Osirak nuclear reactor. Although the Israelis had faced international condemnation for the attack, I believed they deserved our gratitude, and I wanted to thank Ivry. Without Israel's courageous action we may well have had to face a nuclear-armed Saddam Hussein in 1991.

I also called Ronald Reagan. We had won this war with the army, navy, air force, and Marine Corps he had helped build. I thanked him for his unwavering commitment to a strong national defense and his years of support for America's military. I had a chance to visit with the former president the next month when I was in Los Angeles for a USO gala to welcome home the troops. I went to the Reagans' home in Bel Air, where Mrs. Reagan greeted me at the door. She and the president showed me into their living room and directed me to take a seat in a big armchair. President Reagan pulled up a hassock so he could sit close as we talked about what was happening in the world. He concentrated on every detail I had to relate about our victory in the Gulf and he quizzed me about developments in the Soviet Union, which was now a very different place from when he had been in office. It was a great privilege for me to brief him on what I knew, because so much of the change we were seeing came from the U.S. military buildup he had insisted upon. It also came from the moral clarity of his vision. He had not been afraid to call the Soviet Union what it was: an evil empire.

IN ADDITION TO SUCCESSFULLY accomplishing our mission in the Persian Gulf, we'd worked hard to get other nations to contribute. My staff prepared a concept that they jokingly called "Operation Tin Cup" to encourage other countries to share the financial burdens of the war. With President Bush's leadership and the fine help of such cabinet members as Secretary of State James Baker and Secretary of the Treasury Nicholas Brady, the United States received $53.7 billion to offset costs of $61.1 billion.

In the run-up to the war, General Kelly and members of the joint staff had conducted a series of in-depth briefings for me on different facets of the operational aspects of war. After the war was over, we did a series of seminars on lessons learned. They were important sessions that enabled us, for example, to learn about the capabilities of our Apache helicopters by hearing directly from a pilot who had flown one of the missions the first night of the air war in Iraq. One very significant area of advancement from previous wars was in precision-guided munitions, or PGMs. The first major use of these "smart" weapons, which can be guided with great accuracy onto a target using laser or other technology, came in Operation Desert Storm. Although most of the ordnance we dropped in that conflict were the older "dumb" or "gravity" bombs, we saw what PGMs could do. They could be precisely targeted on an enemy's communications networks or electricity grid, enabling us to disable key functions of an adversary's capital city, for example, with minimal collateral damage.

A FEW MONTHS AFTER celebrating the end of the Persian Gulf war, I was standing knee-deep in the waters of the Dean River in British Columbia, just about to cast my fly line and thinking about landing a twenty-pound steelhead. It was August 19, 1991. The fishing had been slow and the water high from late season runoff, but it was starting to clear, and I'd just seen the fisherman next to me hook a magnificent fish.

"Mr. Secretary," I heard someone call. I looked over to the riverbank to see my communications specialist waving me down. "There's been a coup in the Soviet Union!" he shouted. "Deputy Secretary Atwood needs to talk to you." So much for my steelhead. I waded over to the riverbank, climbed out of the water, and walked downriver with the communicator to where a solar-powered satellite phone had been set up that morning. We placed a secure call back to the Pentagon. "Dick, Gorbachev's out," Atwood said—prematurely, as it turned out—when I got him on the phone. "We don't know if the coup is still under way or complete. Things are moving fast." I needed to get back to Washington.

The Dean River is remote, which is why the fishing is so good, and it was complicated to get back to Washington quickly. Some of the guys I'd been camping with on the Dean had a homemade rig, a flat-bottom jet boat built specifically to operate on this river. They took my security agent, communications specialist, and me, along with our gear, in the boat downriver to the head of the falls, where we got out and loaded our stuff into an old school bus for the journey down the rough mountain road around the falls. From there we headed to a nearby airstrip, where a single-engine wilderness charter, with huge rubber tires that enabled it to land on extremely rough runways, waited. It flew us to Prince George, British Columbia, where an air force C-20 was waiting to take us the rest of the way back to D.C.

As the C-20 climbed to altitude over glaciers and sharp peaks, I thought about what the events in the Soviet Union might mean. For the last two years I had been spending time in Saturday sessions in my Pentagon conference room with experts on the Soviet Union from inside and outside the government. I found these sessions extremely useful as a way to gather very smart people together and step back from the rush of daily crisis management in order to think strategically about developments inside our most significant adversary and what they might mean for American defense policy.

I got on a conference call with General Powell, Admiral Mike McConnell, and Lieutenant Colonel John Barry, my junior military assistant. Powell reported on a meeting at the White House that had just wrapped up. He said that the president had been on the phone to world leaders, and although everyone was very concerned, it was clear we shouldn't rule Gorbachev out quite yet. Intelligence reports were indicating that this was not a completed coup. There were military units milling around in Moscow, but they didn't seem to have their act together.

One of the key questions we focused on in the first hours after we learned about the potential coup was the location of the Soviet equivalent of the nuclear "football"—the briefcase that contained the launch codes for the Soviet nuclear arsenal. With Gorbachev apparently in his dacha in the Crimea and the Soviet Minister of Defense Yazov and Marshal Akhromeyev among the coup plotters, it was not at all clear who was in control of the nuclear weapons.

McConnell reported that only three divisions were supporting the coup, and they were all within thirty miles of Moscow. The coup leaders were facing a tough choice, he said: either give up the effort or use force to try to bring it about. Boris Yeltsin, the newly elected president of Russia, was standing up to the coup plotters and calling for popular resistance, McConnell said, and every hour that he stayed free was further indication that the coup plotters were not in control.

I had met Yeltsin on a few occasions, and he'd visited me in my office in the Pentagon in June 1991. By that time he had already left the Communist Party, but it was still startling to hear him declare, as he did in my office, that increasing the Soviet defense budget would be a "crime against the Russian people, who have suffered enough under seventy years of communism." I was intrigued by his emergence and by his political success at getting himself elected president of Russia in 1991.

I talked to Brent Scowcroft after I had hung up with Powell and McConnell, and we agreed that this was potentially an extremely serious event. If the coup succeeded, all our assumptions about reform in the Soviet Union and its impact on our national security planning would be upended. By now we knew that the coup plotters included some key members of the Soviet military command structure. I thought through a list of questions we needed to consider. What exactly do the coup plotters hope to achieve? If he retains power, can Gorbachev hope to resume his reforms? Is there any possibility that this event could lead to a peaceful, orderly progression to a less hostile, demilitarized democratic Soviet Union?

And there were other matters of concern. How secure was the Soviet nuclear arsenal? Could it end up in the hands of the coup plotters or a third party? Were we about to see millions of Soviet refugees flee into Eastern Europe? Would the coup plotters use military force to crush the fledgling independence movements in places such as the Baltics, Georgia, and Armenia?

Within a few days of my return to Washington, the coup had failed, and none of the worst-case scenarios had materialized. Quite the opposite—the changes it hastened were nothing short of historic. Boris Yeltsin, standing on a tank to defy the coup plotters, had seemed to capture a spirit of defiance of old ways and old thinking that was sweeping over the U.S.S.R. During the coup, Lithuania reaffirmed its 1990 declaration of independence, and Estonia and Latvia declared theirs. On August 24, the Ukrainian parliament voted for independence, and on August 25 Byelorussia did the same. August 24 was also the day Mikhail Gorbachev resigned as general secretary of the Communist Party and dissolved the Central Committee, signifying the true end of the Soviet communist era.

On September 5 the Congress of People's Deputies voted to respect the "declarations of sovereignty and acts of independence" adopted in the former Soviet republics, signaling that the end would not be violent. When President Bush convened the National Security Council that day at the White House, it was as though we were at the start of a new and unformed world that we might have the chance to shape. It was breathtaking to think that after so many years of facing down the Soviet nuclear threat and countering their efforts to subjugate people all over the world, we might be watching the Soviet Union disappear peacefully. I thought we needed to move quickly before we lost our chance to influence events, and to my way of thinking our objectives for the former Soviet Union ought to be democracy, demilitarization, economic reform, and independence for the former Soviet republics. These were the same goals the pro-democracy forces inside the Soviet Union were fighting for, and I believed we needed to be firmly and clearly identified with them.

This was not a unanimous view among the president's top advisors. Jim Baker and Brent Scowcroft were both more cautious, urging that we did not necessarily want to see the breakup of the Soviet Union, out of concern for the instability that might generate. I thought we should do everything possible to push as hard as we could to lessen Moscow's control over the former republics. First, I believed as a matter of principle that people should live in freedom. When Lithuania, Latvia, Estonia, and Ukraine all voted for independence, I thought we should stand with them. Second, this was a case where our moral interests and our strategic interests were clearly aligned. It was right that we stand for freedom, and independence for the former republics would weaken our most dangerous adversary. I believed it was time for bold policy initiatives to cement the downfall of the Soviet Union.

The president agreed. He directed us to develop proposals that would demonstrate support for Russia's reformers and show the world we were ushering in a new era. For me and my colleagues at the Defense Department, the obvious place to begin was with our nuclear arsenal.

In my first months as secretary of defense, I had been briefed on the Single Integrated Operational Plan, or SIOP, the targeting plan for the use of our nuclear weapons. Over the years as we had added weapons to our arsenal, the planners had applied them to the same universe of targets. When we added, for example, fifty new Peacekeeper missiles, each with ten warheads, our nuclear target specialists would suddenly have five hundred new weapons they had to direct at a limited list. It seemed to me a commonsense question was in order. Tell me, I said to the planners, how many warheads are going to hit Kiev under the current plan? It was a difficult question to get an answer to because I don't think anybody had ever asked it before, but I finally got a report back that under the current targeting plan, we had literally dozens of warheads targeted on this single city. It was time to rationalize our nuclear targeting. Under Paul Wolfowitz's direction, the policy shop went to work with the joint staff and our nuclear targeting specialists and began to reform our targeting system, which in turn gave us the ability to reduce the size of our nuclear arsenal.

It was a lesson that sometimes the simplest question—how many nuclear weapons are you planning to launch on Kiev?—is the most important one. I appreciated General Powell's description of the significance of what we did. "Cheney and his civilian analysts," he wrote, "reversed four decades of encrusted bureaucratic thinking and put nuclear targeting on a rational basis." And we made it possible, working with Powell and his team on the joint staff, for the president to make bold proposals in response to the historic events unfolding in Moscow. The SIOP review made it clear we could make significant reductions in the size of our nuclear forces and still preserve our deterrent capabilities.

As we pulled our proposals together, I was mindful of avoiding the trap into which so many previous arms control negotiations between the United States and the Soviet Union had fallen. Agonizingly slow, these negotiations usually led to minimal, tit-for-tat reductions. This time we all agreed we should proceed differently. We should announce our intent to make significant real cuts in our nuclear forces and invite the Russians to do the same.

In a speech to the nation on September 27, 1991, President Bush directed that the United States eliminate its entire worldwide inventory of ground-launched short-range nuclear weapons. We would bring home our nuclear artillery shells and short-range ballistic missile warheads from Europe. And he called on the Soviets to do the same. He also announced we would withdraw all tactical nuclear weapons from our surface ships and attack submarines and remove all nuclear weapons from our land-based naval aircraft. And, again, he called on the Soviets to do the same. Then he turned to the issue of our strategic nuclear weapons, which had been the subject of a new treaty, START, signed with President Gorbachev in July 1991. President Bush said he wanted to use that treaty "as a springboard to achieve additional stabilizing changes." Therefore, he ordered all U.S. strategic bombers to immediately stand down from their alert posture. He also pledged to accelerate the destruction of the intercontinental ballistic missile systems scheduled to be eliminated as part of the START talks and announced the termination of the development of the new mobile Peacekeeper ICBM system.

The president also announced that he would be consolidating operational command of our sea-, land-, and air-based strategic nuclear forces in one command, which is now called STRATCOM, headquartered at Offutt Air Force Base. On October 5, 1991, Gorbachev, as president of the Soviet Union, responded to our proposals with an impressive set of cuts the Soviets were willing to make in both their tactical and strategic nuclear arsenals, and he agreed to take Soviet bombers off alert as well. We had succeeded in launching a new approach to arms control—faster, deeper, and more flexible than before.

As we responded to changes in the Soviet Union by offering reductions in our nuclear inventory, we were also thinking about our overall force posture. From the end of World War II until the Soviet Union ceased to exist in 1992, we had planned our defensive and offensive military capabilities primarily around meeting, countering, and defending against a Soviet threat. In late 1989 we had begun to think about cuts that could be made to reflect the emerging new strategic reality, and after months of analysis we had proposed the concept of the "base force," which President Bush had accepted and outlined in a speech in Aspen, Colorado, on August 2, 1990. The speech came only hours after Saddam's tanks rolled into Kuwait, and the attention of the world shifted to the Persian Gulf. Once we had liberated Kuwait, I asked Wolfowitz to take the concept laid out in our base force approach, and using some of the most important lessons we had learned from operations in Desert Storm, put together a new Defense Planning Guidance document that would describe the challenges America faced and the strategic position we should adopt to meet them throughout the 1990s and beyond.

It had been my experience that too often everyday challenges prevent top policymakers from taking the time to think strategically. It is much easier to accede to the moment, blunting crises or responding to opportunities. It takes time and discipline to force yourself and those in the bureaucracy to take a step back and think about America's strategic goals and challenges, but it is essential. You can't hope to adopt the wisest policies without a sense of where the country should be heading and how we should steer the ship to get there. There are places set up to do this in the government, such as the policy planning shop at the State Department and the office of the undersecretary for policy in the Pentagon. But often the individuals in these offices either get drafted to help manage day-to-day crises or their strategic work is so removed from the real-time policymaking that it has little impact.

The Defense Department, in my experience, is better at both strategic policymaking and at producing rigorous "lessons learned" reports than any other agency in government, and the individuals I had in key slots, such as Paul Wolfowitz, Andy Marshall, Scooter Libby, and Eric Edelman, were some of the best strategic thinkers around. It was to this group I looked when I determined that we needed a new defense strategy for the post–Cold War world. Working with retired Lieutenant General Dale Vesser and Zalmay Khalilzad, who were also part of the policy planning shop, they produced the 1992 Defense Planning Guidance, which was a fundamental revision in U.S. defense policy and strategy.

The DPG represented a shift from a focus on the global threat posed by the Soviet Union to defense planning based on regional threats. It also noted that we would work to "preclude hostile, nondemocratic domination of a region critical to our interests" as well as work to preclude the emergence of any hostile powers that could present a global security threat. There was a focus on alliances among democratic nations and the enhanced security that cooperation could bring. We would not only anticipate and plan for a future security environment, but also work to shape it so that we could advance U.S. security objectives.

We would actively encourage former Warsaw Pact countries and, in time, even former Soviet republics to join in the alliances of democratic nations that had so effectively kept the peace. We would strengthen our common defense arrangements. We also recognized the growing threat of proliferation and emphasized that we would work to update our strategy for countering the proliferation of weapons of mass destruction and the means to deliver them.

The 1992 Defense Planning Guidance was very significant in the way that it addressed critical global strategic shifts and set out a sound basis for the United States to continue to enhance its own security and that of its allies in the years to come. As I left office in January 1993, we published the "Regional Defense Strategy," an unclassified strategic plan that incorporated much of the thinking in the Defense Planning Guidance.

The RDS emphasized that U.S. leadership would continue to be crucial in the new defense environment. Our preference was to counter threats whenever possible with friends and allies at our side, but we were clear that America must lead. "Only a nation that is strong enough to act decisively," it said, "can provide the leadership needed to encourage others to resist aggression."

IN RESPONSE TO THE fall of the Berlin Wall I had ordered a review of our major aircraft needs across the military services. I asked the services to look at whether we should move forward in building and buying planes like the B-2, F-22, C-17, and A-12, in light of the changed global security environment. I came into office inclined to support the construction of the A-12, the navy's carrier-based stealth bomber, and in April 1990, I testified in front of the Senate Armed Services Committee in support of moving forward with it. "It's a good system," I said, and "the program appears to be reasonably well-handled." A few months later, when I was informed that the contractor had cost overruns they could not absorb and would not be delivering the planes on time, I was, needless to say, not pleased. I had testified to the Congress in good faith that the program was on track, only to learn later that it wasn't. We launched a review to determine why the information I had received was not accurate. As a result a number of individuals involved with the program inside the Pentagon were disciplined and removed from the program. Ultimately, the undersecretary of defense for acquisition resigned.

Over the coming months it became clear that there were more significant cost overruns, technical problems, and delays. If the program were to proceed, I would have to exercise my authority as secretary of defense to modify the contract to prevent the contractor from being in breach of its obligations to the U.S. government. Modification would result in significant additional cost to the government with no certainty that the program would get back on track. In December I directed the secretary of the navy to show cause why the contract should not be terminated. I said in the show-cause order, "If we cannot spend the taxpayer's money wisely, we will not spend it." I called a meeting in my office on Saturday, January 5, with General Powell, Pentagon Comptroller Sean O'Keefe, Navy Secretary H. Lawrence Garrett, and Donald Yockey, the new undersecretary for acquisition. The group discussed whether I should bail out the contractor. I listened and made my decision.

Two days later I announced that we would not bail them out, a decision that resulted in termination of the program for default. No one could tell me how much more of the taxpayers' money we'd have to spend to procure these planes. My decision not to provide a bailout and to withdraw support for the A-12 sent shock waves through the Pentagon and the defense industry. It was the largest weapons system cancellation in the history of the department, but the decision was the right one. And I am still convinced of that today, even with litigation about the cancellation in its twentieth year.

ON A SATURDAY IN the summer of 1992, I got a call at home from Brent Scowcroft, who was up at Camp David. The president needed a new chief of staff. Sam Skinner, who had taken over from John Sununu, was heading back home to Chicago. Brent wanted to know if I was interested. I wasn't, but I also wasn't completely surprised to get the call. A year earlier when I had traveled with the president to California and Texas, he'd asked me to describe for him some of the problems I'd seen in the way Sununu was running the White House. I thought it was instructive to compare Sununu's approach to Scowcroft's approach, since Brent was running foreign policy for the president and Sununu essentially handled the domestic agenda.

We had talked about the importance of having someone in the chief of staff slot who would be a completely honest broker, as Brent was on the national security side. Those of us in the president's national security team knew that he would give his views to the president privately, but he would make sure to convey accurately all sides of an issue so the president could make an informed decision. And Brent was deeply experienced in the issues he grappled with every day, having already served a term as President Ford's national security advisor.

While I was flattered that Brent thought I might effectively serve as George H. W. Bush's chief of staff, I told Brent I really was not eager to make the move back to the White House. I had already been chief of staff, and I was engaged in critically important issues at the Department of Defense. If the president had asked me directly, I would have done it, but I'm glad that he got Jim Baker to do it instead.

IN OCTOBER 1992 I attended a NATO meeting in northern Scotland, and it was from there that I watched President Bush, Bill Clinton, and Ross Perot compete in the second of the televised presidential debates. As defense secretary, I had no part to play in the presidential election, but I was looking on with enormous interest, and it didn't seem to be going well for our side. The press was pushing a false narrative that had a president who was detached from the lives of most Americans up against a challenger who was younger, more energetic, more empathetic. And unfortunately this was the debate in which the president looked at his watch, a perfectly normal thing to do, but an action that our opponents seized on and wrongly characterized as symbolic of a distracted president. In 1991 George Bush had won a war, but in 1992 he lost the presidency. When the votes were counted in November, it was Bill Clinton 43 percent, George Bush 37 percent, and Ross Perot, 19 percent.

There were many farewells, but the finest was at Fort Myer's ceremonial hall, where the United States military had a chance to say goodbye to the man who had commanded them so ably—and I had a chance to make my farewell too. I noted that it was easy to look back on historic events and regard them as inevitable, but that it mattered who was in command:

> *We are, indeed, fortunate that George Bush was our president when the nation faced the first major crisis of the post Cold War era—the invasion of Kuwait. . . . From the earliest days of the crisis, he refused to ignore or pander to aggression. His clarity of purpose focused the world on the need for action.*

I offered my personal thanks as well. "I will always be grateful to you, Mr. President, for the opportunity you've given me to serve as your Secretary of Defense." George Bush had been a tremendous leader. His wisdom had seen us through changes more significant than any of us could have imagined we would see in our lifetimes. Serving as his secretary of defense was one of the highest honors of my life.

CHAPTER EIGHT

Out of the Arena

As noon approached on Inauguration Day, I gathered my few remaining belongings in the office, said goodbye to my staff, and left the Pentagon for the last time as secretary of defense. Although I would still be secretary for another few hours—until the Senate confirmed Les Aspin and he was sworn in later that afternoon—the moment at which Bill Clinton was taking the presidential oath seemed to be the appropriate time for me to leave.

I was out of public office for the first time in fourteen years, and Lynne and I were moving home to Wyoming. We packed a big U-Haul truck full of furniture and the boxes of my congressional papers, and with help from my new son-in-law, Phil Perry, I strapped a large display case filled with the battle streamers earned by the U.S. military during my time as secretary of defense to the back of the truck. The streamers were a unique and thoughtful farewell gift from the military, but because each one was about four feet long, the glass-fronted display case was too big and too fragile to pack inside the truck with our other belongings.

Phil, who had married Liz just three weeks earlier, would be joining me on the cross-country drive to Wyoming. It takes someone with a strong constitution to agree to make a two-thousand-mile road trip alone with his father-in-law less than a month after joining the family, but Phil stepped up to the task. Luckily he is a man of few words, just as I am, so neither of us worried much about having to make small talk along the way.

When we got to Wyoming, we stopped at the university in Laramie so I could drop off my papers and the battle streamers for safekeeping at the American Heritage Center. The staff seemed surprised when we pulled up in the U-Haul to deliver the materials personally, but it never occurred to me to get them there any other way. Lynne met me that night in Jackson, where we began unpacking and planning for our new life in the private sector.

I KNEW AT LEAST two things for sure: I wanted to spend more time with my family, and I wanted to spend more time fishing. Of course, I also needed to earn a living—hopefully doing useful things—and I wanted to continue to contribute to the major policy and political debates of the day. So, I signed on with the American Enterprise Institute, a think tank in Washington, D.C. I also agreed to join the boards of directors of Procter & Gamble, Union Pacific, US West, and Morgan Stanley. Having spent most of my career in government or academia, I knew I'd learn a lot by serving on the boards of some of the finest corporations in the country.

During that first summer out of office, I had plenty of time to think about the future on an eight-thousand-mile road trip I took alone across the country. I drove from Washington, D.C., to British Columbia, and then doubled back to Wyoming, giving speeches along the way, some paid and some unpaid, and traveling through beautiful country in Wyoming, Idaho, Montana, and the Canadian Rockies, including Banff National Park, with its forests and rivers, and Glacier National Park, with some of the most rugged mountain territory in North America. I also enjoyed some great fishing for rainbow trout in the headwaters of the North Platte and steelhead in the Dean River in British Columbia. It was on this trip that I began seriously to contemplate the possibility of running for president myself in 1996.

The idea of serving as president was very appealing. I had worked in the White House or served in the cabinet of three presidents—Nixon, Ford, and Bush—and I had watched Ronald Reagan from the perspective of my eight years in the House leadership. I had seen presidents succeed and fail. And I believed I knew what it takes to make an effective chief executive.

I also understood the importance of recognizing that no one gets a lot of opportunities to run under circumstances that are right to sustain a presidential campaign. If you don't take your chance when it comes along, you may never get another.

On the other hand, I knew how tough, brutal, and demanding a national campaign can be. It is impossible to preserve even a modicum of privacy for either the candidate or his family under the intense scrutiny that goes with running for president. And fund-raising, which I had never learned to like, demands an enormous commitment of time and energy.

And, of course, there was my health. In 1996 I would be fifty-five years old with an eighteen-year history of coronary artery disease, including three heart attacks and a quadruple coronary bypass. If I decided not to run for president, I wouldn't link the decision to my health, because I didn't want people to think that I was somehow limited in what I could do or that I had decided not to run because I had a "bad heart." But clearly my health history would be an issue in a campaign, and it figured in my thinking as I evaluated the prospects of a grueling presidential run.

Meanwhile, I was itching to get involved in the 1994 midterm elections. As secretary of defense it hadn't been appropriate for me to participate in politics, and now that I was no longer bound by that tradition, I had a lot I wanted to say. I thought Bill Clinton had been let off easy during the 1992 campaign, and I was less than enthusiastic about the way he was managing national security policy. The botched operation in Somalia in October 1993 particularly troubled me. Men were sent on a mission in Mogadishu without being allowed to use the AC-130 gunships that could have helped them succeed. They were denied the armored support they needed—and that their leaders had requested— and eighteen brave Americans lost their lives.

IN DECEMBER 1993 OUR family gathered once again in Jackson, where we had celebrated many happy holidays, but the end of 1993 was filled with great sadness. My mother died the day after Christmas. She had fought Parkinson's disease for years, absolutely refusing to give into it. There would be no assisted living facility for her, she said, because she had to take care of my dad. When the disease began to cause her to lose her balance, she bought a pair of black rubber knee pads to cushion the blows when she fell. And she always picked herself right back up again. I was on a hunting trip in South Texas in the fall when I got word she'd had a stroke. Our friends the True family from Casper sent their plane to pick me up so I could get home as quickly as possible. I got to her bedside, and she knew I was there, but after the stroke she never spoke again.

Five months after Mom died, our lives were filled with joy when our first grandchild, Kate Perry, was born. Today, when I see Kate's skill and athleticism on the softball field, I think of my mother, who loved her ball-playing years with the Syracuse Bluebirds, the team from a little Nebraska town that twice played the Cleveland Bloomer Girls for the national championship. I know Mom would have been so proud of Kate, and all seven of her great-grandchildren.

EARLY IN 1994 WITH a presidential run in mind, I set up a political action committee. The Alliance for American Leadership would contribute money to Republican candidates and finance my own political travels. When I announced the PAC, I explained its purpose this way:

Americans want safety from dangers at home and abroad, the opportunity to pursue a livelihood to support themselves and their

families, and freedom from excessive governmental intrusion. The
Alliance for American Leadership will help achieve those goals by
supporting the election of highly qualified Republican candidates
across the nation.

I kept the PAC simple. I was chairman of the board and two of my
former staffers, Patty Howe and David Addington, were the members. I
hired Addington away from his job as minority staff director and counsel of the Senate Select Committee on Intelligence to make sure the
PAC was run in scrupulous compliance with the complex FEC rules.
Through fund-raising events and direct mail, the PAC raised more than
$1.3 million in less than a year—a significant sum in politics in those
days, particularly for such a small operation—and disbursed it to advance the cause of Republican candidates. I personally did close to 160
campaign events in the 1994 election cycle, traveling the country from
coast to coast.

In September 1994 Lynne and I gathered some close friends with
experience in presidential campaigns and sought their advice: Stu Spencer had been political director in the 1976 Ford campaign; Bob Teeter
was another close friend and our pollster; Terry O'Donnell had been
Ford's personal aide, general counsel of the Defense Department, and
was my private attorney; and Red Cavaney had been lead advance man
for the Ford White House. I knew all of them to be dependably discreet, but also willing to tell me exactly what they really thought. I knew
that none of them would pull punches.

We met in Jackson, and during a couple of gorgeous fall days we
talked about the 1996 campaign, the other prospective candidates,
the pros and cons of a run for the presidency, the prospects for fund-
raising, and what it would take to run and win. Although we didn't
come to any final conclusions, they gave me their best advice on what
I could expect.

THE 1994 MIDTERM ELECTIONS were historic, with Republicans taking control of both houses of Congress for the first time in

forty years. The last time we had had control in the Senate was 1986; in the House, 1954. Even the Democratic Speaker of the House, my friend Tom Foley, lost his seat and became the first Speaker defeated at the polls since the Civil War. It was a stunning result, a clear repudiation of Bill Clinton and his administration. But more than that it represented a revolution in the Congress, particularly in the House. No Republican member of the House then serving had ever served in the majority, chaired a committee or subcommittee, or presided over the House as Speaker. Nineteen ninety-four changed everything—who hired most of the staff, who had the most members on each committee, who controlled the Rules Committee, which set the terms of debate for each bill coming to the floor, and who was given offices in the Capitol. Under the Democrats only three members of the GOP had offices there.

During all those years we spent in the minority, Republicans could never be certain that what we did really mattered. Unless we were willing to sign on and support a Democratic proposal, we rarely had any impact on the floor debate. If we had a good idea, chances were we could advance it only with the approval or permission of some Democratic chairman. Now all of a sudden Republicans were going to be running the show.

Lynne and I hosted an election evening party for some of our close friends, and I don't think I moved from in front of the television the whole night. As I watched the Republicans win control of the Congress, I couldn't help but contemplate what might have been if I had stayed in the House leadership instead of going to the Defense Department. My friend, and successor as House Republican Whip, Newt Gingrich, was about to become Speaker of the House.

I wouldn't have traded my years as secretary of defense for anything—not even presiding over a Republican House of Representatives. And I had to hand it to Newt. Ever since I'd first met him in 1978, he'd been saying the Republicans could win back the majority. Most of us thought that was an unrealistic dream. But not Newt, and he didn't just dream about it. He put together the Contract with America and recruited candidates all across the country to run on the elements of the Contract. Without Newt, a Republican majority might well have stayed a dream.

ONCE THE MIDTERMS WERE over, it was time for me to make a decision about 1996. Did I want to run for president or not? Was I prepared to do all that would be required to mount a successful campaign? At Christmas our family gathered again in Jackson Hole, and as the snow fell outside our windows, we had a running conversation over several days about whether I should run. Although some family members were more enthusiastic than others, I knew I would have everyone's full support for whatever I decided to do.

And what I decided was not to seek the presidency. After stacking up the pros and cons, I looked at it this way: I believed I'd had a great twenty-five-year career in public life, including service as White House chief of staff, secretary of defense, and Wyoming's congressman for ten years. I felt that I was still young enough at fifty-three to have another career in the private sector, and that possibility was certainly more appealing than putting my family through the meat grinder of a national campaign for what would be the long-shot prospect of getting elected president. So, on January 3, 1995, I gave a heads-up to some of my key supporters that I wasn't going to run and then issued this press statement:

> *After careful consideration, I have decided not to become a candidate for the presidency in 1996. I appreciated very much the kind words of encouragement and support I received from many Americans who had urged me to seek the presidency. I look forward to supporting the Republican nominee for President in 1996.*

WITH MY CAREER IN politics now apparently over, I turned my attention back to fishing. I had already been lucky enough to fish some of the world's great waters. During my time at the Defense Department, my counterparts in other countries had invited me to fly-fish while I was visiting. After a NATO meeting in Scotland, while everyone else went golfing at St. Andrews, I was treated to trout fishing with a ghillie, a Scottish fishing guide. The Chileans took me to the wilds of Tierra del Fuego. The Canadian armed forces invited me to the Eagle River in Newfoundland, where I fished for my first Atlantic salmon—big, powerful fish that are very challenging to catch—out of an historic fishing camp that Generals Hap Arnold and George C. Marshall had enjoyed on stopovers as they returned from Europe via the great circle route during World War II. The premier of Newfoundland invited me to fish in the Grand Cascapedia, another of his country's superb salmon rivers.

Now I also had time to go back to places that I loved, such as the Dean River in British Columbia, where Oregon friends had taught me to fish for steelhead—a fish that hatches in fresh water, goes to sea after a couple of years, and then a few years later returns to fresh water to spawn. Rather than dying, they go back to sea and return to spawn again, all the time growing bigger and wilier. They are fast, challenging to hook, tough to land—a real test of skill. And you fish for them in some of the most beautiful parts of North America.

I continued fishing the Snake River in Wyoming and Idaho and the Bighorn in Montana with Wyoming friends as passionate about the sport as I am. My longtime friend Dick Scarlett usually arranged our trips. I made time every year to fish in Pennsylvania with my dear friend Don Daughenbaugh, a retired schoolteacher and coach, who knows more about fly-fishing than anyone I've ever known. I also fished some new territory, going twice to New Zealand, and taking an amazing trip with my daughter Mary and my friend John Robson to fish for Atlantic salmon in the Ponoi River in Russia.

A Canadian businessman, Fred Mannix, invited me to the fabled Ristigouche Salmon Club in New Brunswick. The club was established in 1880, and wealthy American and Canadian members used to make the trip up there in private railway cars to fish for salmon. A. N. Cheney, one of my ancestors, who was far from wealthy, but a noted fly fisherman, used to fish with a friend about six miles above the club for what he called "the grandest of all fish." Together with another friend, Charles Orvis, A. N. Cheney edited *Fishing with the Fly*, a book that has become a fly-fishing classic.

IN 1994 I WAS invited by John Georges, the chairman and CEO of International Paper, to come to the Rocky Brook Salmon Camp on the Miramichi River in New Brunswick. The camp was once part of International Paper's timber holdings, which are mostly sold off now, but the company had the good sense to hold on to this terrific salmon camp. The other guests with me that week were Roger Smith of General Motors; my friend and pollster, Bob Teeter; Patrick Noonan, who was head of the Conservation Fund; and Tom Cruikshank, who was chairman and CEO of Halliburton.

I'd never met Tom Cruikshank before and didn't know he was getting ready to retire and was looking for a replacement. But it wouldn't have mattered if I had, because I wasn't looking for work. I was there to fish, and that's what the group did each morning and late afternoon. At dinner, we'd sit around the fire and have long and sometimes contentious debates about politics and public policy.

A few months after Rocky Brook, I answered the phone one day in my kitchen in Jackson, and it was Tom Cruikshank calling. He told me about his planned retirement and about Halliburton's search. He said they hadn't had any success finding a replacement and that he had mentioned my name as a possible candidate to several members of his board. They were intrigued with the possibility, and he was calling to see if I could fly down to Dallas to meet with them.

I was also intrigued. Halliburton was the second-largest oil services company in the world. They owned Brown & Root, a large construction company with deep roots in Texas and reach around the globe. Altogether, the company had some one hundred thousand employees operating in 130 countries. I agreed to make the trip and landed in the Halliburton plane at Love Field a few days later. I had dinner at Tom Cruikshank's house with several board members, including Anne Armstrong, whom I had known when she was ambassador to the United Kingdom under President Ford. Bob Crandall, the chairman and CEO of American Airlines, was there, as was W. R. Howell, the chairman of JCPenney. We talked about Halliburton and what they were looking for in a CEO. It was a pleasant evening, and they flew me back to Wyoming when it was over.

A few days later Tom called to say they wanted to offer me the job. I accepted, knowing we would have to work out the details, but in principle I was on board. I think part of the reason they wanted me was my international experience. As much as half the company's income was coming from overseas. I had successfully run the Department of Defense, a significant management challenge, and the personal recommendations of board members such as Anne Armstrong helped.

I flew back to Dallas for the public announcement that I was the new CEO and would be reporting for work October 1, 1995. Tom and I would share responsibilities for the first ninety days and then he'd step down and I'd take over January 1, 1996.

During those ninety days, Tom and I traveled the country visiting Halliburton operations. We visited Duncan, Oklahoma, the home of Halliburton—and, as I was to discover, the home of my friend Ambassador Jeane Kirkpatrick, who'd grown up living next door to Erle Halliburton. We also spent time in the field, where I learned about the sophisticated technology that is part of a modern drilling operation. I began to meet Halliburton customers and employees and to learn about the full scope of the business.

AFTER LYNNE AND I moved to Dallas, an old friend from there asked me, "Now that you're in the oil business, what's it going to be— golf, gin rummy, or shooting?" It wasn't a tough call. "Shooting," I said. Texas has some of the greatest quail country in the world, and when Halliburton took over Dresser Industries we acquired a forty-thousand-acre hunting lease on the King Ranch. We got a lot of business done on hunting trips, and it was a heck of a lot of fun.

My favorite place to hunt was the Armstrong Ranch, down in South Texas, about fifty miles from the Gulf of Mexico. Like any Texas ranch worth its salt, the Armstrong is huge, some fifty thousand acres. The quail coveys were as plentiful as any place I know, but the Armstrongs themselves were the real reason to look forward to spending a weekend at the ranch. Anne and Tobin were lovely people, with a sense of hospitality as big as Texas. Their ranch house, as unpretentious as could be, was full of hunting trophies, English antiques (many acquired by Tobin while Anne was ambassador to the Court of Saint James), and hundreds of pictures. They were testimony to many a celebrity having been to the Armstrong, including Prince Charles.

After a hearty ranch breakfast (jalapeño jelly was always on the table), we would load into big Chevy Suburbans and follow caballeros across the prairie until they spotted a covey. Then we'd get out and shoot. We'd have lunch under a huge old oak tree, stop for a siesta, then hunt again, coming back to the ranch in time for drinks and conversation—though the conversation usually depended on getting Tobin to turn the mariachi music down.

I had some wonderful times hunting at the Armstrong, and both Lynne and I really miss Tobin and Anne. He died in 2005 and she in 2008. But the Armstrong was also a place where I knew great sadness. On a hunting trip there while I was vice president, I accidentally shot one of my hunting partners, Harry Whittington.

It was late in the day on February 11, 2006. There were three of us shooting—Harry, Pam Willeford, then U.S. ambassador to Switzerland, and me. The first covey flushed and Harry shot two birds. While he went with his guide and the hunting dogs to find the quail, Pam and I moved on to a second covey. I was on the right and Pam was on my left. I thought Harry had quit shooting and was still looking for his birds from the first covey.

A single bird flushed on my right and I turned to fire. The sun was just starting to set on the horizon, and I did not know that Harry had come up on my right. He was standing in a dip in the ground and the sun was behind him. I didn't see him until it was too late. I will never, as long as I live, forget the sight of Harry falling to the ground after I fired.

We rushed over to him. His face was bloody, and he was stunned.

My Secret Service agents and the military doctors who always traveled with me as vice president were there and treated him immediately. We called for the ambulance that was on the ranch as part of my motorcade. Members of the White House medical unit traveling with me administered first aid to Harry and then got in the ambulance with him. They stopped at ranch headquarters to pick up Harry's wife, Mercedes, and then headed for the hospital in Corpus Christi. I received reports throughout the evening on Harry's condition, and I was able to visit Harry in the hospital the next day.

It was a terrible accident. We had been lucky it wasn't worse. I was using a 28-gauge shotgun that day, which is less powerful than the 20-gauge or the 12-gauge I sometimes used. Harry was wearing shatterproof safety hunting glasses, so his eyes were not hit by any of the pellets. Still, I had shot my friend and he was now lying in a hospital. The last thing on my mind was a press statement, and we didn't issue one that night. In retrospect, we should have.

The following day we issued a statement to the *Corpus Christi Caller-Times*, a local paper that routinely covered that part of Texas, knowing that once they had put out the story it would be reported everywhere. Our choice incensed the White House press pool and the rest of the mainstream media and probably increased the frenzy of their reaction. But, again, the last thing on my mind was whether I was irritating the *New York Times*.

I continued to monitor Harry's condition over the following weeks and months and appreciated the grace with which he handled the situation. He was a true gentleman. As the days passed, the whole incident became great fodder for late-night comedians—and for the president himself. Later in the year, at the annual Gridiron Dinner, where politicians roast themselves, Bush said, "Here I am at thirty-eight percent in the polls, and Dick has to go and shoot the only trial lawyer in Texas who supports us."

When Harry was released from the hospital on February 17, 2006, he spoke to the press and took note of the media frenzy generated by the accident, "My family and I are deeply sorry for all that Vice President Cheney and his family have had to go through this past week," he said. "We send our love and respect to them as they deal with situations that are much more serious than what we have had this week."

I, of course, was deeply sorry for what Harry and his family had gone through. The day of the hunting accident was one of the saddest of my life. And I will never forget Harry Whittington's kindness.

GEORGE W. BUSH BECAME governor of Texas the year before I took over at Halliburton. I had met him briefly when his father was president, but didn't come to know him until we were both working in Texas and I agreed to serve on one of his business advisory councils. I started to see more of him as he began to think about running for president and invited me down to the Governor's Mansion in Austin for one-on-one meetings and sessions with his foreign policy advisory team. The team consisted primarily of Condi Rice, Steve Hadley, Rich Armitage, and Paul Wolfowitz. Scooter Libby also attended some of the sessions. Condi managed the group, helping select topics for discussion and distributing briefing materials ahead of some of the meetings. It was a group of smart, experienced people, all of whom seemed pretty compatible. Had I been running for president myself that year and needed advisors on foreign and defense policy, I probably would have picked the same team.

A meeting of the team was scheduled for February 24, 1999, and I flew down to Austin the night before for dinner with the governor. The next morning I was in my guest room at the mansion getting ready for breakfast when there was a knock at the door. I opened it to find the governor of Texas with a cup of coffee he'd made for me. It was a kind gesture and certainly the highest-ranking room service I'd ever had.

About a month later, Joe Allbaugh, who was helping Bush put together the beginnings of his presidential campaign, visited me in Dallas. We had a good discussion about the mechanics of a run for the presidency and the ins and outs of managing a campaign. We talked about priorities, hiring, scheduling, and how you put the whole thing together. They were just beginning to plot a course to the election of

2000, and I was glad to be as helpful as I could, but my main focus and priority remained my day job running Halliburton.

IN 1998 MY DAD had started to talk about "having his sale," which is an old Nebraska expression for putting your affairs in order before you die. He was eighty-three, and he'd been doing pretty well in the five years since Mom's death in 1993. He'd moved himself into an assisted living facility a year earlier, saying he wanted to do it while he was healthy enough to make the move himself. He still had the house at 505 Texas Place in Casper, and he had been driving out there regularly to check on things. But now he told my sister, Sue, my brother, Bob, and me that he was ready to sell his belongings and the house. We kept telling him not to worry about it, that we'd take care of it. But he wouldn't hear of it. He told us to go through and take whatever we wanted, and then he found an auctioneer to come out and tag everything else for a big sale. He also put the house on the market and found a buyer.

Dad was handling the end the way he had handled so much in his life—with quiet courage and dignity. But there is no denying the pain of closing out a home and life full of memories. One morning after all the furniture and belongings had been moved into the garage and tagged for sale, Sue arrived at the house to find Dad sitting in the garage alone, among the belongings of a lifetime, with tears running down his face.

By the spring of 1999, he had been in the hospital a number of times with the symptoms of congestive heart failure. He had seemed to be on the rebound at the end of May, when he lay down for an afternoon nap and never woke up. Just before he fell asleep, Bob, Sue, and I had all placed calls to him at nearly the same moment. Bob and I both got busy signals, but Susie got through and spoke to him one last time.

Before Dad died, word came that Congress had decided to name the federal building in Casper after me, making it the Dick Cheney Federal Building. He got a big kick out of that. It was a building he'd worked in for a number of years, and now it would have his son's name on it. I thought of my dad and his pride in his long years of service for the federal government as I stood in front of the building for the rededication ceremony in the summer of 1999. I also thought how proud I was to be his son and namesake.

IN THE FALL OF 1999, Lynne and I hosted a party at our home in Dallas for the Barbara Bush Foundation for Family Literacy and its Celebration of Reading programs. Governor Bush and Laura came, and the governor asked if there was a place we could talk for a few minutes. We went into the library, a quiet, paneled room at the back of the house, where he said that he would like me to manage his campaign for the presidency. I told him that I was honored by the request, but that I had to say no. I had a full-time job, and there was no way I could also manage the day-to-day operations of a presidential campaign. I told the governor he had my support and that I'd help in any way I could. But a full-time campaign position just wasn't in the cards for me.

Several months later, in the early spring of 2000, Joe Allbaugh came to see me again. The primary race wasn't completely over, but it was clear George Bush was going to be the Republican nominee. This time Joe wanted to know if I would be willing to be considered as Governor Bush's running mate. Again, I said no. I was very honest with him about it. "Look, Joe," I told him, "that just doesn't make sense for you guys or for me." I went through all the drawbacks, including my three heart attacks and the fact that the governor and I were both oilmen, which our opponents would use against us. In addition, both of us were then living in Texas—which would preclude Texas electors from voting for both of us.

Besides, I was very happy running Halliburton. I'd been there for about four years, and we were involved in energy projects all around the world. Through Brown & Root, we did construction as well, everything from a railroad across the outback of Australia to a baseball stadium for the Houston Astros. We also had a large contract to provide logistical services to the U.S. Army. One of the lessons we'd learned in

Desert Storm was that it is both more effective and cheaper to have a private contractor with the right gear and equipment set up and maintain camps and provide food service and other basics of support than it is to have full-time active-duty military personnel do these jobs. Brown & Root was good at what they did and apparently remains so, because under the Obama administration the army has continued to award the company significant contracts.

I was accomplishing things I was proud of, including the acquisition of Dresser Industries, which made Halliburton the largest energy services company in the world. After being sideswiped by a recession in Asia, our stock was on the way up, and I was a happy man where I was. Moreover, I didn't want to be vice president. I'd known too many unhappy ones to think it was a job worth having. My message to Joe that day was basically thanks, but no thanks.

A few weeks later, Governor Bush came to me with a different request. He wanted to know if I would head his search for a vice presidential running mate. At last it was easy to say yes. I wanted to do whatever I could to help his campaign, and this would be a part-time commitment, something I could do—and accomplish—in a matter of months. When I thought about it, I realized I'd been observing or participating in the vice presidential selection process for nearly a quarter century, so I felt that I had a good sense of how an effective search should work.

In Washington a few days later, I began putting together a small team to run the vice president selection process for me. Liz was home on maternity leave from her law firm, and I asked if she would assist. When she said yes, I'm not sure that she realized her home office would become the nerve center of the operation. I also asked Dave Addington to help out by reviewing the material submitted by each prospective candidate and preparing summaries that I shared with Governor Bush. My son-in-law, Phil Perry, and some other lawyers from his firm worked with Dave to produce the questionnaire we asked each candidate to complete. Dave Gribbin also assisted, particularly with reviewing voting records and public speeches of the candidates. And Jan Baran, a terrific election lawyer, helped us review tax returns and answer questions about election laws in individual states.

It's harder to find a good vice presidential candidate than you might think. You might start off with the idea that it is a very prominent job that thousands of politicians would be dying to have and that a lot would be well qualified for. But when you start looking, you find that everyone has negatives. Everyone has some kind of baggage—whether it's a voting record, a financial problem, or something in his or her personal life.

We started with a list of everyone who should be considered and then began narrowing it down to the truly viable candidates. Sometimes the media refers to the "long" list and the "short" list, but it's really more like the list for public consumption and the real list of possible choices. There are lots of reasons why someone might be put on the list for public consumption. Perhaps you're trying to placate a certain wing of the party, or maybe you want to attract those who supported your opponent in the primaries. And so you mention certain people, although there's not a chance they will be chosen.

I began placing calls to each of the people on the real list and asking if they would agree to be considered. Some, like Senator Connie Mack of Florida, said no way. Connie actually said he'd never speak to me again if I put him on the list. For those who agreed, I explained that we would be sending a questionnaire similar to the paperwork federal employees fill out for employment or for security clearances and warned that it had some intrusive questions on it. I said that I would also be setting up one-on-one interviews. These would be low-profile—with no media attention—and I would have to ask some personal questions. Most candidates who end up on the short list are seasoned enough to know that if they are picked as the nominee, nothing about them will be off-limits and nothing can be counted on to stay secret. The press will start digging, and the other side will unleash opposition researchers. Your whole life will be an open book. Most people understood this and realized how important it was to give us a heads-up about anything that could possibly cause trouble or embarrassment or worse.

We also asked each potential candidate to submit ten years of tax returns; copies of speeches, books, and articles; and videotape of recent TV appearances. We thought long and hard about the best place to receive and store this very sensitive information. We couldn't use campaign headquarters in Austin, where so many curious people came and went every day. Somewhere in the Washington area would be better anyway, because that's where the search team was. Lynne had an office at the American Enterprise Institute, but that was off-limits because you can't conduct political activities on nonprofit premises. In the end, the governor and I figured that no one would guess that all the supersensitive vice presidential selection materials were being kept in locked cabinets in the basement of Liz's house in the D.C. suburbs, so that's where we had everything sent and stored.

On May 10 I had dinner with the governor in Austin to go over the information we had gathered on the first set of prospective candidates. I brought two copies of the binder that contained background information on each. I handed one copy to the governor and kept the other for myself, so I could walk him through it. We had not written down the most sensitive material, so I briefed the governor on it orally. Before we began this first session, I told Governor Bush that what we were about to discuss was highly sensitive, and we had to ensure complete confidentiality. Of course, he agreed, and at the end of each of our meetings to discuss the candidates, he would hand his copy of the briefing book back to me.

Two people not on our list were Colin Powell and John McCain. Both had made it clear that they weren't interested. One candidate who spent a short time on the real list was Don Rumsfeld. Not long after I took on the assignment of managing the selection process, I placed a call to Don and said, "I'm pulling together a list of potential VP candidates, and I'd like to put your name on it. You don't have to say yes, but if you don't say anything, I'm going to put your name on the list." There was silence on the other end of the phone line, so I added Don's name and left him in a position where he could truthfully say he had not asked to be on the list.

His name didn't stay on long, though, and we never went through the vetting with him, because it was pretty clear early in the next session I had with the governor that a Rumsfeld vice presidency just wasn't in the cards. Some in the Bush camp had long believed that back in 1975 Rumsfeld maneuvered George H. W. Bush into the job of CIA director as a way of taking him out of the political arena and precluding him from running as Ford's vice president in 1976. I knew the truth, which was that Democratic senators, in return for Bush's confirmation as CIA director, had required a pledge in writing from President Ford that he wouldn't choose Bush as his running mate in 1976. In fact, George H. W. Bush wanted to be CIA director. I remembered being in the Oval Office when he urged Ford to sign the letter sealing the deal.

One night over dinner in the Governor's Mansion I went through this history with Governor Bush, not because I was pushing him to include Rumsfeld on the ticket but because I wanted him to know the facts as I'd seen them. I told him I was personally convinced that his father's going to the CIA had nothing to do with Rumsfeld. Indeed, if you had to single out one person as responsible, you might point to Elliot Richardson, who had been Ford's first choice for the CIA post. Over the years, Richardson had irritated a number of people, including Henry Kissinger, and it was that kind of resistance to the Richardson choice that led President Ford to move on to nominating George H. W. Bush for the CIA. Governor Bush didn't say a negative word about Rumsfeld, and of course a few months later he picked him to be secretary of defense. But he made it pretty clear that as far as the vice presidency was concerned Rumsfeld wasn't going to be an option.

Over the course of the next few weeks, the governor and I had numerous meetings and phone calls to review the progress of the search for his running mate. He said to me more than once, "Dick, *you're* the solution to my problem." I chose to take the comment as an indication that I needed to redouble my efforts to come up with a candidate.

On July 3 I flew down to Crawford again to brief the governor. We met in the small single-story white frame house he and Laura used on the property before their current place was finished. That morning I sat inside with him and went through the updated binders giving him the latest rundown on everybody. After our meeting Laura joined us for lunch, and then he and I moved outside to the back porch. The porch was basically a concrete pad with a few posts holding up the roof, and it was punishingly hot out there. I remember looking out over the cactus and sagebrush and thinking that this was definitely Texas real estate.

Over the past few months, as I had listened to George Bush talk about what kind of vice president he wanted, I had been impressed. He had a strong sense of his own strengths and weaknesses, and he wasn't looking for someone based on any purely political calculation. He was looking for someone who could help him govern, a person with experience in the kind of national security and foreign policy issues he knew every president must face. And, most important, his pick had to be someone who could step in and become president if the worst happened.

As we sat there looking out at the sunbaked landscape, he said once again, "You know, Dick, you're the solution to my problem." This time I said, "Okay, Governor, I will take a look at what I would have to do in order to be a viable candidate." But I also told him that I needed to come and sit down with him and whomever else he wanted in the room and go through all the reasons he *shouldn't* pick me. I told him he needed to be aware of the negatives about me. As I reflect back on it now, I suspect that George W. Bush had never really accepted my first answer—thanks, but no thanks—when Joe Allbaugh asked if I was willing to be considered. The governor had worked hard to convince me, but I didn't want him to be surprised, and I needed to make sure he vetted the vetter.

I flew back to Washington that afternoon, and the next night Lynne and I went to Alan Greenspan's July Fourth party on the top floor of the Federal Reserve Building. The Fed's white marble headquarters faces the National Mall only a few blocks from the Washington Monument, and the view of the national fireworks from the top floor is spectacular. Alan and his wife, Andrea Mitchell, hosted a buffet dinner for friends and then invited everyone outside on the roof terrace to watch the fireworks.

Lynne and I went through the buffet line and then selected open seats at one of the dinner tables. Washington is a funny place when you're out of power, and that, added to the fact that we had a couple of grandchildren with us, meant that no one rushed to join our little group—except for Bob Woodward. The famed *Washington Post* reporter brought his plate over, sat down beside me, and after some preliminary small talk proceeded to pump me for information about the VP search process and who the pick might be. His instincts were right—there was a big story here—but none of his speculation was focused on me, and I felt no need to broaden his horizons.

After we returned to Dallas, I called Dave Lesar, my chief operating officer at Halliburton, and asked him to come by the house early one morning. I told him what was happening—that there was a possibility George Bush would select me to be his running mate. I told Dave that if that happened I would recommend to the Halliburton board that he take over as chairman and CEO of the company. From my first days as CEO, I had always believed that there should be somebody in the wings ready to take over. Some CEOs don't do that because they think such a person may emerge as competition. They don't want anybody around who would be an obvious successor. I had always operated on the basis that if I got hit by a truck, somebody had to be able to take over—and Dave was the clear choice. I knew that if I did leave Halliburton, the company would be in good hands with Dave, and I wouldn't be walking away leaving them in the lurch.

I also called a meeting of the board of directors. Even though I still considered it to be far from a sure thing, I thought that they needed to know that I might be selected as the Republican vice presidential nominee. Although I had enjoyed excellent relationships with the board, I wasn't sure just how this news would be received. One of the questions that had come up when they'd hired me was whether I was through with politics, and I had assured them I was, because that is what I had believed. Fortunately, the board was supportive. I had given the company five years, and it had been a good five years for Halliburton. I had also picked a strong successor and brought him along. In addition, most of the board understood that when your party's presidential nominee asks you to run with him, it's the right thing to do. It's an obligation.

The board was helpful as I worked to separate myself from the company financially. They even offered to accelerate the exercise dates on all Halliburton options that had been granted to me, so I could exercise them before I was elected, thus eliminating any accusations of a conflict of interest. I declined this offer because I did not want even the appearance that I was getting special treatment. After I left Halliburton I sold the stock I held outright and exercised options that had vested, but that left a significant number of options that had not yet vested. That is, they had been granted to me, but the dates when I could choose to sell them were in the future.

There was no legal requirement that we do so, but in order to sever all our financial ties to Halliburton, Lynne and I set up an irrevocable gift trust agreement that would donate all the after-tax profits from these unvested options to three charities of our choice: the University of Wyoming, George Washington University Hospital, and Capital Partners for Education, which provides scholarships to inner-city children in Washington, D.C. That agreement has resulted in more than $8 million being donated to charity.

I also had deferred income from the company from one year in which I had taken a portion of my salary and asked for the rest of it to be paid out over five years. This was salary that I had already earned, so it was due to me whether the company was doing well or badly. But before I became vice president, so that there would not be even the slightest confusion or suspicion that I had any ongoing connection with Halliburton or any interest or stake in the fortunes of the company, Lynne and I took the extra step of obtaining an insurance policy, for which we paid fifteen thousand dollars, that guaranteed these payments regardless of what happened to the company.

I suppose I shouldn't have been surprised, but after all the steps I had taken to guard against any possible assertion that I had an ongoing stake in the fortunes of the company, it angered me that my critics continued to make false claims about my ties to Halliburton. During the 2004 campaign, the charges were especially outrageous. Early in that campaign summer, Senator Pat Leahy conducted a conference call as a campaign surrogate in which he suggested I was being dishonest and dishonorable and was profiting from Halliburton business while I was vice president. Not long afterward, when I was on the Senate floor for the annual Senate "class photo," Leahy came over and put his arm around me, acting as though we were old buddies. I used a colorful epithet to suggest what he could do to himself and stepped away. It was probably not language I should have used on the Senate floor, but it was completely deserved.

The Kerry-Edwards campaign made a TV ad using the same lies, and I was gratified when the University of Pennsylvania's Public Policy Center analyzed the ad, obtained the relevant documents, including the gift trust agreement, and concluded in a statement on the website FactCheck.org that the ad was "flat wrong."

As I was notifying my board of the possibility that I might be selected as the vice presidential nominee, I also arranged to have a complete physical with my doctors in Washington. After taking a stress test and having an electrocardiogram and a battery of other tests, my doctors spoke with Dr. Denton Cooley, the world-renowned heart surgeon from Texas, who had performed the first heart transplant in the United States. Governor Bush had asked Cooley to assess whether my heart condition was a disqualification.

Lynne was on the board of American Express mutual funds, and once a year the company had a board meeting in Minneapolis to which spouses were invited. That's where I was on the night of July 12, when I was called away from the dinner table to take a call from Governor Bush. He told me that Dr. Cooley had given me a green light on the health front, concluding that there was no reason why I could not run for and serve as vice president. Of course that was good news, but I was still looking ahead to the meeting scheduled for Saturday, July 15, at the Governor's Mansion in Austin, where I intended to lay out the case against myself. And I wouldn't be just going through the motions. There were solid reasons why I didn't think I made sense as George Bush's running mate, and I intended to put them on the table. I was so serious about talking him out of picking me that my family was confident I would come back from the meeting having taken myself off the list.

The governor, his chief strategist, Karl Rove, and I met in the yellow parlor of the Governor's Mansion, a high-ceilinged room with portraits of famous Texans on the wall. I began by going through a list of things about me that I believed the governor should be aware of. First, I told them, I had been arrested twice when I was in my early twenties for driving under the influence, and I'd been kicked out of Yale twice.

I also had health problems. Despite Dr. Cooley's reassurances I wanted to be sure Governor Bush understood how serious they were. At that point I'd had three heart attacks and quadruple bypass surgery. I explained what would happen on the campaign trail if I ever felt chest discomfort or any other symptom. Heart patients have to be vigilant, and I told them that if I ever felt even a twinge in my chest during the campaign, I would go directly to a hospital. It would make no difference if I were in the middle of a speech or in the middle of a debate; minutes could mean the difference between life and death. There was simply no way to judge the impact of such an event on the outcome of a presidential race, but it wasn't likely to be positive.

I also pointed out that the governor and I both had a history in the oil business. Governor Bush had been in the oil business years ago in Midland, and I'd been running Halliburton for five years. It wasn't hard to imagine the negative charges our opponents would level at us based on that common denominator. We also had a potential constitutional problem because we were both living in Texas. The Twelfth Amendment to the Constitution prevents the Electoral College electors from any state from voting for a president and a vice president from their state. In other words, the electors from Texas could not vote for both me and George Bush. Before moving to Texas in 1995, I had been a nearly lifelong resident of Wyoming and still had a home there. But we would need election lawyers to make sure that Governor Bush wasn't giving away Texas's electoral votes by putting me on the ticket.

Finally, I told the governor he needed to understand how deeply conservative I was. He said, "Dick, we know that." And I said, "No, I mean *really* conservative." I had a reputation of being somewhat moderate, partly, I think, because I wasn't a "bomb thrower" like some of my conservative colleagues, and partly because I got along with people all across the political spectrum. I think it was also because I got my start on the national scene working for Jerry Ford, who was a moderate. I needed to make sure the governor understood that my voting record was certainly not moderate.

Karl joined me in vigorously making the case against me as the vice-presidential pick, and the governor listened carefully to both of us. When the meeting broke up, I had no indication whether I had changed Bush's mind, but I was sure that there would be further discussions among his top advisors. We continued to look at one other possibility—former senator Jack Danforth from Missouri. On Tuesday, July 18, I picked up Jack and his wife, Sally, in St. Louis and flew with them to Chicago, where the governor was campaigning. We all met at his hotel downtown to discuss the vice presidency. I stayed for the first part of the meeting and then excused myself so they could talk alone.

During the meeting, the governor's personal aide, Logan Walters, came in the room and told me Liz was on the phone and needed to speak with me. She told me that Pete Williams had called her to say NBC was getting ready to report that I was the governor's pick to be vice president. I told her to tell Pete that no decision had been made yet, which was the truth, as George Bush was right that minute interviewing another potential candidate.

Later in the week I got some very timely advice from election lawyer Jan Baran, who had been one of our advisors in the vice presidential search process. I had asked Jan to look into what the requirements would be for reestablishing my Wyoming residency. Jan explained that there were generally a number of things a court would look at to determine an individual's residency, including where he was registered to vote and whether he had voted in recent elections in his home state. Jan also explained that an important deadline was looming. If I wanted to register to vote ahead of Wyoming's August primary, I would need to do so in person at the Teton County clerk's office no later than that Friday, July 21. I arranged to make the trip home to Jackson and registered in person on that day.

I have always suspected that Pete Williams had a source in the Teton County clerk's office that he shared with his colleague Lisa Myers, because shortly after I registered to vote, she ran it as breaking news on NBC. Suddenly the story was national news and speculation reached a fever pitch.

My voter registration trip even caught many in the campaign's highest ranks by surprise. The process of selecting a vice president had been very closely guarded, and few knew that the governor was as close to picking me as he was. Joe Allbaugh and Bush's communications director, Karen Hughes, who knew Liz had been helping me on the search, got hold of her on her cell phone and asked, "Could you explain to us just what your dad is doing in Wyoming?" Liz, who happened to be getting her hair cut at the time, excused herself, stepped into a utility closet at the salon, and whispered into her cell phone as much as she could about the Twelfth Amendment, the deadline to register in Wyoming, and why I was suddenly all over the news.

EARLY TUESDAY MORNING, I was working out on the treadmill at our house in Dallas when the phone rang. It was George Bush, and he was calling to formally ask me to be his running mate. I said I would be honored.

Ever since the previous Friday when I'd registered to vote in Wyoming, the press had been camped out in front of our house in Dallas. There was a double front door with a large window over the top, and on Monday morning when I walked out of our bedroom in my pajamas, I looked up to see a camera mounted so that it was looking straight in through that window. Another enterprising journalist left a disposable camera on the doorstep, along with a note suggesting that we might use it to take some personal photos of this historic day and then give the camera back to her to develop them.

I drove Lynne and Liz to Love Field, parked the car, and we flew to Austin for the formal announcement that I would be George Bush's running mate. It was the last time I would drive myself for the next eight and a half years. Even though I had held some prominent public positions as White House chief of staff, member of Congress, and secretary of defense, I don't think anything could have prepared me for what was about to happen. When you become your party's vice presidential candidate, you're instantaneously swept into an all-consuming bubble of motorcades, campaign staff, and Secret Service agents, with legions of reporters and cameras following close behind.

After the formal announcement at 2:00 p.m., we headed back to the Governor's Mansion, where photographers for *Time* and *Newsweek* were waiting to take the first official portraits of the newly minted Republican ticket. *Newsweek* ran the photo on the cover with the title "The Avengers: Taking Aim at the Age of Clinton." The headline in the *Washington Post* the next day pretty accurately captured the gist of the coverage of Bush's vice presidential selection: "GOP Hails Cheney's Inclusion on Ticket; Democrats Prepare to Fight Big Oil." A lot of the reaction focused on my experience, particularly in national security, and my twenty-five years of government service, but the Democrats were waiting in the wings, ready to attack.

Of course, the fact that the head of the vice presidential selection committee had ended up as the vice presidential nominee was great material for late-night comedians. And even my family joined in, entertaining themselves by speculating on exactly what I'd told the Halliburton board, offering lines like "So, gentlemen, as you know I've been conducting the vice presidential search process, and I'd like to tell you today that I've picked . . . me."

There was some effort to make a serious charge that I had conducted the search process so that I could position myself to be the nominee, but it ignored a pretty important fact. If I had wanted the job, I could have said yes back in March 2000 when Joe Allbaugh asked if I'd be willing to be considered. It would have been a heck of a lot easier way to end up where I did.

WITH THE CONVENTION LESS than a week away, I had much work ahead of me to get ready for what would be the biggest speech of my political career. Luckily, the campaign assigned the task to two of the best speechwriters I have ever worked with: John McConnell and Matthew Scully. Lynne and I sat with them in the dining room at the Governor's Mansion that afternoon and began to sketch out what I would say. It was Lynne who came up with one of the most memorable parts of my speech. She recalled how Al Gore in 1992 had repeatedly used the phrase "It's time for them to go," referring, of course, to President George H. W. Bush and Vice President Dan Quayle. "Let's turn it back on them," she suggested, and we did.

At the end of the day on which I was announced, Lynne, Liz, and I joined George, Laura, and their eighteen-year-old daughter Jenna for a small family dinner at the mansion. It had been an historic day of such intense media coverage that it wasn't hard to feel as though everyone in the country was focused on the fact that I had just been selected to be George Bush's running mate. Fortunately, there is nothing like a teenager to bring you back down to earth. About halfway through dinner, Jenna turned to me and said, "Hey, what about you? You going to the convention?"

Indeed I was, but before that we had one very special stop to make. The next morning we flew to Casper with the Bushes for our first Bush-Cheney campaign rally, in the gym at Natrona County High School, where Lynne and I had first started dating more than forty years before. Mary flew from her home in Denver to be with us, and the advance team used the green chalkboard in the choir room to diagram the event and brief us before we went on. It was a special moment, to be back in a place that had meant so much to Lynne and to me and to be arriving there as the soon-to-be Republican vice presidential nominee.

Lynne introduced me that day. She talked about our daughters and our great pride in them. She talked about what an honor it was to be joining the Bushes in this historic effort, and she talked about our life together.

> *Dick, when I look back on our more than forty years together, on more changes and adventures than I could ever have imagined when we graduated from NCHS all those years ago, I know that what has sustained me is your deep and abiding kindness and decency and love. . . . So here we are beginning another adventure. . . .*

And what an adventure it would be.

————◄◦►————

CHAPTER NINE

Big Time

The 2000 Republican convention in Philadelphia was a showcase for George W. Bush's "compassionate conservatism," and as much as the mainstream media can ever love a Republican convention, they were fans of this one. They hailed the convention's first-night theme— "Opportunity with a Purpose: Leave No Child Behind"—as something new and welcome from the GOP. When Laura Bush talked about the importance of literacy and Colin Powell spoke about community service and volunteerism, press coverage praised the theme of inclusion, and the convention's "softest of sells."

The Bush campaign communicators had worked hard to put together a convention that would present a moderate face to undecided voters, and they seemed to have succeeded. When they saw a draft of my speech, however, they worried I would undo their months of hard work. One line in particular troubled them, the refrain "It's time for them to go," which purposely echoed the line from Al Gore's 1992 convention address. I was pretty sure that in the context of 2000, it would irritate the heck out of Democrats and thrill Republicans, but some on the Bush staff thought it was too harsh. They didn't want me to attack Clinton and Gore; they believed "red meat" might play well in the hall, but not in people's living rooms.

I think they were hoping for a kinder, gentler Dick Cheney, and I listened to what they had to say, and then I ignored their advice. And to this day I am glad I did. It was important for the Bush-Cheney ticket to reach out to moderates, but we also had to make clear that there were big differences between us and our opponents and that it was time for a change. Watching a tape of the speech now, more than a decade later, I am struck by how well it served that purpose—and how much fun I had giving it.

As a candidate for president, Al Gore was trying his best to distance himself from Bill Clinton and the scandals surrounding him. I tried my best not to let him. Speaking of the two of them that night I said:

Somehow, we will never see one without thinking of the other. . . . They came in together. Now let us see them off together. Ladies and gentlemen, the wheel has turned, and it is time, time for them to go.

Bill Clinton had said that he planned to hold on to power "until the last hour of the last day," and I reminded the crowd that it was his right to do so:

But my friends, that last hour is coming. That last day is near. The wheel has turned, and it is time, time for them to go.

After two nights of compassionate conservatism, the audience in the First Union Center was ready to raise the roof, and raise it they did. They chanted, "Time for them to go! Time for them to go!" before breaking spontaneously into the refrain from a sixties song, "Na na na na, na na na na, hey hey hey, goodbye!" I even got into it myself at one point, signaling like a baseball umpire, "You're outta here!" I'll never forget looking out into the vast crowd and seeing George Shultz, a former secretary of state and one of America's most dignified elder statesmen, swaying back and forth and singing, "Hey hey hey, goodbye!"

I ended my remarks with a reminder to the audience of how lucky we are to live in the United States of America and how great a debt we owe to those who have preserved and protected our great nation. I described a trip I had taken many times as secretary of defense from Andrews Air Force Base to the Pentagon by helicopter. I talked about looking down at the Capitol, where all the great debates that have shaped two centuries of American history have taken place, and then flying along the Mall, where the monument to George Washington, our first president, stands sentinel. To the north was the White House, where John Adams once prayed "that none but honest and wise men may ever rule under this roof." Next came the memorial to Thomas Jefferson, the third president and author of our Declaration of Independence, and then the memorial to Abraham Lincoln, the greatest of presidents, the savior of the Union. Finally, after crossing the Potomac, just before settling down at the Pentagon, I looked down on Arlington National Cemetery. "I never once made that trip," I said,

> *without being reminded of how enormously fortunate we are to be Americans, and what a terrible price thousands have paid so that all of us and millions more around the world might live in freedom. This is a great country, ladies and gentlemen, and it deserves great leadership. Let us go forth from this hall in confidence and courage, committed to restoring decency and honor to our republic.*

At the end of my speech, white banners emblazoned with "Bush-Cheney" in large red letters unfurled from the rafters, and confetti and beach balls showered the crowd. As the celebrations died down, Lynne and I stepped to the side of the stage to listen to one of our favorite singers, Lee Greenwood, end the evening with his great song "God Bless the U.S.A."

There were many amazing moments during the Philadelphia convention. One was when I went with my daughter Mary, who had agreed to serve as my personal assistant during the campaign, to visit my old boss President Gerald Ford. As we arrived in his suite, the eighty-seven-year-old former president walked over to Mary, put his arm around her, and said, "I bet you're proud of your dad, aren't you?" "Yes, sir, Mr. President," she replied. "I sure am." "Good," he said. "Me too." If it hadn't been for President Ford and the trust he placed in me a quarter century before, I wouldn't have been the Republican nominee for vice president, and I was grateful for the opportunity to thank him personally.

The day after Mary and I visited him, he was hospitalized, having suffered a stroke. He would live six more years, time deeply valued by those of us who loved him, and when he died, it was my great, though sad, honor as vice president to eulogize him in the Capitol Rotunda. I remembered his brief presidency, just 895 days, as a time "filled with testing and trial enough for a much longer stay."

> *Even then, amid troubles not of his own making, President Ford proved as worthy of that office as any who had ever come before. He was modest and manful; there was confidence and courage in his bearing. In judgment he was sober and serious, unafraid of decisions, calm and steady by nature, always the still point in the turning wheel.*

A man who never assumed airs and was known for his kindness, Gerald Ford led our nation through one of the greatest constitutional crises in our history.

On the day after the convention, Governor Bush, Laura, Lynne, and I left Philadelphia on a special campaign train, making old-fashioned whistle-stops all across the battleground states of Ohio, Michigan, and Illinois. After that we would spend most of the next nine weeks traveling separately. That way we could double the territory we covered, hold twice as many rallies and town hall meetings, and generate twice the local press coverage.

Unlike many vice presidential candidates who come to their campaigns with a political staff largely in place, I had been gone from politics for seven years, so I used the weeks just after the convention to hire people. My longtime executive assistant, the steady and well-organized Debbie Heiden, came on board and stayed with me through all eight years of my vice presidency. I signed on Dirk VandeBeek, who had handled public relations at Halliburton, to act as my campaign press secretary. I interviewed only one candidate to be my chief of staff, Kathleen Shanahan, who had worked for President Reagan, George H. W. Bush, when he was vice president, and California Governor Pete Wilson. She was extremely competent, tough, smart, and funny, and she fit in right away with the whole Cheney family.

The campaign also assigned a team of three policy people from Austin to take turns traveling with me. I hadn't had time to get up to speed on every one of the issues I might be asked about, so I was going to be learning on the road. These policy advisors knew the governor's position on everything from nuclear waste and education reform, to Social Security and faith-based initiatives, and would make sure my operation and his were always on the same page. Tim Adams was a sharp and reliable hand, who later went on to become undersecretary for international affairs at the Treasury Department. Joel Kaplan was a marine with a law degree from Harvard and a great sense of humor. He came from a family of Democrats, but somewhere along the way he'd figured things out. He later became deputy OMB director and then deputy chief of staff in the White House. And Stuart Holliday combined serious knowledge of every domestic and foreign policy issue that might come up in the campaign with a great ability not to take himself too seriously. Stuart later became an ambassador to the United Nations for special political affairs.

The staff at campaign headquarters in Austin decided my first solo stop on the campaign trail should be in Florida, where I'd participate in what they had dubbed "Education Week." My assignment was to unveil the Bush-Cheney school bonds program at a Fort Lauderdale elementary school, which sounded fine to me, but when I walked into Croissant Park Elementary on the morning of August 31, I realized that my audience was going to be a bunch of third graders. Because I'm a team player I went ahead and gave my speech, covering the complexities of school financing for eight-year-olds sitting cross-legged on a library floor. I'll never forget the confused looks on their faces as I talked about the importance of local bond initiatives. I am sure they were thinking, Who is this guy, what is he talking about, and how much longer before recess?

After the Fort Lauderdale fiasco, I decided to use my own judgment. I'd do what the campaign staff in Austin wanted—but only if I felt right about it. When they sent me a speech about abstinence education to be delivered at another event, I tossed it out. This wasn't a subject I'd pronounced on before, and I couldn't see a compelling reason to begin now.

Governor Bush and I met up again over Labor Day weekend in Illinois, where we spoke at a rally. I introduced him and he made some brief remarks to the enthusiastic crowd. Afterward, as we stood onstage alongside the podium waving to the crowd, we didn't realize that a directional microphone was picking up our words. When the governor recognized a reporter whose coverage had been particularly unfriendly, he pointed him out to me. "There's Adam Clymer," he said, "major-league asshole from the *New York Times.*" I nodded my agreement: "Big time," I said.

Our exchange was played over and over again on TV and radio, totally blocking any other messages we wanted to get out—particularly the one about restoring honor and dignity to the Oval Office. But the story finally died down, and the only lasting result—aside from burnishing Clymer's reputation with his colleagues in the press—was that I became known as "Big Time" around campaign headquarters and beyond.

If you asked my traveling campaign staff, they'd probably tell you that my next Illinois campaign stop was even worse. We went to the Taste of Polonia street festival at the Copernicus Foundation Plaza in Chicago, where I made some brief remarks to the large crowd gathered to celebrate Polish cultural heritage and then handed the microphone back to the Illinois state treasurer, Judy Topinka. She grabbed the mike and enthusiastically announced that "Secretary Cheney will now dance a polka with Miss Polonia!" That was news to me, but I didn't have much time to consider my options because Miss Polonia was right there and ready to dance. So we polkaed—pretty enthusiastically, as I remember. As we whirled around I could see my daughter Mary offstage in the staff section watching in horror. She told me later that her only comfort was the knowledge that Governor Bush's and my description of the *New York Times* reporter at the previous stop would completely overshadow any photos of my polka debut.

September seemed to go from bad to worse. The Gore campaign had enjoyed a major bounce out of their convention, and we were still fighting to catch up. Our effort wasn't helped when the *Dallas Morning News* reported that I had failed to vote in fourteen of sixteen elections that had been held while I was living in Dallas. I can't remember many stories that have surprised me more. As it turned out, individual jurisdictions in Texas often call elections about single issues; they aren't well publicized and draw very few voters. So for most of the elections in question, I hadn't even known I wasn't voting.

Unfortunately, in the high-intensity atmosphere of a presidential campaign, facts don't always matter. You can tell your side of the story, but the press will keep hammering, as will your opponents, who want nothing more than to knock you off message. Any moment I spent explaining why I hadn't voted in fourteen of sixteen elections was a moment I wasn't spending telling people why they should vote for us in this election.

But the press will get off one negative story for another one, and we were able to provide just such a diversion during a campaign stop in Shelton, Connecticut, later the same day that the voting story broke. I was scheduled to speak at an assisted living facility in the 5th Congressional District, where Mark Nielsen was the Republican candidate for Congress. Earlier that day, Nielsen had put a new ad on the air, featuring political figures he believed were "Leaders of Honor and Integrity." These leaders included President George H. W. Bush, Senator John McCain, and Senator Joe Lieberman, my vice presidential opponent. While I couldn't disagree with Nielsen's characterization of my opponent—Senator Joe Lieberman *is* a leader of honor and integrity— we were in the middle of a hard-fought campaign, and it wasn't easy to explain to the press why this Republican congressional candidate was promoting my Democratic opponent.

In anticipation of my arrival at the assisted living center, the advance team turned off the noisy air-conditioning system, and because I was running late, it had been off for quite some time when I got there. The room was so warm that much of my audience was asleep—and I totally understood. Even I had to struggle to stay awake as I slogged through a speech on Medicare reform. My appearance before the audience of senior citizens was a fitting end to a campaign swing that began with a school bond speech to eight-year-olds. Later, my daughter Mary would write a book in which she called my early days of solo campaigning "nine days of hell."

As I began to get my campaign legs back, I realized that the 2000 campaign was actually pretty similar to the Ford campaign twenty-four years earlier. The rallies, the speeches, the whistle-stop train tour were the same kind of events we'd been doing in 1976. Obviously, the technology had improved exponentially, and the news cycle was now twenty-four hours. But it wasn't rocket science, and as I got into the swing of it, it was a lot of fun. We had great events, and I enjoyed the bands and confetti and cheering crowds. Who wouldn't? Still, there were some stories in the press that said I didn't like campaigning. Maybe they were based on the fact that I'm not a traditional, backslapping, glad-handing politician. But nobody ever bothered to ask me—nor, I noticed, did they ever point out that my approach worked. I had actually won every campaign I'd conducted in which my name was on the ballot—six statewide races in Wyoming at that point.

The best part of the campaign was that it was a family effort. Lynne and Mary were on the campaign trail with me nearly every step of the way, and Liz was there most of the time with my three granddaughters in tow. We'd introduce the kids at rallies and then usher them offstage before they stole the whole show. Afterward, we'd gather to recap the highlights—and the lowlights. All these years later, I realize that the disasters often made for the best stories—and the most laughs.

After the convention I knew that my performance at one event in particular, the vice presidential debate, would likely matter more than all the other campaigning I did. The debate was scheduled for October 5, 2000, in Danville, Kentucky. I had spent some time during the Democratic convention that summer watching tapes of Lieberman's debates against Lowell Weicker, the liberal three-term incumbent Republican senator whom Joe had upset in 1988, in no small part because of his superior performance in their televised debates.

Presidential and vice presidential debates are events like no other. First of all, the stakes are unbelievably high, and a single gaffe can derail a candidacy. A mistake can cost an election. And although being able to answer the questions competently is crucial, it isn't nearly enough. A candidate has to have a sense of the most important messages he or she wants to leave with voters and the presence of mind to return to those messages again and again—and then again. It also helps a lot if you can come up with some memorable one-liners. After all is said and done, after all the studying and planning and strategizing, it is likely to be the one-liners that stay with people and determine who wins and who loses a debate. Knowing that I had my work cut out for me, I asked Liz to organize a process for formal debate preparation.

Governor Bush had already participated in numerous debates during the primary campaign, so work had been under way for many months preparing briefing materials and possible questions and answers for him. Gary Edson, who would later become deputy national security and economic advisor to the president, had been in charge of the Bush briefing materials. He came out on the road with us right after the convention, bringing about fifty pounds of briefing books with him. We went through them, and Liz began to prepare briefing books for me, adapting the governor's format and background materials. We also added questions that I was likely to get, about Halliburton, for example, that the governor might not. Gus Puryear, a Nashville lawyer who'd worked with my son-in-law, Phil Perry, on Senate campaign finance hearings, came on board to help with the research and drafting.

I studied the briefing books between campaign stops, and then in early September started having practice sessions with either Phil or Stuart Stevens, a communications consultant with the campaign, playing the role of moderator. They would pepper me with questions, and my job was to hit all the main points we wanted to get across on each key issue within the allotted time for each answer. When I got pretty comfortable with this format, I asked Rob Portman, then a congressman from Ohio, to join our sessions. He played Joe Lieberman, and did a tremendous job. He had spent countless hours listening to tapes of Lieberman's speeches and knew not only the substance of the responses the senator was likely to give, but even the way he was likely to deliver them.

I invited several people I trusted—including Steve Hadley, Paul Wolfowitz, Dave Gribbin, and Scooter Libby—to watch these sessions and give me feedback. At first we stopped after every answer for comments, but this turned out to be pretty frustrating. Everyone had an opinion about how the question should be answered, and I didn't find it particularly helpful to watch my advisors debate each other over the answer I had just given. And I worried we were in danger of missing the big picture—the overall impact of what I was saying. So after a few sessions, I asked everyone to hold their comments to the end.

In late September we moved the debate prep out to Wyoming and instituted a pretty rigorous schedule. Each morning we'd spend three hours going over questions on a particular subject. Each night, at precisely the time the debate would be taking place in Kentucky, we would hold a mock debate. We filmed these prep sessions, and when each session was done, Liz worked with my assembled advisors to summarize their comments on my performance. With their assessments in hand, Liz, Lynne, Rob Portman, and I would review the video and work to improve and hone my responses.

By this time we knew that Lieberman and I would be seated at a round table on the debate stage, and we looked around for some place in Jackson where we could replicate this setup. We settled on the Jackson Hole Playhouse, which not only offered a table and a stage, but came with red velvet curtains and a saloon out front. Photos from one of our practice sessions show a backdrop of branches and vines from the previous evening's performance, and Phil and Rob Portman clowning around in top hats they'd found backstage.

Security is a big issue in presidential and vice presidential debates. While we were getting set up at the Jackson Hole Playhouse, we learned that a staffer working for Mark McKinnon in the Bush debate prep sessions had sent a copy of the governor's briefing book and a tape of one of his practice sessions to a member of Gore's debate team. The materials were immediately turned over to the FBI, but the incident underlined how important it was to be vigilant. Debate preparation sessions already showed up on my schedule as "communications meetings." And the briefing book full of issues and potential questions and answers was neutrally labeled "Secretary Cheney Policy Book." But the Jackson Hole Playhouse, for all its charm, turned out to be a less than secure location. Several reporters, pretending to be tourists who wanted to look around, stopped by the theater one day just before a debate rehearsal began. Fortunately, Liz happened to be in the lobby and was able to send them packing. But after that we decided to relocate and ended up holding most of the practice sessions in our living room, using a rented round table covered with a bedsheet.

The effort that we put into debate preparation was critically important. But if I had to give one piece of advice to future presidential and vice presidential candidates preparing for debates, it would be this: Get some rest. Once you've gone over the issues and know what message you want to convey to the voters, you can do yourself a real favor by just taking a nap. You've got to be relaxed—or at least look like you are—when the moment comes. I think voters figure out pretty quickly that if you can't handle the stress of a political debate, you're not going to be much good in an actual crisis.

Of course, one of my favorite ways to unwind is with a fly rod, and there is no better place to do that than on one of Wyoming's beautiful rivers. Thus it was that I was sitting in a drift boat on the Snake River when I got a call asking if I would accept CNN anchor Bernard Shaw as the moderator for our debate. I said yes with no hesitation. I knew Bernie to be an honest, objective, hardworking journalist, who would study the issues and ask tough questions of us both. He would forever be associated in my mind with the first night of Desert Storm in 1991—a night that turned out to be a tremendous success for the U.S. military. Like so many others around the world, I had watched Bernie broadcasting live from a hotel in downtown Baghdad on January 16 just as the first U.S. air strikes began.

On the final Sunday before my debate, we attended church at St. John's Episcopal Church in Jackson. As I slid into the pew next to my family, I saw quite a few members of my debate prep team scattered throughout the congregation. I am sure that they, like me, figured a prayer or two couldn't hurt.

Suzanne Harris was in the pulpit that morning. Her granddaughter was battling leukemia, and we were all moved as Reverend Harris talked about three-year-old Hannah's strength and courage, beyond what any child should ever have to demonstrate. She talked about what Hannah's life taught about faith—"Our faith is not that bad things won't happen," she said. "Our faith is that when bad things do happen, God can still use that material to make something holy." She reminded us that life is short. "We do not have too much time to gladden the hearts of those who travel the way with us," she said, "so be swift to love and make haste to be kind." In the midst of a hard-fought political campaign, her sermon made all of us pause and reflect. Hannah died a few days later, and Suzanne's words that autumn morning in Jackson are still fresh in my mind as I write this a decade later.

My assignment on October 3 was to travel to a battleground state where the media could cover me watching Governor Bush's first debate with Al Gore. We chose Ohio and took over a restaurant there for a Bush-Cheney debate-watching party. In the lead-up to this first Bush-Gore debate, Gore, who had already demonstrated a propensity for unnecessary overstatement, had made a few quotable remarks that turned out not to be true. First, in order to dramatize a point about the failings of America's health-care system, he said that his mother-in-law paid almost three times as much for the same arthritis medicine that the Gores bought for the family dog. Then, speaking at a Teamsters convention, he claimed that when he was a child, his mother had sung him to sleep with the song "Look for the Union Label." The Gore campaign had to admit that the medicine costs Gore quoted weren't personal at all, but rather from a House Democratic study. And the song Gore claimed his mother had sung to him in the cradle hadn't been written until 1975, when Gore was twenty-seven.

The press, with a little Republican help, of course, sensed a theme, and as we watched from Ohio, Gore locked it in by claiming to have traveled to Texas with Federal Emergency Management Agency Director James Lee Witt when wildfires broke out in Parker County. But as the press discovered, the closest Gore got to the fires was Houston, well over two hundred miles away, and he didn't get there with James Lee Witt—or even meet with him. To this day I can't understand how such a seasoned politician continually got so tangled up in trivial untruths, nor have I ever figured out why he huffed and sighed so audibly that night. It certainly didn't earn him any votes.

The night before my debate, I made sure I got a good night's rest by sleeping in my own bed. We got up early on October 5 and flew to Lexington, Kentucky, then drove to Danville, where our first stop was the official walk-through of the debate site at Centre College. The walk-through was meant to give me a feel for the stage, the auditorium, the table where we would sit, and the "hold room" where I would be just prior to going onstage.

Two of my granddaughters, Kate and Elizabeth, joined us, and having them around certainly helped cut through some of the high anxiety of that day. Elizabeth, three at the time, climbed up into Joe Lieberman's seat at the debate table. While I was listening to a staff briefing about the lights that would time our answers, Elizabeth acquired a pen and set about diligently drawing a dinosaur on Joe's place card. True, dinosaurs were one of the few items in her repertoire at the time, but we all laughed at how well it fit into our campaign theme that the Democratic ticket represented the policies of the past.

While we were doing the walk-through, news was arriving about escalating protests in Serbia. The parliament building in Belgrade was

burning, and it looked as if the brutal and murderous president, Slobo-
dan Milošević, was going to have to yield to the will of his people and
leave office. I told Liz to get a summary of what was happening from
our foreign policy team—Hadley, Wolfowitz, and Libby—and to assign
one of them to give me a five-minute briefing on the latest developments. Then I went in to take a nap.

I'd been prepared for Joe Lieberman to be tough and aggressive, and
I understood later that he had expected the same from me. But our debate that night at Centre College turned out to be a civil and informed
exchange that to this day people cite as an example of thoughtful political discussion. I think it came about because of the respect that Joe
Lieberman and I have for one another and because of Bernie Shaw's
good questions. We discussed everything from military readiness and
the prospect for Middle East peace, to how to fix Social Security and reform education. We didn't agree on much, but our disagreements were
informative. We debated policy and substance and we never descended
into personal attacks.

About two-thirds of the way into the debate, Bernie brought up
the matter of the partisan bickering in Washington. "How would you
elevate the political discourse and purpose?" he asked. I talked about
George Bush's record of bipartisanship in Texas, and Joe talked about
Al Gore's record of bipartisanship in Washington. And then we had
one of those unplanned, unscripted, and totally memorable moments
that can happen in high-stakes debating. In response to my charge
that the Clinton-Gore team hadn't done anything, bipartisan or otherwise, to fix Medicare or Social Security or to improve the nation's
schools, Joe laid out all the ways in which the country was better off
than it had been eight years earlier. Then he turned to me and said,
referring to the extensive news coverage of my most recent financial
disclosure forms, "And I'm pleased to see, Dick, from the newspapers,
that you're better off than you were eight years ago, too." It was a good
line greeted by laughter from the audience. And it gave me the chance
to respond by saying, "And I can tell you, Joe, that the government had
absolutely nothing to do with it," which drew even more applause and
laughter.

If the exchange had ended there it probably would have been pretty much a draw, with each of us scoring a good-natured shot at the other guy's expense. But then, as Bernie got ready to ask his next question, Joe pointed to his wife, Hadassah, in the audience and said, "I can see my wife, and I think she's thinking, 'Gee, I wish he would go out into the private sector.'" It was an opening I couldn't pass up. "Well, I'm going to try to help you do that, Joe." It was completely spontaneous, and it caught Joe off guard. He was experienced enough to know he'd blown it by giving me such a great opening.

Bernie's questions that night covered the political waterfront, including the issue of sexual orientation. He asked, "Should a male who loves a male and a female who loves a female have all the constitutional rights enjoyed by every American citizen?" I had given the issue a lot of thought and answered it from the heart:

> *The fact of the matter is, we live in a free society and freedom means freedom for everybody. We don't get to choose, and shouldn't be able to choose, and say, you get to live free but you don't. That means that people should be free to enter into any kind of relationship they want to enter into. It's really no one's business in terms of trying to regulate or prohibit behavior in that regard. The next step, then, of course, is the question you ask of whether or not there ought to be some kind of official sanction, if you will, of the relationship, or if these relationships should be treated the same way a conventional marriage is. That's a tougher problem. That's not a slam dunk. I think the fact of the matter, of course, is that matter is regulated by the states. I think the different states are likely to come to different conclusions and that's appropriate. I don't think there should necessarily be federal policy in this area.*

I concluded by saying, "I think we ought to do everything we can to tolerate and accommodate whatever kind of relationships people want to enter into." Of course, I had my daughter Mary and her partner, Heather Poe, in my mind, but I was also thinking about what's right for all of us as Americans if we truly believe in freedom.

After Joe and I gave our closing statements, we received a sustained ovation from the audience. I think the applause was for all three of us at the table, an expression of appreciation for the caliber of our discussion and the tone of our debate. As soon as Bernie wrapped the show, Joe leaned over to me and said he was surprised at how quickly the evening had gone. I was, too, and pulled up my sleeve to show him that I hadn't worn a watch. It had been a conscious decision, because I didn't want to be tempted to glance at it.

Lynne, Liz and Phil, Mary, granddaughter Kate, and my sister, Susan, all came up onstage as soon as the debate was done. Al and Ann Simpson were also there, along with our dear friends Dan and Gayle Cook from Dallas, John and Mary Kay Turner, and Dick and Maggie Scarlett from Jackson, and many others. There were lots of hugs all around. After a stop at a very enthusiastic victory rally where I was able to thank everyone who'd worked so hard on all the debate arrangements, we spent the rest of the evening eating takeout pizza, watching reruns of the debate, and enjoying the postdebate analysis—much of which suggested I'd won.

In the next three weeks, we hit most battleground states numerous times and even made it out to California for a bus tour the last weekend of the campaign. I campaigned with an Elvis impersonator in Reno, acquired a purple inflatable space alien in Roswell, New Mexico, and completely lost my train of thought in Green Bay, Wisconsin, when I looked out into the audience and saw Mary standing in the staff section wearing a large foam-rubber cheese head. I grew used to life on a campaign plane, though it did have its trials, and the ride hadn't been without some bumps. Our campaign plane had oozed blue gunk from the latrines all over the luggage hold, been grounded in Maine when Austin forgot to pay the monthly lease, and been the site of more than a few apple and orange bowling contests as well as at least one competition that involved staff members sliding down the aisles on food trays during takeoff.

One characteristic of life aboard a chartered campaign plane is that no one pays much attention to the rules about buckling seat belts and stowing carry-on luggage. Lynne particularly appreciated this since her own campaign-issued cell phone was usually missing. Whenever we came in for a landing cell phones would slip out of purses and bags and it wasn't unusual for one or two to wind up at our feet at the front of the plane. Lynne got used to picking up whichever phone was there and using it for the day. It worked for her, but caused real confusion among campaign staff, who thought they were calling the press secretary or the luggage advance guy and instead got Lynne on the phone.

In the final days of the campaign, with the race uncomfortably close, time became our most precious commodity, and all our attention was concentrated on blanketing the battleground states. We no longer had the luxury of driving from an airport to an event, and by late October nearly every event was a massive airport rally. These were great theater, directed and staged to achieve the maximum impact with each audience. The plane would land and taxi in slowly to a stop right in front of the hangar. Sometimes the advance team would have it timed so the hangar doors would open on cue, and we would walk from the plane into the hangar with the theme from *Rocky* or something equally triumphant blasting over the huge speakers. We did a lot of these events in a lot of different places. In order to avoid the obvious disaster, a staff member was assigned to tape a piece of paper just inside the airplane door, so as I disembarked I would see "Portland, Oregon" or "Everett, Washington" or "Las Vegas, Nevada" and know for sure where we had landed and where I could say I was so glad to be.

Even though the polls were still neck and neck, as the campaign entered the final stretch, I was feeling good about things. I sensed that we had the momentum. Then on Thursday, November 2, five days before the election, we were at a rally in Chicago when we learned a story was breaking that in Maine in 1976, Bush had been cited for driving under the influence. I didn't like the timing of this at all. It looked like the classic "October surprise"—a negative story timed for release at the last minute, when it can do the most damage possible.

I was sure that the news of the governor's DUI would bring up stories of my own DUIs from nearly forty years earlier, but that didn't happen because they had already been written about. They were old news. But this Bush story, even though it was twenty-four years old, was now completely new. The late revelation hurt us. Karl Rove has pointed out that before the story broke we led Gore 40–35 in Maine. One night later Gore was ahead of us 44–40. We ended up losing Maine by 5 percent.

ALTHOUGH THIS OCTOBER SURPRISE was unpleasant, I didn't think it would do us in, and we were in good spirits as we landed at home in Jackson Hole late on the evening of Monday, November 6. We walked through the frigid cold into an airport hangar full of the warmth of friends and family for a final rally. Then we headed home where, too exhausted to sleep, Lynne and I popped popcorn with our granddaughters.

Election Day dawned crisp, clear, and cold. It was one of those late fall mountain mornings I love. We drove the short distance from our house to the Wilson Fire Station to cast our votes. The traveling press corps was there, as was our friend David Kennerly, President Ford's photographer. David always managed to appear at historic moments in our lives, and this certainly was one.

At the fire station Lynne and I stood in line to vote, and I held my granddaughter Kate's hand as the election worker handed me my paper ballot and directed me to the voting booth nearest one of the exits to cast my vote. Photographers and cameramen had been allowed to crowd into the exit doorway, and I could hear the whirring and click-ing of their cameras as I marked the space for George Bush and Dick Cheney on my ballot.

We went directly from the fire station to the airport. Just before boarding the campaign plane for what—one way or the other—was going to be the last time, we took lots of pictures of family and staff on the tarmac. The photos show happy, exhausted folks in front of the plane emblazoned with the big blue Bush-Cheney letters on the side, and in the background the most beautiful mountains in the world, the Grand Tetons.

To help occupy the time on the flight to Austin, some of the staff organized a pool for people to guess what our total number of electoral votes would be. Two hundred and seventy are needed to win and everyone laughed when Liz's sister-in-law, Kristienne Perry, took the decidedly lowball number of 280. Liz and Mary teased her, telling her that she clearly didn't know much about politics if she thought we were going to get only 280 electoral votes.

While we were still in the air, we started to get the first exit poll results. Kathleen Shanahan brought them up to Lynne and me in the front of the plane. They were bad. We were up in Iowa, Missouri, West Virginia, and Wisconsin, but we were down by 3 percent in Florida and 4 percent in Michigan. And the list of states where we were tied was too long for comfort. "It's going to be a long night," Kathleen said. We couldn't have guessed just how long.

As soon as we arrived in Austin, we went to Karl Rove's office at the campaign headquarters. It had a large wall of glass overlooking the hallway, and as we had our meeting, staffers stared in as they walked by, no doubt trying to assess our mood, anxious for any clue as to whether this was going to be a night to celebrate. In fact, we didn't know much more than they did.

Based on the way things seemed to be breaking, Karl said it looked likely to be a long night, but he sketched out the path he saw that could move us to the neighborhood of three hundred electoral votes. Needless to say, Kristienne won the pool and was closer to right than most of the experts.

Lynne and I had invited friends and family to join us at the Four Seasons Hotel to watch the early election returns, before we all headed to the big celebration that had been planned at the state capitol, about a mile away. At six o'clock, when the first results started coming in from the east, it became clear just how close the vote was going to be. Lynne and I left our suite and went downstairs to the big party in the hotel ballroom. Despite the evening's uncertainty, we were buoyed by the love and warmth of our friends.

When we got back upstairs about an hour later, we told Mary,

Heather, Phil, and Liz that they really needed to go down to the party. They said they weren't in a party mood. The networks had already called Florida for Gore, a surprising and irresponsible decision, given that the polling places in the heavily Republican western panhandle of the state hadn't even closed yet. But we exercised our parental prerogative and strongly encouraged the kids to go downstairs. There was nothing they could do except sit in the suite, and all the friends in the ballroom would be so happy to see them. They took our advice, headed downstairs, and were surrounded by hundreds of cheering friends and family a short while later, when the large-screen TVs in the ballroom flashed the news that the networks had reversed the Florida call and returned the Sunshine State to the toss-up column.

With us in our suite that night were our dear friends Al and Ann Simpson, Nick and Kitty Brady, Don and Joyce Rumsfeld, Jim and Susan Baker, Bush-Cheney campaign chairman Don Evans, and Andy and Kathleene Card. A photo from the evening shows Jim Baker sitting next to me with Al Simpson and the Rumsfelds looking over our shoulders. We're all studying the tally that I was keeping on a yellow legal pad. I had clipped an electoral map out of the newspaper that morning and was using it to keep track of which states we needed to win to make it to 270.

It looked to me as if it was indeed going to be a very long night, so about 12:45 a.m. I decided to go into the bedroom to take a nap. I had been asleep only a few minutes when Liz woke me up. "Dad," she said, "you just got elected vice president. The president-elect wants to talk to you." That got my attention. The networks had now called Florida for George Bush, and at 1:30 a.m. Austin time, Al Gore had called Bush to concede. Liz handed me the phone, and Governor Bush got on the line. He told me about Gore's call and suggested that I bring the family over to the Governor's Mansion so we could ride together to the victory celebration at the state capitol, where a large crowd had been standing outside for hours.

As we prepared to leave to join the Bushes, Don Evans was on his cell phone talking to Gore's campaign manager, Bill Daley. "Gore's in talking to his family," he reported. "They are taking it hard, and he's asked us to give him a little while with them before he makes his concession speech." Of course we understood, and we headed over to the Governor's Mansion thinking we would watch Gore's concession speech there.

We left the hotel through the kitchen as we nearly always did when the Secret Service was with us. As we walked through, surrounded by our family, Lynne looked at me and said, "What's wrong? You don't seem as happy as you should be." She read me well. I couldn't say why, exactly, but I thought we were celebrating too soon. "This just doesn't feel right," I told her.

I put those thoughts aside as we walked into the family celebration that was already under way at the Governor's Mansion. President George H. W. Bush and Barbara were there along with Florida Governor Jeb Bush. Al and Ann Simpson had come with us from the hotel. We all crowded around a tiny, antiquated television in the sitting room on the first floor of the ornate old mansion and watched footage of empty stages in Austin and Nashville, where Gore's campaign headquarters was located. The networks were all marking time until Gore made his concession official so that Bush could then make his victory speech. But then there was another phone call for the governor. It was Al Gore, calling to retract his concession.

As the Bush margin in Florida grew smaller and smaller, everyone started looking to Jeb Bush for answers and hope. He was in the corner of the room with my chief of staff, Kathleen Shanahan, huddled over a computer screen. They were logged on to the Florida secretary of state's website trying to follow the vote count directly as it was posted. When the governor of Texas walked into the room looking for information, his brother, the governor of Florida, whispered to Kathleen, "Just don't make eye contact with him," hoping to avoid a barrage of questions he couldn't yet answer.

Everybody was angry and frustrated with Gore. Who *retracts* a concession? In 1976 the election had also been very close, and we had decided to sleep on it and see how things looked in the morning before making any decision about conceding to Carter. I thought that if the

Gore campaign had been any kind of a professional operation, they would have realized how close the vote was and wouldn't have conceded in the first place. But to concede and then take it back was amateur hour. And the fact of the concession hurt Gore, I believe, as we headed into the recount.

It was clear that nothing more was going to be decided that night, but we had a large crowd of supporters still standing in the rain at the state capitol. Don Evans went over to thank them and tell them to go home for the night. The rest of us went to bed.

"NOW WHAT?" MARY ASKED. It was late Wednesday morning in our suite at the Four Seasons, and she addressed her question to the good-sized group that we had assembled: Scooter Libby, Dave Addington, Rob Portman, Paul Wolfowitz, Terry O'Donnell, Steve Hadley, Kathleen Shanahan, and Michael Boskin, a Stanford economist who had been chairman of the Council of Economic Advisers for President George H. W. Bush. Someone had ordered sandwiches, but the plate sat largely untouched on the round table at one end of the room, along-side a book I'd been given, *Hemingway on Fishing*. Enthusiastic as I am about the sport, fishing was about the furthest thing from my mind at that point.

Our sense was that the Gore campaign would not draw things out for too much longer. We anticipated a quick concession. Our hopes were dashed the next day when Gore campaign chairman Bill Daley and former Secretary of State Warren Christopher gave a press conference in Tallahassee. The Gore campaign had sent Christopher to Florida to oversee their recount effort, in much the same way that we had sent former secretary of state Jim Baker. Both sides realized they needed someone with gravitas who didn't appear too partisan or political as the public face of efforts in Florida. But we also knew that we were in a real fight and that we needed seasoned and savvy managers. I was willing to match Jim Baker against Warren Christopher or just about anybody else, any day of the week. He was clearly the best man for this job.

Standing in front of a room full of reporters, Bill Daley announced that the Gore campaign would be requesting hand recounts of the ballots in Palm Beach, Miami-Dade, Volusia, and Broward counties—all solidly Democratic areas. Daley also noted that the Gore campaign was unlikely to stop there and was "still collecting other irregularities." One member of the team watching the press conference with us piped up from the back of the room that the Daley family had been "collecting irregularities" in Chicago for decades. The Gore team was clearly going to do everything they could to overturn the results of election night. We were in for a fight.

It became clear that we were entering on a long course with no predictable end in sight. Although I was confident that we would ultimately prevail, I was concerned about the potential negative impact on our administration of a shortened transition period. Whatever else happened, the forty-third president of the United States was going to be inaugurated at noon on the steps of the U.S. Capitol on Saturday, January 20, 2001. So in the hotel room on the afternoon of November 9, I reached for the nearest piece of paper—which happened to be a Bush-Cheney press release on the situation in Palm Beach County—and flipped it over and began listing what needed to be done in the seventy-one days between now and then. In that time we had to name a cabinet of the highest-caliber individuals we could find. We needed a secretary of state to advise on foreign affairs, a secretary of the Treasury who could oversee the nation's economy, and a secretary of defense who could be entrusted with the nation's security. Along with the attorney general, these are the most prominent cabinet positions, but we also had literally thousands of other jobs to fill, many requiring FBI background checks, financial disclosure, and Senate confirmation. I had personally participated in five previous transitions, and I knew how tough it could be even in the best of circumstances to get everything done in such a short amount of time. We had won the vote in Florida and had therefore won the Electoral College. Although Gore might be trying to overturn the outcome at the ballot box through a series of court challenges, we needed to get moving with preparing to govern.

On November 17 it became clear that the recount was going to drag on much longer than anyone had anticipated. That day the Florida Supreme Court ordered Florida secretary of state Katherine Harris not to certify the election results until it heard arguments about whether the results of the Gore-requested hand recounts must be included in the final certification. There was nothing more we could do in Texas, so, after ten days in Austin, Lynne and I left for Washington.

On Sunday, November 19, Joe Lieberman appeared on *Meet the Press* and I was reminded why I had such respect for him. Despite the fact that the Gore campaign was working hard to disqualify many of the absentee ballots cast by members of the U.S. military stationed overseas, he said he felt that was wrong. He said each campaign should do everything possible to ensure that ballots cast by members of America's armed forces were counted.

A few days later the Florida Supreme Court essentially changed the rules of the election after the election was over by extending the deadline for the completion of the hand recount to November 26. Several hours after we got news of the decision, I awoke in the middle of the night with an uncomfortable sensation in my chest. It wasn't really pain, but I knew it wasn't right. I woke Lynne up and told her we needed to go to the hospital to get it checked out. The trip from our home in McLean to George Washington University Hospital, seven blocks from the White House, took less than fifteen minutes in a speeding black limo driven by the Secret Service down the deserted George Washington Parkway.

At the hospital doctors ran a series of blood tests to determine if my cardiac enzymes were elevated, which is a standard way of checking for a heart attack. The first tests showed no increase in the enzyme level; in other words, no indication that I'd had a heart attack. We passed this information along to campaign headquarters in Austin sometime before I went in for a cardiac catheterization, a procedure that was recommended based on my history and the fact that I had experienced chest discomfort. Dr. Jonathan Reiner inserted a stent made of stainless steel mesh in an artery that was 90 to 95 percent blocked.

When I came back from the procedure about noon, I learned

that a second set of blood tests showed an increase in enzyme levels. It was minimal, such a small elevation that it wouldn't have been detected a few years previously when tests were less sensitive. Nevertheless, the release of enzymes meant I had suffered some heart damage. I'd had a small heart attack, information I was absorbing at the same time that President-elect Bush, operating on earlier information, was telling the press that I hadn't had a heart attack, that "Dick Cheney is healthy."

We notified the Bush camp and told them that doctors would soon be holding a press conference to talk about the second test results. In that briefing, the slightly elevated enzyme levels were the focus, and since in the medical world elevated enzymes are synonymous with *heart attack*, Dr. Alan Wasserman, who held the press conference, didn't use that phrase. Karen Hughes, watching from down in Texas, called to warn us that the press would now be absolutely convinced that the Bush-Cheney campaign was engaged in a cover-up. She told us that the doctors had to go back out and say the words *heart attack*. At my family's urging, the George Washington medical team held a second press conference, using the phrase *heart attack* and explaining that the heart damage I had suffered was minimal. "This would be the smallest possible heart attack that a person can have and still have it classified as a heart attack," Dr. Reiner said. But some members of the press remained suspicious that we were hiding some grave news about my condition. I knew that wasn't true—and I decided not to worry about it. My job was to recuperate.

As a family we did face another immediate challenge: Thanksgiving dinner. I'd be in the hospital Thanksgiving Day, which wouldn't have been such a big deal had I not been the one who always cooked the family's Thanksgiving dinner. No one was in the mood to eat hospital cafeteria food, so we started trying to figure out how to have a traditional feast. Mary, my usual backup cook, was in Colorado, so Liz volunteered. Knowing she was short on experience when it came to turkeys, I wrote out instructions for preparing a Thanksgiving dinner on the back of some recount talking points. They were very clear and complete, beginning with "First, remove plastic wrap from outside of turkey. Second, remove bag of giblets from inside turkey."

We were all relieved when Liz called later to say that Alma Powell, Colin's wife, had offered to cook an entire Thanksgiving dinner for our family. When Liz went to pick up the dinner on Thursday afternoon, she looked around the Powells' kitchen and realized that Alma had, in fact, cooked two entire turkey dinners—one for us and one for her own family. She had probably been up most of the night to get it all done. It was one of the kindest gestures we could imagine and one we'll never forget.

Kathleen Shanahan and some of her friends contributed more food for the occasion, and we were able to enjoy a wonderful, if unique, family Thanksgiving with plenty of turkey to share with the Secret Service agents who were stuck spending the holiday with us in the hospital.

A few days later I was back at home when Katherine Harris finally certified George Bush and me as the winners of the Florida recount. My six-year-old granddaughter, Kate, had fallen asleep on the red couch in our TV room. After the announcement, Lynne whispered in her ear, "Katie, wake up. Grandpa just got elected vice president of the United States." Kate rolled over and gave voice to what many Americans were undoubtedly thinking at that point. "What?" she said. "Again?"

The U.S. Supreme Court had already agreed to hear our challenge to the Florida Supreme Court's decision allowing the hand-recounted ballots. But now that we had been certified as the winners in Florida, our campaign had a major decision to make. We knew that the Gore challenge would continue, but we had to consider whether pushing this to the U.S. Supreme Court now constituted a risk for us. What would happen if they ruled against us? Would that put us in a worse position than we currently occupied, having been certified the winner? Jim Baker and his team in Tallahassee put together a memo laying out the pros and cons of moving ahead, and we had several conference calls going over the possibilities. George Bush listened to the arguments and then made the decision that we would press ahead with the case.

After the certification Governor Bush also announced that I would be chairing the Bush-Cheney transition. For the last several days, we had been operating a skeleton transition from the kitchen table of our home in McLean. Most of the time we had to stand on the back porch to get decent cell phone reception. All of the phones in our house were cordless, and we worried about eavesdropping, so for the most sensitive conversations, Lynne dug an old "princess" style phone out of the attic. This relic from Liz's and Mary's high school days was placed in the middle of the kitchen table. Lynne also found an old bulletin board in the attic, and we leaned it up against the kitchen wall so people could tack up messages.

I scheduled a press conference for November 27, the day after the certification. In my brief, I explained where things stood. I said that even though the Gore team was still contesting the outcome and the General Services Administration was not yet providing us with the transition office space or funds normally available to the president-elect, we felt that we had an obligation to move forward with the business of getting ready to govern. "The transition affects the quality of planning, the building of relationships between the administration and the Congress, the capacity of a new administration to develop and execute a legislative program, and even the ability of the new team to deal with that first crisis when it arises, as it inevitably will," I noted. Every day that we waited to begin the transition was another valuable day lost, and so, I announced, we were setting up a foundation to accept private contributions so that we could begin transition operations.

I also reiterated a point that had been made in the last twenty-four hours by Governor Bush and by Jim Baker:

Governor Bush and I have prevailed at each step of the election process in Florida. Now we have been officially certified, in accordance with the laws of the state of Florida, the winners of the state's twenty-five electoral votes. Every vote in Florida has been counted, every vote in Florida has been recounted. Some have been counted three times. Vice President Gore and Senator Lieberman are appar-

*ently still unwilling to accept the outcome. That's unfortunate in
light of the penalty that may have to be paid at some future date if
the next administration is not allowed to prepare to take the reins of
government.*

*We find ourselves in a unique and totally unprecedented posi-
tion. Never before in American history has a presidential candidate
gone to court to try to change the outcome of an already certified
presidential election. But whatever the vice president's decision, it
does not change our obligation to prepare to govern the nation.*

With that, we began a period of seven weeks of intense work to fill the
most important positions in the U.S. government.

It was important that the American people know that we were preparing to govern, so we arranged regular press briefings to report on
our progress. At first these briefings were held in hotel ballrooms in
downtown D.C., but as soon as we rented office space in McLean for
our transition headquarters, eager volunteers moved heaven and earth
to transform it into a place we could hold such events. I was most impressed when an energetic young advance man gave me a tour of an
area that had been miraculously transformed in twenty-four hours
from an empty space into a professional briefing room with yards and
yards of blue fabric, a stage, a podium, and rows of chairs. I listened as
he explained that the next step would be knocking down a wall so we
could have direct access to the stage without having to walk through the
room. I put the kibosh on that idea. I didn't think we'd want to explain
to the landlord that we needed to knock down walls in what was supposed to be temporary office space. But I was impressed with this young
man's creativity and energy.

On the night of December 12, Liz and Phil were at their house in
McLean, Mary and Lynne were both upstairs fighting the flu, and I
was sitting alone in the kitchen watching the news when there was a
bulletin that the Supreme Court's decision in *Bush v. Gore* was about to
be handed down. The doorbell rang, and I found David Kennerly and
Mike Greene standing on my front porch. David had been having din-

ner with Mike, the AP photographer who covered me throughout the campaign, at a nearby restaurant. When they heard the Supreme Court decision would be announced, they rushed over to my house, figuring photos of me hearing the news—either way—would be historic.

When copies of the decision were made available, television producers grabbed them and sprinted down the steps of the Court building to get the decision into the hands of their on-air reporters. I surfed the channels trying to find a reporter I could trust to be able to skim what might be a very complicated legal document and to report its meaning accurately. When I saw Pete Williams of NBC on the screen, I stopped surfing. I knew that if anyone could analyze the Court's ruling quickly, it would be Pete. And he didn't disappoint. We'd won the case, and we'd won the election. It was time for them to go.

I picked up the phone and called Jim Baker. "Hello, Mr. Vice President–elect," he said. "Thank you, Jim," I said, "and congratulations to you. You did a hell of a job. Only under your leadership could we have gone from a lead of eighteen hundred votes to a lead of one hundred fifty votes." He laughed heartily. He knew and I knew that his leadership in Florida had been vital.

I hung up and looked around. I really was going to be vice president. And the only people there to celebrate the moment with me were David Kennerly and Mike Greene. Pretty soon Liz and Phil showed up with a bottle of champagne. It wasn't the victory party I'd imagined, but it was sweet nonetheless.

The next night we gathered old friends, family, and transition staff at the Sheraton hotel near transition headquarters. As we sat watching Al Gore's concession speech, a small press pool came in to shoot footage. Shortly after they departed, my three-year-old granddaughter, Elizabeth, strolled in dressed in a red and white dress, holding a sippy cup in one chubby hand and a cookie in the other. She stopped in front of the TV and announced loudly, but to no one in particular, "That's Al Gore. We don't like Al Gore." I can't imagine where she picked that up, but I was glad she'd kept her opinion to herself while the press corps was in the room.

As soon as the Supreme Court ruled, the GSA called. They were prepared, they said, to turn over the keys to the official transition space. It
was slightly anticlimactic when, at a press briefing on December 14, the
deputy GSA administrator and I posed for photographers as he finally
handed me a plastic key card on a neck lanyard that would guarantee
my access to the official transition office.

On the day after the Supreme Court's decision was handed down,
five moderate Republican senators—Arlen Specter, Susan Collins, Jim
Jeffords, Olympia Snowe, and Lincoln Chafee—invited me to lunch in
the Capitol. They wanted to talk about how the new Bush administration planned to govern. We had run and been elected on a conservative
agenda of tax cuts, education reform, and a strong national defense.
Since our margin had been historically narrow, my luncheon hosts assumed we would be trimming our sails, moving to the center, and looking for areas of compromise. I suspect they thought that would put
them in a very powerful position. I also suspect that they were surprised
when I made clear that we didn't plan to alter our agenda at all. We
had won, and we would deliver on our campaign promises. We weren't
looking for a fight, but we certainly didn't plan to capitulate preemptively, either.

A few days later we made our first cabinet announcement. I flew
with Colin Powell, the secretary of state-designate, to the Bush ranch
in Crawford. George Bush, General Powell, and I went together to the
local school gym for the announcement. I was proud of the Powell pick
and glad he had agreed to join us. We had worked together well during
my time in the Pentagon, and I was looking forward to the chance to
work with him again.

I introduced George Bush to another old friend when Paul O'Neill
joined us for lunch at the Madison hotel in downtown Washington.
Paul and I had worked together in the Ford administration when Paul
was deputy director of OMB, and now we were considering him to
be secretary of the Treasury. He knew more about the budget and the
budget process than just about anybody else and was one of the most
capable and competent people I'd ever worked with. After a stint in

government, Paul went into the private sector, and we'd crossed paths when I was at Halliburton and he was chairman of Alcoa. He also came highly recommended by former Secretary of State George Shultz and by Federal Reserve Chairman Alan Greenspan. I was key in recruiting Paul to take the job, and I would be the one to call him two years later when the president decided to make a change.

The other top job, of course, was secretary of defense. The president-elect and I interviewed several top candidates. The interviews covered general topics and discussion, but we also asked specific questions—how would you handle a crisis in Taiwan, for example. We had a number of excellent candidates to choose from, but Don Rumsfeld outperformed the others in his interview. Having had the job before and having clearly spent time thinking about what should be done to transform the military into a modern fighting force, he was very impressive in our small meeting. Don would become both the youngest and the oldest man ever to be secretary of defense, and his competence, intelligence, and dedication would serve him and the president well.

We had discussions about bringing in a new director of central intelligence, but decided to leave George Tenet in place. In 1977 Jimmy Carter had replaced George H. W. Bush as CIA director, and I've always assumed that Bush 41 disagreed with that decision, not because it affected him personally, but because he believed that the position should be nonpartisan and shouldn't shift when the presidency changes hands. I imagine that this experience informed President Bush 43's decision to leave George Tenet in place.

We wanted to make sure our cabinet was bipartisan, and we reached out to former Wyoming Governor Mike Sullivan, a Democrat, to see if he would be interested in serving as secretary of interior. Mike had a good record as governor and knew the range of issues the department dealt with very well. When I called to gauge his interest, however, he seemed less than enthusiastic. I don't know if he didn't want to serve in a Republican administration, or perhaps he just wasn't prepared to leave Wyoming and move to Washington. Whatever the reason, we ended up selecting Gale Norton, who was the attorney general of Colorado. She became the first woman to serve as the interior secretary, and she did a terrific job for us at Interior.

One Democrat who served in the cabinet with great distinction was Transportation Secretary Norm Mineta. On September 11, Norm sat with me in the Presidential Emergency Operations Center under the White House and supervised the unprecedented operation of bringing every single commercial airliner out of the sky.

Governor Bush and I had our first intelligence briefings together as president-elect and vice president–elect on December 18 and our first meeting with the Joint Chiefs of Staff in the Pentagon Tank on January 10. I also spent a good deal of time during the transition on Capitol Hill. I would be the only person in the Bush 43 West Wing initially who had previously been a member of Congress, and I enjoyed the chance to renew old friendships. In addition, I knew that we would need good relations on the Hill. As vice president, my constitutional duties—in addition to being prepared to take over should something happen to the president—included breaking tie votes in the U.S. Senate. And the U.S. Senate was split fifty-fifty, so this duty was likely to be more than theoretical.

As the transition drew to a close, I felt very good about all we had accomplished and the team we had put together. I couldn't have imagined then the trials and challenges we would face together or the relationships that would be strained—some to the breaking point—during the eight years ahead.

———◄◦►———

CHAPTER TEN

Angler

The first draft I saw of inaugural events listed "A Tribute to Vice President–Elect Cheney." Having people say nice things about me for an hour or two sounded pretty good, but I had a better idea—to honor America's veterans. On January 19 we gathered together men and women who had served in World War II, Korea, Vietnam, and Desert Storm in the Smith Center at George Washington University, and among those we saluted were nearly a hundred Medal of Honor recipients. One of them, Nicholas Oresko, had single-handedly taken out a German machine-gun bunker during the Battle of the Bulge, and then, despite being wounded, had charged ahead and wiped out a second bunker. He had attended every inauguration since Eisenhower's, I read later. "They've all been wonderful," he said. "But today was one of the greatest because the president and the vice president and the secretary of defense all came by and shook our hands." It was my honor to shake the hands of men like Nicholas Oresko.

The next morning a twelve-car motorcade lined up in the narrow street in front of our McLean town house. Our neighbors came outside to wish us luck and wave goodbye as we pulled away at 8:50 a.m., headed for St. John's Church, across Lafayette Park from the White House. According to protocol, Lynne and I and our family sat in the front pew to the left in the small, historic Episcopal church. President-elect George Bush, Laura, and their daughters were to the right. We sang and prayed and listened to a sermon given by the Reverend Mark Craig, pastor of the Bushes' church in Texas. When the service ended, we climbed back into the motorcade for the two-minute drive to the White House, where we were scheduled to have coffee with the outgoing president and vice president. But instead of pulling away from the curb, our motorcade idled in front of the church. Then it idled some more. We were doing the Inauguration Day equivalent of circling an airport in a holding pattern.

I leaned forward in the limo to ask Tony Zotto, my lead Secret Service agent, what was going on. "President Clinton isn't ready, sir," he said. I knew that President Clinton had a habit of running late, but it was hard to imagine he'd be tardy on this of all days. The clock was ticking, and whether he was ready or not, he would no longer be president in about two hours.

We finally arrived at the White House, and the Bushes, Clintons, Gores, and Cheneys made small talk as we sipped our coffee in the Blue Room. Lynne and I spent time visiting with Hillary Clinton, who had recently been sworn in as the junior senator from New York, and we were both impressed with Chelsea Clinton, who was particularly gracious and warm.

At 10:45 a.m. our motorcade left the White House for the Capitol. As we began the drive up Pennsylvania Avenue, I thought back thirty-two years to September 1968, when I'd traveled nearly the same route on foot my first day on the job as a congressional fellow. And now, here I was, riding up Pennsylvania Avenue in a long black limousine about to be sworn in as the forty-sixth vice president of the United States.

Al Gore rode with me to the Capitol, and he seemed relaxed and in good humor. Looking at his watch, he explained that we'd been kept waiting because President Clinton was signing last-minute pardons. He smiled and wondered aloud, "How many more do you think he can get signed before noon?"

Our motorcade pulled under the portico on the east front of the Capitol. I met Lynne, who had been riding with Tipper Gore, and we walked down the hallway together to room S-106, where we would wait until it was time to walk to the inaugural platform. Our movements at the Capitol were tightly scripted. The schedule for the morning reads, "11:18: Mrs. Cheney and Mrs. Bush announced at Platform Door; 11:20: Vice President–Elect departs Hold Room en route Platform. 11:25: Vice President–Elect is announced at Platform Door."

It is hard to describe the emotion I felt as the announcer said, "Ladies and gentlemen, the Vice President–Elect, Richard Bruce Cheney." I thought of my parents, neither of whom lived to see this day. My mother, who was the family archivist, had documented every important family event for years, taking photos and carefully pasting news clippings into the family scrapbooks. If she had been on the platform, she would have had her camera, and I knew how proud she would have been. My father was a man of few words and a lifelong Democrat, until he switched parties to vote for me in my first Republican congressional primary. He would have taken immense pride—and probably enjoyed a chuckle of disbelief—at seeing his son sworn in as Vice President of the United States.

Four brown leather armchairs were arranged in a semicircle near the podium for George Bush, Bill Clinton, Al Gore, and me. The morning was cold and drizzly, and we had space heaters at our feet. Lynne, Laura Bush, and the Bush girls were seated directly behind us. Mary and Liz were two rows back, seated with Laura Bush's mother, Jenna Welch, and the president's parents, Barbara Bush and President George H. W. Bush.

The family Bible we had chosen for the occasion belonged to my grandfather, Thomas Herbert Cheney, who had signed the first page in pencil, "T. H. Cheney, Sumner, Nebraska 1895." It was a very large Victorian Bible, the kind you could imagine a mother or father reading from as the whole family gathered around a fireplace together. It was so large, in fact, that when Barbara Bush saw Liz holding it on her lap before the ceremony, she said, "Boy, you guys are serious about this, aren't you?"

Shortly before noon I joined Chief Justice William Rehnquist at the podium, raised my right hand, placed my left hand on the Bible, and surrounded by my wife and daughters, became the vice president. It was an emotional moment for all of us, made even more so by the battle of the thirty-seven-day recount. I saw the tears in my daughters' eyes and felt my own emotions well up. We'd been through an election like no other, but here we were. And here was America, once more showing the world the way we peacefully transfer power.

AFTER AN INAUGURAL LUNCH in the Capitol, Lynne and I rode in the inaugural parade down Pennsylvania Avenue, then got out of the car and walked the last few blocks to the White House. Still in our winter coats, we visited my new office in the West Wing. It had been stripped bare. The furniture was gone, the carpets had been pulled up, and the walls were getting a fresh coat of paint. By the next day it would be ready for me to move in. Twenty-four years earlier, on January 20, 1977, I had walked through the West Wing hours before power transferred to a new president. It was nice to be back, on the incoming team this time. My new office stood next door to the one I'd occupied as President Ford's chief of staff when I was just thirty-four. Now I was nearly sixty, and as a helpful staffer pointed out, the oldest guy in the West Wing.

On my sixtieth birthday my family threw a surprise party for me in the vice president's ceremonial office, a beautiful space in the Old Executive Office Building. Each new vice president learns that there is a special drawer in the desk in this office. Pull it open, and under a sheet of Plexiglas you'll find the signatures of every vice president since Harry Truman. On top of this desk, on January 30, 2001, my family unrolled my birthday gift, a hand-painted map showing the battles my great-grandfather Samuel Fletcher Cheney had participated in during the Civil War. For the eight years of my vice presidency, this map would hang behind my desk, surrounded by the American flag, my vice presidential and secretary of defense flags, and the flag of the state of Wyoming.

IN ADDITION TO BEING the oldest guy in the West Wing, I was also the only one the president couldn't fire. As vice president, having been elected and sworn in, I carried my own duties as a constitutional officer. There were only two of them: succeeding the president if he was unable to complete his term and serving as president of the Senate, where I got to cast tie-breaking votes. Beyond that, my role depended on George W. Bush. I had no line responsibility. I wasn't technically in charge of anything. I could only give advice. And the impact of my advice depended first and foremost on my relationship with the president. At the end of the day, it wouldn't have mattered how many years of experience I had or how many other offices I'd held, if the president wasn't interested in what I had to say.

From day one George Bush made clear he wanted me to help govern. He had given a tremendous amount of thought, time, and attention to the issue of what his vice president would do. To the extent that this created a unique arrangement in our history, with a vice president playing a significant role in the key policy issues of the day, it was George Bush's arrangement. For all the eight years we served together, he kept his word that I would have a major role, and I will always be grateful to him for that.

As I think back on what made the relationship work, several things come to mind. First, I made clear early on that I would not be running for president myself in four or eight years. The president never had to worry that I was taking a position with an eye toward how it might be perceived by voters in Iowa or New Hampshire. I also decided to limit my exposure to the press. When I'd been White House chief of staff and secretary of defense, I'd spent a fair amount of time backgrounding reporters and granting interviews, but as vice president I wanted a much lower profile. Members of the press were most often interested in what advice I had given the president on a particular issue, and he needed to know that I wasn't walking out the door of the Oval Office to brief reporters on what I'd just said.

In addition, from the transition onward, there were media stories that I was somehow in charge. They weren't true, and stepping out too much too publicly would only have fed them. I did do a number of memorable and important press interviews, including one with Tim Russert on the Sunday after 9/11, but I was generally much less accessible to the press than I had been in the past. I soon discovered that this was not a strategy for enhancing my image or reputation. For one thing, it limited my response to false charges made against me. But I decided then and believe now that the best way for me to serve the president and the country was to do so without briefing the media every step of the way.

When trouble develops between a president and vice president, it often begins with staff conflict. To avoid that, we decided to integrate our staffs in key areas. Mary Matalin, my communications director, wore two hats. She served as my assistant and as an assistant to the president. This was also true in national security, where Scooter Libby carried both titles. In legal matters, my general counsel, David Addington, worked closely with the lawyers in the White House counsel's office every day. My speechwriter, John McConnell, was also one of the president's top speechwriters. Staff meetings and the policy processes were very well integrated. There were disagreements, of course, but the system worked pretty well most of the time.

SHORTLY AFTER I WAS elected, the Speaker of the House, Denny Hastert, and soon-to-be chairman of the Ways and Means Committee, Bill Thomas, asked to see me. Bill was an old friend and colleague. We'd both been political scientists before being elected in 1978, and now he was about to head one of the most powerful committees in Congress. It was a position that carried with it the rights to some of the best space in the Capitol. Bill and Denny told me that they knew I had an office on the Senate side of the Capitol, but they considered me a man of the House and wanted me to have an office on the House side as well. Bill gave me two offices to choose from, and I picked H-208, just off the House floor. During most of my ten years in Congress, it had been Danny Rostenkowski's office, and I had never seen the inside of it. Now, the space was mine.

To my knowledge, no vice president before or since has had an office on the House side of the Capitol, and I used it for meetings with House members when we were working on key pieces of legislation. I also hosted buffet dinners there before presidential addresses to Congress, including the annual State of the Union. The tight security surrounding a presidential address means that most people who sit in the chamber have to arrive hours before the speech. Lynne and I invited the cabinet and Republican congressional leadership to join us for dinner on these occasions, then shortly before the speech was to start, they could file in to take their seats in the House chamber. This tradition ended in 2006 when the Democrats regained control of the House and Charlie Rangel became the new chairman of the Ways and Means Committee. He reclaimed the office—as I'd expected he would.

Beginning the first Tuesday I was in office, January 23, 2001, I was invited to attend the weekly Senate Republican policy lunch on the Hill, and throughout my eight years as vice president, I tried to make it to this lunch whenever I was in town. I was grateful for the senators' hospitality since as an institution the Senate does not always take kindly to vice presidents, who have a foot in the executive branch as well as in the legislative. When Lyndon Johnson was about to become vice president, he laid out a plan to preside over Democratic caucus meetings in the Senate that infuriated many of his colleagues. "I don't know of any right for a vice president to preside or even be here with senators," one of them declared. In the end, Johnson did not preside—or even attend very often. Harry Reid made it clear that my successor, Senator Joe Biden, would not be welcome—which is too bad. I found these sessions to be important for building relationships and alliances and for getting things done.

I seldom spoke at the caucus lunches, though occasionally, if there was a particularly important issue on the agenda or if I'd been asked by the Republican Senate leadership, I would say a few words. For the most part, I preferred to listen, not to lobby for administration positions. I wanted the Republican senators to view me as an ally in the West Wing—and to continue to invite me to their weekly sessions.

The relationships I had in both houses of Congress meant I was often the first person in the White House to hear if there was a problem. I'd get a call from Speaker Denny Hastert or Senate Majority Leader Trent Lott, for example, giving me a heads-up if a piece of legislation was going off the rails. It was a very effective way, most of the time, to make sure the White House and Republicans on the Hill were on the same page.

Much has been written about my advocacy of a strong executive, and it is true that I am a firm believer in protecting the president's prerogatives, especially when it comes to the conduct of national security policy. But I loved my time in Congress, and I will always consider myself a man of the House. My respect for that institution and my understanding of how Congress works, including the pressures that individual members feel, was important as I worked to get George Bush's legislative agenda enacted.

We needed every Republican vote as the 107th Congress opened in January 2001. Not only had we just triumphed in one of the closest presidential races in history, but the Senate was deadlocked with fifty Republicans and fifty Democrats. My tie-breaking vote as vice president gave the Republicans the majority. Trent Lott, the majority leader, and Tom Daschle, the minority leader, worked out an arrangement for evenly dividing up seats on committees, but each committee was chaired by a Republican.

SECURING TAX RELIEF WAS one of our most important campaign promises, and we proposed reform across the board for what would become the largest tax cut since 1981. It was our belief that taxes ought to be as low as possible, especially when it came to those elements of the tax code that affected savings and investment, economic growth, and job creation. We wanted to reduce rates on capital gains and interest and dividends, as well as lowering overall income tax rates for the American people. We believed, as do most conservatives, that the estate tax should be eliminated or significantly reduced. We saw it as fundamentally unfair, because it represents double taxation for those who have to pay it.

Because there was a significant budget surplus, there was bipartisan support for a tax cut of some size, but the Democrats, particularly in the Senate, wanted a much smaller package than we did. On April 3, 2001, I cast my first tie-breaking vote and stopped a Democratic effort to reduce the size of the tax cuts. On April 5, my tie-breaking vote returned money to the tax cut package for relief of the marriage penalty. I also took part in the negotiations with Senate Republicans and Democrats over the ultimate size of the package. Sitting in Trent Lott's office on April 4, I picked up a napkin imprinted with "Office of the Majority Leader," took out my pen, and wrote out the two numbers representing what we wanted—$1.6 trillion—and what the Democrats wanted—$1.25 trillion. In between the two numbers, I wrote, "1.425 trillion," and I circled it. Ultimately, we would be successful in securing a package of $1.35 trillion in tax relief for the American people. The package included a phased-in reduction of the estate tax, with elimination in 2010. All the tax changes were passed as part of the budget reconciliation process, which exempted them from filibuster, but also provided an expiration date.

As the tax cuts were set to expire in 2010, they were, fortunately, extended for two more years. Although the estate tax was reinstated by President Obama, the current law allows for a five-million-dollar exemption, more than seven times the exemption allowed before President Bush acted.

In the midst of the debate over tax cuts, it looked as though the Republicans might lose their one-vote majority. As we debated the budget resolution throughout the spring of 2001, Senator Jim Jeffords of Vermont made clear that he wanted significantly increased funding for special education programs. Although we were increasing the education budget, we weren't allocating the funds the way Jim wanted, and he threatened to switch parties, which would put the Democrats in control in the Senate.

I know Jim cared deeply about the education program he was proposing, and even though he ended up switching parties, he kept his commitment to us to vote for the final tax cut package. In the end, I think his decision to switch had more to do with the committee chairmanship that Tom Daschle offered him than with anything else. In the Senate committee chairmanships are normally decided purely on seniority—the longest-serving member of the majority party on any committee traditionally becomes the chairman. But it was so important for the Democrats to get Jeffords to switch, Tom Daschle moved him to the head of the line and made him chairman of the Environment and Public Works Committee. With his party shift, every chair of every Senate committee also shifted hands as the Democrats took control.

We worked hard to prevent Jim from switching, and certainly weren't pleased when we failed. But as I look back now, I believe that Jeffords's switch actually contributed to our victory in the 2002 midterm elections. He put the Democrats in control, but their margin was so narrow there was very little they could actually get done. Their inability to show any real accomplishment hurt them and helped us when the voters went to the polls a little over a year later. The president's poll numbers were also high, near 70 percent, and when the midterm results were in, we had increased our majority in the House by eight seats and gained two in the Senate, thus returning that body to Republican control. The last time a president's party had gained seats in both houses of Congress in the first midterm election of his term was when FDR was in office in 1934.

IN 2003 THE PRESIDENT proposed a second major round of tax cuts, and I again spent a good deal of time securing the votes we needed to get them passed. Even though we had enlarged our majority in the House and taken control of the Senate, the task wasn't easy. While all Republicans favored a tax cut, there were a few who didn't want to go with the $550 billion the president was proposing. They were worried about the deficit, a concern I generally appreciated. I have been quoted as saying around this time that "deficits don't matter" and citing Ronald that since Senator Grassley had already staked out a position, he should not be appointed to the conference. There was silence as the group on the balcony calculated the number of improprieties Hastert had just committed. There was, first of all, the House telling the Senate what to do and added to that was the insult of anyone daring to propose that the Senate finance chairman be denied a seat on a tax bill conference. And, then, of course, Senate Finance Chairman Grassley was sitting right there.

I knew that Hastert was doing more than just sending a shot across the bow. He'd phoned in the last couple of days to tell me that House members were saying they wouldn't go to conference with Grassley. They were thinking about sending a bill with a higher number back to the Senate and telling the senators to take it or leave it.

Bill Frist had also called me. Senators were getting their backs up at the idea the House was trying to "jam" them, he said, and personal animosities were running high. Could I step in and help broker a deal?

I was happy to do it. I certainly understood the institutional rivalries at work, and I knew the people involved well. Finance Chairman Grassley and House Ways and Means Chairman Bill Thomas were barely speaking. There was a report that a meeting between them grew so heated that Thomas stomped out of his own office. I liked and admired both men. Chuck is a down-to-earth and decent man who still works his Iowa farm. I remember at least once calling him and reaching him on his cell phone while he was out driving his tractor. He has a stubborn streak, but it has served him and his constituents pretty well over the years. Thomas, who's from Bakersfield, California, loves to legislate, and he brings a very sharp mind to the task. An ex-academic like me, he is famously prickly, but we had known each other since we had both been elected to the House nearly a quarter century before and enjoyed each other's company.

I went to visit Bill in his Ways and Means Committee office on the afternoon of May 21, 2003, and we spent some time reminiscing. We agreed that nobody would have believed it back in 1979 when we were freshman members of Congress that the two of us would be sitting here

Reagan to bolster the case, but of course I thought deficits m
just believed that it was important to see them in context, to
while Ronald Reagan's dramatic increases in the defense budge
historic tax cuts did push the deficit from 2.7 percent of the
mestic product in fiscal year 1980 to 6 percent in fiscal year 1
spending on defense helped put the Soviet Union out of busi
his tax cuts helped spur one of the longest sustained waves of p
in our history. The result was a peace dividend, increased fed
enues, and, eventually, lower deficits.

In 2003, with the deficit just 1.5 percent of the GDP and t
omy in the doldrums, the tax package the president proposed
seemed justified to me, but Senators Olympia Snowe of Ma
George Voinovich of Ohio thought it was too large. Chuck
needing their votes on a budget resolution, agreed to a cap of $
lion on the tax package, a deal to which Majority Leader Bill F
his blessing.

But no one told the House leadership, and they were tho
irritated when the deal became public. House passage of a $55(
tax cut on May 9 did nothing to ease their aggravation, becau
a conference between the House and Senate was looming. Ho
you have a conference, House leaders wanted to know, when on
leading conferees, Senator Grassley, had already announced a lin

The president invited all the players for a drink on the Trum
cony on May 19, 2003. Speaker of the House Denny Hastert
of those who enjoyed the fine view from the balcony that ever
were House Ways and Means Chairman Bill Thomas, Senate M
Leader Bill Frist, and Senate Finance Chairman Chuck Grassl
president talked about his tax cut plan, which would speed up
ductions scheduled for coming years and eliminate the individ
on dividends. The point of it was to promote economic growth,
wanted to get it in place fast, by Memorial Day at the latest.

Denny Hastert, one of the most even-tempered, easygoing m
ever known, then spoke up—and his exasperation with his Sena
leagues was pretty obvious. He recommended to Majority Leade

in 2003, he the chairman of Ways and Means, one of the most powerful positions on the Hill, and I the vice president. Then Bill walked me through where the House was on the tax bill, including the fact that there was great interest in seeing a cut in capital gains included in the final bill. The president's proposal was to eliminate the individual tax on dividends, but Bill didn't think that would fly.

The House had grudgingly come down in its number to a cut of $350 billion and had a tentative deal on that with the Senate, but the bill also included outlays for state assistance and child-credit refunds, which Chuck Grassley thought he needed to get the conference bill through the Senate. That ran the top number up to $382 billion, setting off Senator Voinovich, who decided that the spirit of the $350 billion cap had been violated. I got him to come over to the Ways and Means Committee office, and after what the *Washington Post* correctly called "a tense meeting," there was a deal: tax cuts of $320 billion and reduction of the capital gains tax as well as the individual tax on dividends to 15 percent. That left room for the sweeteners the Senate needed and the whole thing still came in under the $350 billion limit.

I went over to the Senate to get sign-off from Chairman Grassley and Majority Leader Frist and helped work out a few other details that day and the next. By the time I took my seat as president of the Senate on May 23, I felt I had earned my keep. And when I cast the tie-breaking vote to ensure the bill's passage, I was sure I had. On May 28 President Bush signed into law the Jobs and Growth Tax Relief Reconciliation Act of 2003.

The Bush-era tax cuts helped grow the economy and create jobs, and I was glad to see them extended in December 2010 for two more years. If the Obama administration had reversed course and let tax rates rise across the board, the results would have been devastating.

DURING MY FIRST WEEKS as vice president I had another obligation to fulfill. The previous October, as the campaign was winding down, our whole family was out on the road full-time. After one late-night rally, my six-year-old granddaughter, Kate, climbed into the seat next to me on the campaign plane. "Grandpa," she said, "if you win, will you come to school as my show-and-tell?" "You only want me if I win?" I asked. "Yep," she answered. I had to admire the kid's frankness, so we struck a deal, and on a snowy February morning, I was Kate's show-and-tell. My impression was that most of her fellow first graders were more interested in my Secret Service agents than in Kate's old grandpa, but I'll never forget the huge smile on her face as I walked into the classroom.

I SOON SETTLED INTO an early morning routine that varied little during my eight years in office. Around 6:30 a.m. my CIA briefer would arrive with my copy of the President's Daily Brief, or PDB, which contains reports on the most critical intelligence issues of the day. We met in the library on the first floor of the Vice President's Residence, and while I read through the briefing book, the briefer waited, ready to answer questions and to take the book back when I had finished. Scooter Libby, my chief of staff, often joined me for these sessions. Most days, after I received and read through my own copy of the PDB, I would join the president for his briefing. If I was traveling or at an undisclosed location, the president would often be briefed in the White House Situation Room, so I could join by secure videoconference.

During my years as vice president, I had some absolutely first-rate briefers. When a new briefer was assigned to me, we would sit together and go over a list of issues I was particularly interested in following. As a result, my copy of the PDB quickly expanded to two sections. The first section was identical to the president's copy. The second section— "behind the tab," we called it—contained responses to questions I'd asked or items my briefers knew I was interested in. Some mornings I would pull material from my section behind the tab and tell my briefer I thought the president needed to see it. Other times I would raise questions in the session with the president based on items I'd seen behind the tab. On at least one occasion, I asked to have material reinserted in the President's Daily Brief after others on the national security staff decided that he didn't need to see it. In my experience, intelligence was an absolutely crucial element for those in policymaking positions, and if the briefers thought it should be in the PDB, it should go in.

I had spent time on intelligence issues throughout my career, beginning when I was Ford's chief of staff, then when I served on the House Intelligence Committee, and, of course, as secretary of defense. But when I became vice president, I had been away from it for eight years, and I felt it was important to get up to speed. Early on in the administration, I visited various parts of the intelligence community, such as the CIA, the Defense Intelligence Agency, the National Security Agency, and the National Reconnaissance Office. I thought it showed respect to go see people on their turf, and I could meet more of them by visiting an intelligence agency in person.

ONE OF THE CHALLENGES we faced immediately on taking office was the energy crisis in California. The state was experiencing brownouts because it lacked the generating capacity to meet power needs. Over the previous ten years, California's economy had grown 34 percent, and not a single new power plant had been built. Heavy environmental regulations, in particular, discouraged new construction. The state had also, over the years, imposed price caps, so that utility companies facing a significant increase in the price of electricity were unable to pass this cost on to the consumers.

Alan Greenspan, my old friend, who was now the chairman of the Federal Reserve, had been warning us about the looming California crisis since before the inauguration. Now he advised that since California accounted for close to 15 percent of the U.S. economy, the energy shortages there could lead to a nationwide recession. We put in place some short-term emergency orders that required out-of-state utilities to sell their surpluses to California, but we also knew we needed to address the larger problem of our nation's overall energy policy. There would be no overnight fix. Energy shortages are often years in the making, the result of shortsighted solutions too often geared toward a political calendar. We needed to change that.

On January 29, 2001, President Bush announced that he had asked me to chair a task force on the nation's energy situation. In a little more than three months—lightning speed by government standards—we released "Reliable, Affordable, and Environmentally Sound Energy for America's Future," a report that made recommendations to "modernize conservation, modernize our energy infrastructure, increase energy supplies, accelerate the protection and improvement of our environment, and increase our nation's energy security." The report is one I am very proud of. I commend it to anyone looking to understand America's energy challenges still today. The report had its critics, but I've long suspected them of not reading it. They certainly seem to have missed chapters 3 and 4 on the importance of protecting the environment and improving conservation.

The environmental groups that criticized the report are all too often, in my experience, opposed to any increase in the production of conventional sources of energy. They don't want to drill anyplace. They don't want to mine coal anyplace. They seem to believe that we can depend on alternative sources of energy, such as solar or wind. It's my view—and it's the view reflected in the report—that while we should develop alternative sources, in the final analysis, we can't effectively address our energy problems in the near term nor can we remain competitive in the global economy unless we also produce more energy from conventional, domestic sources.

Right now, none of the alternative sources of energy can compete economically with petroleum and coal and other conventional sources. It's also the case that time and again we have found that developing alternative sources has undesirable, unanticipated consequences. The push for ethanol fuel produced from corn, for example, resulted in driving the price of a bushel of corn up significantly. This had a huge impact on people who used corn for purposes other than fuel—purposes that weren't subsidized. Cattlemen, for example, were suddenly faced with significantly higher feed prices. We also saw deforestation in places such as Malaysia as farmers cut down trees in order to plant crops that would bring higher prices during the biofuels craze.

Those who are opposed to producing more energy here at home

sometimes point to conservation as an alternative. As the energy report made clear, conservation is important, but it is nowhere near sufficient to address our energy challenges. In a speech in Toronto in April 2001, I made this point:

> *Now, conservation is an important part of the total effort. But to speak exclusively of conservation is to duck the tough issues. Conservation may be a sign of personal virtue, but it is not a sufficient basis all by itself for sound, comprehensive energy policy. We also have to produce more.*

Critics jumped on this statement, and without ever fully quoting what I'd said, alleged that I was ignoring the importance of conservation. As I look back on the statement now, ten years later, I stand by it 100 percent.

Although all of the formal members of our energy task force were government officials, we sought advice from thousands of outsiders, and it wasn't long after the report was released that several groups, including the Sierra Club and Judicial Watch, filed suit demanding we release the lists of everyone we met with during the course of our work. Democrat Henry Waxman, the ranking member of the Committee on Oversight and Government Reform, also began demanding the lists. Then the General Accounting Office got involved and demanded the lists. We said no, not because we had anything to hide. Every recommendation we made was publicly available, as was the legislation we put forward based on the report. But I believed, and the president backed me up, that we had the right to consult with whomever we chose—and no obligation to tell the press or Congress or anybody else whom we were talking to. If citizens who come to the White House to offer advice have to worry about lawsuits or being called before congressional committees, it would pretty severely curtail the counsel a president and vice president could receive.

There were plenty of people, including some in the White House, who thought we should just turn over the lists. Since there were no nefarious secrets hidden in them, they argued, all we were doing was creating a real political headache for ourselves by refusing to give them up. But I believed something larger was at stake: the power of the presidency and the ability of the president and vice president to carry out their constitutional duties.

We eventually prevailed—on the Hill when the GAO dropped their efforts to get the names and in the United States Supreme Court when the justices ruled 7 to 2 in our favor, remanding the case back to the district court. It was a major victory both for us and for the power of the executive branch. President Bush deserves tremendous credit for standing by me when a lot of people wanted us to take the easy way out. As for the energy report itself, while a number of its recommendations were eventually adopted either through legislation or executive order, our opponents continued to block a more comprehensive approach to the nation's energy challenges.

IN EARLY MAY, A few weeks before we unveiled our national energy policy, President Bush announced another initiative he had asked me to undertake. It concerned our responses to the possibility of weapons of mass destruction—chemical, biological, or nuclear weapons—being used in an attack against our homeland. While we worked to deny such weapons to our enemies, we also needed to be prepared, as the president said, "to defend against the harm they can inflict."

The problem of proliferation of weapons of mass destruction and the possibility that terrorists could acquire such devastating weapons had been a particular concern of mine for some time. The Defense Planning Guidance I issued as secretary of defense in 1992 listed the need to prevent such proliferation as a key objective of the United States. In April 2001, when Nick Lemann of the *New Yorker* magazine asked me about the nature of the threat facing the United States, I said,

> *I think we have to be more concerned than we ever have about so-called homeland defense, the vulnerability of our system to different kinds of attacks. Some of it homegrown, like Oklahoma City.*

Some inspired by terrorists external to the United States—the World Trade Towers bombing, in New York. The threat of a terrorist attack against the U.S., eventually, potentially, with weapons of mass destruction—bugs or gas, biological, or chemical agents, potentially even, someday, nuclear weapons.

Then Lemann asked me what we could do to reduce those threats. I answered, "You need to have very robust intelligence capability if you're going to uncover threats to the U.S., and hopefully thwart them before they can be launched." Intelligence, I said, is our "first line of defense."

When we took office there were numerous federal agencies charged with addressing the consequences of an attack against the United States with weapons of mass destruction. The president asked that I oversee an effort that would study the current system as well as the recommendations made by a number of task forces that had already looked at the issue and suggest ways we could improve our responses.

Members of my staff, including Scooter Libby, retired Admiral Steve Abbot, and Carol Kuntz, who'd been on my Pentagon staff, went to work reviewing studies that had already been completed on this topic. Within a couple of months, they presented me a report that recommended several key steps we could take to improve U.S. preparedness and response to a WMD attack. The list included crafting and implementing a national strategy for preparedness and response; improving the intelligence warning of a WMD attack; clarifying lines of federal authority for counterterrorism and emergency response between FEMA and law enforcement; integrating local, state, and federal emergency response agencies; and improving bioterrorism detection and the public health system's ability to respond to such an attack. The work of my staff on these issues fed directly into efforts we would undertake in the aftermath of 9/11, such as establishing a Department of Homeland Security to coordinate all homeland defense for the nation.

FROM MY TIME IN Congress participating in continuity-of-government exercises, I knew how important it was to ensure we had a plan in place for leadership succession and survival. We had a duty to make sure an enemy attack could not result in decapitation of our government. I asked my general counsel, Dave Addington, to review the formal procedures in place. What happens, for example, if the president becomes ill or is incapacitated? What happens if the vice president can no longer perform his duties? Who should be notified and what steps should be taken to ensure the government can continue to operate in the wake of a national disaster or act of war? These were matters that Addington and I had worked on together before, and we both knew they needed to be addressed before a crisis was at hand. Early in 2001, I asked him to work closely with the White House counsel's office to provide advice and guidance as our administration began its own review.

A few weeks later, David came to see me with a problem he had uncovered. "Mr. Vice President," he said, sitting in the chair next to my desk in my West Wing office, "if you were to become incapacitated, if you were unable to discharge your duties, there is no mechanism by which you could be removed." And there was a second level of complication, he explained, which had to do with the Twenty-Fifth Amendment to the United States Constitution. It provides that "whenever the vice president and a majority of either the principal officers of the executive departments or of such other body as Congress may by law provide, transmit to the president pro tempore of the Senate and the Speaker of the House of Representatives their written declaration that the president is unable to discharge the powers or duties of his office, the vice president shall immediately assume the powers and duties of the office as acting president." A vice president is required in order to carry out the Twenty-Fifth Amendment, in other words, and if I were incapacitated, I might stand in the way of the removal of a president unable to discharge his duties—or I might become an incapacitated acting president. Neither of these was a good outcome for the country.

As David and I were discussing succession, I was mindful of my health. I had a long history of coronary artery disease, and although the doctors had concluded that I was strong enough to serve as vice president, I couldn't discount the possibility of a stroke or another serious heart attack that would leave me unable to function. The example of Woodrow Wilson came to mind. He had suffered a stroke that incapacitated him for the last year and a half of his presidency.

What was needed was a way to remove me from office should I be unable to fulfill my duties, and so I took the extraordinary step of writing a letter of resignation as vice president shortly after I was sworn in. The resignation letter would be effective, as provided by federal law, upon its delivery to the secretary of state. As I signed the letter, I thought about adding instructions concerning when it should be delivered. After all, this was my formal, signed resignation, and it seemed natural that I should set forth the circumstances under which it could be delivered. Addington advised otherwise. He was concerned that any additional notations I made on the letter would muddy the waters should it ever have to be used.

Instead, I took out a piece of my official stationery with the words "The Vice President" written across the top. I wrote the date—March 28, 2001—and then this:

Dave Addington—You are to present the attached document to President George W. Bush if the need ever arises.

—Richard B. Cheney

"Okay, David," I said, looking over the top of my glasses. "I won't give specific instructions about when this letter should be triggered." I pointed at him, still holding the pen I'd used to sign the letter. "But you need to understand something. This is not your decision to make. This is not Lynne's decision to make. The only thing you are to do, if I become incapacitated, is get this letter out and give it to the president. It's his decision, and his alone, whether he delivers it to the secretary of state." "Yes, sir, Mr. Vice President," David said.

I did not want a situation where, should I become incapacitated and there was an effort to remove me from office, my family or my staff stood in the way. The only one who had the right to make that decision was the president of the United States. And he was the only person other than Addington with whom I discussed the letter. I thought it was important that he be aware of it.

Addington double-wrapped the letter in two manila U.S. government envelopes, took it home, and put it in his dresser drawer. He had made a conscious decision not to keep it in his safe at work because he didn't want to find himself unable to get to it in the event the worst did happen and the White House was in crisis mode. When a fire destroyed his home a few years later, David grabbed two things after he got his family out of the house—the folder with his family's financial documents and birth certificates in it and the envelope containing my letter of resignation.

ONE OF THE MOST enduring decisions a president makes is choosing a nominee for the Supreme Court. With lifetime appointments, Supreme Court justices can impact American life long after the president who nominates them is gone from office. The first time I observed a Supreme Court nomination from up close was when President Gerald Ford selected John Paul Stevens, who served on the court for thirty-five years. He is a fine man and a well-regarded jurist, but his record on the court was consistently liberal. The same thing was true of Justice David Souter, appointed by George H. W. Bush. He is a man whom I respect, but he was a predictably liberal vote on the Court.

As we took office we did not know whether there would be a vacancy on the Court during our term, but President Bush wanted to be prepared. He wanted to begin a process to review potential candidates, and I convened a group that included Attorney General John Ashcroft; White House Counsel Alberto Gonzales; Chief of Staff Andy Card; my chief of staff, Scooter Libby; and the president's counselor Karl Rove. When Al Gonzales became attorney general, Harriet Miers joined the group as White House counsel. Gonzales and Miers took the lead in preparing large briefing binders with information about potential candidates that included their experience, their records, how they had ruled on important cases, and how they were viewed by their fellow judges.

We cast our net widely, beginning with appellate court judges, then looking at some district court judges, as well as a small number of state court judges and some lawyers who hadn't served on the bench before, but our focus was certainly on appellate court judges. Other factors such as age also entered into our recommendations. It would be better, all other things being equal, to go with someone in his or her fifties rather than sixties, simply because the younger candidate would be likely to serve longer on the Court.

When Justice Sandra Day O'Connor announced her retirement on July 1, 2005, we were able to move quickly to bring in some of the leading candidates we'd considered for interviews. We conducted these sessions at the Vice President's Residence and in the wardroom of the White House Mess. We covered a broad range of topics with each candidate, trying to learn as much as possible so that we could get a good idea of what kind of justice he or she would be. Track records were important because we believed these were the best indicators of how a judge would rule in the future.

After we'd interviewed the candidates, our group made recommendations to the president, and he conducted interviews with the leading contenders. The preparation we'd done enabled the president to name Judge John Roberts of the U.S. Court of Appeals for the D.C. Circuit less than three weeks after Justice O'Connor's retirement announcement.

While Roberts's nomination was working its way through the Senate, Chief Justice Rehnquist, who had been valiantly fighting cancer, passed away. The president decided to withdraw Roberts's nomination and renominate him to be chief justice. The president then needed to nominate a second individual to fill the O'Connor seat.

Diversity in hiring, both for women and minorities, was an issue about which George Bush cared deeply. He did not just talk the talk. I watched on many occasions as he told the White House personnel team that he wanted to see candidates who reflected the diversity of the nation, and he meant it. When it came time to fill the second Supreme Court slot, the fact that he was replacing the first woman ever to serve on the Court contributed to his commitment to identifying a qualified woman nominee. He decided the best candidate was someone he knew well, his White House counsel, Harriet Miers.

I have a good deal of admiration and respect for Miers. She is an excellent lawyer who served the president well as staff secretary and as White House counsel. She is talented, organized, competent, and no-nonsense. She is completely down-to-earth, something that is sometimes underappreciated in Washington, and she is a pleasure to work with. But she had not been on the list of candidates our group produced for the Supreme Court position.

In late September 2005, the president pulled me aside in the Oval Office to tell me about his decision on the second nominee. "You probably aren't going to agree with this, Dick," he said, "but I've decided to go with Harriet." "Well, Mr. President," I said, "that's going to be a tough sell." But it was his decision to make, and I set about trying to sell it.

Miers ran into trouble with liberals, as any nominee of the president was likely to, but she also ran into trouble with conservatives who felt very strongly that the president should name a justice with a proven track record of judicial conservatism. No matter how much we in the White House made the point that we knew Harriet was conservative, we were not able to convince a number of people on our side of the aisle.

The president later said he was sorry he had put his friend through such a meat grinder. Miers realized this was not a fight we were likely to win and asked that her name be withdrawn. A few days later, on October 31, 2005, President Bush nominated Judge Samuel Alito to the Court. He was confirmed the following January.

President Bush deserves real credit for both the quality of the process he put together to vet nominees and the caliber of the people he named to the Court—Justices John Roberts and Samuel Alito. Thinking back over my forty years in Washington, it is fair to say this was the best method of selecting Supreme Court nominees I'd ever seen.

THE ANTI-BALLISTIC MISSILE TREATY, signed by the United States and the Soviet Union in 1972, put limits on the research and deployment of missile defenses. The treaty was of advantage to the Soviets. They were a superpower because of their offensive capability, and the ABM Treaty prevented the kind of defensive development that could neutralize that advantage. We had been willing to sign the ABM Treaty because in the sometimes strange world of arms control, it was regarded as "stabilizing." The linchpin of Cold War arms control theory was mutually assured destruction, or MAD, meaning that neither the United States nor the Soviet Union would launch a first strike because each side knew they would suffer a devastating counterstrike if they did. A defensive capability played havoc with the idea of MAD. Both sides had to be vulnerable to attack in order for it to work.

After the fall of the Soviet Union and the end of the Cold War, America faced new threats. The number of nations with ballistic missile technology was growing and among them were rogue regimes willing to pass on and potentially use their capabilities. We had to be able to build systems that could intercept incoming missiles if we were to keep the country safe, but the ABM Treaty wouldn't permit us to do it.

I'd been an advocate for a long time of abrogating the ABM Treaty, which we had the right to do, but during the Bush administration's first months it became clear that the State Department had another view. There was concern that withdrawing from the treaty would put unnecessary strain on our relations with Russia, which led Secretary Powell to argue that we should stop short of abrogation and negotiate loopholes in the treaty for developing missile defenses. As I saw it, the State Department had it backward. Rather than compromising on policies that were in our national interest out of concern that we would offend other nations, we should do what served our security best, while undertaking diplomatic efforts to bring our allies and partners along.

President Bush had promised during the campaign to develop and deploy defenses against missiles, and he was good on his word. After lengthy consultations that included the Russians and our European allies, he called Vladimir Putin in December 2001 to formally give six months' notice of our intent to abrogate. All the dire warnings about an adverse Russian reaction turned out to be wrong. Putin accepted the president's decision and reassured him that any negative reaction in Russia would be manageable.

It was during discussions about the ABM Treaty in June 2001 that Presidents Bush and Putin met for the first time. After this meeting President Bush praised Putin and talked about looking into his eyes and getting a "sense of his soul." The president was criticized for the remark, but I think it reflected the hopes of the time that Putin would be a different kind of Russian leader, one who would put his nation on a path to greater freedom. I must say I was never too optimistic about Putin. When I looked into his eyes, I saw an old KGB hand. I didn't trust him and still don't, but then I'm not much given to trusting Russian or Soviet leaders.

President Bush's decision to abrogate the ABM Treaty was exactly the right thing to do. Today, we are faced with a nuclear-armed North Korea experimenting with intercontinental ballistic missiles, an Iran that is trying to acquire nuclear weapons, and a China that is increasing its capabilities. Thanks to George W. Bush—and to the excellent leadership of Secretary of Defense Don Rumsfeld—we have developed and deployed a number of interceptors. And we are safer for it.

AS I WAS SETTLING into the vice presidency, Lynne and I were also settling into the house that would be our home for the next eight years, the Vice President's Residence at the U.S. Naval Observatory. In warm weather, our grandkids swam in the pool, drove their battery-operated cars around the driveway, and roamed the grounds, stopping in to chat with the uniform division Secret Service agents at the guard posts. When it snowed, there were great sledding hills. Most weekends when we were in town, the grandkids would unroll their sleeping bags on the floor of our bedroom for sleepovers. We also shared our home with three wonderful Labs—Davie, who died and is buried there in the shade of a beautiful oak tree; Jackson, who came to live with us after 9/11; and Nelson, who was a bit of a misguided Mother's Day gift for Lynne, but who quickly won a special place in all our hearts.

The vice president's house was a great place to have guests, and we had many events there over our eight years. We had dinners with some of the world's leading experts on the Middle East, people such as Fouad Ajami and Bernard Lewis; parties to celebrate notable authors such as Nathaniel Philbrick, Jay Winik, Edmund Morris, and David McCullough; evenings with great thinkers and analysts such as Charles Krauthammer and Victor Davis Hanson. We had a special evening in June 2001 when we honored President Ford and Betty. He was to have been the first vice president to live in the house but became president before they could move in.

One of my proudest moments at the Vice President's Residence was January 30, 2008, when I managed to surprise Lynne with a party to celebrate the fiftieth anniversary of our first date. I remembered the date all on my own, though it is easy to remember because we went out for the first time on my seventeenth birthday. With help from Cece Boyer, Lynne's chief of staff; Liz Denny Haenle, the social secretary at the Vice President's Residence; Molly Owen Soper, Lynne's personal aide, and many others, I was able to sneak dozens of our friends from high school, along with singer Ronnie Milsap, who provided the evening's entertainment, into the observatory without Lynne guessing anything was up. It was a very special celebration.

Our lives at the observatory were as pleasant as they were largely because of the staff of U.S. Navy enlisted aides who work there. These terrific men and women are consummate professionals. Many of them became like family to us, and we will always be grateful for everything they did.

Lynne and I felt the same way about the Secret Service agents who protected us and our family for more than eight years. After 9/11, their responsibilities and hours increased dramatically. They lived through some pretty tense days with us, did an outstanding job of providing security, and managed kindness and good humor as well.

I am particularly grateful that they had the good sense to understand how important fishing is to me when they selected my Secret Service code name, "Angler." They also picked a great name for Lynne, "Author," and she certainly lived up to it. While I was vice president, she wrote six bestselling books on American history for children and their families and donated well over a million dollars in proceeds to charity.

DESPITE HAVING BEEN ELECTED in one of the closest elections in U.S. history, George Bush and I had major legislative accomplishments in those first months we were in office. The president's education program went into place, we cut taxes, and we proposed an energy policy for the nation. We also dealt with important foreign policy issues in China, Russia, and elsewhere around the globe. We had many achievements to our credit, but the big test of our administration was yet to come. Our time in office would be largely defined by the unprecedented attacks of September 11, 2001.

———◄◦►———

CHAPTER ELEVEN

A Nation at War

On the night of September 11, 2001, the Secret Service evacuated Lynne and me to Camp David, a secure location apart from the president, in case there were further attacks. On Wednesday morning, September 12, we flew back to Washington, now a wartime capital, so that I could attend a National Security Council meeting at 9:30 a.m. I took newspapers with me on the helicopter. The *Washington Post's* banner headlines read, "Terrorists Hijack 4 Airliners; 2 Destroy World Trade Center; 1 Hits Pentagon; 4th Crashes." The *Washington Times'* headline was a single word: "Infamy."

Although we had experienced the fog of war in the first few hours after the attacks, plenty of things were now clear: We had been attacked by a ruthless enemy willing to slaughter innocents in an effort to bring America to her knees. This enemy wasn't a traditional military force, but terrorists who found safe haven wherever they could and operated on a worldwide scale. They had struck us before, blowing a crater five stories deep in the World Trade Center in New York in 1993. Al Qaeda had attacked our embassies in Kenya and Tanzania in 1998, killing hundreds, including twelve Americans. Osama bin Laden, al Qaeda's leader, had personally chosen the operatives who bombed the U.S.S. *Cole* in a Yemeni harbor in 2000. Seventeen crew members had died. During the nineties, the United States had treated terrorist attacks primarily as law enforcement matters, indicting terrorists when we could, trying them, and sending some of them to prison. But that approach hadn't stopped the attacks. Al Qaeda had just delivered the most devastating blow to our homeland in its history.

We needed a new way forward, one based on the recognition that we were at war. We needed to go after the terrorists where they lived, rooting them out before they could attack. And we needed to hold those who gave them sanctuary and support responsible. As the president had said in his address to the nation on the night of September 11, "We will make no distinction between the terrorists who committed these acts and those who harbor them."

In this new kind of war, intelligence would be crucial. We had to find the terrorists so we could take down their networks. We had to stop others from supporting them. And we needed to place high priority on identifying networks and states that were trafficking in weapons of mass destruction so that we could shut down their efforts and prevent terrorists from acquiring those weapons. Terrible as 9/11 had been, the next attack, if it involved nuclear or biological weapons, would be exponentially worse.

In the morning meeting of the National Security Council, we discussed crisis management tasks, figuring out when commercial airline operations should begin again, when the military alert status would return to DefCon 4 from its current elevated level of DefCon 3. We agreed that combat air patrol flights would continue to fly over Washington and New York, and we discussed briefing Congress on the continuing threat.

The NSC meeting that afternoon concentrated more on our military response. The president was determined to use every tool of our national power to defeat the new kind of enemy we faced and to hold those who supported them responsible. I stressed the importance of going after state sponsors of terrorism. By holding them accountable for the acts of the terrorists, we would begin to deny terrorists safe haven and bases from which to operate—two elements they needed to plot, plan, and execute attacks.

We were confident that we would have help in the effort ahead. NATO announced that for the first time in its history, it was prepared to invoke Article V of the NATO Charter, which declares that an attack against one is an attack against all. Other nations would be with us as we responded to 9/11, but it was important, I said, that we not allow our mission to be determined by others. We had an obligation to do whatever it took to defend America, and we needed coalition partners who would sign on for that. The mission should define the coalition, not the other way around. The president made clear that he'd prefer to have allies with us, but we were at war, and if America had to stand alone, she would.

The next day, September 13, we were told that another attack on Washington, D.C., appeared imminent, and the Secret Service recommended that I go to Camp David. Thus Lynne and I missed the prayer service the next day at Washington National Cathedral and the president's eloquent words about grief and justice. Instead on Friday, September 14, we attended a small memorial service at Camp David's Evergreen Chapel. As light from an overcast sky came through the windows, we joined members of the military serving at Camp David in prayers for the lost and those who were suffering and for guidance in the way ahead.

Later that afternoon, members of the National Security Council began arriving at the camp for a series of meetings that the president had called. Don Rumsfeld, Colin Powell, Condi Rice, and I met for dinner that evening in Holly Lodge, which had been the main cabin at the presidential retreat for many years before the newer Laurel Lodge was built. Holly was the place where meetings were held the first time I had visited Camp David as a young Rumsfeld staffer in 1970. As the four of us gathered on the evening of September 14, we talked about the significant challenges ahead.

We were embarking on a fundamentally new policy. We were not simply going to go after the individuals or cells of terrorists responsible for 9/11. We were going to bring down their networks and go after the organizations, nations, and people who lent them support. In 2011 this is a familiar notion, but in 2001 it was all new, and as Rumsfeld, Powell, Rice, and I talked in Holly Lodge on that cool September night, we understood that this would be a long war. There would be no easy, quick victory followed by an enemy surrender. I thought it probable that this was a conflict in which our nation would be engaged for the rest of my lifetime.

WHEN THE NSC CONVENED the next morning, the subject was primarily Afghanistan, where al Qaeda's leadership had plotted the attacks on the United States and trained those who carried them out. Since 1996, Afghanistan had been under the control of the Taliban, who had imposed an extreme form of Islam on the country, closing schools for girls, forbidding music, and carrying out grisly executions. The Taliban had gotten the world's attention earlier in 2001 by blowing up two monumental sixth-century Buddhas at Bamiyan in central Afghanistan on the grounds that they were idols.

George Tenet described what the CIA could accomplish in Afghanistan with increased authority and expanded covert operations, working with the Northern Alliance, a group of fierce fighters opposed to the Taliban. Their leader, Ahmad Shah Massoud, had been assassinated by al Qaeda a few days before 9/11 in an effort to diminish the Northern Alliance's fighting capability.

Outgoing chairman of the Joint Chiefs, General Hugh Shelton, also spoke, laying out a military plan that was not yet fully formed. It gave the president three options: a series of cruise missile strikes, cruise missile strikes plus a bombing campaign, or cruise missile strikes, a bombing campaign, and American forces on the ground in Afghanistan. None of the options was good. It wasn't clear, for example, what mission the troops on the ground would have.

At around noon, the president declared a break for a few hours. I headed back to my cabin and asked the Camp David operator to connect me to Lyzbeth Glick, wife of Jeremy Glick, one of the heroes of United Flight 93. Glick, who had just turned thirty-one, had called his wife from the plane. He told her that hijackers had taken over the aircraft and already killed one passenger. Jeremy wasn't going down without a fight, and he hatched a plot with some of his fellow passengers to try to take the plane back. He spoke final words to his wife, told her to take care of their three-month-old daughter, and then said, "We're going to rush the hijackers." In the battle that followed, the brave passengers aboard Flight 93 gave their lives and saved the lives of so many others. The plane they were on might well have been intended by the hijackers to crash into the Capitol or the White House. Although nothing could provide comfort for her in these terrible days, I wanted Lyzbeth Glick to know that her husband's last act had been one of tremendous bravery and heroism, for which the nation was deeply grateful.

It was only later that we would learn fully of all the acts of heroism that took place on September 11, from the passengers on Flight 93, to the rescue workers who rushed into the burning World Trade Center, to the federal workers who pulled their colleagues out of the rubble of the Pentagon. Out of a day that caused many to wonder at the evil in the world came innumerable acts of goodness and selfless courage.

THE NATIONAL SECURITY COUNCIL convened again that afternoon, and the president went around the table, asking each of us for our thoughts on the road ahead. I spoke last. I stressed that preventing the next attack had to be our top priority. We had to make sure we were leaving no stone unturned in that effort. Improvements in visa procedures, border control, and immigration security were critical, and we had to think more broadly. We had to do everything we could to keep those who would harm us from arming themselves with weapons of mass destruction.

We also had to realize that defending the homeland would require going on the offense. Relying only on defense was insufficient. The terrorists had to break through our defenses only one time to have devastating consequences. We needed to go after them where they lived in order to prevent attacks before they were launched.

Although we had discussed Iraq earlier in the day, I also took time now to say that Afghanistan, where the 9/11 terrorists had trained and plotted, should be first. I believed it was important to deal with the threat Iraq posed, but not until we had an effective plan for taking down the Taliban and denying al Qaeda a safe haven in Afghanistan.

During my years as secretary of defense, I'd seen what our special operations forces were capable of. Paul Wolfowitz made the point that any use of American force in Afghanistan should take advantage of our special operators, and I joined him in urging that we use them extensively. They were a natural choice for rooting out the enemy in some of the harshest terrain in the world.

THE NEXT DAY, SUNDAY, September 16, I left Camp David before 9:00 a.m. for the short trip to Camp Greentop, a National Park Service facility not far from the presidential retreat. Tim Russert of NBC News was waiting in the dining hall to interview me for that morning's *Meet the Press*. I had done Russert's show a number of times over the years, but never under circumstances remotely approaching the ones that prevailed now. The nation was still reeling. People wanted to know how we were going to respond to the attacks and how we would prevent further ones. Nearly nine million viewers tuned in to *Meet the Press* that morning, more than ever before or since.

Tim asked me about the deliberations he knew had been under way at Camp David for the last thirty-six hours. The president had said publicly that Osama bin Laden was the prime suspect, and I talked about al Qaeda, the breadth of its reach, and other terrorist organizations, such as Egyptian Islamic Jihad, with which al Qaeda shared common ideologies. Tim wanted to know what options the president was considering for response. I couldn't talk about specifics, but I did note that nations such as Afghanistan should understand "that if you provide sanctuary to terrorists, you face the full wrath of the United States."

I emphasized how important intelligence would be in this new kind of war. We could not hope to learn about and prevent attacks, to disrupt networks, to defend the nation, without robust intelligence programs. I told Tim we would have to work "the dark side, if you will":

We've got to spend time in the shadows in the intelligence world. A lot of what needs to be done here will have to be done quietly, without any discussion, using sources and methods that are available to our intelligence agencies.

And, yes, I said, when Tim asked, this would mean working with some less than savory characters. Penetrating terrorist networks would require that. "If you're going to deal only with sort of officially approved, certified good guys, you're not going to find out what the bad guys are doing," I said. "We need to make certain we have not tied our hands."

My comments about the "dark side" have been used by critics over the years to suggest something sinister. I don't see it that way. Only five days earlier we had lost nearly three thousand Americans. It was true then and remains true today that defending this nation and preventing another attack require efforts that have to be kept secret and work that goes on in the shadows, sometimes with less than upstanding individuals, in order to save American lives.

Tim and I also talked that morning about the likely duration of the war. I told him that this would be a long-term struggle, one that would take years. We talked about the importance of vigilance and the power of this great nation to face this challenge and prevail.

Tim closed the interview with a remembrance of Father Mychal Judge, the chaplain of the New York City Fire Department. Father Mike was killed at the World Trade Center on 9/11 by falling debris as he administered last rites to a first responder. Tim told of the firefighters who carried Father Mike's body to their firehouse and who together with Father Mike's fellow Franciscans sang the prayer of St. Francis. "May the Lord bless and keep you and show his face to you and have mercy on you." "That," Tim said, "is the way of New York. That is the spirit of

America." The *Meet the Press* crew members stood and applauded at the interview's end.

ON TUESDAY, SEPTEMBER 18, the president signed a joint resolution that had been passed by Congress authorizing the use of military force "against those responsible for recent attacks launched against the United States." That Friday, I joined the president and Secretary Rumsfeld to discuss what that military force might look like. We met in the Treaty Room on the second floor of the White House residence, the same room where the president's father and I had met to discuss my becoming secretary of defense twelve years earlier. General Shelton, the outgoing chairman of the Joint Chiefs, and his successor, General Dick Myers, were both there, as was General Tommy Franks, the CENTCOM commander, and General Dell Dailey, commander of the U.S. Joint Special Operations Command, or JSOC. The Defense Department team had been working since our meetings at Camp David to improve their war plan, and they presented an innovative idea: linking our special operations forces with forces from the Afghan Northern Alliance in a way that would take maximum advantage of our communications and technological capabilities. Our forces would be able, fighting side by side with the Afghans, to call in air strikes on precise targets they'd located together. This approach would effectively utilize our precision-guided munitions. We'd hit the targets identified on the ground with deadly accuracy.

The president asked General Franks and General Dailey when they could begin to operate. They told the president they could go whenever he wanted, displaying an impressive can-do attitude. But I knew from my time at the Pentagon that various factors play into selecting an optimal start date. I also thought that sitting with the president in a room where Abraham Lincoln had held cabinet meetings might not be the situation most likely to elicit that kind of information, so I tried to help out. I knew, for example, that we have a tremendous advantage fighting at night. "Given our night-vision capabilities," I asked, "wouldn't it be better to go during a moonless period?" Yes, said General Dailey, "our advantage is always best when the nights are darkest. General Franks then explained the advantage he hoped to gain from putting special forces into Afghanistan simultaneously with the beginning of air operations. This would take more time, he explained. We couldn't begin within days as we could if we launched air attacks alone. It would be two weeks before special operations forces were staged in Uzbekistan, ready to enter Afghanistan, Franks said. In the immediate aftermath of 9/11, two weeks seemed a long time, but the president went with the best judgment of his military leaders.

THROUGHOUT MUCH OF THIS period, and for a good period of time thereafter, I was often in "undisclosed locations." I was surprised by the intensity of the media interest in this fact. I suppose it was partly the result of presidents and vice presidents never having operated on the assumption that being in the same place was a risk, and the fact that we did operate that way spoke to the concerns of the time. It also became a kind of game to imagine what my undisclosed locations were. One cartoonist imagined an abandoned missile silo, fitted out with a bed, a sink, and a line for my laundry. *Saturday Night Live* featured Darrell Hammond as me in a cave outside Kandahar, Afghanistan. In the skit, I declared myself a "one-man Afghani wrecking crew," then lifted up my shirt to show the audience my "bionic heart," which made me invisible to radar and brewed coffee—a pretty useful combination, I have to admit.

In fact, my undisclosed location was sometimes the Vice President's Residence—we just didn't tell anyone I was there. At other times, it was a city other than Washington where I had an event scheduled. Sometimes the staff and I would work from my home in Wyoming for extended periods. I stayed involved in policy deliberations while I was out of Washington by means of secure video teleconferencing, or SVTS, technology. I could set up a machine that looked like a very large laptop just about anyplace and be wired into meetings going on in the White House Situation Room or anywhere else around the world where the other participants had the same technology.

My most frequent undisclosed location was Camp David. Lynne and I spent many a day there, and sometimes children and grandchildren came, too. During a period of increased threat around Halloween 2001, our granddaughters brought their Halloween costumes, and my staff—Mary Matalin, David Addington, and Scooter Libby—handed out candy at their cabins, as did Lynne's assistant, Laura Chadwick, and the Secret Service agents manning the command posts.

From the beginning, we brought our dog Dave, a hundred-pound yellow Lab, to Camp David. He loved roaming the paths and the woods, and I quickly got used to taking him everywhere with me. One weekend when the president had scheduled a National Security Council meeting at Camp David, I drove with Dave in one of the Camp David golf carts over to Laurel for breakfast. I parked the golf cart, and Dave and I walked down the path toward the big wooden doors of Laurel. I had briefing materials for the day's meetings and the morning newspapers under one arm and opened the door with the other. No sooner had we walked inside than Dave caught sight of the president's dog, Barney, a Scottie, and set off in hot pursuit. I couldn't really blame him. Barney was only slightly larger than the squirrels Dave so much loved chasing, but we didn't want any permanent harm to happen here. I dropped my papers so I could get hold of Dave, who by now had rounded the corner into the dining room. I rounded the same corner to encounter some of the cabinet spouses who had also been invited to Camp David for the weekend. Joyce Rumsfeld, Alma Powell, and Stephanie Tenet, all seated for breakfast, were watching aghast as Dave bounded around the dining table after a furiously scurrying Barney. At about that moment the president appeared. "What's going on here?" he demanded. It was not an unreasonable question. I saw a tray of pastries on the breakfast buffet, grabbed one, and hollered, "Dave, treat!" He stopped in his tracks, then I grabbed him and took him back to Dogwood, the cabin in which Lynne and I were staying. I hadn't been there long when there was a knock at the door. It was the camp commander. "Mr. Vice President," he said, "your dog has been banned from Laurel."

———

THE ATTACKS OF 9/11 had a significant impact on the nation's economy. The airline, tourism, and insurance industries were all badly hit. The stock market remained closed for four trading days—the longest period of time since 1933—and then plunged nearly seven hundred points the first day it was reopened for trading. As we began to plan our response and think broadly about the War on Terror, I sought advice from Federal Reserve Chairman Alan Greenspan about the likely short- and long-term effects of the attacks. Alan came to the Vice President's Residence on Saturday, September 22, for one of the periodic discussions we would have throughout my vice presidency. He said that there was no way in an economy as complex as ours to predict accurately the overall impact of an event like 9/11. He talked about the "million equation model," a paradigm that takes into account the enormous number of factors that have economic impact. All of the million equations that make up our economy had received a huge shock, he said. Citing one example, he talked about the "just in time" inventory system. American manufacturers had moved away from maintaining huge parts inventories and relied instead on a first-rate transportation system, including the airlines, to get them parts when they needed them. The effect of the 9/11 attacks on the airline industry and the disruption in air travel had a big negative impact on this system. He urged that we get the airlines up and running as soon as possible. He also suggested that the government take over airline security, helping to reduce some of the airlines' costs and, even more important, giving passengers the confidence to fly again.

We knew Congress had been focused on what could be done to stimulate the economy in the wake of the attacks, and Alan told me the Senate Finance Committee had asked for a closed-door hearing with him and former Treasury Secretary Robert Rubin. Alan was concerned that Treasury Secretary Paul O'Neill hadn't been included. He asked me to call the ranking Republican on the Senate Finance Committee, Chuck Grassley, on O'Neill's behalf, which I did.

Finally, Alan said it would be important for him to have advance warning, if possible, of any military action. I thought back to Desert

Storm. There was only one person I'd briefed outside the national security team in the days before we commenced operations, and that was Greenspan. He had come to my office in the Pentagon, and I had told him about the timing and the nature of what we planned. Based on our years of friendship and work together, I had confidence that Alan would maintain the secrecy of our operation, and I believed that it was important that the chairman of the Federal Reserve, responsible for the health of the nation's financial institutions, not be surprised. I operated on the same basis now as we prepared to launch military operations in the aftermath of 9/11.

IN A SPEECH TO the nation on the afternoon of October 7, 2001, the president announced the beginning of Operation Enduring Freedom. "The United States military has begun strikes against al Qaeda terrorist training camps and military installations of the Taliban regime in Afghanistan," he said. CIA covert operations teams had already been dispatched to work with the Northern Alliance and other opposition forces. Special operations forces would soon be entering the country.

At an NSC meeting on October 9, George Tenet raised a concern about the Northern Alliance taking Kabul. The Pashtuns who controlled southern Afghanistan would not react well to being governed by tribes from the north, he said, and the result could be civil war. I thought that any argument for holding back the Northern Alliance was misguided. Our objective was to take out al Qaeda, take down the Taliban, and prevent Afghanistan from being used as a base for further operations. The way I saw it, we needed to get these things accomplished fast, before another attack on the homeland. And there was also the weather. After George finished his presentation, I spoke up. As soon as winter hits, I noted, the Northern Alliance is going to be socked in. We need to unleash them soon or accept that we'll have to wait until spring.

In my estimation, we needed to be encouraging the Northern Alliance to advance. "Are there Taliban targets we can hit that would make it easier for them to move?" I asked. Frankly, I thought Kabul couldn't fall soon enough, whether at the hands of the Northern Alliance or otherwise. It would be a visible sign of a new day in Afghanistan.

We were also very focused on getting Osama bin Laden. None of us believed that capturing or killing him would end the terrorist threat, but he was the leader of the organization that had launched the 9/11 attacks, and having him in custody—or dead—would be a powerful symbol of our determination. Tracking him down was certainly one of our top priorities. I was gratified that after years of diligent and dedicated work, our nation's intelligence community and our special operations forces were able on May 1, 2011, to find and kill bin Laden.

AT 1:10 P.M. ON October 18, 2001, Lynne and I boarded Air Force Two for the forty-five-minute flight to New York's LaGuardia Airport. It would be our first visit to the Ground Zero site of the 9/11 attacks. We had been airborne just a short time when Scooter Libby received a call on the plane. There had been an initial positive test result indicating a botulinum toxin attack on the White House. If the result was confirmed, it could mean the president and I, members of the White House staff, and probably scores of others who had simply been in the vicinity had been exposed to one of the most lethal substances known to man. A single gram of botulinum toxin, evenly dispersed and inhaled, can kill a million people. There is an antitoxin, but it does not reverse the paralysis that botulinum causes, although it does keep it from progressing further.

Biological weapons attacks on the homeland were not just the stuff of science fiction. The first attacks with anthrax mailed in letters had occurred just a month before. The most recent case—anthrax mailed to Senator Tom Daschle's office on Capitol Hill—had occurred three days earlier. Against that backdrop, the report of a positive hit for botulinum at the White House had to be taken seriously indeed. When we landed at LaGuardia at 1:55 p.m. to board helicopters headed to Ground Zero, I told Scooter Libby to stay on board the plane, keep working the phones, and get as much information as he could.

As our helicopters neared the southern tip of Manhattan, Ground

Zero came into sight. I felt the same sense of anger and sadness I'd felt on the night of 9/11 when I'd first seen the wreckage at the Pentagon. Viewed from the air, the devastation was staggering. My resolve needed no strengthening after what we had already lived through, but the destruction below made me hope the time for justice would be soon. As the helicopter banked away from Ground Zero, I caught a glimpse of the Statue of Liberty in the distance. On a day as brilliantly sunny as 9/11 had been, there she was, tall and proud in the harbor, a reminder of America's goodness and strength.

I met with Mayor Rudy Giuliani and Governor George Pataki for a briefing on the recovery efforts at Ground Zero, and then we visited the site on foot. A section of the steel frame at the bottom of one of the World Trade towers still stood, wrenched and charred, pointing toward the sky. In front of it, recovery workers from around the country were gathered. They spoke of coming back to the site day after day and working past the point of exhaustion. They spoke of their commitment to continue until the job was done. I walked down the line and thanked each one.

Scooter Libby was waiting for me back at the Waldorf-Astoria hotel, where I was scheduled to give the keynote address at the annual Alfred E. Smith Memorial Foundation dinner in a few hours. He told me there had been two positive hits for botulinum toxin on one of the White House sensors. Tests were being run, he said, and we would have those results by noon the next day.

I put on the white tie and tails required for the evening's speech while a connection to the president, who was in Shanghai, was set up. Then I sat down in front of my secure video screen and delivered the news to him and his traveling party. "Mr. President, we and many others may well have been exposed." In eighteen hours, when the tests came back, we would know.

I went downstairs to the dinner and with the possibility of the botulinum attack weighing on my mind, delivered my remarks. Each of the men and women in the room that night had been touched in some way by the attacks of September 11. The memory was fresh in all our minds,

With my eldest granddaughter, Kate Perry, enjoying an early summer day on the Eastern Shore of Maryland. *Official White House Photo/David Bohrer*

In my West Wing office with granddaughter Grace Perry, who is wearing her Nationals cheerleading uniform in preparation for Opening Day 2007. *Official White House Photo/David Bohrer*

With my first grandson, Philip Perry, at the vice president's residence in the spring of 2006. *Official White House Photo/David Bohrer*

At Andrews Air Force Base with granddaughter Elizabeth Perry and her luggage, getting ready to board Air Force Two. *Official White House Photo/David Bohrer*

Giving grandson Sam a ride on the vice presidential helicopter, Marine Two, with Mary and Heather. *Official White House Photo/David Bohrer*

With our newest grandbaby, Sarah Lynne, in McLean, Virginia, spring 2011. *Photo by David Bohrer*

With my namesake, grandson Richard, on board Air Force Two, summer 2007. *Official White House Photo/David Bohrer*

With President Bush in the Oval Office. In 2000, George W. Bush told me he wanted a vice president who would play an important role in helping to govern the nation, and he was true to his word for the entire eight years we served together. *Official White House Photo/David Bohrer*

With members of the Senate on the steps of the North Portico of the White House. As president of the Senate, I worked hard to develop relationships with my Senate colleagues and with members of the House of Representatives. *Official White House Photo/David Bohrer*

Being evacuated from my office in the West Wing by Secret Service Agent Jim Scott. September 11, 2001. *Official White House Photo/David Bohrer*

In the PEOC, watching the second tower of the World Trade Center collapse. Standing behind me are Josh Bolten, Norm Mineta, Scooter Libby, and Condoleezza Rice. Mary Matalin is seated to my left. *Official White House Photo/David Bohrer*

Early afternoon in the PEOC on 9/11. I had just finished a secure call with the president in which I recommended he begin thinking about a time to return to Washington. *Official White House Photo/ David Bohrer*

Meeting with some of the brave recovery workers at Ground Zero on October 18, 2001. *Official White House Photo/David Bohrer*

Above: With President Bush in the Oval Office in March 2002. We had already toppled the Taliban, and the president asked me to travel to the UK and the Middle East to consult with our allies. *Official White House Photo/David Bohrer*

Right: Outside 10 Downing Street with one of America's most steadfast allies in the War on Terror, Prime Minister Tony Blair, March 2002. *Official White House Photo/David Bohrer; Below:* In Tel Aviv with Prime Minister Ariel Sharon. *Official White House Photo/David Bohrer*

Above: In the desert of Saudi Arabia with King Abdullah. *Official White House Photo/David Bohrer*

In Ramallah, preparing to meet with Palestinian leader Abu Mazen with two of my key foreign policy advisors, John Hannah and Gamal Helal. *Official White House Photo/David Bohrer*

With Pope John Paul II at the Vatican in January 2004. As our meeting ended, the Pope took my hand in both of his and said, "God bless America." *Official White House Photo/David Bohrer*

With Afghan President Hamid Karzai in Kabul for the swearing in of Afghanistan's newly elected parliament, December 19, 2005. *Official White House Photo/David Bohrer*

With Don Rumsfeld in his office in the Pentagon on April 8, 2003, the day before Baghdad was liberated. We had just completed a secure call with General Tommy Franks. *Official White House Photo/David Bohrer*

Former Prime Minister Margaret Thatcher visited the White House on the fifth anniversary of 9/11. It was an honor to give her a tour of the Map Room, where the maps President Roosevelt consulted during World War II are displayed. *Official White House Photo/David Bohrer*

On Air Force Two on July 1, 2004, watching news coverage of the early proceedings in Saddam Hussein's trial in Baghdad. *Official White House Photo/David Bohrer*

In Baghdad with the new Iraqi Prime Minister, Nouri al-Maliki, on March 17, 2008. Gamal Helal, seated between us, is interpreting. *Official White House Photo/David Bohrer*

At Camp Speicher, Iraq, with three of the generals who led us to victory there. Commander of coalition forces General David Petraeus; his deputy and successor, General Ray Odierno; and General Stan McChrystal, who commanded our special operations forces; May 10, 2007. *Official White House Photo/David Bohrer*

At Fort Stewart, Georgia, July 21, 2006, thanking members of the 3rd Infantry Division and the Georgia National Guard's 48th Brigade Combat Team for their service in Iraq. *Official White House Photo/David Bohrer*

With Rob Portman, who played Joe Lieberman and John Edwards in my vice presidential debate preparation sessions in 2000 and 2004, watching video of John Edwards at our house in Wyoming, summer 2004. *Official White House Photo/David Bohrer*

On the campaign trail with Lynne in 2004. *Official White House Photo/ David Bohrer*

Being sworn in for the second time as vice president of the United States, January 20, 2005, with Lynne, Mary, and Liz. My good friend Speaker of the House Denny Hastert administered the oath of office. *Official White House Photo/Susan Sterner*

The most effective way to prepare for a debate—fishing the Snake River in Wyoming.
Official White House Photo/David Bohrer

In one of our regular small group meetings in Steve Hadley's office in the West Wing, where we discussed our most important and sensitive national security policy matters during the second term, with Secretary of Defense Bob Gates, Chairman of the Joint Chiefs Pete Pace, Director of National Intelligence Mike McConnell, Deputy NSC Advisor J. D. Crouch, Secretary of State Condi Rice, and National Security Advisor Steve Hadley. *Official White House Photo/David Bohrer*

Above left: At Camp David on June 13, 2006, with Secretary of Defense Rumsfeld and Secretary of State Rice as we discussed our strategy in Iraq. We are participating in a video conference with President Bush, who had made a surprise visit to Baghdad. *Above right:* With troops in Iraq during one of my last visits as vice president. *Left:* With David Addington, my general counsel and chief of staff, at the vice president's residence in the summer of 2006. The dogs are not impressed with whatever serious topic David and I are discussing. *Official White House Photos/David Bohrer*

Liz and I with Marine Lieutenant Andrew Kinard during a visit to Walter Reed Army Medical Center in June 2007. Andrew, who was wounded in Al Anbar province, Iraq, in 2006, went on to study at Harvard. He is one of the many inspirational warriors I had the honor to know during my time as vice president. *Official White House Photo/David Bohrer*

At Bagram Air Force Base, Afghanistan, March 3, 2008, pinning the Silver Star on Specialist Monica Brown for her bravery in combat. Specialist Brown is only the second woman since World War II to be awarded the Silver Star. *Official White House Photo/David Bohrer*

of my limo to see something completely unexpected and very
—New Yorkers whose cars had been stopped, standing in the
heering and applauding us.

SPECIAL OPERATIONS FORCES were delayed getting into
anistan, not least by treacherous weather. They confronted rain,
, and even sandstorms as they tried to fly helicopters over moun-
s as high as sixteen thousand feet. On October 19, 2001, the first
elve-man team went in near Mazar-e-Sharif in the north, and a unit
two hundred army rangers seized an airfield, code name Rhino, in the
uth, near Kandahar. Another special operations team raided a com-
ound of Mullah Omar, the leader of the Taliban. I have a brick from
his compound that was given to me by some of the special operations
forces who seized it. It sits in my office next to a brick from the house
where special operators killed Abu Musab al Zarqawi, the leader of al
Qaeda in Iraq, in June 2006. Both are reminders of the tremendous
work America's armed forces do in making the world a very dangerous
place for terrorists.

Once we had boots on the ground in Afghanistan and special operators linking up with the Northern Alliance and other opposition
groups, I had expected things would start to move quickly, and I grew
concerned when that didn't happen. On November 2, 2001, the National Security Council had an expanded session with General Franks. I
participated via secure videoconference from the office in Laurel Lodge.
"If you look at the situation from a purely military standpoint, you
would say time is on our side," I said. "Continuing operations against
Taliban targets will weaken them, and the insertion of special forces
and resupply efforts will strengthen the Northern Alliance." But in the
larger strategic context, I said, it was just the opposite. "Time is *not*
on our side." Every day that al Qaeda and its supporters went without
major defeat, the danger to the United States grew. I was at that very
moment operating from an undisclosed location because another attack
was said to be imminent. More attacks were no doubt being planned,
and they could be even more devastating. We knew that al Qaeda had

With Lynne, Liz and Phil, and our granddaughters—Kate, Elizabeth, and Grace—near our
home in Wyoming, my favorite place on earth. *Official White House Photo/David Bohrer*

Hunting in Falfurrias, Texas, with Jim Baker and President George H. W. Bush.
Official White House Photo/David Bohrer

With President-elect Barack Obama and Vice President–elect Joe Biden on inaugural morning 2009 in the Blue Room at the White House. I had strained my back moving boxes into our new house. "Joe," I told Biden, "this is what you're going to look like when your term is up." *Official White House Photo/David Bohrer*

With Lynne and our Lab, Dave, on the porch of the vice president's residence on a beautiful Easter Sunday. *Official White House Photo/David Bohrer*

as I talked about the bravery, generosity, [...] nessed in New York City in the aftermath [...] tice would be delivered to those responsible [...] and in full." Although there would be visib[...] as the one under way in Afghanistan, there w[...] war that would not be so visible. Repeating w[...] sert that first Sunday after the attacks, I talked a[...] intelligence:

> *We are dealing here with evil people who dwell [...]*
> *planning unimaginable violence and destruction. [...]*
> *ternative but to meet the enemy where he dwells. So [...]*
> *means doing business with people you would not like to [...]*
> *next-door neighbor. We must and we will use every me[...]*
> *disposal to ensure the freedom and security of the America[...]*

The response in the room was resounding applause. I have of[...] people from other countries comment on American patrio[...] negatively, but in amazement and admiration that our love [...] country is so deep and abiding. On that night, thinking of th[...] under way, I spoke for all when I said, "We love our country only [...] when she is threatened."

After my speech I received additional information about the bot[...] linum hits. Attorney General John Ashcroft and Homeland Security Advisor Tom Ridge reported that if we had been exposed, we would be showing symptoms by now. It had been fifty-eight hours since the last sensor was tripped. We were all feeling well, and so it looked as though we were off the hook.

Leaving the Waldorf by motorcade, we headed back to LaGuardia. Heightened security precautions meant that the NYPD had shut down all the streets along the motorcade route, backing traffic up for miles. I worried there would be a lot of unhappy New Yorkers. But as my long motorcade, led by police motorcycles and squad cars with lights and sirens, drove through the city streets that night, I looked out the been seeking a nuclear weapon, and they might resort to biological or chemical warfare. People had died in the United States from anthrax spores. The Hart Senate Office Building was closed because anthrax had been mailed to senators. "What do you need to speed it up?" I asked General Franks. The president asked Franks to come back to us as quickly as possible to let us know what we could do to help.

General Franks reported on his recent trip to several key countries in the Middle East and Central Asia. Every leader he visited felt under pressure from public opinion, he said. We weren't getting our story out, but Al Jazeera, the relatively new Arab satellite network, was making sure that al Qaeda's views were broadcast. We'd continue to have the cooperation we needed from the nations Franks had visited, he said, but a number of them wanted to keep their cooperation secret.

When he turned to Afghanistan, Franks reported success working with the CIA to use Predators and AC-130 Spectre gunships to find and take out al Qaeda targets. He noted that the opposition groups, in particular the Northern Alliance, were doing well but were tired and lacked medical care. They needed more support fast, and he intended to make that a priority.

Franks also reported on the campaign under way to destroy the massive cave complexes in which the Taliban lived and hid. He had about 150 caves on a target list, he said, and estimated the count would go to 1,000. He noted that the humanitarian efforts we had begun to drop food and supplies in were going well and were critically important. Finally, Franks listed his goals for the next seven days. They were tasks on the order of enhancing our surveillance capability, getting cold-weather gear to the Northern Alliance, and talking to regional leaders. In fact, what he would deliver within the week was our first major victory.

It started with the CIA, which had contacts in Afghanistan stretching back to the 1980s and knew some of the players well. CIA officers brought our special operators together with the Northern Alliance and other opposition forces, and soon a group of our special forces was traveling on horseback with General Abdul Rashid Dostum and his men and calling in air support to destroy Taliban positions around

Mazar-e-Sharif. As the Taliban fled, American special forces joined in the cavalry charges pursuing them. They called in B-52 strikes to open a crucial pass, and after Mazar-e-Sharif fell on November 9, 2001, they rode with the victorious Northern Alliance into the center of the city. Our special forces gave the first victory of the first war of the twenty-first century a lasting symbol: the man on horseback armed with the ability to call in a five-hundred-pound laser-guided bomb.

After Mazar-e-Sharif, things happened fast. On November 11, 2001, the town of Herat fell to the Northern Alliance. Kabul followed on November 13, and Jalalabad on November 14. The last Taliban stronghold, Kandahar, fell on December 7.

In December the United Nations sponsored a conference in Bonn, Germany, to select an interim leader for liberated Afghanistan. Delegates to the conference chose Hamid Karzai, a Pashtun, who had fought against the Taliban in the south. Karzai, who had grown up in Afghanistan and served briefly in the pre-Taliban Afghan government, had reentered Afghanistan on a motorcycle from Pakistan as the bombing campaign began. With support from our forces, Karzai led the Pashtun troops who took Kandahar. He was inaugurated on December 22, 2001, as chairman of the new Interim Afghan Authority.

In a little over three months, working with the Northern Alliance and allies in the south, we had overthrown the Taliban and liberated 25 million people. We had begun to deny al Qaeda bases from which to plot and train for attacks against us. There were difficult days ahead, but at the end of 2001, we had accomplished much. And we had managed to do all we had done with the number of American troops in Afghanistan never exceeding four thousand.

As we had begun the planning for our military operations in Afghanistan, many worried that we were taking on too formidable a task. As the Soviets could testify, Afghanistan was known as the graveyard of empires for good reason. Any power that would prevail there had to take into account not only the rugged, inhospitable terrain, but the fact that the Afghans were among the toughest, most ruthless fighters in the world. When we launched our efforts, however, it was with forces far superior to those the Soviets had deployed in the 1980s, and we enjoyed a tremendous technological advantage. We also had on our side the kind of creative thinking that freedom encourages. Using the CIA and our special operations forces to marry our technology with Afghan fighters brought about the Taliban's downfall in a remarkably short time. And perhaps the most important distinction was that we were there to liberate, not to occupy; to free, not to oppress the Afghan people.

But, of course, that wasn't the end of it, and as we find ourselves ten years later with nearly one hundred thousand American troops still fighting in Afghanistan, it's important to recognize that in the war in which we are currently engaged, sure and swift victories are likely to be rare. To the extent that Desert Storm led us to expect quick triumphs, it taught us the wrong lesson.

Now we are taking on an enemy scattered throughout many parts of the world and committed to launching mass casualty attacks from any base it can find. The key test in this war is not how long it takes us to complete any particular military operation. The crucial test is whether our policies, including our military operations, are effective at defending the nation from further attack. Critical to that effort is recognizing that our ultimate objective must be ensuring that the Afghan security forces are sufficiently trained and equipped to defend their own people and territory. Our mission will not be complete until the Afghan government and armed forces can, on their own, prevent their nation from once again becoming a safe haven for terrorists.

In my view, the most important lesson to be learned from the Soviet experience in Afghanistan in the 1980s is what happened after the Soviets left. The United States turned its attentions elsewhere, and Afghanistan descended into civil war. The resultant instability and eventual takeover of the country by the Taliban meant that Osama bin Laden and his al Qaeda terrorists were able to find a safe haven there. Throughout the late 1990s, thousands of terrorists were trained in al Qaeda camps in Afghanistan, and it became the base for the attacks of 9/11. When I hear policymakers talk about walking away from Afghanistan, I want to remind them of what the consequences can be.

ONE OF THE FIRST efforts we undertook after 9/11 to strengthen the country's defenses was securing passage of the Patriot Act, which the president signed into law on October 2001. The law, passed by overwhelming, bipartisan majorities in Congress, enabled law enforcement, intelligence officers, and national security personnel to share information about potential terrorist threats. It tore down the wall that had previously prevented this kind of cooperation. It also allowed law enforcement officers to apply tools long used to investigate organized crime to the fight against terrorists.

I also thought it important to be sure the National Security Agency, or NSA, which is responsible for collecting intelligence about the communications of America's adversaries, was doing everything possible to track the conversations of terrorists, so I asked George Tenet whether the NSA had all the authorities it needed. Tenet said he would check with General Mike Hayden, who was then director, and a short time later both of them came to see me in my office in the White House. Hayden explained that he had already made adjustments in the way NSA was collecting intelligence. Those adjustments were possible within NSA's existing authorities, but additional authorities were needed in order to improve the coverage and effectiveness of the program.

The Foreign Intelligence Surveillance Act of 1978 established a court through which NSA was required to seek approval for certain activities. Hayden explained that one of the challenges he faced was that the slow procedures of the court made it impossible to do what needed to be done with speed and agility. He described the kinds of additional activities he could undertake with expanded authorities, and I told him we'd do everything we could to see that he got them.

I reported on our conversation to the president. With his approval, I asked Dave Addington to work with General Hayden and the president's counsel, Alberto Gonzales, to develop a legal process by which we could ensure the NSA got the authorizations Hayden needed. The president was clear that these new authorities had to be signed off on by the attorney general, the secretary of defense, and the director of the CIA before he would grant them. He also said he wanted to keep the program on a short leash and instructed that it should be reauthorized regularly. We were well aware that there is an important balance between protecting privacy and gathering intelligence. The president wanted to make sure the program was used only when needed to defend the nation.

Although parts of the NSA program remain classified, it is now public that a key element involved intercepting targeted communications into and out of the United States where there was a reasonable basis to conclude that at least one party to the communication was associated with al Qaeda or a related terrorist organization. It is hard to imagine a more important kind of communication for us to intercept from the standpoint of our national security than one potentially involving terrorists speaking to someone already in the United States. General Hayden has observed, "Had this program been in effect prior to 9/11, it is my professional judgment that we would have detected some of the 9/11 al Qaeda operatives in the United States and we would have identified them as such."

On October 4, 2001, the president, on the recommendation of the director of central intelligence and the secretary of defense, with the determination of the attorney general that it was lawful to do so, authorized the program for the first time. At the National Security Agency, General Hayden took an extra step. He called in the three most experienced lawyers at the NSA, and, as he has said publicly, they did more than acquiesce in the program. They supported it.

After the initial authorization, every thirty to forty-five days, with a fresh intelligence assessment from the CIA, the same officials made recommendations and gave legal clearance for the president to make a decision whether to continue the program. The program was so sensitive and closely held that Dave Addington carried the authorizing document in a locked classified documents pouch by hand to each of the officials involved.

If the president did not authorize the program every forty-five days, it would stop. It was a tricky task each month getting time on each of the principals' schedules and then getting the document to the president for signature. Once the stars did not align, and the president left for a trip to Asia before the package was ready for him to sign. Al Gonzales and Dave Addington flew to California to get the president's signature, so the program would not stop while he was away.

Wanting to ensure that we were proceeding absolutely within the letter and intent of the law, we also took great care to brief the Congress on the program. Given the extreme fragility and sensitivity of the intelligence sources and methods involved, we briefed only the chairman and ranking member of the House and Senate intelligence committees, a practice that has been followed by both Republican and Democratic administrations when dealing with intelligence programs of this sensitivity. This program was too important and too highly classified for briefings to the whole committees, which, given the rotations of members into those slots, would have resulted in dozens being briefed. The president had to personally approve anyone outside the NSA before they could be read into the program.

I hosted the periodic congressional briefings myself, usually in my West Wing office. Mike Hayden would take the lead in providing detailed information about how the program was functioning and what types of intelligence we were gaining from it.

In the spring of 2004, after Attorney General John Ashcroft had approved the program as lawful approximately twenty times, new lawyers at the Justice Department raised concerns about one aspect of it, and James Comey, who had become deputy attorney general in December 2003, did not want to proceed. In light of this, on March 9, 2004, I met with the professionals who were carrying out the program from the NSA together with the lawyers from the Justice Department who had developed concerns, hoping we could find a way to continue to collect the terrorism intelligence we needed. General Hayden briefed on the details of the program, making its value clear and emphasizing how careful the NSA was about limits and safeguards. But in the end, the lawyers from the Justice Department remained locked in place.

Because it was crucial that the program continue, I held an expanded congressional briefing on March 10, 2004, to discuss whether we needed to seek additional legislative authorities. Seated around the long wooden conference table in the Situation Room were Speaker of the House Denny Hastert, House Minority Leader Nancy Pelosi, Senate Majority Leader Bill Frist, Senate Minority Leader Tom Daschle, Chairman of the House Select Committee on Intelligence Porter Goss and ranking member Jane Harman, and Chairman of the Senate Select Committee on Intelligence Pat Roberts and ranking member Jay Rockefeller. House Majority Leader Tom DeLay was not present, but was briefed later.

After Mike Hayden finished briefing on the program, I put two very clear and specific questions to the group. "First," I said, "we would like to know whether you believe the program should be continued." It was unanimous: Every member agreed that it should continue. "Second," I asked, "should we come to the Congress for an amendment to the FISA statute so that we have additional congressional authority to do what is necessary?" Again, the view around the table was unanimous. The members did not want us to seek additional legislation for the program. They feared, as did we, that going to the whole Congress would compromise its secrecy.

Later that same day, the president called the attorney general, who was in George Washington University Hospital in Washington, D.C., and explained that the program was going to lapse without Department of Justice approval. The attorney general said that he would sign the documents, and the president asked Andy Card and Al Gonzales to take the package to him. Card and Gonzales, with Addington holding the highly classified documents, drove to the hospital, and Card and Gonzales went into the room, where they found Deputy Attorney General Comey already present. It became immediately clear that Ashcroft had changed his mind. He said he would not sign the documents. He also indicated that, because of his health issues, he had delegated all the responsibilities of his office to Deputy Attorney General Comey. Card and Gonzales departed with the unsigned documents in hand.

Soon afterward, the lawyers began to threaten resignation, as did FBI Director Bob Mueller, whom Comey had convinced there was a problem. I had little patience with what I saw happening. The program had been in place more than two years and the attorney general had approved it some twenty times. Most important, we were at war and the program's single purpose was to get intelligence necessary for the defense of the nation. There was a tragic reminder of the threat Islamist terrorism represented the next morning, March 11, 2004, when ten bombs exploded on trains in Madrid, Spain, killing 191 people and wounding more than 1,500.

Faced with threats of resignation, the president decided to alter the NSA program, even though he and his advisors were confident of his constitutional authority to continue the program unchanged.

A few months later we learned that a *New York Times* reporter, James Risen, was preparing to publish a story about the NSA program. Such a story would alert our enemies about the program, making it more difficult for us to continue to collect the intelligence we needed. By explaining that the newspaper would be putting an important national security program at risk, Condi Rice and Mike Hayden convinced Risen and the *Times* to hold the story. But the next year, in December 2005, the paper threatened again to run it. This time Risen had a book about to be published that contained elements of the story, and the *New York Times* wanted to feature it first. We were concerned enough about the damage publication could do to the program that the president had a face-to-face meeting with the publisher and editor of the *Times* to ask them not to go with the story. He explained that making details of the program public would harm our ability to track terrorists' phone calls and might well make it more difficult for us to prevent future attacks. On December 16, 2005, the *Times* published the story anyway, a decision the president called "shameful." I agreed. Moreover, it seemed to me that the *New York Times* had violated Section 798 of Title 18 of the U.S. Code, which prohibits publishing classified information about America's communications intelligence.

Six months later, the *New York Times* published a story that damaged our efforts to track the flow of funding to terrorists. The June 23, 2006, story was headlined "Bank Data Is Sifted by U.S. in Secret to Block Terror." It exposed details about a classified program to track banking transactions, which, of course, was welcome enlightenment to those we were trying to catch. The *Times'* public editor, Byron Calame, at first defended the newspaper's decision to publish on the grounds that the classified program wasn't really much of a secret. After *Times* readers pointed out that the *Times* story had emphasized the program's secrecy, Calame reversed himself, writing, "I don't think the article should have been published."

In the wake of the *New York Times* terrorist surveillance story, Andy Card hosted a meeting in his office that I attended along with some of the president's communications team. Communications Director Dan Bartlett was urging that we be more forthcoming in revealing to the press and the public just what these programs entailed. He said that the president was "just carrying too much baggage" from all the "secret" activities we had under way. I understood it was his job to worry about the president's image, but there were important reasons for our secrecy. "Dan," I said, "we aren't doing these things for our entertainment. We're doing them because we're at war. These programs—and keeping them secret—are critical for the defense of the nation." The president and I and everyone else serving in the administration had one mission: to defend the nation, even if it resulted in negative press stories.

The Terrorist Surveillance Program is, in my opinion, one of the most important success stories in the history of American intelligence. The speed with which the NSA got it up and running, the problems they solved and the way they solved them, the careful attention paid to ensure lawfulness and proper oversight, and the intelligence collected make the program a model of the tremendous work our nation's intelligence community can do. As I think back on all we accomplished in those first post-9/11 months, this program is one of the things of which I am proudest. I know it saved lives and prevented attacks. If I had it to do all over again, I would, in a heartbeat.

NEAR THE TOWN OF Mazar-e-Sharif in Afghanistan there is a nineteenth-century prison fortress called Qala-i-Jangi. In November 2001, when Northern Alliance forces under the command of General Abdul Rashid Dostum captured three hundred Taliban and al Qaeda soldiers, they took their prisoners to the fort. On Sunday morning, November 25, 2001, two CIA officers went to the complex to question the prisoners, meeting with a group of them in an open area outside the cells. Almost immediately one of the officers, Johnny Micheal Spann, found himself surrounded. The prisoners overcame him in a vicious attack, "scrabbling at his flesh with their hands," according to eyewitness accounts, and killing him with weapons they had smuggled in. Spann became the first American combat death in Afghanistan. His companion, a CIA agent known only as Dave, managed to escape the next day. It took two days and heavy American airpower to put down the riot at Qala-i-Jangi.

Many of those being captured in Afghanistan were clearly cold-blooded killers who had committed horrific acts of savagery and welcomed a fight to the death. We needed to find a secure place to hold them away from the field of battle. Defense Department officials settled on the idea of a detention facility at the U.S. naval base at Guantanamo Bay, Cuba, where they had space and support. It was a choice dictated in part by Justice Department advice that keeping detainees off U.S. soil would prevent them from having access to U.S. courts. Holding detainees at Guantanamo also avoided the security concerns that would arise from bringing them into the United States.

In the years since the first enemy combatants were moved to Guantanamo, the facility there and the U.S. servicemen who guard the detainees have been the target of a tremendous amount of unjustified criticism from people with little knowledge about the actual conditions at the camp. It is a model facility—safe, secure, and humane—where detainees have access to television, books, newspapers, movies, their choice of a number of sports and exercise activities, the Koran, healthy food that is in keeping with their religious beliefs, and medical care. It likely provides a standard of care higher than many prisons in European countries where the criticism of Guantanamo has been loudest.

President Bush determined early on in the War on Terror that even though neither al Qaeda nor Taliban detainees qualified for POW status under the Geneva Conventions, the United States armed forces would as a matter of policy treat detainees humanely and "in a manner consistent with the principles of Geneva." And that remained our policy throughout our time in office.

Critics often point to the determination that the Geneva Conventions did not apply to detainees as evidence of our lack of respect for the Conventions. It seems to me to demonstrate the opposite. Geneva is intended to provide protections to those who abide by the laws of war, and among the most important of those is keeping civilians safe. Terrorists intentionally attack civilians, thus putting themselves outside the realm of those whom Geneva is meant to protect. Further, an important incentive to abide by the laws of war is removed if protections are extended to the most egregious violators. When President Reagan rejected a proposal to extend Geneva's protections to terrorists, he rightly observed that doing so would "undermine humanitarian law and endanger civilians in war."

During our time in office, the State Department responded to criticism, particularly from Europe, by looking for ways to shut down the facility. In meeting after meeting we debated Guantanamo. My view was always that it was a safe, secure, humane facility, and we had no better alternative for holding dangerous terrorists. We did in fact move many detainees through Guantanamo and returned some to their home countries. We later learned that a number of the released detainees ended up back on the field of battle, fighting against us and our allies in the War on Terror. By the time we left office, the detainees still remaining in the camp were among the worst of the worst—those too dangerous to be allowed to leave and those whose home countries would not take them back.

It was against this backdrop that President Barack Obama announced on his second day in office that he would close the facility within a year. His administration stepped up efforts to release detainees despite the lesson we had learned about released terrorists returning to terrorism, and the president repeated a number of criticisms that do not bear up under examination. He claimed, for example, that Guantanamo "was probably the number one recruitment tool that is used by" al Qaeda. If that were true, one would expect to see al Qaeda mention Guantanamo frequently, but a review of thirty-four messages and interviews by top al Qaeda leaders issued in 2009 and 2010 shows the word *Guantanamo* appearing in only three. The president has also suggested that Guantanamo should be closed because it is hurting America's image around the world. But it's not Guantanamo that does the harm, it is the critics of the facility who peddle falsehoods about it. Even if, for the sake of debate, one were to accept the image argument, I don't have much sympathy for the view that we should find an alternative to Guantanamo—a solution that could potentially make Americans less safe—simply because we are worried about how we are perceived abroad.

IT HAS BEEN THE case in every major war in which the United States has been engaged that we hold enemy combatants for the duration of the conflict. This war is no different, except that the duration may be longer than any war in which we have previously been involved. As the fighting got under way in Afghanistan, we knew that there would be certain cases where we needed to try detainees. Administration lawyers relied on clear precedent to develop a system of military commissions.

In 1942, a group of eight Nazi saboteurs landed by submarine on beaches in Florida and New York. They were captured, put on trial by a military commission at the direction of President Franklin D. Roosevelt, and convicted. Six of the eight were executed. The Supreme Court unanimously upheld the constitutionality of the order Roosevelt issued establishing the military commissions.

On November 13, 2001, President Bush signed an executive order, based on FDR's order, establishing military commissions to try certain captured detainees. The detainees were foreign enemy combatants engaged in war against the United States. Military commissions were the appropriate place to try them. Our normal Article III court system was not suited for the trial of enemy combatants for a number of reasons. These courts couldn't provide the safeguards in terms of security or protection of classified information that a military commission could. In addition, enemy combatants are not entitled to the rights granted through our civilian court system to criminal defendants. We knew that military commissions were the right place for these trials. We also knew that the model that FDR established had been upheld unanimously by the Supreme Court, and that was the model we chose to follow.

Although the order establishing the commissions had been drafted in coordination with the Office of Legal Counsel at the Department of Justice, three days before the president signed it, Attorney General Ashcroft had come to the White House to express concern that it envisioned no role for the attorney general. But as the long history of military commissions in America reflects, military commissions are an exercise of military authority over enemy combatants and not part of the law enforcement system. Indeed, the Office of Legal Counsel had emphasized that the military commissions should be authorized by the president as commander in chief in a directive to the secretary of defense for military implementation, with minimal involvement of the Department of Justice, which has no military responsibilities.

As it turned out, we also ran into bureaucratic obstacles at the Department of Defense, and the military commissions were very slow to get started. Following a number of court cases and additional legislative action, a military commission system was established that is up and running today. I believe it provides the best forum in which to try enemy combatants of the United States, and I have been gratified to see the Obama administration come around to the same way of thinking.

IN MARCH 2002, PAKISTANI forces raided an al Qaeda safe house in Faisalabad, Pakistan, and captured a terrorist named Abu Zubaydah. A lieutenant of Osama bin Laden, Zubaydah was the highest-ranking al Qaeda member we had captured to date. He had been badly wounded in the firefight that led to his capture, and the CIA officers who had been aiding the Pakistani operation arranged a special flight to bring a doctor from the United States to provide emergency care for him.

Although defiant, Zubaydah provided useful information very early on, disclosing, for example, that the mastermind behind 9/11 had been Khalid Sheikh Mohammed, or KSM. He also provided KSM's code name, Muktar. But then he stopped answering questions, and the CIA, convinced he had information that could potentially save thousands of lives, approached the Justice Department and the White House about what they might do to go further in interrogating him and other high-value detainees. The CIA developed a list of enhanced interrogation techniques that were based on the Survival, Evasion, Resistance, and Escape Program used to prepare our military men and women in case they should be captured, detained, or interrogated. Before using the techniques on any terrorists, the CIA wanted the Justice Department to review them and determine that they complied with the law, including international treaty obligations such as the United Nations Convention Against Torture. Out of that review process, which took several months, came legal opinions advising that the techniques were lawful. The program was approved by the president and the National Security Council.

The techniques worked. Abu Zubaydah gave up information about Ramzi bin al Shibh, who had assisted the 9/11 hijackers, and on the one-year anniversary of the 9/11 attacks, bin al Shibh was captured after a shootout in Pakistan. At the time of his apprehension, he was plotting to use commercial airliners in suicide attacks on Heathrow Airport and other structures in London.

Information from Abu Zubaydah and bin al Shibh led in turn to the capture of KSM, who after being questioned with enhanced techniques became a fount of information. A CIA report, declassified at my request, notes that KSM was the "preeminent source on al-Qa'ida." According to the 2004 report, KSM had become key in the U.S. government's understanding of al Qaeda plots and personalities:

Debriefings since his detention have yielded . . . reports that have shed light on the plots, capabilities, the identity and location of al-Qa'ida operatives and affiliated terrorist organizations and networks. He has provided information on al-Qa'ida's strategic doc-

*trine, probable targets, the impact of striking each target set, and
likely methods of attacks inside the United States.*

In one instance KSM provided information that led us to a terrorist cell
in Karachi, Pakistan. The members of the cell were being groomed by
a terrorist named Hambali, al Qaeda's point person for Southeast Asia,
for operations against the United States, probably to fly a hijacked plane
into the tallest building on the West Coast.

Despite the invaluable intelligence we were obtaining through the
program of enhanced interrogation, in 2005 there was a move on Capitol Hill, led by Senators John McCain and Lindsey Graham, to end it
and require that all U.S. government interrogations be conducted under
the rules of the U.S. Army Field Manual. As one of the CIA interrogators explained to me, the Field Manual is adequate for interrogating
run-of-the-mill enemy soldiers. "If one guy doesn't want to talk to you,
you can say, fine, and move on to the next, until you get to one who will
talk." But a detainee such as Khalid Sheikh Mohammed is different. He
wasn't talking, but there was no one comparable to move on to. For the
safety of the nation we needed him to talk, and that happened after we
put him through the enhanced interrogation program.

In an effort to reach an agreement with Senator McCain and explain to him how damaging his proposed amendment would be, CIA
Director Porter Goss and I met with him in a secure conference room
at the Capitol and tried to brief him about the program and the critical
intelligence we had gained. But John didn't want to hear what we had to
say. We had hardly started when he lost his temper and stormed out of
the meeting. His opinion carried a good deal of weight because he had
been a prisoner of war, but his view of the program was certainly not
unanimous among his fellow former POWs.

Air Force Colonel Leo Thorsness found out he had been awarded the
Medal of Honor while he was a prisoner in Vietnam. The news that he
had received the nation's highest award for valor came to him through
tapping on the prison wall. On Memorial Day 2009, Thorsness, who
was tortured severely by the North Vietnamese, wrote that waterboard-

ing was "harsh treatment but not torture." Although a supporter of Senator McCain, he disagrees with him on using enhanced techniques: "I would not hesitate for a second to use enhanced interrogation, including water boarding, if it would save the lives of innocent people."

Medal of Honor recipient Colonel Bud Day was shot down over North Vietnam, then interrogated and tortured. He managed to escape his prison camp and made it to the Demilitarized Zone, only to be captured again and tortured again. For a time Day shared a cell with McCain, whom he admires, but asked by author Marc Thiessen if he believed waterboarding to be torture, Day replied, "I am a supporter of water boarding. It is not torture. Torture is really hurting someone." Asked what he would say to the CIA officer who interrogated Khalid Sheikh Mohammed, Day replied, "You did the right thing."

Since the beginning of the enhanced interrogation program, the CIA had briefed key members of Congress on the interrogations and on what they were learning. I do not recall in any of the briefings I attended a single member objecting to the program or urging that we stop using these authorized, legal methods. Nonetheless, in the fall of 2005, congressional opinion was not on our side. At one of the weekly Senate Republican policy lunches I regularly attended, I spoke about the importance of the program. I could not reveal much about it. I could not talk about the specific interrogation techniques. I could only urge my colleagues to accept how critically important the program was to our national security. The McCain Amendment passed 90–9. At the president's request, Steve Hadley had tried to negotiate enough flexibility in the language of the amendment to allow the CIA program to continue in a pared-down way. He had secured language he thought the CIA could live with, but after the legislation passed, Porter Goss told Steve that he'd checked with those running the program, and it would have to be shut down.

When former NSA Director Mike Hayden became head of the CIA in May 2006, he reviewed the program and determined that some version of it had to be restarted in order to protect the country. But in June 2006 the Supreme Court handed down its decision in

Hamdan v. Rumsfeld. The decision held that Common Article 3 of the Geneva Conventions, which prohibits any behavior that is "humiliating and degrading" and bans "outrages upon personal dignity," applied to the detainees. The decision seemed to ignore the plain language of Common Article 3, which makes clear that it applies to "armed conflict not of an international character." The War on Terror could hardly be more international, having occurred across countries and continents, but once the Supreme Court handed down its decision, the CIA interrogation program clearly needed new legal underpinning to continue.

The president decided to make aspects of the program public in order to save it. He announced he would bring the terrorists currently in CIA custody to Guantanamo for trial, and he submitted legislation that would provide congressional approval for military commissions and clarify the kinds of questioning that would be allowed under the Detainee Treatment Act.

Congress passed the Military Commissions Act in October 2006 and several months later, in July 2007, the president signed an executive order establishing guidelines for the CIA interrogation program. In 2007 testimony before the Senate Select Committee on Intelligence, General Hayden explained why it would be so damaging to limit CIA interrogations to the methods in the Army Field Manual:

> *We have severely restricted our attempts to obtain timely information from HVDs [high-value detainees] who possess information that will help us save lives and disrupt operations. Limiting our interrogation tools to those detailed in the field manual will increase the probability that a determined, resilient HVD will be able to withhold critical, time-sensitive, actionable intelligence that could prevent an imminent, catastrophic attack.*

"In essence," Hayden concluded, "we would be back to a pre-9/11 posture."

In October 2007 the president spoke about enhanced interrogation at the National Defense University. "This program has produced critical intelligence that has helped us stop a number of attacks," he said, "including a plot to strike the U.S. Marine camp in Djibouti, a planned attack on the U.S. consulate in Karachi, a plot to hijack a passenger plane and fly it into the Library Tower in Los Angeles, California, and a plot to fly passenger planes into Heathrow Airport and buildings in downtown London." Then the president said that critics of the program should be asked: "Which of the attacks I have just described would they prefer we had not stopped?"

WITHIN TWO DAYS OF his inauguration, President Barack Obama signed an executive order that limited interrogations to the Army Field Manual, thus putting us back into the pre-9/11 mode. That decision could be reversed, but within three months of taking office, President Obama also released publicly the legal memos detailing the techniques that had been used in the enhanced interrogation program, meaning that if it ever were reinstated, its effectiveness would be diminished by our having told the world—including our enemies—methods we were likely to use. He released the memos over the objection of his current CIA director and the four previous CIA directors. He also did so despite apparently having been told directly by members of the CIA's clandestine service that the release of this information could endanger our CIA operatives.

President Obama claimed that he wasn't reducing America's tools in fighting the War on Terror because he was setting up a replacement interrogation program: the "High-Value Detainee Interrogation Group," or "HIG." When Umar Farouk Abdulmutallab was apprehended on Christmas Day of 2009 while trying to ignite a bomb he had carried in his underwear onto Northwest Airlines Flight 253, Dennis Blair, director of national intelligence, was asked whether Abdulmutallab had been questioned by the HIG. It turned out he hadn't. Eleven months after the president had shut down the enhanced interrogation program and revealed the techniques in the program publicly, the replacement did not exist. Abdulmutallab was read a Miranda warning.

While the administration moved slowly to establish an interrogation program for terrorists, they were quick to reopen an investigation of the CIA personnel who carried out our enhanced interrogation program. Despite the fact that these officers had already been investigated and cleared by career Justice Department lawyers, Attorney General Eric Holder began threatening them with prosecution. In May 2011, after the U.S. located and killed Osama bin Laden, we learned that intelligence gained by these interrogators through the enhanced interrogation program had helped lead us to him.

AS WE FACED A new kind of enemy in the first war of the twenty-first century, the Bush administration put in place programs that were critical to securing the nation. We went after terrorists in safe havens in Afghanistan and took down the Taliban regime that had sponsored them. We enhanced our ability to intercept terrorist communications and track the money that financed them. And we developed a program to gain intelligence from detained terrorists that saved lives and prevented future attacks. As time passed after the 9/11 attacks and the threat of another attack seemed to recede in people's minds, criticism of what we had done mounted, and no program was more bitterly condemned than the CIA's procedures for interrogating high-value detainees. Amid the heated rhetoric some basic points tended to be ignored. The program was safe, legal, and effective. It provided intelligence that enabled us to prevent attacks and save American lives. Above all else, it was part of a broad effort that enabled us, for seven and a half years, to prevent any further mass casualty attacks against the United States.

———◄◦►———

CHAPTER TWELVE

Liberating Iraq

Saddam Hussein's willingness to use weapons of mass destruction was well-known to the world. He had used chemical weapons not only against his enemies, but against his own people. In 1988 during the Iran-Iraq War, he attacked the Kurdish town of Halabja with mustard gas and nerve gas, killing thousands of innocents. Villagers died as they were going about their daily tasks. Mothers died, holding their children.

Saddam was determined to add nuclear weapons to his arsenal, and after the 1991 Gulf War, we learned that his program to develop them was far more advanced than we had thought. The judgment of an International Atomic Energy Agency report was that Saddam could have had a nuclear device by late 1992, had his efforts not been derailed by Desert Storm.

After the Gulf War the United Nations Security Council demanded that Iraq declare and give up the components of its nuclear program as well as chemical and biological weapons and the capacity to produce them. UN Resolution 687 further required that Saddam destroy any ballistic missiles with a range greater than one hundred fifty miles and permit a regime of on-site inspections aimed at making sure he carried through. It also extended a program of tough and comprehensive sanctions.

But Security Council resolutions had little impact on Saddam. A 1993 National Intelligence Estimate assessed that international support for sanctions was eroding, but judged that even if they remained in place, Saddam Hussein would "continue reconstituting Iraq's conventional military forces" and "will take steps to reestablish Iraq's WMD programs." In a 1994 Joint Atomic Energy Intelligence Committee report, the intelligence community agreed "that the Iraqi government is determined to covertly reconstitute its nuclear weapons program."

In 1995 Saddam's son-in-law, Hussein Kamel al-Majid, his brother Saddam, and their families defected to Jordan. Hussein Kamel had been in charge of portions of Iraq's WMD programs, and the revelations that followed his defection led inspectors to realize that Saddam was deceiving them, particularly when it came to his biological and nuclear efforts. Saddam lured Hussein Kamel, his brother, and their families back to Iraq and then had Kamel and his brother murdered, along with their father, their sister, and her children, not long after their return.

In 1998 Saddam Hussein insisted that international weapons inspectors stop work and leave Iraq. In response, Congress passed and President Clinton signed into law the Iraq Liberation Act, making regime change in Iraq the policy of the United States government and approving nearly $100 million to fund Iraqi opposition groups working for Saddam's ouster.

That December, President Clinton launched Operation Desert Fox, a four-day air strike campaign meant to diminish Saddam's weapons capabilities. "If Saddam defies the world and we fail to respond, we will face a far greater threat in the future," Clinton said. "Mark my words, he will develop weapons of mass destruction. He will deploy them, and he will use them."

There was bipartisan support for the operation. Among the Democrats who spoke out was Congresswoman Nancy Pelosi, then a member of the House Intelligence Committee. "Saddam Hussein has been engaged in the development of weapons of mass destruction technology which is a threat to countries in the region," she said, "and he has made a mockery of the weapons inspections process." A number of senators, including Democrats John Kerry, Carl Levin, and Tom Daschle, wrote to President Clinton urging that he "take necessary actions (including, if appropriate, air and missile strikes on suspect Iraqi sites) to respond effectively to the threat posed by Iraq's refusal to end its weapons of mass destruction programs." Senator Joe Biden, writing in the *Washington Post* two months before the strikes, noted the limitation of any policy that left Saddam in power. "Ultimately, as long as Saddam Hussein is at the helm, no inspectors can guarantee that they have rooted out the entirety of Saddam Hussein's weapons program," he wrote, and he observed that "the only way to remove Saddam is a massive military effort, led by the United States."

Saddam Hussein did not find Desert Fox persuasive. In 1999 he began firing on U.S. and British planes that were enforcing the no-fly zones in northern and southern Iraq. The United States together with the United Kingdom and France had established the zones to prevent Saddam from oppressing the Kurds in the north and the Shia in the south. Meanwhile, as we would later learn, Saddam was using the oil-for-food program, intended for the people of Iraq, to enrich himself, bribe others, and purchase improvements for facilities that had the potential to be used for WMD development.

In 1999 the U.S. intelligence community assessed that Saddam had revitalized his biological weapons program. In 2000 a National Intelligence Estimate on worldwide biological weapons threats contained this key judgment:

> *Despite a decade-long international effort to disarm Iraq, new information suggests that Baghdad has continued and expanded its offensive BW program by establishing a large scale, redundant, and concealed BW agent production capability. We judge that Iraq maintains the capability to produce previously declared agents and*

probably is pursuing development of additional bacterial and toxin
agents. Moreover, we judge that Iraq has BW delivery systems avail-
able that could be used to threaten US and Allied forces in the Per-
sian Gulf region.

There was also consistent reporting that Saddam had in place the personnel and the infrastructure for a nuclear weapons program and that he was continuing to acquire technologies that had the potential for either nuclear or nonnuclear use.

One of the first intelligence reports that George Bush and I received in late 2000 before we were sworn in was a far-ranging assessment of Iraq's activities concerning weapons of mass destruction. Although the report itself remains classified, the title does not. It was called *Iraq: Steadily Pursuing WMD Capabilities.* As there had been in the preceding decade, there would be over the next twenty-seven months a steady drumbeat of intelligence warnings about the threat posed by Saddam.

THERE WERE ALSO BY this time sixteen United Nations Security Council resolutions aimed at mitigating the danger arising from Iraq. Saddam repeatedly violated them, ignoring requirements related to weapons of mass destruction as well as those that had to do with terrorism. Resolution 687, passed in 1991, had declared that Iraq must not commit or support terrorism, or allow terrorist organizations to operate in Iraq. But in 1993 the Iraqi Intelligence Service (IIS) attempted to assassinate former President George H. W. Bush, and throughout the 1990s, the IIS participated in terrorist attacks. Saddam provided safe haven to Abdul Rahman Yasin, the Iraqi bomb maker who supplied the bomb for the first attack on the World Trade Center, in 1993. He also provided sanctuary to Abu Abbas, the Palestinian terrorist who led the 1985 hijacking of the cruise ship *Achille Lauro* and the killing of an American passenger, and to Abu Nidal, who had killed a number of civilians in attacks on El Al ticket counters at airports in Rome and Vienna.

In the wake of 9/11, after the United States had gone into Afghanistan in Operation Enduring Freedom, CIA Director George Tenet told the Senate Select Committee on Intelligence, "We have solid evidence of the presence in Iraq of al Qaeda members, including some that have been in Baghdad." The CIA had "solid reporting" of senior-level contacts between Iraq and al Qaeda and "credible reporting" that al Qaeda was seeking contacts in Iraq that could help them acquire capabilities in weapons of mass destruction. Saddam Hussein was by this time providing $25,000 payments to the relatives of Palestinian suicide bombers, and, Director Tenet noted, "Iraq's increasing support to extremist Palestinians, coupled with growing indications of a relationship with al-Qa'ida, suggest that Baghdad's links to terrorists will increase, even absent U.S. military action."

In Senate testimony in 2003, Director Tenet also noted that Iraq was providing safe haven to Abu Musab al Zarqawi, a Jordanian-born terrorist who had trained in Afghanistan and become a key al Qaeda lieutenant. He had arrived in Iraq in 2002, spent time in Baghdad, and then supervised camps in northern Iraq that provided a safe haven for as many as two hundred al Qaeda fighters escaping Afghanistan. At one of those camps, called Khurmal, Zarqawi's men tested poisons and plotted attacks to use them in Europe. From his base in Iraq, Zarqawi also directed the October 2002 killing of Laurence Foley, a U.S. Agency for International Development officer, in Jordan.

For a period extending back to the first Gulf War, the U.S. intelligence community had been providing detailed assessments concerning Saddam Hussein's efforts to develop nuclear weapons, carry on biological and chemical weapons programs, and support terror. The National Intelligence Estimate that we received in 2002 was a continuation of earlier evaluations, and sobering as its judgments were, what the president and I read in our daily briefings was even "more assertive," as Director Tenet would later write.

After 9/11 no American president could responsibly ignore the steady stream of reporting we were getting about the threat posed by Saddam Hussein. We had experienced an unprecedented attack on our homeland. Three thousand Americans, going about their everyday lives, had been killed. The president and I were determined to do all we could to prevent another attack, and our resolution was made stronger by the awareness that a future attack could be even more devastating. The terrorists of 9/11 were armed with airplane tickets and box cutters. The next wave might bring chemical, biological, or nuclear weapons.

When we looked around the world in those first months after 9/11, there was no place more likely to be a nexus between terrorism and WMD capability than Saddam Hussein's Iraq. With the benefit of hindsight—even taking into account that some of the intelligence we received was wrong—that assessment still holds true. We could not ignore the threat or wish it away, hoping naïvely that the crumbling sanctions regime would contain Saddam. The security of our nation and of our friends and allies required that we act. And so we did.

THE PRESIDENT AND I spoke about Iraq privately in the weeks following 9/11. I was aware that Secretary Rumsfeld had set up a process to review all Department of Defense war plans, and I suggested to the president that it would be useful to make certain that Rumsfeld had assigned priority to planning for possible military action against Saddam Hussein. I knew from my experience as secretary of defense during Desert Storm that good military planning takes time. Instructing Rumsfeld to have the military update our Iraq war plans was the best way for the president to ensure that he would have effective, responsible options should military action become necessary. I also suggested that our planning be undertaken at Central Command headquarters in Tampa, Florida. CENTCOM, under the command of General Tommy Franks, was responsible for the Middle East, including Iraq, and planning we did there was much less likely to leak than planning we did in Washington.

On December 28, 2001, I sat in my second-floor study at our home in Wyoming. Outside my window, snow covered the ground. On the desk in front of me was the secure videoconference monitor that allowed me to participate remotely in classified meetings with the president and other members of the NSC. For the meeting that morn-

ing, the president was at his ranch in Crawford, Texas, with General
Franks. Don Rumsfeld was joining the meeting from his home in Taos,
New Mexico; various others, including Colin Powell, Condi Rice, and
George Tenet, joined from D.C.

After updating us on the situation in Afghanistan, Franks turned to
the briefing he had prepared on Iraq. The current war plan, Op Plan
1003, was essentially the same as the one that we had gone to war with
in 1991. Pentagon planners had been revising it, but it still called for
more than four hundred thousand troops; required a six-month, very
public buildup; and failed to take account of the way the world had
changed. Saddam's military, though formidable, was about half the size
it had been during the first Gulf War. Our military was also smaller,
but its capabilities had increased, largely because of advances in precision weaponry and the ability to coordinate air strikes with ground
operations. Franks presented the beginnings of a reconceptualized war
plan, one that would allow us to move faster by simultaneously targeting multiple centers of power within Iraq. He laid out several assumptions, a primary one of which was that Iraq would use weapons of mass
destruction against our troops, and we needed to prepare for that. He
also noted that should we go to war against Iraq, other parts of the U.S.
government would have important roles to play. The State Department,
which had worked with the international community to establish a provisional government in Afghanistan, would need to undertake a similar
effort for Iraq.

All of us in the meeting were aware of the success we had just had in
Afghanistan with CIA operatives working with special operations forces
and Afghan fighters. George Tenet cautioned that Iraq would be a different matter.

I knew that Saddam Hussein's regime was a hard target to penetrate,
but I wanted a better understanding of just what the CIA could do inside Iraq, and so I asked Tenet to set up a briefing. On January 3, 2002,
Tenet and two of his top officers, including the director of the Iraq
Operations Group, came to my West Wing office to meet with me and
Scooter Libby. The IOG director, whose name remains classified, began
with a short history of agency involvement in Iraq, including a botched

operation in the mid-1990s that Saddam had crushed. Then he moved on to a discussion of what lessons the agency had learned from its Iraq operations. At the top of his list, he emphasized that covert action could accomplish a good deal, but it could not, by itself, oust Saddam. Any U.S. covert action should be part of overall U.S. policy, and all elements of that policy needed to point to the same goal in a coordinated fashion. Second, it would be important to have a clear understanding of what we were willing to do militarily. Covert action would be much more effective with military support. Third, we needed a process for timely decision making. The success or failure of operations—and the lives of the people involved—might depend upon getting a fast answer from policymakers in Washington.

One of his most important points was the need to rebuild trust between the United States and the Iraqi people. They remembered that we had encouraged them to rise up during Desert Storm and then stood by while Saddam's gunships slaughtered thousands and put down the uprising. They were terrified of Saddam and doubted our word. When CIA officers attempted to recruit sources inside Iraq, they were most often met with skepticism about our seriousness in wanting to oust Saddam. If we wanted to establish an effective covert action program inside Iraq, we would need to convince the Iraqis that this time we meant it.

This task was complicated, the IOG director said, by our "bifurcated strategy"—working through the United Nations for sanctions and inspections while simultaneously pursuing regime change. His point was well taken, but the dual-track policy was intentional. The best way to get Saddam to come into compliance with UN demands was to convince him we would use force if he didn't comply. I understood that international meetings, resolutions, and negotiations might convey uncertainty about our willingness to use military force, but for now there was no alternative.

THAT SPRING THE PRESIDENT asked me to travel to the Middle East. I was scheduled to visit twelve countries in ten days for discussions on a range of issues, including not only our operations in Afghanistan but also our ongoing efforts in the worldwide War on Terror. I planned to discuss the next phases in the War on Terror, which meant talking about the threat posed by Saddam Hussein. I knew that at each stop I would also be discussing the Israeli-Palestinian conflict, which had been marked by terrible violence in the last year and a half.

This was my first trip overseas as vice president, and I was aware my office carried with it certain demands of ceremony and protocol, but I asked that these be kept to a minimum. I had previously traveled to all of the countries on my schedule, with the exception of Yemen. I'd known most of their leaders for more than a decade, and I knew my time would be best spent in frank and direct conversations with them.

I began my trip with a stop in London to visit one of America's closest and best allies in the War on Terror, British Prime Minister Tony Blair. I have tremendous respect for Prime Minister Blair. He is a Labour Party liberal and I am a conservative Republican, and we didn't always agree on strategy or tactics. But America had no greater ally during our time in office. His speeches about the war were some of the most eloquent I've been privileged to hear. I particularly recall sitting in the vice president's chair behind the podium in the chamber of the House of Representatives in July 2003 as the prime minister addressed a joint session of Congress. He knew that critics in America were asking why we had to take the lead in liberating Iraq and confronting terror, and he gave the answer: "Because destiny put you in this place in history, this moment in time, and the task is yours to do." But America wouldn't be alone, he pledged. "We will be with you in this fight for liberty."

As we met in March 2002 at Number 10 Downing Street, the prime minister and I discussed our ongoing efforts in Afghanistan, including plans to rebuild the Afghan National Army, expand the NATO mission, and get the international community more engaged in helping to rebuild that troubled country. I told Blair that the president had not decided yet about military action against Saddam Hussein and that we wanted to consult widely with our allies as the process unfolded. I also told the prime minister, as I did other leaders on this trip, that if war came, there should be no doubt about the outcome. The president wanted it to be absolutely clear that if he decided to go to war, we would finish the job. We would remove Saddam Hussein, eliminate the threat he posed, and establish a representative government.

We also discussed the upcoming meeting of the Arab League in Beirut, where the topic would be the Israeli-Palestinian conflict. The Israelis were threatening to bar Yasser Arafat from leaving his Ramallah compound to travel to the summit. I told the prime minister that we were encouraging the Israelis to allow Arafat to attend, but if he continued to incite Palestinian violence while he was gone, we would urge Israel not to allow him back into the West Bank.

In truth, by this time I was skeptical that Arafat could ever be a partner for peace. I believe the president shared my concerns. Just a few months before, Israeli commandos had stormed a freighter on the Red Sea, the *Karine-A*, and found millions of dollars of Iranian-produced weapons bound for terrorists in Gaza. There was no doubt in my mind that Arafat and his colleagues were behind the purchase. Their real interest was in the *Karine-A*'s cargo of Katyusha rockets and C-4 explosive, not in peace.

Still, I stressed to Prime Minister Blair that the United States would certainly remain engaged in attempting to find a solution to the Israeli-Palestinian crisis, but we would not do so at the expense of the War on Terror. I was not as confident as Blair that solving this crisis would take the steam out of the terrorist threat. I believed then, and do now, that were the Israeli-Palestinian crisis solved tomorrow, the terrorists would simply find another rationale for their continuing jihad.

At a press conference following our session, the prime minister was unhesitating in describing the threat that his intelligence, as well as ours, indicated that Saddam represented:

> *Let's be under no doubt whatever, Saddam Hussein has acquired weapons of mass destruction over a long period of time. He's the only leader in the world that's actually used chemical weapons against his own people. He is in breach of at least nine UN Security Council resolutions about weapons of mass destruction.*

Blair concluded, "That there is a threat from Saddam Hussein and the weapons of mass destruction that he has acquired is not in doubt at all." I added that in the context of what we had learned about al Qaeda's efforts to acquire nuclear, biological, and chemical capability, we needed to be very concerned "about the potential marriage, if you will, between a terrorist organization like al Qaeda and those who hold or are proliferating knowledge about weapons of mass destruction."

That afternoon Lynne and I took a brief side trip to visit Winston Churchill's war rooms, the underground complex used by the prime minister and his cabinet during World War II. The modest rooms, their walls hung with yellowed maps, were a powerful reminder of Churchill's brave leadership and the heroic fight of the Allies against Hitler. I remembered first reading Churchill's account of World War II nearly forty years before when I'd been building power line in Wyoming during the day and reading his volumes by a Coleman lantern at night.

I FLEW FROM LONDON to Amman, Jordan, for meetings with King Abdullah II. During the first Gulf War, King Abdullah's father, the late King Hussein, had sided with Saddam Hussein, but now Jordan was a close ally in the War on Terror. I thanked the king for Jordan's help in combatting terror and then walked him through our concerns about Iraq, none of which surprised him. Iraq's neighbors were keenly aware of the threat Saddam posed, but they were apprehensive about the consequences of military action. I made clear that military action was not imminent, but could become necessary. If so, it would be decisive, with no question about the outcome.

I told the king that if it came to war, there were a number of fronts on which we would likely request Jordanian assistance. I advised him as well that the president was very interested in consulting with him in the weeks and months ahead. We realized that any military action could have serious economic and political consequences, and we wanted to do what we could to mitigate them.

The king pressed for us to redouble our efforts on the peace process, and I assured him of President Bush's commitment, noting that

he had dispatched retired General Anthony Zinni to the region to do what he could to get the peace process back on track. I observed that even though we did not support some of the key elements of the initiative recently announced by Saudi Crown Prince Abdullah, such as the requirement that Israel return to its pre-1967 borders, we were hopeful that the initiative might provide a way for the parties at least to get back to the negotiating table. I also said, though, that we could not lose focus on the War on Terror. Attempts to reach a lasting peace between the Israelis and Palestinians had been under way for over fifty years with little progress to show. We could not afford to conduct the War on Terror on a similar timetable.

My next stop was Sharm el Sheikh, an Egyptian resort on the Red Sea, for meetings with Hosni Mubarak, a man I had known for many years. Mubarak, too, expressed his concerns about the Israeli-Palestinian crisis, warning in private that continued violence was playing into the hands of extremists in the region and putting tremendous pressure on moderate Arab leaders like himself. I told him I would relay his concerns to the president.

When we discussed Iraq and the threat it posed to the region, I again conveyed the message that the president had not decided on military action and was very interested in getting advice and guidance from our friends. Should it come to war, we would need some specific assistance from Egypt, such as overflight rights and logistics support. President Mubarak said that he was willing to consider the full gamut of our requests.

My security detail was very concerned about my next flight. We were going to Sanaa, Yemen, and there was particular worry about someone using a shoulder-fired missile to take down our airplane as we came in for a landing. The Secret Service came up with a diversionary plan. During the trip I had been flying in the large 747 that is normally the backup for Air Force One. Parked next to it that morning at the Sharm el Sheikh airport was a C-17 military transport aircraft that usually moves large equipment or troops. Lynne and I approached the stairs to the 747 together, but only she got on. Together with a small group

of staff members, I walked past the 747 and boarded the rear ramp of the C-17.

Lynne and most of the staff flew in the 747 directly to Oman, while I took the C-17 into Yemen. For an additional diversion, the 757 I normally used as Air Force Two made an approach into the Sanaa airport immediately ahead of us—coming in as though to land, but instead pulling up and flying north to Oman. The C-17 executed a tight corkscrew maneuver to evade surface-to-air threats, and we landed safely at the airport. President Ali Abdullah Saleh, there to greet me, seemed unfazed by my unusual arrival.

At this stop and others in the region, I was conscious that Arab leaders had relations with Saddam and that it was likely some of my messages would get back to him. I felt it was important that Saddam hear our resolve and that we do everything possible to make him understand that the president was determined to see Iraq comply with UN resolutions and that if it came to war, the United States would prevail.

I flew from Yemen to Oman, where I had a working dinner with Sultan Qaboos, a gracious host, whose country was making significant contributions to the War on Terror. The next day, March 15, I visited American sailors on the U.S.S. *Stennis* in the Arabian Sea. Fighter jets being launched off the *Stennis's* enormous carrier deck were conducting operations in Afghanistan, and I had a chance to thank the young Americans on board for their service—and to talk about what lay ahead. "Our next objective," I said, "is to prevent terrorists and regimes that sponsor terror from threatening America or our friends and allies with weapons of mass destruction." I went through the cafeteria line and had lunch with some of the sailors of the *Stennis*. I came away impressed, as I always was after I visited with our troops, by the commitment and competence of the men and women of America's armed forces. I told the press corps traveling with me that my visit to the *Stennis* was the highlight of my trip—and I meant it.

My next stop was the United Arab Emirates, where I met with President Zayed and some of his top aides, including Sheikh Mohammed bin Zayed, then chief of staff of the UAE armed forces and one of the

most insightful and direct leaders in the Middle East. I then flew on to see Crown Prince Abdullah in Jeddah, Saudi Arabia. King Fahd was still alive, but infirm, and the crown prince was the de facto ruler of the country. I had first met Abdullah twelve years earlier when I had flown to Saudi Arabia the first weekend after Saddam invaded Kuwait to secure basing rights for American forces. Although I did not always agree with him on policy, I had come to trust and respect him over the years as a plainspoken, honest man of deep faith.

In a practice we would repeat numerous times over the next six years, we had dinner together with members of our staffs and then moved to another room to meet privately, with only my professional and trusted interpreter, Gamal Helal, in attendance. I laid out for Abdullah the enormous impact of the 9/11 attacks on America. With three thousand Americans dead, we could not wait for terrorists to attack again and then deal with them after the fact. As the president had said, waiting for threats to fully materialize was waiting too long. Saddam, his pursuit of weapons of mass destruction, and his ties to terrorist groups, including al Qaeda, were of great concern. We intended to pursue a diplomatic resolution, but if we couldn't achieve one, we would be compelled to act. And if war did come, I assured the crown prince, we would prevail.

The crown prince was concerned about Saddam but skeptical about U.S. military action. He wanted more reassurance that we would, in fact, see it through. At the president's request I conveyed an invitation for the crown prince to visit the president at his Texas ranch, and I offered to have Secretary of Defense Don Rumsfeld and Joint Chiefs Chairman General Richard Myers meet him in Texas to brief him about our planning prior to his meeting with the president. Abdullah accepted my offer.

The crown prince also wanted to talk about the initiative he had put forth to advance the peace process. I told the crown prince we welcomed his initiative, and we hoped it would give impetus to the peace process at the upcoming Arab summit in Beirut and beyond. But, I cautioned, we viewed Arafat as a serious problem. Abdullah was not naïve about Arafat, but he saw him as the leader of the Palestinians, someone who should be treated as a partner.

Following stops in Bahrain, Qatar, and finally Kuwait, I headed for Israel. On the way, I called a meeting in the plane's conference room to discuss the Arab-Israeli situation. The State Department representative on my trip, Assistant Secretary for Near Eastern Affairs Bill Burns, lobbied for me to meet with Arafat. He argued that it would be wrong for such a senior U.S. official to travel to Jerusalem and meet only with the Israelis. Members of my staff—John Hannah, Eric Edelman, and Scooter Libby—objected to such a meeting. They argued that it would be seen as rewarding Arafat, who was still trafficking in terror. At a minimum, they suggested, if I agreed to meet, it would have to be in exchange for some positive action on Arafat's part.

Tony Zinni, our envoy for the Israeli-Palestinian conflict, was waiting for me on the tarmac in Tel Aviv, and we conferred in my limo about Arafat. Zinni had been working to get him to agree to key security steps on the path to a cease-fire. Would it be helpful, I asked, to offer up a meeting with me as an inducement for Arafat's cooperation? Zinni said that it would, and so I offered to meet with Arafat provided he agreed to the conditions Zinni had set forth. Zinni was confident the meeting could take place before I was scheduled to leave the next day.

That night at the King David Hotel, in a room overlooking the Old City of Jerusalem, Israeli Prime Minister Ariel Sharon told me he wanted to help General Zinni, that he wanted to secure a ceasefire and get back to negotiations. He was willing, he said, to begin reducing the Israeli presence in the West Bank, but he needed Arafat to take steps of his own. And he left no doubt that he would respond to further terrorist attacks with an iron fist. Sharon was a tough old soldier who had fought in Israel's war of independence in 1948, the Suez war in 1956, the Six Day War in 1967, and the Yom Kippur war of 1973. He didn't mince words, and I believed that ultimately peace would only come through a strong leader like Sharon. He would drive a tough bargain, but his word counted—and he would defend his nation against terrorists and extremists who had no interest in peace.

As the hour for my departure from Israel approached, there was still no agreement from Arafat. I said I'd be more than willing to come back the following week. I would make a special trip to see Arafat if he met Zinni's conditions. Instead, one week after my return to Washington, on March 27, 2002, a Palestinian suicide bomber walked into the Park Hotel in Netanya, Israel, during Passover Seder, and killed thirty people. In the days that followed, Prime Minister Sharon sent Israeli army units deeper into the West Bank to hunt down the terrorists responsible.

From Israel, I headed to Turkey, a country that had long been a friend of the United States. Turkey had stood with us in Korea and, as a NATO member, been an invaluable ally during the Cold War. We had major military facilities at Incirlik Air Base, from which we had conducted operations during Desert Storm and in the aftermath, when we provided humanitarian relief to Kurdish refugees in northern Iraq. But by 2002 a worrisome change was under way, and my visit with Turkish leaders, though cordial, was far different from the one I had made in 1990, when we were seeking allies to expel Saddam Hussein from Kuwait. In fact, all of my visits in the region were different this time. All of our friends were nervous. But something deeper was happening in Turkey. In November 2002 the Islamist AKP party would win a majority in parliament, making Recep Erdogan, leader of the party, prime minister the following March. The newly elected parliament would reject our request to deploy the U.S. Army's 4th Infantry Division through Turkey when it came time to begin operations against Saddam Hussein, and we would ultimately send it through Kuwait.

In general, I think we failed to understand the magnitude of the shift that was taking place in Turkey. The significance of an Islamist government taking power in one of America's most important NATO allies was in a sense obscured because of all the other challenges we faced. Today, Turkey appears to be in the middle of a dangerous transition from a key NATO ally to an Islamist-governed nation developing close ties with countries like Iran and Syria at the expense of its relations with the United States and Israel.

As I ended my trip and headed for Washington, I thought about what I would report to the president. As I saw it America had to pursue three broad objectives in the region simultaneously: vigorously prosecuting the war against terrorism, confronting Iraq about its support for terror and pursuit of WMD, and managing the Israeli-Palestinian conflict. I did not believe, as many argued, that the Israeli-Palestinian conflict was the linchpin of every other American policy in the Middle East. I saw instead a complicated region in which issues are interrelated and couldn't be compartmentalized. We did not have the luxury of dealing with them sequentially, waiting until the Israeli-Palestinian conflict was resolved before we dealt with the threat that terrorism posed to the United States.

It would have been wrong to push the Israelis to make concessions to a Palestinian Authority controlled by Yasser Arafat, who we knew was supporting, encouraging, and funding terror. At the same time it seemed clear to me that if military action became necessary in Iraq, we would need Arab support, and it would be easier to get such support if we could reduce the tensions between the Israelis and Palestinians.

ON APRIL 4, 2002, President Bush expressed concern for the "mounting toll of terror" and announced he was sending Secretary of State Powell back to the region to focus on the Israeli-Palestinian conflict. On April 12, with Powell in the Middle East, the National Security Council convened to discuss conditions for a possible Powell meeting with Arafat. In the middle of the discussion, an NSC staffer entered the Situation Room with news that there had been another suicide bombing in Jerusalem. There were six dead and over a hundred injured.

Nevertheless, at a press briefing in Israel, Secretary Powell decided to float the idea of an international conference on the Israeli-Palestinian issue. The president had not agreed to this, and it was a bad idea. Giving Arafat a place on the world stage would only legitimize him at a moment he was making it clear that he had chosen the path of terror. Secretary Powell repeated the offer again a few weeks later, making a similar announcement in a press briefing in Washington with some of his European and UN counterparts. When I heard this I called National

Security Advisor Rice from Air Force Two and suggested she needed to let Secretary Powell know that he was once more out of line with the president's policy. We had all discussed next steps in the Middle East with the president in the Oval Office that morning, and he had not authorized Colin to announce we would participate in an international conference. I'm not sure what transpired between Condi and Colin, but the next day, when the Principals Committee—the NSC minus the president—met to discuss the Middle East, Colin apologized. He said he had "exceeded his brief" and gone beyond what the president wanted him to say.

My concern as we discussed the peace process and next steps was that we all needed to remember our number-one priority was winning the War on Terror. I argued that we would benefit from a limited or interim Israeli-Palestinian agreement that would allow a cooling-off period and give time for new leadership to emerge on the Palestinian side. But it was critically important that we not launch high-profile international conferences or summit meetings in futile pursuit of a final settlement agreement that Arafat showed no willingness to embrace on any reasonable terms. Bill Clinton had made that mistake at the end of his second term with a high-profile, high-expectations, and high-stakes maneuver that brought Arafat and Israeli Prime Minister Ehud Barak to Camp David for a series of talks that failed tragically and led to the renewed intifada. There was no way we could afford to repeat that train wreck if we wanted successfully to pursue the War on Terror.

Looking back, I believe that Secretary Powell's trip to the Middle East in the spring of 2002 was a watershed moment in relations between the State Department and the White House. Both Powell and his deputy, Richard Armitage, seemed to take the fact that the White House had been compelled to walk back Powell's announcement of a Middle East conference as a personal affront to the secretary. I had built many relationships over the thirty-four years since I had first come to Washington, and it was about this time that I began hearing from a number of former and current high-ranking government officials that Secretary Powell and Deputy Secretary Armitage were not only failing to support the president's policies, but were openly disdainful of them. I knew that Powell had been stung by press reports that he was not a strong secretary, but now it was as though a tie had been cut.

THAT SPRING WE HAD a visitor from another part of the world: Chinese Vice President Hu Jintao. As a matter of protocol, he and I were counterparts, and I had him out to the Vice President's Residence for lunch. Of all the lunches I hosted over the years for visiting dignitaries, this one may have had the highest-ranking U.S. delegation. Flanking me on the U.S. side of the table were Colin Powell, Treasury Secretary Paul O'Neill, Commerce Secretary Don Evans, Labor Secretary Elaine Chao, National Security Advisor Condi Rice, and Deputy Defense Secretary Paul Wolfowitz.

I was interested in finding a way to pull Hu aside so that the two of us could have a private conversation. He had been rigidly scripted in every one of his meetings with U.S. officials, never deviating from his talking points. I thought that if the two of us could talk alone, he might loosen up and we could have a real exchange. My plan was to take him into the library on the first floor of my residence after lunch.

The Chinese delegation wasn't on board with our plan. Moments after Hu and I had seated ourselves in the library, the doors flew open and Li Zhaoxing, a senior Communist Party member close to Hu's boss, President Jiang Zemin, burst in. He had blown past my staff as they tried to explain politely that this was a one-on-one meeting, and now he seated himself between Hu and me. It was clear this was the minder reporting back to Beijing. Hu didn't skip a beat and continued to deliver the scripted answers he'd been giving in other meetings.

My relations with Hu were capped off by the visit I had with him two years later when I was in China in early 2004. By that time Hu had ascended to the presidency, and I had a sensitive message President Bush had asked me to convey in a one-on-one session. We agreed that a small meeting would occur after our larger session. The meeting went fine, I thought, and I had conveyed the message without any minder pushing his way in.

As I left the meeting room I was surprised to learn from my staff that the conversation I thought had been private had actually been broadcast into an adjacent room, where Hu's staff gathered around a speaker to listen. The Chinese, apparently, aren't fans of one-on-one meetings.

DON RUMSFELD AND Tommy Franks came to the White House on May 10, 2002, with a status report on the military planning process. Part of the discussion focused on timing. The logistics of any major military operation are exceedingly complex, and though we were still hopeful that war would not be necessary, we worried that Saddam might launch an attack on us or our allies before we had sufficient forces in place. No one wanted us to be embroiled in a conflict at a time of Saddam's choosing rather than ours.

I was concerned about a number of contingencies. How did our war plan deal with weapons of mass destruction? How did we intend to discourage Saddam from using these weapons, and what preparations were we making to protect our troops if he did? If we were successful at getting the inspectors back into Iraq, how effective did we believe they could be? Could we insist on placing U.S. inspectors on the teams? How could we deny Iraq the ability to launch Scud missiles at Israel, as Saddam had done during the first Gulf War? How was Saddam likely to respond to our actions? What would it take for us effectively to defend the Kurds against the Iraqi forces massed in the north?

Throughout the process Congress would be very important, and I wanted to know if we had a strategy to ensure that key members were briefed on how we would conduct the war if it came. We also needed to ensure that Congress and the American public understood the consequences of an unconstrained Saddam. With his tremendous oil resources and the fraying sanctions, failure to bring him under control or act against him would simply give him time to advance his WMD programs and perhaps develop a nuclear weapon.

THROUGHOUT MAY AND MUCH of June, we debated our policy toward the Israeli-Palestinian crisis. In meetings of the Principals

Committee and the National Security Council, I urged that we move beyond Yasser Arafat. The record was clear, in my view, that he could not be part of trying to establish peace.

Our policy debates culminated in the president's Rose Garden speech on June 24, 2002, in which the United States called for the first time for new Palestinian leadership. The president said that the Palestinian people needed to elect new leaders "not compromised by terror" if they were to achieve the independent state that they deserved. He called on the Israelis to withdraw to their September 2000 positions as the Palestinians made security improvements and said that "Israeli settlement activity in the occupied territories must stop." It was a bold and courageous speech that committed America to active leadership toward the goal of peace—but only if the Palestinian people chose new leaders who renounced terror.

BY THE SUMMER OF 2002, the anthrax attacks that had followed shortly after 9/11 had not been solved, and I had received numerous reports about terrorist interest in dangerous biological and chemical substances. In Principals Meetings we had discussed threats that might emanate from Russia's former biological weapons program, whether from loose stockpiles of biological warfare agents or unemployed scientists. The war in Afghanistan had given us access to sites in that country that showed al Qaeda's work on biological weapons to be further along than had been suspected.

My staff and I spent significant time on response measures, such as whether and how to produce, stockpile, and administer vaccines for anthrax and smallpox. We discussed vaccination against bioterrorist threats, a very controversial subject, even when applied to a well-defined segment of the population—such as the American military. There had been only limited use of the anthrax vaccine during the first Gulf War, and critics claimed it risked adverse side effects. I was among those who believed the risk was well worth taking, particularly for troops going into areas where the development of biological weapons had been reported. It seemed to me, however, that if the men and women of our armed forces were going to have to act on that belief, I should, too, and I received the vaccine series. I received a smallpox vaccine, as well.

Smallpox was a concern not only because it is disfiguring and deadly but because so many Americans were unprotected. Routine vaccination had ceased in 1972 after the disease was eradicated in the United States, but even those who had been vaccinated before were not necessarily safe because acquired immunity gradually declines.

During our first months in office, Scooter Libby and others on my staff had studied the results of an exercise, called "Dark Winter," that had simulated the effect of a smallpox attack on the United States. A group of distinguished Americans acted the parts of the National Security Council, with former Georgia Senator Sam Nunn playing the president. The scenario they were given posited terrorist attacks with smallpox in Oklahoma City, with the infection spreading rapidly around the country and beyond. Despite the best efforts of exercise participants, sixteen thousand people were infected within two weeks, with seventeen thousand more expected to fall ill in the twelve days after that. These numbers represented just the first two generations of the disease. In the fourth generation, it was estimated, there might be as many as three million infected, with as many as one million dying.

One of the primary problems faced by exercise participants was a shortage of vaccine, which was, in fact, the situation in the United States in early 2001. My office began pressing the Department of Health and Human Services to get more vaccine produced and to make plans for its distribution. In October 2001 the department announced plans to increase the stockpile of U.S. smallpox vaccine to 300 million doses—one for every American.

On July 17, 2002, I flew to Atlanta with Scooter and my homeland security advisor, Carol Kuntz, for a daylong series of briefings at the Centers for Disease Control and Prevention. I met with the CDC smallpox experts, toured their anthrax laboratory, and received a briefing on biological warfare countermeasures. The men and women of the CDC, including the new director, Dr. Julie Gerberding, were an impressive group and would play an important role in fighting terrorism during the time I was in office. I also came to have great respect for the knowledge and wisdom of Dr. Anthony Fauci, head of the National Institute of Allergy and Infectious Diseases. He, too, was a key figure in improving the security of the country against biological attacks.

At the end of my visit to the CDC I spoke to staff members gathered in the auditorium. I thanked them for the tremendous contribution they were making in defending the nation. I wanted to make sure they knew they had an advocate in the White House.

ON AUGUST 5 WE had a National Security Council meeting to review the latest iteration of the war plan. Tommy Franks was refining and modifying the plan in order to shorten lead times. We were all more comfortable with a plan that gave Saddam less time to plan and prepare counterattacks. In a discussion about postwar planning, there was a brief exchange about the military requirements for postwar security operations. The president looked at CIA Director Tenet and asked him point-blank what the Iraqi people's reaction would be to an American military overthrow of Saddam Hussein. Tenet didn't skip a beat: "Most Iraqis will rejoice when Saddam is gone," the CIA director responded.

I WORKED OUT OF Wyoming for a good part of August, attending meetings back in Washington by SVTS, with the equipment set up in my upstairs office. On August 10 I was scheduled to confer via SVTS with a visiting delegation of Iraqi exiles opposed to Saddam Hussein. They had gathered in the ornate Cordell Hull Conference Room in the Old Executive Office Building, across the street from the White House. All of them had taken their places and were waiting for me to appear on the screen, when, unbeknownst to me, my four-year-old granddaughter, Elizabeth, wandered into my office. The Iraqis were treated to images of Elizabeth jumping around in a pink princess outfit and making faces at herself as she watched her performance reflected back on the two-way video hookup. She was hustled off by my personal aide, Brian McCormack, before I arrived on the scene. I sat down in front of the camera and Scooter Libby sat down just outside of view. Unaware of the performance that had just taken place, I said to the delegation: "Greetings from Wyoming. I'm here with my chief of staff." It was only after the meeting that someone explained why the Iraqis found that so funny.

Since January 2002 Scooter had been urging the State Department to get the major Iraqi opposition groups together for an international conference to begin planning for a post-Saddam government, but a conference had been repeatedly delayed while Secretary Powell and Deputy Secretary Armitage warned about too much engagement with Saddam's opponents. They were "externals," or so the argument went, who had left Iraq during Saddam's reign and would not have credibility with Iraqis who had stayed. Therefore, the State Department argued, they should not be actively involved in our postwar planning. I've reflected on this assessment and its consequences many times in the years since as I have watched so-called externals play a crucial role in Iraq's democratic government. The prime minister of Iraq today, Nouri al Maliki, lived in exile until 2003, as did Ayad Allawi, whom Maliki narrowly defeated in the 2010 national elections.

The idea that we shouldn't work closely with opponents of Saddam who were living in exile slowed us down. I think we would have done a better job in the wake of Saddam's ouster if we had had a provisional government, made up of externals and internals, ready to take over as soon as Saddam fell. This would have put Iraqis in charge of Iraq and helped avoid the taint of occupation that we began to experience under the Coalition Provisional Authority.

A question that came up early and often in our discussions of a government to follow Saddam was whether we were committed to establishing a democracy in Iraq. I believed we had no alternative. Any provisional government would have to agree to early, free, and fair elections. Critics on the left have accused the United States of attempting to impose democracy at the point of a gun, but I see it differently. If the United States took military action and removed Saddam from power, we had an obligation to ensure that what followed reflected our values and belief in freedom and democracy. It may well have been easier simply to handpick another Iraqi strongman and install him in one of Saddam's palaces, but that would have been inconsistent with American values and, in my view, immoral.

IN MID-AUGUST FORMER National Security Advisor Brent Scowcroft wrote an op-ed in the *Wall Street Journal* urging us not to attack Iraq. "It is beyond dispute that Saddam is a menace," he wrote, noting that Saddam brutalized his own people and had launched wars on two of his neighbors. Scowcroft also thought it a settled matter that Saddam had weapons of mass destruction, but he thought it "unlikely" that Saddam would provide WMD to terrorists, overlooking the fact that Iraq had already provided safe haven, training, and material support to terrorists. Brent went on to argue that we could rely on the UN Security Council and international inspections to contain the threat posed by Saddam, overlooking the fact that Saddam had repeatedly ignored the United Nations since Brent and I served together eleven years earlier in the first Bush administration.

As I read Brent's piece, I found myself thinking that it reflected a pre-9/11 mind-set, the worldview of a time before we had seen the devastation that terrorists armed with hijacked airplanes could cause. We had to do everything possible to be sure that they never got their hands on weapons that could kill millions.

Brent was very close to the president's father, and he and I had been good friends since the Ford administration. He'd had a hand in recommending me to be secretary of defense in the previous Bush administration. He obviously had major disagreements with the policies of the second Bush administration, and he didn't hesitate to express those differences publicly.

Brent was quoted later saying he believed I had changed since we'd worked together in the first Bush administration. In reality, what had happened was that after an attack on the homeland that had killed three thousand people, the world had changed. We were at war against terrorist enemies who could not be negotiated with, deterred, or contained, and who would never surrender. This was not the world of superpower tensions and arms control agreements in which Brent had served.

––––––

DURING AUGUST I BECAME concerned that too much emphasis was being placed on getting UN inspectors back into Iraq. One proposal talked about in the White House was for an "aggressive" inspection regime—a set of inspections so intrusive they might result in toppling Saddam. National Security Advisor Rice advanced this idea, and the president and Tony Blair discussed it. I didn't buy it. It seemed fanciful to me. Saddam Hussein, who had faced so much worse, was not going to be ousted by teams of UN inspectors, no matter how insistent they might be.

Inspections, I thought, could too easily be a source of false comfort, allowing us to think that we were doing something significant about the threat Saddam posed, when, in fact, we were not. I decided to press the issue in a speech I gave to the Veterans of Foreign Wars on August 26, 2002. Saddam had "made a science out of deceiving the international community," I said to the audience assembled in Nashville, Tennessee. I recalled how surprised analysts were after the Gulf War to find that he was perhaps within a year of acquiring a nuclear weapon. I also cited what had happened in the spring of 1995:

> *The inspectors were actually on the verge of declaring that Saddam's programs to develop chemical weapons and longer-range ballistic missiles had been fully accounted for and shut down. Then Saddam's son-in-law suddenly defected and began sharing information. Within days the inspectors were led to an Iraqi chicken farm. Hidden there were boxes of documents and lots of evidence regarding Iraq's most secret weapons program.*

Inspectors subsequently discovered that Saddam had deceived them "about the extent of his program to mass produce VX, one of the deadliest chemicals known to man," I said. And he had not shut down his prohibited missile programs, but had "continued to test such missiles, almost literally under the noses of UN inspectors."

Given this record, a return of inspectors to Iraq did not ensure Saddam's compliance with UN resolutions, but it would give him time to plot and plan and eventually acquire "the whole range of weapons of mass destruction." I emphasized the need, in facing such a threat, to proceed with "care, deliberation, and consultation with our allies." And we should keep in mind, I said, that for all the dangers we were facing, there were also opportunities:

> *With our help, a liberated Iraq can be a great nation once again. Iraq is rich in natural resources and human talent, and has unlimited potential for a peaceful, prosperous future. Our goal would be an Iraq that has territorial integrity, a government that is democratic and pluralistic, a nation where the human rights of every ethnic group are recognized and protected.*

All who sought justice and dignity in Iraq, I concluded, "can know they have a friend and ally in the United States of America."

WHEN THE NATIONAL SECURITY Council met at Camp David on Saturday, September 7, 2002, one of the topics on which we spent a good deal of time was the president's upcoming speech at the United Nations. He was going there, as presidents often do, for the opening of the General Assembly. I was a strong advocate of using the speech to challenge the United Nations. The president should point out that the Security Council had passed sixteen resolutions aimed at removing the danger posed by Saddam. When he repeatedly violated them, the UN had responded with yet more resolutions. I argued that the time had come to confront the United Nations, hold the organization accountable, and make clear that if the Security Council was unwilling to impose consequences for violations, the UN would become irrelevant. What I hoped we wouldn't do was what we'd done for the last twelve years—simply adopt yet one more meaningless resolution.

Underlying the debate over the speech and UN resolutions was the issue of military force itself. The president had not yet made a decision, but in neither this meeting nor any other I attended did any of the president's advisors argue against using military force to remove Saddam from power. Nor did anyone argue that leaving Saddam in power, with all the risks and costs associated with that course, was a viable option.

When we finished our NSC meeting, the president hosted Tony Blair in his office in Laurel Lodge. I joined the two of them, and we talked through the need for United Nations involvement. Blair was tough. He understood the stakes and the importance of acting against Saddam, and he was clear that he would be with us no matter what—and that was likely to include strong opposition from within his own party.

Blair argued that a UN resolution was necessary to achieve maximum international cooperation. He was very persuasive, and I understood that the president wanted to support his friend. There was no legal obligation for us to pursue a resolution, but there were some in the United States and many more in Europe who felt it would legitimize military action, and a resolution would also speak to their concerns. The president told the prime minister he would go forward with a resolution.

I knew the president was no more interested than I was in an endless round of inspections and deception in Iraq, and in the days that followed, I recommended inserting into the resolution a requirement for Saddam to submit within thirty days a declaration disclosing his WMD capacity and holdings. This would lay down a marker, set a deadline for assessing one final time whether action against Saddam was required.

AS WORK WENT FORWARD at the United Nations, we also sought congressional authorization for the use of force. Several members of Congress requested that the intelligence community produce a National Intelligence Estimate, a document that reflects the consensus view of U.S. intelligence agencies. The judgments contained in the 2002 NIE were of a piece with the briefings the president and I had been receiving. "Iraq has continued its weapons of mass destruction programs in defiance of UN resolutions and restrictions," the report said. "Baghdad has chemical and biological weapons as well as missiles with ranges in excess of UN restrictions; if left unchecked, it probably will have a nuclear weapon during this decade." Most agencies assessed that "Baghdad started reconstituting its nuclear program about the time that UNSCOM inspectors departed—December 1998," and that "if Baghdad acquires sufficient fissile material from abroad it could make a nuclear weapon within several months to a year."

The judgment that Iraq was reconstituting its nuclear program was based in part on aluminum tubes the Iraqis had ordered. Most of the intelligence community believed they were intended for centrifuges to be used in uranium enrichment. There was a minority view in the NIE, which Director Tenet later emphasized, that the tubes were for another purpose, possibly the production of artillery rockets. But that was not the CIA's position at the time, and in 2002 Tenet conducted briefings using one of the tubes. He would reach down on the floor, pick up an aluminum tube that was at least three feet long, and place it on the table. With this very impressive prop in place, he would explain with great confidence why the tubes were compelling evidence that Iraq was reconstituting a program to enrich uranium.

In the lead-up to the vote in Congress, various members explained their positions. Senator John Kerry said, "When I vote to give the president of the United States the authority to use force, if necessary, to disarm Saddam Hussein, it is because I believe that a deadly arsenal of weapons of mass destruction in his hands is a threat, and a grave threat, to our security." Senator Hillary Clinton gave a speech on the floor of the Senate, parts of which I could have given myself. Among the reasons she would vote to give the president the authority to go to war, she declared, was that "Saddam Hussein is a tyrant who has tortured and killed his own people" and "used chemical weapons on Iraqi Kurds and Iranians, killing over 20,000 people." Senator Clinton noted that since inspectors left Iraq in 1998, "Intelligence reports show that Saddam Hussein has worked to rebuild his chemical and biological weapons stock, his missile delivery capability, and his nuclear program." She cited his connection to terrorism, noting that he "has also given aid, comfort, and sanctuary to terrorists, including al Qaeda members." She argued that if Saddam Hussein were left unchecked, he would "continue to increase his capability to wage biological and chemical warfare" and "keep trying to develop nuclear weapons."

One of the most eloquent statements of the necessity of removing Saddam came from Senator Jay Rockefeller, the vice chairman of the Senate Intelligence Committee. He acknowledged the "unmistakable evidence that Saddam Hussein is working aggressively to develop nuclear weapons and will likely have nuclear weapons within the next five years." He noted that "Saddam's government has contact with many international terrorist organizations that likely have cells here in the United States," and he talked about the lesson our country had learned in September 2001:

> September 11 changed our world forever. We may not like it, but it is the world in which we live. When there is a grave threat to Americans' lives, we have a responsibility to take action to prevent it.

A few months later in an appearance on CNN, Senator Rockefeller expanded on Saddam's connection to terrorism: "The fact that Zarqawi certainly is related to the death of the USAID officer [Laurence Foley] and that he is very close to bin Laden puts to rest, in fairly dramatic terms, that there is at least a substantial connection between Saddam and al Qaeda."

On October 10, the House passed the resolution authorizing the use of force in Iraq by a vote of 296–133, forty-six more votes in favor than had been the case for Desert Storm in 1991. Shortly after midnight the Senate approved the resolution 77–23, a much larger margin than for the Gulf War.

ON NOVEMBER 8, 2002, the Security Council unanimously approved Resolution 1441. It gave Iraq "a final opportunity to comply with its disarmament obligations," demanded immediate and unrestricted access for UN inspectors, and required that Iraq provide a "complete declaration of all aspects" of its weapons of mass destruction programs and delivery systems. On December 7 Iraq submitted a twelve-thousand-page declaration, which, a few weeks later, British Foreign Secretary Jack Straw called "an obvious falsehood." Hans Blix of Sweden, the head of the UN inspection effort, reinforced that idea when he reported to the Security Council in January. He said that the Iraqi declaration was mostly "a reprint of earlier documents" and that among the items it failed to account for were 6,500 chemical bombs, containing some one thousand tons of chemical agent. He noted that inspectors had indications that Iraq had weaponized VX, a deadly nerve gas, which conflicted with the account Iraq had given. He observed that "there are strong indications that Iraq produced more anthrax than it declared" and no convincing evidence that any of it had been destroyed. Missiles declared by Iraq had been "tested to a range in excess of the permitted range of 150 kilometers," Blix said, and he noted that inspectors had discovered unarmed chemical warheads that Iraq had failed to declare. They were in a bunker that was relatively new and had probably been placed there within the past few years.

EVEN WHEN WAR AND peace are on the table, other matters have to be dealt with, and at the end of 2002, it was the Treasury Department. The president had decided he wanted to make a change. Paul O'Neill wasn't working out. I felt somewhat responsible since I had recommended him for the job. I had gotten to know O'Neill during the Ford administration when he was the senior civil servant at OMB. He had been a superb budget analyst, a real star of the Ford administration, and after that, he had entered the business world, where he eventually became the well-regarded CEO of Alcoa. My friend Alan Greenspan was also a great fan of O'Neill and had thought he'd be a superb Treasury secretary.

In retrospect the problems were evident early on. When we were trying to reform tax policy and get the economy moving again, O'Neill often seemed more concerned with the accident record at Treasury. He also dedicated himself to the problem of bringing clean water to Africa—an important goal to be sure—but one better suited for the portfolio of the director of the Agency for International Development than for that of the Treasury secretary.

And there were some structural problems. Economic policy was being run out of the White House, and meetings to make big decisions often did not include the Treasury secretary. O'Neill should have demanded—as Hank Paulson would later demand—to be included in any White House meeting about economic policy. On the other hand, either the president or I could have said, "Where's O'Neill? We should not be having this meeting without the Treasury secretary."

On December 6 I called O'Neill. "Paul, the president has decided to make a change in his economic team," I said, "and he wants you to come over so he can talk to you in person." After initially agreeing to come to the White House, Paul called me back and canceled. He had someone drop off his resignation letter and left town.

ON DECEMBER 21, WITH the White House decorated for Christmas, a group including George Tenet, Condi Rice, Scooter Libby, Andy Card, and me met in the Oval Office with the president to review a briefing prepared by the CIA on Iraq's weapons of mass destruction and the threat posed by Saddam. Although we had already secured congressional authorization and a UN resolution, we knew we would have to explain the threat Saddam posed to the American public. George Tenet's deputy, John McLaughlin, had put together the briefing, and as he presented it in a dry, academic fashion, none of us was very impressed. When he had finished, the president, seated in one of the chairs in front of the fireplace, turned to George, who was on the sofa to his right. "Just how good is our case on Iraq WMD?" he asked. "It's a slam dunk, Mr. President," Tenet said. "It's a slam dunk."

The president wanted a better presentation. What he envisioned, he said, was a case against Saddam that was like a closing argument in a trial. Thinking that lawyers might be best suited for the job, he directed Libby and Hadley to take the CIA material we had on Saddam and turn it into a brief that strongly presented the evidence against him.

After Christmas the president asked Colin Powell to make the public case against Saddam at the UN. The work Scooter and Steve had done, coordinating with a CIA officer detailed to the National Security Council and drawing from intelligence community reports, was forwarded to Powell for him to use as he prepared his remarks. I called Colin, told him the package he had received had good material in it, and encouraged him to take a look. Powell and members of his staff said later that they threw Steve's and Scooter's documents out and spent several days and nights at the CIA, where they personally confirmed with George Tenet every piece of information that went into his speech.

A few days later, Powell sat in the United States chair in the Security Council, with George Tenet behind him, and presented the case against Iraq. "My colleagues," he said, "every statement I make today is backed up by sources, solid sources. These are not assertions. What we're giving you are facts and conclusions based on solid intelligence."

Later, when it turned out that much of what Powell said about weapons of mass destruction was wrong, I think embarrassment caused him and those around him to lash out at others. Libby seemed to be a particular target of their ire. They excoriated the material that he and the National Security Council staff had provided, while at the same time boasting that they had thrown it in the garbage. As it happened much of what they discarded focused on Saddam's ties to terror and human rights violations, charges that would stand the test of time.

ON SATURDAY, JANUARY 11, 2003, at the president's request, I invited Prince Bandar, the Saudi ambassador to Washington, to my West Wing office for a briefing about our concept for military operations in Iraq. Thirteen years earlier Colin Powell and I had conducted a similar briefing for Bandar at the round table in my Pentagon office. This time it was Joint Chiefs Chairman Dick Myers and Secretary of Defense Don Rumsfeld who outlined our thinking and explained why we needed Saudi help. Being able to operate out of bases in the Kingdom would be crucial to us for an operation in Iraq.

I knew that Bandar was concerned about our commitment to see this thing through, and with the president's approval, I intended to reassure him. I'd done that on the eve of Desert Storm, when I made two commitments to King Fahd. I had told him the United States would send sufficient forces to defend Saudi Arabia and liberate Kuwait, and I had assured him that when the job was done, we'd bring our troops home. And we'd kept our commitments.

But Saddam had survived, and he had managed simply by surviving to portray himself as the victor. None of his neighbors wanted to see that happen again. It might make him even more dangerous. If the United States was going to conduct a military operation, we needed to ensure that Saddam didn't remain in power.

General Myers gave Bandar a good look at what we had in mind. Bandar, who had been a fighter pilot, understood the strategy and jargon, and there was no doubt he was impressed. But he wanted to know if there would be a way out for Saddam. Don assured him that Saddam would not be left in power. Bandar asked again, directly, "Is Saddam going to survive this time?" I had quietly listened through most of the briefing, but now I spoke out. "Bandar," I said, "once we start this, Saddam is toast."

Bandar was convinced. He wanted to be able to tell the crown prince that he had heard this directly from the president, and so when he left my office, I conveyed his message to the president. He met with Bandar the following Monday.

TONY BLAIR RETURNED TO Washington at the end of January, arguing that we needed yet another UN resolution. Colin Powell, Condi Rice, Don Rumsfeld, and I were all in agreement that this was a mistake. We'd managed one resolution, no one believed we needed a second, and it would be very hard to get. French Foreign Minister Dominique de Villepin had already declared that "nothing today justifies envisaging military action" against Iraq. I was also concerned that going after a second resolution and failing to get it would give our critics a chance to say we were acting alone—though, in fact, we had assembled a coalition of several dozen countries. Many made small contributions, to be sure, but the historical significance was immense of having not only long-standing allies like the United Kingdom and Australia with us, but also countries such as the Czech Republic, from the former Soviet bloc. I also thought that going to the UN again would make us look hesitant and uncertain, but Blair saw a second resolution as a political necessity for him at home. Although he had a huge margin in Parliament, he couldn't count on his fellow Labour Party members, and he foresaw the possibility of not only losing a vote on the war, but even bringing down his government. Britain was our major ally, and when the president decided to try for a second resolution, I understood his reasons. But our efforts to gather support for the resolution were unsuccessful, and on Monday, March 17, we pulled it down. That night the president addressed the nation and gave Saddam Hussein forty-eight hours to leave Iraq.

The next day, Tuesday, Blair won his vote in Parliament. A majority of Labour members supported him, and he got an even larger share of the Conservatives' votes. At the request of the British, I had called a number of the Tories, including Iain Duncan Smith, the Conservative leader. He was, on this issue, a rock of support for Blair.

On Wednesday, as the military operation was ready to begin, I made calls to a series of world leaders, letting them know that diplomacy had run its course. My schedule shows that I talked to the leaders of Egypt, Israel, Hungary, Bulgaria, Romania, and South Korea. The Syrian president, Bashar Assad, was also on my call list, but when my office reached his, word came back that he was "unavailable."

Somewhere during the series of phone calls, I was called down to the Oval Office. The president's national security team was gathering to hear George Tenet, who had come to report that CIA sources inside Iraq believed they knew where Saddam Hussein would be that night. The agency had eyewitness accounts, George said, that Saddam and his two sons had been at a compound called Dora Farms and were likely to return. Amid a frenzy of activity, with new information coming in real time and staffers and principals hurrying in and out, Secretary Rumsfeld and Joint Chiefs Chairman Myers talked about our military options. If, in fact, Saddam was there, we had the possibility of striking a decapitation blow in the first moments of the war. But we had to act fast, and there were risks. We would need bunker-busting bombs on the target, and that meant planes flying close to Baghdad before its air defenses had been destroyed.

We thoroughly discussed the pros and cons, and eventually the president kicked everyone else out of the Oval Office, looked at me, and said, "Dick, what do you think we ought to do?" I told him I thought we should launch. If the intelligence was right, we had the chance to shorten the war significantly by killing Saddam up front. I thought that was worth the risk. The president agreed. He called the others back into his office and told them to launch. Shortly after the deadline for Saddam to leave Iraq expired, two F-117 stealth fighters bombed Dora Farms.

The next day we got initial reports that the strike might have worked. An eyewitness reported a man looking like Saddam had been dragged from the rubble and left lying on a stretcher in the open air. It didn't take long, however, to find out those first reports were wrong.

IN THE EARLY DAYS and weeks of Operation Iraqi Freedom, I received nearly daily briefings on our progress. Tommy Franks also gave regular updates via SVTS from his forward headquarters in Qatar. He did so on the morning of March 30, and the news was encouraging. The oil fields had been taken intact, western Iraq was no longer a base for launching missiles against Iraq's neighbors, and our air strikes were significantly degrading Iraq's forces. We were already operating from Iraqi airfields; Khurmal, the al Qaeda poisons camp, had been destroyed; and humanitarian supplies were arriving in Iraq. Our forces had closed to within sixty miles of Baghdad on multiple fronts and were still over 90 percent combat capable. The list went on and on. Tommy concluded: "The regime is in trouble and they know it."

One of our biggest concerns was that Saddam might concentrate his best forces around the city, use chemical or biological weapons against our troops, and then create a fortress for himself inside Baghdad. We worried we'd have to deal with a siege of the city that would be extremely costly in lives and casualties. To avoid getting bogged down on the road to Baghdad, our commanders orchestrated and executed an operation that emphasized speed. They raced for the capital. Like millions of Americans, I watched news reports on television night after night as journalists embedded with the troops reported on the rapid advance toward the heart of Saddam's regime.

At a briefing on the progress of the war on April 2, the Defense Department reported that in Najaf, people were "receiving us as liberators." At an April 5 briefing, the report was "crowds beginning to turn out to welcome us." On April 9, the day we marched into Baghdad, the conclusion was "situation really, really positive." Banner headlines in the *Washington Post* reported, "U.S. Forces Move Triumphantly through Capital Streets, Cheered by Crowds Jubilant at End of Repressive Regime." A few weeks before on *Meet the Press*, I had told Tim Russert that "from the standpoint of the Iraqi people, my belief is we will, in fact, be greeted as liberators." There were certainly difficult days ahead, but contrary to subsequent assertions by war critics, my assessment had been on target. We were greeted as liberators when we freed the Iraqi people from Saddam's grip.

With improvements in technology and equipment, our forces had capabilities we could only have dreamt of during Desert Storm. Our ground forces had improved their combat power and increased the range and accuracy of their weapons. Every one of our air-to-ground fighters could now put a laser-guided bomb to the target, compared with only 20 percent in Desert Storm. In Desert Storm, we had only one kind of unmanned aerial vehicle. In Iraqi Freedom, we had ten different types, ranging from tactical systems that would allow our soldiers to look over the next hill to strategic systems that operated at high altitudes.

In 1991 Saddam had time to set Kuwait's oil fields ablaze. In 2003 our special operations forces were sent in early to protect the six hundred oil wells in southern Iraq. During Desert Storm Saddam had fired Scud missiles at Israel and Saudi Arabia. In Iraqi Freedom our special operations forces seized control of the missile launch baskets in western Iraq and prevented their use.

The plan put together by General Franks and Secretary Rumsfeld for the liberation of Iraq was bold, impressive, and effective. By moving with astonishing speed, going with a small force, and without preceding air bombardment, they achieved tactical surprise. With less than half of the ground forces and two-thirds of the air assets used in Desert Storm, they achieved a far more difficult objective in less time and with fewer casualties.

On April 9 Lynne and I were visiting the D-Day Museum in New Orleans. Watching television in our hotel before I went onstage to speak, we saw the statue of Saddam in central Baghdad pulled down by Iraqis and American marines. We knew we were watching the end of Saddam's regime.

Just before the statue came down, a young marine draped an American flag over Saddam's face. Watching the scene on television, I completely understood. We all wanted to see an Iraqi flag up there soon, but our troops had just accomplished a stunning military victory. They had earned the right to plant the stars and stripes anyplace they wanted.

At the end of the day, back in the White House, my guest was Kanan Makiya, an Iraqi dissident who had stood against Saddam for decades. A gentle, soft-spoken man, he had documented the atrocities of Saddam's regime. It was an emotional meeting, and I'll never forget Kanan's words that evening: "Thank you," he said, "for our liberation."

CHAPTER THIRTEEN

Intelligence and Politics

During the spring of 2003, stories began to appear in the press that a former U.S. ambassador had been sent to Africa in 2002 after I had asked questions about a report that Iraq had tried to acquire uranium from Niger. According to the articles the unnamed ambassador told the CIA upon his return that the report was wrong. His assessment was of interest to the media because it seemed to contradict a sixteen-word statement that President Bush had made in his 2003 State of the Union speech. "The British government," he had said, "has learned that Saddam Hussein recently sought significant quantities of uranium from Africa."

I was surprised by the stories about the ambassador. Well over a year before, when I had read a Defense Intelligence Agency report about Iraq possibly trying to acquire uranium from Niger, I had done what I often did and asked for further information. What was the CIA's opinion of the report? What did the CIA think were the implications for Iraq's nuclear program? A few days later, around Valentine's Day 2002, I received a CIA memo saying that Iraq had existing stockpiles of yellowcake, or unenriched uranium ore, two hundred tons of which had previously been acquired from Niger, but that these stockpiles were in sealed containers that the International Atomic Energy Agency inspected annually. This was interesting information, since it indicated that if Saddam intended to restart his nuclear program, he was going to have to acquire uranium clandestinely—and he had a history with Niger. The mid-February memo said the agency was seeking to clarify and confirm the reporting on recent efforts by Iraq to acquire Niger uranium.

Fifteen months had passed and I hadn't gotten an answer from the CIA, yet now I was reading in the newspapers that the agency had sent someone on a mission to Niger, an unnamed ambassador, who was intent on providing the results of his trip, which had never been provided to me, to members of the press, and he was doing so in order to call our truthfulness into question. In all my years working with the intelligence community—as White House chief of staff, as a member of the House Intelligence Committee, as secretary of defense supervising such intelligence organizations as the Defense Intelligence Agency, the National Reconnaissance Office, and the National Security Agency—I had never seen anything like this, and after I had read a couple of the stories, I picked up the secure phone on my desk and punched the button that gave me a direct line to CIA Director George Tenet out at CIA headquarters in Langley. "What the hell is going on, George?" I asked when he picked up the phone.

Tenet sounded embarrassed and seemed not to know much more than I did. He said neither he nor his deputy, John McLaughlin, had been aware of an envoy being sent to Niger. He did add one fact, though. He said they had learned that the wife of the fellow who went to Niger "worked in the unit that sent him." George said he'd get to the bottom of it and get back to me. I shook my head as I hung up. It sounded like amateur hour out at the CIA.

On July 6, 2003, the retired ambassador, Joe Wilson, apparently tired of anonymity, wrote an op-ed for the *New York Times* titled "What I Didn't Find in Africa." Wilson said that in response to my request for more information, the CIA had sent him to Niger, paying his expenses, but not for his time, which he donated "pro bono." As a result of his trip, he said, he concluded that the story about Iraq trying to acquire uranium in Niger was false, and he asserted that I surely must have been told that by the CIA. To round things out, Wilson brought up the president's statement in the State of the Union address and accused the administration of twisting intelligence in order to justify the war.

I often clipped pieces out of newspapers, and that's what I did with Wilson's op-ed. I wrote a few comments in the margin that expressed my consternation: "Have they done this sort of thing before? Send an ambassador to answer a question? Do we ordinarily send people out pro bono to work for us? Or did his wife send him on a junket?"

After the op-ed appeared, there was a debate inside the White House, and at least one discussion in the Oval Office, about whether we should apologize for the inclusion of "the sixteen words" in the president's State of the Union speech. The CIA had cleared the president's address; but now with a spotlight on the words, Director Tenet was saying that they didn't rise to an appropriate level of certainty. Some on the president's senior staff believed that if we issued an apology, the story would go away. I strongly opposed the idea. An apology would only fan the flames, and why apologize when the British had, in fact, reported that Iraq had sought a significant amount of uranium in Africa? *The sixteen words were true.*

It is worth noting at this point in a complicated story that when the British government later investigated prewar intelligence on Iraq, they confirmed their reporting. "Iraqi officials visited Niger in 1999," the Butler Review noted, and "the British Government had intelligence from several different sources indicating that this visit was for the purpose of acquiring uranium." The British not only stood by their intelligence, they concluded that the statement in President Bush's State of the Union speech was "well-founded."

I was under the impression that the president had decided against a public apology, and was therefore surprised a few days later when National Security Advisor Condoleezza Rice told the White House press pool, "We wouldn't have put it in the speech if we had known what we know now." The result was the conflagration I had predicted. The media immediately wanted to know who was responsible. Suddenly the White House staff was consumed with reviewing drafts of the President's State of the Union speech, going over communications with the CIA about the speech, and poring through previous speeches to determine how the sixteen words got into the speech. First George Tenet and later Steve Hadley, the deputy national security advisor, issued statements accepting the blame. It was a ridiculous situation—particularly in light of the fact that the sixteen words were, as the British put it, "well-founded."

Rice realized sometime later that she had made a major mistake by issuing a public apology. She came into my office, sat down in the chair next to my desk, and tearfully admitted I had been right. Unfortunately, the damage was done. George Tenet was furious at having had to apologize. He would later write that after the sixteen words "my relationship with the administration was forever changed." As Tenet would also recount in his book, while he was still smarting from making an apology, Colin Powell invited him over to his house in McLean and told him that although he, Tenet, still had support in the White House, he also had people trying to pull the rug out from under him and that I was chief among them.

This was not the case. I was a strong supporter inside the White House of what Tenet and the CIA were trying to do. When there were suggestions after 9/11 that we have a group similar to the Warren Commission investigate intelligence failures, I had argued against it, saying it would too easily turn into a witch hunt and that what we needed to do was focus on preventing the next attack. As for the sixteen words, I hadn't thought George or anyone else should apologize, particularly after I learned what struck me as a pretty startling fact. Despite what Joe Wilson was saying in the press, he had brought back information from Africa that supported the sixteen words. He had told CIA debriefers about a conversation he'd had with a former prime minister of Niger, who said that in 1999 he had met with an Iraqi delegation to discuss "expanding commercial relations" between Iraq and Niger. Since Niger's chief export is uranium ore, the prime minister assumed the Iraqis wanted to buy yellowcake.

On July 14, 2003, Bob Novak wrote a column identifying Wilson's wife, Valerie Plame, as an "operative" at the CIA and suggesting she may have recommended him for the trip to Niger. Soon thereafter, as I later learned, the CIA notified the Justice Department that the leak to Novak of where Wilson's wife worked was a possible violation of criminal law, and the agency subsequently made a formal request for a criminal investigation. George Tenet later told me that there were close to four hundred reports of possible criminal violations involving classified information pending at the Justice Department and that they were seldom pursued. There were just too many of them, and they often involved the press, which the Justice Department was not eager to take on. But this referral involved the White House, and someone leaked news of it to Andrea Mitchell of NBC News, who on September 26, 2003, reported, "The CIA has asked the Justice Department to investigate allegations that the White House broke federal laws by revealing the identity of one of its undercover employees in retaliation against the woman's husband, a former ambassador who publicly criticized President Bush's since-discredited claim that Iraq had sought weapons-grade uranium from Africa."

A criminal referral was a big story in any case, but I couldn't help but note that we had made it bigger. By apologizing we had given reporters such as Mitchell grounds for saying that the president had been mistaken, although he had not been. *Mistaken* soon evolved into *lied*, and, of course, Joe Wilson was pushing the story line along. He "confirmed" for two reporters that the CIA had circulated his report to my office and told them that the administration "knew the Niger story was a flat-out lie." He wrote a book, appeared in magazines, and continued to fabricate, claiming on behalf of Senator John Kerry's presidential campaign, for example, that his "report" had exposed the "lie" in President Bush's State of the Union speech. Senator Pat Roberts, chairman of the Senate Select Committee on Intelligence, noted in the committee's 2004 report that Wilson admitted at least twice to committee staff that he drew "on either unrelated past experiences or no information at all" for some of his claims. Wrote Roberts, "The former ambassador, either by design or through ignorance, gave the American people and, for that matter, the world a version of events that was inaccurate, unsubstantiated, and misleading."

ON SEPTEMBER 30, 2003, the Justice Department announced it had launched an investigation. Attorney General John Ashcroft recused himself from the case, and Deputy Attorney General James Comey took over the matter. He decided to appoint a special counsel and chose Patrick Fitzgerald, an old friend of his, who was U.S. Attorney for the Northern District of Illinois, to investigate and possibly prosecute the case. Fitzgerald was appointed on December 30, 2003.

Among the many things that should give a thinking person pause about this whole sad story is that Patrick Fitzgerald knew from the outset who had leaked the information about Wilson's wife to Bob Novak. It had been Deputy Secretary of State Rich Armitage, who told the Justice Department that he had leaked the information to Novak, but kept what he had done from the White House. Armitage would later admit that he had even earlier told journalist Bob Woodward about Wilson's wife's employment. Indeed, on Bob Woodward's tape of the June 13, 2003, conversation, Armitage can be heard leaking the fact that Wilson's wife worked at the CIA four separate times.

Despite knowing Armitage's role, Fitzgerald spent more than two years conducting what the *Washington Post* called "a lengthy and wasteful investigation." For the latter part of 2003, all of 2004, and a good part of 2005, members of the White House staff produced box after box of documents, were interviewed by the FBI, hauled before a grand jury, and repeatedly questioned about these events.

Meanwhile, over at the State Department, Armitage sat silent. And, it pains me to note, so did his boss, Colin Powell, whom Armitage told he was Novak's source on October 1, 2003. Less than a week later, on October 7, 2003, there was a cabinet meeting. At the end of it, the press came in for a photo opportunity, and there were questions about who had leaked the information that Wilson's wife worked at the CIA. The president said he didn't know, but wanted the truth. Thinking back, I realize that one of the few people in the world who could have told him the truth, Colin Powell, was sitting right next to him.

I participated in two lengthy sessions with the special counsel. The first was in my West Wing office in May 2004. The second was in Jackson Hole, Wyoming, in August 2004. The second session was conducted under oath so that my testimony could be submitted to the grand jury. The president himself was questioned by Fitzgerald in a session in the Oval Office.

At the end of it all, the special counsel did not charge anyone with leaking information about Wilson's wife. The only charges brought were against my chief of staff, Scooter Libby, one of the most competent, intelligent, and honorable people I have ever met. Libby had worked for me at the Defense Department, where I had been very impressed by his performance. I had been delighted when he agreed to leave his successful law practice and come into the White House as vice presidential chief of staff and national security advisor. He did important work for me and for the nation.

On October 28, 2005, Scooter was indicted on one count of obstructing justice, two counts of perjury, and two of making false statements. In 2007, during a time of intense public debate and anger about the war in Iraq, Libby's trial took place at the federal courthouse in Washington, D.C. He was convicted on four counts, none of which were based on leaking Valerie Plame's name or CIA employment to the press. Instead the counts turned essentially on what Scooter recalled about a telephone conversation he'd had with Tim Russert of NBC News in 2003. The issue wasn't whether a public official had leaked Plame's CIA employment to a reporter. The special counsel had left that subject far behind and was now focused on whether a reporter, Russert, had mentioned Wilson's wife to a public official, Libby. Russert said he had not brought her up. Scooter said Russert had.

I believed that Scooter was innocent and should never have been indicted, much less convicted. It was hardly surprising that two busy men would disagree about what happened in a telephone conversation that occurred months before. Even if you decided that one version was more accurate than the other, it wasn't right to insist that the second version was a lie rather than the result of a faulty memory. During the trial there were many examples of witnesses forgetting important events, but their fates didn't hang on the accuracy of their recall.

I'd watched before as independent or special counsels assigned to investigate public figures went on and on, and even when they failed to find an underlying crime, they caused plenty of human wreckage. Once an independent or special counsel has been appointed, there is pressure to indict someone for something. Without a trial and conviction, it is very difficult to justify the amounts of time and taxpayer dollars expended—and they are enormous. Under the old Independent Counsel Act or in the case of a special counsel given the full power of the Attorney General of the United States, as Patrick Fitzgerald was, there are no time constraints, no budgetary limits, and no oversight. You very quickly end up with an unaccountable organization armed with the full power of the state to go after public officials.

In 1992, after investigating for six years and spending more than $40 million, Lawrence Walsh, the independent counsel for Iran-Contra, indicted former Secretary of Defense Caspar Weinberger for not mentioning notes he had on file in the Library of Congress. Walsh brought the indictment on the eve of the hotly contested 1992 presidential election. The following month I observed on *Meet the Press* that the Weinberger indictment was a "travesty." Noting that I had been the senior House Republican on the Iran-Contra committee, I pointed out that Weinberger had been *opposed* to the Iran-Contra operation. "Now, six years after the fact . . . ," I said, "on a fairly slim reed, the special prosecutor who has yet really to nail anybody, and who's spent millions of dollars, is out trying to prosecute Cap Weinberger." I concluded by calling the indictment an "outrage."

After the 1992 election I was among those whom President George H. W. Bush consulted about issuing pardons for individuals involved in Iran-Contra. He summoned James Baker and me into the private study next to the Oval Office in the closing days of 1992 and asked our opinion. Jim and I both supported the idea of pardons. I believed that the individuals in question were good men who hadn't thought they were doing anything wrong. They were CIA and administration officials who'd gotten in the way of the independent counsel juggernaut, and in the case of Weinberger, politics was clearly at work. Pardons were the right thing, and the president issued them on Christmas Eve 1992, putting the matter to rest.

President George W. Bush commuted Scooter's sentence so he would not have to go to prison. While that was appreciated, I felt strongly that Scooter deserved a pardon, and I broached the subject on numerous occasions with the president. We talked about what the president's father had done before he left office, and I was of the impression that the president agreed with me that Libby should be pardoned, although he made no commitments. We had small meetings with a group of senior staff members in the Oval Office near Thanksgiving and Christmas 2008 to discuss cases that were pending and pardons that would be issued then. The president said he planned to do some of the more controversial pardons nearer to the end of his term.

Just before George W. Bush and I left office, we had the last of our private lunches, and he told me he had changed his mind about an additional round of pardons. There were not going to be any more, which meant there would be none for Libby. I was deeply disappointed. I understood that a pardon for Libby was unlikely to be well received in the mainstream media and that it wouldn't be of short-term help to those around the president who were focused on generating positive press about his last days in office. But in the long term, where doing the right thing counts, George W. Bush was, in my view, making a grave error. "Mr. President," I said, "you are leaving a good man wounded on the field of battle."

George Bush made courageous decisions as president, and to this day I wish that pardoning Scooter Libby had been one of them.

ON SATURDAY, DECEMBER 13, 2003, I flew to New York for a political fund-raiser. As Air Force Two landed at Stewart International

Airport in Newburgh around 3:30 in the afternoon, I got word that I should call President Bush. We connected at 3:43 p.m. and he said, "Dick, it looks like we've captured Saddam Hussein." He explained that elements of the 4th Infantry Division operating near Tikrit, working with a special operations unit specializing in hunting high-value targets, had pulled a man who appeared to be Saddam out of a small spiderhole. We knew Saddam had body doubles, so although this man had tattoos and scars that appeared to match those we knew Saddam had, we were proceeding cautiously. The president told me the prisoner was being escorted to Baghdad under heavy guard.

Almost as soon as I hung up, Don Rumsfeld called. He said the man in custody had been identified by a witness as Saddam, and there were plans to do a comparison of the prisoner's DNA with DNA from one of Saddam's late sons. If news of Saddam's capture didn't leak, he told me, an announcement would be made the next morning at 7:00 a.m. D.C. time.

Capturing Saddam was a major accomplishment. The next day at a Baghdad press conference, when Paul Bremer, head of the Coalition Provisional Authority, announced simply, "We got him," Iraqi journalists jumped to their feet, joyfully applauding and cheering. We hoped that having Saddam in custody would give the Iraqi people confidence that he and his Baathist regime were not coming back.

But we still had not found the stockpiles of chemical or biological weapons we had believed Saddam possessed.

AFTER WE LIBERATED IRAQ, we had set up the Iraq Survey Group, an organization made up of American, British, and Australian weapons experts, who were to hunt for Saddam's WMD stockpiles and programs. David Kay, who had participated in the search for banned weapons in Iraq after the first Gulf War, was selected to lead the group. He reported directly to George Tenet, and throughout 2003 Kay updated us on the investigation's progress.

In late July, Kay came to the White House to brief us on his investigation. He expressed confidence that he'd find weapons of mass destruction and confirmed the existence of research programs involving chemical and biological weapons. He was confident we'd find chemical weapons, but was less sure about biological weapons stockpiles. The footprint of a biological weapons program was very small and easy to hide or destroy.

In October, when Kay went before the House and Senate intelligence committees, he reported that while the Iraq Survey Group had not yet found "stocks of weapons," they had discovered "dozens of WMD-related program activities and significant amounts of equipment that Iraq concealed from the United Nations during the inspections that began in late 2002," including "a clandestine network of laboratories and safehouses within the Iraqi Intelligence Service that contained equipment subject to UN monitoring and suitable for continuing chemical and biological weapons research" and "a prison laboratory complex, possibly used in human testing of biological warfare agents, that Iraqi officials working to prepare for UN inspections were explicitly ordered not to declare to the UN."

But by the time Kay resigned in January 2004, he said he no longer expected that we would find stockpiles of weapons of mass destruction. He did not dismiss the threat Iraq had represented. "I actually think what we learned during the inspections made Iraq a more dangerous place, potentially, than in fact we thought it was even before the war," he said. Kay also said that Saddam had the intention of pursuing WMD activities, a conclusion echoed in the report of his successor, Charles Duelfer. According to Duelfer, "Saddam wanted to re-create Iraq's WMD capability . . . after sanctions were removed." Duelfer cited Iraqi diplomat Tariq Aziz's opinion that Saddam would have restarted WMD programs, beginning with the nuclear program, after sanctions and noted that Saddam had purposely retained the men and women who knew how to do so. He also had dual-use infrastructure readily at hand that he could use to reestablish a biological weapons program and produce chemical weapons within months.

But there were no stockpiles of weapons of mass destruction. That was the big news, and it came at the beginning of a presidential election year. The Democrats did not, apparently, want to admit that they too had accepted and relied on faulty intelligence. Instead they decided to blame us for "misleading" the country, for "lying" the nation into war. This was the most blatant hypocrisy, since they had seen the intelligence—and reached the same conclusions we had. When John Kerry accused the president of trafficking in "untruth," he was guilty of exactly what he accused the president of doing.

One part of the attack was aimed specifically at me. It was said that I pressured CIA analysts so that they exaggerated the threat that Saddam represented. It wasn't a charge that made any sense, since the judgments the CIA arrived at were essentially the same as those produced by the agency during the Clinton years. Intelligence services in other countries had also reached similar conclusions. It became something of a journalistic sport during my time in office to portray me as the all-powerful vice president, but not even the most aggressive versions of this story suggested that my influence reached to MI6 or BND, the British and German intelligence services.

The charge seemed to arise out of my visits to the CIA, which began with George Tenet and a few senior analysts briefing me and quickly expanded to include more junior regional or topic experts. We would sit around a conference table where Tenet or his deputy would introduce topics and analysts. I would then ask questions and the analysts could report on what they knew. I found these sessions immensely valuable, and I believe the analysts, who often work long hours in obscurity removed from policymakers, did as well.

The Robb-Silberman Commission and the Senate Select Committee on Intelligence produced bipartisan reports on our intelligence failures regarding stockpiles of weapons of mass destruction, and both concluded that there was no politicization of intelligence or inappropriate pressure from policymakers. The Robb-Silberman report urged, in fact, that "policymakers actively probe and question analysts." I asked tough questions, no doubt about that. And I asked a lot of them. I pushed hard to get information that would help us develop policies that would ensure America wasn't attacked again. If I had not been as thorough as I was, I would not have been fulfilling my obligations and responsibilities as a senior official. In light of subsequent revelations, such as the mistakes in the 2002 National Intelligence Estimate on Iraqi WMD, I wish I'd been even tougher.

One line of questioning I pursued had to do with the relationship between al Qaeda and Saddam. It was important to know what the association was in the wake of 9/11, as many besides myself recognized. Senator Evan Bayh, in a closed hearing, parts of which were later made public, asked about Iraqi links to al Qaeda. George Tenet responded in a letter dated October 7, 2002, with a list that included these points:

- *We have solid reporting of senior level contacts between Iraq and al Qaeda going back a decade.*
- *Credible information indicates that Iraq and al Qaeda have discussed safe haven and reciprocal non-aggression.*
- *Since Operation Enduring Freedom, we have solid evidence of the presence in Iraq of al Qaeda members, including some that have been in Baghdad.*
- *We have credible reporting that al Qaeda leaders sought contacts in Iraq who could help them acquire WMD capabilities. The reporting also stated that Iraq had provided training to al Qaeda members in the areas of poisons and gases and making conventional bombs.*

Despite such statements coming from the agency's highest levels, I'd find the CIA sometimes seemed hesitant to use the words *al Qaeda* and *Iraq* in the same sentence. In early 2003, for example, I received an intelligence report about Egyptian Islamic Jihad's activities in Iraq. It described safe houses, for example, that were being established in Baghdad. But by this time EIJ, which was the organization of Ayman Zawahiri, Osama bin Laden's number two, had merged with al Qaeda, so I asked my briefer if it wouldn't be correct, given the merger, to attribute the reported activities to al Qaeda rather than EIJ. It took several weeks for the answer to come back, but finally I was told that yes, they are interchangeable here. Tenet publicly acknowledged that EIJ and al Qaeda were "indistinguishable" from each other, but finished intelligence reports continued to refer to them as separate entities.

As George Tenet and others have noted since, there was a dispute inside the CIA between the terrorism analysts, who looked at the reporting and judged there to be a relationship between Saddam and al Qaeda, and the regional Middle East experts, who didn't believe there could be a connection between the secular Saddam and the radical Islamist bin Laden. I have long suspected that because of this split, the CIA came up with the phrase "no authority, direction, or control." The terrorism experts would make their judgments about a connection between Saddam and al Qaeda, but then to satisfy the regional analysts, a higher-up at the agency would intone that Saddam had "no authority, direction, or control." The phrase turned out to be handy for administration critics, because it seemed to say that Saddam had no responsibility for terrorism while we were asserting he did. We had the facts on our side. He harbored terrorists, and he sponsored them. He didn't have to be in control of al Qaeda in order to be in violation of United Nations resolutions that forbade Iraq's giving terrorists safe haven. He didn't have to have authority over al Qaeda—any more than the Taliban had—to be in violation of the Bush Doctrine, which held, in the president's words, that "any nation that continues to harbor or support terrorism will be regarded by the United States as a hostile regime."

WHEN I APPEARED ON *Meet the Press* on the Sunday after 9/11, Tim Russert asked me whether we had any evidence linking Saddam Hussein or the Iraqis to the 9/11 attacks. "No," I answered. But shortly afterward, George Tenet brought me information that suggested the possibility: The CIA had a report that Mohammed Atta, the lead hijacker of 9/11, had met with a representative of the Iraqi Intelligence Service in Prague prior to the attacks. I was subsequently shown a photograph said to have been taken in Prague and told that there was a high probability that the man in the photo was Mohammed Atta. Thus when I sat down with Tim Russert on December 9, 2001, I mentioned a report, "pretty well confirmed," that Atta had gone to Prague and met with a senior Iraqi intelligence official. Colin Powell, apparently shown the same information, went even further, telling Wolf Blitzer on CNN's *Late Edition,* "Certainly those meetings took place."

In the summer of 2002, having been told that the case for Mohammed Atta's Prague meeting was weakening, I began to alter my statements. I said to Tim Russert on September 8 that the meeting was "unconfirmed at this point." The next year, following along with what the CIA was reporting, I told Tim, "We've never been able to develop any more of that yet, either in terms of confirming it or discrediting it. We just don't know." I was careful with what I said—and disappointed when Director Tenet later erroneously wrote that I continued to claim the story was "pretty well confirmed" after the CIA began to doubt it.

I was also disappointed on June 2, 2004, when Tenet, citing personal reasons, told the president he would be leaving. The Senate Intelligence Committee was soon to issue a report that many thought would be critical of Tenet, and I suspected that entered into his thinking. The president had kept Tenet on when we came into office, a move I had supported. Throughout the intelligence mistakes of Tenet's tenure, the president and I had backed him. For him to quit when the going got tough, not to mention in the middle of a presidential campaign, seemed to me unfair to the president, who had put his trust in George Tenet.

THE RELATIONSHIP BETWEEN POLICYMAKERS and the intelligence community has long been complicated. Faulty intelligence in the Bay of Pigs operation infuriated President Kennedy and eventually led to the resignation of CIA head Allen Dulles. The exposure of unsavory intelligence activities during the Vietnam era led to the congressional Pike and Church committees and the public airing of some of the CIA's most sensitive secrets. During the investigation in the 1980s of covert arms sales to Iran and diversion of proceeds to aid the Nicaraguan Contras, dedicated intelligence professionals doing what they thought they were supposed to do ended up as targets of an independent counsel, and few were the policymakers defending them. Taking a long-term perspective, it's easy to see why both sides had become wary of one another.

What we are asking of our intelligence community in today's world is exceedingly challenging. Compare it, for example, to their task during the Cold War. What mattered then wasn't so much the activities of individuals. The Soviets posed a massive military threat, which meant divisions and tanks, artillery and missiles, things you could count that were hard to conceal from satellites—and even then we didn't always get it right because intelligence is such a tough business. The intelligence requirements of the War on Terror are entirely different and in some ways much more difficult. It's very hard to detect and track nineteen men with box cutters who intend to fly airplanes into buildings. Technology was on our side during the Cold War, but the situation has in some ways shifted. Now it is possible for an individual or a handful of people to acquire the technological means—a dirty bomb or weaponized anthrax—to kill on a massive scale.

The intelligence that Saddam had stockpiles of WMD was wrong, and this intelligence failure would have an impact on policy during subsequent years of our administration. But I recognized the magnitude of the task the intelligence community faced in trying to predict how far along a secretive, rogue regime was in its most highly sensitive top secret programs.

Intelligence is by its very nature an extremely difficult business, and the public almost never hears about intelligence successes—of which there have been many, very many, particularly in the War on Terror. I have tremendous respect for the men and women who serve our nation in America's intelligence services. Thousands upon thousands of them go to work every day committed to doing all they can to defend the nation from our enemies, and their commitment is unchanged regardless of which party is in power. Their work has saved countless American lives.

THREE TIMES BEFORE THE 2004 campaign got under way I offered to the president to take myself off the Republican ticket. I had become a lightning rod for attacks from the administration's critics, and given the challenges we were facing in the War on Terror, in particular, it was critically important that George Bush be reelected. If President Bush felt he had a better chance to win with someone else as his running mate, I wanted to make sure he felt free to make the change.

The first two times I suggested that he might consider replacing me, he brushed it off. So I brought it up again and emphasized the seriousness with which he should consider the matter. He went away and thought about it. A few days later, he told me he wanted me to run with him again. I was honored to do so. We had a record of accomplishment during our first term in office that I was proud to take before the American people.

As I thought about the case we would present to the voters in the 2004 election, I found it useful to think back to what the world had looked like when we took office in January 2001. Unbeknownst to us, planning for 9/11 was well under way. The hijackers had been recruited, funds raised, training was ongoing, and some of the hijackers were already in the United States. In Afghanistan, the Taliban controlled most of the country and provided a major operations base and sanctuary for al Qaeda. Training camps were in operation, and twenty thousand terrorists passed through the camps between 1996 and September 11, 2001.

Pakistan was on edge. There were major problems in U.S.-Pakistani relations. President Pervez Musharraf's hold on power was tenuous and he had al Qaeda sympathizers in key slots in his government. Pakistan's radical Islamic movement was strong and areas of the country were hosting al Qaeda operating bases. Pakistan's stability was a major concern. If radicals managed to take control, they would also control the country's nuclear arsenal.

In Iraq, Saddam Hussein remained in power. He'd started two wars and produced and used WMD against the Kurds and the Iranians. He was providing safe haven and financial support to terrorists and twenty-five-thousand-dollar payments to encourage suicide bombers in Israel. His was one of the bloodiest regimes of the twentieth century and a dangerous potential link between terrorists and WMD capability.

Abdul Qadeer Khan, the father of Pakistan's nuclear program, was in 2001 selling nuclear weapons technology and equipment to rogue states like Iran, North Korea, and Libya. Libyan dictator Muammar Qaddafi was Khan's biggest customer.

And throughout the 1980s and 1990s, terrorists had learned two dangerous lessons from America's weak response to previous attacks— on our embassy and Marine barracks in Beirut, in Somalia, on the World Trade Center in 1993, on the military training facilities in Riyadh and at the Khobar Towers housing complex, on our embassies in East Africa, and on the U.S.S. *Cole*. First, terrorists came to believe they could strike with impunity, that the U.S. response was likely to be inconsequential. Second, they learned that if they did attack U.S. assets or personnel, we might well change our policy or withdraw.

By 2004 the world looked very different. The attacks of 9/11 had changed everything. We had strengthened our homeland defense, including improvements to our defenses against biological weapons, and created the Department of Homeland Security. We had also gone after the terrorists' financial networks, improved our intelligence capabilities, and gone on the offense, implementing the Bush Doctrine.

We had driven the Taliban from power in Afghanistan, killing or capturing hundreds of al Qaeda fighters. Osama bin Laden and his deputies were on the run, hampering al Qaeda's ability to plan attacks against the United States. A new government had been established in Afghanistan, a constitution had been written, and presidential elections would be held in the fall of 2004. Violence levels were down, the military was making progress, Afghan security forces were growing, and we were working closely with Hamid Karzai and the Afghan government. Afghanistan seemed on a positive trajectory.

In Pakistan President Musharraf had signed up with the United States after 9/11 and was providing significant support for our operations in Afghanistan. The Pakistanis had helped us capture or kill hundreds of al Qaeda terrorists in Pakistan, including the mastermind of 9/11, Khalid Sheikh Mohammed.

In Iraq Saddam Hussein was no longer in power. His sons were dead. He was in jail. We had established an interim government, transferred sovereignty, and begun training Iraqi security forces so they could take on increasing responsibility. Though much hard work remained, the world was clearly safer with Saddam gone.

Libyan leader Muammar Qaddafi watched the U.S. action in Afghanistan and preparations for Iraq and decided he didn't want to be next. As we launched into Iraq, we received a message that Qaddafi might be willing to give up his nuclear program. Senior U.S. intelligence officials worked with British counterparts to conduct nine months of negotiations with the Libyans. Then, six days after Saddam was captured, Qaddafi announced he would turn over all his WMD materials. His centrifuges, uranium hexafluoride, weapon design, and associated materials were shipped to the United States. Libya was out of the nuclear business as a direct result of U.S. action in Afghanistan and Iraq.

In Pakistan, again due to tremendous work by our intelligence professionals, A. Q. Khan had also been put out of business. We had taken down his network. On February 4, 2004, he'd gone on Pakistani TV and confessed to his illegal nuclear proliferation activities. He was under house arrest, and we had stopped one of the world's worst proliferators of nuclear weapons technology.

Finally, terrorists around the world now understood that the United States would strike at those who intended us harm. We had done all these things—and kept the American people safe from another attack.

ON MAY 10, 2004, President Bush and I went to the Pentagon to view photos that had recently been made public, as well as some that hadn't been released, of American soldiers abusing Iraqi detainees at Abu Ghraib prison. The photos were deeply disturbing. The behavior recorded in them was cruel and disgraceful and certainly not reflective of U.S. policy. Secretary Rumsfeld had testified in front of the Senate and House armed services committees a few days before our visit to the Pentagon. He apologized, took full responsibility, and promised a complete investigation. He had also tried to resign on May 5. He believed someone had to be held accountable, and since the behavior had occurred on his watch, he offered the president his letter of resignation. The president hadn't accepted it.

As our May 10 Pentagon meeting came to a close, Don asked to see the president alone, and as President Bush told me when we got back to the White House, Don tried to resign for the second time, saying this time his mind was made up. The president asked me to talk to him, to explain how much we needed him, and to convince him to stay.

The next day, Tuesday, after the weekly Republican Senate Policy Lunch at the Capitol, I headed to the Pentagon to talk to Don. As my motorcade crossed the Potomac, I thought back thirty years to the day in 1975 when Jerry Ford had directed me to contact Rumsfeld to persuade him to accept the job of secretary of defense. How could I have ever imagined that five presidents later, I would be urging him not to resign from that office—which in the interim I had held myself?

I took a seat at the small round table around which I'd held nightly senior staff sessions when I was secretary. Don was by the standing desk he kept near the window. I told him I understood why he had submitted his letter of resignation, but that he was wrong on this one. We were in the midst of a war against a very tough and determined enemy, and his departure would undermine our policies in Iraq and Afghanistan. I told him that I believed his resignation would do serious, perhaps irreparable, harm and asked him to reconsider. In the end, he agreed to stay.

Ultimately those responsible for the abuses at Abu Ghraib were reprimanded, relieved of duty, and, where appropriate, prosecuted. There were a dozen independent investigations conducted of detainee policy on Rumsfeld's watch, and none found any evidence that abuse was either ordered, authorized, or condoned by military authorities or senior officials at the Department of Defense. One of my greatest regrets about Abu Ghraib is the focus it put on a relatively small group whose actions were in such marked contrast to the deep and enduring commitment to duty and honor that I have observed time and again in the men and women of America's military. The wanton abuse committed by those few soldiers did lasting damage to America's image, but they do not represent our country or the men and women who defend it.

MY FIRST MAJOR POLITICAL speech of the 2004 campaign was at the Ronald Reagan Presidential Library in Simi Valley, California. Mrs. Reagan could not have been more gracious, the audience was friendly, and the day before I made the speech, Senator John Kerry had provided me with some very good material. Asked about his vote against an $87 billion bill to provide material support to our troops, he replied, "I actually did vote for the $87 billion before I voted against it." I quoted the line, and it brought down the house—as it would every time I used it.

I wasn't on the road in 2004 as much as in 2000, since now I had a full-time job, but when I did campaign, it was a family affair. Lynne traveled with me, and our daughter Mary, who was in charge of my campaign, was almost always with us. Liz, who had her fourth child and our first grandson, Philip, in July, didn't do much traveling during the summer, but managed my preparation for the vice presidential candidates' debate. We frequently took our three granddaughters on the road. Kate, who was ten, threw out the first baseball for the Altoona Curve, a minor-league baseball team in Pennsylvania; Grace, four, rode at the front of the bus on bus tours and shouted "Four more years!" into a microphone; and Elizabeth, seven, dressed up as the Grim Reaper for Halloween. At our campaign stops that day, we introduced her as John Kerry's health plan.

One place I spoke was at Cabela's, a large sporting goods store, in East Grand Forks, Minnesota. We held a town hall meeting in front of a large array of stuffed mountain sheep, and, best of all, I got to do some shopping afterward. I later found out that great as the event was, we were in the wrong location. The Bush-Cheney campaign higher-ups had wanted us to hit the Fargo media market, which covers northwest Minnesota, but a snafu in logistics sent us to the Grand Forks media market—and Cabela's—instead. But I thoroughly enjoyed the stop, and I'm not sure anyone at campaign headquarters ever figured out that we'd done the event eighty miles away from where we were supposed to—or if they did, they never said anything to me about it.

As I got ready to debate the Democratic vice presidential nominee, Senator John Edwards of North Carolina, I got my old debate prep team back together, with then Congressman Rob Portman of Ohio again serving as my sparring partner. All the buildup around Edwards and his skill as a trial lawyer led me to expect a formidable opponent when we met on October 5, 2004, at Case Western Reserve University in Cleveland. I came away from our session that evening feeling he hadn't done much to prepare for the most important event either of us would participate in during the 2004 campaign.

There was one subject on which he had clearly done some planning. A little over halfway through the debate, moderator Gwen Ifill asked us about the president's proposal for a constitutional ban on same-sex marriages. Edwards opened his answer this way: "Let me say first that I think the vice president and his wife love their daughter. I think they love her very much. And you can't have anything but respect for the fact that they're willing to talk about the fact that they have a gay daughter, the fact that they embrace her. It's a wonderful thing. And there are millions of parents like that who love their children." I was furious with his response. What gave him the right to make pronouncements about my family? But you never want to let the other guy get under your skin, so I kept my anger in check. When Ifill asked me if I'd like to respond, I said, "Well, Gwen, let me simply thank the senator for the kind words he said about my family and our daughter. I appreciate that very much." "That's it?" Gwen said. "That's it," I said.

My favorite line of attack on Edwards was to call him "Senator Gone," which is what his hometown newspaper had dubbed him since he was so frequently absent from the Senate. I further observed:

In my capacity as vice president, I am president of the Senate, the presiding officer. I'm up in the Senate most Tuesdays when they're in session. The first time I ever met you was when you walked on the stage tonight.

I later found out that I had crossed paths with Edwards once before, at a prayer breakfast in downtown D.C. in 2001. But our meeting clearly hadn't left much of an impression and didn't take the edge off my charge: This guy was a less than serious senator.

I enjoyed listening to the after-debate commentary. MSNBC's Chris Matthews, who usually turns red in the face and starts shouting at the mere mention of my name, paid me a compliment, describing the debate between Cheney and Edwards as the howitzer versus the water pistol. Mike Barnicle of the *Boston Herald* was also kind. The only thing that surprised him, he said, was "that at the end of the debate, at the end of ninety minutes, Dick Cheney did not turn to John Edwards and say, 'By the way, give me the car keys too.'"

At the presidential debate a week later, moderator Bob Schieffer of CBS asked John Kerry, "Do you believe homosexuality is a choice?" Kerry answered, "We're all God's children, Bob. And I think if you were to talk to Dick Cheney's daughter, who is a lesbian, she would tell you that she's being who she was, she's being who she was born as."

Now it was obvious that there was a concerted effort by the Kerry-Edwards campaign to remind viewers that my daughter Mary was gay, to bring her into the debate and into the campaign. I don't recall another instance of a candidate for the presidency attempting to use the child of an opponent for political gain. Later that evening, when Fox's Chris Wallace asked Kerry's campaign manager, Mary Beth Cahill, about the remark, she replied that my daughter was "fair game."

Lynne was furious. She hadn't been scheduled to speak at the post-debate rally we were attending, but she took the podium anyway, and let John Kerry have it. "The only thing I can conclude," she said, "is that he is not a good man. I'm speaking as a mom. What a cheap and tawdry political trick." She was exactly right, and I told the crowd I sure was glad she was on our side.

Most of America reacted the same way we had. It didn't matter where you came down on the issue of gay marriage or whether you identified yourself as a Republican or Democrat. Seeing a candidate for president be so obviously opportunistic did not inspire feelings of confidence. In fact, it had quite the opposite effect, and the Bush-Cheney campaign got a bump in the polls. We all started referring to it as the "Mary Cheney bounce."

We ended the campaign with a huge swing that took us to Wisconsin, Michigan, Pennsylvania, Ohio, Iowa, New Mexico, Hawaii, Colorado, Nevada, and finally to Jackson, Wyoming, on November 1, where an airport hangar full of friends greeted us. The next morning Lynne and I voted at the fire station near our home in Jackson and headed back to Washington, D.C. The exit polls were bad; so bad, in fact, that I knew they were wrong. I was sure we were going to win.

We didn't have our victory celebration that night, but the next afternoon instead, in the auditorium of the Reagan Building. Screaming Bush-Cheney supporters were hanging over railings and maybe even from the rafters. We had won 51 percent of the popular vote to Kerry's and Edwards's 48 percent and 286 electoral votes to their 251. Wednesday, November 3, 2004, was a very nice day.

AS WE GOT READY for the second term, it was clear the president wanted to make big changes in personnel. Although I tended to get involved in personnel matters with less frequency than I had at the beginning of our time in office, I felt strongly that major change was needed in the national security team. Getting a new secretary of state was a top priority.

Like the president I had believed that Colin Powell would be an effective secretary of state. I had long admired his talents and had personally selected him for appointment by George H. W. Bush to be chairman of the Joint Chiefs of Staff. He was superb in that job. But it was not the same when he was at the State Department. I was particularly disappointed in the way he handled policy differences. Time and again I heard that he was opposed to the war in Iraq. Indeed, I continue to hear it today. But never once in any meeting did I hear him voice objection. It was as though he thought the proper way to express his views was by criticizing administration policy to people outside the government. I'd been sorry in 1992 when Bill Clinton's election brought an end to my working relationship with Powell at the Pentagon, but when President Bush, after his reelection in 2004, accepted Powell's resignation, I thought it was for the best.

IN DECEMBER 2004 LYNNE and I traveled to Afghanistan for the inauguration of Hamid Karzai, the nation's first democratically elected president. Before the ceremony, we had breakfast with U.S. troops stationed at Bagram Air Base, outside Kabul. When I spoke to the men and women who were gathered, I reflected on the fact that we were meeting that morning in a nation that had just held the first free elections in its five-thousand-year history:

> *Just eight months earlier the United Nations hoped that six and a half million Afghans would register to vote. The number turned out to be more than 10 million, and on election day, they showed up at twenty-two thousand polling stations across the country. Near one of these stations, a coalition officer told of seeing a line of people two miles long, all walking down a road on their way to the polls. He spoke of old people walking and being ferried in goat carts, amputees on crutches, droves of people moving toward the polling booths, and then, late in the evening, aged adults running to beat the deadline to get in line in order to vote.*

It was a time of great promise and hopefulness in Afghanistan, and I thanked the American soldiers and airmen at Bagram for the enormous part they had played in defending America and securing freedom for the Afghan people.

A few hours later, Lynne and I arrived at Afghanistan's presidential palace, which still bore the marks of the years of fighting the Afghans had lived through. President Karzai and I met to discuss the ongoing military operations and his work to set up a new government. At our press conference immediately afterward, he made clear his gratitude to the American people:

Whatever we have achieved in Afghanistan—the peace, the election, the reconstruction, the life that the Afghans are living today in peace, the children going to school, the businesses, the fact that Afghanistan is a respected member of the international community—is from the help that the United States of America gave us. Without that help, Afghanistan would be in the hands of terrorists—destroyed, poverty-stricken, and without its children going to school or getting an education. We are very, very grateful, to put it in simple words that we know, to the people of the United States of America for bringing us this day.

After the press conference, Lynne and I headed to another building in the presidential compound for the inauguration itself. President Karzai arrived with Afghanistan's last king, the elderly Mohammad Zahir Shah, who had been living in exile. The ceremony was both solemn and joyful. Prayers were followed by songs from schoolgirls wearing colorful embroidered robes. When Karzai, in a coat of green and blue, rose to speak, there was enthusiastic applause. One official in the crowd of turbaned Afghan men recognized me. Sibghatullah Mojaddedi, chairman of the Loya Jirga, the assembly that had approved Afghanistan's 2003 constitution, remembered we had met eighteen years earlier. In 1986, he was one of the mujahideen fighting the Soviets, and I was a member of the House Intelligence Committee. We'd had dinner near the Khyber Pass, and here we were now, eighteen years later, and he, like me, was a gray-haired public servant.

AFTER SPENDING CHRISTMAS IN Wyoming with our family, Lynne and I left the United States again, this time for Krakow, Poland. I led the U.S. delegation to the commemoration of the sixtieth anniversary of the liberation of the Auschwitz-Birkenau death camps. The Polish government had invited a number of world leaders, including Russian President Vladimir Putin, to Krakow for the commemoration ceremonies.

As I sat in a meeting with Polish President Aleksander Kwasniewski in Wawel Castle the evening before the ceremonies began, a member of his staff brought in a note. Kwasniewski read it and then translated it for me. President Putin, who was scheduled to meet with Kwasniewski within the hour, had not yet left Moscow. He wouldn't be making the meeting, it seemed.

Putin's rudeness was thought by many to be calculated. The Poles were charting an independent course, and Moscow was not happy about it. Among the errors of the Poles, as Moscow saw it, was supporting the Orange Revolution in Ukraine, which had come about when the Moscow-backed candidate for the presidency of Ukraine had tried to steal the election. Crowds in Kiev's Independence Square had forced a new vote, and reform candidate Viktor Yushchenko had emerged triumphant. I had long believed that the United States should play a more active role in integrating Ukraine and other former Soviet states into the West, and I took the opportunity in Krakow to meet privately with Yushchenko, whose face still bore the scars of an assassination attempt, in which someone—rumors were it was the Russians—had poisoned him with dioxin.

The next day, as we gathered in the ornate nineteenth-century Juliusz Slowacki Theater in Krakow's old town for the first event commemorating the liberation of Auschwitz, Putin still had not arrived. He still wasn't there when his turn came to speak. The Poles gave his slot to Yushchenko, and the program continued, speeches interspersed with memorial readings and music. Forty-five minutes or so into the event, there was a commotion at the side door of the theater. Burly Russian security agents burst in, followed by President Putin, who strode up the side aisle and immediately onto the stage. Ignoring the fact that someone else was speaking, he began delivering his remarks, seemingly intent on showing our Polish hosts how little regard he had for them. Watching his behavior that day reminded me why Russia's leaders are still so disliked by their neighbors and why we were right to expand NATO and offer membership to former Soviet client states like Poland and Romania.

My ten-year-old granddaughter, Kate, had asked to come with us on this trip. We explained to her that coming face-to-face with the evil of the Holocaust would be very difficult, but she said she knew that and wanted to come. In the theater that day in Krakow, there were many Holocaust survivors. Kate was one of the few children. Before the ceremony a woman spotted Kate sitting with our daughter Liz. She walked across the theater, introduced herself, and asked Kate how old she was. Then she pulled a black-and-white photo from her purse. It showed young children in the striped pajamas of Auschwitz prisoners. "This little girl is me, when I was ten," she said, pointing to one of the children in the photo. She wanted to bear witness, to impress the tragedy of the Holocaust on someone young so that it will not be forgotten. And Kate will never forget.

IN THE SUMMER OF 2005, we were at our home in Jackson, Wyoming, when Hurricane Katrina made landfall in Florida on August 25. Four days later, on the morning of August 29, after picking up steam in the Gulf of Mexico, Katrina made landfall in Louisiana. The eye of the storm passed forty miles east of New Orleans, causing massive destruction along the Gulf coast in Mississippi. First reports suggested that New Orleans had escaped the worst of the storm and the levees were holding. It wasn't until early on Tuesday, August 30, that we began to hear they weren't. I participated by secure videoconference in a briefing on the hurricane damage at 6:30 a.m. Wyoming time on August 31 and realized that the situation was much, much worse than we had ever expected. I headed back to Washington the next morning.

Even before Katrina made landfall, the president had signed an emergency declaration. More than four thousand National Guard troops, under the command of state governors, were deployed; the Federal Emergency Management Agency had prepositioned food, water, and rescue teams; the U.S. Coast Guard was calling in reinforcements from around the country and preparing its helicopters for search and rescue. But the failure of the levees meant that more was needed. Eighty percent of New Orleans was under six to twenty feet of water. Thousands of people who did not evacuate before landfall sought refuge in the Superdome and the New Orleans Convention Center, where there was insufficient food and water. Looting and violence were breaking out.

The president wanted to deploy immediately tens of thousands of U.S. troops, but if they were to have law enforcement authority, Louisiana Governor Kathleen Blanco would have formally to request that the president federalize the response to Katrina, which she refused to do. That left the president with the option of acting against her wishes and declaring Louisiana in a state of insurrection in order to bring in troops. That is the requirement imposed by posse comitatus, an 1878 law that makes a declaration of insurrection necessary if the U.S. military is to be used for domestic law enforcement. The president was understandably reluctant to take the extreme step of assuming control in a state without the governor's acquiescence, and he also faced resistance from Pentagon leaders, who were reluctant to send troops trained for combat to restore domestic order. But as Governor Blanco continued to dither, the president decided to send in the troops anyway—though they would not have law enforcement powers. It was a risky decision. One can easily imagine scenarios in which U.S. troops are helpless in the face of violence. But the idea was that National Guardsmen, who are not covered by posse comitatus, could act with state and local authorities to take law enforcement responsibility. And it was an idea that worked.

Shortly after the president's announcement, Andy Card told me the president was thinking of setting up a senior-level task force to oversee the relief efforts and wanted to know if I would be willing to chair it. I told him I would, but only if the task force had real responsibility. I would need the authority to hire and fire people and to move in and really get things done. It didn't take me long to figure out that the task force idea had originated with the communications staff and would put me in a role that was primarily symbolic. I would be a figurehead without the ability really to do anything about the performance of the federal agencies involved. This wouldn't be helping. It would be creating a distraction, and I let Card know that I wasn't enthusiastic. The matter was dropped.

At the president's request I traveled to the Gulf coast on September 8 to get a firsthand look at the situation. Lynne and I traveled first to Gulfport, Mississippi, where Michael Chertoff, the extremely competent secretary of homeland security, came on board Air Force Two to brief us, then accompanied us to the National Guard center where the emergency response was being coordinated. We met with state and local officials, including Governor Haley Barbour, then walked through the Second Street Gulf Shore neighborhood. Nothing was left of some of the homes but jumbled piles of lumber. Other homes were still standing, and we talked with the families who were cleaning up the debris and doing their best to try to recover whatever they could. One man took us into his redbrick bungalow. The water had receded but the damage was great. He was nevertheless resolved that he was going to get it fixed and live in his home again. The sense I got in Gulfport was of devastation mixed with a determination to rebuild and get moving again. This sentiment seemed to flow from the top, where a resilient Governor Barbour was handling the disaster with efficiency and competence.

Our next stop was the U.S.S. *Iwo Jima* for a briefing from Coast Guard Admiral Thad Allen, who would soon be in charge of all Katrina relief efforts. He was rightly proud of the performance of the Coast Guard. They were rescuing people stranded in trees, in boats, and on roofs. In the end they would save more than thirty thousand lives.

We flew by helicopter to a levee overlooking New Orleans's Ninth Ward, where we saw complete devastation. As far as the eye could see, fetid water covered everything, except the tops of houses. We met with Lieutenant General Russ Honoré, a native of Louisiana. The commander of Joint Task Force Katrina, Honoré combined authority and ability with a true compassion for what his fellow Louisianans were going through. And he knew how to get things done. He drove Lynne and me through the center of New Orleans in his Humvee to a site where the Coast Guard was loading huge sandbags—the size of sofas— and transporting them by helicopter in an effort to plug the breaches in the levees.

We in the Bush administration took a severe pounding for our response to Hurricane Katrina, and no doubt we could have done things better at all levels. President Bush has written that he should have sent in U.S. troops earlier, which may be true, but which to my mind lets state authorities off the hook too easily. To this day I'm not sure why Governor Blanco refused to request a federalized response to Katrina. I did think she made a wise decision when she determined in 2007 not to run for a second term as Louisiana's governor.

It is also important to recognize that many people—Mike Chertoff, Thad Allen, and Russ Honoré among them—did tremendous work in the aftermath of one of the worst natural disasters ever to hit the United States. And among those whose efforts ought to be recognized is President George Bush. In the days, weeks, and months after Katrina, he personally dedicated hundreds of hours not only to ensuring an effective federal response, but to reaching out to people who needed to know that their government cared about them.

AS 2005 DREW TO a close, the American military and our partners in the multinational coalition had accomplished a great deal. We had removed one of the world's worst dictators. We had captured Saddam. We had handed responsibility for Iraq back to the Iraqis, and over the next twelve months they would hold three national elections, produce a constitution, and elect a parliament and prime minister. Our forces had captured and killed many of the leaders of the insurgency and provided security for the Iraqi people when they cast their votes and began to build a democracy.

In our prewar planning for the postwar period, we had anticipated a number of dangerous contingencies that failed to materialize. Saddam did not use weapons of mass destruction. The Republican Guard did not make a stand at Baghdad and force our troops into a siege or house-by-house fighting. Saddam was not able to set his oil fields ablaze or launch missiles into Israel.

There were also some things we failed to anticipate. Based on intelligence reports, we believed we would be able to rely on the Iraqi police to keep the peace and provide security. That turned out not to be true.

The Iraqi police were among the least trusted, most infiltrated institutions in Iraqi society. We also thought that once we removed the top Baathist leaders from Saddam's government, we'd be able to get things up and running relatively quickly, but we discovered that many people were so accustomed to acting only on orders from the top that they were paralyzed without them. I was told of a shoe factory that had not been damaged by the fighting. It still had plenty of basic materials and supplies to operate and people eager and willing to go to work. Yet it continued to sit idle. When the owner of the factory was asked why it wasn't operating, he said that no one had told him he could start it. Worse, however, was the fact that the society had been completely and totally brutalized for thirty years. It is fair to say that we underestimated the difficulty of rebuilding a traumatized and shattered society.

We also underestimated the extent to which the Shia felt betrayed by the United States after Desert Storm. In 1991 we had encouraged them to rise up against Saddam. When they did, Saddam slaughtered thousands of them and we did not, for the most part, come to their aid. They were understandably fearful that we would abandon them again.

Much has been written about the internal debates we had in the period when the Coalition Provisional Authority was running Iraq. I tend to think that hindsight in this area is twenty-twenty. We had tremendously talented people working hard in Baghdad—military and civilian—to accomplish an exceedingly difficult task. They didn't always get it right. And we didn't always get it right in Washington. It is possible, for example, that we could have avoided the impression of an American occupation had we established a provisional Iraqi government from the outset.

Once we had turned over sovereignty in June 2004, we looked toward political milestones, such as elections and the adoption of a constitution, in the belief that they would be followed by reduced levels of violence. As the Iraqis took control of their own country, we believed the terrorists and insurgents would have difficulty continuing to fight. They would be seen as attacking Iraqis who were simply trying to run their own country. When violence increased, we thought the enemy was lashing out in final acts of desperation, last efforts to terrorize and destroy before a self-governing Iraq made such attacks futile, even counterproductive. That was the context of my comment in May 2005 that the insurgents were "in the last throes." I believed they were.

At the end of the day, it's important to remember that the ultimate blame for the violence and bloodshed in Iraq after liberation lies with those who created it—the terrorists and those who were supporting them, primarily al Qaeda and Iran. They were a determined and ruthless enemy, committed to causing mass casualties among Iraqi civilians and American soldiers. They wanted to create chaos, break our will, and force us to leave. In January 2004 American forces had captured an al Qaeda courier who was carrying a letter from Abu Musab al Zarqawi to al Qaeda leaders. The letter detailed Zarqawi's plan to foment sectarian violence between Shia and Sunni in Iraq by "targeting and striking [Shiite] religious, political, and military symbols" and "dragging them into a sectarian war." He went on to declare that "fighting the Shia is the way to take the nation to battle." He also made clear how much al Qaeda feared democracy, writing that when "the sons of this land will be the authority . . . we will have no pretext. We can pack up and leave and look for another land."

The Shia refused to be dragged into sectarian violence for over two years. Then at dawn on February 6, 2006, explosions destroyed the golden dome of the Askariya Mosque in Samarra, one of the holiest sites for Shiite Islam. Planned by Zarqawi, the bombing had the effect he intended, inflaming the Shia and plunging the country into a deeper sectarian conflict. Understanding that Iraq was the central front in the War on Terror, al Qaeda was intent on victory. We had to decide whether we would stick with a strategy that emphasized transferring responsibility to Iraqis and getting our troops out, or whether we, too, would fight to win.

—◄◦►—

CHAPTER FOURTEEN

Surge

I left my home in St. Michaels, Maryland, early on Monday, June 12, 2006, for the fifty-minute helicopter flight to Camp David. The national security team was gathering for a review of our Iraq war strategy, and as the Camp David landing zone came into sight, I thought through some of the questions we needed to address: Is there more we could be doing to defeat the insurgency? Do we need more troops? Are the Iraqis convinced that we'll see this through? What does it take to win?

In the conference room at Laurel Lodge we all sat on one side of the table facing the video monitors on the wall, where Generals John Abizaid and George Casey and Ambassador Zal Khalilzad began the brief with an update of our operations on the ground in Iraq. We'd had a major success on June 7, when American forces located and killed Abu Musab al Zarqawi, the leader of al Qaeda in Iraq. General Stan McChrystal had built a top-notch special operations unit that had been tracking senior al Qaeda operatives and taking down terrorist networks. McChrystal's men had been tracking Zarqawi for some time when they received confirmation he was staying in a house near Baqubah, Iraq.

An F-16 dropped two five-hundred-pound bombs on the house, killing Zarqawi. After the attack, U.S. forces raided seventeen other locations in and around Baghdad, where they found valuable intelligence information.

This was good news. Zarqawi, who had found refuge in Iraq after 9/11, had led a campaign of violence in Iraq—kidnappings, suicide bombings, public beheadings—and with the bombing of the mosque at Samarra, he had launched a frenzy of sectarian bloodletting. Killing him was an important achievement, but as I listened to Abizaid and Casey brief on our operations, I had a nagging concern. They were carrying out a strategy that defined success based on turnover of responsibility to the Iraqis, and there was a danger, in a setting that had grown so violent, of withdrawing prematurely—before Iraqi military and police were capable of defending and securing their own sovereign territory.

We were confronting an extraordinarily complex set of forces inside Iraq. At the heart of much of the bloodshed was al Qaeda's strategy, which was to kill as many Shia and Americans as possible—and the more ruthlessly the better, so that the Shia would strike back and we would respond to the mayhem by leaving. Disaffected Sunnis, fearful of their future in an Iraq run by a coalition government of Shia and Kurds and worried that Shia were using their power in the new government to exact sectarian revenge, filled the ranks of the insurgency. They joined in the killing of American and Iraqi security forces, as well as Iraqi civilians. As the violence dragged on, Shiite militia and death squads became increasingly active, targeting Sunnis and battling one another for power. Tens of thousands had become part of the Jaysh al Mahdi militia, which was controlled by Muqtada al Sadr, a radical anti-American Shiite leader. Our forces had seriously degraded the capabilities of Sadr's militia in engagements in Najaf and Karbala in 2004, but particularly after the dome of the Askariya mosque was reduced to rubble, he and his army contributed significantly to the violence in Iraq.

The Iranians were playing a deadly role, providing support to a number of the Shiite militias, including Muqtada al Sadr's. The Iranian

aimed to clear Baghdad's most violent neighborhoods and keep the extremists out while building up essential services and infrastructure. On August 17 General Casey, using secure video hookup from Iraq, briefed the National Security Council. Most of the group gathered in the Roosevelt Room because renovations were under way in the White House Situation Room. I attended, using secure video hookup from Wyoming. Casey reported that the U.S. forces who had participated had been very effective and performed well and said that he thought we would see continued improvement in the Iraqi Security Forces. He said he would like to be able to turn over Baghdad security to the Iraqis by the end of 2006.

I respected General Casey, but I couldn't see a basis for his optimism. Violence was ongoing—and, in fact, in the months ahead it would escalate dramatically. The neighborhoods that had been cleared would be reinfiltrated, and Operations Together Forward would be widely regarded as failures. I asked what we could do to reduce the number of attacks and suggested we consider having U.S. forces take on a bigger role. This was a concept General Casey continued to resist, in large part because he and General Abizaid, as well as some in the Pentagon civilian leadership, assumed that U.S. forces were an irritant that inflamed the insurgency and made the violence worse. They continued to argue that the solution was to "take our hand off the bicycle seat" and put the Iraqis in charge as quickly as we could.

ON AUGUST 24, 2006, I asked Colonel Derek Harvey, a retired army intelligence officer, to come to the Vice President's Residence to brief me. Colonel Harvey was then working at the Defense Intelligence Agency and was one of the very best sources on the nature of the enemy we faced. He had spent a great deal of time working in Iraq, studying the insurgency and its networks. John Hannah, my national security advisor, kept in touch with Derek as he provided regular updates for me on the situation on the ground in Iraq. Derek had briefed me several times over the previous years and also provided his in-depth analysis to the National Security Council. As we looked for a way forward, I felt his assessment of the causes of the insurgency and the role played by former elements of Saddam's regime was key to understanding how we might change our strategy to defeat the enemy.

As I looked for alternatives to our current strategy, I kept hearing about Colonel H. R. McMaster, a veteran of the first Gulf War. He had been awarded a Silver Star for his leadership in the famed tank battle of 73 Easting in the southeastern desert of Iraq. McMaster and his unit had destroyed several Iraqi Revolutionary Guard units while suffering no casualties of their own. McMaster had also had a remarkable success in the war in which we were currently engaged. In 2005, in command of the 3rd Armored Cavalry Regiment, he had succeeded in bringing stability to the town of Tal Afar, where Sunnis had been kidnapping and killing Shia and Shia were leaving the beheaded corpses of Sunnis in the streets. McMaster, on his own initiative, had employed a classic counterinsurgency strategy, isolating the insurgents from the townspeople and providing security while helping the local population to establish political and economic institutions.

I asked for a briefing from Colonel McMaster, and he came to the Vice President's Residence on September 28, 2006. An accomplished soldier with a Ph.D. in history, McMaster joined me in the library on the main floor of the vice president's house and gave me his assessment of where things stood in Iraq and what we needed to do to win.

Despite the success of the enemy in inciting sectarian violence, he said, we could make tremendous progress—but not if we withdrew prematurely from critical areas. He urged that we avoid the trap of considering handoff to the Iraqis an end in itself. Instead, we should define the conditions we wanted to achieve before transitioning authority. These should include defeating the insurgency in any area we were handing over, so that economic and political development could move ahead, and ensuring that the Iraqi army and border police were capable of sustained independent security operations. The rule of law had to be established, and the Iraqi police had to be able to enforce it. It was also crucial that local governing authorities be capable of meeting the basic needs of the population.

McMaster's track record was encouraging, and his case was thoughtful and convincing. I also knew the strategy he described was being worked on by one of the brightest minds in the military. In January 2006, during a stop at Fort Leavenworth, Kansas, I had visited with General David Petraeus, an army three-star with a Princeton Ph.D. Petraeus got highest marks from many people, including Don Rumsfeld and Paul Wolfowitz, then Rumsfeld's deputy at the Defense Department. Petraeus had just returned from Iraq, where he had been in charge of training Iraqi security forces and was beginning work on revising the army's counterinsurgency manual. After Petraeus completed his manual, I received a draft, and it was as clear and cogent as Petraeus himself. I realized that changing the mission in Iraq to emphasize counterinsurgency would require a greater American troop presence, but I thought the idea deserved serious consideration.

Chairman of the Joint Chiefs of Staff Pete Pace had been impressed with Colonel McMaster's work in Tal Afar and brought him and several other colonels back to Washington for a ninety-day assignment to do some creative thinking and make recommendations to the Joint Chiefs of Staff for the way ahead in Iraq. The group came to be known as the Council of Colonels and worked inside the Pentagon to develop a strategy for victory.

That fall, at least three other reviews of our policy were under way. At the direction of the president, Deputy National Security Advisor J. D. Crouch was overseeing a process for Steve Hadley that brought together senior officials from the State Department, Defense Department, the joint staff, the intelligence community, and the NSC to conduct a review to provide recommendations directly to the president. John Hannah and Robert Karem represented my office in the process. Outside the government, retired four-star general and former Vice Chief of Staff of the Army Jack Keane and Fred Kagan, formerly a professor of military history at West Point, were working at the American Enterprise Institute, a Washington, D.C., think tank, on a proposal for a counterinsurgency strategy and troop surge. And the bipartisan Iraq Study Group, created by Congress, had been working since March to come up with a new approach.

Not only was the increased violence in Iraq leading to real concern in Washington; it was also putting a strain on our relations with the new Iraqi government. Prime Minister Nouri al Maliki and other Iraqi Shiite leaders believed that the violence being caused by the Shiite militias was simply a response to Sunni attacks—which, he noted, the Americans had failed to prevent. I knew that many Iraqis viewed the Americans as powerful enough to do whatever we wanted, and so when we didn't stop attacks, they suspected there was a reason. Was Maliki thinking we had bought into the Sunni idea that the Shia militias were the primary enemy in Iraq? Did he think we were turning our back on the Shia?

We discussed this issue at length in our October 21 secure videoconference with our team in Baghdad. If we were going to get the Iraqis into the fight and help them stand up and take responsibility for governance and their own security, we had to avoid a rift with the Maliki government. We needed to be working hand in glove with them, as we trained their forces and helped them carry out what should be a coordinated effort. General Casey agreed that we needed to continue to manage the relationship with the Shia very carefully.

TEN DAYS LATER, ON October 31, 2006, after the president and I had finished our morning briefings in the Oval Office, he said, "Dick, can I talk to you for a second?" We went down the small hallway that leads to the private dining room where we held our weekly lunches. "I've decided to make a change at Defense," the president said, "and I'm looking at Bob Gates to replace Rumsfeld." He was informing me of his decision, not soliciting my views. He already knew them, since twice before I had argued against replacing Rumsfeld. Just after the 2004 election, when he reviewed the entire cabinet and decided to move Powell out at State, he also considered moving Rumsfeld out at Defense. I made the case that Rumsfeld was doing a tremendous job, that he was carrying out administration policy, and that replacing him would signal dissatisfaction with the strategy the president himself had set. I'd made the same arguments in 2005 when the issue came up again.

This time the president didn't wait around after he told me he had made up his mind. He turned and was out the door fast. He knew I'd be opposed, and I suspect he didn't want to hear the arguments he knew I'd make.

In my view Don Rumsfeld was a formidable secretary of defense. He engaged more directly in managing the building than any before or since. He got things done. Maybe he didn't have the best bedside manner in the world, but he is one of the most competent people I've ever met. He brought vast experience, endless energy, and total loyalty to the president to the job. He would argue passionately for what he believed in, but once the president made a decision, he would salute smartly and make it happen.

But it was clear that the president thought it was time for a fresh set of eyes on the situation in Iraq, and I didn't think Don would disagree. He had come to see me in March 2006 to make sure I knew that he would do whatever he could to help ensure our success in the wars in Iraq and Afghanistan. He was very specific with me—he was prepared, he said, to step down anytime the president believed he should.

On Sunday, November 5, I was working in the upstairs family room at the Vice President's Residence when I took a call from the president. He said he'd offered the secretary of defense job to Bob Gates, and Gates had accepted. "Dick, would you like to be the one to tell Don, or should I ask Josh Bolten to make the call?" he asked. "I'll do it, Mr. President," I said. "I owe Don an awful lot and he should hear the news from me."

When I reached him and told him that the president had decided he wanted to make a change at Defense, Don handled it like the consummate professional he is. "Okay. I got it," he said. Then he repeated something he'd told me before, that he had been giving serious thought to resigning if the Democrats managed to take the House or the Senate in the upcoming election. "I'm just too much of a target," he said. He worried that if Democrats won a majority in either house, he would be forced to spend all his time testifying and justifying the decisions of the last five and a half years, rather than focusing on the challenges we still faced. We had critically important work to do, and Don was concerned his staying on could diminish our ability to do it.

LATE IN THE AFTERNOON of November 9, the president, Steve Hadley, Secretary Rice, and I met in the White House residence for an in-depth discussion about the way forward in Iraq. We had a wide-ranging conversation that covered the global implications for the United States and our allies if we failed to see things through. Two days earlier, on November 7, we had lost our Republican majorities in both the House and the Senate, and we also talked about the U.S. political environment and the message being sent by the public debates about the war and the ongoing deliberations of the Iraq Study Group.

I went through a series of recent events I feared might signal to the Iraqis that the Americans had lost the will to see this through. The press was portraying the Republican loss in the midterms as a referendum on Iraq policy. The new Speaker of the House, Nancy Pelosi, and the new majority leader of the Senate, Harry Reid, had been very clear that they would push for withdrawal of American forces from Iraq. Senator Joe Lieberman had essentially been purged from Democratic ranks because of his support for the war. U.S. public opinion polls had gone south on Iraq and were now pretty consistently showing a majority opposed to continued military action there. And the president had announced Don Rumsfeld's departure. All these events were giving an overall impression to anyone paying attention that the Americans might well be getting ready to bail on Iraq. I was very concerned, especially about how all this would be read by Iraqis who wanted the United States to stand with them to secure their country. I maintained contact with a number of Iraqis, and increasingly they were voicing concern to me about the security situation and America's will to prevail.

The next morning, when we had our weekly secure videoconference with our military commanders and our ambassador in Iraq, the president asked Ambassador Khalilzad what the mood was there. Zal said people were worried that America was getting ready to leave. He confirmed some of my worst concerns about the situation.

I was also worried about the message we were sending to our troops and their families. They were the constituency that mattered more than any other, and this was the first time since we'd created the all-volunteer force that our soldiers had been committed in an unpopular war. Their morale and that of their families was crucial, and as criticism mounted, we had to be absolutely clear, internally and publicly, that we would not compromise our fundamental mission for political reasons. There is a sacred trust between our soldiers and their civilian leaders, and no matter how loudly we were being criticized in the press or how vehemently the Democrats were attacking us, we had to remember what mattered—giving our troops a mission they could carry out to fight and win in Iraq.

BY THE FALL OF 2006 we had lost over 2,500 brave Americans in Afghanistan and Iraq. If we adopted a counterinsurgency strategy and surged more forces, our troops would be going into the enemy's strongholds, moving out of their forward operating bases. Increased contact with the enemy was the only way to win, but our generals had been clear—this new strategy would likely bring more casualties, at least in the near term. Sending American troops into harm's way is the toughest decision that a commander in chief has to make, and as I thought about a surge, which George W. Bush might be deciding on soon, I thought about our soldiers and their families and the deep gratitude our nation owes them. Over the course of my vice presidency, I met many families of the fallen. Most often, through their unimaginable pain, their message to me was, Don't let our son have died in vain. Finish the job.

Our soldiers understand, sometimes better than the politicians in Washington, why they are fighting. I remember the wife of a member of one of our special operations units telling me that on every one of his missions, her husband carried with him a patch from the New York City Fire Department—he was fighting for those who had died on 9/11. Her husband's missions were secret, and he couldn't talk about them, but she said she wished she could somehow reach out to the wives and loved ones of the firefighters and policemen and all those who were killed on

9/11 and tell them her husband and thousands of others were hunting down the terrorists responsible for those attacks.

Many of our wounded soldiers are hospitalized at Walter Reed Army Medical Center in Washington, D.C. I never came away from my visits there without being moved beyond words at the courage and the dedication of the warriors. Countless times, the only request they made when I asked if there was anything we could do for them was that they be allowed to return to their units.

Organizations like Fisher House do wonderful work providing support and a place for families of these soldiers to stay. Diane Bodman, wife of Energy Secretary Sam Bodman, dedicated herself to making sure the young men and women who were well enough to leave the hospital for even a brief time had places to go and things to see. Lynne and I were honored to invite them to the Naval Observatory. We had barbecues and some outstanding country and western music. Singers such as Charlie Daniels and Rodney Atkins regarded entertaining at these events as a privilege—and we felt the same way about hosting them.

The wounded warriors are exemplary of the tremendous caliber of men and women who make up America's armed forces. They are the greatest fighting force—and the greatest force for good—the world has ever known. And we must never lose sight of the fact that they are the reason we, and many millions more all around the world, live in freedom today.

THE IRAQ STUDY GROUP, co-chaired by Lee Hamilton and Jim Baker, came to the White House to brief us on their report on December 6. Hamilton, whom I had known since we were in the House together, opened the presentation. He said the goal of the Iraq Study Group was to recommend a way to achieve a reduction of the U.S. commitment to Iraq over time without setting a specific timetable. He talked about shifting the role of U.S. forces to be more focused on training. He suggested we needed conditions for the Iraqis to meet, as well as a broad diplomatic effort in the region. My friend Jim Baker spoke next. He said the military effort should shift from efforts to suppress sectarian violence to a mission of training, equipping, and supporting Iraqi forces. He believed a new diplomatic initiative was necessary and should include direct talks with the Syrians and Iranians.

Other members of the group followed, with several urging that we restart the Israeli-Palestinian peace process. Chuck Robb, former Democratic senator from Virginia and a veteran of Vietnam, stressed how important it was that we not withdraw immediately and raised the possibility of a surge if we decided it was needed. When my Wyoming friend Al Simpson spoke, he said that the group understood the difference between a committee making recommendations—even a committee as prestigious as this one—and those of us in power making decisions. He said he was praying for us.

I appreciated the work this bipartisan group had done. They had taken their responsibilities seriously and worked hard to come up with sound recommendations. But I was troubled as I listened to their suggestions and later as I read the report. The only place the word *victory* appeared in the document was in connection with the chances for an al Qaeda victory. This was not a strategy for winning the war.

While we all knew that ultimately the Iraqis would have to stand up and take on responsibility themselves for securing their nation, the ISG failed to recognize the stakes for the United States if we withdrew before the Iraqis were capable of defending themselves. The report's focus on political reconciliation and finding political solutions to the nation's problems left out the importance of a secure environment in which reconciliation could occur and political agreements could be reached. I was also disappointed with the group's suggestions with respect to Iran and Syria. The group recommended that we open a dialogue with each nation, asserting that neither had an interest in seeing a chaotic Iraq—but both Iran and Syria were working hard to encourage precisely that.

The next morning we had our Oval Office intelligence brief earlier than normal because the president and Prime Minister Tony Blair were having breakfast at 8:00 a.m., followed by a joint press conference. As the intelligence briefing wrapped up, a staffer came in with a copy of the president's opening remarks for the press conference. I didn't usually get involved with drafts of presidential speeches, but a quick glance at this one sent up a red flag. I'd seen an earlier version and it had the word *victory* in it. Someone had taken it out of the remarks.

For some time, Dan Bartlett, the director of communications, and Josh Bolten, the chief of staff, had been arguing that the president shouldn't say "victory." They viewed that as the equivalent of arguing to stay the course. They were concerned the press would hear it and write that the president hadn't understood the message of the midterms we'd just lost. They worried it would lead to stories that the president was "stubborn" and "wasn't listening." They urged repeatedly that for optics' sake, we make clear we had a changed strategy—and that meant deleting references to "victory."

I disagreed. Our national security depended on victory in Iraq. That was simply the truth, and the president should be clear about it. I also thought about our soldiers and their families and what they would think when they heard the president's remarks. The commander in chief could not be sending men and women into harm's way if we weren't fighting to win.

"Mr. President," I said, holding up the proposed remarks, "you can't refuse to talk about winning. That will be a huge signal that you no longer believe in victory." The president understood immediately, and a few hours later when he appeared with Prime Minister Blair, he said, "We agree that victory in Iraq is important; it's important for the Iraqi people, it's important for the security of the United States and Great Britain, and it's important for the civilized world." It could not have been any clearer.

At four that afternoon the president's principal national security advisors met in the secure conference room in the Old Executive Office Building, across West Executive Avenue from the White House, to discuss Iraq. Secretary Rice and I had a vigorous debate. She argued that Iraq was experiencing the kind of sectarian violence that American forces should not be in the middle of. Our troops should stand back, she said, and engage only if they think they are witnessing a massacre, the kind of violence that had happened in 1995 when Serbian forces had slaughtered thousands of Bosnians in Srebrenica. I did not think this was realistic. My view was that we had to stay actively and aggressively engaged in the fight, that the outcome mattered too much for us to simply pull back and watch the Iraqis battle it out.

By the next morning, when we gathered in the Roosevelt Room for a meeting on this topic with the president, much of the distinction between Secretary Rice's view and mine had been airbrushed away. Instead of two crisply drawn options for the president, the NSC staff presented what they described as "an emerging consensus." They were following a practice for managing conflicting views that Rice had started when she was national security advisor. I'd never been a fan of it, but I was particularly concerned that in the case of Iraq the president should be presented with clear choices, not halfway measures, not policy recommendations that split the difference.

I spoke up. "These aren't the options we discussed last night. The distinction has been blurred here." There was a big difference between letting the Iraqis fight it out and staying engaged to defeat the enemy, and I observed that attempting to find some sort of compromise position, some view that made everyone happy around the table, might in fact produce policy that was incomprehensible and impossible to implement as a military strategy.

The chairman of the Joint Chiefs, Pete Pace, followed up, pointing to the suggestion that U.S. troops get involved only if there were a massacre on the order of Srebrenica. "How do I write that into an order for the troops?" he asked. "Hold your fire unless you think it looks like Srebrenica?" That just doesn't work, he said. "Either we're in or we're not in. Either we're operating or we're not operating."

THE PRESIDENT WANTED TO hear from outside experts and get their thoughts on a new strategic approach for Iraq, and so a group gathered in the Oval Office on the afternoon of December 11. Retired four-star general Barry McCaffrey, who had played a major role during Desert Storm as commander of the 24th Infantry Division, was there. Wayne Downing, a retired four-star who had been teaching at West

Point, was another member of the group. When I was secretary of defense, he had commanded the Joint Special Operations Command that oversees our special operations forces worldwide. Several civilian experts were also at the session, including Eliot Cohen and Stephen Biddle. The group was united in the notion that we were in trouble in Iraq and needed to clean it up, but they weren't united in recommending a course of action. Jack Keane, the retired vice chief of staff of the army, was the most direct and had the best developed concept. Keane made the point that Iraq was in crisis, but that we were a long way from having to accept defeat. He said that Baghdad was the key, and we needed our troops in the neighborhoods around the clock. He also urged that we not be distracted by the Shiite militias. "They are not the issue," he said. We needed to keep our energies focused on defeating al Qaeda and the Sunni insurgents, who were at the heart of the security problem across Iraq.

When the meeting with the president concluded, Jack came back to my office, and Fred Kagan, the military historian with whom Jack had been working, joined us. Their basic idea was a shift to a counterinsurgency strategy, where the primary focus would be protecting the population, since their cooperation and the intelligence they could provide were crucial to success. Under this strategy troops would secure Baghdad by hitting targeted areas, putting up a cordon, then going house to house, arresting and capturing the enemy. Our troops would be in the neighborhoods 24/7, no longer going back at night to the large and sometimes isolated forward operating bases. The increase in forces and our increased visibility and contact with the local population would, Keane and Kagan believed, convey the notion that we were in it to win and would stay until the enemy was defeated.

Without this change of strategy, simply adding more troops would not bring a victory, but this new strategy could not be successful without more troops. To achieve the increase, Keane and Kagan proposed to speed up the deployment of troops getting ready to go to Iraq and then delay bringing some troops home, so that there would be a surge of as many as seven extra brigades into Baghdad. They also recommended sending a Marine Regimental Combat Team, the equivalent of roughly another brigade, to Al Anbar Province, a stronghold of the Sunni insurgency.

We would also work very closely with the local forces, making sure they understood that even when the combat operation was over, we would leave some troops behind to secure the area and maintain order. Assisting Iraqi forces in holding these areas until they were capable of operating without us would be manpower intensive, which was one of the reasons a surge was crucial. A surge would also give us additional capability to speed up and improve the effectiveness of the Iraqi forces.

Keane and Kagan had the full package: a new strategy and the way to implement it. The next day I described for the president in general terms what they were proposing and what they believed was feasible, which led us to a conversation about the Joint Chiefs of Staff. They knew there was a strategy review under way and that there was talk of a surge, and they were concerned that it would have a negative impact on overall force readiness and troop morale. But it was pretty clear, as the president observed, that the worst thing for troop morale would be losing the war.

The president was scheduled to see the chiefs at the Pentagon the next day, December 13, and I told him I thought it was important to have an in-depth discussion. We rode over together, along with Steve Hadley, went in through the River Entrance, and after a couple of left turns, were in the chiefs' windowless conference room, the Tank.

General Pace opened the meeting, summarizing the chiefs' recommendations. Their emphasis was on expanding the U.S. advisory effort, shifting the U.S. focus to developing the Iraqi Security Forces, and transitioning to Iraqi control. "The question is when do you shift to advising," the president said. "You don't want to do it too early." Pace responded that General Casey did not believe that the Iraqi forces would fall apart if we shifted now. "We need to get the Iraqi Security Forces in charge," he said.

Then I spoke. I emphasized the importance of winning in Iraq and said that the chiefs' plan seemed to put the burden on the Iraqi people and the Iraqi Security Forces at a time when they weren't ready. "We're betting the farm on Iraqi Security Forces," I said, and I wanted to know why, given the importance of prevailing in Iraq, we were willing to do that. "Wouldn't it be better to make a major push with our own forces to get it done?" I also talked about the consequences of losing, the way it would destabilize the entire region and frighten off the moderates in countries like Afghanistan and Pakistan who had signed on with us. "Suddenly it will be very dangerous to be a friend of the United States," I said. "There's an awful lot riding on this."

The resistance to a surge that the president and I heard that day was in part a product of the chiefs' mission as mandated by the 1986 Goldwater-Nichols Act. That legislation essentially took the chiefs out of the war-fighting business and put them in charge of raising and sustaining our military forces. The chiefs don't take our forces to war, and they aren't in the chain of command. They nurture, prepare, train, and equip the force, but then it gets turned over to a combatant commander to fight and win wars. So, when you go into the Tank and talk to the chiefs, they have responsibilities that go beyond what's happening on the ground in Baghdad. They are also focused on supporting and sustaining our overall military readiness. Surging forces in Iraq could make that more difficult.

Of course, if the president gives a mission to the chiefs, they will salute smartly and get it done. But they have an obligation to point out consequences, and the president needs to hear the arguments so that he understands the trade-offs.

The most articulate spokesman of the chiefs' viewpoint that day in the Tank was General Pete Schoomaker. A graduate of the University of Wyoming, where he played football and joined ROTC, Pete was involved in Desert One, the failed attempt in 1980 to rescue American hostages in Iran. He then became part of the original special operations teams that were formed in response to that failure. I'd had a hand in recruiting him from retirement to become army chief of staff, and he had done a terrific job.

By the end of 2006, Schoomaker's concern was that we were putting huge stress on the force. On a daily basis he was dealing with long deployments, multiple deployments, and what that meant for soldiers and their families. He was facing recruiting and retention challenges, as well as a host of other problems that resulted from our ongoing operations in Iraq and Afghanistan. In addition, in these conflicts we'd deployed individual reservists and National Guard members to fill in where needed in Afghanistan and Iraq. This meant that when it was time to deploy these reserve and Guard units as a whole, key members had already been deployed and weren't available. We no longer had the kind of reserve and Guard units we had anticipated having.

The pace of operations also took a toll on equipment. Humvees, for example, were normally driven about eight thousand miles a year in peacetime exercises. Some of them were now being driven forty thousand miles a year. Add to that the fact that the Humvee was never intended to be an armored vehicle. It was designed as a soft-sided, all-purpose vehicle for the military, but because of the IED threat in Iraq, we put special armor on many of them to protect the troops. A Humvee without armor weighs about 6,500 pounds, and that's the amount of weight its transmission and suspension systems were designed for. When we up-armored them, as we had to do, we added another three to four thousand pounds. The wear and tear was significant, and that meant significant additional cost to repair and replace equipment.

When the chiefs argued that now was not the time to surge forces, I think that part of their objective was to get the notion across to the president that if he was going to order a surge in troops, he was going to have to make a significantly larger investment in our military. It was a point well taken, and in his next budget, the president included funding to increase the size of both the army and the Marine Corps.

One argument the chiefs made that didn't go far was the notion that we ought not commit more forces to Iraq because we needed to maintain a reserve force to deploy in the event of an unforeseen contingency somewhere else in the world. The president wasn't persuaded. He told them his priority was to win the war we were fighting, not hold back out of concern for some potential future war.

———

THROUGHOUT THIS PERIOD, Jack Keane brought important perspective to the matter of what our forces could bear and how far we could push the chiefs. He knew that they would be legitimately concerned about the stress on the force, but he also pointed out that in an all-out global War on Terror, you do what you have to do to win. If you've got to go to fifteen-month deployments or eighteen-month deployments or stop-loss orders for the entire force or doubling the size of the force, whatever you've got to do you do because the one thing you can't afford is defeat. With thirty-seven years of service in the army and his experience as vice chief of staff, he was for me personally a real anchor and a source of wisdom. His advice carried a good deal of weight. His view that it was absolutely possible to do what needed to be done without breaking the force went a long way toward giving me and other policymakers a sense that a surge was doable.

THE PRESIDENT WANTED THE new secretary of defense, Bob Gates, to have a chance to visit Iraq and meet with Generals Casey and Abizaid before any public announcement of a new war strategy. After Gates returned from Iraq, the National Security Council gathered at the president's ranch in Crawford on December 28, 2006. Bob explained that General Casey had agreed to a surge, but that he wanted no more than two brigades, with additional brigades in the pipeline for deployment if needed. This looked like the kind of compromise solution we had been trying to avoid, and the president decided against it.

By this time, he had also decided on new military leadership in Iraq. He was going to make General Casey army chief of staff and nominate General David Petraeus to replace him. I thought Petraeus was a superb choice, tough, bright, and competent. Jack Keane, who didn't offer praise lightly, was one of his biggest fans. The two had been close since 1991, when they had been watching a training exercise at Fort Campbell, Kentucky, and a high-velocity round had accidentally struck Petraeus in the chest. Keane stayed by him, helicoptering with Petraeus to the Vanderbilt Medical Center in Nashville, where a cardiothoracic surgeon named Bill Frist—who would later become Senate majority leader—operated on him for nearly six hours.

Petraeus made it clear that he needed five brigades. So did the general whom the president was nominating to be second in command in Iraq, Ray Odierno, a brilliant, no-nonsense army three-star who would implement the new strategy. Petraeus and Odierno would be joined in Iraq by an extremely talented new ambassador, Ryan Crocker.

On January 10, 2007, the president announced in a speech to the nation that he was committing twenty thousand additional troops—five brigades—to Iraq, and most of them would go to Baghdad. He was also increasing American forces in Anbar, the home base of al Qaeda in Iraq, by four thousand. The brigades would deploy over time so that it would be summer before we reached full strength.

The president's decision was particularly courageous against the drumbeat of criticism we were facing from outside the administration. On December 17, 2006, former secretary of state Colin Powell had said that America was "losing in Iraq" and a "surge cannot be sustained." Days after the president's speech, Republican Senator Chuck Hagel declared the surge "a waste of our troops and a waste of our treasure," and Senator Barack Obama predicted that rather than solving sectarian violence, the surge would increase it.

Shortly after the additional troops began arriving in Iraq, critics declared that the surge had failed. Perhaps most memorably, in April 2007 Senator Harry Reid said, "This war is lost, and the surge is not accomplishing anything." While even members of his own party thought Reid had gone too far in declaring America's defeat, there was certainly hand-wringing on both sides of the aisle, especially among members worried about reelection and concerned that we weren't seeing results quickly enough.

Inside the White House and the Pentagon, senior officials began to look for ways to placate the Congress and a hostile media. Although the president had just signed up for the surge, some of his advisors were already talking about bringing at least one brigade home by the end of the year. This was a political recommendation, totally divorced from the situation on the ground, which according to Generals Petraeus and Odierno would require the surged brigades well into 2008.

On Tuesday morning, May 22, a David Ignatius column appeared in the *Washington Post* titled "After the Surge: The Administration Floats Ideas for a New Approach in Iraq." It quoted administration officials on the need to revamp policy in order to attract bipartisan support and to take into account the fact that the surge might not have the stabilizing effect we had hoped. I was very concerned when I read the piece, and I raised it with the president in the Oval Office. "Whoever is leaking information like this to the press is doing a real disservice, Mr. President," I said, "both to you and to our forces on the ground in Baghdad." We shouldn't be suggesting that our war policy was being tailored for political purposes, pieced together to include elements simply because they would attract Democratic support, I said. And we shouldn't be cutting our commanders off at the knees, suggesting that their strategy would fail before the forces were even in place. "We have to correct this," I said, "particularly with our generals in the field. They have to know they have the full backing of the president and his top officials and that we will not start pulling troops out before the mission is complete."

A short time later Steve Hadley came into my office and closed the door. He told me that he was the source for Ignatius and that he'd talked to him at the instruction of the president. That gave me a moment's pause, but then I thought it was just as well I hadn't known. I might have been less forceful about making a case that deserved to be made forcefully. This wasn't a time for mixed messages.

A little before 7:00 a.m. on Saturday, May 26, 2007, I boarded Air Force Two for the short flight to New York, where I was scheduled to deliver remarks at the U.S. Military Academy's commencement ceremonies. The day's papers were laid out on the table in my cabin, and as I scanned the front-page headlines, a story by David Sanger in the *New York Times* caught my attention. "White House Is Said to Debate '08 Cut in Iraq Combat Forces by 50%," it read. In language making clear that key people inside the administration were sources for the article, the story laid out an administration plan to begin withdrawing well before commanders on the ground thought was wise and to "greatly scale back the mission that President Bush set for the American military when he ordered it in January to win back control of Baghdad and Anbar Province." It was another major story suggesting that the surge in forces—which was still not complete—would not succeed. The story also indicated that the administration was trimming back because of "growing political pressure."

A few hours later under a hazy blue sky I helped present diplomas to the impressive young cadets of the West Point Class of 2007. Their class motto was "Always Remember. Never Surrender." I found myself wishing that we in Washington could speak so clearly.

On May 30, toward the end of our weekly secure videoconference with our team in Iraq, the president asked our new ambassador Ryan Crocker and General Petraeus whether they had anything they wanted to add before signing off. General Petraeus, to his great credit, raised the issue of the press reports suggesting that the administration thought the surge might fail and was looking for ways to bring troops home early. He said that he and General Odierno had been sitting out there in Baghdad reading these reports, looking at each other across the table, and wondering what was going on back in Washington. Bringing up the news stories was a gutsy thing to do, and he did it in a way that was direct but totally nonconfrontational. Exactly right.

The president was getting some bad advice from those on the staff urging a political compromise for our Iraq strategy. I thought it would be helpful if he spent some time with Jack Keane. On Thursday, May 31, when I'd been scheduled to have my regular weekly lunch with the president, I suggested bringing Jack along, and I asked Steve Hadley to join us as well.

Jack traveled to Iraq frequently, and he and I had an informal arrangement that he'd stop by my office after he got back from a trip. I wanted to be sure he had the opportunity to pass along information he thought the president should have. Because of ongoing resistance inside the Pentagon and at Central Command to the surge strategy, I also wanted to ensure that General Petraeus's thoughts and concerns made it all the way up the chain of command.

Jack was just back from his second trip to Iraq since General Petraeus took over, and as we sat around the table in the president's private dining room, Jack began by talking about how proud he was of the caliber of our forces. They were the most competent and capable military force in history, he said, and they believed deeply in what they were doing. And even though the president's decision to surge forces meant longer deployments, more time away from home and families, and higher casualty rates initially, the sense of duty and commitment and pure competence among our forces in the field were just superb.

In 2006, he said, the enemy had the momentum, but now because of the surge, we had it. He pointed to what was happening in Anbar Province among the Sunni sheikhs. They were forming their own groups, which came to be known as Concerned Local Citizens, or CLCs, and signing on with the Americans to fight al Qaeda. One of the first questions the CLCs were asking our troops was "Are you here to stay this time?" When they believed we were, they got into the fight with us to restore safety and security in their own towns.

Keane said it was clear that the surge was working, but leaks like those in the *New York Times* the previous weekend weren't helpful. To the military leadership in the field such stories looked like a signal that the civilians were getting ready to pull the plug. The president explained that his staff was simply working on options, looking for ways to deal with the political problem we had on the Hill. Steve noted that although the president had just won a war-funding vote by threatening a veto, there was concern that the Democrats might succeed in passing other measures to tie our hands. That's why we needed to be ready with a new plan, a new direction.

I made the point that talking about "a new direction" isn't cost-free. You can't suggest a shift in strategy in Washington without it having an impact on our troops in the field, I said.

Jack said that what motivates generals like Petraeus and Odierno is duty. The president gave them a mission. He told them to surge, extend the deployments, and defeat the insurgents. Those generals carry out that mission out of a sense of duty. Now, he said, they may hear from folks back here in Washington who don't like the policy, and they may hear criticism or skepticism from visiting members of Congress. But it was critically important that they not hear it from their civilian leaders. He stressed the importance of keeping the chain of command knitted together and moving forward with the mission. He said that our troops in the field wouldn't be much affected by "Plan B" talk, but for our senior commanders it could be corrosive if they thought that civilian leadership had lost confidence in the mission.

A WEEK LATER SECRETARY GATES announced that he was withdrawing the nomination of Pete Pace for a second term as chairman of the Joint Chiefs of Staff. His nomination, which should have been routine, was pulled after Secretary Gates asked the Democratic chairman of the Senate Armed Services Committee, Carl Levin of Michigan, to survey other Democratic senators and let Gates know how the nomination would be received. Not surprisingly, Levin reported back that the confirmation hearings would focus on the last four years of the war. Gates decided to pull the nomination rather than have a fight. When he chose Admiral Mike Mullen to be the next chairman of the Joint Chiefs, it meant that Gates's original choice for vice chairman, Admiral Ed Giambastiani, would have to step aside since those positions can't both be occupied by individuals from the same service. As a result Gates's decision not to fight for Pete Pace resulted in the loss of two terrific officers who had served the nation with honor during a time of war. I thought it was a bad call.

On one of my first visits to Walter Reed to spend time with our wounded warriors, I had invited Pete Pace to come with me. We spent a morning together going room to room, and there was an emotional connection between Pete and those young soldiers and marines that I'd never seen with any other senior officer. His connection to these young men and his enormous admiration and respect for them were deep and sincere and returned to him many times over.

I had first met Admiral Giambastiani when I was on the House Intelligence Committee and he was head of an important submarine command. Extremely smart and highly effective at dealing with both the civilian and military leadership at the Pentagon, Ed had managed through a career of high achievement to maintain a down-to-earth modesty. Secretary Gates got it right at Admiral Giambastiani's farewell ceremony when he noted that Ed had made an art form of combining distinction and humility.

I would have fought to keep both of them.

I WAS ON AIR FORCE TWO flying to Washington on Sunday, July 8, when I got a call from Steve Hadley. The president had called Steve back to Washington from a family vacation, Steve said. He, Dan Bartlett, Ed Gillespie, Karl Rove, and Josh Bolten had been having a series of meetings at the president's request to try to come up with a change in strategy to satisfy some of the growing opposition on the Hill. I had been in Wyoming for the Fourth of July holiday while the meetings had been going on, but I'm not sure I would have been invited if I had been in town, since I was so opposed to temporizing on the surge in order to placate the Democrats. Not only was this the absolute wrong time to send a message that we were wavering; it wasn't even good politics. In trying to pacify opponents, we'd drive away supporters who understood the stakes, and in the end the Democrats wouldn't be appeased. They would simply demand more withdrawals.

The next morning, I picked up my copy of the *New York Times* to find another front-page story by David Sanger, this one titled "In White House, Debate Is Rising on Iraq Pullback." It opened by saying that "White House officials fear that the last pillars of political support among Senate Republicans for President Bush's Iraq strategy are collapsing around them." It reported that while the president and his aides once thought that decisions about the surge could wait until after General Petraeus and Ambassador Crocker made a mid-September report on the effectiveness of the strategy, now some aides were recommending the president "announce plans for a far more narrowly defined mission for American troops that would allow for a staged pullback."

As we sat in the Oval Office a few hours later for the daily communications session, no one challenged the substance of the piece, though there was speculation about who had leaked it. I made the case that the group was misreading the Congress. I didn't think the situation was as grim as they thought it was. I went back to my office and called Trent Lott, the Senate Republican whip, who was not at all pessimistic. He said he thought the degree to which Republicans were falling away from the president had been hyped by the press. The situation wasn't nearly as dire as the *New York Times* described it. Trent said he wanted to do a formal whip count before giving me a solid answer on the question of how many Republicans we could count on for any Iraq war vote. He told me he would run the traps and get back to me.

That afternoon, as White House discussions of the strategy continued, I again made the point that compromising now, before Petraeus had a chance to report back, was foolish. The Democrats would simply pocket whatever concessions we made and demand more later.

I also had an interesting visit from Henry Kissinger that day. He told me that he'd been approached by a couple of Republican senators who asked him if he would take a public position on Iraq, something different from the White House position, to give the Republicans something to endorse. He said they'd told him as many as ten Republican senators were prepared to embrace a new position so long as it was different from the White House view and one that Henry recommended. Henry had refused. He supported the president's policy.

The next day, Tuesday, July 10, 2007, I attended the weekly Republican Senate Policy Lunch, and Iraq was the focus. John McCain was just back from Iraq and gave a terrific presentation about why we were on the right course and why it was so important to stay on it. When he finished I was asked to say a few words. My normal practice was just to listen at these lunches, but given the stakes of the Iraq war debate and the indications of dissatisfaction in the Republican Senate ranks, I decided to speak. I echoed John's assessment that we needed to continue to back Petraeus. I talked about the consequences of failure for the United States and for our allies and the costs of premature withdrawal or retreat. I also reiterated the point that we could not in good conscience compromise on what we knew to be the right policy simply because of political pressure.

That night Lynne and I hosted some key Republican senators for dinner at the Vice President's Residence. Trent and Tricia Lott were there, and Trent pulled me aside. He'd done his whip count and said, "You know, I think we're going to be okay on the votes. I think we can win them all." He anticipated we'd lose seven or eight Republicans, but he couldn't see the Democrats getting the sixty votes they needed to block a filibuster on any measure they might put forward to tie our hands or change the strategy.

As dinner broke up, Republican Minority Leader Mitch McConnell walked over to me. Mitch had been one of the most concerned of the Republicans. He was up for reelection and had suggested to the president that he needed to begin a withdrawal in order to avoid massive defection of Republican senators. "Dick," McConnell said, "I may have been wrong. Tell the president that I think we may well be able to win these votes and hold the Senate Republicans for the month of July." That would get us through to the August recess and into September, when Dave Petraeus and Ryan Crocker were scheduled to testify. That was all we needed.

Ambassador Crocker and General Petraeus spent sixteen or seventeen hours testifying in front of Congress on September 10 and 11, 2007. They did a tremendous job, delivering their honest, unvarnished assessment of the situation in Iraq. They exhibited professionalism and competence under some intensely partisan attacks, particularly from senators who were gearing up to run for the Democratic presidential nomination.

A few nights later, as the president prepared to address the nation to sum up the progress Petraeus and Crocker had reported on, I found myself once again intervening in the speech-drafting process. Despite the fact that the president's surge strategy was a repudiation of the Baker-Hamilton report, Steve Hadley had inserted a reference to the group into the speech. I am sure Steve thought he was working to forge consensus, but it didn't make any sense. "Mr. President, you can't refer to Baker-Hamilton," I said. "Our strategy is Petraeus-Crocker, not Baker-Hamilton." He agreed and removed the reference.

Given the opposition of politicians and the public to putting more troops into Iraq, George Bush was truly courageous to order a new strategy and the surge of troops to carry it out. The next ten months ratified his brave decision. Our troops, together with the Iraqis, defeated the insurgency, dealt a severe blow to al Qaeda, and created a secure environment so that the Iraqi political process could begin to take hold. When historians look back, George Bush's decision will stand out as one that made a difference for millions and put history on a better track.

AS I REFLECT BACK on why the surge worked so well, the first credit for its success goes to our troops in the field, the men and women of the U.S. military, some of whom gave their lives securing this victory for our nation. The colonels who led these troops and were among the first to understand the importance of counterinsurgency also deserve tremendous credit, as do the generals who led them and one tremendously skilled American diplomat. General David Petraeus was the strategic visionary. Deeply knowledgeable about counterinsurgency doctrine, he took over command in some of Iraq's darkest days and turned things around with his determination to prevail. General Ray Odierno, commander of the multinational corps in Iraq under Petraeus, took the Petraeus doctrine and made it operational. He designed and commanded simultaneous and sustained offensive operations that denied the enemy any place to hide. Generals Petraeus and Odierno were aided immeasurably by the tireless work of Ambassador Ryan Crocker, the U.S. ambassador in Iraq from 2007 to 2009. The surge would not have succeeded without Crocker's historic efforts to knit diplomatic and military strategies together and to work with the Iraqi government to forge a new relationship between two sovereign nations.

Finally, what we accomplished in Iraq would not have been possible without the work of General Stan McChrystal and America's special operations forces. Their skill and bravery made it exceedingly dangerous to be an al Qaeda leader in Iraq. America's special ops forces are among the most valiant warriors the world has ever known, and I was honored to join some of them at a dinner in 2008. Their chaplain, a young man from Wyoming, said this in his invocation:

We are soldiers, God, agents of correction. May our world see the power of faith. May our nation know the strength of selfless service. And may our enemies continue to taste the inescapable force of freedom.

I am aware of no greater example of selfless service than America's special operations forces. Someday when the full history of this period can be written, all Americans will know the contributions they made to defend our freedom and our way of life.

———◄◦►———

CHAPTER FIFTEEN

Setback

In the fall of 2006, as violence in Iraq was still escalating, North Korea conducted its first nuclear test, setting off an explosion at the Punggye test site some two hundred forty miles northeast of Pyongyang. When the blast was detected, it was Sunday evening, October 8, in Washington, D.C. The next morning President Bush went before the cameras in the Diplomatic Reception Room to condemn the test and issue a warning:

> *The North Korean regime remains one of the world's leading proliferators of missile technology, including transfers to Iran and Syria. The transfer of nuclear weapons or material by North Korea to states or non-state entities would be considered a grave threat to the United States, and we would hold North Korea fully accountable for the consequences of such action.*

Six months later we received intelligence that a threat of this nature had materialized. I learned about it in detail one afternoon in mid-April

2007, in National Security Advisor Steve Hadley's office. I was seated in one of Steve's large blue wing chairs and he was to my left. Two Israeli officials were on the sofa to my right. Meir Dagan, director of Mossad, the Israeli intelligence service, pulled materials from his briefcase and spread them on the coffee table in front of us. For the next hour, Dagan showed us photos of a building in the Syrian desert at a place called al-Kibar. It was a nuclear reactor.

Additional photographs, which the intelligence community would later make public, showed key parts of the reactor as it was being built, vertical tube openings in the top for control rods and refueling, a reinforced concrete reactor vessel with a steel lining. Satellite imagery showed pipes that would supply water from the Euphrates for the cooling process. The Syrians had tried to hide what they were doing, locating the plant in a wadi, or valley, so it couldn't be seen from the ground, constructing unnecessary walls and false roofs so that its purpose wouldn't be clear from the air. But Israeli intelligence knew what it was: a gas-cooled, graphite-moderated nuclear reactor.

Important clues about the reactor's intended purpose came from what the photographs didn't show. There were no power lines coming out of it, none of the switching facilities that would be present if its purpose were to produce electricity. It was not near any power grid.

What the Israelis, and later our own intelligence agencies, did see was a striking resemblance to the North Korean reactor located at Yongbyon, sixty miles north of Pyongyang, which the North Koreans used to produce plutonium for nuclear weapons. The Syrian reactor was similar in size and capacity. Side-by-side photographs showed the vertical tubes in the Syrian reactor arranged in ways strikingly similar to those in Yongbyon. The fact that the North Koreans were the only ones who had built such a gas-cooled, graphite-moderated reactor in the past thirty-five years pointed to them as the source for what the Syrians were building in the desert.

According to a briefing by senior U.S. intelligence officials, "sustained nuclear cooperation between North Korea and Syria" likely began "as early as 1997." There had been multiple visits by senior North

Koreans from Yongbyon to Syria before construction began at al-Kibar in 2001, and, according to the intelligence community, subsequent contacts as well. In a briefing provided for the press on April 24, 2008, senior U.S. intelligence officials explained:

> *In 2002, North Korean officials were procuring equipment for an undisclosed site in Syria. North Korea, that same year, sought a gas-cooled reactor component we believe was intended for the Syrian site. A North Korean nuclear organization and Syrian officials involved in the covert nuclear program reportedly were involved in a cargo transfer from North Korea to probably al-Kibar in 2006.*

Over the last several years I had seen intelligence reports of officials with ties to North Korea's nuclear program making repeated visits to Damascus, and I had asked questions. Are the North Koreans and the Syrians cooperating on nuclear technology? We know the North Koreans are assisting the Syrians in the area of ballistic missile technology. How do we know that they aren't also providing nuclear assistance? We believed that the North Koreans provided uranium hexafluoride, the basic feedstock from which enriched uranium can be created, to the Libyans. Why wouldn't they do the same for the Syrians?

The answers I got back were inconclusive. I kept hearing that there was "no evidence" of nuclear cooperation. Listening to Dagan tell the story of the reactor at al-Kibar on that April afternoon in the West Wing, I realized that not only was there evidence, but it was actually very solid.

In addition to information about the facility, there were also photographs of some of the people involved. One, taken in Syria, showed the man in charge of North Korea's nuclear reactor fuel manufacturing plant at Yongbyon standing next to the leader of the Syrian Atomic Energy Commission. A second photo showed the same North Korean official in his country's delegation at the six-party talks—the talks we initiated in 2003 as a multilateral effort to get the North Koreans to give up their nuclear program. It was pretty remarkable—even for the North Koreans—for a member of their negotiating team to be spending time, when he wasn't at the negotiating table, proliferating nuclear technology to Syria.

The discovery of the reactor sparked an in-depth policy debate inside the White House about what our response should be. The Israelis were requesting that we launch an air strike to destroy the plant, an idea I supported. I believed an American military strike on the reactor would send an important message not only to the Syrians and North Koreans, but also to the Iranians, with whom we were attempting to reach a diplomatic agreement to end their nuclear program. An American strike to destroy the Syrian reactor would demonstrate that we were serious when we warned—as we had for years—against the proliferation of nuclear technology to terrorist states. The Syrian plant was isolated from any civilian population center, and it was a clear and distinct target standing out in the eastern desert. We certainly had the capacity to take it out with ease, and doing so would go a long way toward reminding our adversaries that we would not, as the president had said, "permit the world's most dangerous regimes to threaten us with the world's most destructive weapons." I believed that our diplomacy would have a far greater chance of being effective if the North Koreans and Iranians understood that they faced the possibility of military action if the diplomacy failed.

Most of our discussions about the al-Kibar reactor took place in the weekly small group meetings that Steve Hadley had begun hosting in his office during the second term. The sessions were similar to the weekly breakfasts Brent Scowcroft had hosted when he was President George H. W. Bush's national security advisor with Secretary of State Jim Baker and me. The Hadley sessions were larger, with the chairman of the Joint Chiefs of Staff, the director of national intelligence, and the head of the CIA present, as well as Secretaries Rice and Gates, Hadley, and me. We met without staff and had some of the best policy discussions of our time in office. We exchanged ideas and debated without worrying that our deliberations would leak, as they sometimes did when there were more people in the room.

In a session in Hadley's office in the spring of 2007, as we discussed options for a response to the discovery of the Syrian reactor, those who opposed any military action expressed the view that a U.S. or Israeli strike could launch a wider regional war. There was also concern that the Syrians might take retaliatory action against American troops in Iraq. My view was that these concerns were not well founded. I believed the dangers of allowing the North Korean–Syrian nuclear project to go forward were far greater than the prospect of a wider conflict. The worst outcome would be one in which no action was taken and the Syrians were allowed to become a nuclear power.

Much of our conversation focused on the bad intelligence we had received about Iraq's stockpiles of weapons of mass destruction. That experience made some key policymakers very reluctant to consider robust options for dealing with the Syrian plant. I found that regrettable. In this instance there was no question based on the information we were getting from the Israelis and now from our own intelligence services that what we were looking at in the Syrian desert was a clandestine nuclear reactor, built by two terrorist-sponsoring states.

I thought back to the history of World War II. U.S. intelligence had failed to predict the Japanese surprise attack on Pearl Harbor in 1941. A few months later, when Admiral Chester Nimitz, commander of the Pacific Fleet, received intelligence that the Japanese fleet was headed for Midway, he did not hesitate to act. He could have questioned the accuracy of the intelligence or ignored it, based on the error at Pearl Harbor, but he didn't. He sent what was left of the American Pacific Fleet to intercept the Japanese, sank four of their frontline carriers, and turned the tide of the war in the Pacific. Had Admiral Nimitz refused to act on intelligence warnings in the aftermath of the intelligence failure at Pearl Harbor, the outcome of the war in the Pacific may well have been different. I was afraid we were doing just that in this case. Although the evidence about the Syrian nuclear reactor was solid, the intelligence community's failure on Iraq was still affecting our decision making.

At our weekly private lunch on June 14, 2007, the president and I talked about the danger of nuclear proliferation. I noted that it was still our biggest long-term security challenge. It was clearly the ultimate threat to the homeland. Since taking office we had made significant progress on stopping the spread of nuclear weapons technology to rogue states or terrorist organizations. We had removed Saddam Hussein and the threat he posed. Libya had handed over its program, encouraged in large part by watching what happened to Saddam. We had taken down the A. Q. Khan network, which had been a source of centrifuges, uranium feedstock, and weapons design for Libya, North Korea, and Iran. But North Korea's robust program continued. Estimates were that they now possessed enough plutonium for six to twelve warheads, and they had conducted their first nuclear test on our watch. They had admitted having a program to enrich uranium, a second path to obtaining the material needed for a nuclear weapon, and we believed that they had provided a key ingredient in the enrichment process—uranium hexafluoride—to Libya. We now also knew they were proliferating nuclear technology to the Syrians.

The picture on Iran was no better. They had a robust program under way based on uranium enrichment centrifuge technology. Estimates were they could have three thousand centrifuges in operation by the end of 2007.

Syria and Iran, both working to develop nuclear capability, were two of the world's leading state sponsors of terror. Syria was facilitating the flow of foreign fighters into Iraq, where they killed U.S. soldiers. Iran was providing funding and weapons for exactly the same purpose, as well as providing weapons to the Taliban in Afghanistan. They were both involved in supporting Hezbollah in its efforts to threaten Israel and destabilize the Lebanese government. They constituted a major threat to America's interests in the Middle East.

I told the president we needed a more effective and aggressive strategy to counter these threats, and I believed that an important first step would be to destroy the reactor in the Syrian desert. He was well aware of the dangers we faced and decided he wanted to hear more from all of his advisors as he considered the next steps on Syria. We gathered in the Yellow Oval Room on the second floor of the White House residence at 6:30 p.m. on Sunday, June 17, 2007.

The first question was, how good was the intelligence? Mike McConnell, the very professional director of national intelligence, said, "It's about as good as it gets." He noted the intelligence community had "high confidence" this was a nuclear reactor.

We discussed two possible paths of response. One was diplomatic. We would make news of the reactor public, go to the United Nations and the International Atomic Energy Agency, and try to build international consensus to force the Syrians to shut the reactor down. I was skeptical. The UN and IAEA record on forcing rogue states to give up their nuclear programs was not impressive, and I had no reason to believe this approach would work here. The other option, which I favored, was military. Either we or the Israelis take the Syrian plant out.

Two days later Israeli Prime Minister Ehud Olmert was in town for meetings. I participated in his lunch with the president, and the prime minister asked to see me separately as well. He was staying in Blair House, across Pennsylvania Avenue from the White House, and I joined him there for dinner on June 19, 2007. After dinner we kicked our staff members out and had a lengthy one-on-one meeting. He was very focused both on the threat from Iran and on the Syrian nuclear facility. The existence of a secret nuclear reactor in Syria posed an existential threat to Israel, and the proliferation involved in its construction was a direct threat to America's national security. Olmert urged that the United States take military action to destroy the facility and made clear Israel would act if we did not.

At another session later that month with most of the National Security Council present, I again made the case for U.S. military action against the reactor. Not only would it make the region and the world safer, but it would also demonstrate our seriousness with respect to nonproliferation. It would enhance our credibility in that part of the world, taking us back to where we were in 2003, after we had taken down the Taliban, taken down Saddam's regime, and gotten Qaddafi to turn over his nuclear program. But I was a lone voice. After I finished, the president asked, "Does anyone here agree with the vice president?" Not a single hand went up around the room. I had done all I could, and I'm not sure the president's mind would have been changed if the others had agreed with me. He had decided to recommend to the Israelis that we take the diplomatic path. How, he asked, were the Israelis likely to respond to that decision? Secretary Rice told him she believed that the Israelis would accept the offer of diplomacy. She thought Prime Minister Olmert would go along with the idea of taking the information to the United Nations and working for multilateral action to shut down the facility.

I told the president that the Israelis would destroy the reactor at al-Kibar if we did not. Ehud Olmert, whom I had known for years, meant what he said about taking action. I also remembered 1981, when the Israelis had ignored world opinion and launched an air strike to destroy a nuclear reactor Saddam Hussein was building at Osirak in Iraq.

In mid-July the president placed a call to Prime Minister Olmert to tell him we wanted to go the diplomatic route. Olmert, disappointed, said that wouldn't work for Israel. He could not place the fate of Israel in the hands of the UN or the IAEA. And time was growing short. The reactor had to be destroyed before it "went hot," before the nuclear fuel was loaded, or there would be the potential for significant radioactive contamination.

Under cover of darkness on September 6, 2007, Israeli F-15s crossed into Syrian airspace and within minutes were over the target at al-Kibar. Satellite photos afterward showed that the Israeli pilots hit their target perfectly. There was not a single crater except where the nuclear reactor once stood.

In the days that followed the strike, the Israeli government asked that we not reveal what we knew about the target they'd struck in the desert. They believed that widespread public discussion about the nuclear plant or the fact that the Israelis had launched the strike might force Syrian President Bashar Assad to respond, launching a wider conflict. For the Syrians and the North Koreans, though, the private message was clear—Israel would not tolerate this threat. We agreed to maintain secrecy in the near term about the plant and the operation to take it out.

Assad decided to keep quiet as well. A North Korean delegation showed up in Syria shortly after the attack, probably to advise on the way forward, and the Syrians subsequently demolished the reactor building, covered the site with soil, and erected a metal structure over it.

What had happened in the desert might, for a short time, remain a secret. But all of us on the National Security Council knew the truth: that the North Koreans had proliferated nuclear technology to Syria, one of the world's worst state sponsors of terror. The North Koreans and the Syrians were clearly violating the red line drawn by President Bush on October 9, 2006, in the wake of North Korea's first nuclear test.

BY THE TIME WE came into office, the North Koreans had an established pattern of behavior. They would make an agreement about their nuclear sites, pocket the benefits of the agreement, and then continue on with their weapons programs. They were masters of brinksmanship—creating problems, threatening their neighbors, and expecting to be bribed back into cooperation. It had usually worked for them. In 1994, with Bill Clinton in the White House, they agreed to freeze their plutonium production program in exchange for 500,000 metric tons of fuel oil a year and two reactors of a type that cannot easily be used to produce weapons material. But they secretly pursued a second route. In 2002, with the North Koreans having received millions of tons of fuel oil and with the al-Kibar reactor construction under way, an American delegation confronted them with evidence of their deception, and they admitted they had been developing a second way to produce nuclear weapons—by enriching uranium.

It was with the intention of breaking this pattern of deceit and deception that President Bush in 2003 established the six-party talks made up of the United States, South Korea, North Korea, Japan, China, and Russia. The idea was to move away from the bilateral, or one-on-one, negotiations that had failed in the past and to bring into the diplomatic process other nations that had an interest in preventing North Korea from developing nuclear weapons. China was particularly important, because as North Korea's economic lifeline, China had considerable influence over the isolated and insular North Korean government. We knew that the Chinese were concerned about the regional instability that could arise from a nuclear-armed North Korea, particularly given the likelihood that nations like Japan and others would feel the need to follow suit.

By 2006, however, we were clearly slipping back into the old pattern. An early indication came at the end of October, just three weeks after North Korea tested a nuclear weapon. Assistant Secretary of State Christopher Hill, who was leading our delegation to the six-party talks, decided to participate in an hours-long, private meeting with North Korean envoy Kim Gye Gwan in Beijing. As Hill well knew, President Bush's policy was to take a regional approach to North Korea's nuclear programs, thus bringing the combined pressure of several nations to bear, but the North Koreans had been demanding that the United States meet with them one-on-one, in the way that had proved so fruitful for them in the past. Hill, against instructions from Secretary Rice, obliged, cutting our six-party allies, the Japanese and South Koreans, out of the negotiations and providing the North Koreans what can only have looked to them like a reward for bad behavior. Two and a half months later, with Secretary Rice's approval, Assistant Secretary Hill and the American delegation held a bilateral meeting with the North Korean delegation in Berlin. On the evening of January 16, 2007, the Americans provided a lavish meal, supplied large amounts of liquor, and proposed friendly toasts. Said one member of the delegation, "We pulled out all the stops because we wanted to demonstrate that we were serious and sincere." The North Koreans had crossed one of the brightest of bright lines—they had tested a nuclear weapon—and we were hosting them at a banquet.

Worse was to follow as Hill and Rice made concession after concession to the North Koreans and turned a blind eye to their misdeeds. As I watched the course the State Department was taking, I concluded that our diplomats had become so seized with cutting a deal, any deal, with the North Koreans that they had lost sight of the real objective, which was forcing the North to give up its weapons. I do not believe that the president ever lost sight of the ultimate goal, however. I heard him repeatedly ask both Rice and Hill if we were truly on a path to denuclearization. Unfortunately, the reassurances he received did not reflect reality.

MANY OF OUR DIPLOMATIC failures would be played out against an action plan that participants in the six-party talks agreed to in February 2007. It provided for the North Koreans to halt operations at Yongbyon and to admit UN inspectors within sixty days in exchange for 50,000 tons of fuel oil. North Korea would then provide a complete declaration of all of its nuclear programs, disable all its existing facilities, and in return receive another 950,000 tons of fuel oil. The United States would also begin the process of removing North Korea from the list of states that sponsor terrorism and lift the economic sanctions of the Trading with the Enemy Act.

At the next convening of the six-party talks, in March 2007, the North Koreans played the game they had played so often and effectively before. They walked out of the talks and refused to participate further unless $25 million in North Korean funds frozen in a Macaubased bank were returned to them. The funds had been frozen in September 2005, when the U.S. Treasury Department designated Banco Delta Asia as a "primary money laundering concern," charging that the bank had circulated U.S. currency counterfeited in North Korea and laundered money for a variety of North Korean criminal activities, including drug trafficking. The designation essentially prevented the bank from conducting international transactions in U.S. currency. Now the North Koreans were demanding the money before they would participate in nuclear negotiations.

The State Department urged that we agree to the demand and began looking for ways to get the funds returned to the North Koreans. Their efforts were complicated when international banks refused to transfer the money, fearing being caught up in a transaction that involved illicit funds. Finally, a Russian bank agreed to participate, and the Federal Reserve Bank of New York wired the money into a North Korean account at the Russian bank. By June 2007, as a result of our pressuring the banks involved, the North Koreans had gotten $25 million in illicit funds unfrozen and wired to them. With the money in hand, they said they would shutter the Yongbyon plant—which they were supposed to have done two months previously.

By mid-August 2007, we had known for four months that the North Koreans were proliferating nuclear technology to the Syrians. Although I was sure the Israelis would take out the plant, nothing had happened as yet, and we had not come up with an effective strategy to leverage the knowledge we had of the reactor at al-Kibar. Secretary Rice's approach was to downplay the existence of the reactor out of concern for the six-party talks. Although the reactor made a mockery of the talks up until then, further talks, she reasoned, might be disrupted if the Syrian plant became public. The president would soon be traveling to Australia for the annual Asia-Pacific Economic Cooperation meetings, where he would be seeing Chinese President Hu Jintao, and I urged him to take a presentation on the North Korean–Syrian reactor and have a heart-to-heart with Hu. The Chinese could exert far more pressure than they had so far, and showing them the results of failing to stop the North Korean nuclear program might motivate them. But the president was not persuaded.

The North Koreans were supposed to provide a complete declaration of all their nuclear activities by the end of 2007, but they did not, and as we discussed their missing another deadline, Secretary Rice argued that North Korea's final declaration need not include any mention of uranium enrichment. Although they had once admitted to such a program and although we knew they had one, she urged that we not require them to declare it.

I failed to see how accepting a false declaration from North Korea advanced the objective of complete, verifiable, irreversible destruction of the North Korean nuclear program, which had long been the Bush administration's stated goal. To the contrary, by letting them avoid admitting their enrichment program in what was supposed to be a *complete* declaration, we were helping them hide what they were doing. And to make matters worse, we were promising rewards for their duplicity.

But Secretary Rice urged that we view a North Korean declaration that was solely about their plutonium program as a "first step." She said there was no need to be concerned about their uranium enrichment program because in a side conversation between Chris Hill and his North Korean counterpart, the counterpart had admitted to the uranium program. There was no official record of this conversation, but the very fact that it had occurred, said the secretary, meant that it wasn't necessary for the North Koreans to include the uranium enrichment program in their final declaration.

This was an approach to arms control I had never seen before. Not only were we going to accept a false declaration, but we were supposed to be reassured because the other side had whispered an admission of the declaration's falsehood in Chris Hill's ear. The secretary repeatedly assured the president that he shouldn't worry. Everything was fine. But clearly it wasn't.

BY DECEMBER 2007 I was not just concerned about where we stood on North Korea. We faced a number of critical foreign policy challenges at the very same time that the power of the president and the administration to solve them was waning. It is a natural phenomenon that most administrations face as they get down to the end of their time in office: The president's ability to do big things diminishes on an almost weekly basis in the final year of his presidency.

The Iranians were continuing their nuclear efforts, and although we had been working to find a diplomatic solution, the president made it very clear that all options were on the table and that we could not accept a nuclear-armed Iran. Within the last few months, however, our commander in the Middle East, Admiral Fox Fallon, had been interviewed on the record criticizing what he called "bellicose" comments from Washington as "unhelpful" and suggesting that no planning for any military option was under way. A foreign diplomat posted in Washington said to me a few days later, "If you guys are going to take the military option off the table, couldn't you at least have your secretary of state do it?" People expected the top diplomat to make such statements,

he said, "but when the CENTCOM commander does it, they take notice." After making similar comments again in early 2008, Fallon would
resign.

A few months earlier, while Secretary Gates and Secretary Rice were
on a visit to Saudi Arabia, I had received a panicked phone call from
a member of their traveling party. Secretary Gates had apparently just
informed the king that the president would be impeached if he took
military action against Iran. The president had not decided what the
next steps were on Iran, and it was inappropriate for key officials to
suggest either publicly or with important allies that his options were
limited. We had to tell the Saudis that Secretary Gates was speaking for
himself and not reflecting U.S. policy. Statements like those by Gates
and Fallon removed a key element of our leverage and convinced allies
and enemies we were less than serious about addressing the threat. This,
in turn, made a diplomatic solution more difficult.

On December 3, 2007, the director of national intelligence declassified key findings from a new National Intelligence Estimate on Iran.
The first key judgment in the report asserted: "We judge with high
confidence that in the fall of 2003, Tehran halted its nuclear weapons
program." Only if you went to a footnote did you understand that by
"nuclear weapons program," the intelligence community meant "Iran's
nuclear weapon design and weaponization work and *covert* uranium
conversion-related and uranium enrichment-related work" (emphasis
added). The community chose not to consider Iran's very significant
declared enrichment efforts in its dramatic opening statement.

As the NIE indicated, there are three parts to making a nuclear
weapon: weapons design, weaponization of the nuclear material, and
production of the nuclear material—whether plutonium or enriched
uranium. The NIE judged that Iran had halted the first two activities,
which are easily resumed, and had made "significant progress" in the
third area, involving "declared centrifuge enrichment activities." But it
took careful reading to get to this understanding, and there were few
careful readers, especially in the media. The report was read as providing
assurance that we need no longer worry about Iran's nuclear program.

Director of National Intelligence Mike McConnell later testified that he would have presented the key findings differently if he had it to do over again. As it was, the NIE clearly gave a false impression. The story of the production of the 2007 Iran NIE is in part a reflection of the continued impact of the bad intelligence we had received about Iraq's WMD stockpiles. After the charges of politicizing intelligence that filled the air beginning in 2003, policymakers were hesitant to urge edits or suggest that the presentation and structure of the report were misleading. When I was briefed on the report just before its release, I made sure to have two staff members with me, and I said very little. This was the way to avoid being accused of pressuring anyone. But it is not a good way to make policy.

Once it was released, I heard from leaders in the Arab world that they believed the NIE either was prepared at George Bush's instruction so he would not have to take military action or was put together by a disloyal CIA to ensure that the president did not take military action. Neither was true, but such perceptions hurt us. The NIE itself precluded us from considering as robust a range of options as we might have otherwise.

Secretary Rice had determined that she would not only get a deal with the North Koreans before we left office but would also get an agreement on final-status issues aimed at resolving the decades-old Israeli-Palestinian problem. Although clearly laudable as a goal, neither side nor many experts believed it was possible during our remaining time in office, given the complex set of issues, entrenched hatreds, ongoing violence, and the Hamas-controlled government in Gaza. Moreover, launching a major effort had an impact on other policy priorities. The secretary's determination to launch a multilateral peace initiative led her to believe she had to get the Syrians to the table to participate. This meant ignoring their efforts to build a covert nuclear reactor. It also meant overlooking the foreign fighters who were crossing the border from Syria into Iraq and killing Americans. It was my view that the Syrians needed to be held accountable, not sent a personal letter from Secretary Rice inviting them to the Annapolis Conference on Middle East peace.

Secretary Rice's outreach to Syrian dictator Bashar Assad came at a difficult moment for the people of Lebanon. As they tried to form a new democratically elected government, they were under enormous pressure from Syria, which had occupied Lebanon for nearly thirty years. After the assassination of former Lebanese Prime Minister Rafik Hariri in 2005, popular uprisings had caused Syria to withdraw its troops, but car bombings and assassinations of anti-Syrian politicians and intellectuals in Lebanon continued. Iran, meanwhile, was engaged in efforts to destabilize Lebanon, primarily through its sponsorship of the terrorist group Hezbollah, whose members were demanding an ever-larger role in the government. In July 2006 after Hezbollah fired rockets into Israel and crossed the border, attacking and taking Israeli soldiers hostage, war broke out between Israel and Lebanon. Hezbollah had survived the war, and by the end of 2007 they, along with their ally Syria and their patron Iran, were ascendant in Lebanon. We could have done much more to support the democratic aspirations of the people of Lebanon and thus helped to counter the growing regional prominence of Iran and Syria, had an unrealistic effort to solve the Israeli-Palestinian conflict not absorbed so much of our attention.

Moreover, as we entered our final year in office, we still had much work to do in Afghanistan and Pakistan. In Afghanistan there was a continued need for diplomatic heavy lifting as we supported Hamid Karzai's effort to extend the central government's authority throughout the country and continued to fight the Taliban. We also had much to do in Pakistan, where President Musharraf had provided key support, but had an increasingly weak hold on power over a government whose loyalties were at times divided.

In Iraq, there was good news. The surge of troops and the shift to a counterinsurgency strategy were showing signs of success. Security was returning to large parts of the country, including Baghdad. But as General Petraeus noted, the gains were "fragile and reversible." We needed to continue the fight and follow through on our efforts to aid the Iraqi people in solidifying their political progress. Our relationship with the Iraqis was evolving, from one where we had been in complete control of the country to one where key treaties would govern the relations be-

tween our two sovereign nations. We were working on a status of forces
agreement, or SOFA, that would govern our military relations, as well
as a strategic framework agreement that would establish our diplomatic,
security, and economic relations. These agreements, which would establish American relations with Iraq for many years to come, deserved
the highest levels of diplomatic attention. They would highlight one
of the most significant accomplishments of George Bush's presidency—
the liberation of Iraq and the establishment of a true democracy in the
Arab world.

ON JANUARY 4, 2008, the director of national intelligence, Mike
McConnell, came into the Oval Office for our regular morning intelligence briefing. He surprised us by bringing three analysts with him,
experts on North Korea. A National Security Council meeting on that
subject was scheduled for 8:35, and as I later understood, there had been
some skirmishing about how much intelligence would be provided in
the memo that went to NSC members ahead of time. The State Department had been trying to keep it to a minimum, so McConnell apparently decided to bring the latest thinking on the subject of North Korea
directly to the president. President Bush grilled the analysts, homing in
on a central question: Were the North Koreans likely to give up their
nuclear weapons as a result of the negotiations going on through the
six-party talks? The experts were not optimistic.

We walked from the Oval Office to the newly renovated Situation
Room, where the National Security Council meeting was being held.
The high-tech meeting room was packed. Every seat at the table and
against the outer wall was filled. The president ignored the agenda and
dove right in. Directing his questions to Chris Hill, who was seated
against the wall behind Secretary Rice, the president asked, "What is
the status of the talks? Will they lead to the North Koreans giving up
their weapons?" Rice said, "I got this," and stepped in to respond. She
emphasized the importance of getting the North Koreans to dismantle
the reactor at Pyongyang and of doing whatever we could to make that
happen. It was a first step, she said, only a first step.

Then the president called on me. The North Koreans were not living up to their end of the bargain, I said. They had so far refused to admit to their uranium enrichment activity. They denied proliferating to the Syrians. If the declaration they provide is false, and we accept it, we won't be accomplishing anything except helping the North Koreans cover up their nuclear activity. I said I realized the State Department was working hard on this, but I was becoming increasingly concerned that the six-party talks were now a convenient way for the North Koreans to hide what they were really doing, and we were not only complicit, but were in fact rewarding them for it by offering benefits and concessions in exchange for missed deadlines and false declarations. I reminded the group that eventually the work the North Koreans were doing in Syria would be public, and then we would have to explain why we had looked the other way.

Then I asked what was to me the bottom-line question about our negotiations. "Is it accurate to say that there will be no lifting of our designation of North Korea as a terrorist state and no removal of the Trading with the Enemy Act sanctions unless they present a comprehensive and complete declaration of their programs?" The president said, "Absolutely." Secretary Rice concurred. I pressed further: "I assume that their failure to admit they've been proliferating to the Syrians would be a deal killer." Secretary Rice agreed, although seeming reluctant. The president emphasized that was his position.

Rice had been working to convince the president that the process she and Chris Hill were working would lead to the North Koreans giving up their nuclear weapons. My view—and the view the president heard in the Oval Office that morning from the intelligence experts—was that there was nothing we could offer them by way of concessions that was worth as much to them as their nuclear weapons. They were convinced the survival of their regime depended upon the weapons. I believed that the only way diplomacy would work was if the Chinese and our other partners in the six-party talks understood we were through playing games and were deadly serious about the threat we all faced.

A few days later, Jay Lefkowitz, the State Department envoy for human rights issues in North Korea, gave a speech at the American Enterprise Institute in which he said, "It is increasingly clear that North Korea will remain in its present nuclear status when the administration leaves office in one year." North Korea, he said, "is not serious about disarming in a timely manner" and "its conduct does not appear to be that of a government that is willing to come in from the cold." The next day the State Department issued a statement distancing itself from Lefkowitz's remarks, saying that he was the envoy for human rights issues and not "somebody who speaks authoritatively about the six-party talks." He sounded pretty authoritative to me.

At the end of the month, Assistant Secretary Hill gave a speech at Amherst College that made it sound as though we were on our way to ruling out a North Korean uranium program. Yes, he said, North Korea had acquired aluminum tubes "to construct centrifuges," but "we've seen that these tubes are not being used for the centrifuge program":

> *We've had American diplomats go and look at this aluminum that was used and see what they're actually using it for. We actually had American diplomats, people like myself, carry this aluminum back in their suitcases to verify that this is the precise aluminum that the North Koreans had actually purchased for this purpose and so what has emerged is the fact that they are not using it for uranium enrichment.*

Hill neglected to note that the tubes the North Koreans had turned over to us contained traces of highly enriched uranium.

In Senate testimony the next week, Hill acknowledged that the North Koreans had purchased key components for enriching uranium, but again emphasized that they had showed us examples of their using the components for nonnuclear purposes. "More work will be done on that," he said, "so that we can clearly say at some point in the future that we can rule out that they have any on-going program for uranium enrichment." Getting to that point would prove to be impossible, however. Months later, when the North Koreans began to deliver documents to us concerning activities at their plutonium reactor at Yongbyon, the documents themselves contained traces of highly enriched uranium.

There was a period in the spring when it looked as though we might be able to get off the path that Rice and Hill had put us on. Hill was in Geneva negotiating what would be in the North Korean declaration, and Steve brought a draft of the proposed language into the Oval Office during our morning meeting on March 14, 2008. The president said he didn't want to see it. "I'm not going to sign anything until the vice president has signed off on it," he said. "You go over it with Dick. When he's happy with it, I'm happy with it."

Steve came back to my office, and we looked at the document. "Steve," I said, "this just isn't going to fly." It had the United States presenting information about North Korea's enriching uranium and efforts to build a nuclear reactor in Syria. And it had the North Koreans saying they understood the concerns—not admitting to enriching or proliferating, but saying they understood that the idea they might have troubled us. This was not by any stretch the full and complete declaration the North Koreans were committed to making, which was, I suspected, why Rice and Hill were calling it a "sideletter" and advising that it not be made public.

Concerned that it would damage the six-party talks, Secretary Rice was also still working to keep what we knew about the North Korean–built Syrian nuclear reactor from being made public, long after the period during which the Israelis had expressed concern. She successfully delayed an announcement for several months. Finally, at the end of April, senior intelligence officials conducted a briefing, complete with video, telling the story of al-Kibar.

By late May, Secretary Rice had decided that she ought to go to Pyongyang to meet with North Korean President Kim Jong Il. At one of our small group meetings in Steve Hadley's office, Steve said the president had asked him to solicit the views of the group about this idea. Condi argued that if we wanted to keep the North Koreans at the table in the six-party talks, we had a choice between lifting the terrorism designation or sending her personally to Pyongyang. Steve asked if anyone had any response to this suggestion. I signaled that I did, which I'm sure was no surprise to Steve. I said this would be yet one more example of our responding to North Korea's refusal to keep their commitments by making another preemptive concession. The North Koreans still hadn't provided a full and complete declaration of their nuclear activities, I pointed out, and now, suddenly we would be sending the secretary of state to Pyongyang? It was a bad idea. A much better option would be to insist they keep their commitments.

Steve called on Secretary of Defense Gates, who didn't come down one way or the other. Gates called on Joint Chiefs Chairman Admiral Mike Mullen, who was sitting slouched in his chair, listening to all this with his head in his hand. He didn't say a word, just pointed at me, signaling that he was signing on with my view. I think a number of us were getting tired of refighting the same battles in meeting after meeting where it seemed we had to argue against yet another misguided approach from the State Department.

Steve brought the meeting to a close and said he and Condi would report the group's views back to the president. A short while later, I was sitting in my office, when one of the president's senior advisors came through the door, holding a copy of that week's *Weekly Standard.* The cover story was titled "In the Driver's Seat: Condoleezza Rice and the Jettisoning of the Bush Doctrine." Pointing to the cover, the senior advisor said, "Yet another reason why Condi should not go to North Korea."

A few days later the president and I had our weekly lunch, and as we sat out on his private patio he encouraged me to keep challenging policy that I thought was mistaken. He did not say he agreed with me, but I think he believed the debates would make for a better outcome in terms of his decision making. I hadn't planned to stop arguing anyway. I feared we were headed for a train wreck.

ON JUNE 26, THE North Koreans provided a declaration to the Chinese that failed to describe either their uranium enrichment program or their proliferation activities. It did not even fully describe their plutonium activities. Despite this, within hours President Bush was in the Rose Garden announcing that he was lifting provisions of the Trading with the Enemy Act and notifying Congress of his intent to take North Korea off the list of state sponsors of terror.

I was disappointed, and not just because I disagreed with the president. It was his call. But the process and the decision that followed had seemed so out of keeping with the clearheaded way I'd seen him make decisions in the past. The president said we would use the next forty-five days—the notice period for Congress before the North Koreans could formally be removed from the terrorism list—to develop a "comprehensive and rigorous" protocol for verifying the North Korean declaration. As I listened to the president's remarks I wondered how, exactly, we were going to go about verifying what we already knew to be a false declaration.

On June 27, 2008, the North Koreans called in the television cameras and blew up the cooling tower of the nuclear reactor at Yongbyon. It was 1950s technology, a device they could easily afford to give up. By that point they had produced enough plutonium for a store of weapons, and, besides, as President Obama's director of national intelligence would later confirm, they had a robust ongoing uranium enrichment operation that could also produce material for nuclear weapons.

Two months later, when North Korea decided that we had not taken them off the terrorist list in a timely enough fashion, they announced that they had stopped dismantling the Yongbyon complex. Three weeks after that, Pyongyang announced it was restarting the reprocessing plant and began reattaching equipment that had been removed earlier in the year.

On October 9, 2008, Secretary Rice, Steve Hadley, and I met with the president in the Oval Office to discuss the verification protocol Chris Hill was negotiating. As I listened I realized that despite the president's insistence on a "comprehensive and rigorous" verification protocol a few months earlier, there was actually no written agreement at all. There was a document the Chinese had proposed, which Rice was calling the verification agreement, but, in fact, the North Koreans had not agreed to the document. There were also some notes Chris Hill had taken of conversations he'd had with his North Korean counterpart, which we were now supposed to regard as part of a formal protocol. At an interagency meeting that week, the State Department handed out a fact sheet explaining that "agreement on verification measures has been codified in a joint document between the United States and North Korea and has been reaffirmed through extensive consultation." In reality, there was no joint document—just Chris Hill's notes.

Looking for a way to explain this situation, Rice said, "Mr. President, this is just the way diplomacy works sometimes. You don't always get a written agreement." The statement was utterly misleading, totally divorced from what the secretary was doing, which was urging the president, in the absence of an agreement, to pretend to have one—with a nuclear-armed, terrorist-sponsoring state that we knew to be lying about their nuclear program and proliferating nuclear technology to at least one other terrorist-sponsoring state.

"Look, Condi," he said to her, "I just need more time on this. I need to think about it." Steve Hadley asked her if she could provide a paper for the president to read as background on the proposal. Was there something he could review? "No," she said, although she was sitting on the sofa reading from a document describing the purported agreement.

The issue of Japan came up. We had known for some time that the Japanese government was very unhappy that we might lift the terrorism designation. They were concerned in particular about Japanese citizens, many of them children, who had been abducted by the North Koreans decades earlier. I had met with some of their families during my trip to Asia in 2007, and the stories of lost children were heartbreaking. Now, the Japanese perceived we might be contemplating removing North Korea from the terrorism list without a resolution of this issue, and their diplomats had been in repeatedly to see my deputy national security advisor, Samantha Ravich, and others on my national security staff. The Japanese were also troubled by our apparent willingness to take the North Koreans at their word, to trust this rogue regime. Secretary Rice denied there was any objection from the Japanese and told the president they had simply asked for a delay of twenty-four hours so they could "handle their political situation." This was inaccurate. Later that day I received a message from our ambassador in Japan, Tom Schieffer, which I would pass on to the president. Schieffer, who had been one of the president's partners when he owned the Texas Rangers, had grown increasingly concerned about our North Korean policy and was now reporting that the Japanese found the "verification proposal" unacceptable as presented. Schieffer also passed along a warning from the prime minister of Japan: Given North Korea's history of duplicity, it was essential to get any agreement with them in writing.

As the October 9, 2008, meeting was drawing to a close, Steve Hadley tried to restore some orderliness to how we were proceeding. "Condi," he said, "there are some questions that have to be answered here before we can go ahead." One option we discussed was sending Chris Hill back to Pyongyang to get written assurances. If this agreement was so important, and if Secretary Rice was so confident in the North Korean assurances, why not get a proper agreement? She did not want to do that. And, it turned out, she didn't have to.

The next day, October 10, 2008, I got word that the president had agreed to allow Secretary Rice to sign the document removing North Korea from the terrorist list, which she did on October 11. It was a sad moment because it seemed to be a repudiation of the Bush Doctrine and a reversal of so much of what we had accomplished in the area of nonproliferation in the first term. The president had been right when he had denounced the failed approach of the Clinton era. Now we seemed to be embracing it.

By the end of October the North Koreans announced that "verification" would be limited only to the plutonium reactor site at Yongbyon. On November 12, they announced that inspectors could not take soil or nuclear waste samples from the site. On December 11, the North Koreans made clear they did not feel bound by any "oral agreement" Hill thought he had with them, and the negotiations came to a standstill. An article in the *Washington Post* the next morning contained this: "U.S. officials acknowledge now that most of the purported agreements announced two months ago were simply oral understandings between Hill and his North Korean counterparts." It was not our finest hour.

I could see the North Koreans hitting the rewind button in mid-January 2009, shortly before President Obama was sworn into office, when they demanded that the United States normalize relations with them before they would consider abandoning their nuclear weapons:

- In April 2009 they tested a Taepodong 2 intercontinental ballistic missile.
- In May 2009 they tested a second nuclear weapon.
- In September 2009 they announced they were in the final stages of enriching uranium and weaponizing plutonium.
- In March 2010 a North Korean submarine torpedoed and sank a South Korean vessel, killing forty-six sailors.
- In November 2010 they invited a visiting American delegation to view their uranium enrichment program, unveiling two thousand gas centrifuges operating at the Yongbyon facility, site of the old plutonium reactor on which we had been so focused.
- In November 2010, days after they unveiled their centrifuge operation, North Korea launched a massive artillery barrage at a South Korean island, killing two South Korean marines and two civilians.
- And in February 2011, Director of National Intelligence Jim Clapper said in testimony to the Senate Select Committee on Intelligence that the North Koreans did indeed have a uranium enrichment facility at Yongbyon, a disclosure that "supports the United States' longstanding assessment that the DPRK [Democratic People's Republic of Korea] has pursued a uranium-enrichment capability."

In addition, Clapper said that given the "scale of the facility and the progress the DPRK has made in construction, it is likely North Korea has been pursuing enrichment for an extended period of time. If so,

there is a clear prospect that the DPRK has built other uranium enrichment related facilities in its territory."

AS I HAVE NOTED before, we accomplished a great deal in our
first years in office in slowing the proliferation of nuclear materials
and technology. As we dealt with North Korea, particularly throughout 2007 and 2008, the president would sometimes refer to one of
those accomplishments—getting the Libyans to turn over their nuclear
materials—and say he was looking for the North Koreans to have their
"Qaddafi moment." That is what we all hoped to achieve, and I don't
believe the president himself ever lost sight of that as the objective. But
I think Secretary Rice and Assistant Secretary Hill did. For them, the
agreement seemed to become the objective, and we ended up with a
clear setback in our nonproliferation efforts.

In early 2001 the president had it exactly right when he decided to
set a new course for dealing with North Korea and made other countries, most importantly China, a part of the negotiations. When our
diplomats began meeting bilaterally with the North Koreans again,
sometimes in contravention of their instructions, China was essentially
sidelined, as were our allies the Japanese and the South Koreans. We
missed a number of important opportunities to use our leverage to get
them to play a more constructive role. There is no question but that the
challenge of North Korea's nuclear program was one of the toughest we
faced during our time in office. As we worked to meet this challenge,
I wish the president had been better served by his State Department
team.

THE STORY OF OUR diplomacy with North Korea, particularly in
the second term of the Bush presidency, carries with it important lessons for American leaders and diplomats of the future. First is the importance of not losing sight of the objective. In this case, the president
had made clear that our goal was getting the North Koreans to give up
their nuclear weapons program. However, as negotiations proceeded,
the State Department came to regard getting the North Koreans to

agree to something, indeed anything, as the ultimate objective. That mistake led our diplomats to respond to Pyongyang's intransigence and dishonesty with ever greater concessions, thereby encouraging duplicity and double-dealing. And in the end it led them to recommend we accept an agreement that didn't accomplish the president's goal and even set it back. A good model for future leaders is Ronald Reagan's approach at the Reykjavik Summit with Gorbachev in 1986. He wasn't so desperate for an agreement that he would take whatever he could get. He would not concede America's right to missile defense, and when the Soviets refused to grant that point, he ended the talks.

This leads to the second and related lesson. The most effective diplomacy happens when America negotiates from a position of strength. If we remember that our ultimate goal is the substantive one of denuclearization and we are willing to walk away rather than accept a partial, untrue, or damaging agreement, we are in a much stronger position. At the same time, if our adversaries understand we will not compromise on fundamental principles and that we will use military force if necessary, they are much more likely to do business at the negotiating table. That is why I argued that we should have taken action ourselves to destroy the North Korean–built nuclear reactor in the Syrian desert. It would have sent an unmistakable message to the Syrians, the Iranians, and the North Koreans that our words meant something, that we would not tolerate the proliferation of nuclear technology. Such a message might well have encouraged those nations to take advantage of the opportunity to reach a diplomatic agreement rather than risk military action. The effect of U.S. military action was seen clearly, for example, when Muammar Qaddafi watched the United States liberate Iraq and then called to say he'd like to give up his nuclear weapons program.

The third lesson is that red lines must mean something. In the aftermath of 9/11, President Bush put in place an effective nonproliferation policy that yielded results. We dedicated ourselves to preventing terrorists and terror-sponsoring states from acquiring weapons of mass destruction. When the North Koreans tested a nuclear weapon in October 2006, President Bush warned that we would hold them fully accountable for the consequences of any proliferation, especially to states like Syria and Iran. Six months later, when we discovered they were proliferating to Syria, we should have held them accountable and did not. The lesson for other rogue nations might unfortunately be that they need not worry about threats from America. When our actions don't match our rhetoric, diplomacy becomes much more difficult, and ultimately it becomes more likely that terror-sponsoring states will feel they can defy the will of the United States with impunity.

Fourth, effective diplomacy requires that we think strategically. The president did just this when he insisted in 2001 that we get the Chinese engaged in our efforts to convince the North Koreans to give up their nuclear program. We also brought in the Russians, the Japanese, and the South Koreans. The president saw that North Korea was already so isolated and under such extensive sanctions that the United States alone had little ability to bring significant pressure to bear. However, a multilateral approach that included China might well have the ability to pressure Pyongyang. We lost opportunities to encourage the Chinese to play a more constructive role. In the immediate aftermath of North Korea's nuclear test in October 2006, for example, the Chinese were upset, particularly because Pyongyang gave them only an hour's notice of the test. We should have used that moment of leverage to bring our partners in the six-party talks together—with the Chinese in the lead—to put true pressure on the North Koreans. Another moment of maximum leverage was when we discovered the existence of the nuclear reactor that the North Koreans were building in Syria. Again, we should have immediately taken the information to the Chinese and worked together with them to develop a strategic plan to accomplish our objective. Instead, with Assistant Secretary Chris Hill determined to have bilateral discussions with the North, we sidelined the Chinese, ensuring that they would not be as effective a partner for us as they could have been.

Fifth, America's position in the world is strengthened when we stand with allies. In this instance we failed to do that, instead sidelining two key allies—the Japanese and the South Koreans—in our bilateral dealings with the North. Accepting a fundamentally flawed "agreement" also meant that we turned our back on an issue of critical importance to the Japanese, one that we had committed to helping them resolve: the return of their lost children.

Finally, effective diplomacy requires that our diplomats study and learn from our history. In this case, recent history with North Korea was a pretty effective guide to how they would behave. They signed the Agreed Framework in 1994 during the Clinton administration and immediately began violating its terms, demanding payment and looking for ways to use the negotiations to blackmail the United States. We now know the North was actively working to enrich uranium and proliferating with the Syrians while they were party to the Agreed Framework. They behaved the same way with us and have brought out all their threats and demands again for the Obama administration. They have learned now, through Republican and Democratic administrations, that this is an effective way to operate. It yields concessions from the West while they continue to develop nuclear weapons. I hope a future president and secretary of state will break the cycle. This is particularly important because in the area of nonproliferation, as in so much else, the United States must lead. If we do not hold the line, few others will.

History in a broader sense is also important. In every administration, Republican and Democrat, there is often an inclination on the part of the State Department to make preemptive concessions to bad actors in the hope that their behavior will change. I often wondered what historical lessons or examples my State Department colleagues were drawing on as they advocated such policies. If they had been able to point to something, to say, well, here is where it worked in the past, I might have viewed their efforts differently. Sadly, the history is clear. Policies that ignore or reward dangerous behavior by our adversaries do not work. Concessions delivered out of desperation in the naive hope that despots will respond in kind tend not to enhance the security of the United States.

———◄◦►———

CHAPTER SIXTEEN

Endings

According to the Constitution, the vice president is also president of the Senate, and in the early days of the country, that gave the vice president quite a lot to do. The first vice president, John Adams, even participated in debate on issues that came before the Senate, although after a friend advised him that his lengthy disquisitions were stoking resentment, he eased off. By my time, the position of Senate president had pretty much boiled down to casting tie-breaking votes—a job not to be disdained. My ability to cast those votes gave Americans the Bush tax cut that they still enjoy as I write.

In 2008, I found something else I could do as president of the Senate. It all began when the U.S. Court of Appeals for the D.C. Circuit struck down the District of Columbia's ban on handguns. In an eloquent decision written by Judge Laurence Silberman, the court held that the right to bear arms guaranteed by the Second Amendment is an individual right and that the D.C. handgun ban violated that right. The Supreme Court had agreed to hear the case and the Justice Department filed an amicus brief, which was no surprise, but the position that the department took was unexpected. Instead of affirming the Court of Appeals decision, the Justice Department argued that it was too broad and asked that the Supreme Court send the case back to the lower courts. This stance seemed inconsistent with the president's previous position on the Second Amendment, and it was certainly inconsistent with my view.

One evening in early February, David Addington got a call from Senator Kay Bailey Hutchison's office. A staff person told Addington that a number of members of the House and Senate were preparing to file an amicus brief in support of the D.C. Circuit decision and wondered if, by any chance, I might be interested in signing on. Addington had the brief sent over, read it, and then called to see what I'd like to do. It wasn't a hard decision. I signed on, joining fifty-five senators and 250 House members, as "President of the United States Senate, Richard B. Cheney."

When the brief arrived at the court, the fact that I had joined it was pretty big news. It generated a front-page story in the *Washington Post* headlined, "Cheney Joins Congress in Opposing D.C. Gun Ban: Vice President Breaks with Administration." White House chief of staff Josh Bolten wasn't happy. He came to my office to tell me he needed to tell Addington that we'd committed a "process foul." I wasn't sure what that meant but told Josh to be my guest. Addington, who was always careful to protect the institution of the vice presidency, listened and then explained to Josh, with a smile, I'm sure, that he worked for the vice president, not the president's chief of staff, and that the Senate functions of the vice president were the vice president's business.

Most others around the West Wing seemed pleased. Barry Jackson, who had replaced Karl Rove as the president's political advisor, said he was delighted to see that I'd taken a firm position in support of the Second Amendment. The president never said a word to me about it. I don't know to this day whether he'd signed off on the Justice Department position or left it to Josh Bolten. But it was a mistake. There was no reason for us to back off our strong support of the Second Amendment. And the Supreme Court agreed, affirming the Court of Appeals decision on June 26, 2008. Justice Antonin Scalia later joked that the

Court was unsure how to rule until, thankfully, "the vice president's brief showed up."

AT 3:00 P.M. ON Thursday, March 20, 2008, my helicopter touched down at Bagram Air Base, twenty-seven miles north of Kabul. Built primarily during the Soviet invasion, Bagram is today one of America's largest military bases in Afghanistan. I joined some of our troops for dinner that night. Often when I was visiting troops in the field, I would participate in reenlistment and award ceremonies. It was an honor to watch young soldiers on the front lines raise their hands and take an oath to support and defend the Constitution of the United States. In the awards ceremonies I was often asked to pin medals on soldiers who had demonstrated exemplary bravery and courage under fire. No ceremony I participated in as vice president was more memorable than the one at Bagram Air Base that evening.

On April 25, 2007, Specialist Monica Brown, a nineteen-year-old army medic from Lake Jackson, Texas, had been traveling in a convoy at dusk in Afghanistan's Paktika Province, when the vehicle behind her struck an improvised explosive device, seriously injuring all five soldiers inside. The convoy immediately came under small-arms fire. Without hesitation, Brown and her platoon sergeant, Staff Sergeant Jose Santos, jumped from their vehicle and ran back to the burning Humvee. As vehicles in the convoy attempted to maneuver to provide cover for Brown to care for the patients, the insurgents began firing mortar rounds. Under heavy fire, Brown, with no regard for her own safety, loaded the wounded into a vehicle to move them a short distance away and directed other soldiers to assist her in stabilizing them and preparing them for evacuation. One of the injured soldiers, Specialist Jack Bodami, said this about her: "To say she handled herself well would be an understatement. It was amazing to see her keep completely calm and take care of our guys with all that going on around her. Of all the medics we've had with us throughout the year, she was the one I trusted the most."

For her bravery, Specialist Brown became only the second woman since World War II to be awarded a Silver Star. After her citation was read, I pinned the medal on Specialist Brown. Her commanders were lined up nearby, and there wasn't a dry eye among them. I noticed that my lead Secret Service agent, Pat Caldwell, also had tears in his eyes. He whispered something to his number two, Special Agent Dale Pupillo, and left the dining hall, putting Dale in charge. Pat had been awarded a Silver Star in Vietnam when he, too, was nineteen years old. As David Addington explained to Specialist Brown, watching another young American soldier in a combat zone receive the same award was understandably emotional for Caldwell. When he came back inside, Brown walked over and embraced him. They shared a bond that crossed generations.

A few days after the actions for which Specialist Brown won her Silver Star, the army transferred her, because army regulations prohibit women from participating in combat missions. As secretary of defense and as vice president, I had supported the ban on women in combat units. Increasingly, though, soldiers like Monica Brown find themselves on the front lines, and her heroism made me think our policy ought to be adjusted. It needs to reflect the changing nature of twenty-first-century war, in which combat and noncombat, frontline and rear, are not always so easy to delineate. Brown's own commander said this about her: "Our regular medic was on leave at the time. We had other medics to choose from, but Brown had shown us that she was more technically proficient than any of her peers." I thought it was a mistake that she was pulled out of her unit.

THIS VISIT IN MARCH 2008 was my fourth trip to Afghanistan as vice president. Since the beginning of Operation Enduring Freedom in October 2001, the U.S. military, our coalition partners, and the Afghan people had accomplished much, overthrowing the Taliban, denying al Qaeda the bases from which they had planned the attacks of 9/11, and capturing or killing many of al Qaeda's top leaders. The Afghan people had elected a president and a parliament. The United States and our allies had delivered billions of dollars in economic assistance to support Afghanistan's new leadership and their efforts to build a free, secure, and sovereign nation.

Despite these many accomplishments, by 2006 we were seeing a very worrisome trend. Violence, which decreased during the winter months, when the weather made fighting difficult, increased significantly in the spring and summer, and each year brought more attacks than the one before. Al Qaeda and the Taliban had retaken key strongholds, and at the end of 2006, President Bush had ordered a troop increase from 21,000 to 31,000 over two years.

In early 2007, I had traveled to the region for talks with Presidents Karzai and Musharraf. I brought CIA Deputy Director Steve Kappes with me to Pakistan in 2007, and we discussed with Musharraf the matter of the tribal areas on the Pakistani side of the border with Afghanistan, which both the Taliban and al Qaeda were using to regroup and rearm before crossing the border to attack again. Musharraf had tried to work out a deal whereby he would agree that Pakistani troops would not interfere in the Federally Administered Tribal Areas if the tribal leaders would deny safe haven to al Qaeda and the Taliban. The deal did not work. And although Musharraf continued to express support for our efforts in our private meetings, increasingly his commitments were not translating into action from his government.

I left Islamabad on February 26 and flew into Bagram Air Base. Shortly after I landed, a storm rolled in, making it impossible for me to fly the thirty miles to Kabul. For security reasons, I couldn't go by car. I would either have to cancel my meeting with President Karzai or spend the night at Bagram, hoping the weather would clear by morning. Given the critical importance of the relationship, skipping the meeting was not an option. So we stayed overnight.

The next morning, I was reading through my morning briefing materials, when I heard a blast—loud, though clearly some distance away. The Secret Service moved me into a concrete shelter, and I soon learned that a suicide bomber had struck at the front gate, killing twenty-three, including an American soldier. The Taliban later claimed responsibility and said they were aiming at me. Whether or not that was true, the attack itself was, tragically, typical of the violence happening in Afghanistan.

When I met President Karzai in Kabul, he expressed his gratitude for American support. He told me of the time he had spent as a refugee, living in a camp in Pakistan and traveling across the border into Afghanistan, trying to convince the tribal leaders to take on the Taliban regime. He said the one question they always asked was "Have you got the Americans with you?" He said the tribal leaders would take on the fight when they knew they could count on us to back them. He felt that President Bush's decision to increase troop levels as well as commit close to $11 billion in additional reconstruction aid sent a very clear signal that we were with him. Karzai had his difficulties, however, some of his own making and many not.

There were several reasons for the significant challenges we faced and continue to face in Afghanistan. First, the country's geography, history, tribal society, and extreme poverty all combine to make it a very difficult place to govern. Second, it is the largest producer of heroin in the world, single-handedly meeting the demand in Europe. The poppy industry generates cash that funds warlords and encourages corruption. Third, extreme poverty makes the task of building a sovereign, free, secure nation much more difficult in many ways than it was in Iraq, where there is more than a 100 billion–barrel oil reserve. In recent months there has been a significant discovery of mineral deposits in Afghanistan. I am hopeful that this find can someday provide the resources Afghanistan needs to thrive. Fourth, our multilateral method of operating in Afghanistan carries with it both strengths and weaknesses. We have had many courageous allies fighting alongside us, but some of the rules of engagement imposed on their forces by home governments have made it difficult to count on them in a pinch. I remember one colonel explaining to me the dismay of American troops when they called in air strikes only to have a French Mirage jet conduct the equivalent of an unarmed flyover.

It is also the case that arrangements we had agreed to in 2002 for dividing up the responsibilities for reconstruction turned out to be less effective than we had hoped. Some governments failed to follow through on their commitments, which left large segments of the reconstruction undone or underfunded.

Finally, and most important, is the problem of Pakistan. It is worth remembering that before 9/11, it was one of only three governments in the world that recognized the Taliban. Musharraf formally cut those ties, and the Pakistanis worked with us to capture some of the most important leaders in the War on Terror, including Khalid Sheikh Mohammed and Abu Zubaydah. But a large and active extreme Islamist segment of the population was incensed by Pakistan's cooperation with the United States, and Musharraf became an assassination target. He survived two attempts on his life within eleven days in December 2003. Within the Pakistani government, there were also some who continued to support the Taliban, which, among other things, hindered efforts to clear out the tribal areas. Al Qaeda had its sympathizers, too, as Osama bin Laden's presence in Abbottabad for some six years seems to suggest.

After my visit with Musharraf in 2007, his position grew increasingly weak. He suspended the chief justice of Pakistan's Supreme Court, which brought thousands of protestors into the streets. In November 2007, he suspended Pakistan's constitution and declared emergency rule. He lifted it on December 15, promising to go ahead with free and fair elections. Then, on December 27, 2007, former Prime Minister Benazir Bhutto, who had returned to Pakistan to lead her party in the parliamentary elections, was assassinated. The following year, Musharraf was voted out of office. He was succeeded by Asif Ali Zardari, the widower of Benazir Bhutto.

Our efforts in Afghanistan continued to be hindered by the safe haven that the Taliban and al Qaeda found in Pakistan. We ramped up our use of armed drones—unmanned aerial vehicles—and the president asked his national security team to conduct a review of Afghanistan, similar to the one we had done for Iraq in 2006. The results of the review, which was completed after the 2008 election, called for more resources and a focus on counterinsurgency. The president asked Steve Hadley to talk to General Jim Jones, his counterpart in the incoming Obama administration, to tell him about the review and to let him know we could either release the results publicly or pass them quietly to the incoming team so they could use them without politics getting in the way. General Jones asked that we pass along the report quietly,

would be for the year, and the panel, made up of the White House chief of staff, the director of the OMB, and me, was a place where they could appeal. The panel worked well, and did not have to meet very often, particularly after one cabinet member made an appeal that resulted in her budget numbers being lowered.

THE REASONS FOR THE financial crisis of 2008 are likely to be long debated. Many of the analyses I've read or watched on TV strike me as oversimplified, more interested in pointing out villains—greedy bankers or feckless deregulators—than in coming to a true understanding. One analysis I have found particularly thoughtful is the minority view in the *Financial Crisis Inquiry Report* of 2011. In it, commissioners Keith Hennessey and Douglas Holtz-Eakin and commission vice chairman Bill Thomas note a complexity of factors, including a surge in housing prices that was accompanied by a surge in mortgage lending. Convinced that housing prices would continue to escalate, both lenders and borrowers were willing to enter into mortgage agreements that were not sustainable. The idea was that the growth of home equity would enable buyers to refinance into loans they could carry for the long term. Mortgage lenders were particularly encouraged to discount the risk involved because they sold the mortgages and did not ultimately have to bear whatever losses they produced.

Government-sponsored entities Fannie Mae and Freddie Mac, along with companies in the private sector, combined mortgages, many of them high-risk, into mortgage-backed securities. Credit agencies gave these securities unduly high ratings, and too many institutions and investors failed to inquire as diligently as they should have into the risk they were assuming. Some institutions made big bets on mortgage-backed securities, and when the housing bubble burst, they suffered massive losses. Such losses, combined with heavy leveraging, brought the investment bank Bear Stearns to the edge of bankruptcy in March 2008. JPMorgan agreed to step in and acquire Bear Stearns, but only after Treasury Secretary Hank Paulson, working with Tim Geithner, then head of the Federal Reserve Bank of New York, and Ben Bernanke, chairman of the Federal Reserve, agreed to a $30 billion loan as part of the sale.

Mortgage giants Fannie Mae and Freddie Mac were also in trouble. For years Alan Greenspan had been warning about the unwarranted risks they were taking and the potential fallout. Small-town banks all over America held paper issued by Fannie Mae and Freddie Mac to meet their capital requirements. If Fannie and Freddie failed, there would be a systemic failure. It was also the case that Fannie's and Freddie's mortgage-backed securities were held around the world by investors who believed they were guaranteed by the United States government. Should Fannie or Freddie fail, an international crisis would ensue. In 2003, the administration had put forward legislation, which was blocked by Barney Frank, Democratic chairman of the House Banking Committee, that would have reformed these institutions and strengthened governmental regulations of their activities. We put forward similar legislation again in 2005, and again it was blocked by Fannie Mae and Freddie Mac lobbyists and supporters, particularly in the Democratic caucus on Capitol Hill.

Finally, in July 2008, with the financial crisis looming, legislation that provided for regulation was passed, and it brought about a careful examination of Fannie's and Freddie's books. Treasury Secretary Paulson recommended taking both institutions into government conservatorship, the president approved, and on September 7, the government took control.

But there seemed no end to the crisis. Lehman Brothers, another major American financial institution, was on the brink of collapse, and we had to decide whether to step in and keep it afloat. The key was finding an interested buyer, but it turned out there wasn't one. Lehman declared bankruptcy on September 15, 2008. Some have charged that letting Lehman go under was a grave error that somehow caused the financial crisis, but as Hank Paulson and others have pointed out, there was no legal, workable way to save Lehman. Moreover, the events of September 2008 followed upon one another in such rapid succession that no single event can be said to have precipitated them.

On the weekend of the Lehman failure, Merrill Lynch agreed to be purchased by Bank of America on the following Tuesday, in order to prevent the failure of American International Group, a huge international insurance and financial firm that had insured mortgage-backed obligations. The Federal Reserve stepped in with an $85 billion loan, in exchange for which the U.S. government assumed ownership of nearly 80 percent of AIG.

It was clear that what we were facing called for more than individual interventions, particularly as it became apparent that America's credit markets were shutting down. Huge companies with top credit ratings, such as General Electric, were unable to meet their short-term capital requirements. One money market fund "broke the buck"—was unable to return at least a dollar for every dollar invested. And the ramifications were economy-wide. People often talk about the difference between Wall Street and Main Street, but in this instance, credit was becoming a problem for everyone from GE to the businesswoman who owned a McDonald's franchise. This crisis was going to affect not only CEOs, but also retirees depending on their 401(k)s. I thought of my great-grandfather, Samuel Fletcher Cheney, who in 1896 had lost his homestead when he couldn't borrow money. I thought of my grandfather who'd lost almost everything when his bank failed at the beginning of the Great Depression. What the United States was facing in September 2008 had the potential to devastate Americans in all walks of life, just as the Great Depression had.

The country was fortunate that the president had such an outstanding economic team to work the crisis that confronted us. Eddie Lazear, chairman of the Council of Economic Advisers, was the kind of creative thinker who's always appreciated, but never more so than in the unprecedented situation we faced. Ben Bernanke, chairman of the Federal Reserve, was a cool and thoughtful presence. He was a scholar of the Great Depression, and when he told you that the situation we were in might be even worse than that, you listened. I thought he had been a very effective chairman of the Council of Economic Advisors, and when I'd interviewed him as we were looking for a Federal Reserve chairman to take over when Alan Greenspan left, I had been impressed. I was even more impressed during the crisis of 2008. His quiet manner may have obscured the very aggressive actions to which he committed the Fed in order to pull us away from the abyss. The role he played has, I think, been generally underappreciated.

Treasury Secretary Hank Paulson was a booming presence whose experience as chairman and chief executive officer of Goldman Sachs gave him a hands-on knowledge of Wall Street that no one else in the administration could match. It was invaluable as trouble piled upon trouble. As I watched Paulson work, I was also struck by the physical and emotional toll the crisis was taking on him. He described in the book he later wrote how lack of sleep caused him to have dry heaves several times a day. He sometimes stood in meetings because he was afraid if he sat down his back would spasm. Whatever the challenges he had faced running Goldman Sachs—and he had been an enormous success there—dealing with a crisis that affected the nation and the world was bigger.

I remember thinking how grounded the president was through the whole economic ordeal. He kept perspective and was very good at handling pressure. He dealt effectively with some of the most difficult and complex economic issues any president has had to face.

On Thursday, September 18, I was traveling when the president's economic team was scheduled to present the rescue plan they had devised. Keith Hennessey, assistant to the president for economic policy, and Neil Patel, my chief domestic policy advisor, called me on Air Force Two to brief me on the details: a guarantee for money market deposits, an initiative to restore liquidity to the commercial paper market from the Federal Reserve, and the centerpiece, a plan to buy $700 billion of the mortgage-backed securities that were dragging down major institutions and causing credit to seize up. I had long been an advocate of keeping government intervention in the private sector to a minimum. What we were talking about now was the largest such intervention in the history of the republic, and I was a strong supporter. I told Hennessey he could tell the president I was behind the package, and I reinforced that point in a private meeting with the president in the Oval Office the next morning. There was no other option.

I knew the Congress would be wary of such a plan. Republicans who were facing tough reelection battles would not be eager to cast a vote that looked like a Wall Street bailout at precisely the moment when so many Main Street businesses were severely hurting. We briefly contemplated not seeking congressional authority. When the Federal Deposit Insurance Corporation Act had been passed in 1991, it included language that would allow for a major injection of funds directly into the banking system with the approval of the president, the secretary of the Treasury, and a majority of the Federal Reserve Board should there be a threat to the integrity of our financial system. Ben Bernanke made clear, however, that he would feel much more comfortable with congressional approval, so we went to work trying to secure it.

Hank Paulson worked very well with congressional Democrats and spent much time with Speaker Pelosi, House banking chairman Barney Frank, and Majority Leader Steny Hoyer trying to put the package together. House Republicans felt out of the loop and were soon so angry that they were refusing to participate in meetings with Secretary Paulson. I got a call from House Minority Leader John Boehner asking me to come up to the Hill to brief the Republicans.

On Tuesday, September 23, I left the West Wing at 8:45 on my way to the Capitol. I had Keith Hennessey and Kevin Warsh, a member of the Federal Reserve board of directors, with me. When we walked into the large meeting room in the Capitol, the House Republican conference had already gathered and they gave me a very warm welcome, a standing ovation. They expressed the same support, giving me another ovation, as I left. But in between my coming and going, many members made it quite clear that they would not support the $700 billion Troubled Assets Relief Program, or TARP, as it was known. There were a number of problems, but the biggest was that we had allowed the package to be described as a "Wall Street bailout," leaving the impression that we were giving taxpayer money to Wall Street fat cats rather than trying to prevent a total financial collapse. In addition, I don't think we had adequately conveyed to the public how serious the consequences of not acting could be. Joe Barton, an old friend and Republican member from Texas, stood up at the caucus meeting and after praising me to the skies blasted the TARP. He told me he'd had over four hundred calls into his district office on this issue and only four callers had urged him to support the bill. His experience was representative of what other Republican members were facing, and I understood their frustration and that of their constituents. So many people had paid so little attention to the risks they were assuming—and now the taxpayers were on the hook. I left the session thinking that if the vote had been held that day, we'd have been lucky to have fifty Republicans with us.

I went back up to the Hill a few hours later for the weekly Senate Republican conference lunch. We had opposition to the TARP on the Senate side as well. Senator Jeff Sessions of Alabama, normally a solid supporter of the administration, spoke out strongly against the bill. But we also had support, and Sessions was followed by Judd Gregg of New Hampshire, Tom Coburn of Oklahoma, Mike Enzi of Wyoming, and Kit Bond of Missouri—all of whom spoke about why the bill was so important. I sat quietly and kept track. Eventually six senators spoke in favor and there'd been only one negative statement. I decided I didn't need to say anything.

ON SEPTEMBER 24, 2008, Republican presidential nominee John McCain announced he was suspending his presidential campaign to come back to Washington to deal with the financial crisis. It was a move that frankly surprised many of us in the White House. After all, there really wasn't much John could actually do, and it seemed pretty risky to announce the campaign suspension and head back to Washington without being clear about what you could actually deliver. But we wanted McCain to win, so when he asked the president to convene the congressional leadership in the Cabinet Room of the White House to discuss the financial crisis, the president did it. He called Senator Obama, McCain's opponent, and asked him to be there as well. What unfolded that day in the West Wing was likely unique in the annals of American presidential contests.

The congressional leaders were assembled when the president and I walked into the Cabinet Room from the Oval Office. He went around to the right to his seat, greeting people on his way. I went around to the left to take my seat across the table from him. I'd been there just a few minutes when Senator Obama came around to shake hands and say hello. It was a thoughtful gesture, and he seemed very much at ease and in command of the situation. The president called on Speaker Pelosi to open the session for the Democrats, and she, in turn, deferred to Senate Majority Leader Harry Reid, who said, "Mr. President, we've decided that Senator Obama speaks for all of us." Reid turned the floor over to Senator Obama, a step that immediately put the Democratic presidential nominee on a par with the most senior leaders in the room—and made him the president's counterpart. Obama was eloquent, saying that we had to get the bill passed, emphasizing how serious the situation was, and offering to lend whatever support he could. He needled the Republicans a little for hanging back, not enough to give offense, but sufficient to put the ball back in our court.

When the president turned to Senator McCain to speak, he passed. Since he had called for the meeting in the first place, that was a surprise. After a few other people expressed their opinions, most of them negative, the president came back to McCain. This time he spoke, but only for himself. It was a marked contrast with Obama, whose words carried the authority of all the Democrats in the room. Senator McCain added nothing of substance. It was entirely unclear why he'd returned to Washington and why he'd wanted the congressional leadership called together. I left the Cabinet Room when the meeting was over thinking the Republican presidential ticket was in trouble.

The president and I kept working the phones, making calls to individual members of Congress, trying to convince them of the importance of this piece of legislation. I was successful in persuading Congresswoman Barbara Cubin, Wyoming's sole member of the House, to agree to support the bill. Of course, she was retiring and didn't have to worry about reelection. But I was happy to report to the president that I'd gotten 100 percent of the Wyoming House delegation to sign on. He hadn't swayed anyone in the Texas delegation, a highly unusual situation.

When the vote was held on September 29, we got only 65 Republican votes, and the TARP package was defeated 205–228. The stock market fell 777 points that afternoon, the largest single-day drop in history.

Bills that involve raising revenue have to originate in the House. Since the House had just killed the TARP package, we needed a way to start over in the Senate, where we knew we would have more support. We were able to use a tax bill that had already passed the House as a vehicle to try again. Watching the stock market slide nearly eight hundred points had an impact on a number of members who had voted no the first time around. It made clear the very real costs of a loss of confidence in America's financial sector and drove home the imperative to act. On Wednesday, October 1, the Senate passed legislation that would enable the purchase of troubled assets, and the House passed it on Friday, October 3, by a vote of 263–171. Not long after passage, Secretary Paulson, Chairman Bernanke, and New York Fed Chairman Geithner recommended using $250 billion of the TARP for direct infusions of capital into the banking system. I agreed with this approach. We were facing a situation where the value of the troubled assets could have been as much as $5 trillion, and we did not want to run the risk of having our $700 billion disappear with no impact. On the other hand, if we put $1 into a bank, they could leverage that amount by ten to multiply the impact of the money.

TARP has remained controversial and was indeed an issue that many successful candidates used against incumbents who had supported it in the 2008 elections. But as I write this in 2011, it is clear that TARP was a success. According to economist Robert Samuelson, of the $245 billion invested in banks, Treasury has already recovered approximately $244 billion. Treasury expects ultimately to record an overall profit from the bank investments portion of TARP of approximately $20 billion.

Within a few weeks of the passage of the $700 billion program, General Motors informed us that without significant government intervention, they wouldn't survive. There was language in the TARP legislation that would allow us to use a portion of the funds for a loan package for the automobile companies, but I had reservations about doing so.

Early in my congressional days, I had opposed the 1979 Chrysler loan guarantee, and I had continued throughout my career to be philosophically opposed to bailing out specific companies or industries. I believed our intervention in the financial sector was justified, because the federal government was responsible for maintaining the strength and viability of our economy, including our financial system and currency. Providing sufficient support to avoid the collapse of our banking system was something only the federal government could do. But, all things considered, companies in the private sector should be judged in the marketplace. Having the government intervene was not, in my opinion, a good idea.

The General Motors crisis came at the end of our administration and within a few weeks of our handover of power to the Obama-Biden team. The president decided that he did not want to pull the plug on General Motors as we were headed out the door. He wanted to give the incoming team time to decide on their policy options and therefore came up with a short-term package to keep GM afloat until the new administration had a chance to review the situation. Although I understood the reasoning, I would have preferred that the government not get involved and was disappointed—but not surprised—when the Obama administration significantly increased the government intervention in the automobile industry shortly after taking office.

AFTER HAVING BEEN HEAVILY involved in campaigning for many previous election cycles—midterms and presidential campaigns—I essentially sat out the campaign of 2008. I didn't like being sidelined, but understood the reasoning behind it. After eight years there certainly was a sense of Bush-Cheney fatigue among the voters, and the McCain campaign wanted to distance their candidate from the White House and our policies. This made for some awkward moments. After the campaign's tracking polls began to nosedive, for example, they quit sharing them with us. It also meant, though, that the American people didn't get a chance to hear a solid defense of many of our policies, particularly concerning the War on Terror. Although Senator McCain was a solid supporter of what we were doing in Iraq and Afghanistan, he didn't defend our terrorist surveillance program with nearly the same enthusiasm, and he opposed the enhanced interrogation program. I thought Senator Obama's views in these areas were misguided, and I regretted that no one was making the argument on the other side.

Since I wasn't campaigning, I had more time for other activities, such as appreciating two grandsons who had been born since the last presidential election: Liz's and her husband Phil's fifth child, Richard Perry, and Mary's and her partner Heather Poe's first child, Sam. I was also able to be of use to my granddaughters. In August 2008, I got a call from Liz, who needed a favor. "Do you think you could request a meeting with the Jonas Brothers tomorrow?" she asked. "The who?" I asked. She explained that a musical group called the Jonas Brothers was filming a public service announcement at the White House. Her three daughters, who were big Jonas Brothers fans, had heard about the taping and asked if they could come watch. Liz had called a friend in the first lady's office, but was told it was a closed set. That's why she was calling me.

"Trust me," she said. "If you get your granddaughters a meeting with the Jonas Brothers, they'll think you're the coolest grandfather in history." Apparently, though, the boys were in such high demand that the only way this would happen is if I made the request myself. Although I was frankly unsure what I was getting myself into, if it would make my granddaughters happy I was willing to give it a shot. I buzzed my assistant, Debbie Heiden, and asked her to call over to Mrs. Bush's office and tell them I'd like to meet some people called the Jonas Brothers. "And I'm going to need some bios," I added.

The next day, my delighted granddaughters helped me show the Jonas Brothers and their family the West Wing. They were impressive and polite young men, who hid well whatever surprise they might have felt at hearing that Dick Cheney wanted to see them.

IN SEPTEMBER, LYNNE AND I left on a trip that included stops in several former Soviet republics, including Georgia. We arrived in the capital of Tbilisi on September 4, just a few weeks after a cease-fire had been negotiated to put an end to a conflict between Georgia and Russia. The fighting had been centered initially in two "breakaway" republics inside Georgia: South Ossetia and Abkhazia. These territories, though part of Georgia geographically, had large Russian populations and had been trying to assert their independence. In August South Ossetian forces under the command of Russian commanders, fired on Georgian villages in South Ossetia. Mikheil Saakashvili, the president of Georgia, had ordered a response, which seemed to give Russian leader Vladimir Putin the excuse he'd been looking for to launch an aggressive military action against the Georgians.

After first moving to defeat Georgian forces inside the two republics, Russian forces began moving into Georgia proper, first to Gori, a major transportation hub, and then toward Tbilisi. They moved with the kind of speed that strongly suggested significant advance planning, leaving the impression that Putin had been planning such an attack for some time. That, together with the fact that the Russian response was far in excess of what was required if the goal was simply to protect Russians in South Ossetia and Abkhazia, suggested to me and many others that Putin was intent on reasserting Russian influence in its former republics.

For some time, there had been growing tension between the government in Moscow and President Saakashvili's government in Tbilisi. Saakashvili, who had studied in the United States and wanted to orient Georgia toward the West, made no secret of his view that Georgia should join NATO. Putin viewed this as a direct threat to Russia inside what he considered Russia's sphere of influence.

As we discussed these developments in National Security Council meetings in the days just after the Russian invasion, I suggested that we needed to view this as more than a question of the independence of South Ossetia or Abkhazia. This was Putin trying to reverse the trend of the last twenty years. He now had the forces and the wealth—primarily from oil—to be able to begin to re-exert Russian influence not just in Georgia, but across the "near abroad," countries such as Moldova, Ukraine, the Baltic nations, and the former Central Asian republics. He had been quoted saying that he regarded the demise of the Soviet Union as "the greatest geopolitical catastrophe of the century," which couldn't have been further from my point of view. I viewed the collapse of the Soviet Union as the greatest forward step for human liberty in the last sixty years. As I analyzed the situation, Putin wanted to turn back the clock and do whatever possible to restore Russian power and influence.

Shortly after the Russian invasion of Georgia, Poland had agreed to host missile interceptors, one part of a defense system that we had designed to stop missiles fired from the Middle East from hitting either Europe or the United States. Senior Russian military officials let the Polish government know that if it went ahead with the deployment of the missile defense system, Poland could expect to become a nuclear target. The Czechs had agreed to host the radar component of the defense system, and about the time the announcement was made, Russia cut back on oil deliveries to the Czech Republic.

I always felt in my dealings with Putin that it was important to remember his background. He was part of the Soviet KGB, and in many ways his actions as the leader of Russia reflected that. One Russian economist who used to work for Putin and then had a falling-out described it to me this way: "All authoritarian regimes have security services. But today's Russia is really the first state where the security service has become the state." While America and Western Europe had moved beyond the divisions of the Cold War, Putin seemed to long for them.

During my visit to Georgia, I voiced American support for Georgia's sovereignty. I also announced that the United States would provide over $1 billion in economic and humanitarian assistance. Before returning to the United States, I attended the Ambrosetti Forum, an annual economic conference held in Italy, where I denounced Russia's invasion of Georgia and its heavy-handed dealings with Poland and the Czech Republic. As for Georgia and Ukraine, the time had come, I said, to begin action to make them members of NATO.

I was disappointed to see the Obama administration in its early months decide to halt the missile defense project with Poland and the Czech Republic. I suspect the Russians put the same kind of pressure on them as they had put on us. I was glad to see my successor, Vice President Joe Biden, endorse the idea of NATO membership for Georgia and Ukraine, but progress in achieving that has been disappointingly slow.

In the end, we need to make clear to the Russians and our friends and allies that we will be aggressive in expanding the borders of the free world and that the Russian government has to make a choice. It cannot continue to reap the benefits of a free world economy while simultaneously blackmailing other governments, attempting to use military force to unilaterally redraw sovereign boundaries, and imprisoning anyone who poses a threat to Putin's leadership. For our part, we have to be careful not to let our desire for a changed Russia color our analysis of what's actually happening. In 1982, when Yuri Andropov became general secretary of the Soviet Communist Party, I recall getting reports that he liked jazz and drank scotch, both supposedly signaling that he was a reformer. Similarly, when Vladimir Putin transferred authority to Dmitri Medvedev, some Russia analysts saw this as heralding a new day of openness and increased commitment to reform and democracy. It wasn't true of Andropov, and it wasn't true of Medvedev. We need to be very careful on whom we pin our hopes.

ON OCTOBER 22, LYNNE and I joined President Bush and Laura for a dinner in the White House residence in honor of the Supreme Court. It was a very special evening. The president and Laura gave everyone a tour of the second floor of the residence. They were impressive guides and had both clearly spent a good deal of time reading the history of the house and its previous occupants. I had been in the rooms many times before, but I always learned something new when I joined a tour given by the Bushes. They would walk through and describe each room—the Lincoln Bedroom, the Queen's Bedroom—and what the house had looked like in past administrations.

Over the course of the last few years we had had some serious disagreements with a number of the Supreme Court's decisions, particularly as they related to the War on Terror. But on this evening those disputes were not in view. It was a wonderful evening of camaraderie, and Justice John Paul Stevens spoke for all of us when he congratulated the president on making two great appointments to the court—Justices Roberts and Alito. Lynne made a special toast to Laura at the dinner, thanking her for all she had done to restore and maintain the beauty of the White House and of Camp David. We were especially grateful, Lynne said, for her work at Camp David, which had so often been our "undisclosed location."

ON NOVEMBER 4, 2008, Barack Obama was elected president of the United States. I called Senator Joe Biden, congratulated him, and offered to do whatever I could to help ease his transition into office. Lynne and I were pleased to host the vice president–elect and his wife, Jill, at the Naval Observatory. We showed them around what would soon be their home and introduced them to some of the outstanding people who work there.

As an administration, we worked hard to conduct a smooth and helpful transition. I had been part of a number of them through the years, incoming and outgoing, and this was the best I had seen. I think all of us on both sides of this one understood the stakes. With a nation at war, it was particularly important to put politics aside and hand over power and policies smoothly. In some ways, though, I'm not sure it's really possible to prepare someone to take office. One of my former national security staffers, Eric Edelman, who was serving as the under-secretary of defense for policy at the end of our administration, pointed out how much the velocity of issues a policymaker had to face daily had changed. Some of those coming into office had served during the Clinton years, and though any experience was helpful, the sheer volume and speed of decisions had increased exponentially since then. The best we could do was offer our assistance, provide briefings, and maybe venture a little advice along the way.

Josh Bolten decided to host a unique session for the incoming chief of staff, Rahm Emanuel, during our last weeks in office. Josh gathered all the living former chiefs of staff, about a dozen of us. Don Rumsfeld

was there, Howard Baker, Jack Watson, John Sununu, and Leon Panetta, among others, and we met around the table in the office we had
all once inhabited. Josh went around and asked each of us to give Rahm
our most important piece of advice. By this time, of course, there'd been
years of stories about how I was the evil genius controlling the Bush
administration from behind a curtain, so when it came my turn I advised Rahm, "Whatever you do, make sure you've got the vice president
under control." It was one of my better lines.

There were lots of goodbyes over the following weeks, as we thanked
so many people who had done so much for us and for the country over
the last eight years. One group that worked largely in anonymity was
the White House Medical Unit. For eight years, Dr. Lewis Hofmann
had been by my side. He'd spent countless hours in hold rooms, on
airplanes, and in vans. He'd spent so much time in the back end of a
fishing boat that he'd taken up fly-fishing with a passion. My family and
I will always be grateful to Lew for his friendship and for all he did for
us. The president and I gathered the group together in the Rose Garden
for one last goodbye after the election. The president put it this way:
"You all have been just great. Miracle workers, actually. When I picked
the vice president I never expected him to survive, but you pulled him
through." While I'd had more optimism about my outlook, I couldn't
argue with his gratitude for the docs.

JANUARY 20, 2009, DAWNED cold and sunny. We joined the
Bidens, Bushes, and Obamas at the White House for the traditional
pre-inaugural coffee. I was in a wheelchair, having strained my back
moving boxes over the weekend, and as my successor, Joe Biden, and
I greeted each other that morning, I warned him, "Joe, this is how
you're liable to look when your term is up." Then we made the drive up
Pennsylvania Avenue to the Capitol, and I took my seat on the inaugural platform. As I looked out over the massive crowds gathered that
morning, I thought back to my first days in Washington in 1968. I
had arrived a few months after a section of the city had been in flames,
engulfed in the race riots that followed Dr. Martin Luther King, Jr.'s

murder. Now, here we were, united as Americans, inaugurating our first African-American president. Barack Obama had not been my candidate, and I would disagree deeply with many of the decisions he would make as president, but I, like most Americans, felt tremendous pride that morning at the historic nature of this moment.

I could never have imagined when I first came to Washington that I would be leaving as vice president so many years later. I thought about all I had seen and been a part of during a span of time when Americans had seen great change and sadness, joy and triumph. And yet for all the life that filled those forty years, they seemed to have passed in the blink of an eye.

The path I had traveled was partly due to the circumstances of my birth. Not that I had been born into a powerful or privileged family; I wasn't. But I was born an American, a blessing surely among life's greatest. I had parents who loved me and taught me the importance of sacrifice and hard work. I was privileged to have chances—and second chances—of the kind that may be possible only in our great nation. On that inaugural morning, as the wheel turned and it was time for us to go, I thought finally of my grandchildren. I cannot begin to imagine all the opportunities they will have and the ways in which their lives will unfold. They, too, have the blessings of love and the opportunities and freedoms only America can provide, and they have a grandfather who will be watching with great interest.

On the afternoon of January 20, 2009, as the president was getting ready to depart for Texas, I introduced him to supporters who had gathered at Andrews Air Force Base by saying that my eight years of service with him had been a special honor. He had made it possible for me to participate in momentous events, and as I looked back on what we had accomplished, nothing was more important than having kept the nation safe after the devastating attacks of 9/11. In that fight, he had been an outstanding leader, making tough decisions and inspiring others with the determination required for the war against a new kind of enemy. He had been a visceral and forthright commander, a president who strengthened all of us with his conviction. Few who experienced 9/11 will ever forget that September day when he stood at Ground Zero and promised "the people who knocked these buildings down will hear all of us soon."

He had made some decisions I didn't agree with, but he had paid me the high honor of listening to my views, which, of course, he did not have to do. History is full of examples of vice presidents who were kept far from the center of power. Indeed, I've known a few personally. But at the beginning George W. Bush had said that I would be part of governing. He had been—as I had known he would be—a man of his word.

For all of us who gathered at Andrews Air Force Base on January 20, it was the kind of event that completes one time in our lives and signals that another has begun. And except for a veteran reporter or two, the Cheneys had to be the only ones at Andrews that afternoon who could remember being in the same place to see off another president thirty-two years earlier. Back then our daughters were little girls, and the president I had served had been voted out of office. Now Liz and Mary had children of their own, and this time the president was departing on his own terms, after eight years in office.

Being vice president certainly had its benefits, but I liked picking up where our family had left off in normal life. I got a new car, and it was good to be a driver again. I wanted to drive all the way to Wyoming, just as I had done in 1993 after leaving the Pentagon, but Lynne didn't think that was such a great idea. I acquired a BlackBerry, began to do a little emailing, and even sent a text message or two. Instead of the intelligence briefings that used to begin the day, I had to make do again with the morning newspapers. As it turned out, they were still filled with stories and commentaries critical of the Bush administration's national security record. I could read all of this and accept it in silence, but only for so long.

On his second full day in office, President Obama signed an executive order directing that the detainment facility at Guantanamo Bay, Cuba, be closed within a year. He also ordered an end to the use of enhanced interrogation techniques, all of this in keeping with his many repeated and categorical pledges on the matter during the 2008 campaign. As a candidate, he had cast the issue in terms of constitutional imperatives, basic American values, and elementary standards of human rights—often in a tone suggesting that we in the Bush administration had not considered any of these, or, indeed, had violated them. Senator Obama had not really been challenged on such assertions during the presidential race. His opponent, Senator John McCain, actually agreed with Obama on some crucial points. And John's preference, in any case, was that President Bush and I lie low and let him frame the election in his own way. Personally, I felt that a straightforward defense by the president and me would be better than no rebuttal at all from the White House, but it was John's campaign and he deserved to run it the way he wanted.

Even so, in those early days of the Obama administration, my first instinct was to let the criticism pass. But the subject kept coming up, and the president and members of his administration were making assertions about the program and its value that were inaccurate. I remembered two documents in particular that I had seen as vice president. They were CIA reports, one of which specified what we had learned from Khalid Sheikh Mohammed, after he had been subjected to enhanced interrogation. The other reported on the pivotal role that detainee questioning had played in our battle against al Qaeda. It seemed to me that if the American people were going to have an informed debate about Bush administration counterterrorism policies, and enhanced interrogation in particular, they should have the facts about the intelligence we gained—and the attacks we prevented—through the program.

I wanted another look at the documents, so on March 31, 2009, I took a trip to the National Archives in downtown D.C. and reviewed them in a secure reading room. The reports were just as I recalled, and I filled out a form making an official request that they be declassified. Before I had a response to my request, the president decided to declassify a different set of documents. These were the memos produced by the Bush administration Justice Department that explained the legal rationale supporting enhanced interrogation and also detailed the particular methods involved. At about the same time, President Obama and his attorney general, Eric Holder, signaled the possibility that the lawyers who prepared these memos and the intelligence officers who conducted enhanced interrogations might face professional sanction or even criminal prosecution.

I was appalled that the new administration would even consider punishing honorable public servants who had carried out the Bush administration's lawful policies and kept the country safe. I was also deeply concerned about the selective fashion in which sensitive information was being declassified and made public. The administration had just revealed to the world, including our enemies, methods used to question detainees thought to have information about future attacks. Yet the information in the memos I had requested—detailing all we had learned, and the attacks we had stopped through the enhanced interrogation program—was being kept secret. A few weeks after President Obama released the legal memos, I heard from CIA Director Leon Panetta, a colleague and friend from my days in the House. He wrote to tell me that my request was being denied.

I had scheduled a speech on these matters for Thursday, May 21, 2009, at the American Enterprise Institute, a Washington, D.C., think tank with which I have been long affiliated. On Monday of that week, the White House announced that President Obama would also be giving a speech that day at about the same time. I think his speech was meant to preempt mine, but I was happy to slide the time for mine back so that he could speak first. The result was what the media called "dueling speeches."

In his speech, President Obama reaffirmed his pledge to follow the "imperative" of closing Guantanamo within a year, adding that the facility had "likely created more terrorists around the world than it ever detained." Indeed, he said, "By any measure, the costs of keeping it open far exceed the complications involved in closing it." On the matter of enhanced interrogation, he said, "I categorically reject the assertion that these are the most effective means of interrogation," and called the techniques we had authorized "torture." Such methods, the president explained, had all arisen from the "expedience" of the previous administration, at an unacceptable cost to conscience and to the fundamental values of our country: "They are not who we are, and they are not America."

When my turn came, I recalled the days after 9/11 and the absolute determination of the Bush administration to make sure our nation never again faced such a day of horror. The key to ensuring that was intelligence, and we gave our intelligence officers the tools and lawful authority they needed to gain information, some of it known only to the worst of the terrorists, through tough interrogation, if need be. The interrogations had the sole purpose of gaining specific information that would save American lives and did in fact yield such information. I called again for the release of the memos that would prove just that.

To describe what we had done as a program of torture, I said, "is to libel the dedicated professionals who have saved American lives and to cast terrorists and murderers as innocent victims." I also challenged the whole assumption that American values were abandoned, or even compromised, in the fight against terrorists:

> For all that we've lost in this conflict, the United States has never lost its moral bearings. And when the moral reckoning turns to the men known as high-value terrorists, I can assure you they were neither innocent nor victims. As for those who asked them questions and got answers: they did the right thing, they made our country safer, and a lot of Americans are alive today because of them.

In my long political career I had seen politicians run for the hills when things got tough, trying to distance themselves from those on the ground when subpoenas started arriving. I had no intention of turning my back on honorable public servants. To the contrary, I counted it a privilege to speak in their defense.

Two years later, as I write in the spring of 2011, I am happy to note that for President Obama the "imperative" of closing Guantanamo has evolved into the necessity of keeping it open. The memos I asked for were eventually released. They are available on the Internet, and I used them in writing this book.

On May 1, 2011, President Obama announced that we had located and killed Osama bin Laden in a compound an hour or so outside Islamabad, Pakistan. Through years of hard work by our intelligence professionals and our military, we were able to track down the world's most wanted terrorist. It was a moving day for all Americans, and President Obama deserves credit for making the call to send our special forces in to act on the intelligence. He should honor all the brave Americans who helped make this mission possible, including the men and women of the CIA interrogation program, who obtained some of the intelligence we relied on to find bin Laden. They do not deserve to be the targets of ongoing investigations and possible prosecution. They deserve to be decorated.

The exchange I had with the president in the spring of 2009 was an unexpected detour. There were plenty of younger Republican leaders to carry on in the cause, and I hardly aspired to be Barack Obama's principal adversary. I also had a book to get moving on and a few other concerns that wouldn't wait.

One of them was a new turn in some old health issues. I'd had an amazing run since my first heart attack in 1978. All along the way I had benefited from advances in medical research and technology—and fabulous doctors. After my fourth heart attack in 2000, my cardiologist, Dr. Jonathan Reiner of George Washington University Hospital in Washington, D.C., advised that I have an implantable cardioverter-defibrillator, or ICD, placed in my chest. It's a device that shocks the heart back to normal rhythm if necessary. Mine didn't go off for the eight years I was in office, but around Christmas 2009, while I was backing my car out of the garage of our house in Wyoming, everything went blank. I had gone into ventricular fibrillation. Somebody else would likely be telling the story right now if the ICD hadn't kicked in to do exactly what it's supposed to do.

By the summer of 2010, I was rapidly descending into end-stage heart failure. Dr. Reiner recommended that I consider a left ventricular assist device, or LVAD, which is essentially a battery-operated pump that helps the heart push blood to the body. I entered Inova Fairfax Hospital in Falls Church, Virginia, which has an outstanding LVAD program, on July 6 for surgery two days later, but declined so rapidly that the doctors decided they needed to go in right away. In long overnight surgery, the LVAD was implanted.

It was not easy surgery and I was in the intensive care unit for many weeks. I received wonderful medical attention and love and care from Lynne, Liz, and Mary. The mind is an amazing thing, and during the weeks I was unconscious, I had a prolonged dream, more vivid than any I've ever had, about a beautiful place in Italy. It was in the countryside, a little north of Rome, and it really seemed I was there. I can still describe the villa where I passed the time, the little stone paths I walked to get coffee or a batch of newspapers. It was a lengthy and very pleasant stay, far preferable to a daily awareness of where I really was and what was really happening.

My Italian holiday ended about the time I came off the ventilator and my eyes focused on the face of a doctor calling my name. When he saw that I was coming to, he said, "How do you feel, Mr. Cheney? You're looking good." I knew enough to doubt him and am afraid I did not reply as graciously as I should have. But my rather rude response got a laugh from the doctor and everyone else in the room. I was on my way back.

Like a lot of people who face life-threatening illness and walk in the sunshine again, I couldn't dismiss the possibility that more than the skill of doctors, the luck of the draw, or my own will to live had pulled me through. I do know that my cause was pleaded in some earnest prayers. On the phone with my old friends John and Mary Kay Turner in Wyoming, Liz asked them to light a candle for me. "We'll do more than pray," John told her. "We'll storm Heaven."

I have some medical choices to make in the future, but I'm doing well for now. I've gotten used to the various contraptions that are always with me, and I'm working and traveling, I've hunted a time or two, and I have some fishing planned. My forward strategy is to assume an abundance of good days ahead. Since the age of thirty-seven, when I first learned I had coronary artery disease, my attitude has been to place all bets on a long future and so far it's worked. But however many tomorrows there are, I know well how fortunate I am to have had the years I've had. I have reached the biblical three score and ten, and a man who can look back on the things I have seen and the people I have known has no grounds for complaint.

In my time, I have known and even been saluted by men given far shorter lives who gave far more in service to their country. What a privilege it was to have spent so much of my career in the company of the men and women of the United States armed forces. As a young man, and again half a lifetime later, I had a place in the room when great issues were debated and big questions decided. That chance was more than I expected when I headed to Washington more than forty years ago. And how lucky I am to have had Lynne, Liz, and Mary as my companions on that journey and now my grandchildren as well. A seventh has joined us now, Mary and Heather's daughter Sarah Lynne, the apple of her grandmother's eye. I've seen some high-achieving people go far in the world more at the expense of their families than with their families, and to do that is to miss out on one of life's finest experiences. As a family we've shared the work, the joys, and the laughter, the setbacks and the successes, and for that I am a grateful man.

I am a firm believer in America and its work in the world. Our political battles are messy, shrill, and sometimes cruel, and yet for all of that, the system has a way of producing courageous and compassionate action when it is needed most. We have stood firm in the face of evil and defied history in the selfless way we have done it. Instead of seeking empire, we have sought freedom for others.

There have been nearly ten generations since the country's founding, and each succeeded in overcoming great challenges. All that I have seen in my time tells me that we will as well—but it is not inevitable. We hear warning after well-founded warning that we are living beyond our means, but we have not shown the political will to change that. Therein lies a danger not only for us but for generations to come whom we are burdening in ways our forebears would never have thought to burden us. And the technology that has eased our lives—indeed, that has saved mine—has a deadly downside. It has always been easy for those who are evil to kill, but now it is possible for a few to do so on an unimaginable scale. This is a danger all too easy to put out of mind, but one we simply cannot grow careless about.

The key, I think, is to choose serious and vigilant leaders, to listen to the men and women who want us to entrust them with high office and judge whether they are saying what they think we want to hear or whether they have the larger cause of the country in mind. It's not always easy to move beyond pleasing promises, but in the case of

America, the greater good is so grand. We're not a perfect country, but our founding ideals, right and true, have allowed human potential to unfold and creativity to thrive in ways never before seen on earth. We are so fortunate to be Americans. And we have a duty as clear as any I know to pass on this great nation, its possibilities undimmed, to the rising generations.

ACKNOWLEDGMENTS

My daughter Liz was my collaborator and the CEO of our book team. Working with her has been a joy. I deeply appreciated her energy and enthusiasm for the project, her talent, her knowledge, and her sense of humor. It is a rare blessing to have reason to spend so many hours of quality time telling your daughter about your life and work. My wife, Lynne, and my daughter Mary helped with the book as well, making this truly a family project, as so much of my public life has been. Lynne and Mary know my story and are both accomplished writers, which made their editorial suggestions invaluable.

Liz assembled an outstanding team to assist her. Robert Karem, who served on my national security team during my time as vice president, did stellar work researching, editing, and fact-checking, as well as ably keeping me up to speed on today's national security issues. Alexandra Jajonie, a recent graduate of Virginia Tech, kept us all organized, oversaw much of the fact-checking, and demonstrated an ability to juggle tough assignments in a cool and collected manner that belied her years. Jim Steen, who lived through many of the chapters of this book, was invaluable in answering questions—in particular, about my days in Congress and as secretary of defense. His recall and ability to produce obscure documents instantaneously was singularly impressive. John McConnell and Matthew Scully, two of the best speechwriters I have ever known, provided valuable assistance for this book, and I would like to thank them for all they have added to it. I am also grateful for their assistance over the years. In my speeches as vice president, they helped me capture crucial aspects of an historic time. Frank Gannon, whom I first met during the Nixon administration and who is a wonderful storyteller, was a wise and steady hand as I worked on this book. He brought the experience of having worked on previous memoirs as well as knowledge and memories of what Washington was like in the turbulent years of the early 1970s. I also want to thank Peter Long, who served as my assistant at the American Enterprise Institute and was an important part of the book team; Cara Jones, a former navy officer and graduate student at Johns Hopkins, who helped immensely in the research and fact-checking of the secretary of defense and vice presidency chapters; and Will Speicher, who also provided assistance checking facts in the early stages of the manuscript. Victoria Coates also provided key research assistance, particularly for the Nixon and Ford chapters of the book.

At the National Archives, our work was aided tremendously by Nancy Smith and Stephannie Oriabure, who answered questions, procured photos, and tracked down information from presidential libraries. Christian C. Goos at the Gerald R. Ford Presidential Library and historian Donald A. Ritchie of the U.S. Senate Historical Office Staff also provided important research assistance. I want to thank them, and also Bill Leary of the National Security Council, who was instrumental in reviewing and expediting clearances for this book.

Mary Matalin has lived this project since its inception and her contributions are too numerous to list. We all treasure her wise counsel and her friendship. I am also grateful that Kara Ahern, who helped manage my vice presidential campaign in 2004, came back to help oversee events and travel for me. She has once again become a key member of the Cheney team.

A number of people reviewed early versions of parts of this book and made many useful suggestions. Even when I did not heed their advice, I was often prompted to rethink and rewrite, and I'm grateful for the inspiration provided by David Addington, Eric Edelman, John Hannah, Scooter Libby, Terry O'Donnell, Neil Patel, Samantha

Ravich, Pete Williams, and Paul Wolfowitz. Many of the photos in the book were taken by David Bohrer, vice presidential photographer for eight years, and I am grateful not only for his amazing work but for his help in overseeing the photo selection process for *In My Time.* I appreciate as well Pete Williams's assistance in helping us choose photos. David Kennerly, who has taken incredible shots at key moments of our lives over many years, is also well represented in this book, and I am grateful for his talent and friendship.

I'd like to thank the American Enterprise Institute, with which I've been long associated, and its outstanding and visionary president Arthur Brooks for the many forums the organization has provided over the years for debate about the most important policy issues of our times. Both Lynne and I are grateful for Cristina Allegretti's skillful attention to detail in managing our AEI office. Debbie Heiden, who worked for me at the White House, continues to help keep my life in order. Gus Anies also played an important role in keeping me organized through the process of writing this book.

Bob Barnett was a skillful representative as we launched this project, and we have benefited from his sage counsel every step of the way. I would also like to thank the terrific team at Simon & Schuster, starting with CEO Carolyn Reidy, whose interest in this project was evident from day one. Our outstanding editor, Mitchell Ivers, made a number of trips to Washington to read the manuscript and make important edits. Louise Burke, Anthony Ziccardi, Jennifer Robinson, and Jean Anne Rose have all made it a pleasure to work with Simon & Schuster. I am also appreciative of the efforts of Sally Franklin, Al Madocs, Tom Pitoniak, Lisa Litwack, Michael Nagin, and Natasha Simons.

While I was campaigning for the vice presidency and serving in office, I was lucky to have a number of talented and dedicated personal aides. My daughter Mary was the first of these during the 2000 campaign. Brian McCormack, Jen Field, Charlie Durkin, and Lucy Tutwiler all served in this post during my vice presidency. I want to thank them for their tireless work handling any and all tasks thrown their way. I also want to acknowledge my longtime friend Ron Walker, who got on the plane with us in 2000 and helped us get our campaign legs back.

It is somewhat unusual, I realize, to thank medical teams for their help, but in my case, it would be a serious oversight if I failed to do so. I am grateful to the doctors at George Washington University Hospital for their tremendous care over the years, and I particularly want to thank Dr. Jonathan Reiner and Dr. Jehan El-Bayoumi. Dr. Lew Hofmann traveled with me around the world several times when I was vice president and I would like to thank him, as well as Dr. Sean O'Meara and the group at Guardian 24/7 that has provided me such useful guidance since. I am also indebted to the team at Inova Fairfax Hospital in Falls Church, Virginia, particularly Dr. Shashank Desai, Dr. Nelson Burton, Dr. Anthony Rongoni, Dr. Jason Vourlekis, and the coordinators Lori Edwards, Tonya Elliott, and Carolyn Rosner.

Lynne and I have been blessed with a loving family, our parents, our brothers, my sister, our children, and our grandchildren, and I see this book as a tribute to them all. Lynne and I are also grateful for the many friends with whom we have shared our lives in Wyoming, Washington, and around the world. Many are mentioned in this book, but too briefly to reflect the depths of our gratitude, and I would like to conclude by acknowledging to all of them how much their support has meant. We are fortunate to have such friends.

NOTES

All links were active as of June 26, 2011

2   *shortly before 10:00 a.m.:* Many timelines have been constructed for 9/11, and there is variation among them. The times in the Prologue are based on *The 9/11 Commission Report* (New York: W. W. Norton & Company, 2004), notes taken that day by Lynne Cheney, and my recollections.

60   *wigs and toupees: Federal Register,* vol. 36, no. 220, November 13, 1971, p. 21789.

62   *effort to freeze prices:* Allen J. Matusow, *Nixon's Economy: Booms, Busts, Dollars, & Votes* (Lawrence: University Press of Kansas, 1998), p. 231.

87   *in the Oval Office:* Rumsfeld Papers, Memorandum for Don Rumsfeld from Dick Cheney, July 8, 1975, http://library.rumsfeld.com/doclib/sp/158/07-08-1975%20From%20Dick%20Cheney%20re%20Solzhenitsyn.pdf.

90   *pretty frank document:* Rumsfeld Papers, Memorandum for the President from Donald Rumsfeld and Richard Cheney, October 24, 1975, http://library.rumsfeld.com/doclib/sp/174/1975-10-24%20To%20Gerald%20Ford%20re%20Re-election%20and%20Rumsfeld%20and%20Cheney%20Resignations.pdf.

219   *pilots called it "tank plinking":* Rick Atkinson, *Crusade: The Untold Story of the Persian Gulf War* (New York: Houghton Mifflin Company, 1993), p. 264.

220   *from using its WMD:* Keith Payne, *Deterrence in the Second Nuclear Age* (Lexington: University Press of Kentucky, 1996), pp. 83–84.

221   *"too dear and too high":* Ibid.

233   *"on a rational basis":* Colin Powell, *My American Journey* (New York: Random House, 1995), p. 541.

235   *DPG represented a shift:* For more on the 1992 Defense Planning Guidance and our post–Cold War defense posture, see chapters by Paul Wolfowitz and Eric Edelman in *In Uncertain Times: American Foreign Policy after the Berlin Wall and*

9/11, eds. Melvyn P. Leffler and Jeffrey W. Legro (Ithaca: Cornell University Press, 2011).

269 *"softest of sells":* Ronald Brownstein, "A Strong Case for Change Is Played Down," *Los Angeles Times,* August 1, 2000.

276 *"nine days of hell":* Mary Cheney, *Now It's My Turn: A Daughter's Chronicle of Political Life* (New York: Threshold Editions, 2006), p. 64.

286 *by 5 percent:* Karl Rove, *Courage and Consequence: My Life as a Conservative in the Fight* (New York: Threshold Editions, 2010), p. 193.

301 *"shook our hands":* Linda D. Kozaryn, "President Hosts Nation's Combat Heroes," American Forces Press Service, January 23, 2001, http://www.defense.gov/specials/outreachpublic/hosts.html.

307 *attend very often:* Robert A. Caro, *The Years of Lyndon Johnson: Master of the Senate* (New York: Alfred A. Knopf, 2002), p. 1038.

316 *"nation's energy security":* National Energy Policy Development Group, *National Energy Policy: Reliable, Affordable, and Environmentally Sound Energy for America's Future,* May 16, 2001, http://www.ne.doe.gov/pdffiles/nationalenergypolicy.pdf.

316 *during the biofuels craze:* Michael Grunwald, "The Clean Energy Scam," *Time,* March 27, 2008.

319 *"first line of defense":* Nicholas Lemann, "The Quiet Man: Dick Cheney's Discreet Rise to Unprecedented Power," *The New Yorker,* May 7, 2001.

326 *right thing to do:* See Richard B. Cheney, Remarks at the Heritage Foundation Dinner Commemorating the 25th Anniversary of President Reagan's Strategic Defense Initiative, March 11, 2008, http://georgewbush-whitehouse.archives.gov/news/releases/2008/03/print/20080311–9.html.

346 *never exceeding four thousand:* Douglas J. Feith, *War and Decision: Inside the Pentagon at the Dawn of the War on Terrorism* (New York: HarperCollins, 2008), p. 88.

348 *was collecting intelligence:* Michael V. Hayden, Address to the National Press Club: What American Intelligence & Especially the NSA Have Been Doing to Defend the Nation, January 23, 2006, http://www.dni.gov/speeches/printer_friendly/20060123_speech_print.htm.

349 *a related terrorist organization:* For additional information on the terrorist surveillance program, see Michael V. Hayden, Hearing Before the Senate Select Committee on Intelligence, May 18, 2006, http://intelligence.senate.gov/109808.pdf.

349 *"identified them as such":* Hayden, Address to the National Press Club.

350 *lawful approximately twenty times:* Letter from Shannen Coffin, Counsel to the Vice President, to Senator Patrick Leahy, August 20, 2007; Authorizations for the program dated October 4, November 2, and November 30, 2001; January 9, March 14, April 18, May 21, June 24, July 30, September 10, October 15, and

November 18, 2002; January 8, February 7, March 17, April 22, June 11, July 14, September 10, October 15, and December 9, 2003; January 14, 2004.

353 *"should have been published":* Byron Calame, "Banking Data: A Mea Culpa," *New York Times,* October 22, 2006.

354 *riot at Qala-i-Jangi:* Alex Perry, "Inside the Battle at Qala-i-Jangi," *Time,* December 1, 2001.

354 *and medical care:* Thomas Joscelyn, "The Real Gitmo: What I Saw at America's Best Detention Facility for Terrorists," *Weekly Standard,* December 28, 2009.

355 *"endanger civilians in war":* Ronald Reagan, Message to the Senate Transmitting a Protocol to the 1949 Geneva Conventions, January 29, 1987, http://www.reagan.utexas.edu/archives/speeches/1987/012987B.HTM.

356 *appearing in only three:* Thomas Joscelyn, "Gitmo Is Not al Qaeda's 'Number One Recruitment Tool,'" *Weekly Standard,* December 27, 2010, http://www.weeklystandard.com/blogs/gitmo-not-al-qaedas-number-one-recruitment-tool_524997.html.

357 Abu Zubaydah capture and interrogation: George W. Bush, Address to the Na-
–58 tion, September 6, 2006; Michael V. Hayden, Classified Statement for the Record before the Senate Select Committee on Intelligence, April 12, 2007 (since declassified); George Tenet, *At the Center of the Storm: My Years at the CIA* (New York: HarperCollins, 2007), pp. 145–47 and 241–43.

359 *building on the West Coast:* Central Intelligence Agency, "Khalid Shaykh Muhammad: Preeminent Source On Al-Qa'ida," July 13, 2004, http://www.washingtonpost.com/wp-srv/nation/documents/Khalid_Shayhk_Muhammad.pdf.

360 *"lives of innocent people":* Marc A. Thiessen, *Courting Disaster: How the CIA Kept America Safe and How Barack Obama Is Inviting the Next Attack* (Washington, D.C.: Regnery Publishing), pp. 159–60. For Thorsness Medal of Honor citation, see http://www.militarytimes.com/citations-medals-awards/recipient.php?recipientid=2195.

360 *"the right thing":* Thiessen, *Courting Disaster,* pp. 158 and 162. For Day Medal of Honor citation, see http://militarytimes.com/citations-medals-awards/recipient.php?recipientid=1075.

360 *what they were learning:* Hayden, Statement for the Record, April 12, 2007.

362 *endanger our CIA operatives:* Evan Thomas, "Why Is This Spy Smiling?" *Newsweek,* May 16, 2009.

364 *derailed by Desert Storm:* International Atomic Energy Agency, *The Implementation of United Nations Security Council Resolutions Relating to Iraq,* August 12, 1996.

365 *"reestablish Iraq's WMD programs":* Director of Central Intelligence, National In-

telligence Estimate, "Prospects for Iraq: Saddam and Beyond," December 1993, p. vii, http://www.foia.cia.gov/docs/DOC_0001188931/DOC_0001188931.pdf.

365 *"its nuclear weapons program":* quoted in Charles S. Robb and Laurence H. Silberman, *The Commission on the Intelligence Capabilities of the United States Regarding Weapons of Mass Destruction, Report to the President of the United States,* March 31, 2005, part 1, p. 54, http://www.gpoaccess.gov/wmd/pdf/full_wmd_report.pdf.

365 *after their return:* Charles Duelfer, *Comprehensive Report of the Special Advisor to the DCI on Iraq's WMD,* vol. 1, Regime Strategic Intent, Realizing Saddam's Veiled WMD Intent, September 30, 2004, https://www.cia.gov/library/reports/general-reports-1/iraq_wmd_2004/chap1.html#sect7.

366 *for WMD development:* Duelfer, *Comprehensive Report,* vol. 1, Regime Strategic Intent, Key Findings, September 30, 2004, https://www.cia.gov/library/reports/general-reports-1/iraq_wmd_2004/chap1.html#sect1.

366 *his biological weapons program:* Statement by Director of Central Intelligence George J. Tenet on the 2002 National Intelligence Estimate on Iraq's Continuing Programs for Weapons of Mass Destruction, August 11, 2003, https://www.cia.gov/news-information/press-releases-statements/press-release-archive-2003/pr08112003.htm.

367 *"the Persian Gulf region":* quoted in Senate Select Committee on Intelligence, *Report on the U.S. Intelligence Community's Prewar Intelligence Assessments on Iraq,* July 7, 2004, p. 144, http://www.intelligence.senate.gov/108301.pdf.

367 *nuclear or nonnuclear use:* Senate Select Committee on Intelligence, *Report on Whether Public Statements Regarding Iraq by U.S. Government Officials Were Substantiated by Intelligence Information,* June 5, 2008, pp. 6–7, http://intelligence.senate.gov/080605/phase2a.pdf.

367 *President George H. W. Bush:* Central Intelligence Agency, "Iraq: Baghdad Attempts to Assassinate Former President Bush," July 12, 1993, http://www.foia.cia.gov/docs/DOC_0000756378/DOC_0000756378.pdf.

367 *participated in terrorist attacks:* Senate Select Committee on Intelligence, *Report on Prewar Intelligence,* July 7, 2004, pp. 315–16.

368 *"absent U.S. military action":* Letter from George Tenet to Bob Graham, October 7, 2002, *Congressional Record,* October 9, 2002, p. S10154.

368 *Development officer, in Jordan:* George Tenet, Hearing before the Senate Select Committee on Intelligence, February 11, 2003, p. 78, http://intelligence.senate.gov/108161.pdf; Senate Select Committee on Intelligence, *Report on Prewar Intelligence,* pp. 337 and 353; Tenet, *Center of the Storm,* pp. 350–54.

368 *Tenet would later write:* Tenet, *Center of the Storm,* p. 370; See also Robb-Silberman Report, p. 14.

384 *than had been suspected:* Robb-Silberman Report, pp. 267–70.

385 *one million dying:* Tara O'Toole, Mair Michael, and Thomas V. Inglesby, "Shining Light on 'Dark Winter,' " *Clinical Infectious Diseases,* vol. 34, issue 7, April 1, 2002, pp. 972–83, http://cid.oxfordjournals.org/content/34/7/972.full#sec-2.

392 *"several months to a year":* National Intelligence Council, National Intelligence Estimate, "Iraq's Continuing Programs for Weapons of Mass Destruction," October 2002, http://www.dni.gov/nic/special_keyjudgements.html. The assistant secretary of state for intelligence and research had an alternative view, judging that while Saddam was "pursuing at least a limited effort to maintain and acquire nuclear weapons-related capabilities," he did not have "an integrated and comprehensive approach," which made it impossible to predict when he could acquire a nuclear weapon.

394 *"an obvious falsehood":* "Britain: Iraq Statement an 'Obvious Falsehood,' " Associated Press, December 18, 2002.

394 *within the past few years:* Hans Blix, *An Update on Inspection,* January 27, 2003, http://www.un.org/Depts/unmovic/Bx27.htm.

404 *speech was "well-founded":* Committee of Privy Counsellors, *Review of Intelligence on Weapons of Mass Destruction,* July 14, 2004, pp. 123–25, http://news.bbc.co.uk/nol/shared/bsp/hi/pdfs/14_07_04_butler.pdf.

405 *chief among them:* Tenet, *Center of the Storm,* p. 469.

406 *wanted to buy yellowcake:* Senate Select Committee on Intelligence, *Report on Prewar Intelligence,* pp. 43–46.

406 *"a flat-out lie":* Spencer Ackerman and John B. Judis, "The First Casualty," *New Republic,* June 30, 2003.

406 *State of the Union speech:* web chat sponsored by Kerry campaign, October 29, 2003, quoted at http://www.factcheck.org/article222.html.

407 *"unsubstantiated, and misleading":* Senate Select Committee on Intelligence, *Report on Prewar Intelligence,* p. 445.

407 *four separate times:* Michael J. Sniffen, "Journalists Say CIA Agent's ID Was Offered Freely," Associated Press, February 13, 2007; For Bob Woodward recording of Armitage interview, http://www.youtube.com/watch?v=FoPG1PVic10.

407 *on October 1, 2003:* David Johnston, "Leak Revelation Leaves Questions," *New York Times,* September 2, 2006.

409 *accuracy of their recall:* For the issue of memory in the Libby trial, see Stan Crock, "'Fair Game' Glamorizes Distortions and Perpetuates Myths," *World Affairs,* September/October 2010, http://www.worldaffairsjournal.org/articles/2010-SeptOct/full-Crock-SO-2010.html.

412 *"declare to the UN":* Central Intelligence Agency, Statement by David Kay on the Interim Progress Report on the Activities of the Iraq Survey Group, October 2, 2003,

https://www.cia.gov/news-information/speeches-testimony/2003/david_kay_100 22003.html.

412 *"before the war":* Interview with David Kay, *Weekend Edition,* National Public Radio, January 25, 2004.

412 *"after sanctions were removed":* Duelfer, *Comprehensive Report,* vol. 1, Regime Strategic Intent, Key Findings, September 30, 2004, https://www.cia.gov/library/reports/general-reports-1/iraq_wmd_2004/chap1.html#sect1.

412 *chemical weapons within months:* Duelfer, *Comprehensive Report,* vol. 1, Regime Strategic Intent, Realizing Saddam's Veiled WMD Intent, September 30, 2004, https://www.cia.gov/library/reports/general-reports-1/iraq_wmd_2004/chap1.html#sect7. For knowledge base and dual use, see key findings for chemical, biological, nuclear in vols. 2 and 3.

414 *"making conventional bombs":* Letter from George Tenet to Bob Graham, October 7, 2002, *Congressional Record,* October 9, 2002, p. S10154.

415 *"indistinguishable" from each other:* Tenet, Hearing before the Senate Select Committee on Intelligence, p. 78, http://intelligence.senate.gov/108161.pdf.

421 *the Department of Defense:* Donald Rumsfeld, *Known and Unknown: A Memoir* (New York: Sentinel, 2011), p. 552.

427 *"bringing us this day":* Stephen F. Hayes, "Present at the Creation: With Dick Cheney at the Inauguration of Afghanistan's First Elected President," *Weekly Standard,* December 20, 2004.

466 Information and quotations about the al-Kibar nuclear reactor and Syrian-North
–68 Korean cooperation: "Background Briefing with Senior U.S. Officials on Syria's Covert Nuclear Reactor and North Korea's Involvement," April 24, 2008, http://www.dni.gov/interviews/20080424_interview.pdf.

473 *metal structure over it:* Ibid.

474 *"serious and sincere":* Mike Chinoy, *Meltdown: The Inside Story of the North Korean Nuclear Crisis* (New York: St. Martin's Press, 2008), p. 318.

477 *military option was under way:* Demetri Sevastopulo, Daniel Dombey, and Andrew Ward, "US Strike on Iran 'Not Being Prepared,' " *Financial Times,* November 12, 2007.

478 *dramatic opening statement:* Director of National Intelligence, National Intelligence Estimate, "Iran: Nuclear Intentions and Capabilities," November 2007, http://www.dni.gov/press_releases/20071203_release.pdf.

479 *to do over again:* See Mark Mazzetti, "Intelligence Chief Says Al Qaeda Improves Ability to Strike in U.S.," *New York Times,* February 6, 2008, and Michael McConnell, Annual Threat Assessment Hearing of the Senate Armed Services Committee, February 27, 2008.

483 *traces of highly enriched uranium:* Glenn Kessler, "Uranium Traces Found on N. Korean Tubes," *Washington Post,* December 21, 2007.

484 *traces of highly enriched uranium:* Glenn Kessler, "New Data Found on North Korea's Nuclear Capacity," *Washington Post,* June 21, 2008.

489 *"his North Korean counterparts":* Glenn Kessler, "N. Korea Doesn't Agree to Written Nuclear Pact; Earlier Assurances Contradicted, U.S. Says," *Washington Post,* December 12, 2008.

496 Descriptions and quotations regarding Specialist Monica Brown's Silver Star:
–97 http://ourmilitaryheroes.defense.gov/profiles/brownm.html.

501 *left them with no plan:* Richard B. Cheney, Speech to the Center for Security Policy, October 21, 2009, http://www.centerforsecuritypolicy.org/p18209.xml?genre _id=1004.

503 *whatever losses they produced:* "Dissenting Statement of Commissioner Keith Hennessey, Commissioner Douglas Holtz-Eakin, and Vice Chairman Bill Thomas," *The Financial Crisis Inquiry Report,* January 2011, pp. 411–39, http://www .gpoaccess.gov/fcic/fcic.pdf.

510 *approximately $20 billion:* Robert J. Samuelson, "Why TARP Has Been a Success Story," *Newsweek,* March 28, 2011.

514 *Putin seemed to long for them:* Richard B. Cheney, Remarks at the 2006 Vilnius Conference, May 4, 2006, http://georgewbush-whitehouse.archives.gov/news/ releases/2006/05/20060504–1.html.

514 *make them members of NATO:* Richard B. Cheney, Remarks at the Ambrosetti Forum, September 6, 2008, http://georgewbush-whitehouse.archives.gov/news/ releases/2008/09/20080906–1.html.

523 *in writing this book:* Central Intelligence Agency, "Khalid Shaykh Muhammad: Preeminent Source on Al-Qa'ida," July 13, 2004, http://www.washingtonpost .com/wp-srv/nation/documents/Khalid_Shayhk_Muhammad.pdf; Central Intelligence Agency, "Detainee Reporting Pivotal for the War Against Al-Qa'ida," June 3, 2005, http://www.washingtonpost.com/wp-srv/nation/documents/Detainee _Reporting.pdf.

INDEX